A RETURN TO VISION

A RETURN TO VISION

RICHARD L. CHERRY
ROBERT J. CONLEY
NORTHERN ILLINOIS UNIVERSITY

BERNARD A. HIRSCH
UNIVERSITY OF ILLINOIS

HOUGHTON MIFFLIN COMPANY · BOSTON
New York · Atlanta · Geneva, Illinois · Dallas · Palo Alto

Library of Congress Catalog Card Number: 70–139210
ISBN: 0–395–11221–4

ACKNOWLEDGMENTS

GORDON W. ALLPORT, "Prejudice: Linguistic Factors." From Gordon W. Allport, *The Nature of Prejudice*, 1954, Addison-Wesley, Reading, Mass.

MARGOT ASTROV, "The Magic Creativeness of the Word." Copyright © 1946 by Margot Astrov. Reprinted from *The Winged Serpent* by Margot Astrov by permission of The John Day Company, Inc., publisher.

W. H. AUDEN, "The Unknown Citizen." Copyright 1940 and renewed 1968 by W. H. Auden. Reprinted from *Collected Shorter Poems 1927–1957*, by W. H. Auden, by permission of Random House, Inc.

AZTEC, A Song by Nezahualcoyotl." From Daniel G. Brinton, *Ancient Nahuatl Poetry*, p. 123, Library of American Aboriginal Literature, Vol. 7, Philadelphia, 1887.

JAMES BALDWIN, "Sonny's Blues." Copyright © 1957 by James Baldwin. Reprinted from *Going to Meet the Man* by James Baldwin by permission of the publisher, The Dial Press.

DANIEL BERRIGAN, "The Funeral Oration of Thomas Merton as Pronounced by the Compassionate Buddha." Reprinted from *Catholic Worker* with the permission of Dorothy Day, editor.

BYRON BLACK, "I, the Fake Mad Bomber and Walking It Home Again." Reprinted from the Summer, 1961 issue of *Prairie Schooner* with the permission of the University of Nebraska Press.

BLACKFOOT, "A Prayer to the Sun." Clark Wissler, *Ceremonial Bundles of the Blackfoot Indians*, p. 253. Papers of the American Museum of Natural History, Vol. 7, 1912.

R. P. BLACKMUR, "The Artist as Hero: A Disconsolate Chimera." Copyright, 1951, by Richard P. Blackmur. Reprinted from his volume, *The Lion and the Honeycomb* by permission of Harcourt Brace Jovanovich, Inc.

KENNETH BOULDING, "The Role of Ideology in the Great Transition." From *The Meaning of the Twentieth Century: The Great Transition* by Kenneth E. Boulding. Copyright © 1964 by Kenneth Ewart Boulding. Reprinted by permission of Harper & Row, Publishers, Inc.

CLAUDE BROWN, "The Language of Soul." Reprinted from the April, 1968 issue of *Esquire*. Copyright © 1968 by Claude Brown. Reprinted by permission of the Sterling Lord Agency.

LARRY BRYANT, "Black America's Own Language." Reprinted with the permission of United Press International.

JAMES BRANCH CABELL, "We Await." Reprinted from *Beyond Life,* published by the Robert M. McBride Company.

JOSEPH CAMPBELL, "Out of the Void—Space" and "The Hero Today." From *The Hero With A Thousand Faces,* Joseph Campbell, Bollingen Series XVII (copyright © 1949 by Bollingen Foundation) Princeton University Press. Reprinted by permission of Princeton University Press.

ALBERT CAMUS, "The Artist and His Time." From *The Myth of Sisyphus and Other Essays,* by Albert Camus, translated by Justin O'Brien. Copyright © 1955 by Alfred A. Knopf, Inc. Reprinted by permission.

LOUIS W. CARTWRIGHT, "The New Hero." From *To Make a Difference,* edited by Otto Butz. Copyright © 1967 by Otto Butz. Reprinted by permission of Harper & Row, Publishers, Inc.

CHIPPEWA, "A Song of Healing" and "Song Sung Over a Dying Person." Frances Densmore, *Chippewa Music I,* Bureau of American Ethnology, Bulletin 45 (Washington D.C., 1910), p. 73 and p. 95.

ELDRIDGE CLEAVER, "Political Struggle in America." Reprinted from the March 16, 1968 issue of *The Black Panther* with the permission of the Black Panther Party.

NORMAN COUSINS, "The Environment of Language." Reprinted from the April 8, 1967 issue of *Saturday Review*. Copyright 1967 Saturday Review, Inc.

COUNTEE CULLEN, "Incident." From *On These I Stand* by Countee Cullen. Copyright, 1925 by Harper & Row, Publishers, Inc.; renewed, 1953 by Ida M. Cullen. Reprinted by permission of Harper & Row, Publishers, Inc.

E. E. CUMMINGS, "next to of course god america i." Copyright, 1944, by E. E. Cummings. Reprinted from his volume, *Poems 1923–1954* by permission of Harcourt Brace Jovanovich, Inc.

RENÉ DUBOS, "The New Pessimism." Reprinted with the permission of Charles Scribner's Sons from *So Human an Animal,* pp. 9–22, by René Dubos. Copyright © 1968 René Dubos.

FRIEDRICH DÜRRENMATT, "The Tunnel." Copyright 1961 by Friedrich Dürrenmatt. Reprinted by permission of Kurt Hellmer, Author's Agent.

IRWIN EDMAN, "A Reasonable Life in a Mad World." Reprinted from the March, 1949 issue of *Atlantic Monthly*. Copyright © 1949, by The Atlantic Monthly Company, Boston, Mass. Reprinted with permission.

T. S. ELIOT, "The Hollow Men." From *Collected Poems 1909–1962* by T. S. Eliot, copyright, 1936, by Harcourt Brace Jovanovich, Inc.; copyright © 1963, 1964, by T. S. Eliot. Reprinted by permission of the publisher.

RALPH ELLISON, "Mister Toussan." Reprinted from the November 4, 1941 issue of *New Masses*. Reprinted by permission of William Morris Agency, Inc. Copyright © 1941 by Ralph Ellison.

PETER FARB, "Man at the Mercy of His Language" and "Messiahs: Indian and Others." *Excerpted in part* from the book *Man's Rise to Civilization as Shown by the Indians of North America from Primeval Times to the Coming of the Industrial State* by Peter Farb. Copyright, © 1968 by Peter Farb.

WILLIAM FAULKNER, "Speech of Acceptance Upon the Award of the Nobel Prize for Literature." From *The Faulkner Reader,* Copyright 1954 by William Faulkner (Random House, Inc.).

E. M. FORSTER, "The Celestial Omnibus." From *The Collected Tales of E. M. Forster.* Published 1947 by Alfred A. Knopf, Inc. Reprinted by permission.

SIR JAMES G. FRAZER, "Human Sacrifices for the Crops." Reprinted with permission of The Macmillan Company from *The Golden Bough* by Sir James George Frazer. Copyright 1922 by The Macmillan Company, renewed 1950 by Barclays Bank, Ltd.

ROBERT FROST, "Desert Places" and "Mending Wall." From *The Poetry of Robert Frost* edited by Edward Connery Lathem. "Desert Places" copyright 1936 by Robert Frost. Copyright © 1964 by Lesley Frost Ballantine. Copyright © 1969 by Holt, Rinehart and Winston. Reprinted by permission of Holt, Rinehart and Winston, Inc. "Mending Wall" copyright 1930, 1939, © 1969 by Holt, Rinehart and Winston, Inc. Copyright © 1958 by Robert Frost. Copyright © 1967 by Lesley Frost Ballantine. Reprinted by permission of Holt, Rinehart and Winston, Inc.

WILLIAM H. GRIER AND PRICE M. COBBS, "Black Rage." Chapter X of *Black Rage* by William H. Grier and Price M. Cobbs, © 1968 by William H. Grier and Price M. Cobbs, Basic Books, Inc., Publishers, New York.

EDITH HAMILTON, "East and West." Reprinted from *The Greek Way* by Edith Hamilton. By permission of W. W. Norton & Company, Inc. Copyright 1930, 1943 by W. W. Norton & Company, Inc. Copyright renewed 1958 by Edith Hamilton. "Introduction to Norse Mythology." Copyright 1942, by Edith Hamilton. From *Mythology* by Edith Hamilton, by permission of Little, Brown and Co.

S. I. HAYAKAWA, "Art and Tension" and "Language and Survival." From *Language in Thought and Action,* Second Edition, by S. I. Hayakawa, copyright, 1941, 1949, © 1963, 1964, by Harcourt Brace Jovanovich, Inc. and reprinted with their permission.

TOM HAYDEN, "The Terror." From *Rebellion in Newark,* by Tom Hayden. Copyright © 1967 by Tom Hayden. Reprinted by permission of Random House, Inc.

HINDU, "The Isa Upanisad." Translated by P. Lal. Reprinted with the permission of P. Lal.

LANGSTON HUGHES, "Let America Be America Again." Reprinted by permission of Harold Ober Associates Incorporated. Copyright 1938 by Langston Hughes. Copyright renewed.

ALDOUS HUXLEY, "Words and Their Meanings." Reprinted with the permission of Laura Huxley.

SHIRLEY JACKSON, "The Lottery." Reprinted with the permission of Farrar, Straus & Giroux, Inc. from *The Lottery* by Shirley Jackson, copyright 1948, 1949 by Shirley Jackson.

ROBINSON JEFFERS, "Apology for Bad Dreams." Copyright 1925 and renewed 1953 by Robinson Jeffers. Reprinted from *The Selected Poetry of Robinson Jeffers* by permission of Random House, Inc.

C. E. M. JOAD, "How Religion Arose, and Why It Flourished." Reprinted from *The Present and Future of Religion* with the permission of Ernest Benn Limited and the executors of the estate of C. E. M. Joad.

LEROI JONES, "Expressive Language." From *Home: Social Essays* by LeRoi Jones. Reprinted by permission of William Morrow and Company, Inc. Copyright © 1963, 1966 by LeRoi Jones.

C. S. LEWIS, "What Christians Believe." Reprinted with permission of The Macmillan Company from *The Case for Christianity* by C. S. Lewis. Copyright 1952 by The Macmillan Company.

ARCHIBALD MACLEISH, "The End of the World." Reprinted from *Collected Poems 1917–1952* by Archibald MacLeish with the permission of Houghton Mifflin Company, Publishers.

CLAUDE MCKAY, "Outcast." From *Selected Poems of Claude McKay,* copyright 1953 by Bookman Associates, Inc.

HUEY P. NEWTON, "A Message." Reprinted from *Black Fire,* Volume III, Number 12, May 3, 1969, published by the Black Student Union of San Francisco State College.

FREDERICK NIETZSCHE, "Zarathustra's Prologue, Sections 1–3" and "On the New Idol." From *The Portable Nietzsche* translated and edited by Walter Kaufmann. Copyright 1954 by The Viking Press, Inc. Reprinted by permission of The Viking Press, Inc.

GEORGE ORWELL, "Politics and the English Language." From *Shooting an Elephant and Other Essays* by George Orwell, copyright, 1945, 1946, 1949, 1950, by Sonia Brownell Orwell. Reprinted by permission of Harcourt Brace Jovanovich, Inc. "The Principles of Newspeak." From *Nineteen Eighty-Four* by George Orwell. Harcourt, Brace & World, Inc. Copyright, 1949 by Harcourt, Brace and Company, Inc. Reprinted by permission of Brandt & Brandt.

OSAGE, "Myth of Creation." From Alice Fletcher and Francis LaFleche, *The Omaha Tribe,* p. 63, 27th Annual Report of the Bureau of American Ethnology, Washington, 1911.

CARL SANDBURG, from "I Am the People, the Mob" (6 lines reprinted in Louis W. Cartwright: "The New Hero"). From *Chicago Poems* by Carl Sandburg. Copyright 1916 by Holt, Rinehart and Winston, Inc. Copyright 1944 by Carl Sandburg. Reprinted by permission of Holt, Rinehart and Winston, Inc.

ALVIN A. SAXON, JR., "Watts." Reprinted by permission of The World Publishing Company from *From the Ashes: Voices of Watts* edited by Budd Schulberg. An NAL book. Copyright © 1967 by New American Library, Inc.

HUGH J. SCHONFIELD, from *The Passover Plot.* Chapters 1 and 2 reprinted by permission of Bernard Geis Associates. Copyright © by Hugh Schonfield.

SENECA, "Red Jacket and the Missionary." From a pamphlet published in 1809 by James D. Bemis entitled "Indian Speeches; Delivered by Farmer's Brother and Red Jacket, Two Seneca Chiefs, pp. 4–8. The pamphlet was printed at Canandaigua, N.Y.

ARTHUR L. SMITH, "Toward a Revolutionary Rhetoric." From Arthur L. Smith, *Rhetoric of Black Revolution,* p. 1–23, Copyright © 1969 by Allyn and Bacon, Inc., Boston. Reprinted by permission of the publisher.

W. T. STACE, "Man Against Darkness." Copyright © 1948, by The Atlantic Monthly Company, Boston, Mass. Reprinted with permission.

GEORGE STEINER, "The Hollow Miracle" and "The Retreat from the Word." From *Language and Silence,* Essays on Language, Literature, and the Inhuman by George Steiner. Copyright © 1961, 1958 by George Steiner. Reprinted by permission of Atheneum Publishers.

STAN STEINER, "The Case of the Deerslayer." From *The New Indians* by Stan Steiner. Copyright © 1968 by Stan Steiner. Reprinted by permission of Harper & Row, Publishers, Inc.

DON C. TALAYESVA, "The Return to the Old Gods." From *Sun Chief: The Autobiography of a Hopi Indian,* edited by Leo W. Simmons. Copyright © 1942 by Yale University Press.

JOHN UPDIKE, "A & P." Copyright © 1962 by John Updike. Reprinted from *Pigeon Feathers and Other Stories,* by John Updike, by permission of Alfred A. Knopf, Inc. First appeared in *The New Yorker.*

WILLIAM BUTLER YEATS, "The Second Coming" (included as a selection and also within Louis W. Cartwright: "The New Hero") and "To a Friend Whose Work Has Come to Nothing." Reprinted with permission of The Macmillan Company from *Collected Poems* by William Butler Yeats. "The Second Coming" copyright 1924 by The Macmillan Company, renewed 1952 by Bertha Georgie Yeats. "To a Friend Whose Work Has Come to Nothing" copyright 1916 by The Macmillan Company, renewed 1944 by Bertha Georgie Yeats.

BILOINE W. YOUNG, "The American Indian: Citizen in Captivity." Reprinted from the December 11, 1965 issue of *Saturday Review* with the permission of the author. Copyright 1965 Saturday Review, Inc.

ZUNI, "Creation Myth." From Frank Cushing, *Outlines of Zuni Creation Myths,* pp. 379ff., 13th Annual Report of the Bureau of American Ethnology, Washington, 1892.

CONTENTS

Part One: The Fear

which is at the heart of all fears—the fear of chaos

Part Two: The Word

which is the primary means of articulating the fear and thereby attaining some measure of control over it

Part Three: Toward Oneness

**where man attempts to perceive order in the world
and in himself through a given mythology or world-view**

Part Four: With What We Have

**as institutions of social order, and how they sometimes
become forces that frustrate the development
of human goals, desires and thought**

xiv

Part Five: A Return to Vision

**where literature and the arts provide the highest expression
of the individual's experience and convey
the universality of this experience**

ALTERNATE TABLE OF CONTENTS

Essays
Rhetorical Principles

Short Stories
Dominant Themes

Poems
Modes and Stylistic Devices

INTRODUCTION

Ultimately the goal of all education must be to enable a person to develop his own intellectual and imaginative capacities to the highest degree possible. When we consider that all intellectual and imaginative endeavors depend primarily on two basic abilities—the ability to perceive relationships at various levels between people, objects, ideas, situations, systems, historical circumstances, and so forth; and the ability to generalize validly from given data—we can see a definite direction in which to proceed to attain this goal. But we cannot attain it by isolating our present situation from the rest of human experience. By focusing entirely on *our* time, *our* war, and *our* revolution, we obscure the larger social and cultural context in which these issues exist and thereby prevent ourselves from seeing why we are where we are and why certain universal problems so perniciously defy solution. Thus, *A Return to Vision* provides an awareness of this larger context, some of the background necessary to objectively view the major issues and a perspective from which to rationally evaluate varying points of view which are brought to bear on them. No solutions are offered here, no systems, no ideologies. Our concerns are human needs, human fears, and how human beings express them and attempt to come to terms with them. We hope *A Return to Vision* affords some necessary insights into the human experience. It is the reader's task to use and thereby to develop his abilities to perceive relationships, and to generalize effectively to apply them to his own circumstances and to the state of his world. Yet, we have not left the reader alone in this task. *A Return to Vision* is organized to aid in the development of these basic intellectual skills.

The plan of *A Return to Vision* involves an interrelated thematic approach in which five themes are related through their basic characteristics and through the nature of the selections which develop each one. The first part, "The Fear," treats chaos, disorder, and man's response to it. The fear of chaos has traditionally been man's most profound fear, and his attempt to eliminate chaos by imposing order on life is at the heart of all human experience. However, as man exists on different levels and must function within different spheres of existence, we deal with this attempt more specifically in the remaining sections of the book.

Part Two, "The Word," deals with language, not as a science, but as the expression of man's experience and ultimately as a shaping force of that experience. The primary purpose of this part is to present language as man's attempt to order his responses so that he can communicate them to others, thereby giving rise to a culture which is, in the last analysis, the result of man's need to discern meaning in life. Man uses language not only to impose order on experience, but to make sense of his world through his pursuit of "universal truths." It is through a given social order that he must consider these truths. Thus, the third part, "Toward Oneness," is concerned with man's search for universal truths which, of necessity, takes place on the "spiritual" (moral? philosophical?) plane of existence. Part Four, "With What We Have," is concerned with society insofar as it reflects man's attempt to give these truths a concrete shape and thereby make them a part of his everyday life. Parts Three and Four will also consider how society attempts to subjugate the individual for the sake of this preconceived order and how many individuals will unknowingly accept this regimentation rather than risk additional change, disorder, and chaos. The final part, "A Return to Vision," concerns itself with art as a medium through which the artist attempts to impose order on man's emotional and intellectual experiences. This brings the book full circle in that the artist, through his art, is attempting on a higher plane what all men attempt within the framework of their lives: that is, somehow to identify themselves by articulating perceptions of and responses to experience, to find understanding through the search for certain "truths," and to embody these truths within a given mode of artistic expression.

Richard L. Cherry
Robert J. Conley
Bernard A. Hirsch

A RETURN TO VISION

PART ONE

The Fear

When man speaks of his relationship to his environment, to the world, or to the universe, he is concerned with an act of defining; for as a human being, he establishes identity through his relationships to things outside himself. These things may range from friends to ideologies and institutions, and they all help him to arrive at some idea of who he is. His values and beliefs define him as a person much the same way that institutions and ideals define a nation.

Therefore when life threatens to render his values unworkable or to destroy the ideological foundations of his institutions, he becomes afraid. These things are essential to his definition of himself. He takes meaning from them. If they are meaningless, what is he?

This section, then, is concerned with the fear at the heart of all fears—that of chaos. "The established order of things," René Dubos tells us in "The New Pessimism," appears to be threatened by technological and social forces that increasingly dominate the world, just as it was threatened by the raiding Norsemen and Saracens ten centuries ago." Yeats, in "The Second Coming," is even more apocalyptic: "Things fall apart; the centre cannot hold;/ Mere anarchy is loosed upon the world. . . ." Nor is ours the first age to understand this fear. Those "raiding Norsemen," Edith Hamilton tells us, envisioned a heaven ". . . unlike any other heaven men have dreamed of. No radiancy of joy is in it, no assurance of bliss. It is a grave and solemn place, over which hangs the threat of inevitable doom." The Aztecs of Mexico, despite a highly developed culture, profoundly felt this fear: "I foresaw, being a Mexican, that our rule began to be destroyed, I went forth weeping that it was to bow down and to be destroyed." ("A Song by Nezahualcoyotl")

Nations and societies are not alone in experiencing the fear of chaos. The individual, beset by a world which consistently erodes his ever-diminishing store of certainties, feels it most profoundly. The narrator in Robert Frost's poem is terrified of his own "desert places." "I want my life," implores James Branch Cabell, "to have symmetry, or, in default of that, at least to acquire some clarity." But this, all too often, is denied us. In a world in which "The best lack all conviction, while the worst/ Are full of passionate intensity" (Yeats), where ". . . Ralph the lion was engaged in biting/ The neck of Madam Sossman while the drum/ Pointed . . ." (MacLeish), all may seem, in the final analysis—nothing.

1

THE NEW PESSIMISM

René Dubos

As the year 2000 approaches, an epidemic of sinister predictions is spreading all over the world, as happened among Christians during the period preceding the year 1000. Throughout the tenth century, Norsemen and Saracens incessantly raided Western Europe, disorganizing daily life and secular institutions, pillaging churches and monasteries. The rumor spread that the year 1000 would mark the end of the world and that a new spiritual universe would come into existence. Even those who did not believe that the world would come to an end probably assumed that living conditions would be corrupted by the barbaric invaders.

Prophets of gloom now predict that mankind is on a course of self-destruction, or that, in the unlikely event of its survival, it will progressively abandon the values and amenities of Western civilization. Nuclear warfare, environmental pollution, power blackouts, the progressive erosion of public services constitute direct and obvious threats to human existence. Furthermore, social regimentation and loss of privacy may soon reach levels incompatible with the traditional ways of civilized life. The established order of things appears to be threatened by technological and social forces that increasingly dominate the world, just as it was threatened by the raiding Norsemen and Saracens ten centuries ago.

Many observers of the contemporary scene would agree with the following words by the American journalist James Reston in the most influential daily newspaper of the most prosperous city in the world: "The old optimistic illusion that we can do anything we want is giving way to doubt, even to a new pessimism." Newspaper headlines daily seem to confirm the belief that the problems of the cities, the races, and the nations are beyond our control.

Apprehension is most widespread and expresses itself most clearly with regard to nuclear warfare, threats to health, the rise of automation, and other ill-defined consequences of scientific technology. Popular articles entitled "The Truth About . . ." almost uniformly refer to the dangers of technological or medical innovations. The new pessimism, however, has other determinants which transcend the fear of annihilation and affect the quality of life. In particular, science is being accused of destroying religious and philosophic values without substituting other guides to behavior or providing a meaningful picture of the universe. The disintegrating effect of loss of belief was pungently expressed a generation ago by the American philosopher John Dewey in his warning that a culture which permits science to destroy traditional values, but which distrusts its power to create new ones,

2

is destroying itself. Man finds it difficult to live without ultimate concern and faith in the significance of his destiny.

The malaise has now extended to the scientific community itself. While all scientists still believe that the opportunities for the extension of knowledge are boundless, many are beginning to doubt the wisdom and safety of extending much further some of the applications of knowledge. In addition, there have been claims that limitations inherent in the very structure of the physical world may soon slow down, then interrupt altogether, the development of the scientific technologies which have resulted in the most spectacular achievements of our age. Airplanes cannot practically fly much faster than at the present supersonic speeds; electronic computers are approaching theoretical limits of speed and efficiency; high-energy accelerators cannot long continue to become larger and more powerful; even space travel will have achieved its human possibilities within a very few decades.

The most important factor in dampening the euphoria that until recently was universal in scientific circles is the social and economic necessity of imposing directions and limitations to many technological developments. The current discussions concerning the advisability of devoting large resources to the manned space program have brought to light difficulties in reconciling the demands of certain technologies with more traditional human needs.

A few years ago, American scientists could state, "We *must* go to the moon, for the simple reason that we *can* do it"—echoing President John F. Kennedy, who in turn had echoed the statement by the English mountain climber George Mallory that Mount Everest *had* to be climbed, simply because it was there. Such statements are admirable to the extent that they express man's determination to accept difficult challenges, whenever and wherever there is some chance that the effort will lead to spectacular feats. But dashing expressions do not constitute an adequate substitute for the responsibility of making value judgments.

There are many good scientific reasons for accepting the staggering human, financial, and technological effort required to explore space and to land a man on the moon. There are equally good reasons, however, for undertaking other kinds of difficult and challenging tasks—such as exploring the earth itself or the depths of the oceans, probing into the nature of matter and energy, searching for the origins of man and his civilizations, controlling organic and mental disease, striving for world peace, eliminating city slums, preventing further desecration of nature, or dedicating ourselves to works of beauty and to the establishment of an harmonious equilibrium between man and the rest of creation.

Laymen as well as scholars can think of many projects at least as important and interesting as space travel or lunar exploration, and just as likely to succeed. But limitations of resources make it impossible to prosecute all worthwhile projects at the same time. Hence, the statement that we *must* do something because we *can* do it is operationally and ethically meaningless; it is tantamount to an intellectual abdication. Like other responsible human beings, scientists and sociologists must discriminate; their choice of goals must be made on the basis of value judgments.

The problem of choice is greatly complicated by the fact that techno-logical advances endlessly create new dilemmas, since every innovation has unforeseen consequences. Social regimentation, traffic jams, environmental pollution, constant exposure to noise and other unwanted stimuli are but a few of the undesirable accompaniments of economic and technological growth. Indeed, many innovations that have enhanced the wealth and power of our society in the past threaten to paralyze it at a later date. Abundance of goods, excess of comfort, multiplicity of means of communication are generating in the modern world situations almost as distressing as the ones that used to result from shortages of food, painful physical labor, and social isolation. We are creating new problems in the very process of solving those which plagued mankind in the past.

During recent years experts in the natural and social sciences have re-peatedly pointed out that the erratic and misguided growth of technology and urban conditions now poses as serious a threat as the undisciplined growth of the world population. Economic affluence and scientific break-throughs appear paradoxically to remove man still further from the golden age.

The new pessimism derives in large part probably from the public's disen-chantment at the realization that science cannot solve all human problems. Furthermore, the public is beginning to realize that whenever scientists make claims for support of their activities in the name of relevance to industrial technology, they are in fact making value judgments concerning the im-portance of technology in human life, judgments for which they have no spe-cial competence. A few spectacular technological failures might suffice to generate a bankruptcy of science.

Phrases such as the classical age, the age of faith, the age of reason, or the romantic age may not correspond to historical realities, but they convey nevertheless mankind's nostalgic longing for certain qualities of life that most people, rightly or wrongly, associate with the past. In contrast, we prosaically designate our own times the atomic age, space age, age of auto-mation, antibiotic age—in other words, the age of one or another tech-nology. These terms are used approvingly by technologists and disparag-ingly by humanists. The one term which has received almost universal acceptance is age of anxiety.

Social and technological achievements have spread economic affluence, increased comfort, accelerated transportation, and controlled certain forms of disease. But the material satisfactions thus made possible have not added much to happiness or to the significance of life. Not even the medical sci-ences have fulfilled their promises. While they have done much in the pre-vention and treatment of a few specific diseases, they have so far failed to increase true longevity or to create positive health. The age of affluence, technological marvels, and medical miracles is paradoxically the age of chronic ailments, of anxiety, and even of despair. Existentialist nausea has found its home in the most affluent and technologically advanced parts of the world.

Present-day societies abound in distressing problems, such as racial conflicts, economic poverty, emotional solitude, urban ugliness, injustice in all its forms, and the collective lunacy that creates the threat of nuclear warfare. But modern anxiety has deeper roots that reach into the very substance of each person's individuality. The most poignant problem of modern life is probably man's feeling that life has lost significance. The ancient religious and social creeds are being eroded by scientific knowledge and by the absurdity of world events. As a result, the expression "God is dead" is widely used in both theological and secular circles. Since the concept of God symbolized the totality of creation, man now remains without anchor. Those who affirm the death of God imply thereby the death of traditional man—whose life derived significance from his relation to the rest of the cosmos. The search for significance, the formulation of new meanings for the words God and Man, may be the most worthwhile pursuit in the age of anxiety and alienation.

Alienation is a vague word, but it denotes an attitude extremely widespread at present in affluent societies. Feeling alienated is an ancient experience which has taken different forms in the course of history. Many in the past experienced forlornness because the cosmos and the human condition appeared to them meaningless and pointless. Jean Jacques Rousseau, in the eighteenth century, traced alienation to the estrangement of man from nature that in his view resulted from artificial city life. Karl Marx, in the nineteenth, coined the word *Entfremdung*—rendered as "alienation" by his translators —to denote both the plight of the industrial worker deprived of the fruits of his production, and the depersonalization of labor in mechanized industries.

Many forms of alienation now coexist in our communities. The social and cultural malaise affects not only disenchanted intellectuals, industrial labor, and the poor classes, but also all those who feel depersonalized because circumstances compel them to accept mass standards which give them little chance to affirm their identity. Alienation is generated, furthermore, by the complete failure of even the most affluent societies to achieve harmonious relationships between human life and the total environment. The view that the modern world is absurd is no longer limited to the philosophical or literary avant-garde. It is spreading to all social and economic groups and affects all manifestations of life.

Psychologists, sociologists, and moralists tend to attribute anxiety and despair to the breakdown of intimate social relationships, with the attendant personal loneliness so pervasive in modern cities. The breakdown, however, is not limited to the interplay between human beings. It extends to the interplay between man and the natural forces that have shaped his physiological and mental self and to which his most fundamental processes are still bound. Chaos in human relationships has the same origin as chaos in the relationships between man and his environment.

In all countries of Western civilization, the largest part of life is now spent in an environment conditioned and often entirely created by technology.

Thus one of the most significant and disturbing aspects of modern life is that man's contacts with the rest of creation are almost always distorted by artificial means, even though his senses and fundamental perceptions have remained the same since the Stone Age. Modern man is anxious, even during peace and in the midst of economic affluence, because the technological world that constitutes his immediate environment, by separating him from the natural world under which he evolved, fails to satisfy certain of his unchangeable needs. In many respects, modern man is like a wild animal spending its life in a zoo; like the animal, he is fed abundantly and protected from inclemencies but deprived of the natural stimuli essential for many functions of his body and his mind. Man is alienated not only from other men, not only from nature, but more importantly from the deepest layers of his fundamental self.

The aspect of the new pessimism most commonly expressed is probably the belief that decrease in individual freedom is likely to result from increasing densities of population and the consequent need to accept a completely technicized urban environment. A heavy and repetitious anthology could be composed of writings by all kinds of scholars lamenting the sacrifice of personality and freedom at the altar of technological regimentation. As society becomes ever more highly organized, the individual will progressively vanish into the anonymous mass.

In his book *The Myth of the Machine,* the American critic Lewis Mumford predicts a future in which man will become passive and purposeless —a machine-conditioned animal designed and controlled for the benefit of depersonalized, collective organizations.

Former Secretary of State Dean Acheson expresses a similar concern in his recently published memoirs. He puts the golden age of childhood "quite accurately between the last decades of the nineteenth century and the first half of the 1920s . . . before the plunge into a motor age and city life swept away the freedom of children and dogs, put them both on leashes and made them the organized prisoners of an adult world."

The new pessimism considers it almost inevitable that the complexity of social structures will result in social regimentation and that freedom and privacy will come to be regarded as antisocial luxuries. Under these conditions, the types of men more likely to prosper will be those willing to accept a sheltered but regimented way of life in a teeming and polluted environment from which both wilderness and fantasy will have disappeared. The world may escape catastrophic destruction, but if present trends continue our descendants will find it difficult to prevent a progressive decadence of the social order of things. The tide of events will bring about simultaneously, paradoxical as it may seem, the fragmentation of the person and the collectivization of the masses.

Naturally there are some optimists among the modern soothsayers, but the new Jerusalem they envision is little more than a dismal and grotesque magnification of the present state of affairs. They predict for America a gross national product of many trillions of dollars and an average family income so large that every home will be equipped with more and more power equipment and an endless variety of electronic gadgets. Drugs to control the operations of the body and the mind, complicated surgery, and organ transplantations will make it commonplace to convert ordinary citizens into "optimen." The working day will be so short and the life span so long that countless hours will be available for the pursuit of entertainment—and eventually perhaps merely for the search for a *raison d'etre.*

Most modern prophets, in and out of the academies, seem to be satisfied with describing a world in which everything will move faster, grow larger, be mechanized, bacteriologically sterile, and emotionally safe. No hand will touch food in the automated kitchen; the care and behavior of children will be monitored electronically; there will be no need to call on one's friends because it will be possible to summon their voices, gestures, shapes, and complexions on the television-paneled walls of the living room; life will be effortless and without stress in air-conditioned houses romantically or excitingly lighted in all sorts of hues according to one's moods; exotic experiences will be safely and comfortably available in patios where artificial insect sounds and the proper degree of heat and moisture will create at will the atmosphere of a tropical night or a New England summer day. Actual examples of the dismal life that technological prophets envision for the future can be found increasingly in periodicals and books, notably the recently published *The Year 2000. . . .*

Admittedly, modern prophets also have visions reaching beyond the mere provision of effortless comfort and entertainment. But what they then imagine has the absurd quality of supersonic planes so rapid that travelers are back where they started from before having finished their first cocktail. As to the prophecies concerning space travel, or life on the bottom of the oceans, their chief purpose would seem to be to provide images of new environments in which boy meets girl and where good guy overcomes bad guy —in other words, where human beings behave exactly as they do on earth. Young people in lovers' lanes and desperadoes with their big hats and guns seem to be as essential to the unbelievable world of the future as to the old-fashioned dime novels and Western scenarios.

Science-fiction writers, abetted by not a few distinguished scientists, have indulged in a game of overpromise, which will inevitably lead to a letdown when it becomes obvious that the promises cannot be fulfilled. There exists in the modern world a pathological trend to view man's future from Mount Olympus, assiduously averting the eyes from the valleys of want, sorrow, and tears. Oddly enough, the natural sciences today provide the easiest and cheapest roads of escape from reality.

The word "unbelievable" (or its equivalent "incredible") is ambiguous. As commonly used, it denotes events or situations so extraordinary that they are difficult to believe but are nevertheless true. The present writings about all the marvels of the "unbelievable future" intend to convey this sense of impossible but true. Etymologically, however, unbelievable has a much more negative meaning, and it is in the sense of actual impossibility that the word will be used here. The "opti-man" imagined by the prophets of dismal optimism turns out to be not only a hollow man, but also a pseudo-man; not only would he be devoid of the attributes that have given its unique value to the human condition, but he would not long survive because he would be deprived of the stimuli required for physical and mental sanity.

The kind of life so widely predicted for the twenty-first century is unbelievable in the etymological sense because it is incompatible with the fundamental needs of man's nature. These needs have not changed significantly since the Late Stone Age and they will not change in the predictable future; they define the limits beyond which any prediction of the future becomes literally unbelievable.

Whatever scientific technology may create, *l'homme moyen sensuel* will continue to live by his senses and to perceive the world through them. As a result, he will eventually reject excessive abstraction and mechanization in order to reestablish direct contact with the natural forces from which he derives the awareness of his own existence and to which he owes his very sense of being.

The one possible aspect of the future seldom discussed by those who try to imagine the world-to-be is that human beings will become bored with automated kitchens, high-speed travel, and the monitoring of human contacts through electronic gadgets. People of the year 2000 might make nonsense of the predictions now being published in the proceedings of learned academies and in better-life magazines, simply by deciding that they want to regain direct contact with the natural forces that have shaped man's biological and mental being. The visceral determinants of life are so permanent, and so demanding, that mankind cannot long safely ignore them. In my opinion, the world in the year 2000 will reflect less the projections of technologists, sociologists, and economists than the vital needs and urges of biological man.

At the end of his *Education,* written in 1905, the American historian Henry Adams gloomily predicted that the cult of the Dynamo was to be the modern substitute for the cult of the Virgin. The present scene appears to confirm his prediction, but the future may still prove him wrong. One begins to perceive disenchantment among the worshipers of the Dynamo, and, more importantly, there are encouraging signs of unrest in the younger generation. Frequently in the past the son rejected what the father had taken for granted, and civilization thus took a step forward. Beatniks, hipsters, teddy boys, provos, hooligans, *blousons noirs,* and the countless other types of rebellious youths are probably as ignorant, foolish, and irresponsible as conventional people believe them to be. But conventionality rarely has the knack of guessing who will shape the future. The substantial citizen of Imperial Rome and the orthodox Jews of the synagogue looked down on the small tradesmen, fishermen, beggars, and the prostitutes who followed Jesus as he preached contempt for the existing order of things. Yet Imperial Rome and the Temple collapsed, while Jesus' followers changed the course of history.

The vision of the future, as seen in the light of the new intellectual pessimism or of the dismal optimism of some technologists, would be terribly depressing if it were not for the fact that it so much resembles visions of the future throughout history. Pessimists have repeatedly predicted the end of the world, and utopians have tried to force mankind into many forms of straitjackets. Those who did not live before 1789, wrote the French statesman Talleyrand, have not known the *douceur de vivre*. This melancholy belief did not prevent Talleyrand from living very successfully to the age of eighty-four. When he died in 1838, the storming of the Bastille was half a century past. The Industrial Revolution had begun, and the world certainly looked uncouth and dark to many genteel souls. But we now realize that it was a beginning rather than an end. Like Talleyrand, and like society after the Industrial Revolution, we too shall probably manage to find an acceptable formula for our times. Fortunately, the creativeness of life always transcends the imaginings of scholars, technologists, and science-fiction writers.

THE SECOND COMING

William Butler Yeats

Turning and turning in the widening gyre
The falcon cannot hear the falconer;
Things fall apart; the centre cannot hold;
Mere anarchy is loosed upon the world,
The blood-dimmed tide is loosed, and everywhere
The ceremony of innocence is drowned;
The best lack all conviction, while the worst
Are full of passionate intensity.

Surely some revelation is at hand;
Surely the Second Coming is at hand.
The Second Coming! Hardly are those words out
When a vast image out of *Spiritus Mundi*
Troubles my sight: somewhere in sands of the desert
A shape with lion body and the head of a man,
A gaze blank and pitiless as the sun,
Is moving its slow thighs, while all about it
Reel shadows of the indignant desert birds.
The darkness drops again; but now I know
That twenty centuries of stony sleep
Were vexed to nightmare by a rocking cradle,
And what rough beast, its hour come round at last,
Slouches towards Bethlehem to be born?

INTRODUCTION TO NORSE MYTHOLOGY

Edith Hamilton

The world of Norse mythology is a strange world. Asgard, the home of the gods, is unlike any other heaven men have dreamed of. No radiancy of joy is in it, no assurance of bliss. It is a grave and solemn place, over which hangs the threat of an inevitable doom. The gods know that a day will come when they will be destroyed. Sometime they will meet their enemies and go down beneath them to defeat and death. Asgard will fall in ruins. The cause the forces of good are fighting to defend against the forces of evil is hopeless. Nevertheless, the gods will fight for it to the end.

Necessarily the same is true of humanity. If the gods are finally helpless before evil, men and women must be more so. The heroes and heroines of the early stories face disaster. They know that they cannot save themselves, not by any courage or endurance or great deed. Even so, they do not yield. They die resisting. A brave death entitles them—at least the heroes—to a seat in Valhalla, one of the halls in Asgard, but there too they must look forward to final defeat and destruction. In the last battle between good and evil they will fight on the side of the gods and die with them.

This is the conception of life which underlies the Norse religion, as somber a conception as the mind of man has ever given birth to. The only sustaining support possible for the human spirit, the one pure unsullied good men can hope to attain, is heroism; and heroism depends on lost causes. The hero can prove what he is only by dying. The power of good is shown not by triumphantly conquering evil, but by continuing to resist evil while facing certain defeat.

Such an attitude toward life seems at first sight fatalistic, but actually the decrees of an inexorable fate played no more part in the Norseman's scheme of existence than predestination did in St. Paul's or in that of his militant Protestant followers, and for precisely the same reason. Although the Norse hero was doomed if he did not yield, he could choose between yielding or dying. The decision was in his own hands. Even more than that. A heroic death, like a martyr's death, is not a defeat, but a triumph. The hero in one of the Norse stories who laughs aloud while his foes cut his heart out of his living flesh shows himself superior to his conquerors. He says to them, in effect, You can do nothing to me because I do not care what you do. They kill him, but he dies undefeated.

This is stern stuff for humanity to live by, as stern in its totally different way as the Sermon on the Mount, but the easy way has never in the long run commanded the allegiance of mankind. Like the early Christians, the Norsemen measured their life by heroic standards. The Christian, however, looked forward to a heaven of eternal joy. The Norseman did not. But it would appear that for unknown centuries, until the Christian missionaries came, heroism was enough.

The poets of the Norse mythology, who saw that victory was possible in death and that courage was never defeated, are the only spokesmen for the belief of the whole great Teutonic race—of which England is a part, and ourselves through the first settlers in America. Everywhere else in northwestern Europe the early records, the traditions, the songs and stories, were obliterated by the priests of Christianity, who felt a bitter hatred for the paganism they had come to destroy. It is extraordinary how clean a sweep they were able to make. A few bits survived: *Beowulf* in Engand, the *Nibelungenlied* in Germany, and some stray fragments here and there. But if it were not for the two icelandic Eddas we should know practically nothing of the religion which molded the race to which we belong. In Iceland, naturally by its position the last northern country to be Christianized, the missionaries seem to have been gentler, or, perhaps, they had less influence. Latin did not drive Norse out as the literary tongue. The people still told the old stories in the common speech, and some of them were written down, although by whom or when we do not know. The oldest manuscript of the *Elder Edda* is dated at about 1300, three hundred years after the Christians arrived, but the poems it is made up of are purely pagan and adjudged by all scholars to be very old. The *Younger Edda,* in prose, was written down by one Snorri Sturluson in the last part of the twelfth century. The chief part of it is a technical treatise on how to write poetry, but it also contains some prehistoric mythological material which is not in the *Elder Edda*.

The *Elder Edda* is much the more important of the two. It is made up of separate poems, often about the same story, but never connected with each other. The material for a great epic is there, as great as the *Iliad,* perhaps even greater, but no poet came to work it over as Homer did the early stories which preceded the *Iliad*. There was no man of genius in the Northland to weld the poems into a whole and make it a thing of beauty and power; no one even to discard the crude and the commonplace and cut out the childish and wearisome repetitions. There are lists of names in the *Edda* which sometimes run on unbroken for pages. Nevertheless the somber grandeur of the stories comes through in spite of the style. Perhaps no one should speak of "the style" who cannot read ancient Norse; but all the translations are so alike in being singularly awkward and involved that one cannot but suspect the original of being responsible, at least in part. The poets of the *Elder Edda* seem to have had conceptions greater than their skill to put them into words. Many of the stories are splendid. There are none to equal them in Greek mythology, except those retold by the tragic poets. All the best Northern tales are tragic, about men and women who go steadfastly forward to meet death, often deliberately choose it, even plan it long beforehand. The only light in the darkness is heroism.

A SONG BY NEZAHUALCOYOTL

Aztec

1

The sweet-voiced *quetzal* there, ruling the earth, has intoxicated my soul.

2

I am like the quetzal bird, I am created in the one and only God; I sing sweet songs among the flowers; I chant songs and rejoice in my heart.

3

The fuming dewdrops from the flowers in the fields intoxicate my soul.

4

I grieve to myself that ever this dwelling on earth should end.

5

I foresaw, being a Mexican, that our rule began to be destroyed, I went forth weeping that it was to bow down and to be destroyed.

6

Let me not be angry that the grandeur of Mexico is to be destroyed.

7

The smoking stars gather against it; the one who cares for flowers is about to be destroyed.

8

He who cared for books wept, he wept for the beginning of the destruction.

THE HOLLOW MEN

T. S. Eliot

Mistah Kurtz—he dead.
A penny for the Old Guy.

I

We are the hollow men
We are the stuffed men
Leaning together
Headpiece filled with straw. Alas!
Our dried voices, when
We whisper together
Are quiet and meaningless
As wind in dry grass
Or rats' feet over broken glass
In our dry cellar

Shape without form, shade without color,
Paralyzed force, gesture without motion;

Those who have crossed
With direct eyes, to death's other Kingdom
Remember us—if at all—not as lost
Violent souls, but only
As the hollow men
The stuffed men.

II

Eyes I dare not meet in dreams
In death's dream kingdom
These do not appear:
There, the eyes are
Sunlight on a broken column
There, is a tree swinging
And voices are
In the wind's singing
More distant and more solemn
Than a fading star.

Let me be no nearer
In death's dream kingdom
Let me also wear
Such deliberate disguises
Rat's coat, crowskin, crossed staves
In a field
Behaving as the wind behaves
No nearer—

Not that final meeting
In the twilight kingdom

III

This is the dead land
This is cactus land
Here the stone images
Are raised, here they receive
The supplication of a dead man's hand
Under the twinkle of a fading star.

Is it like this
In death's other kingdom
Waking alone
At the hour when we are
Trembling with tenderness
Lips that would kiss
Form prayers to broken stone.

IV

The eyes are not here
There are no eyes here
In this valley of dying stars
In this hollow valley
This broken jaw of our lost kingdoms

In this last of meeting places
We grope together
And avoid speech
Gathered on this beach of the tumid river

Sightless, unless
The eyes reappear
As the perpetual star
Multifoliate rose
Of death's twilight kingdom

The hope only
Of empty men.

V

Here we go round the prickly pear
Prickly pear prickly pear
Here we go round the prickly pear
At five o'clock in the morning.

Between the idea
And the reality
Between the motion
And the act
    Falls the Shadow
                    For Thine is the Kingdom

Between the conception
And the creation
Between the emotion
And the response
Falls the Shadow
                        Life is very long

Between the desire
And the spasm
Between the potency
And the existence
Between the essence
And the descent
Falls the Shadow

                    For Thine is the Kingdom
For Thine is
Life is
For Thine is the

This is the way the world ends
This is the way the world ends
This is the way the world ends
Not with a bang but a whimper.

WE AWAIT

James Branch Cabell

... I ask of literature precisely those things of which I feel the lack in my own life. I appeal for charity, and implore that literature afford me what I cannot come by in myself. ... For I want distinction for that existence which ought to be peculiarly mine, among my innumerable fellows who swarm about earth like ants. Yet which one of us is noticeably, or can be appreciably different, in this throng of human ephemeræ and all their millions and inestimable millions of millions of predecessors and oncoming progeny? And even though one mote may transiently appear exceptional, the distinction of those who in their heydays are "great" personages—much as the Emperor of Lilliput overtopped his subjects by the breadth of Captain Gulliver's nail—must suffer loss with time, and must dwindle continuously, until at most the man's recorded name remains here and there in sundry pedants' libraries. There were how many dynasties of Pharaohs, each one of whom was absolute lord of the known world, and is to-day forgotten? Among the countless popes who one by one were adored as the regent of Heaven upon earth, how many persons can to-day distinguish? And does not time breed emperors and czars and presidents as plentiful as blackberries, and as little thought of when their season is out? For there is no perpetuity in human endeavor: we strut upon a quicksand: and all that any man may do for good or ill is presently forgotten, because it does not matter. I wail to a familiar tune, of course, in this lament for the evanescence of human grandeur and the perishable renown of kings. And indeed to the statement that imperial Cæsar is turned to clay and Mizraim now cures wounds, and that in short Queen Anne is dead, we may agree lightly enough; for it is, after all, a matter of no personal concern: but how hard it is to concede that the banker and the rector and the traffic-officer, to whom we more immediately defer, and we ourselves, and the little gold heads of our children, may be of no importance, either! ... In art it may so happen that the thing which a man makes endures to be misunderstood and gabbled over: yet it is not the man himself. We retain the *Iliad,* but oblivion has swallowed Homer so deep that many question if he ever existed at all. ... So we pass as a cloud of gnats, where I want to live and be thought of, if only by myself, as a distinguishable entity. And such distinction is impossible in the long progress of suns, whereby in thought to separate the personality of any one man from all others that have lived, becomes a task to stagger Omniscience. ...

I want my life, the only life of which I am assured, to have symmetry or, in default of that, at least to acquire some clarity. Surely it is not asking very much to wish that my personal conduct be intelligible to me! Yet it is forbidden to know for what purpose this universe was intended, to what end it was set a-going, or why I am here, or even what I had preferably do while here. It vaguely seems to me that I am expected to perform an allotted task, but as to what it is I have no notion. . . . And indeed, what have I done hitherto, in the years behind me? There are some books to show as increment, as something which was not anywhere before I made it, and which even in bulk will replace my buried body, so that my life will be to mankind no loss materially. But the course of my life, when I look back, is as orderless as a trickle of water that is diverted and guided by every pebble and crevice and grass-root it encounters. I seem to have done nothing with premeditation, but rather, to have had things done to me. And for all the rest of my life, as I know now, I shall have to shave every morning in order to be ready for no more than this! . . . I have attempted to make the best of my material circumstances always; nor do I see to-day how any widely varying course could have been wiser or even feasible: but material things have nothing to do with that life which moves in me. Why, then, should they direct and heighten and provoke and curb every action of life? It is against the tyranny of matter I would rebel,—against life's absolute need of food, and books, and fire, and clothing, and flesh, to touch and to inhabit, lest life perish. . . . No, all that which I do here or refrain from doing lacks clarity, nor can I detect any symmetry anywhere, such as living would assuredly display, I think, if my progress were directed by any particular motive. . . . It is all a muddling through, somehow, without any recognizable goal in view, and there is no explanation of the scuffle tendered or anywhere procurable. It merely seems that to go on living has become with me a habit. . . .

And I want beauty in my life. I have seen beauty in a sunset and in the spring woods and in the eyes of divers women, but now these happy accidents of light and color no longer thrill me. And I want beauty in my life itself, rather than in such chances as befall it. It seems to me that many actions of my life were beautiful, very long ago, when I was young in an evanished world of friendly girls, who were all more lovely than any girl is nowadays. For women now are merely more or less good-looking, and as I know, their looks when at their best have been painstakingly enhanced and edited. . . . But I would like this life which moves and yearns in me, to be able itself to attain to comeliness, though but in transitory performance. The life of a butterfly, for example, is just a graceful gesture: and yet, in that its loveliness is complete and perfectly rounded in itself, I envy this bright flicker through existence. And the nearest I can come to my ideal is punctiliously to pay my bills, be polite to my wife, and contribute to deserving charities: and the programme does not seem, somehow, quite adequate. There are my books, I know; and there is beauty "embalmed and treasured up" in many pages of my books, and in the books of other persons, too, which I may read at will: but this desire inborn in me is not to be satiated by making marks upon paper, nor by deciphering them. . . . In short, I am enamored of that flawless beauty of which all poets have perturbedly divined the existence somewhere, and which life as men know it simply does not afford nor anywhere foresee. . . .

And tenderness, too—but does that appear a mawkish thing to desiderate in life? Well, to my finding human beings do not like one another. Indeed, why should they, being rational creatures? All babies have a temporary lien on tenderness, of course: and therefrom children too receive a dwindling income, although on looking back, you will recollect that your childhood was upon the whole a lonesome and much put-upon period. But all grown persons ineffably distrust one another. . . . In courtship, I grant you, there is a passing aberration which often mimics tenderness, sometimes as the result of honest delusion, but more frequently as an ambuscade in the endless struggle between man and woman. Married people are not ever tender with each other, you will notice: if they are mutually civil it is much: and physical contacts apart, their relation is that of a very moderate intimacy. My own wife, at all events, I find an unfailing mystery, a Sphinx whose secrets I assume to be not worth knowing: and, as I am mildly thankful to narrate, she knows very little about me, and evinces as to my affairs no morbid interest. That is not to assert that if I were ill she would not nurse me through any imaginable contagion, nor that if she were drowning I would not plunge in after her, whatever my delinquencies at swimming: what I mean is that, pending such high crises, we tolerate each other amicably, and never think of doing more. . . . And from our blood-kin we grow apart inevitably. Their lives and their interests are no longer the same as ours, and when we meet it is with conscious reservations and much manufactured talk. Besides, they know things about us which we resent. . . . And with the rest of my fellows, I find that convention orders all our dealings, even with children, and we do and say what seems more or less expected. And I know that we distrust one another all the while, and instinctively conceal or misrepresent our actual thoughts and emotions when there is no very apparent need. . . . Personally, I do not like human beings because I am not aware, upon the whole, of any generally distributed qualities which entitle them as a race to admiration and affection. But toward people in books—such as Mrs. Millamant, and Helen of Troy, and Bella Wilfer, and Mélusine, and Beatrix Esmond,—I may intelligently overflow with tenderness and caressing words, in part because they deserve it, and in part because I know they will not suspect me of being "queer" or of having ulterior motives. . . .

And I very often wish that I could know the truth about just any one circumstance connected with my life. . . . Is the phantasmagoria of sound and noise and color really passing or is it all an illusion here in my brain? How do you know that you are not dreaming me, for instance? In your conceded dreams, I am sure, you must invent and see and listen to persons who for the while seem quite as real to you as I do now. As I do, you observe, I say! and what thing is it to which I so glibly refer as I? If you will try to form a notion of yourself, of the sort of a something that you suspect to inhabit and partially to control your flesh and blood body, you will encounter a walking bundle of superfluities: and when you mentally have put aside the extraneous things,—your garments and your members and your body, and your acquired habits and your appetites and your inherited traits and your prejudices, and all other appurtenances which considered separately you recognize to be no integral part of you,—there seems to remain in those pearl-colored brain-cells, wherein is your ultimate lair, very little save a faculty for receiving sensations, of which you know the larger portion to be illusory. And surely, to be just a very gullible consciousness provisionally existing among inexplicable mysteries, is not an enviable plight. And yet this life—to which I cling tenaciously,—comes to no more. Meanwhile I hear men talk about "the truth"; and they even wager handsome sums upon their knowledge of it: but I align myself with "jesting Pilate," and echo the forlorn query that recorded time has left unanswered. . . .

Then, last of all, I desiderate urbanity. I believe this is the rarest quality in the world. Indeed, it probably does not exist anywhere. A really urbane person—a mortal open-minded and affable to conviction of his own shortcomings and errors, and unguided in anything by irrational blind prejudices, —could not but in a world of men and women be regarded as a monster. We are all of us, as if by instinct, intolerant of that which is unfamiliar: we resent its impudence: and very much the same principle which prompts small boys to jeer at a straw-hat out of season induces their elders to send missionaries to the heathen. The history of the progress of the human race is but the picaresque romance of intolerance, a narrative of how—what is it Milton says?—"truth never came into the world but, like a bastard, to the ignominy of him that brought her forth, till time hath washed and salted the infant, declared her legitimate, and churched the father of his young Minerva." And I, who prattle to you, very candidly confess that I have no patience with other people's ideas unless they coincide with mine: for if the fellow be demonstrably wrong I am fretted by his stupidity, and if his notion seem more nearly right than mine I am infuriated. . . . Yet I wish I could acquire urbanity, very much as I would like to have wings. For in default of it, I cannot even manage to be civil to that piteous thing called human nature, or to view its parasites, whether they be politicians or clergymen or popular authors, with one half the commiseration which the shifts they are put to, quite certainly, would rouse in the urbane. . . .

So I in point of fact desire of literature, just as you guessed, precisely those things of which I most poignantly and most constantly feel the lack in my own life. And it is that which romance affords her postulants. The philtres of romance are brewed to free us from this unsatisfying life that is calendared by fiscal years, and to contrive a less diastrous elusion of our own personalities than many seek dispersedly in drink and drugs and lust and fanaticism, and sometimes in death. For, beset by his own rationality, the normal man is goaded to evade the strictures of his normal life, upon the incontestable ground that it is a stupid and unlovely routine; and to escape likewise from his own personality, which bores him quite as much as it does his associates. So he hurtles into these very various roads from reality, precisely as a goaded sheep flees without notice of what lies ahead. . . .

And romance tricks him, but not to his harm. For, be it remembered that man alone of animals plays the ape to his dreams. Romance it is undoubtedly who whispers to every man that life is not a blind and aimless business, not all a hopeless waste and confusion; and that his existence is a pageant (appreciatively observed by divine spectators), and that he is strong and excellent and wise: and to romance he listens, willing and thrice willing to be cheated by the honeyed fiction. The things of which romance assures him are very far from true: yet it is solely by believing himself a creature but little lower than the cherubim that man has by interminable small degrees become, upon the whole, distinctly superior to the chimpanzee: so that, however extravagant may seem these flattering whispers to-day, they were immeasurably more remote from veracity when men first began to listen to their sugared susurrus, and steadily the discrepancy lessens. To-day these things seem quite as preposterous to calm consideration as did flying yesterday: and so, to the Gradgrindians, romance appears to discourse foolishly, and incurs the common fate of prophets: for it is about to-morrow and about the day after to-morrow, that romance is talking, by means of parables. And all the while man plays the ape to fairer and yet fairer dreams, and practise strengthens him at mimickry. . . .

THE TUNNEL

Friedrich Dürrenmatt

The young man who boarded his usual train that Sunday afternoon was twenty-four years old and fat. He was fat in order to protect himself, for anything he perceived out of the ordinary terrified him. Indeed, this clarity of vision was probably the only real ability he possessed, and even this was a burden to him. Although his fat gave a general protection to his body, he found it necessary to stuff every sort of hole in his body through which the terrifying influences might reach him. He smoked cigars (Ormond Brazil 10). He wore a pair of sunglasses over his ordinary glasses. He even stuffed his ears with wads of cotton wool. At twenty-four he was still dependent on his parents, a consequence of rather nebulous studies at the University. And the University was two hours away from home by train. Departure time five-fifty. Arrival at seven twenty-seven.

And so this student, fat and twenty-four years old, boarded his usual Sunday train to attend a seminar the following day. The fact that he had already decided to skip class was irrelevant. As he left his home town the afternoon sun shone from a cloudless summer sky. It was pleasant weather for a trip he knew almost by heart. The train's route lay between the Alps and the

Juras, past rich villages and towns, over a river and, after some twenty minutes further travel, into a little tunnel just beyond Burgdorf. The train was overcrowded and he had entered at one of the front cars. With considerable difficulty he worked his way toward the rear. Perspiring, and with two pairs of glasses, he offered an oafish appearance. All the travellers were sitting closely packed, some even on suitcases. All the second-class compartments were occupied, and only the first-class compartments were relatively empty. The young man fought through the melee of families and recruits, students and lovers, falling against this one or that one as the train swayed, stumbling against stomachs and breasts until he came to a seat in the last car. At last he had found space enough to have a bench to himself, a pleasant surprise, since third-class coaches are seldom divided into compartments with benches. Opposite him, playing a solitary game of chess, he noted a man even fatter than himself, and on the same bench, near the corridor, sat a red-haired girl reading a novel. The young man gratefully chose the window seat on the empty bench. He had just lit an Ormond Brazil 10 when the train entered the little tunnel. Of course he had travelled this stretch many times before, almost every Saturday and Sunday throughout the past year, but he had never found the opportunity to examine the tunnel closely. He had, in fact, been only vaguely aware of it. Several times he had intended to give it his full attention, but each time he had been thinking of other matters, and each time the brief plunge into darkness had passed unnoticed, so fast was the train and so brief its plunge into the darkness of the little tunnel.

And even this time he had not been thinking of the tunnel and so had forgotten to take off his sunglasses. Outside the tunnel the sun had been shining with all its force, flooding the hills and woods and the distant chain of the Juras with golden evening light. Even the little houses of the town through which they had just passed had seemed built of gold. This abrupt passage from light to darkness must then be the reason why the tunnel seemed so much longer than usual. He waited patiently in the dark compartment for the return to daylight. At any moment the first pale shimmer of daylight would gleam on his window-pane, widen as quickly as a flash of lightning, then close in powerfully with its full yellow brightness. Nevertheless, the darkness lasted. He took off his sunglasses. At about the same time the girl lit a cigarette. As her match flared orange he thought he detected a grim annoyance in her face. No doubt she resented the interruption in her perusal of her novel. He looked at his wrist watch. The luminous dial said six-ten.

He leaned back, settling himself in the corner between window and compartment wall, and directed his thoughts to the complications of his studies. No one really believed he was studying at all. He thought of the seminar he had to attend the next day, and which he would not attend. Each of his activities seemed a pretext designed to achieve order behind the facade of routine pursuits. Perhaps what he sought was not order itself, but only a semblance of order. The art of an actor who used his fat, his cigars and his cotton wool as make-up for a genteel comedy, while all the while he knew himself to be a part of some monstrous farce. When he next looked at his watch the time was six-fifteen. The trains was still in the tunnel. He felt confused. At last the light bulbs flickered and the compartment brightened. The red-haired girl returned to her novel and the fat gentleman resumed his solitary chess game. The whole compartment now appeared reflected in the window. But outside, on the other side of the window, the tunnel was still there.

He stepped into the corridor in which a tall man was walking up and down restlessly. He observed the light raincoat and the black scarf around the gentleman's neck. Surely there was no need for a scarf in this weather? A black scarf? He peered into the other compartments in the rear coach. The passengers were reading their newspapers or chatting. Normal. He returned to his corner and sat down. The tunnel must come to an end any minute now. At any second? His wrist watch read six-twenty. He felt an obscure annoyance with himself for not having paid more attention to the tunnel on previous trips. They had been in the tunnel for a quarter of an hour now. And surely, allowing for the speed of the train, it must be one of the longest tunnels in Switzerland. Or perhaps he had taken the wrong train. But he could recall no other tunnel of such length and importance within twenty minutes of his home. On impulse he asked the fat chess player if the train were indeed bound for Zurich. The man confirmed this. The student ventured again that he hadn't known that there was such a long tunnel on this part of the journey. The chess player was more than a little annoyed to have his difficult considerations interrupted a second time. He replied testily that in Switzerland there were a great many tunnels, in fact, an extraordinary number of tunnels, that he was actually travelling in Switzerland for the first time, but that an affluence of tunnels was the first thing one noticed about Switzerland, and indeed, his statistical almanac confirmed the fact that no country possessed such a positive abundance of tunnels as Switzerland! And he added that now he must excuse himself; he was very sorry, really, but a most difficult chess problem in regard to the Nimzowitsch Defence occupied his mind and he could afford no further diversions. The last remark was polite, but firm. It was evident that no further conversation could be expected from the chess player and, in any event, he could be of little use, since the route was new to him.

At that moment the conductor appeared, and the student had high hopes that his ticket would be refused. The official was pale and scrawny. He gave an impression of nervousness as he remarked to the girl near the door that she would have to change trains at Olten. Although Olten was also a regular stop on the Zurich run, the young man did not give up hope of being on the wrong train, so complete was his conviction that he had mistaken trains in boarding. He didn't doubt that he would have to pay extra fare, but he accepted the expense with equanimity. The return to daylight would be cheap at the price. He therefore handed his ticket to the conductor and said that his destination was Zurich. He accomplished the speech without once removing the Ormond Brazil 10 from his mouth.

"But the gentleman is on the right train," replied the conductor as he inspected the ticket.

"But we're going through a tunnel!" The young man had spoken with considerable anger. He was determined to put an end to the confusion. The official replied that they had just passed Herzogenbuchsee and would soon approach Langenthal where the train was due at six-twenty. The young man looked at his watch. Six-twenty. But they had been travelling through the tunnel for the past twenty minutes, he persisted. The conductor raised his brows.

"This is the Zurich train," he said, now looking for the first time toward the window. "Six-twenty," he said again, uneasily. "We'll be in Olten soon. Arrival time six thirty-seven. We must have gone into some bad weather suddenly. A storm. Yes. That's why it's dark."

The gentleman with the Nimzowitsch Defence problem entered the conversation now. He had been holding out his ticket (and holding up his game) for some time, but the conductor had not yet noticed him. "Nonsense," he interjected. "Nonsense! We're travelling through a tunnel. I can see the rock clearly. Looks like granite. Switzerland has more tunnels than all the rest of the world put together. Read it in a statistical almanac."

The conductor relieved him of his ticket, and repeated pleadingly that this was truly the Zurich train. Unmollified, the young man demanded to speak to the Chief Conductor. The ticket collector now felt his dignity to have been abused. He directed the student to the front of the train, but reiterated huffily that the train was going to Zurich, that the time was now six twenty-five, that in twelve minutes time (according to the summer schedule) the train would arrive in Olten, and that the young man should have no further doubts on that point. *He* travelled this train at least twelve times a month.

Nevertheless the young scholar set off to find the Chief Conductor. Movement through the crowded train now seemed even more difficult than before. The train must be travelling exceedingly fast. In any event, it was making a frightful racket. He stuffed the wads of cotton a little more firmly into his ears, for he had loosened them in order to speak to the ticket collector. The passengers were behaving calmly. This train was no different from any other Sunday afternoon train, and no one appeared worried. In the second-class compartments he came upon an Englishman standing by the corridor window. "Simplon," he was saying, as he tapped the pane with his pipe and beamed inanely.

Things were very much as usual in the dining car too. No seats were vacant, and neither waiters nor diners, occupied with Wiener Schnitzel and rice, made any comment on the tunnel. But there, near the exit of the dining car, he recognized the red bag of the Chief Conductor.

"What can I do for you, sir?" The Chief Conductor was a tall man, quiet behind a carefully groomed black mustache and neat rimless glasses.

"We have been in a tunnel for twenty-five minutes."

The Conductor did not look toward the windows, as the young man might have expected, but turned to a nearby waiter. "Give me a packet of Ormond 10," he said. "I smoke the same brand as the gentleman here." The waiter, however, indicated that the brand was not in stock, and the young man, glad of an opportunity for further conversation, proffered a Brazil.

"Thank you," returned the Conductor. "In Olten I shall hardly have time to buy any. You are doing me a great favor. Smoking is a most important business. Will you come this way, please?"

Mystified, the young man followed him into the freight car ahead of the diner.

"The next car is the locomotive," offered the official. "This is the front of the train."

A sickly yellow light burned amid the baggage. Most of the car lay in total darkness. The side doors were barred, as was the small window beside them, and through its irons the greater blackness of the tunnel seeped in. The trunks, many decorated with hotel stickers, the bicycles and the baby carriage that composed the cargo of the coach seemed haphazardly arranged. The Chief Conductor, an obviously precise man, hung his red bag on a near-by hook.

"What can I do for you?" he asked again, without, however, looking at the student. Instead, he began to enter neat columns in a book he had taken from his pocket.

"We have been in a tunnel since Burgdorf," answered the young man with determination. "There is no such enormous tunnel on this line. I know. I travel back and forth every week on this train."

The Chief Conductor continued to write. "Sir," he said, stepping close to his inquisitor, so close that their bodies almost touched, "sir, I have little to tell you. I have no idea how we got into this tunnel. I have no explanation for it. But I ask you to consider this. We are moving along on tracks: therefore this tunnel leads somewhere. We have no reason whatever to believe that anything is wrong with this tunnel, except, of course, that there seems to be no end to it." The Chief Conductor still held the unlit Ormond Brazil 10 between his lips. He had spoken extremely quietly, yet with such dignity and clarity, and with such assurance, that his words were audible despite the increased noise of the baggage car.

"Then I must ask you to stop the train," said the young man impatiently. "I really don't understand you. If there's something wrong with this tunnel —and it seems you can't explain even its existence—then your duty is to stop this train at once."

"Stop the train?" returned the older man slowly. It seemed he had already thought of that, but, as he informed his companion, it was a serious matter to stop a train. With this, he shut the book and laid it in the red bag which was swaying to and fro on its hook. Then he carefully lit the Ormond 10. The young man offered to pull the emergency brake overhead, and was on the point of releasing the lever, when suddenly he staggered forwards and was sent crashing against the wall. At the same moment, the baby carriage rolled toward him and several trunks slid by. The Chief Conductor swayed strangely and began to move, hands outstretched, through the freight car.

"We are going downhill!" he announced as he joined the young man now leaning against the wall. But the expected crash of hurtling train against granite tunnel did not occur. There was no shattering of telescoped coaches. Once again the train seemed to be running on a level. The door opened at the other end of the car. In the bright light of the diner, until the door swung to again, they could see the passengers merrily toasting one another's health.

"Come into the locomotive." At this point the Chief Conductor was peering throughtfully, almost menacingly at the student. He opened the door nearby. As he did so a rush of tempestuous heat-laden air struck the pair with such force that they were driven back against the wall. At the same moment a frightful clatter resounded through the almost empty freight car.

"We'll have to climb over to the engine," he cried into the younger man's ear. Despite his shouting, his voice was hardly audible. He then disappeared through the right-angle of the open doorway. The student followed cautiously in the direction of the swaying and brightly lit engine. He didn't know why he was climbing, but at this point determination had overcome reason. He found himself on a pitching platform between the two cars, and clung desperately to the iron rails on both sides. Although the terrific draught moderated but slightly as he inched his way up to the locomotive, he dreaded the wind less than the immediate nearness of the tunnel walls. They were hidden from him in the blackness, but were nevertheless frighteningly close. It was necessary to focus all his attention on the engine ahead, yet the pounding of the wheels and the hissing vibrating push of air against him gave him the feeling of careening, at the speed of a falling star, into a world of stone.

A board just wide enough to walk on crossed the gap between the cars and ran the length of the engine. Above and parallel to it, a curving metal rod served as railing. To reach the plank he would have to make a jump of nearly a yard. He braced himself, leapt, and pushed himself along the board. His progress was slow, since he had to press close to the outside of the engine to keep his foothold. It was not until he reached the long side of the engine and was fully exposed to the roaring hurricane of wind and to the menacing cliff walls now brilliantly illuminated by the engine lights that he began to realize his fear. But just then he was rescued by the Chief Conductor who pulled him through a small door into the engine. Exhausted, the young man lay against the wall. He was grateful for the sudden quiet. With the engine door shut, the steel walls of the giant locomotive deadened the noise almost completely.

"Well, we've lost the Ormond Brazil too," said the Conductor. "It wasn't a very sensible idea to light one before starting the climb, but they break so easily in one's pocket. It's their unusual length."

The young man was delighted to converse normally again. The close and terrifying rock walls had reminded him uncomfortably of his everyday world, of its ever similar days and years. The thought occurred to him that their boring similitude had perhaps been only a preparation for the present moment: that this was a moment of initiation, of truth, this departure from the surface of the earth and precipitous descent into the womb of the earth. He took another brown package from his right coat pocket and offered the Chief Conductor a new cigar. He took one himself, and carefully they lit their Brazils from the Conductor's lighter.

"I am very fond of these Ormonds," said the older man, "but one must pull very hard on them. Otherwise they go out so easily."

For some reason these words made the student suspicious. Was the Conductor as uncomfortable as he about the tunnel? For the tunnel still ran on interminably, and his mind persisted in the thought that surely the tunnel must stop, even as a dream can end, all of a sudden.

"Six-forty," he said, consulting his watch. "We should be in Olten now." Even as he spoke, he thought of the hills and woods radiant only a short while ago in the late golden sun. The thought could have been present in both their minds. Nevertheless, the two men stood and smoked and leaned against their wall.

"Keller is my name," announced the Conductor as he puffed at his Brazil. The student refused to change the topic of conversation.

"The climb to the engine was very dangerous, didn't you think? At least it was for me. I'm not used to that sort of thing. Anyway, I'd like to know why you've brought me here."

"I don't know," said Keller. "I wanted time to consider."

"Time to consider?"

"Yes," returned the Chief Conductor. "That's right." And he went on smoking. Just then the engine reeled over at a still steeper angle.

"We could go into the engineer's cabin," suggested Keller. He did not, however, leave his position against the wall. Annoyed by his companion's indecisiveness, the young man stepped briskly along the corridor to the driver's cabin, then abruptly stopped.

"Empty!" he said to the Conductor who had now moved up behind him. "The driver's seat is empty!" They went into the cabin. It was swaying too, for the engine was still tearing through the tunnel at enormous speed, bearing the train along with it, as though the weight of the coaches behind no longer counted.

"Allow me," said the Chief Conductor. He pressed some levers and pulled the emergency brake. There was no change. "We tried to stop the engine earlier. As soon as we noticed the alteration in the tracks. It didn't stop then either."

"It certainly isn't stopping now," said the other. He pointed to the speed indicator. "A hundred. Has the engine ever done a hundred before?"

"Good heavens! It has never gone so fast. Sixty-five at the most."

"Exactly. And the speed is increasing. Now the speedometer says a hundred and five. We must be falling." He went up to the window, but he couldn't keep his balance. He was pressed with his face against the glass, so fantastic was their speed. "The engine driver?" he shouted as he stared at the rock masses streaking towards him in the glare of the arc lights, disappearing above him and below him on either side of the engineer's cabin.

"He jumped off," Keller yelled back. He was now sitting on the floor, his back against the controls.

"When?" The student pursued the matter obstinately. Keller hesitated a while. He decided to relight his Ormond, an awkward task, for his legs were then at the same height as his head while the train continued its roll to one side.

"Five minutes after the switch. No use thinking to save him. Freight car man abandoned the train too."

"And you? asked the student.

"I am in charge of this train. I, too, have always lived without hope."

"Without hope," repeated the young man. By then he was lying on the glass pane, face pressed against glass. Glass and engine and human flesh were pressed together above the abyss. "Back in the compartment," he thought, "we had entered the tunnel, but we didn't know that even then everything was already lost. We didn't think that anything had changed, and yet the shaft of the depths had already received us, and we had entered our abyss."

"I'll have to go to the rear," shouted the Chief Conductor. "The coaches will be in a panic. Everyone will be trying to get to the rear of the train."

"That's true." The student thought of the chessplayer and of the red-haired girl with her novel. He handed Keller his remaining packages of Ormond Brazil. "Take them. You'll lose your cigar again when you climb over."

"Aren't you coming?" The Conductor was once more on his feet and with difficulty he had begun to clamber up the funnel of the corridor. The student gazed at the useless instruments, at the useless ridiculous levers and switches shining silver-like in the glare of the cabin lights.

"A hundred and thirty," he called. "I don't think you'll be able to get to the coaches above us at this speed."

"It's my duty," shouted Keller over his shoulder.

"Certainly," returned the young man. He didn't bother turning his head to watch the other's senseless efforts.

"At least I have to try," yelled the Conductor. He was already far over the head of the fat young man. He braced elbows and thighs against slippery walls and seemed, indeed, to be making some progress. But just then the engine took a further turn downwards. It hurtled towards the interior of the earth, goal of all things, in its terrible plunge. Keller now was directly over his friend who lay face downwards on the silver gleaming window at the bottom of the driver's cabin. His strength gave. Suddenly he fell, crashed against the control panel and came to rest on the window beside his companion.

"What are we to do?" he cried, clinging to the young man's shoulders and shouting into his ear. The very fact that it was now necessary to shout alarmed him. The noise of the unrushing walls had destroyed even the quiet of the engine.

The younger man lay motionless on the pane of glass which separated him from the depths below. His fat body and weighty flesh were of no further use to him, no protection now.

"What are we to do?" persisted the Chief Conductor.

"Nothing," came the merciless reply. Merciless, yet not without a certain ghostly cheerfulness. Now, for the first time, his glasses were gone and his eyes were wide open. Greedily he sucked in the abyss through those wide-open eyes. Glass and metal splinters from the shattered control panel now studded his body. And still he refused to tear his thirsting eyes from the deadly spectacle below. As the first crack widened in the window beneath them, a current of air whisted into the cabin. It seized his two wads of cotton wool and swept them upwards like arrows into the corridor shaft overhead. He watched them briefly and spoke once more.

"Nothing. God let us fall. And now we'll come upon him."

DESERT PLACES

Robert Frost

Snow falling and night falling fast, oh, fast
In a field I looked into going past,
And the ground almost covered smooth in snow,
But a few weeds and stubble showing last.

The woods around it have it—it is theirs.
All animals are smothered in their lairs.
I am too absent-spirited to count;
The loneliness includes me unawares.

And lonely as it is, that loneliness
Will be more lonely ere it will be less—
A blanker whiteness of benighted snow
With no expression, nothing to express.

They cannot scare me with their empty spaces
Between stars—on stars where no human race is.
I have it in me so much nearer home
To scare myself with my own desert places.

A REASONABLE LIFE
IN A MAD WORLD

Irwin Edman

That the world is mad has been the judgment of self-denominated sane philosophers from the Greeks to the present day. It is not a discovery of our own age that both the public and private lives of human beings are dominated by folly and stupidity. Philosophers pressing the point have brought such charges not against human nature only—that is, the world of human relations—but against that larger universe in which the world of human relations is set. As far back as the Book of Job and probably much further back, for there must have been at least gruntingly articulate Jobs in prehistory, it is not only men who have been declared mad: by any standards of rationality the universe itself has been called irrational, pointless, meaningless, with incidental, unintended overtones of cruelty and injustice.

With the provincialism of each generation, ours imagines that the causes of cynicism and despair are new in our time. There have, of course, been modern improvements and refinements of stupidity and folly. No previous generation has been by way of organizing itself with insane efficiency for blowing the whole race to smithereens. It does not take a particularly logical mind at the present moment to discover that the world is quite mad, though a great many critics apparently think that the cruel absurdity of technical efficiency combined with moral bankruptcy is a discovery that it took great wit on their part to turn up.

Reputations are being made by reiterating, to the extent of four or five hundred pages, that collective modern man is a technical genius merged with a moral imbecile.

The first encouragement I can bring is the reminder that the kind of madness which we all realize to be the present state of the world is not something new. It is, just like everything else in the modern world, bigger and more streamlined, if not better. It is a pity some of the great satirists are dead; Swift and Voltaire would have given their eyeteeth for the present situation. And Aristophanes would scarcely have believed it. But the essential charges they would bring against the present time and the essential absurdities they would show up are not different in essence now from what they were.

Neither nature nor man appears reasonable by reasonable human standards. So acutely does this seem to many people to be true that in almost exuberant desperation they decide to march crazily in the insane procession. Existentialists make a cult of anxiety and despair and find a kind of wry comfort in saying, Since the world is absurd, let absurdity and irony be our

29

standards. There are others who say—and the currency of an ersatz theological literature shows how epidemic they are—that since the world and mankind at present seem so palpably absurd it simply can't be true, and history, as Toynbee now assures us, moves delightfully and progressively to fulfillment in the Church of God—a kind of quiet, English Church incorporating the best of Islam, Buddhism, Confucianism, and a little, even, of the Hebrew prophets and the secular sciences.

The excitements and confused urgencies of the present time may seem to make hysteria or mystical narcosis or hedonistic excitement tantamount to a philosophy. But the still, small voice of rationality persists. And the question still remains the same as that propounded by the Greeks long ago: How, in a world certainly not at first acquaintance rational-appearing, is it possible to lead a rational life?

It seems mad now to say that anyone could believe, as the Fabians did (including such unsentimental people as George Bernard Shaw and Sidney and Beatrice Webb and Graham Wallas and later H. G. Wells), that the world could be transformed into a livable, beautiful, reasonable place by the co-operation of reasonable men. It is not simply that the violent external events of the past generation have revealed to us how precarious were security and comfort, and for how few it obtained at all.

But the psychological sciences have revealed to us the deep sources of violence, confusion, hysteria, and madness in ourselves. What perhaps a generation ago seemed a melodramatic aphorism when Santayana uttered it seems now to be a hitting of the nail on the head: "The normal man holds a lunatic in leash." The definition needs to be amended. In the light of the past twenty-five years, the normal man no longer *does* hold a lunatic in leash. The fact that even talk about a third world war has become standard has practically made lunacy respectable. It is now become a stamp of madness to talk as if one seriously believed that a peaceful and just world were possible.

And yet the sentiment of rationality persists and the hope persists also that it is not impossible, at least in imagination, to dream and in organized effort to work for what seems "an ordered, coherent world society." The most ardent workers for such a world, however, realize that there is plenty of madness left, out of which a third world war may come.

II

The persistence of power politics, the greed for privilege, the insane clutching of wealth, the pathological tribalisms of nations, of class, and of race; it is this world in which we are actually living, and the human problem for anyone in it is to discover what is a reasonable life in such a world.

Is it to forget as far as possible and to live only in the moment and to make that moment as brief and bright as possible? Is it to surrender any hope for pleasure or happiness now and give one's dedicated and ruthless devotion to work for a more reasonable world? Is it to seek Nirvana or to seek some salvation in another world? There seems to be some sense in each answer, but which answer one chooses will depend ultimately on how one answers a basic question: Is the world always and necessarily mad? Is it completely mad now, and is it possible even now to understand the madness and, through understanding, to endure or change it?

Let us try as simply as possible to deal with some of these questions. First, is the world always and necessarily mad? By "the world," of course, one means both the processes of nature and the activities of human beings. For "world" in the first sense one had perhaps better use the word "universe." A thoroughly rational universe would be one which was achieving a purpose set down in advance, a purpose which in human terms made sense and which by human standards made moral sense. A rational universe might be one such as the Deists conceived in the eighteenth century, in which nature was simply reason incarnate or reason embodied in the vast machinery of things.

In one respect at least the advance of knowledge of the physical world has not made the world seem more irrational. It has made it seem orderly and regular. But in another respect an understanding of the causes and consequences of nature by conventional standards made nature seem wholly irrational. "I am what I am," said Jehovah in the Old Testament, as if that announcement were sufficient explanation of his wrathful ways. "It is what it is and it does what it does" may be said to be the conclusions of empirical physical science. It is maddening to rational creatures to discover they were born into a world which is not particularly interested in human purposes, which perhaps permits and sustains these purposes but is innocent of any solicitude concerning them. The rain notoriously falls on the just and the unjust, and the just feel highly put upon. Death is no respecter of persons; plagues fell the virtuous. The most generous and devoted enterprises are washed away by floods along with the conspiracies of the sinister and hateful.

Theologians have spent a good deal of time trying to gloss away the irrationalities of the universe, explaining that God moves in a mysterious or at least salutary way, his morally therapeutic wonders to perform. Job was not greatly impressed by his comforters, and neither are we. But if exasperated humans have criticized the world in general, they have been especially critical of the madness of their fellow men. Voltaire found his greatest weapon of satire in treating cruelty, barbarism, and superstition not as evil but as absurd.

The most serious and damaging charge we can bring against civilization is that by the very standards of civilization it is a ridiculous failure. It takes a high degree of sophistication and technical resources to make such an international shambles as we seem fated to do. It takes something like genius in folly to have millions starving in the midst of plenty, to have technological magic whose fruits are poverty, squalor, anarchy, and death; it takes a refinement of absurdity to use the most generous aphorism of the highest religions to justify or rationalize intolerance, violence, and our established international disorder.

Now about the first irrationality: that of the universe itself. Perhaps the only reasonable attitude is that of resignation and endurance of it. Perhaps it is only the persistence of our childhood wishes and expectations that has led to an assumption that the universe must conform to human purposes and that it is shockingly unreasonable of it not so to conform. We can, within the limits of a world not made for us, make it conform to ideals and values which flower out of nature itself. Part of the life of reason is a contemplation of the unchanging and unchangeable elements in the world of nature; part of it is a sedulous attempt to discover the ways of changing the world in the interest of human values.

With respect to the world of human activities there has been an accelerated desperation at the present time. In the old days when humor could still flourish in Central Europe it used to be said that the difference between the temper of Berlin and Vienna could be stated as follows: In Berlin when things went wrong it was remarked: "The situation is serious but not hopeless"; in Vienna with smiling deprecation the Viennese used to say: "The situation is hopeless but not serious." The Berlin version seems of late more greatly to have impressed the world.

Though Existentialism may be said to describe the world as being both hopeless and trivial, if one so conceives the realm of human affairs the Epicurean prescription for a reasonable life is perhaps the best that one can find. However clouded and uncertain the future, there is at least possible for the lucky and the prudent a brief, bright interval in which they may find luster and to which their refined sensibilities may give luster. In a world without meaning they may find exquisite nuances of meaning in the arts, in friendship, in love.

The trouble with the Epicurean solution and abdication is that it is always haunted by a scruple of conscience and the shadow of despair. There is something already tarnished in a brightness that declares itself both ultimately meaningless and transient. Sorrow and inhibition and regret dog the footsteps of the Epicurean in a world where folly is no longer a joke but a terrifying threat to all mankind.

There are those, therefore, in our own age who jump to the other extreme. One insists that one *must* give up any hope for present happiness and give one's dedicated and ruthless devotion to work for a better world. I have friends, especially in social or government work or in the social sciences, who regard humor, irony, urbanity, or relaxation with something of the same moral impatience with which a missionary might watch the natives of the Fiji Islands dance or lounge in the sun. There is so little time; it is later than you think; there is no time for comedy. Urbanity is a form of evasion, and laughter is a form of bourgeois or decadent callousness. Let us gird our loins and work together rapidly for the common good or we shall all in common be destroyed. The psychiatric departments of hospitals number among their patients a good many people who in their earnest haste to save the world from destruction ended up by destroying their equilibrium and almost themselves. The tension of moral earnestness, the refusal to permit the enjoyment of even such goods as are possible in a chaotic world, is one of the diseases of our civilization, not a sign of its health. If Epicureanism leads to dismay, unrelieved moral dedication leads to fanaticism. Neither the playboy nor the zealot is a true or adequate incarnation of the life of reason.

Those who recognize the disillusion of a pleasure philosophy or the destructiveness of a moral fanaticism have begun in our age, as they have in other ages, to turn to otherworldly philosophies. They have tried to seek an inward light unquenchable by external circumstances. They have tried in spirit to follow the Indian saint into the wilderness or the monk into his cell or the mystic into his remote meditation. They have sought Nirvana, or a Oneness with the One, or an Aloneness with the Alone. The follies of society are not cured by the incantations of pure mysticism, and the search for oblivion is really a pathological attempt simply to become oblivious to the actual and remediable conflicts and disorders in society.

There are still others than the pleasure-lovers, the Nirvana-seekers, the devotees of such mystics, who have sought to make a prescription for a reasonable life. Among those others now epidemic are followers of historians and zoologists who with the theological wave of a wand discover that a palpably absurd world is somehow moving toward a cozy fulfillment where, as I heard Mr. Toynbee say, "God is Love." It would seem a strange moment to detect the course of history as the operations of universal love when the world is being filled with universal hate.

No, I do not think any of these ersatz solutions will do. The pressure of events simply confirms again what the life of reason does consist in: a brave contemplation of what things are discoverably like and a resolute attempt to improve the lot of man in the conditions into which he finds himself born. The life of reason must always have a stoic element because there is no sign that either the follies of humanity or the uncaring order of nature will ever be magically transformed.

The life of reason must also contain an element of hope, for it is quite clear, as the history of every improvement in man's estate has shown us, that human intelligence accompanied by human goodwill may profoundly improve the life of mankind. The life of reason must include the pleasure principle also, for what else gives life meaning if not joy and delight of life, and what a folly it would be not to cherish and embrace, not to nourish then, even in a sick society, that which yields the fruit of a quickened, multiplied awareness, the substance of vision and of joy. The universe may be pointless, but there are many good points in it. Our urgencies may be intense, but the world does not end with us or even with our own civilization; nor, if we do not quench intelligence and generosity in ourselves, is it a foregone conclusion that our civilization must end. And the best insurance, perhaps, of maintaining both is to reaffirm the quality of life itself, of its possibility of beauty and its intimations of order and of justice.

THE END OF THE WORLD

Archibald MacLeish

Quite unexpectedly as Vasserot
The armless ambidextrian was lighting
A match between his great and second toe
And Ralph the lion was engaged in biting
The neck of Madame Sossman while the drum
Pointed, and Teeny was about to cough
In waltz-time swinging Jocko by the thumb—
Quite unexpectedly the top blew off:

And there, there overhead, there, there, hung over
Those thousands of white faces, those dazed-eyes,
There in the starless dark, the poise, the hover,
There with vast wings across the canceled skies,
There in the sudden blackness, the black pall
Of nothing, nothing, nothing—nothing at all.

PART TWO

The Word

Language is of such primary importance to man that many cultures ascribe to it an independent existence which predates even the gods which created the universe. The Uitoto's story of the creation, for example, opens in this way: "In the beginning, the word gave origin to the Father." The word, then, especially in primitive culture, is often thought to have a magic creative power of its own. As Margot Astrov points out in "The Magic Creativeness of the Word," the utterance of the word strengthens the gods, cures sickness, protects one in battle—in other words gives one control over the incalculable forces of one's environment. The word gives order to all being.

In our more sophisticated, ostensibly more rational society we have come to discount not only the magic qualities of the word but also the power of the word—the ability of the word to order and communicate knowledge and experience. We have come to take language for granted and very seldom think about the words we use or the way we use them. We think of language as being mere words, mere rhetoric, of no particular value in themselves since they are merely symbols arbitrarily selected to stand for certain objects or ideas. This attitude, according to S. I. Hayakawa, Aldous Huxley, George Orwell, and George Steiner, is affecting our ability to cope with our experiences effectively.

Granted, the word is not magic, at least not in the way early societies thought it was, but, in a very real sense, the word does have a creative power of its own; not over inanimate nature, but over men. In "Words and Their Meanings," Aldous Huxley says, "Words are magical in the way they affect the minds of those who use them . . . words have power to mold men's thinking, to canalize their feeling, to direct their willing and acting." Language is the primary force of civilization, of culture. Without language, man would be even less than the larger apes, if he existed at all. Language is the primary tool of man—that which gives him an edge over the physically superior beings inhabiting this planet with him. Language is the carrier of man's collective knowledge, his collective truths, his collective experiences.

Experience, truth, and man's understanding of his environment differ from one culture or society to the next, and language both molds and reflects these differing perceptions. In "Man at the Mercy of His Language" Peter

Farb tells us: "Language directs the perceptions of its speakers to certain things; it gives them ways to analyze and categorize experience." As Norman Cousins says, then, language is an environment having "as much to do with the philosophical and politic conditioning of a society as geography or climate." When we deny the importance or validity of the language or dialect of another, we are denying the importance of the culture that is expressed and shaped through this language or dialect. And when we deny the importance or power of our language, we have begun to move toward the reality of that final fear, the disintegration of our way of life, because we will have denied ourselves the only means by which we can effectively order our perceptions and we will have denied the total validity of our culture. And those few who have the ability and the will to manipulate language, to hide reality in the web of imprecise words and aphorisms, to soothe fears and give concreteness to certain abstract truths, will then control us through this artificial reality. Language dies when it can no longer express the truth, the reality, the experience of its speakers. And when language dies, with it dies the civilization, for, in the words of George Steiner, "It is language that has been the vessel of human grace and the prime carrier of human civilization."

THE RETREAT FROM THE WORD

George Steiner

The Apostle tells us that in the beginning was the Word. He gives us no assurance as to the end.

It is appropriate the he should have used the Greek language to express the Hellenistic conception of the *Logos,* for it is to the fact of its Greek-Judaic inheritance that Western civilization owes its essentially verbal character. We take this character for granted. It is the root and bark of our experience and we cannot readily transpose our imaginings outside it. We live inside the act of discourse. But we should not assume that a verbal matrix is the only one in which the articulations and conduct of the mind are conceivable. There are modes of intellectual and sensuous reality founded not on language, but on other communicative energies such as the icon or the musical note. And there are actions of the spirit rooted in silence. It is difficult to *speak* of these, for how should speech justly convey the shape and vitality of silence? But I can cite examples of what I mean.

In certain Oriental metaphysics, in Buddhism and Taoism, the soul is envisioned as ascending from the gross impediments of the material, through domains of insight that can be rendered by lofty and precise language, toward ever deepening silence. The highest, purest reach of the contemplative act is that which has learned to leave language behind it. The ineffable lies beyond the frontiers of the word. It is only by breaking through the walls of language that visionary observance can enter the world of total and immediate understanding. Where such understanding is attained, the truth need no longer suffer the impurities and fragmentation that speech necessarily entails. It need not conform to the naïve logic and linear conception of time implicit in syntax. In ultimate truth, past, present, and future are simultaneously comprised. It is the temporal structure of language that keeps them artificially distinct. That is the crucial point.

The holy man, the initiate, withdraws not only from the temptations of worldly action; he withdraws from speech. His retreat into the mountain cave or monastic cell is the outward gesture of his silence. Even those who are only novices on this arduous road are taught to distrust the veil of language, to break through it to the more real. The Zen *koan*—we know the sound of two hands clapping, what is the sound of one?—is a beginner's exercise in the retreat from the word.

The Western tradition also knows transcendences of language toward silence. The Trappist ideal goes back to abandonments of speech as ancient as those of the Stylites and Desert Fathers. St. John of the Cross expresses the austere exaltation of the contemplative soul as it breaks loose from the moorings of common verbal understanding:

> *Entréme donde no supe,*
> *Y quedéme no sabiendo,*
> *Toda sciencia trascendiendo.* *

But to the Western point of view, this order of experience inevitably carries a flavor of mysticism. And, whatever our lip service (itself a revealing term) to the sanctity of the mystic vocation, the commanding Western attitude is that of Cardinal Newman's quip, that mysticism begins in mist and ends in schism. Very few Western poets—perhaps only Dante—have persuaded the imagination of the authority of transrational experience. We accept, at the lambent close of the *Paradiso,* the blindness of eye and understanding before the totality of vision. But Pascal is nearer the mainstream of classic Western feeling when he says that the silence of cosmic space strikes terror. To the Taoist that selfsame silence conveys tranquillity and the intimation of God.

The primacy of the word, of that which can be spoken and communicated in discourse, is characteristic of the Greek and Judaic genius and carried over into Christianity. The classic and the Christian sense of the world strive to order reality within the governance of language. Literature, philosophy, theology, law, the arts of history, are endeavors to enclose within the bounds of rational discourse the sum of human experience, its recorded past, its present condition and future expectations. The code of Justinian, the *Summa* of Aquinas, the world chronicles and compendia of medieval literature, the *Divina Commedia,* are attempts at total containment. They bear solemn witness to the belief that all truth and realness—with the exception of a small, queer margin at the very top—can be housed inside the walls of language.

LANGUAGE AND SURVIVAL

S. I. Hayakawa

What Animals Shall We Imitate?

People who think of themselves as tough-minded and realistic, among them influential political leaders and businessmen as well as go-getters and hustlers of smaller caliber, tend to take it for granted that human nature is selfish and that life is a struggle in which only the fittest may survive. According to this philosophy, the basic law by which man must live, in spite of his surface veneer of civilization, is the law of the jungle. The "fittest" are

---

* I entered where I did not know, and I remained not knowing, all knowledge transcending.

those who can bring to the struggle superior force, superior cunning, and superior ruthlessness.

The wide currency of this philosophy of the "survival of the fittest" enables people who act ruthlessly and selfishly, whether in personal rivalries, business competition, or international relations, to allay their consciences by telling themselves that they are only obeying a law of nature. But a disinterested observer is entitled to ask whether the ruthlessness of the tiger, the cunning of the ape, and obedience to the law of the jungle are, in their *human* applications, actually evidences of *human* fitness to survive. If human beings are to pick up pointers on behavior from the lower animals, are there not animals other than beast of prey from which we might learn lessons in survival?

We might, for example, point to the rabbit or the deer and define fitness to survive as superior rapidity in running away from our enemies. We might point to the earthworm or the mole and define it as the ability to keep out of sight and out of the way. We might point to the oyster or the housefly and define it as the ability to propagate our kind faster than our enemies can eat us up. If we are looking to animals for models of behavior, there is also the pig, an animal which many human beings have tried to emulate since time immemorial. (It will be remembered that in the *Odyssey* Circe gave ingenious and practical encouragement to those inclined this way.) In Aldous Huxley's *Brave New World,* we see a world designed by those who would model human beings after the social ants. The world, under the management of a super-brain-trust, might be made as well-integrated, smooth, and efficient as an ant colony and, as Huxley shows, just about as meaningless. If we simply look to animals in order to define what we mean by "fitness to survive," there is no limit to the subhuman systems of behavior that can be devised: we may emulate lobsters, dogs, sparrows, parakeets, giraffes, skunks, or the parasitical worms, because they have all obviously survived in one way or another. We are still entitled to ask, however, if *human* survival does not revolve around a different kind of fitness from that of the lower animals.

Because of the wide prevalence of the dog-eat-dog, survival-of-the-fittest philosophy in our world (although the H-bomb has awakened *some* people to the need for a change in philosophy), it is worth while to look into the present scientific standing of the phrase "survival of the fittest." Biologists distinguish between two kinds of struggle for survival. First, there is the *interspecific* struggle, warfare between different species of animals, as between wolves and deer, or men and bacteria. Second, there is the *intraspecific* struggle, warfare among members of a single species, as when rats fight other rats, or men fight other men. A great deal of evidence in modern biology indicates that those species which have developed elaborate means of intraspecific competition often unfit themselves for interspecific competition, so that such species are either already extinct or are threatened with extinction at any time. The peacock's tail, although useful in sexual competition against other peacocks, is only a hindrance in coping with the environment or competing against other species. The peacock could therefore be wiped out overnight by a sudden change in ecological balance. There is evidence, too, that strength and fierceness in fighting and killing other animals, whether in interspecific or intraspecific competition, have never been enough of themselves to guarantee the survival of a species. Many a mammoth reptile, equipped with magnificent offensive and defensive armaments, ceased millions of years ago to walk the earth.[1]

If we are going to talk about human survival, one of the first things to do, even if we grant that men must fight to live, is to distinguish between those qualities that are useful to men in fighting the environment and other species (for example, floods, storms, wild animals, insects, or bacteria) and those qualities (such as aggressiveness) that are useful in fighting other men.

The principle that if we don't hang together we shall all hang separately was discovered by nature long before it was put into words by man. Cooperation within a species (and sometimes with other species) is essential to the survival of most living creatures. Man, moreover, is the *talking* animal—and any theory of human survival that leaves this fact out of account is no more scientific than would be a theory of beaver survival that failed to consider the interesting uses a beaver makes of its teeth and flat tail. Let us see what talking—human communication—means.

Cooperation

When someone shouts at you, "Look out!" and you jump just in time to avoid being hit by an automobile, you owe your escape from injury to the fundamental cooperative act by which most of the higher animals survive, namely, communication by means of noises. You did not see the car coming; nevertheless, someone did, and he made certain *noises to communicate* his alarm to you. In other words, although your nervous system did not record the danger, you were unharmed because another nervous system did. You had, for the time being, the advantage of someone else's nervous system in addition to your own.

Indeed, most of the time when we are listening to the noises people make or looking at the black marks on paper that stand for such noises, we are drawing upon the experiences of others in order to make up for what we ourselves have missed. Obviously the more an individual can make use of the nervous systems of others to supplement his own, the easier it is for him to survive. And, of course, the more individuals there are in a group cooperating by making helpful noises at each other, the better it is for all—within the limits, naturally, of the group's talents for social organization. Birds and

[1] "For example, the brain of the massive [about two tons] stegosaur weighed only about 70 grams, or 2½ ounces. . . . By contrast, even the brain of the sheep—which is not a particularly brilliant animal—weighs 130 grams, greater both in absolute size and even more relatively to body size. . . . So far as strength is concerned, nothing could stop one of the great dinosaurs when it was on its way; but while it is all very well to be able to go where you are going, the reasons for going and what is seen and understood on the way are even more important." Weston La Barre, *The Human Animal* (1954), pp. 24–25.

animals congregate with their own kind and make noises when they find food or become alarmed. In fact, gregariousness as an aid to survival and self-defense is forced upon animals as well as upon men by the necessity of uniting nervous systems even more than by the necessity of uniting physical strength. Societies, both animal and human, might almost be regarded as huge cooperative nervous systems.

While animals use only a few limited cries, however, human beings use extremely complicated systems of sputtering, hissing, gurgling, clucking, cooing noises called *language,* with which they express and report what goes on in their nervous systems. Language is, in addition to being more complicated, immeasurably more flexible than the animal cries from which it was developed—so flexible indeed that it can be used not only to report the tremendous variety of things that go on in the human nervous system but also *to report those reports.* That is, when an animal yelps, he may cause a second animal to yelp in imitation or alarm; the second yelp, however, is not *about* the first yelp. But when a man says, "I see a river," a second man can say, "He says he sees a river"—which is a statement about a statement. About this statement-about-a-statement further statements can be made—and about these, still more. *Language, in short, can be about language.* This is a fundamental way in which human noisemaking systems differ from the cries of animals.

The Pooling of Knowledge

In addition to having developed language, man has also developed means of making, on clay tablets, bits of wood or stone, skins of animals, and paper, more or less permanent marks and scratches which *stand for* language. These marks enable him to communicate with people who are beyond the reach of his voice, both in space and in time. There is a long course of evolution from the marked trees that indicated Indian trails to the metropolitan daily newspaper, but they have this in common: They pass on what one individual has known to other individuals, for their convenience or, in the broadest sense, instruction. Many of the lopstick trails in the Canadian woods, marked by Indians long since dead, can be followed to this day. Archimedes is dead, but we still have his reports on what he observed in his experiments in physics. Keats is dead, but he can still tell us how he felt on first reading Chapman's Homer. From our newspapers and radios we learn with great rapidity facts about the world we live in. From books and magazines we learn how hundreds of people whom we shall never be able to see have felt and thought. All this information is helpful to us at one time or another in throwing light on our own problems.

A human being, then, is never dependent on his own experience alone for his information. Even in a primitive culture he can make use of the experience of his neighbors, friends, and relatives, which they communicate to him by means of language. Therefore, instead of remaining helpless because of the limitations of his own experience and knowledge, instead of having to discover what others have already discovered, instead of exploring the false trails they explored and repeating their errors, he can *go on from where they left off.* Language, that is to say, makes progress possible.

Indeed, most of what we call the human characteristics of our species are expressed and developed through our ability to cooperate by means of our systems of making meaningful noises and meaningful scratches on paper. Even people who belong to backward cultures in which writing has not been invented are able to exchange information and to hand down from generation to generation considerable stores of traditional knowledge. There seems, however, to be a limit both to the amount and to the trustworthiness of knowledge that can be transmitted orally.[2] But when writing is invented, a tremendous step forward is taken. The accuracy of reports can be checked and rechecked by successive generations of observers. The amount of knowledge accumulated ceases to be limited by people's ability to remember what has been told them. The result is that in any literate culture of a few centuries' standing, human beings accumulate vast stores of knowledge—far more than any individual in that culture can read in his lifetime, let alone remember. These stores of knowledge, which are being added to constantly, are made widely available to all who want them through such mechanical processes as printing and through such distributive agencies as the book trade, the newspaper and magazine trade, and library systems. The result is that all of us who can read any of the major European or Asiatic languages are potentially in touch with the intellectual resources of centuries of human endeavor in all parts of the civilized world.

A physician, for example, who does not know how to treat a patient suffering from a rare disease can look up the disease in the *Index Medicus,* which will send him in turn to medical journals published in all parts of the world. In these he may find records of similar cases as reported and described by a physician in Rotterdam, Holland, in 1913, by another physician in Bangkok, Siam, in 1935, and by still other physicians in Kansas City in 1954. With such records before him, he can better handle his own case. Again, if a person is worried about ethics, he is not limited to the advice of the pastor of the Elm Street Baptist Church; he may go to Confucius, Aristotle, Jesus, Spinoza, and many others whose reflections on ethical problems are on record. If he is worried about love, he can get insights not only from his mother or best friend but from Sappho, Ovid, Propertius, Shakespeare, Havelock Ellis, or any of a thousand others who knew something about it and wrote down what they knew.

Language, that is to say, is the indispensable mechanism of human life— of life such as ours that is molded, guided, enriched, and made possible by the accumulation of the *past* experience of members of our own species. Dogs and cats and chimpanzees do not, so far as we can tell, increase their wisdom, their information, or their control over their environment from one

---

[2] This is so despite the fact that preliterate people often exhibit remarkable feats of memory, such as the ability to remember every landmark and detail of a journey that may extend for hundreds of miles, or the ability to recall verbatim folk tales and sagas that may take days to recite. Literate people, who rely on notebooks and reference books, have relatively very poor memories.

generation to the next. But human beings do. The cultural accomplishments of the ages, the invention of cooking, of weapons, of writing, of printing, of methods of building, of games and amusements, of means of transportation, and the discoveries of all the arts and sciences come to us as *free gifts from the dead*. These gifts, which none of us has done anything to earn, offer us not only the opportunity for a richer life than our forebears enjoyed but also the opportunity to add to the sum total of human achievement by our own contributions, however small they may be.

To be able to read and write, therefore, is to learn to profit by and take part in the greatest of human achievements—that which makes all other achievements possible—namely, the pooling of our experiences in great cooperative stores of knowledge, available (except where special privilege, censorship, or suppression stand in the way) to all. From the warning cry of primitive man to the latest newsflash or scientific monograph, language is social. Cultural and intellectual cooperation is the great principle of *human* life.

This is by no means an easy principle to accept or to understand—except as a kind of pious truism that we should like, because we are well-meaning people, to believe. We live in a highly competitive society, each of us trying to outdo the other in wealth, in popularity or social prestige, in dress, in scholastic grades or golf scores. As we read our daily papers, there is always news of conflict rather than of cooperation—conflict between labor and management, between rival corporations or movie stars, between rival political parties and nations. Over us all hangs the perpetual fear of another war even more unthinkably horrible than the last. One is often tempted to say that conflict, rather than cooperation, is the great governing principle of human life.

But what such a philosophy overlooks is that, despite all the competition at the surface, there is a huge substratum of cooperation *taken for granted* that keeps the world going. The coordination of the efforts of engineers, actors, musicians, cameramen, utilities companies, typists, program directors, advertising agencies, writers, and hundreds of others is required to put on a single television program. Hundreds of thousands of persons cooperate in the production of motor cars, including suppliers and shippers of raw materials from different parts of the earth. Any organized business activity whatsoever is an elaborate act of cooperation, in which every individual worker contributes his share. A lockout or a strike is a *withdrawal of cooperation:* things are regarded as "back to normal" when cooperation is restored. We may indeed as individuals compete for jobs, but our function in the job, once we get it, is to contribute at the right time and place to that innumerable series of cooperative acts that eventually result in automobiles being manufactured, in cakes appearing in pastry shops, in department stores being able to serve their customers, in the trains and airlines running as scheduled. And what is important for our purposes here is that all this coordination of effort necessary for the functioning of society is *of necessity achieved by language or else it is not achieved at all.*

The Niagara of Words

And how does all this affect Mr. T. C. Mits?[3] From the moment he switches on an early-morning news broadcast until he falls asleep at night over a novel or a magazine, he is, like all other people living in modern civilized conditions, swimming in words. Newspaper editors, politicians, salesmen, disc jockeys, columnists, luncheon-club speakers, and clergymen; colleagues at work, friends, relatives, wife and children; market reports, direct-mail advertising, books, and billboards—all are assailing him with words all day long. And Mr. Mits himself is constantly contributing to that verbal Niagara every time he puts on an advertising campaign, delivers a speech, writes a letter, or even chats with his friends.

When things go wrong in Mr. Mits' life—when he is worried, perplexed, or nervous, when family, business, or national affairs are not going as he thinks they should, when he finds himself making blunder after blunder in personal or financial matters—he blames a number of things as responsible for his difficulties. Sometimes he blames the weather, sometimes his health or the state of his nerves, sometimes his glands; if the problem is a larger one, he may blame his environment, the economic system he lives under, a foreign nation, or the cultural pattern of his society. When he is pondering the difficulties of other people, he may attribute their troubles too to causes such as these, and he may add still another, namely, "human nature." (He doesn't blame his own "human nature" unless he is in a very bad way indeed.) It rarely, if ever, occurs to him to investigate, among other things, the nature and constituents of that daily verbal Niagara as a possible source of trouble.

Indeed, there are few occasions on which Mr. Mits thinks about language as such. He pauses from time to time over a grammatical point. Sometimes he feels an uneasiness about his own verbal accomplishments, and so begins to consider improving his vocabulary. Occasionally, he runs into advertisements on "how to increase your word power," and wonders if he shouldn't take steps to become a more effective persuader—and he may buy a book or take a course, which may make him feel better for a while. Confronted by the Niagara of words—the magazines he hasn't time to keep up with and the books he knows he should read—he wonders if it wouldn't help to take a course in speed-reading.

Once in a while he is struck by the fact that some people (although he never includes himself among these) twist the meanings of words, especially during the course of arguments, so that words are often very tricky. Occasionally, too, he notices, usually with irritation, that words sometimes mean different things to different people. This condition, he feels, could be corrected if people would only consult their dictionaries oftener and learn the "true meanings" of words. He knows, however, that they will not—at least,

---

[3] Lillian and Hugh Lieber, of Long Island University, are responsible for christening this gentleman, "The Celebrated Man In The Street." Mits' wife's name is, of course, Wits. See *The Education of T. C. Mits* (1944) and *Mits, Wits, and Logic* (1960).

not any oftener than he does, which is not very often—so that he puts this failure down as another instance of the weakness of human nature.

This, unfortunately, is about the limit of Mr. Mits' linguistic speculations. And here Mr. Mits is representative not only of the general public, but also of many scientific workers, publicists, and writers. Like most people, he takes words as much for granted as the air he breathes, and gives them about as much thought. (After all, he has been talking ever since he can remember.) Mr. Mits' body automatically adjusts itself, within certain limits, to changes in climate or atmosphere, to shifts from cold to warm, from dry to moist, from fresh to foul; no conscious effort on his part is required to make these adjustments. Nevertheless, he is ready to acknowledge the effect that climate and air have upon his physical well-being, and he takes measures to protect himself from unhealthy air, either by getting away from it, or by installing air-conditioning systems to purify it. But Mr. Mits, like the rest of us, also adjusts himself automatically to changes in the verbal climate, from one type of discourse to another, from one set of terms to another, from the listening habits of one kind of social occasion to those of another kind of social occasion, without conscious effort. He has yet, however, to acknowledge the effect of his verbal climate on his mental health and well-being.

Nevertheless, Mr. Mits is profoundly involved in the words he absorbs daily and in the words he uses daily. Words in the newspaper make him pound his fist on the breakfast table. Words his superiors speak to him puff him out with pride, or send him scurrying to work harder. Words about himself, which he has overheard being spoken behind his back, worry him sick. Words which he spoke before a clergyman some years ago have tied him to one woman for life. Words written down on pieces of paper keep him at his job, or bring bills in his mail every month which keep him paying and paying. Words written down by other people, on the other hand, keep them paying him month after month. With words woven into almost every detail of his life, it seems amazing that Mr. Mits' thinking on the subject of language should be so limited.

Mr. Mits has also noticed that when large masses of people, for example under totalitarian regimes, are permitted by their governments to hear and read only carefully selected words, their conduct becomes so strange that he can only regard it as mad. Yet he has observed that some individuals who have the same educational attainments and the same access to varied sources of information as he has, are nevertheless just as mad. He listens to the views of some of his neighbors and he cannot help wondering, "How can they think such things? Don't they see the same things happening that I see? They must be crazy!" "Does such madness," he asks, "illustrate again the 'inevitable frailty of human nature'?" Mr. Mits, who, as an American, likes to regard all things as possible, does not like the conclusion that "nothing can be done about it," but often he can hardly see how he can escape it. Occasionally, timidly, Mr. Mits approaches one more possibility: "Maybe I'm crazy myself. Maybe we're all nuts!" Such a conclusion leads to so complete an impasse, however, that he quickly drops the notion.

One reason for Mr. Mits' failure to get any further in his thinking about language is that he believes, as most people do, that words are not really important; what is important is the "ideas" they stand for. But what is an "idea" if it is not the *verbalization* of a cerebral itch? This, however, is something that has rarely, if ever, occurred to Mr. Mits. The fact that the implications of one set of terms may lead inevitably into blind alleys while the implications of another set of terms may not; the fact that the historical or sentimental associations that some words have make calm discussion impossible so long as those words are employed; the fact that language has a multitude of different kinds of use, and that great confusion arises from mistaking one kind of use for another; the fact that a person speaking a language of a structure entirely different from that of English, such as Japanese, Chinese, or Turkish, may not even think the same thoughts as an English-speaking person—these are unfamiliar notions to Mr. Mits, who has always assumed that the important thing is always to get one's "ideas" straight first, after which the words would take care of themselves.

Whether he realizes it or not, however, Mr. Mits is affected every hour of his life not only by the words he hears and uses, *but also by his unconscious assumptions about language.* If, for example, he likes the name Albert and would like to christen his child by that name but superstitiously avoids doing so because he once knew an Albert who committed suicide, he is operating, whether he realizes it or not, under certain assumptions about the relationship of language to reality. Such unconscious assumptions determine the effect that words have on him—which in turn determines the way he acts, whether wisely or foolishly. Words—the way he uses them and the way he takes them when spoken by others—largely shape his beliefs, his prejudices, his ideals, his aspirations. They constitute the moral and intellectual atmosphere in which he lives—in short, his *semantic environment.* . . . Human "fitness to survive" means the ability to talk and listen and read in ways that increase the chances for you *and fellow-members of your species* to survive *together.*

THE TOWER OF BABEL

The Old Testament

Book of Genesis

Chapter 11

1 And the whole earth was of one language, and of one speech.

2 And it came to pass, as they journeyed from the east, that they found a plain in the land of Shi'när; and they dwelt there.

3 And they said one to another, Go to, let us make brick, and burn them throughly. And they had brick for stone, and slime had they for morter.

4 And they said, Go to, let us build us a city and a tower, whose top *may reach* unto heaven; and let us make us a name, lest we be scattered abroad upon the face of the whole earth.

5 And the LORD came down to see the city and the tower, which the children of men builded.

6 And the LORD said, Behold, the people *is* one, and they have all one language; and this they begin to do: and now nothing will be restrained from them, which they have imagined to do.

7 Go to, let us go down, and there confound their language, that they may not understand one another's speech.

8 So the LORD scattered them abroad from thence upon the face of all the earth: and they left off to build the city.

9 Therefore is the name of it called Bā'bĕl; because the LORD did there confound the language of all the earth: and from thence did the LORD scatter them abroad upon the face of all the earth.

THE MAGIC CREATIVENESS OF THE WORD

Margot Astrov

The singing of songs and the telling of tales, with the American Indian, is but seldom a means of mere spontaneous self-expression. More often than not, the singer aims with the chanted word to exert a strong influence and to bring about a change, either in himself or in nature or in his fellow beings. By narrating the story of origin, he endeavors to influence the universe and to strengthen the failing power of the supernatural beings. He relates the myth of creation, ceremonially, in order to save the world from death and destruction and to keep alive the primeval spirit of the sacred beginning. Above all, it seems that the word, both in song and in tale, was meant to maintain and to prolong the individual life in some way or other—that is, to cure, to heal, to ward off evil, and to frustrate death. Healing songs, and songs intended to support the powers of germination and of growth in all their manifestations, fairly outnumber all other songs of the American Indian.

The word, indeed, is power. It is life, substance, reality. The word lived before earth, sun, or moon came into existence. Whenever the Indian ponders over the mystery of origin, he shows a tendency to ascribe to the word a creative power all its own. The word is conceived of as an independent entity, superior even to the gods. Only when the word came up mysteriously in the darkness of the night were the gods of the Maya enabled to bring forth the earth and life thereon. And the genesis of the Uitoto opens, characteristically enough, in this way: "In the beginning, the word gave origin to the

Father." The word is thought to precede the creator, for the primitive mind cannot imagine a creation out of nothingness. In the beginning was the thought, the dream, the word.

The concept of the word as Creative Potency lives on, even in the simplest song of hunting or of harvest, of battle, love, or death, as sung by the contemporary Indian.

It is this conscious certainty of the directing and influencing power of the word that gives a peculiar urging force to the following war song as heard by Robert H. Lowie among the Crow Indians:[1]

> Whenever there is any trouble,
> I shall not die but get through.
> Though arrows are many, I shall arrive.
> My heart is manly.

By chanting these words the singer raises himself to a higher level of achieving power; it is the magic quality of these words that will render him invulnerable.

It is not the herb administered to the sick which is considered the essential part of the cure, rather the words recited over that herb before its use. When a Hupa Indian is sick, the priest recites over him the account of a former cure whose central incident is the travel of some mythical person to the ends of the world to find release from his ailment. It is sufficient, says Goddard in his fine book on the Hupa, that the priest tell how one went: the spirit of the suffering person will follow the words even if he does not comprehend them.

A considerable number of songs of the Indian can be understood only from this firm belief in the word's power to bring about the desired result upon which the singer has fixed his mind.[2]

The word not only engenders courage and power of endurance, but it also is the ultimate source of material success. "I have always been a poor man. I do not know a single song," thus the Navajo informant of W. W. Hill began his account of agricultural practices.

> It is impossible [continues Dr. Hill] to state too strongly the belief as illustrated by that statement. It summed up in a few words the whole attitude of the Navaho toward life and the possibility of success. With respect to agriculture, it was not the vicissitudes of environment that made for successful crops or failures, but the control of the natural forces through rituals.[3]

And, quite logically, the Eskimo hunters think it a mistake to believe that women are weaker than men. For were it not for the incantations sung by

[1] R. H. Lowie, *Crow Religion, Anthropological Papers of the American Museum of Natural History,* XXV (1922), 410.

[2] Of course, it should be kept in mind that the tune which carries the word is of equal importance and may emanate as much magical power. Poetry, with the American Indian, is not an independent art but exists only in connection with music—that is, as song.

[3] W. W. Hill, *The Agricultural and Hunting Methods of the Navaho Indians,* Yale University Press, 1938, p. 52.

the women left behind, the hunter would return without game. Said one hunter to Bogoras: "In vain man walks around, searching; but those that sit by the lamp are really strong, for they know how to call the game to the shore. . . ."

A SONG OF HEALING

Chippewa

You will recover; you will walk again.
It is I who say it; my power is great.
Through our white shell
I will enable you to walk again.

SONG SUNG OVER A DYING PERSON

Chippewa

You are a spirit,
I am making you a spirit,
In the place where I sit
I am making you a spirit.

A PRAYER TO THE SUN

Blackfoot

Okōhe! okōhe! natosi! iyo! Sun, take pity on me; take pity on me. Old age, old age, we are praying to your old age, for that I have chosen. Your children, morningstar, seven stars, the bunched stars, these and all stars, we can call upon them for help. I have called upon all of them. Take pity on me; take pity on me that I may live a good life. My children now, I have led them to old age. That which is above, now I choose, take pity on me. Iyo! Now then, you people, I have called upon you sincerely for help. Especially for this, take pity on me. Good days and happy nights, for that take pity on me. Good days and happy nights is what I have called upon you for. You must listen to me. Iyo! Old age let me lead my children to it. Let me get a stock of many horses and other things. Take pity on me and grant all this. Then take pity on me that I may get the full pay for all my work. Iyo! Take pity on me; take pity on me; take heed.

WORDS AND THEIR MEANINGS

Aldous Huxley

For a long time past, thinking men have tended to adopt a somewhat patronizing attitude towards the words they use in communicating with their fellows and formulating their own ideas. "What do you read, my lord?" Polonius asked. And with all the method that was in his madness Hamlet scornfully replied, "Words, words, words." That was at the beginning of the seventeenth century; and from that day to this the people who think themselves realists have gone on talking about words in the same contemptuous strain.

There was a reason for this behavior—or at least an excuse. Before the development of experimental science, words were too often regarded as having magical significance and power. With the rise of science a reaction set in, and for the last three centuries words have been unduly neglected as things having only the slightest importance. A great deal of attention has been paid, it is true, to the technical languages in which men of science do their specialized thinking, particularly, of course, to mathematics. But the colloquial usages of everyday speech, the literary and philosophical dialects in which men do their thinking about the problems of morals, politics, religion and psychology—these have been strangely neglected. We talk about "mere matters of words" in a tone which implies that we regard words as things beneath the notice of a serious-minded person.

This is a most unfortunate attitude. For the fact is that words play an enormous part in our lives and are therefore deserving of the closest study. The old idea that words possess magical powers is false; but its falsity is the distortion of a very important truth. Words *do* have a magical effect—but not in the way that the magicians supposed, and not on the objects they were trying to influence. Words are magical in the way they affect the minds of those who use them. "A mere matter of words," we say contemptuously, forgetting that words have power to mold men's thinking, to canalize their feeling, to direct their willing and acting. Conduct and character are largely determined by the nature of the words we currently use to discuss ourselves and the world around us. The magician is a man who observes that words have an almost miraculous effect on human behavior and who thinks that they must therefore be able to exercise an equal power over inanimate nature. This tendency to objectify psychological states and to project them, thus objectified, into the external world is deeply rooted in the human mind. Men have made this mistake in the past, men are making it now; and the results are invariably deplorable. We owe to it not only the tragic fooleries of black magic, but also (and this is even more disastrous) most of the crimes and lunacies committed in the name of religion, in the name of patriotism, in the name of political and economic ideologies. In the age-long process by which men have consistently stultified all their finest aspirations, words have played a major part. It was, I believe, the realization of this fact that prompted the founders of the two great world religions to insist upon the importance of words. In the Christian gospels the reference to this matter is contained in one of those brief and enigmatic sayings which, like so many of the *logia,* unfortunately lend themselves to a great variety of interpretations. "But I say unto you, that every idle word that men shall speak, they shall give account thereof in the day of judgment. For by thy words thou shalt be justified, and by thy words thou shalt be condemned." It is possible to interpret this utterance in terms of a merely magical theory of the significance of language. It is equally possible to put another construction on the saying and to suppose that what Jesus was referring to was what may be called the psychological magic of words, their power to affect the thinking, feeling and behavior of those who use them. That it was the intention of the Buddha to warn men against such psychological magic the surviving documents leave us in no doubt whatever. "Right speech" is one of the branches of the Buddhist's Eightfold Path; and the importance of restraint in the use of words for intellectual purposes is constantly stressed in all those passages in the Pali Scriptures, where Gotama warns his followers against entangling themselves in the chains of metaphysical argument.

It is time now to consider a little more closely the mechanism by which words are able to exercise their psychological magic upon the minds of men and women. Human beings are the inhabitants, not of one universe, but of many universes. They are able to move at will from the world, say, of atomic physics to the world of art, from the universe of discourse called "chemistry" to the universe of discourse called "ethics." Between these various universes philosophy and science have not as yet succeeded in constructing any bridges. How, for example, is an electron, or a chemical molecule, or even a living cell related to the G minor quintet of Mozart or the mystical theology of St. John of the Cross? Frankly, we don't know. We have no idea how thought and feeling are related to physical events in a living brain and only the very vaguest notions about the way in which a brain is related to the charges of electrical energy which appear to be its ultimate components. So far as we are concerned, the only connection between these various universes consists in the fact that we are able to talk about all of them and in some of them to have direct intuitions and sensuous experiences. The various universes we inhabit all belong to *us;* that is the only thing that unites them. Logical and scientific bridges are nonexistent; when we want to pass from one to another, we have to jump.

Now, all these various universes in which we live are members of one or other of two super-universes; the universe of direct experience and the universe of words. When I look at this paper in my hand I have a direct sensuous experience. If I choose to, I can keep my mouth shut and say nothing about this experience. Alternatively, I may open my mouth and, making use of a certain system of signs, called the English language, I may impart the information that my experience consisted of whiteness mitigated by rows of black marks which I recognize as belonging to the alphabetical system by means of which spoken language can be rendered in terms of a visible equivalent.

To discuss the formal mechanism by which the world of immediate human experience is related to the various languages of mankind is a task which, even if I had the time, I should be quite incompetent to perform. And fortunately it is not necessary for our present purposes that it should be performed. It is enough, in this context, to point out that, between the world of immediate experience and the world of language, between things and words, between events and speech, certain relations have in fact been established; and that these relations are governed by rules that are in part purely arbitrary, in part dictated by the nature of our common experiences. The form of the rules varies from language to language. We are not, however, concerned with these variations. For our present purposes, the significant fact is that all human societies use some kind of language and have done so from the remotest antiquity.

Human behavior as we know it, became possible only with the establishment of relatively stable systems of relationships between things and events on the one hand and words on the other. In societies where no such relationship has been established, that is to say, where there is no language, behavior is nonhuman. Necessarily so; for language makes it possible for men to build up the social heritage of accumulated skill, knowledge and wisdom, thanks to which it is possible for us to profit by the experiences of past generations, as though they were our own. There may be geniuses among the gorillas; but since gorillas have no conceptual language, the thoughts and achievements of these geniuses cannot be recorded and so are lost to simian posterity. In those limited fields of activity where some form of progress is possible, words permit of progress being made.

Nor is this all. The existence of language permits human beings to behave with a degree of purposefulness, perseverance and consistency unknown among the other mammals and comparable only to the purposefulness, perseverance and consistency of insects acting under the compulsive force of instinct. Every instant in the life, say, of a cat or a monkey tends to be irrelevant to every other instant. Such creatures are the victims of their moods. Each impulse as it makes itself felt carries the animal away completely. Thus, the urge to fight will suddenly be interrupted by the urge to eat; the all-absorbing passion of love will be displaced in the twinkling of an eye by a no less absorbing passion to search for fleas. The consistency of human behavior, such as it is, is due entirely to the fact that men have formulated their desires, and subsequently rationalized them, in terms of words. The verbal formulation of a desire will cause a man to go on pressing forward towards his goal, even when the desire itself lies dormant. Similarly, the rationalization of his desire in terms of some theological or philosophical system will convince him that he does well to persevere in this way. It is thanks to words and to words alone that, as the poet says:

> Tasks in hours of insight willed
> May be in hours of gloom fulfilled.

And let us remember incidentally that by no means all of our tasks are willed in hours of insight. Some are willed in hours of imbecility, some in hours of calculating self-interest; some under the stress of violent emotion, some in mere stupidity and intellectual confusion. If it were not for the descriptive and justificatory words with which we bind our days together, we should live like the animals in a series of discrete and separate spurts of impulse. From the psychological point of view, a theology or a philosophy may be defined as a device for permitting men to perform in cold blood and continuously actions which, otherwise, they could accomplish only by fits and starts and when the impulse was strong and hot within them. It is worth remarking, in this context, that no animals ever make war. They get into individual squabbles over food and sex; but they do not organize themselves in bands for the purpose of exterminating members of their own species in the name of some sacred cause. The emphasis here must be placed on the word "name." For, of course, animals have no lack of sacred causes. What could be more sacred to a tiger than fresh meat or tigresses? What is lacking in the animal's world is the verbal machinery for describing and justifying these sacred causes. Without words, perseverance and consistency of behavior are, as we have seen, impossible. And without perseverance in slaughter and consistency in hatred there can be no war.

For evil, then, as well as for good, words make us the human beings we actually are. Deprived of language we should be as dogs or monkeys. Possessing language, we are men and women able to persevere in crime no less than in heroic virtue, capable of intellectual achievements beyond the scope of any animal, but at the same time capable of systematic silliness and stupidity such as no dumb beast could ever dream of.

It is time now that I gave a few typical instances of the way in which words have power to modify men's thought, feeling and conduct. But before doing so, I must make a few more remarks of a general nature. For our present purposes, words may be divided into three main classes. The first class consists of words which designate definite and easily recognizable objects or qualities. Table, for example, is an easily recognizable object and brown an easily recognizable quality. Such words are unambiguous. No serious doubts as to their meaning exist. The second class contains words which designate entities and qualities less definite and less easily recognizable. Some of these are highly abstract words, generalizing certain features of many highly complex situations. Such words as "justice," "science," "society," are examples. In the same class we must place the numerous words which designate psychological states—words such as "beauty," "goodness," "spirit," "personality." I have already mentioned the apparently irresistible human tendency to objectify psychological states and project them, on the wings of their verbal vehicle, into the outer world. Words like those I have just mentioned are typical vehicles of objectification. They are the cause of endless intellectual confusion, endless emotional distress, endless misdirections of voluntary effort.

Our third class contains words which are supposed to refer to objects in the outer world or to psychological states, but which in fact, since observation fails to reveal the existence of such objects or states, refer only to figments of the imagination. Examples of such words are the "dragon" of the Chinese and the "death instinct" of Freudian psychologists.

The most effective, the most psychologically magical words are found in the second category. This is only to be expected. Words found in the second class are more ambiguous than any others and can therefore be used in an almost indefinite number of contexts. A recent American study has shown that the word "nature" has been used by the philosophers of the West in no less than thirty-nine distinct senses. The same philosopher will give it, all unconsciously of course, three or four different meanings in as many paragraphs. Given such ambiguity, any thesis can be defended, any course of action morally justified, by an appeal to nature.

Ambiguity is not the only characteristic which makes these words peculiarly effective in determining conduct. Those which stand for generalizations and those which designate psychological states lend themselves, as we have already seen, to objectification. They take verbal wings and fly from the realm of abstraction into the realm of the concrete, from the realm of psychology into the external universe.

The objectification and even the personification of abstractions is something with which every political speech and newspaper article has made us familiar. Nations are spoken of as though they were persons having thoughts, feelings, a will and even a sex, which, for some curious reason, is always female. This female, personal nation produces certain psychological effects on those who hear it (or rather her) being talked about—effects incomparably more violent than those that would be produced if politicians were to speak about nations as what in fact they are: organized communities inhabiting a certain geographical area and possessing the means to wage war. This last point is crucially important. California is an organized community; but since it does not possess an army and navy, it cannot qualify for a place in the League of Nations.

Another familiar entity in political speeches is the pseudo-person called "Society." Society has a will, thoughts and feelings, but, unlike the Nation, no sex. The most cursory observation suffices to show that there is no such thing as Society with a large S. There are only very large numbers of individual societies, organized in different ways for different purposes. The issue is greatly complicated by the fact that the people who talk about this nonexistent Society with a big S, tend to do so in terms of biological analogies which are, in many cases, wholly inapplicable. For example, the so-called philosophical historians insist on talking of a society as though it were an organism. In some aspects, perhaps, a society does resemble an organism. In others, however, it certainly does not. Organisms grow old and die and their component cells break down into inanimate substances. This does not happen to a society, though many historians and publicists loosely talk as though it did. The individuals who compose what is called a decadent or collapsed society do not break down into carbon and water. They remain alive; but the cells of a dead organism are dead and have ceased to be cells and become something else. If we want to talk about the decline and fall of societies in terms of scientific analogies, we had better choose our analogy from psychics rather than biology. A given quantity of water, for example, will show least energy, more energy, most energy according to its temperature. It has most energy in the form of superheated steam, least in the form of ice. Similarly, a given society will exhibit much energy or little energy according to the way in which its individual members live their lives. The society of Roman Italy, for example, did not die; it passed from a high state of energy to a lower state of energy. It is for historians to determine the physiological, psychological, economic and religious conditions accompanying respectively a high and a low degree of social energy.

The tendency to objectify and personify abstractions is found not only among politicians and newspaper men, but also among those who belong to the, intellectually speaking, more respectable classes of the community. By way of example, I shall quote a paragraph from the address delivered by Clerk Maxwell to the British Association in 1873. Clerk Maxwell was one of the most brilliantly original workers in the whole history of physics. He was also what many scientists, alas, are not—a highly cultivated man capable of using his intelligence in fields outside his particular specialty. Here is what he could say before a learned society, when at the height of his powers.

"No theory of evolution," he wrote, "can be formed to account for the similarity of molecules." (Throughout this passage, Maxwell is using the word "molecule" in the sense in which we should now use the word "atom.") "For evolution necessarily implies continuous change, and the molecule is incapable of growth or decay, of generation or destruction. None of the processes of Nature, from the time when Nature began, have produced the slightest difference in the properties of any molecule. We are therefore unable to ascribe either the existence of the molecules or the identity of their properties to any of the causes which we call natural. Thus we have been led along a strictly scientific path very near to the point at which Science must stop. . . . In tracing back the history of matter Science is arrested when she assures herself, on the one hand that the modecule has been made and, on the other, that it has not been made by any of the processes which we call natural."

The most interesting point that emerges from these lines is the fact that, like the Nation, but unlike Society, Science has a sex and is a female. Having recorded this item in our text books of natural history, we can go on to study the way in which even a mind of the caliber of Clerk Maxwell's can be led into absurdity by neglecting to analyze the words which it uses to express itself. The word "science" is current in our everyday vocabulary. It can be spelt with a capital S. Therefore it can be thought of as a person; for the names of persons are always spelt with capital letters. A person who is called Science must, *ex hypothesi,* be infallible. This being so, she can pronounce without risk of contradiction, that "none of the processes of Nature, since the time when Nature began" (Nature is also spelt with a capital letter and is of course also a female), "have produced the slightest difference in the properties of any molecule." Twenty-three years after the date of Maxwell's speech, Becquerel observed the radioactivity of uranium. Two years after that Mme. Curie discovered radium. At the turn of the new century Rutherford and Soddy demonstrated the fact that the radium atom was in a process of rapid disintegration and was itself derived from uranium whose atoms were disintegrating at a much slower rate.

This cautionary story shows how fatally easy it is for even the greatest men of science to take the particular ignorance of their own time and place, and raise it to the level of a universal truth of nature. Such errors are particularly easy when words are used in the entirely illegitimate way in which Maxwell employed the word "Science." What Maxwell should have said was something like this, "Most Western scientists in the year 1873 believe that no process has ever modified the internal structure of individual atoms. If this is so (and of course the beliefs of 1873 may have to be modified at any moment in the light of new discoveries), then perhaps it may be legitimate to draw certain inferences of a theological nature regarding the creation of matter."

How was it possible, we may ask ourselves, that a man of Clerk Maxwell's prodigious intellectual powers, should have committed a blunder so monstrously ridiculous, so obvious, when attention is called to it, to people of even the most ordinary mental capacities? The question demands a double answer—the first on the purely intellectual level, the second in terms of feeling and will. Let us deal with these in order. Maxwell made his mistake, first of all, out of a genuine intellectual confusion. He had accepted the English language without question or analysis, as a fish accepts the water it lives in. This may seem curious in the light of the fact that he had certainly not accepted the technical language of mathematics without question or analysis. We must remember, however, that nontechnical language is picked up in infancy, by imitation, by trial and error, much as the arts of walking and rudimentary cleanliness are acquired. Technical languages are learned at a later period in life, are applied only in special situations where analysis is regarded as creditable and the ordinary habits of daily living are in abeyance. Children and young people must be deliberately taught to analyze the nontechnical language of daily life. With very few exceptions, they will never undertake the task on their own initiative. In this respect, Maxwell was not exceptional. He turned his intensely original and powerful mind on to the problems of physics and mathematics, but never on those of everyday, untechnical language. This he took as he found it. And as he found in it such words as "Science" with a capital S and a female sex, he made use of them. The results, as we have seen, were disastrous.

The second reason for Maxwell's error was evidently of an emotional and voluntary nature. He had been piously brought up in the Protestant tradition. He was also, as the few letters to his wife which have been printed seem to indicate, a practising mystic. In announcing that "Science" with the capital S and the female sex had proved that atoms had not evolved, but had been created and kept unchangingly themselves by nonnatural forces, he had a specifically religious purpose in view. He wanted to show that the existence of a demiurge after the pattern of Jehovah, could be demonstrated scientifically. And he wanted also, I suspect, to prove to himself that the psychological states into which he entered during his moments of mystical experience could be objectified and personified in the form of the Hebraic deity, in whose existence he had been taught to believe during childhood.

This brings us to the threshold of a subject, profoundly interesting indeed, but so vast that I must not even attempt to discuss it here; the subject of God and of the relations subsisting between that word and the external world of things and events, between that word and the inner world of psychological states. Shelley has sketched the nature of the problem in a few memorable sentences. "The thoughts which the word, 'God,' suggests to the human mind are susceptible of as many varieties as human minds themselves. The Stoic, the Platonist and the Epicurean, Polytheist, the Dualist and the Trinitarian, differ infinitely in their conceptions of its meaning. . . . And not only has every sect distinct conceptions of the application of this name, but scarcely two individuals of the same sect, who exercise in any degree the freedom of their judgment, or yield themselves with any candor of feeling to the influencings of the visible world, find perfect coincidence of opinion to exist between them." Such, I repeat, is the problem. No complete solution of it is possible. But it can at least be very considerably clarified by anyone who is prepared to approach it armed with equipment suitable to deal with it. What is the nature of this suitable equipment? I would assign the first place to an adequate vocabulary. Students of religion have need of a language sufficiently copious and sufficiently analytical to make it possible for them to distinguish between the various types of religious experience, to recognize the difference between things and words, and to realize when they are objectifying psychological states and projecting them into the outside world. Lacking such a language they will find that even a wide knowledge in the fields of theology, of comparative religion and of human behavior will be of little use to them. It will be of little use for the simple reason that such knowledge has been recorded, up to the present time, in words that lend themselves to the maximum amount of intellectual confusion and the minimum of clarity and distinctness.

Words and their meanings—the subject is an enormous one. "Had we but world enough and time" as the poet says, we could continue our discussion of it almost indefinitely. But unfortunately, or perhaps fortunately, world and time are lacking, and I must draw to a close. I have been able in this place to let fall only a few casual and unsystematic remarks about those particular aspects of the science of signs which Charles Morris has called the semantic and pragmatic dimensions of general semiosis. I hope, however, that I have said enough to arouse an interest in the subject, to evoke in your minds a sense of its profound importance and a realization of the need to incorporate it systematically into the educational curriculum.

Any education that aims at completeness must be at once theoretical and practical, intellectual and moral. Education in the proper use of words is complete in the sense that it is not merely intellectual and theoretical. Those who teach, teach not only the science of signs, but also a universally useful art and a most important moral discipline. The proper use of language is an important moral discipline, for the good reason that, in this field as in all others, most mistakes have a voluntary origin. We commit intellectual blunders because it suits our interests to do so, or because our blunders are of such a nature that we get pleasure or excitement from committing them. I have pointed out that one of the reasons for Maxwell's really monstrous misuse of language must be sought in that great man's desire to reconcile his scientific ideas with the habits of religious belief he had contracted in childhood. There was a genuine confusion of thought; but a not entirely creditable wish was very definitely the father of this confusion. And the same is true, of course, about those who for propagandist purposes, personify such abstractions as "Society" or "the Nation." A wish is father to their mistaken thought—the wish to influence their hearers to act in the way they would like them to act. Similarly, a wish is the father of the mistaken thought of those who allow themselves to be influenced by such preposterous abuses of language—the wish to be excited, to "get a kick," as the phrase goes. Objectified in the form of a person, the idea of a nation can arouse much stronger feelings than it can evoke when it is spoken of in more sober and accurate language. The poor fools who, as we like to think, are helplessly led astray by such machiavellian demagogues as Hitler and Mussolini are led astray because they get a lot of emotional fun out of being bamboozled in this way. We shall find, upon analysis, that very many of the intellectual

errors committed by us in our use of words have a similar emotional or voluntary origin. To learn to use words correctly is to learn, among other things,
the art of foregoing immediate excitements and immediate personal triumphs.
Much self control and great disinterestedness are needed by those who would
realize the ideal of never misusing language. Moreover, a man who habitually speaks and writes correctly is one who has cured himself, not merely
of conscious and deliberate lying, but also (and the task is much more difficult and at least as important) of unconscious mendacity.

When Gotama insisted on Right Speech, when Jesus stressed the significance of every idle word, they were not lecturing on the theory of semiosis;
they were inculcating the practice of the highest virtues. Words and the
meanings of words are not matters merely for the academic amusement of
linguists and logisticians, or for the aesthetic delight of poets; they are matters of the profoundest ethical significance to every human being.

MAN AT THE MERCY OF HIS LANGUAGE

Peter Farb

Linguistically speaking, man is not born free. He inherits a language full
of quaint sayings, archaisms, and a ponderous grammar; even more important, he inherits certain fixed ways of expression that may shackle his
thoughts. Language becomes man's shaper of ideas rather than simply his
tool for reporting ideas. An American's conventional words for directions
often limit his ability to read maps: It is an apt youngster indeed who can
immediately grasp that the *Upper* Nile is in the *south* of Egypt and the
Lower Nile is in the *north* of Egypt. Another example: English has only
two demonstrative pronouns ("this" and "that," together with their plurals)
to refer either to something near or to something far away. The Tlingit Indians of the Northwest Coast can be much more specific. If they want to
refer to an object very near and always present, they say *he; ya* means an
object also near and present, but a little farther away; *yu* refers to something
still farther away, while *we* is used only for an object so far away that it is
out of sight. So the question arises whether even the most outspoken member of American society can "speak his mind." Actually, he has very little
control over the possible channels into which his thoughts can flow. His
grammatical mind was made up for him by his culture before he was born.

The way in which culture affects language becomes clear by comparing
how the English and Hopi languages refer to H_2O in its liquid state. English,
like most other European languages, has only one word—"water"—and
it pays no attention to what the substance is used for or its quantity. The

Hopi of Arizona, on the other hand, use *pahe* to mean the large amounts of water present in natural lakes or rivers, and *keyi* for the small amounts in domestic jugs and canteens. English, though, makes other distinctions that Hopi does not. The speaker of English is careful to distinguish between a lake and a stream, between a waterfall and a geyser; but *pahe* makes no distinction among lakes, ponds, rivers, streams, waterfalls, and springs.

A Hopi speaker, of course, knows that there is a difference between a geyser, which spurts upward, and a waterfall, which plunges downward, even though his vocabulary makes no such distinction. Similarly, a speaker of English knows that a canteen of water differs from a river of water. But the real point of this comparison is that neither the Hopi nor the American uses anywhere near the possible number of words that could be applied to water in all of its states, quantities, forms, and functions. The number of such words is in the hundreds and they would hopelessly encumber the language. So, to prevent the language from becoming unwieldy, different kinds of water are grouped into a small number of categories. Each culture defines the categories in terms of the similarities it detects; it channels a multitude of ideas into the few categories that it considers important. The culture of every speaker of English tells him that it is important to distinguish between oceans, lakes, rivers, fountains, and waterfalls—but relatively unimportant to make the distinction between the water in a canteen in his canoe and the water underneath the same canoe. Each culture has categorized experience through language in a quite unconscious way—at the same time offering anthropologists commentaries on the differences and similarities that exist in societies.

The possibility of such a relationship between language and culture has been formulated into a hypothesis by two American linguists, Sapir and Whorf. According to Sapir, man does not live in the midst of the whole world, but only in a part of it, the part that his language lets him know. He is, says Sapir, "very much at the mercy of the particular language which has become the medium of expression" for his group. The real world is therefore "to a large extent unconsciously built up on the language habits of the group . . . The worlds in which different societies live are distinct worlds, not merely the same world with different labels attached." To Sapir and Whorf, language provides a different network of tracks for each society, which, as a result, concentrates on only certain aspects of reality.

According to the hypothesis, the differences between languages are much more than mere obstacles to communication; they represent basic differences in the "world view" of the various peoples and in what they understand about their environment. The Eskimo can draw upon an inventory of about twenty very precise words for the subtle differences in a snowfall. The best a speaker of English can manage are distinctions between sticky snow, sleet, hail, and ice. Similarly, to most speakers of English, a seal is simply a seal, and they have only that one word to describe it; if they want to say anything else about the seal, such as its sex or its color, then they have to put an adjective before the word "seal." But the Eskimo has a number of words with which to express various kinds of sealdom: "a young swimming seal," "a male harbor seal," "an old harbor seal," and so forth. A somewhat similar situation exists in English with the word "horse." This animal may be referred to as "chestnut," "bay mare," "stallion," and other names that one would not expect to find in the vocabulary of the horseless Eskimo.

The Eskimo, of course, is preoccupied with seals, a primary food source for him, whereas some speakers of English seem to be taken up with the exact particulars of the domesticated horse. The real question is: Do these different vocabularies restrict the Eskimo and the speaker of English, and do they force the speakers of different languages to conceptualize and classify information in different ways? Can an Eskimo look at a horse and in his own mind classify it as "a bay mare"? Or, because he lacks the words, is he forever blind to the fact that this kind of animal exists? The answer is that with a little practice an Eskimo can learn to tell apart the different kinds of horses, just as an American can learn about the various seals, even though the respective languages lack the necessary vocabularies. So vocabulary alone does not reveal the cultural thinking of a people.

But does the *totality* of the language tell anything about the people who speak it? To answer that, look at the English verb "grab." An English speaker says, "I grab it," "I grabbed it," "I will grab it," and so on. Only the context of the situation tells the listener what it is that is being grabbed and how it is being done. "I grab it" is a vague sentence—except in one way. English is remarkably concerned about the tense of the verb. It insists on knowing whether I grab it now, or grabbed it some time in the past, or will grab it at a future time. The English language is preoccupied with time, and so is the culture of its speakers, who take considerable interest in calendars, record-keeping, diaries, history, almanacs, stock-market forecasts, astrological predictions, and always, every minute of the waking day, the precise time.

No such statement as "I grab it" would be possible in Navaho. To the Navaho, tense is of little importance, but the language is considerably more discriminating in other ways. The Navaho language would describe much more about the pronoun "I" of this sentence; it would tell whether the "I" initiated the action by reaching out to grab the thing, or whether the "I" merely grabbed at a horse that raced by. Nor would the Navaho be content merely with "grab"; the verb would have to tell him whether the thing being grabbed is big or little, animate or inanimate. Finally, a Navaho could not say simply "it"; the thing being grabbed would have to be described much more precisely and put in a category. (If you get the feeling that Navaho is an exceedingly difficult language, you are correct. During World War II in the Pacific, Navaho Indians were used as senders and receivers of secret radio messages because a language, unlike a code, cannot be broken; it must be learned.)

Judging by this example and by other linguistic studies of Navaho, a picture of its speakers emerges: They are very exacting in their perception of the elements that make up their universe. But is this a true picture of the Navaho? Does he perceive his world any differently from a White American? Anthropological and psychological studies of the Navaoh show that he does.

He visualizes himself as living in an eternal and unchanging universe made up of physical, social, and supernatural forces, among which he tries to maintain a balance. Any accidental failure to observe rules or rituals can disturb this balance and result in some misfortune. Navaho curing ceremonies, which include the well-known sandpainting, are designed to put the individual back into harmony with the universe. To the Navaho, the good life consists of maintaining intact all the complex relationships of the universe. It is obvious that to do so demands a language that makes the most exacting discriminations.

Several words of caution, though, about possible misinterpretations of the Sapir–Whorf Hypothesis. It does not say that the Navaho holds such a world view because of the structure of his language. It merely states that there is an interaction between his language and his culture. Nor does the hypothesis maintain that two cultures with different languages and different world views cannot be in communication with each other (the Navaho and the White American are very much in communication today in Arizona and New Mexico). Instead, the hypothesis suggests that language is more than a way of communicating. It is a living system that is a part of the cultural equipment of a group, and it reveals a culture at least as much as do spear points, kinship groups, or political institutions. Look at just one of the clues to culture that the Sapir–Whorf Hypothesis has already provided: Shortly after the hypothesis was proposed, it was attacked on the basis that the Navaho speak an Athabaskan language and the Hopi a Uto-Aztecan one, yet they live side by side in the Southwest and share a culture. So, after all, asked the critics, what difference can language make in culture? Instead of demolishing the hypothesis, this comparison actually served to reveal its value. It forced anthropologists to take another look at the Navaho and the Hopi. As the hypothesis had predicted, their world views are quite far apart —and so are their cultures.

The Sapir–Whorf Hypothesis has alerted anthropologists to the fact that language is keyed to the total culture, and that it reveals a people's view of its total environment. Language directs the perceptions of its speakers to certain things; it gives them ways to analyze and to categorize experience. Such perceptions are unconscious and outside the control of the speaker. The ultimate value of the Sapir–Whorf Hypothesis is that it offers hints to cultural differences and similarities among peoples. . . .

THE ENVIRONMENT OF LANGUAGE

Norman Cousins

The words men use, Julian Huxley once said, not only express but shape their ideas. Language is an instrument; it is even more an environment. It has as much to do with the philosophical and political conditioning of a society as geography or climate. The role of language in contributing to men's problems and their prospects is the subject of an imaginative and valuable study now getting under way at Pro Deo University in Rome, which is winning recognition in world university circles for putting advanced scholarship to work for the concept of a world community.

One aspect of the Pro Deo study, as might be expected, has to do with the art of conveying precise meaning from one language to another. Stuart Chase, one of America's leading semanticists, has pointed out that when an English speaker at the United Nations uses the expression "I assume," the French interpreter may say "I deduce" and the Roman interpreter may say "I consider." When Pope Paul VI sent a cable to Prime Minister Alexei Kosygin and Party Chairman Leonid Brezhnev on their accession to office, he expressed the hope that the historic aspirations of the Russian people for a fuller life would be advanced under the new leadership. As translated into Russian by the Vatican's own interpreter, the Pope's expression of hope came out in a way that made it appear that the Pope was making known his endorsement of the new regime. The eventual clarification was inevitably awkward for all concerned.

The Pro Deo study, however, will not be confined to problems of precise translation. The major emphasis of the study has to do with something fundamental: the dangerous misconceptions and prejudices that take root in language and that undermine human values. The color of a man's skin, for example, is tied to plus-or-minus words that inevitably condition human attitudes. The words "black" and "white," as defined in Western culture, are heavily loaded. "Black" has all sorts of unfavorable connotations; "white" is almost all favorable. One of the more interesting papers being studied by the Pro Deo scholars is by Ossie Davis, the author and actor. Mr. Davis, a Negro, concluded on the basis of a detailed study of dictionaries and *Roget's Thesaurus* that the English language was his enemy. In *Roget's,* he counted 120 synonyms for "blackness," most of them with unpleasant connotations: blot, blotch, blight, smut, smudge, sully, begrime, soot, becloud, obscure, dingy, murky, threatening, frowning, foreboding, forbidden, sinister, baneful, dismal, evil, wicked, malignant, deadly, secretive, unclean, unwashed, foul, blacklist, black book, black-hearted, etc. Incorporated in the same listing were words such as Negro, nigger, and darky.

In the same *Roget's,* Mr. Davis found 134 synonyms for the word "white," almost all of them with favorable connotations: purity, cleanness, bright, shining, fair, blonde, stainless, chaste, unblemished, unsullied, innocent, honorable, upright, just, straightforward, genuine, trustworthy, honest, etc. "White" as a racial designation was, of course, included in this tally of desirable terms.

No less invidious than black are some of the words associated with the color yellow: coward, conniver, baseness, fear, effeminacy, funk, soft, spiritless, poltroonery, pusillanimity, timidity, milksop, recreant, sneak, lily-livered, etc. Oriental peoples are included in the listing.

As a matter of factual accuracy, white, black, and yellow as colors are not descriptive of races. The coloration range of so-called white people may run from pale olive to mottled pink. So-called colored people run from light beige to mahogany. Absolute color designations—white, black, red, yellow —are not merely inaccurate; they have become symbolic rather than descriptive. It will be argued, of course, that definitions of color and the connotations that go with them are independent of sociological implications. There is no getting around the fact, it will be said, that whiteness means cleanliness and blackness means dirtiness. Are we to doctor the dictionary in order to achieve a social good? What this line of argument misses is that people in Western cultures do not realize the extent to which their racial attitudes have been conditioned since early childhood by the power of words to ennoble or condemn, augment or detract, glorify or demean. Negative language infects the subconscious of most Western people from the time they first learn to speak. Prejudice is not merely imparted or superimposed. It is metabolized in the bloodstream of society. What is needed is not so much a change in language as an awareness of the power of words to condition attitudes. If we can at least recognize the underpinnings of prejudice, we may be in a position to deal with the effects.

To be sure, Western languages have no monopoly on words with connotations that affect judgment. In Chinese, whiteness means cleanliness, but it can also mean bloodlessness, coldness, frigidity, absence of feeling, weakness, insensitivity. Also in Chinese, yellowness is associated with sunshine, openness, beauty, flowering, etc. Similarly, the work black in many African tongues has connotations of strength, certainty, recognizability, integrity, while white is associated with paleness, anemia, unnaturalness, deviousness, untrustworthiness.

The purpose of Pro Deo University in undertaking this study is not just to demonstrate that most cultures tend to be self-serving in their language. The purpose is to give educational substance to the belief that it will take all the adroitness and sensitivity of which the human species is capable if it is to be sustained. Earth-dwellers now have the choice of making their world into a neighborhood or a crematorium. Language is one of the factors in that option. The right words may not automatically produce the right actions but they are an essential part of the process.

EXPRESSIVE LANGUAGE

LeRoi Jones

Speech is the effective form of a culture. Any shape or cluster of human history still apparent in the conscious and unconscious habit of groups of people is what I mean by culture. All culture is necessarily profound. The very fact of its longevity, of its being what it is, *culture,* the epic memory of practical tradition, means that it is profound. But the inherent profundity of culture does not necessarily mean that its *uses* (and they are as various as the human condition) will be profound. German culture is profound. Generically. Its uses, however, are specific, as are all uses . . . of ideas, inventions, products of nature. And specificity, as a right and passion of human life, breeds what it breeds as a result of its context.

Context, in this instance, is most dramatically social. And the social, though it must be rooted, as are all evidences of existence, in culture, depends for its impetus for the most part on a multiplicity of influences. Other cultures, for instance. Perhaps, and this is a common occurrence, the reaction or interreaction of one culture on another can produce a social context that will extend or influence any culture in many strange directions.

Social also means *economic,* as any reader of nineteenth-century European philosophy will understand. The economic is part of the social—and in our time much more so than what we have known as the spiritual or metaphysical, because the most valuable canons of power have either been reduced or traduced into stricter economic terms. That is, there has been a shift in the actual meaning of the world since Dante lived. As if Brooks Adams were right. Money does not mean the same thing to me it must mean to a rich man. I cannot, right now, think of one meaning to name. This is not so simple to understand. Even as a simple term of the English language, *money* does not possess the same meanings for the rich man as it does for me, a lower-middle-class American, albeit of laughably "aristocratic" pretensions. What possibly can "money" mean to a poor man? And I am not talking now about those courageous products of our permissive society who walk knowledgeably into "poverty" as they would into a public toilet. I mean, The Poor.

I look in my pocket; I have seventy cents. Possibly I can buy a beer. A quart of ale, specifically. Then I will have twenty cents with which to annoy and seduce my fingers when they wearily search for gainful employment. I have no idea at this moment what that seventy cents will mean to my neighbor around the corner, a poor Puerto Rican man I have seen hopefully watching my plastic garbage can. But I am certain it cannot mean the same

65

thing. Say to David Rockefeller, "I have money," and he will think you mean something entirely different. That is, if you also dress the part. He would not for a moment think, "Seventy cents." But then neither would many New York painters.

Speech, the way one describes the natural proposition of being alive, is much more crucial than even most artists realize. Semantic philosophers are certainly correct in their emphasis on the final dictation of words over their users. But they often neglect to point out that, after all, it is the actual importance, *power,* of the words that remains so finally crucial. Words have users, but as well, users have words. And it is the users that establish the world's realities. Realities being those fantasies that control your immediate span of life. Usually they are not your own fantasies, *i.e.,* they belong to governments, traditions, etc., which, it must be clear by now, can make for conflict with the singular human life all ways. The fantasy of America might hurt you, but it is what should be meant when one talks of "reality." Not only the things you can touch or see, but the things that make such touching or seeing "normal." Then words, like their users, have a hegemony. Socially —which is final, right now. If you are some kind of artist, you naturally might think this is not so. There is the future. But *immortality* is a kind of drug, I think—one that leads to happiness at the thought of death. Myself, I would rather live forever . . . just to make sure.

The social hegemony, one's position in society, enforces more specifically one's terms (even the vulgar have "pull"). Even to the mode of speech. But also it makes these terms an available explanation of any social hierarchy, so that the words themselves become, even informally, laws. And of course they are usually very quickly stitched together to make formal statutes only fools or the faithfully intrepid would dare to question beyond immediate necessity.

The culture of the powerful is very infectious for the sophisticated, and strongly addictive. To be any kind of "success" one must be fluent in this culture. Know the words of the users, the semantic rituals of power. This is a way into wherever it is you are not now, but wish, very desperately, to get into.

Even speech then signals a fluency in this culture. A knowledge at least. "He's an educated man," is the barest acknowledgment of such fluency . . . in any time. "He's hip," my friends might say. They connote a similar entrance.

And it is certainly the meanings of words that are most important, even if they are no longer consciously acknowledged, but merely, by their use, trip a familiar lever of social accord. To recreate instantly the understood hierarchy of social, and by doing that, cultural, importance. And cultures are thought by most people in the world to do their business merely by being hierarchies. Certainly this is true in the West, in as simple a manifestation as Xenophobia, the naïve bridegroom of anti-human feeling, or in economic terms, Colonialism. For instance, when the first Africans were brought into the New World, it was thought that it was all right for them to be slaves because "they were heathens." It is a perfectly logical assumption.

And it follows, of course, that slavery would have been an even stranger phenomenon had the Africans spoken English when they first got here. It would have complicated things. Very soon after the first generations of Afro-Americans mastered this language, they invented white people called Abolitionists.

Words' meanings, but also the rhythm and syntax that frame and propel their concatenation, seek their culture as the final reference for what they are describing of the world. An A flat played twice on the same saxophone by two different men does not have to sound the same. If these men have different ideas of what they want this note to do, the note will not sound the same. Culture is the form, the overall structure of organized thought (as well as emotion and spiritual pretension). There are many cultures. Many ways of organizing thought, or having thought organized. That is, the form of thought's passage through the world will take on as many diverse shapes as there are diverse groups of travelers. Environment is one organizer of *groups,* at any level of its meaning. People who live in Newark, New Jersey, are organized, for whatever purpose, as Newarkers. It begins that simply. Another manifestation, at a slightly more complex level, can be the fact that blues singers from the Midwest sing through their noses. There is an explanation past the geographical, but that's the idea in tabloid. And singing through the nose does propose that the definition of singing be altered . . . even if ever so slightly. (At this point where someone's definitions must be changed, we are flitting around at the outskirts of the old city of Aesthetics. A solemn ghost town. Though some of the bones of reason can still be gathered there.)

But we still need definitions, even if there already are many. The dullest men are always satisfied that a dictionary lists everything in the world. They don't care that you may find out something *extra,* which one day might even be valuable to them. Of course, by that time it might even be in the dictionary, or at least they'd hope so, if you asked them directly.

But for every item in the world, there are a multiplicity of definitions that fit. And every word we use *could* mean something else. And at the same time. The culture fixes the use, and usage. And in "pluralistic" America, one should always listen very closely when he is being talked to. The speaker might mean something completely different from what we think we're hearing. "Where is your pot?"

I heard an old Negro street singer last week, Reverend Pearly Brown, singing, "God don't never change!" This is a precise thing he is singing. He does not mean "God does not ever change!" He means "God don't never change!" The difference, and I said it was crucial, is in the final human reference . . . the form of passage through the world. A man who is rich and famous who sings, "God don't never change," is confirming his hegemony and good fortune . . . or merely calling the bank. A blind hopeless black American is saying something very different. He is telling you about the extraordinary order of the world. But he is not telling you about his "fate." Fate is a luxury available only to those fortunate citizens with alternatives. The view from the top of the hill is not the same as that from the bottom of the hill. Nor are most viewers at either end of the hill, even certain that, in fact, there is any other place from which to look. Looking down usually eliminates the possibility of understanding what it must be like to look up. Or try to imagine yourself as not existing. It is difficult, but poets and politicians try every other day.

Being told to "speak proper," meaning that you become fluent with the jargon of power, is also a part of not "speaking proper." That is, the culture which desperately understands that it does not "speak proper," or is not fluent with the terms of social strength, also understands somewhere that its desire to gain such fluency is done at a terrifying risk. The bourgeois Negro accepts such risk as profit. But does *close-ter* (in the context of "jes a close-ter, walk wi-thee") mean the same thing as *closer?* Close-ter, in the term of its user is, believe me, exact. It means a quality of existence, of actual physical disposition perhaps . . . in its manifestation as a *tone* and *rhythm* by which people live, most often in response to common modes of thought best enforced by some factor of environmental emotion that is exact and specific. Even the picture it summons is different, and certainly the "Thee" that is used to connect the implied "Me" with, is different. The God of the damned cannot know the God of the damner, that is, cannot know he is God. As no Blues person can really believe emotionally in Pascal's God, or Wittgenstein's question, "Can the concept of God exist in a perfectly logical language?" Answer: "God don't never change."

Communication is only important because it is the broadest root of education. And all cultures communicate exactly what they have, a powerful motley of experience.

MISTER TOUSSAN

Ralph Ellison

Once upon a time
The goose drink wine
Monkey chew tobacco
And he spit white lime.
            —RHYME USED AS A PROLOGUE TO NEGRO SLAVE STORIES.

"I hope they all gits rotten and the worms git in 'em," the first boy said.

"I hopes a big wind storm comes and blows down all the trees," said the second boy.

"Me too," the first boy said. "And when ole Rogan comes out to see what happened I hope a tree falls on his head and kills him."

"Now jus' look a-yonder at them birds," the second boy said, "they eating all they want and when we asked him to let us git some off the ground he had to come calling us little nigguhs and chasing us home!"

"Doggonit," said the second boy, "I hope them birds got poison in they feet!"

The two small boys, Riley and Buster, sat on the floor of the porch, their bare feet resting upon the cool earth as they stared past the line on the paving where the sun consumed the shade, to a yard directly across the street. The grass in the yard was very green and a house stood against it, neat and white in the morning sun. A double row of trees stood alongside the house, heavy with cherries that showed deep red against the dark green of the leaves and dull dark brown of the branches. They were watching an old man who rocked himself in a chair as he stared back at them across the street.

"Just look at him," said Buster. "Ole Rogan's so scared we gonna git some his old cherries he ain't even got sense enough to go in outa the sun!"

"Well, them birds is gitting their'n," said Riley.

"They mocking birds."

"I don't care what kinda birds they is, they sho in them trees."

"Yeah, old Rogan don't see *them*. Man, I tell you white folks ain't got no sense."

They were silent now, watching the darting flight of the birds into the trees. Behind them they could hear the clatter of a sewing machine: Riley's mother was sewing for the white folks. It was quiet and as the woman worked, her voice rose above the whirring machine in song.

"Your mamma sho can sing, man," said Buster.

"She sings in the choir," said Riley, "and she sings all the leads in church."

"Shucks, I know it," said Buster. "You tryin' to brag?"

As they listened they heard the voice rise clear and liquid to float upon the morning air:

> I got wings, you got wings,
> All God's chillun got a-wings
> When I git to heaven gonna put on my wings
> Gonna shout all ovah God's heaven.
> Heab'n, heab'n
> Everybody talkin' 'bout heab'n ain't going there
> Heab'n, heab'n, Ah'm gonna fly all ovah God's heab'n. . . .

She sang as though the words possessed a deep and throbbing meaning for her, and the boys stared blankly at the earth, feeling the somber, mysterious calm of church. The street was quiet and even old Rogan had stopped rocking to listen. Finally the voice trailed off to a hum and became lost in the clatter of the busy machine.

"Wish I could sing like that," said Buster.

Riley was silent, looking down to the end of the porch where the sun had eaten a bright square into the shade, fixing a flitting butterfly in its brilliance.

"What would you do if you had wings?" he said.

"Shucks, I'd outfly an eagle, I wouldn't stop flying till I was a million, billion, trillion, zillion miles away from this ole town."

"Where'd you go, man?"

"Up north, maybe to Chicago."

"Man, if I had wings I wouldn't never settle down."

"Me, neither. Hecks, with wings you could go anywhere, even up to the sun if it wasn't too hot. . . ."

". . . I'd go to New York. . . ."

"Even around the stars. . . ."

"Or Dee-troit, Michigan. . . ."

"Hell, you could git some cheese off the moon and some milk from the Milkyway. . . ."

"Or anywhere else colored is free. . . ."

"I bet I'd loop-the-loop. . . ."

"And parachute. . . ."

"I'd land in Africa and git me some diamonds. . . ."

"Yeah, and them cannibals would eat the hell outa you too," said Riley.

"The heck they would, not fast as I'd fly away. . . ."

"Man, they'd catch you and stick soma them long spears in your behin'!" said Riley.

Buster laughed as Riley shook his head gravely: "Boy, you'd look like a black pin cushion when they got through with you," said Riley.

"Shucks, man, they couldn't catch me, them suckers is too lazy. The geography book says they 'bout the most lazy folks in the whole world," said Buster with disgust, "just black and lazy!"

"Aw naw, they ain't neither," exploded Riley.

"They is too! The geography book says they is!"

"Well, my ole man says they ain't!"

"How come they ain't then?"

" 'Cause my ole man says that over there they got kings and diamonds and gold and ivory, and if they got all them things, all of 'em cain't be lazy," said Riley. "Ain't many colored folks over here got them things."

"Sho ain't, man. The white folks won't let 'em," said Buster.

It was good to think that all the Africans were not lazy. He tried to remember all he had heard of Africa as he watched a purple pigeon sail down into the street and scratch where a horse had passed. Then, as he remembered a story his teacher had told him, he saw a car rolling swiftly up the street and the pigeon stretching its wings and lifting easily into the air, skimming the top of the car in its slow, rocking flight. He watched it rise and disappear where the taut telephone wires cut the sky above the curb. Buster felt good. Riley scratched his initials in the soft earth with his big toe.

"Riley, you know all them African guys ain't really that lazy," he said.

"I know they ain't," said Riley, "I just tole you so."

"Yeah, but my teacher tole me, too. She tole us 'bout one of them African guys named Toussan what she said whipped Napoleon!"

Riley stopped scratching in the earth and looked up, his eyes rolling in disgust:

"Now how come you have to start lying?"

"Thass what she said."

"Boy, you oughta quit telling them things."

"I hope God may kill me."

"She said he was a *African?*"

"Cross my heart, man. . . ."

"Really?"

"Really, man. She said he come from a place named Hayti."

Riley looked hard at Buster and seeing the seriousness of the face felt the excitement of a story rise up within him.

"Buster, I'll bet a fat man you lyin'. What'd that teacher say?"

"Really, man, she said that Toussan and his men got up on one of them African mountains and shot down them peckerwood soldiers fass as they'd try to come up. . . ."

"Why good-God-a-mighty!" yelled Riley.

"Oh boy, they shot 'em down!" chanted Buster.

"Tell me about it, man!"

"And they throwed 'em off the mountain. . . ."

". . . Goool-leee! . . ."

". . . And Toussan drove 'em cross the sand. . . ."

". . . Yeah! And what was they wearing, Buster? . . ."

"Man, they had on red uniforms and blue hats all trimmed with gold, and they had some swords all shining what they called sweet blades of Damascus. . . ."

"Sweet blades of Damascus! . . ."

". . . They really had 'em," chanted Buster.

"And what kinda guns?"

"Big, black cannon!"

"And where did ole what-you-call-'im run them guys? . . ."

"His name was Toussan."

"Toussan!" Just like Tarzan. . . ."

"Not *Taar*-zan, dummy, *Toou*-zan!"

"Toussan! And where'd ole Toussan run 'em?"

"Down to the water, man. . . ."

". . . To the river water. . . ."

". . . Where some great big ole boats was waiting for 'em. . . ."

". . . Go on, Buster!"

"An' Toussan shot into them boats. . . ."

". . . He shot into em. . . ."

". . . Shot into them boats. . . ."

"Jesus!! . . ."

"With his great big cannons. . . ."

". . . Yeah! . . ."

". . . Made a-brass. . . ."

". . . Brass. . . ."

". . . An' his big black cannon balls started killin' them peckerwoods. . . ."

". . . Lawd, Lawd. . . ."

". . . Boy, till them peckerwoods hollowed *Please, Please, Mister Toussan, we'll be good!*"

"An' what'd Toussan tell em, Buster?"

"Boy, he said in his big deep voice, *I oughta drown all a-you bastards.*"

"An' what'd the peckerwoods say?"

"They said, Please, Please, *Please, Mister Toussan.* . . ."

". . . We'll be good," broke in Riley.

"Thass right, man," said Buster excitedly. He clapped his hands and kicked his heels against the earth, his black face glowing in a burst of rhythmic joy.

"Boy!"

"And what'd ole Toussan say then?"

"He said in his big deep voice: *You all peckerwoods better be good, 'cause this is sweet Papa Toussan talking and my nigguhs is crazy 'bout white meat!*"

"Ho, ho, ho!" Riley bent double with laughter. The rhythm still throbbed within him and he wanted the story to go on and on. . . .

"Buster, you know didn't no teacher tell you that lie," he said.

"Yes she did, man."

"She said there was really a guy like that what called hisself Sweet Papa Toussan?"

Riley's voice was unbelieving and there was a wistful expression in his eyes which Buster could not understand. Finally he dropped his head and grinned.

"Well," he said, "I bet thass what ole Toussan said. You know how grown folks is, they cain't tell a story right, 'cepting real old folks like grandma."

"They sho cain't," said Riley. "They don't know how to put the right stuff to it."

Riley stood, his legs spread wide and stuck his thumbs in the top of his trousers, swaggering sinisterly.

"Come on, watch me do it now, Buster. Now I bet ole Toussan looked down at them white folks standing just about like this and said in a soft easy voice: Ain't I done begged you white folks to quit messin' with me? . . ."

"Thass right, quit messing with 'em," chanted Buster.

"But naw, you-all all had to come on anyway. . . ."

". . . Jus' 'cause they was black. . . ."

"Thass right," said Riley. "Then ole Toussan felt so damn bad and mad the tears come a-trickling down. . . ."

". . . He was really mad."

"And then, man, he said in his big bass voice: Goddamn you white folks, how come you-all cain't let us colored alone?"

". . . An' he was crying. . . ."

". . . An' Toussan tole them peckerwoods: I been beggin' you-all to quit bothering us. . . ."

". . . Beggin' on his bended knees! . . ."

"Then, man, Toussan, got real mad and snatched off his hat and started stompin' up and down on it and the tears was tricklin' down and he said: You-all come tellin' me about Napoleon. . . ."

"They was tryin' to scare him, man. . . ."

"Said: I don't give a damn about Napoleon. . . ."

". . . Wasn't studyin' 'bout him. . . ."

". . . Toussan said: Napoleon ain't nothing but a man! Then Toussan pulled back his shining sword like this, and twirled it at them peckerwoods' throats so hard it z-z-z-zinged in the air!"

"Now keep on, finish it, man," said Buster. "What'd Toussan do then?"

"Then you know what he did, he said: I oughta beat the hell outa you peckerwoods!"

"Thass right, and he did it too," said Buster. He jumped to his feet and fenced violently with five desperate imaginary soldiers, running each through with his imaginary sword. Buster watched him from the porch, grinning.

"Toussan musta scared them white folks almost to death!"

"Yeah, thass 'bout the way it was," said Buster. The rhythm was dying now and he sat back upon the porch, breathing tiredly.

"It sho is a good story," said Riley.

"Hecks, man, all the stories my teacher tells us is good. She's a good ole teacher—but you know one thing?"

"Naw; what?"

"Ain't none of them stories in the books! Wonder why?"

"Hell, you know why, Ole Toussan was too hard on them white folks, thass why."

"Oh, he was a hard man!"

"He was mean. . . ."

"But a good mean!"

"Toussan was clean. . . ."

". . . He was a good, clean mean," said Riley.

"Aw, man, he was sooo-preme," said Buster.

"Riiiley!!"

The boys stopped short in their word play, their mouths wide.

"Riley, I say!" It was Riley's mother's voice.

"Ma'am?"

"She musta heard us cussin'," whispered Buster.

"Shut up, man. . . . What you want, Ma?"

"I says I wants you-all to go round in the backyard and play, you keeping up too much fuss out there. White folks says we tear up a neighborhood when we move in it and you-all out there jus' provin' them out true. Now git on round in the back."

"Ah, ma, we was jus' playing, ma. . . ."

"Boy, I said for you-all to go on."

"But, ma . . ."

"You hear me, boy!"

"Yessum, we going," said Riley. "Come on, Buster."

Buster followed slowly behind, feeling the dew upon his feet as he walked upon the shaded grass.

"What else did he do, man?" Buster said.

"Huh? Rogan?"

"Hecks, naw! I'm talkin' 'bout Toussan."

"Doggone if I know, man—but I'm gonna ask that teacher."

"He was a fightin' son-of-a-gun, wasn't he, man?"

"He didn't stand for no foolishness," said Riley reservedly. He thought of other things now, and as he moved along he slid his feet easily over the short-cut grass, dancing as he chanted:

> Iron is iron,
> And tin is tin,
> And that's the way
> The story . . .

"Aw come on man," interrupted Buster. "Let's go play in the alley. . . ."

> And that's the way . . .

"Maybe we can slip around and git some cherries," Buster went on.

> . . . the story ends, chanted Riley.

BLACK AMERICA'S OWN LANGUAGE

Larry Bryant

"It was a man named Nicodemus. He was a leader of the Jews.

"Jesus, he tell Nicodemus say, 'This ain't no jive; if a man ain't born over again, ain't no way he gonna get to know God.'

"Then Nicodemus, he ask him, 'How a man gonna be born when he already old? Can't nobody go back inside his mother and get born.'

"So Jesus tell him, 'This ain't no jive, this the truth. The onliest way a man gonna get to know God, he got to get born regular and got to get born from the Holy Spirit.'"

This is an excerpt from a translation of the Bible, John 3:1–5, into what many linguists call "black English."

They contend that black English is a separate form of English and should be treated as such.

Alfred S. Hayes of the Center for Applied Linguistics in Washington, D.C., says it should come as no surprise that American blacks have developed their own language.

"Given centuries of 'ghettoization' and separation, it's not remarkable that they should have developed not only distinctive ways of behaving, but different ways of speaking," Hayes says.

Center linguists call black English a fully formed linguistic system in its own right, with its own grammatical rules and history.

Ralph W. Fasold, one of the center's staff members, explains: "The distinctiveness of Negro dialect lies in certain features that it alone among English dialects has, and also in the combination of grammatical features that occur in the dialect."

In an article written with Walter A. Wolfram, Fasold says some of the differences between standard English and black English, though seemingly small, have important consequences for the communication of a message.

He says many of the most significant features of these systems are to be found in their verb and tense systems, and especially their treatment of the verb "to be."

A sentence such as "he be at work" is a well-known stereotyped characteristic of black English. Fasold stresses that this function of the word "be" has a habitual meaning for the black English speaker.

"There is no equivalent category in standard English and such a meaning can only be conveyed by a circumlocution—'He is at work all the time.' Thus, we see a clear-cut difference between the two grammatical systems," Fasold wrote.

Fasold cites many basic differences in the speech patterns of the two systems:

The "s" suffix does not exist in the verb systems of black English. As a result, the equivalent of the standard English sentence "He doesn't go" is "He don't go."

There is, in black English, an absence of the "-ed" suffix in the past forms of verbs. There are sentences such as "He miss a bus yesterday" and "He had miss it yesterday."

Some verbs that have irregular past forms in standard English have the same form for past and present tenses in black English, such as: "He come every day" and "He come yesterday."

In black English, contractions of the forms of the verb "have" are dropped. The sentences "I've been here for hours" and "He's gone home already" would read "I been here for hours" and "He gone home already."

The negative forms of "is", "am", "has" and "have" become "ain't" in black English. It also corresponds to the standard English "didn't." When a black child says "I ain't like that," one might suppose he means, "I'm not like that." However, the actual translation is "I didn't like that."

A Howard University masters candidate, Maxine Legall, says the history of black English can be traced to Africa.

Miss Legall, who specializes in black English, says the West African languages Hausa and Yoruba have had a great influence. Many American terms, including yam, pickaninny, mamma and nanny are derivatives of such languages.

There is no time element in black English, she says. There is a concept of time, but the language itself is not time-oriented.

"Black English is not chronological documentation of life, as is standard English. It is an extension of the whole way of life of black people."

Another linguist, William A. Stewart, says the origin of black English can be traced to Caribbean-area creole.

He says the first English learned by black slaves was a pidginized one. It became established as their language, and was passed on to succeeding generations of blacks, for whom it was their native tongue.

According to Stewart, present-day black English results from a process called "decreolization." The original creole language has been lost through its gradual merger with the British-derived English dialect.

Teachers, black and white, have responded to black English by declaring it "bad" and banning it from the classroom.

Malcolm X College President Charles G. Hurst says teachers just don't understand the problem.

"Full integration of the disadvantaged person into the society in which he must play a respected role is heavily dependent upon teachers who have the information and the kind of awareness so vital to understanding the student," he says.

Roger Shuy of the Washington Linguistics Center says he would like black children to possess "bi-dialectism"—control over both black and standard English.

Shuy is opposed to current methods of teaching English. He calls them "Bonnie-and-Clyde" techniques.

"Bonnie and Clyde eradicated, without discrimination, those who stood between them and their goals," Shuy says. "English teachers try to completely wipe out all traces of a kid's right to continue speaking the dialect of his home."

"Start where the learner is and communicate to him through channels he has at that point, in language familiar to him and with concepts with which he is familiar.

"We must consider the reaction of a child when he is told that the language he speaks, the language of his parents and friends, is deficient. There are enough ways for students to be alienated and intimidated by the school system without our needing to insult his language.

"The teacher's job is not to eradicate black English—or any kind. Instead, teachers should help children to make the switch comfortably from one setting to another."

Hayes agrees. "Let's look at children as they come into school," he says. "Every child speaks a highly developed human language, a language with a complex sound system, complex grammar—a language that is generally related to the language of his surroundings." To continue "suppressing" black English in favor of standard English represents one of the worst forms of discrimination, he contends.

Hayes says a widespread "other-side-of-the-tracks" reaction exists in today's schools.

He explains that if a child talks or dresses a certain way, these things may trigger certain implications about the person, "all of which are unjust and have absolutely nothing to do with this person's potential, which may be great or small on quite other grounds."

Shuy says even a bright child may remain silent in class as a defense mechanism, because to use the only language he knows (black English) is to risk criticism or at least correction.

"School is a game in which one is supposed to be right as often as possible and wrong as seldom as possible," Shuy notes. "If opening one's mouth leads to being wrong, then there are two solutions: either one learns to do what is right or one keeps one's mouth shut."

However important it may be for students to learn standard English, he says, it is not so important that it should endanger the entire educational process by causing children to retreat to silence in order to keep from being wrong.

If teachers degrade the language the child is using when he enters the classroom, this destroys his confidence in his oral communication, Shuy says. Teachers must try to build up the child's confidence, he argues, for without it there is no way of teaching him.

Hayes cites cases in which black children regarded as "slow readers" were able to read passages of black English with amazing speed and accuracy. The first few lines of "The Night Before Christmas" would be translated as:

> *It's the night before Christmas,*
> *And all through the house,*
> *Ain't nobody moving.*
> *Not even a mouse.*
> *There go them stockings,*
> *Hanging up on the wall,*
> *So Santa Claus can full them up,*
> *If he pays our house a call . . .*

Ideally, Hayes said, the teacher could control which language is used at a given time, and the student would be required to switch back and forth at the teacher's direction.

A Howard University student leader, Q. T. Jackson, contends that black English is another manifestation of black power.

"Just as the Afro hair styles, the Afro dress and the way blacks address each as 'brother and sister' have given black people a greater amount of racial pride, black English will also work to unify American blacks," Jackson says.

"A lot of the problem lies with the more affluent, educated Negroes. They feel that since they were held back so long by their inability to speak standard English, they will never speak it again."

THE LANGUAGE OF SOUL

Claude Brown

Perhaps the most soulful word in the world is "nigger." Despite its very definite fundamental meaning (the Negro man), and disregarding the deprecatory connotation of the term, "nigger" has a multiplicity of nuances when used by soul people. Dictionaries define the term as being synonymous with Negro, and they generally point out that it is regarded as a vulgar expression. Nevertheless, to those of chitlins-and-neck-bones background the word nigger is neither a synonym for Negro nor an obscene expression.

"Nigger" has virtually as many shades of meaning in Colored English as the demonstrative pronoun "that," prior to application to a noun. To some Americans of African ancestry (I avoid using the term Negro whenever feasible, for fear of offending the Brothers X, a pressure group to be reckoned with), nigger seems preferable to Negro and has a unique kind of sentiment attached to it. This is exemplified in the frequent—and perhaps even excessive—usage of the term to denote either fondness or hostility.

It is probable that numerous transitional niggers and even established ex-soul brothers can—with pangs of nostalgia—reflect upon a day in the lollipop epoch of lives when an adorable lady named Mama bemoaned her spouse's fastidiousness with the strictly secular utterance: "Lord, how can one nigger be so hard to please?" Others are likely to recall a time when that drastically lovable colored woman, who was forever wiping our noses and darning our clothing, bellowed in a moment of exasperation: "Nigger, you gonna be the death o' me." And some of the brethren who have had the precarious fortune to be raised up, wised up, thrown up or simply left alone to get up as best they could, on one of the nation's South Streets or Lenox Avenues, might remember having affectionately referred to a best friend as "My nigger."

The vast majority of "back-door Americans" are apt to agree with Webster—a nigger is simply a Negro or black man. But the really profound contemporary thinkers of this distinguished ethnic group—Dick Gregory, Redd Foxx, Moms Mabley, Slappy White, etc.—are likely to differ with Mr. Webster and define nigger as "something else"—a soulful "something else." The major difference between the nigger and the Negro, who have many traits in common, is that the nigger is the more soulful.

Certain foods, customs and artistic expressions are associated almost solely with the nigger: collard greens, neck bones, hog maws, black-eyed peas, pigs' feet, etc. A nigger has no desire to conceal or disavow any of these favorite dishes or restrain other behavioral practices such as bobbing his head, patting his feet to funky jazz, and shouting and jumping in church. This is not to be construed that all niggers eat chitlins and shout in church, nor that only niggers eat the aforementioned dishes and exhibit this type of behavior. It is to say, however, that the souful usage of the term nigger implies all of the foregoing and considerably more.

The Language of Soul—or, as it might also be called, Spoken Soul or Colored English—is simply an honest vocal portrayal of black America. The roots of it are more than three hundred years old.

Before the Civil War there were numerous restrictions placed on the speech of slaves. The newly arrived Africans had the problem of learning to speak a new language, but also there were inhibitions placed on the topics of the slaves' conversation by slave masters and overseers. The slaves made up songs to inform one another of, say, the underground railroads' activity. When they sang *Steal Away* they were planning to steal away to the North, not to heaven. Slaves who dared to speak of rebellion or even freedom usually were severely punished. Consequently, Negro slaves were compelled to create a semi-clandestine vernacular in the way that the criminal underworld has historically created words to confound law-enforcement agents. It is said that numerous Negro spirituals were inspired by the hardships of slavery, and that what later became songs were initially moanings and coded cotton-field lyrics. To hear these songs sung today by a talented soul brother or sister or by a group is to be reminded of an historical spiritual bond that cannot be satisfactorily described by the mere spoken word.

The American Negro, for virtually all of his history, has constituted a vastly disproportionate number of the country's illiterates. Illiteracy has a way of showing itself in all attempts at vocal expression by the uneducated. With the aid of colloquialisms, malapropisms, battered and fractured grammar, and a considerable amount of creativity, Colored English, the sound of soul, evolved.

The progress has been cyclical. Often terms that have been discarded from the soul people's vocabulary for one reason or another are reaccepted years later, but usually with completely different meaning. In the Thirties and Forties "stuff" was used to mean vagina. In the middle Fifties it was revived and used to refer to heroin. Why certain expressions are thus reactivated is practically an indeterminable question. But it is not difficult to see why certain terms are dropped from the soul language. Whenever a soul term becomes popular with whites it is common practice for the soul folks to relinquish it. The reasoning is that "if white people can use it, it isn't hip enough for me." To many soul brothers there is just no such creature as a genuinely hip white person. And there is nothing more detrimental to anything hip than to have it fall into the square hands of the hopelessly unhip.

White Americans wrecked the expression "something else." It was bad enough that they couldn't say "sump'n else," but they weren't even able to get out "somethin' else." They had to go around saying *something else* with perfect or nearly perfect enunciation. The white folks invariably fail to perceive the soul sound in soulful terms. They get hung up in diction and grammar, and when they vocalize the expression it's no longer a soulful thing.

In fact, it can be asserted that spoken soul is more of a sound than a language. It generally possesses a pronounced lyrical quality which is frequently incompatible to any music other than that ceaseless and relentlessly driving rhythm that flows from poignantly spent lives. Spoken soul has a way of coming out metered without the intention of the speaker to invoke it. There are specific phonetic traits. To the soulless ear the vast majority of these sounds are dismissed as incorrect usage of the English language and, not infrequently, as speech impediments. To those so blessed as to have had bestowed upon them at birth the lifetime gift of soul, these are the most communicative and meaningful sounds ever to fall upon human ears: the familiar "mah" instead of "my," "gonna" for "going to," "yo" for "your." "Ain't" is pronounced 'ain' "; "bread" and "bed," "bray-ud" and "bay-ud"; "baby" is never "bay-bee" but "bay-buh"; Sammy Davis Jr. is not "Sammee" but a kind of "Sam-eh"; the same goes for "Eddeh" Jefferson. No matter how many "man's" you put into your talk, it isn't soulful unless the word has the proper plaintive, nasal "maee-yun."

Spoken soul is distinguished from slang primarily by the fact that the former lends itself easily to conventional English, and the latter is diametrically opposed to adaptations within the realm of conventional English. Police (pronounced pō′lice) is a soul term, whereas "The Man" is merely slang for the same thing. Negroes seldom adopt slang terms from the white world and when they do the terms are usually given a different meaning. Such was the case with the term "bag." White racketeers used it in the Thirties to refer to the graft that was paid to the police. For the past five years soul people have used it when referring to a person's vocation, hobby, fancy, etc. And once the appropriate term is given the treatment (soul vocalization) it becomes soulful.

However, borrowings from spoken soul by white men's slang—particularly teen-age slang—are plentiful. Perhaps because soul is probably the most graphic language of modern times, everybody who is excluded from Soulville wants to usurp it, ignoring the formidable fettering to the soul folks that has brought the language about. Consider "uptight," "strung-out," "cop," "boss," "kill 'em," all now widely used outside Soulville. Soul people never question the origin of a slang term; they either dig it and make it a part of their vocabulary or don't and forget it. The expression "uptight," which meant being in financial straits, appeared on the soul scene in the general vicinity of 1953. Junkies were very fond of the word and used it literally to describe what was a perpetual condition with them. The word was pictorial and pointed; therefore it caught on quickly in Soulville across the country. In the early Sixties when "uptight" was on the move, a younger generation of soul people in the black urban communities along the Eastern Seaboard regenerated it with a new meaning: "everything is cool, under control, going my way." At present the term has the former meaning for the older generation and the latter construction for those under thirty years of age.

It is difficult to ascertain if the term "strung-out" was coined by junkies or just applied to them and accepted without protest. Like the term "uptight" in its initial interpretation, "strung-out" aptly described the constant plight of the junkie. "Strung-out" had a connotation of hopeless finality about it. "Uptight" implied a temporary situation and lacked the overwhelming despair of "strung-out."

The term "cop," (meaning "to get"), is an abbreviation of the word "copulation." "Cop," as originally used by soulful teen-agers in the early Fifties, was deciphered to mean sexual coition, nothing more. By 1955 "cop" was being uttered throughout national Soulville as a synonym for the verb "to get," especially in reference to illegal purchases, drugs, pot, hot goods, pistols, etc. ("Man, where can I cop now?") But by 1955 the meaning was all-encompassing. Anything that could be obtained could be "copped."

The word "boss," denoting something extraordinarily good or great, was a redefined term that had been popular in Soulville during the Forties and Fifties as a complimentary remark from one soul brother to another. Later it was replaced by several terms such as "groovy," "tough," "beautiful" and, most recently, "out of sight." This last expression is an outgrowth of the former term "way out," the meaning of which was equivocal. "Way out" had an ad hoc hickish ring to it which made it intolerably unsoulful and consequently it was soon replaced by "out of sight," which is also likely to experience a relatively brief period of popular usage. "Out of sight" is better than "way out," but it has some of the same negative, childish taint of its predecessor.

The expression, "kill 'em," has neither a violent nor a malicious interpretation. It means "good luck," "give 'em hell," or "I'm pulling for you," and originated in Harlem from six to nine years ago.

There are certain classic soul terms which, no matter how often borrowed, remain in the canon and are reactivated every so often, just as standard jazz tunes are continuously experiencing renaissances. Among the classical expressions are: "solid," "cool," "jive" (generally as a noun), "stuff," "thing," "swing" (or "swinging"), "pimp," "dirt," "freak," "heat," "larceny," "busted," "okee doke," "piece," "sheet" (a jail record), "squat," "square," "stash," "lay," "sting," "mire," "gone," "smooth," "joint," "blow," "play," "shot," and there are many more.

Soul language can be heard in practically all communities throughout the country, but for pure, undiluted spoken soul one must go to Soul Street. There are several. Soul is located at Seventh and "T" in Washington, D.C., on One Two Five Street in New York City; on Springfield Avenue in Newark; on South Street in Philadelphia; on Tremont Street in Boston; on Forty-seventh Street in Chicago, on Fillmore in San Francisco, and dozens of similar locations in dozens of other cities.

As increasingly more Negroes desert Soulville for honorary membership in the Establishment clique, they experience a metamorphosis, the repercussions of which have a marked influence on the young and impressionable citizens of Soulville. The expatriates of Soulville are often greatly admired by the youth of Soulville, who emulate the behavior of such expatriates as Nancy Wilson, Ella Fitzgerald, Eartha Kit, Lena Horne, Diahann Carroll, Billy Daniels, or Leslie Uggams. The result—more often than not—is a trend away from spoken soul among the young soul folks. This abandonment of the soul language is facilitated by the fact that more Negro youngsters than ever are acquiring college educations (which, incidentally, is not the best treatment for the continued good health and growth of soul); integration and television, too, are contributing significantly to the gradual demise of spoken soul.

Perhaps colleges in America should commence to teach a course in spoken soul. It could be entitled the Vocal History of Black America, or simply Spoken Soul. Undoubtedly there would be no difficulty finding teachers. There are literally thousands of these experts throughout the country whose talents lie idle while they await the call to duty.

Meanwhile the picture looks dark for soul. The two extremities in the Negro spectrum—the conservative and the militant—are both trying diligently to relinquish and repudiate whatever vestige they may still possess of soul. The semi-Negro—the soul brother intent on gaining admission to the Establishment even on an honorary basis—is anxiously embracing and assuming conventional English. The other extremity, the Ultra-Blacks, are frantically adopting everything from a Western version of Islam that would shock the Caliph right out of his snugly fitting shintiyan to anything that vaguely hints of that big, beautiful, bountiful black bitch lying in the arms of the Indian and Atlantic Oceans and crowned by the majestic Mediterranean Sea. Whatever the Ultra-Black is after, it's anything but soulful.

INCIDENT

Countee Cullen

Once riding in old Baltimore,
   Heart-filled, head-filled with glee,
I saw a Baltimorean
   Keep looking straight at me.

Now I was eight and very small,
   And he was no whit bigger,
And so I smiled, but he poked out
   His tongue, and called me, "Nigger."

I saw the whole of Baltimore
   From May until December;
Of all the things that happened there
   That's all that I remember.

PREJUDICE: LINGUISTIC FACTORS

Gordon W. Allport

Without words we should scarcely be able to form categories at all. A dog perhaps forms rudimentary generalizations, such as small-boys-are-to-be-avoided—but this concept runs its course on the conditioned reflex level, and does not become the object of thought as such. In order to hold a generalization in mind for reflection and recall, for identification and for action, we need to fix it in words. Without words our world would be, as William James said, an "empirical sand-heap."

Nouns That Cut Slices

In the empirical world of human beings there are some two and a half billion grains of sand corresponding to our category "the human race." We cannot possibly deal with so many separate entities in our thought, nor can we individualize even among the hundreds whom we encounter in our daily round. We must group them, form clusters. We welcome, therefore, the names that help us to perform the clustering.

The most important property of a noun is that it brings many grains of sand into a single pail, disregarding the fact that the same grains might have fitted just as appropriately into another pail. To state the matter technically, a noun *abstracts* from a concrete reality some one feature and assembles different concrete realities only with respect to this one feature. The very act of classifying forces us to overlook all other features, many of which might offer a sounder basis than the rubric we select. Irving Lee gives the following example:

> I knew a man who had lost the use of both eyes. He was called a "blind man." He could also be called an expert typist, a conscientious worker, a good student, a careful listener, a man who wanted a job. But he couldn't get a job in the department store order room where employees sat and typed orders which came over the telephone. The personnel man was impatient to get the interview over. "But you're a blind man," he kept saying, and one could almost feel his silent assumption that somehow the incapacity in one aspect made the man incapable in every other. So blinded by the label was the interviewer that he could not be persuaded to look beyond it.[1]

Some labels, such as "blind man," are exceedingly salient and powerful. They tend to prevent alternative classification, or even cross-classification.

[1] I. J. Lee, *How Do You Talk about People?,* Freedom Pamphlet (New York, Anti-Defamation League, 1950), p. 15.

Ethnic labels are often of this type, particularly if they refer to some highly visible feature, e.g., Negro, Oriental. They resemble the labels that point to some outstanding incapacity—*feeble-minded, cripple, blind man.* Let us call such symbols "labels of primary potency." These symbols act like shrieking sirens, deafening us to all finer discriminations that we might otherwise perceive. Even though the blindness of one man and the darkness of pigmentation of another may be defining attributes for some purposes, they are irrelevant and "noisy" for others.

Most people are unaware of this basic law of language—that every label applied to a given person refers properly only to one aspect of his nature. You may correctly say that a certain man is *human, a philanthropist, a Chinese, a physician, an athlete.* A given person may be all of these; but the chances are that *Chinese* stands out in your mind as the symbol of primary potency. Yet neither this nor any other classificatory label can refer to the whole of a man's nature. (Only his proper name can do so.)

Thus each label we use, especially those of primary potency, distracts our attention from concrete reality. The living breathing, complex individual —the ultimate unit of human nature—is lost to sight. The label magnifies one attribute out of all proportion to its true significance, and masks other important attributes of the individual.

. . . a category, once formed with the aid of a symbol of primary potency, tends to attract more attributes than it should. The category labeled *Chinese* comes to signify not only ethnic membership but also reticence, impassivity, poverty, treachery. To be sure, . . . there may be genuine ethnic-linked traits making for a certain *probability* that the member of an ethnic stock may have these attributes. But our cognitive process is not cautious. The labeled category, . . . includes indiscriminately the defining attribute, probable attributes, and wholly fanciful, nonexistent attributes.

Even proper names—which ought to invite us to look at the individual person—may act like symbols of primary potency, especially if they arouse ethnic associations. Mr. Greenberg is a person, but since his name is Jewish, it activates in the hearer his entire category of Jews-as-a-whole.

The anthropologist Margaret Mead has suggested that labels of primary potency lose some of their force when they are changed from nouns into adjectives. To speak of a Negro soldier, a Catholic teacher, or a Jewish artist calls attention to the fact that some other group classifications are just as legitimate as the racial or religious. If George Johnson is spoken of not only as a Negro but also as a *soldier,* we have at least two attributes to know him by, and two are more accurate than one. To depict him truly as an individual, of course, we should have to name many more attributes. It is a useful suggestion that we designate ethnic and religious membership where possible with *adjectives* rather than with *nouns.*

Emotionally Toned Labels

Many categories have two kinds of labels—one less emotional and one more emotional. Ask yourself how you feel, and what thoughts you have, when you read the words *school teacher,* and then *school marm.* Certainly the second phrase calls up something more strict, more ridiculous, more disagreeable than the former. Here are four innocent letters: m-a-r-m. But they make us shudder a bit, laugh a bit, and scorn a bit. They call up an image of a spare, humorless, irritable old maid. They do not tell us that she is an individual human being with sorrows and troubles of her own. They force her instantly into a rejective category.

In the ethnic sphere even plain labels such as Negro, Italian, Jew, Catholic, Irish-American, French-Canadian may have emotional tone for a reason that we shall soon explain. But they all have their higher key equivalents: nigger, wop, kike, papist, harp, cannuck. When these labels are employed we can be almost certain that the speaker *intends* not only to characterize the person's membership, but also to disparage and reject him.

Quite apart from the insulting intent that lies behind the use of certain labels, there is also an inherent ("physiognomic") handicap in many terms designating ethnic membership. For example, the proper names characteristic of certain ethnic memberships strike us as absurd. (We compare them, of course, with what is familiar and therefore "right.") Chinese names are short and silly; Polish names intrinsically difficult and outlandish. Unfamiliar dialects strike us as ludicrous. Foreign dress (which, of course, is a visual ethnic symbol) seems unnecessarily queer.

But of all these "physiognomic" handicaps the reference to color, clearly implied in certain symbols, is the greatest. The word Negro comes from the Latin *niger,* meaning black. In point of fact, no Negro has a black complexion, but by comparison with other blonder stocks, he has come to be known as a "black man." Unfortunately *black* in the English language is a word having a preponderance of sinister connotations: the outlook is black, blackball, blackguard, blackhearted, black death, blacklist, blackmail, Black Hand. . . .

There is thus an implied value-judgment in the very concept of *white race* and *black race.* One might also study the numerous unpleasant connotations of *yellow,* and their possible bearing on our conception of the people of the Orient.

Such reasoning should not be carried too far, since there are undoubtedly, in various contexts, pleasant associations with both black and yellow. Black velvet is agreeable, so too are chocolate and coffee. Yellow tulips are well liked; the sun and moon are radiantly yellow. Yet it is true that "color" words are used with chauvinistic overtones more than most people realize. There is certainly condescension indicated in many familiar phrases: dark as a nigger's pocket, darktown strutters, white hope (a term originated when a white contender was sought against the Negro heavyweight champion, Jack Johnson), the white man's burden, the yellow peril, black boy. Scores of everyday phrases are stamped with the flavor of prejudice, whether the user knows it or not.[2]

---

[2] L. L. Brown, "Words and White Chauvinism," *Masses and Mainstream* (1950), 3, pp. 3–11. See also *Prejudice Won't Hide! A Guide for Developing a Language of Equality* (San Francisco, California Federation for Civic Unity, 1950).

Members of minority groups are often understandably sensitive to names given them. Not only do they object to deliberately insulting epithets, but sometimes see evil intent where none exists. Often the word Negro is spelled with a small *n,* occasionally as a studied insult, more often from ignorance. (The term is not cognate with white, which is not capitalized, but rather with Caucasian, which is.) Terms like "mulatto" or "octoroon" cause hard feeling because of the condescension with which they have often been used in the past. Sex differentiations are objectionable, since they seem doubly to emphasize ethnic difference: why speak of Jewess and not of Protestantess, or of Negress and not of whitess? Similar overemphasis is implied in terms like Chinaman or Scotchman; why not American man? Grounds for misunderstanding lie in the fact that minority group members are sensitive to such shadings, while majority members may employ them unthinkingly.

The Communist Label

Until we label an out-group it does not clearly exist in our minds. Take the curiously vague situation that we often meet when a person wishes to locate responsibility on the shoulders of some out-group whose nature he cannot specify. In such a case he usually employs the pronoun "they" without an antecedent. "Why don't they make these sidewalks wider?" "I hear they are going to build a factory in this town and hire a lot of foreigners." "I won't pay this tax bill; they can just whistle for their money." If asked "who"? the speaker is likely to grow confused and embarrassed. The common use of the orphaned pronoun *they* teaches us that people often want and need to designate out-groups (usually for the purpose of venting hostility) even when they have no clear conception of the out-group in question. And so long as the target of wrath remains vague and ill-defined specific prejudice cannot crystallize around it. To have enemies we need labels.

Until relatively recently—strange as it may seem—there was no agreed-upon symbol for *communist.* The word, of course, existed but it had no special emotional connotation, and did not designate a public enemy. Even when, after World War I, there was a growing feeling of economic and social menace in this country, there was no agreement as to the actual source of the menace.

A content analysis of the *Boston Herald* for the year 1920 turned up the following list of labels. Each was used in a context implying some threat. Hysteria had overspread the country, as it did after World War II. Someone must be responsible for the postwar malaise, rising prices, uncertainty. There must be a villain. But in 1920 the villain was impartially designated by reporters and editorial writers with the following symbols:

alien, agitator, anarchist, apostle of bomb and torch, Bolshevik, communist, communist laborite, conspirator, emissary of false promise, extremist, foreigner, hyphenated-American, incendiary, IWW, parlor anarchist, parlor pink, parlor socialist, plotter, radical, red, revolutionary, Russian agitator, socialist, Soviet, syndicalist, traitor, undesirable.

From this excited array we note that the *need* for an enemy (someone to serve as a focus for discontent and jitters) was considerably more apparent than the precise *identity* of the enemy. At any rate, there was no clearly agreed-upon label. Perhaps partly for this reason the hysteria abated. Since no clear category of "communism" existed there was no true focus for the hostility.

But following World War II this collection of vaguely interchangeable labels became fewer in number and more commonly agreed upon. The out-group menace came to be designated almost always as *communist* or *red*. In 1920 the threat, lacking a clear label, was vague; after 1945 both symbol and thing became more definite. Not that people knew precisely what they meant when they said "communist," but with the aid of the term they were at least able to point consistently to *something* that inspired fear. The term developed the power of signifying menace and led to various repressive measures against anyone to whom the label was rightly or wrongly attached.

Logically, the label should apply to specifiable defining attributes, such as members of the Communist Party, or people whose allegiance is with the Russian system, or followers, historically, of Karl Marx. But the label came in for far more extensive use.

What seems to have happened is approximately as follows. Having suffered through a period of war and being acutely aware of devastating revolutions abroad, it is natural that most people should be upset, dreading to lose their possessions, annoyed by high taxes, seeing customary moral and religious values threatened, and dreading worse disasters to come. Seeking an explanation for this unrest, a single identifiable enemy is wanted. It is not enough to designate "Russia" or some other distant land. Nor is it satisfactory to fix blame on "changing social conditions." What is needed is a human agent near at hand: someone in Washington, someone in our schools, in our factories, in our neighborhood. If we *feel* an immediate threat, we reason, there must be a near-lying danger. It is, we conclude, communism, not only in Russia but also in America, at our doorstep, in our government, in our churches, in our colleges, in our neighborhood.

Are we saying that hostility toward communism is prejudice? Not necessarily. There are certainly phases of the dispute wherein realistic social conflict is involved. American values (e.g., respect for the person) and totalitarian values as represented in Soviet practice are intrinsically at odds. A realistic opposition in some form will occur. Prejudice enters only when the defining attributes of "communist" grow imprecise, when anyone who favors any form of social change is called a communist. People who fear social change are the ones most likely to affix the label to any persons or practices that seem to them threatening.

For them the category is undifferentiated. It includes books, movies, preachers, teachers who utter what for them are uncongenial thoughts. If evil befalls—perhaps forest fires or a rocket explosion—it is due to communist saboteurs. The category becomes monopolistic, covering almost anything that is uncongenial. On the floor of the House of Representatives in 1946, Representative Rankin called James Roosevelt a communist. Con-

gressman Outland replied with psychological acumen, "Apparently everyone who disagrees with Mr. Rankin is a communist."

When differentiated thinking is at a low ebb—as it is in times of social
crisis—there is a magnification of two-valued logic. Things are perceived as
either inside or outside a moral order. What is outside is likely to be called
"communist." Correspondingly—and here is where damage is done—whatever is called communist (however erroneously) is immediately cast outside
the moral order.

This associative mechanism places enormous power in the hands of a
demagogue. For several years Senator [Joseph] McCarthy managed to discredit many citizens who thought differently from himself by the simple
device of calling them communists. Few people were able to see through
this trick and many reputations were ruined. But the famous senator had no
monopoly on the device. . . .

Verbal Realism and Symbol Phobia

Most individuals rebel at being labeled, especially if the label is uncompli-
mentary. Very few are willing to be called *fascistic, socialistic,* or *anti-
Semitic.* Unsavory labels may apply to others; but not to us.

An illustration of the craving that people have to attach favorable symbols
to themselves is seen in the community where white people banded together
to force out a Negro family that had moved in. They called themselves
"Neighborly Endeavor" and chose as their motto the Golden Rule. One
of the first acts of this symbol-sanctified band was to sue the man who sold
property to Negroes. They then flooded the house which another Negro
couple planned to occupy. Such were the acts performed under the banner
of the Golden Rule.

When symbols provoke strong emotions they are sometimes regarded no
longer as symbols, but as actual things. The expressions "son of a bitch"
and "liar" are in our culture frequently regarded as "fighting words." Softer
and more subtle expressions of contempt may be accepted. But in these particular cases, the epithet itself must be "taken back." We certainly do not
change our opponent's attitude by making him take back a word, but it
seems somehow important that the word itself be eradicated.

Such verbal realism may reach extreme lengths.

> The City Council of Cambridge, Massachusetts, unanimously passed a
> resolution (December, 1939) making it illegal "to possess, harbor, seques-
> ter, introduce or transport, within the city limits, any book, map, magazine,
> newspaper, pamphlet, handbill or circular containing the words Lenin or
> Leningrad.[3]

Such naïveté in confusing language with reality is hard to comprehend
unless we recall that word-magic plays an appreciable part in human thinking.

[3] S. I. Hayakawa, *Language in Action* (New York, Harcourt, Brace & World, Inc.,
1941), p. 29.

TOWARD A REVOLUTIONARY RHETORIC

Arthur L. Smith

Every revolution has rhetoric that attempts to justify the claims and legitimize the aspirations of the revolutionists; the black revolution is no exception. During the American Revolution, for example, the dissident voices of Samuel Adams, James Otis, and Patrick Henry verbalized the sentiments and moods of a people suffering the violence of oppression. In much the same way, the contemporary black social revolution possesses a unique rhetoric that speaks to and for the black masses.

The terms employed must signify unity and aggressiveness for the revolutionists' rhetoric. A revolutionary rhetoric must possess an offensive stance if it is to mold the beliefs of the masses into a tight compact against the *status quo* opinion. Thus, all revolutionary rhetoric is essentially aggressive rather than defensive. The aggression inherent in revolutionary rhetoric becomes a unifying force that gives revolutionists a mien of tremendous energy.

Rhetoric of revolution, then, is distinguished by a fluidity that depends on the linguistic components of the language as much as the grievances of the revolutionists. Indeed, the one is partly dependent on the other. Without grievance, distress, and political or social discomfort, a revolution lacks the necessary fuel on which to base its power. Thus, all effective revolutions have been for equality, justice, and dignity.

In an article in the *William and Mary Quarterly,* Gordon S. Wood expresses a belief that revolutions must be based on genuine grievances.[1] But what people believe their situation to be is a crucial factor in their susceptibility to revolutionary rhetoric. As long as the revolutionists believe that grievances exist, for rhetorical purposes they do exist. As Wood indicates, the American colonists were probably not the most persecuted people of their time, either economically, politically, or socially.[2] Yet the American colonists had a violent revolution. It was a revolution, then, created in part by the articulation of grievances in a dynamic linguistic aggression that tended to exaggerate the colonists' complaints.

Despite its fluidity, revolutionary rhetoric has some features of any other rhetoric. Rhetoric is concerned with the communication of ideas, values, opinions, and beliefs in an effort to elicit the approval or acceptance of others. Within his particular situation, the rhetor attempts to discover means with which to show the aptness of his message. Insofar as the revolutionist

[1] Gordon S. Wood, "Rhetoric and Reality in the American Revolution," William and Mary Quarterly, XXIII, ser. 3, (1966), p. 4.
[2] *Ibid.*

seeks to find the means of persuasion within a given rhetorical situation, he functions as a rhetor.

The present rhetoric of black revolution first appeared after the Montgomery bus boycott and the Supreme Court School Decision of 1954, *Brown vs. Board of Education.* Before these events, the policies of the NAACP and the eloquence of Martin Luther King, Jr., had directed and inspired the black masses. After these events, black nationalists, black Muslims, and their sympathizers increasingly preached revolution as the panacea of the black predicament. Their rhetoric, essentially different from that of King and the Montgomery Improvement Association, is reminiscent of David Walker, W. E. B. Du Bois and to a lesser extent, Marcus Garvey.[3]

The early rhetoric of black revolution was characterized by aggression against whites, who were portrayed as the conveyors of racist attitudes and values. Simultaneously, this rhetoric tried to create black unity. Externally, the outlook was aggressive; internally the search was for unity. Little attempt was made to appeal to white America in the traditional rhetorical context. The black revolutionists did not seek the approval or acceptance of their ideas by their white audiences. Contrarily, they seemed to seek rejection by the white audience. White rejection, however, usually guaranteed black unity, and this was precisely the revolutionist's aim. For example, some black revolutionists asked that blacks be left alone to set up their own state, to seek their own economic development, and to assert their manhood. It should not be suggested that it was a rhetoric pleading for acceptance, for the black revolutionists were calling for the effective separation and even alienation of the two races.

The message of these black revolutionists is both frightening and hopeful. The terrifying fact is the futility of the rhetorical aim of those seeking a separate land for blacks. In one speech, Malcolm X voiced the sentiment, "We want our own land right here in America."[4] But what is contained in that sentence is an impossibility inherent in America. To grant blacks a separate state or states in America would be to destroy America. Even though it may be possible to understand the despair, alienation, and anxiety that bring on the land demands by black revolutionists, their rhetoric fails insofar as it seeks intrinsically impossible demands of the nation. Yet the rhetors' indictment of white America is that it could not and would not relinquish any land without a loss of national purpose. Part of the American mythology involves the impossibility of the separate states assertion. What is intricately included in this impossibility is the notion of a national destiny, or dream, or goal of a new and more equitable world order. To allow separate states for blacks within the boundary of the United States would nullify

[3] David Walker, author of the 1829 pamphlet *"An Appeal to the Coloured Citizens of the World,"* was the first militant black to have a significant impact on white America. W. E. B. Du Bois challenged Booker T. Washington's social philosophy by insisting on full social, economic, and political equality for blacks. Marcus Garvey led the largest mass movement of Afro-Americans during the 1920's. His rhetoric emphasized black dignity, self-respect, and a return to Africa.

[4] Malcolm X, "Message to the Grass Roots," long playing record published by the Afro-American Broadcasting and Recording Company, Detroit, 1965. (The speech was given to the Northern Negro Grass Roots Leadership Conference, Detroit, November 20, 1963.)

united in the national term and destroy the nation's social and political mythology. Since no rhetoric can be successful unless it is consistent with or effectively overcomes the listener's mythology, this aspect of the black nationalists' rhetoric is profoundly unconvincing to most Americans.

The conjecture can be made that the black nationalists who made land demands anticipated rejection, despite their vehement agitation. Indeed, it seems unlikely that the rhetors expected the American nation to grant their radical demands, if only because of the verbal commitment to fraternity among the American peoples by the recent Federal administrations. But the black nationalists also knew that with their rhetoric they had placed the spotlight on a basic American dilemma, exposing a festering sore in the nation's body politic.

A dilemma that the black nationalists verbalize for white Americans is: How can we divorce ourselves from the blacks and at the same time maintain our national integrity? The nationalists have consistently argued that America does not want the blacks integrated in the nation. During the 1968 national elections, black nationalists were heard saying, "Most whites want to vote for Wallace; even if they don't, they want to."[5] But the difficulty of the dilemma as stated can be appreciated when it is realized that many blacks consider themselves American and believe the national mythology as firmly as do other persons. More significant than expected rejection is the fact that the black nationalists posed the question in the first place. This indicates that they were aware of the impending impasse for white Americans. The aggressiveness of their rhetoric was demonstrated: once they perceived the essential contradiction in American society, they heightened the dilemma by voicing their separate states suggestion. Whatever else may have been their intentions, the black nationalists succeeded in showing that whites were not willing to go forward (in their terms) one way or the other. Of course, the black nationalists were attempting to prove that if anything could be said concerning white America, it was that there existed unanimity only on one issue: the social *status quo*.

Because their rhetoric contains both the language of aggression and unification, the black nationalists have issued a specialized call for community. No effort is made to unify America; all energy is expended for inducing unity among black Americans. The black nationalists contend that the unity of black Americans is a necessary step for the eventual unity of the nation.[6] Thus, such phrases as black is beautiful, let's get ourselves together, and most important Black Power have become common in the black community as rallying expressions for unity.

Meant for black people as a unifying rhetoric, these phrases and slogans like them seem to have been taken by the press and other media as particularly terrifying. Perhaps, terrifying because they are aggressive terms that contradict white America's view of the docile Negro. But if these phrases produce a certain dissonance for white Americans, for blacks they signal the

[5] Speech given by Walter Bremond at University of Southern California, Los Angeles, August, 1968.

[6] Malcolm X, *Malcolm X Speaks,* edited by George Breitman, New York: Merit, p. 21.

dawn of a new era. In the words of one black nationalist, "They are black words and phrases defined by blacks for blacks."[7] In 1967 in Los Angeles, Stokely Carmichael was pressed by two white reporters for his definition of Black Power. Carmichael insisted that he would not define the terms, that they had meaning for black people, and that if white people did not understand them, then that was their hang-up.[8] Obviously if these words are understood by blacks and suspected as something devious or sinister by whites, the nationalists have again become aggressors and unifiers. Black nationalists insist that white Americans are terrified when "black" is combined with "power." When Black Power is mentioned, whites tend to conjure up scenes of violence, which causes the black nationalists to ask, what has White Power meant? A black student at a California state college complained recently that the white advisor of their black student organization had confided to him that he would feel more comfortable with the "Negro Club" than with the Black Students Action Group. For blacks, the word "Negro" is hopelessly stereotyped; but for whites, it is comfortable. With this rhetoric of definition and redefinition, the black nationalists have succeeded in getting most whites off balance in their effort to force white Americans to see this nation's social predicament.

In the practice of this rhetoric, keeping the opponent off balance becomes a key strategy. Like the other rhetors of the black revolution, the black nationalists attack; they seldom defend. A good offensive rhetoric is considered a good measure of defense because the opposition must use his energy to refute the charges pressed against him.

For example, the black rhetor says, "The whites are hated all around the world," or "LBJ is a buffoon," or "America is a racist country."[9] These charges keep the opposition in motion to deny, to defend, to support, and to safeguard, while the black revolutionist is free to launch new attacks in different socio-political areas. The rhetorical strategy is based on this rationale of movement: Anything that facilitates black unity is good; anything that indicts white America is good.

These rhetorical moves are apparently calculated to terrify the whites and to unify the blacks. On the one hand, they are terrifying because of their mystery, indefiniteness, and even, vagueness; on the other, unifying because they give blacks their own power words and terms. One black rhetor remarked after President Johnson's civil rights speech in which he said, "We shall overcome," that the president "wouldn't dare get on TV and say, 'We want Black Power.' "[10] The effect of these terms and phrases seems to be to give coherence to a confused despair and to canalize the sentiments and emotions of black people toward an object outside themselves.

The fluidity of this rhetoric is sensed when the revolutionists insist on redefining their situational culture in a way that liberates them while it im-

---

[7] Interview given by Stokely Carmichael, Los Angeles, May 1967. (The author was present during this interview.)

[8] *Ibid.*

[9] See Charles Lomas, *The Agitator in American Society,* Englewood: Prentice-Hall, 1968, pp. 135–151.

[10] Speech given by Maulana Karenga at Purdue University, December 9, 1968.

prisons the whites. Specifically, the black revolutionists are concerned with identity, black identity in a white world. Their rhetoric also becomes a rhetoric or redefinition as they grapple with terms like *Negritude,* Negro, Afro-Americans, black, natural, and brother. In the identity crisis, each revolutionist has to hew out his own definition from the forest of cultural possibilities in an effort to elicit response from his audience when he appeals to them on the basis of this new definition. For example, Maulana Karenga's "Negro" may not come off as menacingly as H. Rap Brown's, and yet the term is repugnant to each of them. Redefinition means a reshaping of the black man's universe to upgrade black people.

Of course, the question of the white man's place will have to be answered before the black universe can achieve stability. But the rhetoric of most black revolutionists attempts to avoid that question. "We have no time to be concerned with the white man's problems," the black revolutionist is often heard to say.[11] The Black Muslims have tried to answer the question of the white man in a black universe by defining the white man as a "devil" created by an evil black scientist. Their metaphysics have failed to impress many blacks who must deal with the "devil" every day.

What redefinition means to the black revolutionists is that the whites will have to bargain on black terms and understand the world as constructed by blacks. Thus, whites are often entangled in a quandary of definition: black power, soul brother, and *Negritude.*

To the unsophisticated white audiences, these terms suggest a unique separateness on the part of the black man, maybe even prejudice. Other whites view these terms, whether defined or not, as a search for identity and relationship. And yet the imprisonment of the whites is accomplished in either case, for now they are doing the viewing, rather than the defining. Some whites are uncomfortable because the definitions are no longer being provided by their stereotype of the "Negro." Furthermore, the basis is established for a better rhetoric because it is the first time that a significant number of blacks have addressed themselves so engagingly to their total liberation. Proposing new vocabularies, seeking white attitudinal reform, and calling for a restructuring of our national concerns, the black revolutionists have questioned the essence of the American experience. And for a rhetoric to be relevant, it must go beyond the superficial and strike at reality. Perhaps this explains the reluctance of the nation to accept or believe the revolutionists. No one can continue to accept the American experience without first reckoning with the rhetoric of the black rhetors. To suggest that this is an egalitarian country or that all people share in the American promise is an absurdity in the light of the overwhelming data, experienced and cited by the votarists of the black movement. Clearly this is a new era in the American socio-political experience because large numbers of blacks have begun to speak to the essential American paradoxes for which white America has few resolutions.

The situation in which whites held the key even to the black man's defini-

[11] Speech given by Minister Franklin Florence at Purdue University, October, 1968.

tion of himself no longer exists. As one black revolutionist puts it, "Those cats gave us Negro, black in Spanish; but since we speak English, baby, we're going to be black in English. They can't get 'nigger' from that like they could from 'Negro.' Now they will have to be satisfied with our blackness."[12] Blacks seem to believe that there is some truth in the old adage, "the namer of names is always the father of things." To be defined by whites is to remain a slave, and slavery is anything but a pleasant memory to the black race. Thus his rhetoric shows new assertiveness, movement, aggressiveness, as he refuses to allow the white man to define his identity.

Since the black revolutionists see the search for black identity as depending on complete acceptance of blackness, they tell their audiences to get African names for their children, to wear *dashikis,* to wear the *au naturel* haircuts, and to help themselves by refusing to accept white handouts.

The re-emergence of black nations in Africa has considerably influenced the rhetoric of the black revolution. African travel rather than European travel is urged on the black masses. For example, a few years ago, a glance through *Jet* magazine would have revealed very few blacks traveling to Africa; but there was seldom an issue that did not have a story of a black person touring the European capitals. The rhetoric of the black revolutionists has seemingly influenced a rediscovery of the black Americans' African heritage. Evidence of this is also seen in the popularity of Afro-American as a name for black Americans. This term takes into account both African heritage and American nationality.

Essentially, the black revolutionists' aim is to preach pride, self-respect, and self-assertion. Because of this stance, bleaching creams, processed hair, and even the conventional Western hair comb have become despicable symbols of black slavery to white values. While I was doing research for this book [*Rhetoric of Black Revolution,* Boston: Allyn and Bacon, Inc., 1969,] a young black lady said to me, "The white people made the forks in the combs close together for their hair, not for ours." The revolutionist assumes that bleaching creams and processed hair destroy the power of any black self-assertion because the black man becomes a seeker of white values. Karenga (who changed his name from Ron Everett) decries the black man who goes to an integrated party and tries to speak like the whites. To Karenga, this is a clear case of 'copping out.' Nor does he take kindly to the black man who refuses to see the value of wearing African dress. Thus, Karenga's organization US has started making Afro-American outfits to be sold in black communities. Pride and self-respect are the twin concepts that keep the rhetoric in motion in the black communities.

Even the churches have been affected by the secularistic emphasis on racial pride, where heretofore the churches concentrated on preaching the deliverance of God. Black values are enhanced by the rhetoric, and a sense of coherence is presented for the black community.

By asking the black community to find its salvation within itself, the black revolutionist gives a sense of independence that was never produced, nor could ever be produced by white rhetoric regardless of how liberal that

---

[12] *Ibid.*

rhetoric appeared to be. Its support, however earnest and honest, carried with it the sting of paternalism. Whether the rhetoric was uttered by a president or a mayor made little difference to the black revolutionists, except as it may have been a method for restraining white racism. Even though it was clear that blacks could not make social progress without the relaxation of white discrimination, the black revolutionists also understood that the black masses had to 'get themselves together.' The possibility of black success resides largely with the white community. But even without massive support from the white community, the rhetoric of the black revolutionists makes powerful medicine and might lead to recovery of black pride.

Even more dramatic and significant than black unity is the black revolutionists' insistence that the black people are the only salvation of the nation. Black rhetors see in the intrigues of international politics the need for a rending of the fabric of America. Haranguing crowds of depressed and oppressed people, the rhetors proclaim the doom of America if the black people fail to save the nation. Furthermore, the world will only escape destruction by the efforts of the colored peoples (as opposed to the colorless peoples) because the whites are too degenerate.

The rhetors insist that redefinition plays a significant role in the nation's salvation. Karenga, particularly, is fond of saying that when the whites define the peoples of the world, they put all other peoples on the defensive. To say 'nonwhite' is abominable to the rhetors of black revolution because to accept nonwhite is to be defined by whites. On the other hand, Karenga argues that the colored peoples of the world, including Mexican-Americans, Japanese, and Malayans, must refuse to be defined by the white man.[13] Some black rhetors have asked their audiences, "What would the white man think if we started referring to him as nonblack?" While this appears to be a game, it is nonetheless a serious attempt by the black man to transcend the slavery experience.

It is this optimism within the present upsurge in black identity that validates the rhetoric that seeks to destroy and construct. Throughout the anxious speeches and activities of the black revolutionists, this tension is brought on by a mission to tear down and at the same time to build. To whites, Stokely Carmichael and H. Rap Brown appeared to be spokesmen of destruction. But to most black audiences, their message is one of restoration that has been needed so long and so desperately. Even though their rhetoric is seldom associated with violence, it does suggest the need to destroy racist institutions; this is the threat of violence.

Until the black revolutionists began pronouncing their prescriptions for what they called a sick society, most Americans were content with the token accomplishments of social legislation. When the black revolutionists came with a different rhetoric from that of Martin Luther King, Jr., Bayard Rustin, and Roy Wilkins, their voices were like prophets of doom from the wilderness. In a nation where King, Rustin, and Wilkins were considered radicals, the black revolutionists, who called for a more authentic revolution, were

[13] Speech given by Maulana Karenga to the United Mexican American Students at University of California, Los Angeles, May, 1968.

anathema. Whereas Martin Luther King, Jr., had been content with the gradual change brought about through protest and social legislation, the black revolutionists saw the immediate deliverance of the black masses in political leverage, economic control of the ghettoes, and self-assertion. They argued that the black man could never be free until he accepted and asserted his freedom even in the face of physical death.

The black revolutionists introduced a new dynamism identified by pride and self-respect into the black community. Now blacks were speaking of "our brothers in Africa" when only a few years before they would have scorned the suggestion. The black masses had been galvanized by the strange message of black identity, and as Karenga has said, this was their ultimate reality.[14] No longer seeking to receive, they wanted to be able to give. Tired of begging, they intended to earn or take, as circumstances dictated.

Involved in the black man's new awareness was an acceptance of things black, an acceptance of the Dark Continent, the epitome of blackness. Given the American situation with political juggling of social legislation, disdain for the black man's cry of police brutality, the South's lack of will to enforce the 1954 Supreme Court School Desegregation Decision, *Brown vs. Board of Education,* white backlash, and many other injustices, the black revolutionists decided that the white man had no intention to move until the black man did. Thus, only in this grasping for black awareness could the black masses really come to grips with themselves and their American predicament.

The message of the revolutionists to the masses was that they had to retrod their dismal past until they arrived, beyond slavery and exploitation, to the land where black men were born free. In seeing this, the black revolutionists were more advanced in their concept of social action than was Martin Luther King, Jr., because they knew that America was not yet able to provide them with a rationale for identity sufficient for liberation. Bombarded by Shakespeare, Milton, Emerson, and Poe, the blacks now believed that they also needed Phillis Wheatley, Paul Laurence Dunbar, and Countee Cullen, Americans of African descent.[15] Confronted with European cultures that had never really accepted the black man, the revolutionists now saw the need for emphasis on African cultures. Had the American people respected the African's heritage, schools would have taught courses dealing with African cultures as well as with European cultures. But American education has all but ignored the existence of the black man, except during slavery. To make up for this omission, the black revolutionists have sought to reindoctrinate the black masses with their history. Thus, acceptance of kinky hair, broad nose, and black skin, coupled with a knowledge of black history, in short, an identification and association with Africa and blackness, have produced a new consciousness of black manhood.

[14] Maulana Karenga, *The Quotable Karenga,* edited by Clyde Halisi and James MTume, Los Angeles: US Organization, 1967, p. 3.

[15] In 1773, Phillis Wheatley, a Boston slave, published the first volume of verse by an Afro-American. Paul Laurence Dunbar was the first black poet to be recognized as a major creative artist. He published hundreds of poems in dialect and literary English. Countee Cullen was a leader of the Black Renaissance that swept Harlem during the 1920's and '30's.

More than an accusation against the American society, this rhetoric of manhood initiated by the black revolutionists was an indictment of white liberal rhetoric in America. The rhetoric of white America was bound to fail because it could not appropriate satisfaction for white Anglo-Saxon Protestants and also for blacks up from slavery.

Inasmuch as rhetoric must have an audience because communication is a reciprocal process, the black revolutionists needed receivers for their message. To an extent, they inherited a ready-made audience. The audience of Martin Luther King, Jr., was especially susceptible to the rhetoric of the black revolutionists. He had prepared them intellectually and emotionally for acceptance for their dignity and manhood by demonstrating that they could get results by unity. Taking their cue from this point, the black revolutionists declared that freedom had always come when men asserted themselves. Understandably it was not a great distance between "We shall overcome" and "We want Black Power." In saying that Dr. King's audience was prepared for the black revolutionists, I am not contending that the revolutionists did not have audiences of their own. But the masses who listened to King gradually swayed to the music of the black revolutionists.

Because the message of the black revolutionists is primarily for blacks and only indirectly for whites, the majority of Americans fail to understand the rhetoric. If the black rhetor has effect on whites then he has accomplished through language what he hoped to accomplish through black unity. Having seen the extensive camera coverage of the civil rights movement of the early 1960's, however, the black revolutionist is not unaware of his greater audience. Thus, the use of a circuitous strategy actually could be effective on the white audience. For example, the rhetor might open his address to a black audience with the television cameras recording the proceedings by suggesting that the blacks should consider burning down the white-owned businesses in the black ghetto.

Perhaps the white Americans could understand the rhetoric more readily if it was directly addressed to them. Unable to make an objective evaluation of a rhetoric that they seem to hear by chance, the majority of white Americans are confused and frightened by it. It is analogous to a man overhearing part of a conversation between persons next door about injuring him or his property. He is filled with intense anxiety because he cannot unravel the mystery that includes him in its center. But the black rhetor's message often affects those who overhear as much, though not in the same way, as those who hear directly.

In being receptive to the message, the black man discovered new awareness of and strength in his past by accepting his heritage and by understanding the slave. What the people of this audience could not do, and the black revolutionists told them they must not do, was to accept *slave-think*. Out of this refusal to accept *slave-think* evolved the black revolutionists' doctrine against the welfare system. They view the welfare system as deviously contributing to the undermining of black heritage, home, attitude, and dignity. Furthermore, the rhetoric suggests that the great dispenser of *slave-think* is the white American. Consequently, when blacks tried to gain their liberty and freedom in ways similar to those used by the early American revolutionaries, white Americans found it difficult to accept black assertiveness. In this connection, the black rhetors attempt to demonstrate that white Americans are not only involved in *slave-think* in America, but also deal in it in other parts of the world.

Favorite passages of the black rhetors cite the conspiratorial designs of the white man to assign *slave-think* to other peoples of the world. Usually the audience is prepared for the charge against the whites with an argumentative question, such as "Why did America drop the Bomb on Japan rather than Germany?" or, "Who installed Tshombe as leader of the Congo?" or, "Do you think America will fight for black liberation in South Africa?" The questions often are presented in a rhetorical way because for most black audiences the answers are self-evident. Answers are seldom given and explanations are not accepted; the assertion in the question becomes indictment enough.

Occasionally, a speaker or writer will allude to the paradox that occurred during World Wars I and II where blacks died for other people's rights, yet did not have those rights in their own land. Having prepared the audience for the contemporary situation, the black rhetor might end with the incisive retort, "If the white man plays Nazi, we ain't playing Jews."[16] Stokely Carmichael has made especially effective rhetorical use of this line for closing a speech. The statement has been used primarily by Carmichael and Brown, but lesser rhetors have joined the chant, thereby making what was a classic line worn and dull. I might remark here that the evolution of this retort is a good example of why there has been no truly eloquent black revolutionist since Malcolm X. Only Malcolm X spoke from the real convictions and experiences of life; there was nothing theatrical or sophistic about his rhetoric. That is not to say, however, that the other black revolutionists have not had real experiences and do not now have true convictions, but rather that they have not yet articulated their realities.

The black man's present susceptibility to the rhetoric of black revolution will be fully exposed only when the black forefathers are understood. Despite the hardships imposed upon them during and after slavery, these illiterate and semi-literate blacks told their children that times would be better. These are the people whom the black revolutionists, on cue from Malcolm X, have begun to vindicate. The field Negro, according to Malcolm X, never really gave up his manhood. In understanding this, it is fairly easy to see the children's need to witness those better times. Reconstruction merely remade the South into what it had been before the Civil War; only the names of processes, experiences, situations, and relationships were changed. Booker T. Washington captured the spirit of the new South by understanding that it was essentially the same South. After Washington, no black man stood so high in the public mind, until Dr. Martin Luther King, Jr.

If one were to give the requirements for a black charismatic leader, he could do little better than the life, experiences, education, and temperament of Martin Luther King, Jr. King was born in the South. He was the son of

[16] Speech given by Stokely Carmichael to a Black Power rally in South Park, Los Angeles, November 26, 1966.

a Baptist preacher and was himself a preacher. Inasmuch as the vast majority of blacks in the South were active or nominal Baptists, this was a valuable asset. King could speak the language of the small town southern blacks when he invoked the prophets or the words of Jesus. Often speaking in the same melodious cadence black preachers had been using for years, King could captivate his audience by dropping the vocal pitch to give a sense of foreboding to the tone. He was the epitome of the black preacher.

History probably will record that he fulfilled a strategic mission in the black man's struggle for dignity, for after King's Montgomery encounter other rhetors using his style began appearing in cities having a large black population. If King could do it, they seemed to say, so can we. Even more important was the fact that even though he was educated, he could still speak the language of the small town preacher. There was a certain pride that ran through black communities whenever King was speaking or being interviewed on radio or television because he represented for many blacks the race at its best. There was a natural response to an educated Southern-born black man who spoke the language of the preachers. With the debut of Martin Luther King, Jr., a prophetic urgency gripped America as demonstrations of grievances were mounted throughout the nation. King and the Montgomery Improvement Association, which was later succeeded by the Southern Christian Leadership Conference, started a movement that would gain momentum with each succeeding year until finally it seemed to exhaust itself.

Only when the society did not appear to be responding to King's non-violent strategy did the black revolutionists seize the opportunity to preach self-assertiveness. Malcolm X said in the speech, "Message to the Grass Roots" on November 10, 1963, "When Martin Luther King failed to desegregate Albany, Georgia, the civil-rights struggle in America reached its low point. King became bankrupt, almost, as a leader."[17]

King's movement had been based on a fundamental belief in the goodness of man. He insisted that America had the moral courage to correct the injustices perpetrated on the black man. Beyond that, he believed that America would redress the grievances if those injustices were amply shown. With the extensive news coverage of the difficulties that blacks were having in getting accommodations, housing, and voting privileges, it was clear that America must now know what the black man faced. When the blacks of King's movement had amply dramatized the situation, they hoped for an outburst of national indignation.

But with King's demonstrations, including pray-ins, ride-ins, sit-ins, and sleep-ins, America saw children pelted with rocks, students pulled from lunch counters, dogs unleashed by policemen on small children, and baseball bats brandished. With the deaths associated with the civil rights movement, the romanticism, partly induced by the rhetoric of Martin Luther King, Jr., turned sour. The demonstrators were greeted as outside agitators, disrupters of race relations, and lawbreakers. The expected reserve of national

[17] *Malcolm X Speaks,* p. 13.

will to do what was right and honorable did not pay off in white America's consciences, although some important civil rights bills were passed by Congress.

Other than the blacks themselves, only idealistic white youth with a sense of national and personal will to correct years of injustices responded. Their response was visceral and genuine, and they too helped to create the "new black." It was their ideals and deeds of national concern that defined the magnitude of the problem. It was a realization of their impotence against what they called the establishment that convinced blacks like Stokely Carmichael of the need for a more radical means of persuasion.

The angry young blacks wished to take communication out of the realm of suggestion and put it into a more immediate and direct relationship. To do this, the black revolutionists insisted on alleviating the elements that kept the black masses helpless. Believing that enslavement can only be accomplished through force and superstition, the rhetors of black revolution attempted to liberate the black masses by using a militant rhetoric to change the black man's self-concept. With the emancipation of the slaves, force, for the most part, was eliminated as an instrument of slavery; but superstition continued to enslave the black man. The rhetoric seeks to deliver the black man from the humiliating image he has had of himself.

It is a rhetoric of exaggeration, to some extent, and that is another reason for its lack of total success. Black heritage and identity can be based on the true nature of African history without the obvious tall tales propagated by some nationalists and the Black Muslims. Elijah Muhammad taught his coterie of black nationalist preachers that a black scientist created the white man by mistake thousands of years ago. While the attempt by Muhammad's preachers to persuade the black masses never really succeeded, the exaggeration did teach the masses something about myth-making. Convinced that the white man had dominated other peoples of the world because his myths were stronger, the black rhetors saw an opportunity to re-direct and re-structure reality. An example of the re-structuring of reality with the black man at its center is the black revolutionist's description of his ethnic characteristics. Whereas most anthropological and sociological works by white authors describe the black man in comparison to the white man, the black revolutionists reverse the process. Their rhetoric suggests that compared to the black man, the average white man exhibits the following physical traits: head slightly less elegant, nose less well-developed, lips not so full, and hair stringy. The intent of this rhetoric is to get on the offensive by defining one's world in relationship to one's self, as indeed, the black revolutionists insist the white man has done for five hundred years.

With the emergence of the new black rhetoric in the late 1960's also came a refinement of the tools of protest speaking. The black revolutionists utilized the techniques of agitational rhetoric with a greater degree of sophistication than had Martin Luther King, Jr., Roy Wilkins, Bayard Rustin, or Whitney Young in their effort to liberate the black masses from superstition and white oppression.

Even though King's message did not contain the threat of violence committed by himself or his followers, the message of the black revolutionists was always "or else." The only times that King's rhetoric even hinted of violence were when he pleaded with America to accept his nonviolent approach because rejection could only lead to violence. But he never intimated that he would be a party to or a preacher of violence. The message of Martin Luther King, Jr., was that of a preacher pleading with his congregation to repent of their sins lest evil times befall them. Calling America to higher purposes and seeking moral goals, King tried to persuade a whole nation of the beauty of justice, compassion, and love.

Where King's rhetoric was a request, the black revolutionists' is a demand. The black revolutionists warn that if their demands are not met, they have but one alternative for their complete freedom, violence. They employ few qualifiers in their language. They speak with certainty and directness about their intentions if the society fails to respond to their ultimatums. To show determination and promise, the black revolutionists often use "will" without modifiers. Instead of calling for moral understanding, the revolutionists say, "we will burn this town down if things do not change." But the phrase, "if things do not change" only appears to be an escape hatch. The black revolutionists usually are certain that things will not change, and they know that many in their audience will feel the same sense of futility. Of course, the directness and certainty of the language add to the rhetoric's dimension of urgency. The society is faced with a challenge from the black revolutionists, but at the same time the challengers are forced to make a decision. They cannot fail to "burn the town down," or "sack the corner grocery store" and still maintain their ethos in the black community. As an observation, it seems that those agitational movements that have repeatedly failed to produce actions comparable to their pronouncements have always been exhausted.

Futhermore, it is the strategy of the black revolutionists to particularize all grievances. In statements such as "No people has ever been denied free access to education and jobs like we have," "The Man consigns us, defines us and intimidates us, when other people would have died before they submitted," and "LBJ wants us to kill for them (whites), but if we kill, we gon' decide who we gon' kill," the aim is to get the audience to feel specifically persecuted by using words that isolate the hearers from others within the society.[18] Thus even with all of its aggressive characteristics, the rhetoric of black revolution is isolationistic. In search of definitions and limits, it seeks to carve out an area that the black audience can call its own. Whether in politics, art, music, language, or heroes the task is to find a sphere sufficiently free of white intervention to call black.

But this is an essential paradox of the black revolutionists' rhetoric, that it cannot completely divorce itself from the white world. Ultimately, black revolutionary rhetoric is a creation of white society, for without the severities of white society the rhetoric would be unneeded. Even the Spirituals, which

[18] Carmichael, Los Angeles, November 26, 1966.

the black revolutionists rightly say were a black thing, were inspired by white oppression. Soul and all that it implies becomes a black thing in response to the white world.

Yet the constant goal of the black revolutionist is to occupy a moral or psychological territory that he can call his own. In the speeches made before black audiences, the attempt is made to stake out a position from which to charge the white society. It is both similar to and more than youth seeking to establish their own turfs and perimeters. Words are marshalled to canalize the opinions, beliefs, and emotions of the black masses into an offensive against the establishment.

You may have decided that the rhetoric possesses a militaristic outlook; indeed the style of the rhetoric does indicate reliance on military terminology. The rhetors have appropriated the language of revolution, whether revolution comes or not, to attain their rhetorical purpose. In the rhetoric of black revolution, sloganizing is nothing less than a form of rhetorical aggression. To state a complex or intricate concept in a few simple emotional words is effectively to agitate: WE WANT BLACK POWER; MOVE ON OVER OR WE WILL MOVE OVER YOU; HELL NO, WE WON'T GO. The rhetorical impact on the audience is related to the degree of assertiveness contained within the slogan. From the slogans, society tends to acquire impressions of the revolutionists as "militant," "violent," "belligerent," "self-assertive," or "dominating." The actions of the rhetors may not be violent, although their followers may react to their speeches by engaging in violence. But the stigma of militancy or being violent is not necessarily dependent on physical actions. Primarily, it is in the use of language that the rhetor of revolution becomes identified as militant. In much the same way as a slogan's degree of assertiveness affects the society by causing people to form impressions of the sloganizer, the intensity of the assertion also figures in a slogan's ability to galvanize a given audience. However, the more assertive a slogan is, the fewer its adherents. Some people who accepted WE SHALL OVERCOME could not subsequently shout WE WANT BLACK POWER or MOVE ON OVER OR WE WILL MOVE OVER YOU. The last slogan contains the agitational *or* that suggests an alternative unfavorable to the agitator's opposition. As a rhetorical device, it contains a threat of violence, and therefore must be considered an emotional addition to the linguistic composition of a rhetorical discourse. Thus the slogan becomes what it was originally as a Scottish war cry—a call to militancy.

In the volatile context of social relationships, changing mores, interrelated and unrelated life patterns, the stage is prepared for the black revolutionist who exploits the inadequacies of the social system. The black masses may see the system as anything from the weekly service bills to the inability of a parent to supply a child with lunch money. The system is even more violent because of their blackness. Where others may speak of social slights or stupid prejudices of white America, the revolutionists see everything in terms of a design to undermine the dignity of black people.

The revolutionist exploits the black masses' belief that the white man's system is evil; he also dwells on the disillusionment caused by that system.

The theme of disaffection with America is prevalent in the rhetoric of the black revolutionist. It is present in such statements as, "What do we have to lose if the country is burned down," and "America has always been racist and has always given us a bad deal," and, "we should be fighting in South Carolina rather than in South Vietnam."

Commonly, the rhetor of this rhetoric uses the chronological pattern of organization to bring his audience up to the present time on racial matters. Once this is accomplished, he usually asks his audience, "Now, what has America done for you?" The black audiences immediately make a negative mental response to the question. Capitalizing on the various military campaigns the black American has fought in, the revolutionist wants to know, Why give your life for the yellow man's freedom when you don't have your own? By his affirmations, the black revolutionist thus strengthens the masses' disillusionment with white society. The rhetorical context, then, is one of diverse social and moral patterns that allow the black revolutionists the opportunity to exploit the grievances of the masses, whether political, social, economic or cultural.

POLITICAL STRUGGLE IN AMERICA

Eldridge Cleaver

I think the first thing we have to realize, really get into our minds, is that it is a reality when you hear people say that there's a "black colony" and a "white mother country." I think you really have to get that distinction clear in your minds in order to understand that there are two different sets of political dynamics functioning in this country. If you don't make that distinction, then a lot of the activities going on in this country will be non-sensical. For instance, if there's a homogeneous country and everyone here is a citizen of that country, when it comes to participating in the politics of this country, it makes a lot of sense to insist that black people participate in electoral politics and all the other forms of politics as we have known them. But if you accept the analysis that the black colony is separate and distinct from the mother country, then a lot of other forms of political struggle are indicated.

I think that most black revolutionaries or militants or what have you have generally accepted this distinction. A lot of people seem reluctant to accept this distinction. I know that in your education you were given to believe the melting pot theory, that people have come from all over the world and they've been put into this big pot and they've been melted into American citizens. In terms of the white immigrants who came to this country, this is more or less true. But in this stew that's been produced by these years and years of stirring the pot, you'll find that the black elements, the black components have not blended well with the rest of the ingredients. And this is so because of the forms of oppression that have been generated—black people have been blocked out of this, and blocked out of that, and not allowed to participate in this, and excluded from that. This has created a psychology in black people where they have now turned all the negative exclusions to their advantage.

I mean the same things that were used to our disadvantage are now being turned around to our advantage. The whole thing about condemning blackness and developing an inferior image of everything black has now been turned completely around because I think the slogan of Black Power was a recognition of the change in the psychology of black people, that in fact they have seized upon their blackness and rallied around the elements or the points at which they were oppressed. They have turned the focal point of the oppression into the focal point of the struggle for national liberation.

Now, when people decide in their own minds that they are going to separate themselves from a country or from a political situation, a lot of dynamics and a lot of directions flow from that basic distinction. For example, people are talking these days about going to the United Nations and seeking membership in the United Nations for Afro-America. And when you look at the criteria for nationhood, you'll find that the only place that black people fall short in terms of this standard is the one where the land question comes up. They say that a nation is defined as a people sharing a common culture, a common language, a common history, and a common land situation. Now, that land question was a hang-up for a long time, simply because the black people in this country were dispersed throughout the population of the mother country. People couldn't begin to deal with the question of how to build a nation on someone else's land. It presents a very sticky problem.

In the history of the liberation struggle in this country, the two outstanding efforts that we remember in history were the Marcus Garvey movement and the Nation of Islam under Elijah Muhammed. I consider their fundamental mistake was that they projected goals that they were unable to fulfill. Marcus Garvey said that he was going to take black people back to Africa. In fact, he wasn't in a position to do that, technically speaking in terms of resources. It falls down to a question of resources, because I think that if Marcus Garvey had been able to come over here with enough ships and enough technical resources, he would have succeeded, because he did have a very tight grip on the minds and imaginations of black people, and he could have had enough of them with him to make his dream a reality. Elijah Muhammed said that he wanted to have a part of this country, that he would accept some of these states. Well, the way he approached the question I think, was sure to doom it to be unfulfilled because he was asking the white power structure to give him several states. He offered no alternative means of obtaining these states other than come down from the sky and give them to us. Well, black people have been waiting for help to come from abroad and from the sky, from underground, and from anywhere, and it hasn't come. So that we began to feel that we were in a bag where nothing could happen.

The beautiful thing about the slogan Black Power was that it implemented the dictum laid down by Kwame Nkrumah, in which he said, "Seek ye first the political kingdom, and other things will be added unto you." It's very important to realize that in moving to gain power, you do not conceal or repudiate the land question, you hold it in abeyance. What you're saying is that we must first get ourselves organized, and then we can get some of this land. It's very important to realize that 20,000,000 people or 30,000,000 people, what have you—we're going to have to take a count because the government has been lying to us about everything else they do so we can assume that they are lying about that, so we can say that there might be 30,000,000, 40,000,000 we might even be a majority, I don't know; but I am quite sure that there are more than the 20,000,000 that the government wants to give us. But, we can say that it's possible to organize 20,000,000 or 30,000,000 people right here. Even though we are dispersed throughout the mother country, it is possible to set up political forms where we can have representatives in the full sense of the word, like ambassadors going to other countries.

You can see from the experience of Malcolm and from the experience of Stokely that govenments around the world are hip enough to the political realities of our situation to recognize and to accept our representatives in every sense of the word. I mean, Stokely Carmichael, when he went to Havana, received the same respect, or maybe even a little more, as delegates from other countries. Black people recognize this and they know that there is a way through the international machinery to cope with the situation.

I think it's very important to realize that there is a way to move. So that today black people are talking about going to the United Nations, asking the United Nations for a UN supervised plebiscite throughout the colony. Black people have never been able through any mechanism to express what their will is. People have come along and spoken in the name of black people; they have said that black people want to be integrated; they have said black people want to be separated; but no where at no time have black people been given the chance to register their own position. I think it's very important that we decide this once and for all, because as black people we are able to wage a campaign on this subject: do you want to be a part of America, do you want to be integrated into America, or do you want to be separated from America, do you want to be a nation, do you want to have your ambassadors, your representatives seated in the United Nations, as a full member of the General Assembly, do you want to have your ambassadors accepted around the world? I think it would be very hard for the black people to say no, particularly when the argument of the government is going to be that black people don't need those things because they are already American citizens. Because then we come back and say, Well, if we're citizens, what about this, and what about that? And, at the very least, what it will do is to put tremendous pressure on the Babylonians, and they need all the pressure we can give them.

Now, a lot of people don't want to see this country and its structure basically change. They want to think the United States of America is an eternal entity. When you look at history, you'll find that great empires have had their boundaries changed, have had their political structures rearranged, and some of them, like Rome, lasted for 500, 600 years, and the people thought nothing could ever destroy this. It's gone. The Egyptian Empire—all the empires as you look down through history, you will find that a day of reckoning came down and the whole situation was rearranged. Americans cannot envision a situation where the same thing could happen here. I think that black people have already envisioned that this, in fact, could happen, because if we were to get organized in this fashion and then be able to bring international leverage against the United States, we could have those questions decided in our favor in an international forum. I think that by then Mao Tse-tung would be at the UN, I think he would vote for us, I don't think he would sustain LBJ's argument. I think that Fidel Castro would vote for us. I think Charles De Gaulle may say something about that. I don't think he would just turn thumbs down on us, so that there are a lot of areas that we have to get into and explore. Now what that means is that there are realities out here today and will be in the future.

One thing about the coalition with the Peace and Freedom Party: we approached this whole thing from the point of view of international relations. We feel that our coalition is part of our foreign policy. That is how we look at it, that is how we are moving on it and thinking about it.

A lot of people feel just as Mike Parker said: We are endangering them as well as ourselves by coalescing with the white radicals, particularly here in Berkeley. Berkeley, as far as we can see, has a foul reputation among a lot of black cats, especially black cats associated with the NCNP. Bobby Seale, myself, and several other members of the Black Panther Party spent about a week in Los Angeles, and we were put through a lot of changes by black cats who didn't relate to the Peace and Freedom Party. They told us rather frankly that we had become tools of the white racists who had refused to accept the 50% bit in Chicago and they wanted to know what we were trying to do, were we trying to undercut what other blacks were trying to do around the country? Our reply to that was that we had made a functional coalition with the Peace and Freedom Party and that we feel that we have 100% say so over our affairs. I mean we don't allow Mike Parker and Bob Avakian to come in and dictate to us what is going to happen in terms of what we want to do. They have not tried to do that, and they are not going to try, and they had better not try. And in the same way, we do not come in and try to dictate to them what they are going to do, although we have been accused of that, but that is not the way it goes.

We recognize that we have a powerful interest in seeing a white radical movement develop into something that we can relate to. There are many things that we cannot do by ourselves. And then, there are many things that the white radical movement cannot do by itself. So we recognize that, and we are not going to be running around trying to stab each other in the back, or put each other in trickbags. It is not going to work from our point of view and we hope it won't work from your point of view because we have an interest in seeing that you develop a stable organization and a stable movement.

Now, one very important thing that we are working towards is how to unify the black population in this country within a national structure. The structure has to be inclusive enough to pull in all black people. In the past, when a new organization came on the scene, it sought to eliminate existing organizations. It was going to move every other organization out and it was going to take over and do this thing. We say that this is a mistake. What we have done is worked out a merger with SNCC. The Black Panther Party for Self-Defense and SNCC are going to merge into a functional organization that can move nationally. We are moving into a period now where the Black Panther Party for Self-Defense has consolidated enough of a base to move things nationally. SNCC has already established national contact as well as international contact.

It is very important to realize that SNCC is composed virtually of black hippies, you might say, of black college students who have dropped out of the black middle class. And because that is their origin and that is where they came from, they cannot relate to the black brother on the block in a political fashion. They can relate to him, they can talk to him, they can communicate with him much better than, say, Roy Wilkins ever could. But, they are not able to move him *en masse* to the point where he could be organized and involved in political functions.

Now, the beauty and the genius of what Bobby Seale and Huey Newton have done is that they are able to move the last man on the totem pole. That is very important, because until that man can move, we really can't do that thing. SNCC has seen that the Black Panther Party is able to get to that man. So what they have done is made their apparatus available to us and there's no hangup; we can move into that. Most people don't know this, but a lot of the rhetoric you hear from Stokely Carmichael and Rap Brown these days, especially when Rap Brown first started speaking, was adopted precisely because they had come to the West Coast and spent a little time with the Black Panthers out here. That is very important, and if you see them you ask them to tell you about that, that they were greatly influenced by the Panthers. I mean that their lines were already moving in that direction because of the political pressures they were forced to deal with, but they hadn't yet made that step, they hadn't taken that leap. But coming out here and seeing the Panthers moving, seeing brothers carrying guns on the street, talking about the gun, violence, and revolution had a certain impact on their minds and they went back talking about that. So now we can say that SNCC— actually, I shouldn't even be going into this until February 17th at the Oakland Auditorium. This is when we are going to do this officially. I think it is very important that you be there so that you can see and hear for yourself what these people have to say, unless you want to depend on the newspapers, and you really don't want to get into that. So, let's just say that we are involved in trying to create models in the vanguard set so that people around the country will see how we can move.

Now, we have done two important things, I think. One, we have made this coalition with the Peace and Freedom Party; and two, we have merged with SNCC. When people look at that they can say that in the Era of Black Power, we have got to merge and merge into larger units until we have a national structure. In terms of our relationship with the white community, we can move with functional coalitions.

It is very important that we all hold up our end of the bargain—and don't think that by using us you can get away with something, because, in fact, you will only destroy what you are trying to build for yourself. Black people have only one way to protect themselves, particularly politically, and that is to be capable of implementing and inflicting a political consequence. If we cannot inflict a political consequence, then we will in fact become nothing. So, that if the Peace and Freedom Party ever tries to misuse us, we have to be in a position to hurt the Peace and Freedom Party. We have to keep the political relationship such that if we were to pull out of it, that would be very costly to the Peace and Freedom Party. We must maintain that, we must be able to inflict a consequence, and we intend to be able to do that, and it is very important that that happens. White radicals who are like the vanguard in the white community should recognize that and then move to help us get in that position—because without that you are not going to be able to convince people that they should even relate to this whole effort.

As Mike Parker said, we are also catching a lot of hell—the word is purgatory, rather, it is not hell—about this coalition. Because a lot of people have begun to feel that we can be trusted, they have taken a wait-and-see attitude to find out how this coalition comes down, to see if we, in fact, do become puppets. People all around the country are asking—if you could look at our mail or listen to our phone calls—you would know about all the people who have asked, "Hey, what is this you are doing out there? What do you think you're doing, man, explain that to me." We feel that we are able to explain that, and as I said, Bobby is going to be going on a nation-wide tour and is going to be explaining that, I am going on a nation-wide tour and other members of the Party are going to be going on these tours. We are going to be explaining it and SNCC is going to be explaining it, and I think that we are going to be able to do it. It is very important that the Peace and Freedom Party be able to relate to that, because when we move nationally we will have to talk about the Peace and Freedom Party and then they will have grounds for moving into areas that we have already organized. So it is going to become extremely important that we realize what we are doing. And the thing that we need from the white mother country is technical assistance—technical assistance to the colony, dig it?

I think we have a good thing going. I want to see it continue to develop and broaden and deepen because we are all involved in this and there is no way out. We have got to do it, because time is against us, a lot of people are against us, and I know that I am out of time, so I think I will cool it right here.

POLITICS AND THE ENGLISH LANGUAGE

George Orwell

Most people who bother with the matter at all would admit that the English language is in a bad way, but it is generally assumed that we cannot by conscious action do anything about it. Our civilization is decadent and our language—so the argument runs—must inevitably share in the general collapse. It follows that any struggle against the abuse of language is a sentimental archaism, like preferring candles to electric light or hansom cabs to aeroplanes. Underneath this lies the half-conscious belief that language is a natural growth and not an instrument which we shape for our own purposes.

Now, it is clear that the decline of a language must ultimately have political and economic causes: it is not due simply to the bad influence of this or that individual writer. But an effect can become a cause, reinforcing the original cause and producing the same effect in an intensified form, and so on indefinitely. A man may take to drink because he feels himself to be a failure, and then fail all the more completely because he drinks. It is rather the same thing that is happening to the English language. It becomes ugly and inaccurate because our thoughts are foolish, but the slovenliness of our language makes it easier for us to have foolish thoughts. The point is that the process is reversible. Modern English, especially written English, is full of bad habits which spread by imitation and which can be avoided if one is willing to take the necessary trouble. If one gets rid of these habits one can think more clearly, and to think clearly is a necessary first step toward political regeneration: so that the fight against bad English is not frivolous and is not the exclusive concern of professional writers. I will come back to this presently, and I hope that by that time the meaning of what I have said here will have become clearer. Meanwhile, here are five specimens of the English language as it is now habitually written.

These five passages have not been picked out because they are especially bad—I could have quoted far worse if I had chosen—but because they illustrate various of the mental vices from which we now suffer. They are a little below the average, but are fairly representative samples. I number them so that I can refer back to them when necessary:

> (1) I am not, indeed, sure whether it is not true to say that the Milton who once seemed not unlike a seventeenth-century Shelley had not become, out of an experience ever more bitter in each year, more alien [*sic*] to the founder of that Jesuit sect which nothing could induce him to tolerate.
>
> Professor Harold Laski
> (Essay in *Freedom of Expression*)

(2) Above all, we cannot play ducks and drakes with a native battery of idioms which prescribes such egregious collocations of vocables as the Basic *put up with* for *tolerate* or *put at a loss* for *bewilder.*

Professor Lancelot Hogben (*Interglossa*)

(3) On the one side we have the free personality: by definition it is not neurotic, for it has neither conflict nor dream. Its desires, such as they are, are transparent, for they are just what institutional approval keeps in the forefront of consciousness; another institutional pattern would alter their number and intensity; there is little in them that is natural, irreducible, or culturally dangerous. But *on the other side,* the social bond itself is nothing but the mutual reflection of these self-secure integrities. Recall the definition of love. Is not this the very picture of a small academic? Where is there a place in this hall of mirrors for either personality or fraternity?

Essay on psychology in *Politics* (New York)

(4) All the "best people" from the gentlemen's clubs, and all the frantic fascist captains, united in common hatred of Socialism and bestial horror of the rising tide of the mass revolutionary movement, have turned to acts of provocation, to foul incendiarism, to medieval legends of poisoned wells, to legalize their own destruction of proletarian organizations, and rouse the agitated petty-bourgeoisie to chauvinistic fervor on behalf of the fight against the revolutionary way out of the crisis.

Communist pamphlet

(5) If a new spirit *is* to be infused into this old country, there is one thorny and contentious reform which must be tackled, and that is the humanization and galvanization of the B.B.C. Timidity here will bespeak canker and atrophy of the soul. The heart of Britain may be sound and of strong beat, for instance, but the British lion's roar at present is like that of Bottom in Shakespeare's *Midsummer Night's Dream*—as gentle as any sucking dove. A virile new Britain cannot continue indefinitely to be traduced in the eyes or rather ears, of the world by the effete languors of Langham Place, brazenly masquerading as "standard English." When the Voice of Britain is heard at nine o'clock, better far and infinitely less ludicrous to hear aitches honestly dropped than the present priggish, inflated, inhibited, schoolma'amish arch braying of blameless bashful mewing maidens!

Letter in *Tribune*

Each of these passages has faults of its own, but, quite apart from avoidable ugliness, two qualities are common to all of them. The first is staleness of imagery; the other is lack of precision. The writer either has a meaning and cannot express it, or he inadvertently says something else, or he is almost indifferent as to whether his words mean anything or not. This mixture of vagueness and sheer incompetence is the most marked characteristic of modern English prose, and especially of any kind of political writing. As soon as certain topics are raised, the concrete melts into the abstract and no one seems able to think of turns of speech that are not hackneyed: prose consists less and less of *words* chosen for the sake of their meaning, and more and more of *phrases* tacked together like the sections of a prefabricated henhouse. I list below, with notes and examples, various of the tricks by means of which the work of prose-construction is habitually dodged:

Dying metaphors. A newly invented metaphor assists thought by evoking a visual image, while on the other hand a metaphor which is technically "dead" (e.g., *iron resolution*) has in effect reverted to being an ordinary word and can generally be used without loss of vividness. But in between these two classes there is a huge dump of worn-out metaphors which have lost all evocative power and are merely used because they save people the trouble of inventing phrases for themselves. Examples are: *Ring the changes on, take up the cudgels for, toe the line, ride roughshod over, stand shoulder to shoulder with, play into the hands of, no axe to grind, grist to the mill, fishing in troubled waters, on the order of the day, Achilles' heel, swan song, hotbed.* Many of these are used without knowledge of their meaning (what is a "rift," for instance?), and incompatible metaphors are frequently mixed, a sure sign that the writer is not interested in what he is saying. Some metaphors now current have been twisted out of their original meaning without those who use them even being aware of the fact. For example, *toe the line* is sometimes written *tow the line.* Another example is *the hammer and the anvil,* now always used with the implication that the anvil gets the worst of it. In real life it is always the anvil that breaks the hammer, never the other way about: a writer who stopped to think what he was saying would be aware of this, and would avoid perverting the original phrase.

Operators or *verbal false limbs.* These save the trouble of picking out appropriate verbs and nouns, and at the same time pad each sentence with extra syllables which give it an appearance of symmetry. Characteristic phrases are *render inoperative, militate against, make contact with, be subjected to, give rise to, give grounds for, have the effect of, play a leading part (role) in, make itself felt, take effect, exhibit a tendency to, serve the purpose of, etc., etc.* The keynote is the elimination of simple verbs. Instead of being a single word, such as *break, stop, spoil, mend, kill,* a verb becomes a *phrase,* made up of a noun or adjective tacked on to some general-purpose verb such as *prove, serve, form, play, render.* In addition, the passive voice is wherever possible used in preference to the active, and noun constructions are used instead of gerunds (*by examination of* instead of *by examining*). The range of verbs is further cut down by means of the *-ize* and *de-* formations, and the banal statements are given an appearance of profundity by means of the *not un-* formation. Simple conjunctions and prepositions are replaced by such phrases as *with respect to, having regard to, the fact that, by dint of, in view of, in the interests of, on the hypothesis that;* and the ends of sentences are saved by anticlimax by such resounding commonplaces as *greatly to be desired, cannot be left out of account, a development to be expected in the near future, deserving of serious consideration, brought to a satisfactory conclusion,* and so on and so forth.

Pretentious diction. Words like *phenomenon, element, individual* (as noun), *objective, categorical, effective, virtual, basic, primary, promote, constitute, exhibit, exploit, utilize, eliminate, liquidate,* are used to dress up simple statements and give an air of scientific impartiality to biased judgments and give an air of scientific impartiality to biased judgments. Adjectives like *epoch-making, epic, historic, unforgettable, triumphant, age-old, inevitable, inexorable, veritable,* are used to dignify the sordid processes of international politics, while writing that aims at glorifying war usually takes on an archaic color, its characteristic words being: *realm, throne, chariot, mailed fist, trident, sword, shield, buckler, banner, jackboot, clarion.* Foreign words and expressions such as *cul de sac, ancien régime, deus ex machina, mutatis mutandis, status quo, gleichschaltung, weltanschauung,* are used to give an air of culture and elegance. Except for the useful abbreviations *i.e., e.g.,* and *etc.,* there is no real need for any of the hundreds of foreign phrases now current in English. Bad writers, and especially scientific, political, and sociological writers, are nearly always haunted by the notion that Latin or Greek words are grander than Saxon ones, and unnecessary words like *expedite, ameloriate, predict, extraneous, deracinated, clandestine, subaqueous,* and hundreds of others constantly gain ground from their Anglo-Saxon opposite numbers.[1] The jargon peculiar to Marxist writing (*hyena, hangman, cannibal, petty bourgeois, these gentry, lackey, flunkey, mad dog, White Guard,* etc.) consists largely of words and phrases translated from Russian, German, or French; but the normal way of coining a new word is to use Latin or Greek root with the appropriate affix and, where necessary, the size formation. It is often easier to make up words of this kind (*deregionalize, impermissible, extramarital, nonfragmentary* and so forth) than to think up the English words that will cover one's meaning. The result, in general, is an increase in slovenliness and vagueness.

Meaningless words. In certain kinds of writing, particularly in art criticism and literary criticism, it is normal to come across long passages which are almost completely lacking in meaning.[2] Words like *romantic, plastic, values, human, dead, sentimental, natural, vitality,* as used in art criticism, are strictly meaningless, in the sense that they not only do not point to any discoverable object, but are hardly ever expected to do so by the reader. When one critic writes, "The outstanding feature of Mr. X's work is its living quality," while another writes, "The immediately striking thing about Mr. X's work is its peculiar deadness," the reader accepts this as a simple difference of opinion. If words like *black* and *white* were involved, instead of the jargon words *dead* and *living,* he would see at once that language was being used in an improper way. Many political words are similarly abused. The word *Fascism* has now no meaning except in so far as it signifies "something not

[1] An interesting illustration of this is the way in which the English flower names which were in use till very recently are being ousted by Greek ones, *snapdragon* becoming *antirrhinum, forget-me-not* becoming *myosotis,* etc. It is hard to see any practical reason for this change of fashion: it is probably due to an instinctive turning away from the more homely word and a vague feeling that the Greek word is scientific.

[2] Example: "Comfort's catholicity of perception and image, strangely Whitmanesque in range, almost the exact opposite in aesthetic compulsion, continues to evoke that trembling atmospheric accumulative hinting at a cruel, an inexorably serene timelessness. . . . Wrey Gardiner scores by aiming at simple bull's-eyes with precision. Only they are not so simple, and through this contented sadness runs more than the surface bittersweet of resignation." (*Poetry Quarterly.*)

desirable." The words *democracy, socialism, freedom, patriotic, realistic, justice,* have each of them several different meanings which cannot be reconciled with one another. In the case of a word like *democracy,* not only is there no agreed definition, but the attempt to make one is resisted from all sides. It is almost universally felt that when we call a country democratic we are praising it: consequently the defenders of every kind of régime claim that it is a democracy, and fear that they might have to stop using the word if it were tied down to any one meaning. Words of this kind are often used in a consciously dishonest way. That is, the person who uses them has his own private definition, but allows his hearer to think he means something quite different. Statements like *Marshal Pétain was a true patriot, The Soviet press is the freest in the world, The Catholic Church is opposed to persecution,* are almost always made with intent to deceive. Other words used in variable meanings, in most cases more or less dishonestly, are: *class, totalitarian, science, progressive, reactionary, bourgeois, equality.*

Now that I have made this catalogue of swindles and perversions, let me give another example of the kind of writing that they lead to. This time it must of its nature be an imaginary one. I am going to translate a passage of good English into modern English of the worst sort. Here is a well-known verse from *Ecclesiastes:*

> I returned and saw under the sun, that the race is not to the swift, nor the battle to the strong, neither yet bread to the wise, nor yet riches to men of understanding, nor yet favour to men of skill; but time and chance happeneth to them all.

Here it is in modern English:

> Objective considerations of contemporary phenomena compel the conclusion that success or failure in competitive activities exhibits no tendency to be commensurate with innate capacity, but that a considerable element of the unpredictable must invariably be taken into account.

This is a parody, but not a very gross one. Exhibit (3), above, for instance, contains several patches of the same kind of English. It will be seen that I have not made a full translation. The beginning and ending of the sentence follow the original meaning fairly closely, but in the middle the concrete illustrations—race, battle, bread—dissolve into the vague phrase "success or failure in competitive activities." This had to be so, because no modern writer of the kind I am discussing—no one capable of using phrases like "objective consideration of contemporary phenomena"—would ever tabulate his thoughts in that precise and detailed way. The whole tendency of modern prose is away from concreteness. Now analyze these two sentences a little more closely. The first contains forty-nine words but only sixty syllables, and all its words are those of everyday life. The second contains thirty-eight words of ninety syllables: eighteen of its words are from Latin roots, and one from Greek. The first sentence contains six vivid images, and only one phrase ("time and chance") that could be called vague. The second contains not a single fresh, arresting phrase, and in spite of its ninety syllables it gives only a shortened version of the meaning contained in the first. Yet without a doubt it is the second kind of sentence that is gaining ground in modern English. I do not want to exaggerate. This kind of writing is not yet universal, and outcrops of simplicity will occur here and there in the worst-written page. Still, if you or I were told to write a few lines on the uncertainty of human fortunes, we should probably come much nearer to my imaginary sentence than to the one from *Ecclesiastes*.

As I have tried to show, modern writing at its worst does not consist in picking out words for the sake of their meaning and inventing images in order to make the meaning clearer. It consists in gumming together long strips of words which have already been set in order by someone else, and making the results presentable by sheer humbug. The attraction of this way of writing is that it is easy. It is easier—even quicker, once you have the habit—to say *In my opinion it is not an unjustifiable assumption that* than to say *I think*. If you use ready-made phrases, you not only don't have to hunt about for words; you also don't have to bother with the rhythms of your sentences, since these phrases are generally so arranged as to be more or less euphonious. When you are composing in a hurry—when you are dictating to a stenographer, for instance, or making a public speech—it is natural to fall into a pretentious, Latinized style. Tags like *a consideration which we should do well to bear in mind* or *a conclusion to which all of us would readily assent* will save many a sentence from coming down with a bump. By using stale metaphors, similes, and idioms, you save much mental effort, at the cost of leaving your meaning vague, not only for your reader but for yourself. This is the significance of mixed metaphors. The sole aim of a metaphor is to call up a visual image. When these images clash—as in *The Fascist octopus has sung its swan song, the jackboot is thrown into the melting pot*—it can be taken as certain that the writer is not seeing a mental image of the objects he is naming; in other words he is not really thinking. Look again at the examples I gave at the beginning of this essay. Professor Laski (1) uses five negatives in fifty-three words. One of these is superfluous, making nonsense of the whole passage, and in addition there is the slip—*alien* for akin—making further nonsense, and several avoidable pieces of clumsiness which increase the general vagueness. Professor Hogben (2) plays ducks and drakes with a battery which is able to write prescriptions, and, while disapproving of the everyday phrase *put up with,* is unwilling to look *egregious* up in the dictionary and see what it means; (3), if one takes an uncharitable attitude towards it, is simply meaningless: probably one could work out its intended meaning by reading the whole of the article in which it occurs. In (4), the writer knows more or less what he wants to say, but an accumulation of stale phrases chokes him like tea leaves blocking a sink. In (5), words and meaning have almost parted company. People who write in this manner usually have a general emotional meaning—they dislike one thing and want to express solidarity with another —but they are not interested in the detail of what they are saying. A scrupulous writer, in every sentence that he writes, will ask himself at least four questions, thus: What am I trying to say? What words will express it?

What image or idiom will make it clearer? Is this image fresh enough to have an effect? And he will probably ask himself two more: Could I put it more shortly? Have I said anything that is avoidably ugly? But you are not obliged to go to all this trouble. You can shirk it by simply throwing your mind open and letting the ready-made phrases come crowding in. They will construct your sentences for you—even think your thoughts for you, to a certain extent—and at need they will perform the important service of partially concealing your meaning even from yourself. It is at this point that the special connection between politics and the debasement of language becomes clear.

In our time it is broadly true that political writing is bad writing. Where it is not true, it will generally be found that the writer is some kind of rebel, expressing his private opinions and not a "party line." Orthodoxy, of whatever color, seems to demand a lifeless, imitative style. The political dialects to be found in pamphlets, leading articles, manifestoes, White papers and the speeches of undersecretaries do, of course, vary from party to party, but they are all alike in that one almost never finds in them a fresh, vivid, homemade turn of speech. When one watches some tired hack on the platform mechanically repeating the familiar phrases—*bestial atrocities, iron heel, bloodstained tyranny, free peoples of the world, stand shoulder to shoulder*—one often has a curious feeling that one is not watching a live human being but some kind of dummy: a feeling which suddenly becomes stronger at moments when the light catches the speaker's spectacles and turns them into blank discs which seem to have no eyes behind them. And this is not altogether fanciful. A speaker who uses that kind of phraseology has gone some distance toward turning himself into a machine. The appropriate noises are coming out of his larynx, but his brain is not involved as it would be if he were choosing his words for himself. If the speech he is making is one that he is accustomed to make over and over again, he may be almost unconscious of what he is saying, as one is when one utters the responses in church. And this reduced state of consciousness, if not indispensable, is at any rate favorable to political conformity.

In our time, political speech and writing are largely the defense of the indefensible. Things like the continuance of British rule in India, the Russian purges and deportations, the dropping of the atom bombs on Japan, can indeed be defended, but only by arguments which are too brutal for most people to face, and which do not square with the professed aims of political parties. Thus political language has to consist largely of euphemism, question-begging and sheer cloudy vagueness. Defenseless villages are bombarded from the air, the inhabitants driven out into the countryside, the cattle machine-gunned, the huts set on fire with incendiary bullets: this is called *pacification*. Millions of peasants are robbed of their farms and sent trudging along the roads with no more than they can carry: this is called *transfer of population* or *rectification of frontiers*. People are imprisoned for years without trial, or shot in the back of the neck or sent to die of scurvy in Artic lumber camps: this is called *elimination of unreliable elements*. Such phraseology is needed if one wants to name things without calling up mental pictures of them. Consider for instance some comfortable English professor defending Russian totalitarianism. He cannot say outright, "I believe in killing off your opponents when you can get good results by doing so." Probably, therefore, he will say something like this:

"While freely conceding that the Soviet regime exhibits certain features which the humanitarian may be inclined to deplore, we must, I think, agree that a certain curtailment of the right to political opposition is an unavoidable concomitant of transitional periods, and that the rigors which the Russian people have been called upon to undergo have been amply justified in the sphere of concrete achievement."

The inflated style is itself a kind of euphemism. A mass of Latin words falls upon the facts like soft snow, blurring the outlines and covering up all the details. The great enemy of clear language is insincerity. When there is a gap between one's real and one's declared aims, one turns as it were instinctively to long words and exhausted idioms, like a cuttlefish squirting out ink. In our age there is no such thing as "keeping out of politics." All issues are political issues, and politics itself is a mass of lies, evasions, folly, hatred, and schizophrenia. When the general atmosphere is bad, language must suffer. I should expect to find—this is a guess which I have not sufficient knowledge to verify—that the German, Russian and Italian languages have all deteriorated in the last ten or fifteen years, as a result of dictatorship.

But if thought corrupts language, language can also corrupt thought. A bad usage can spread by tradition and imitation, even among people who should and do know better. The debased language that I have been discussing is in some ways very convenient. Phrases like *a not unjustifiable assumption, leaves much to be desired, would serve no good purpose, a consideration which we should do well to bear in mind,* are a continuous temptation, a packet of aspirins always at one's elbow. Look back through this essay, and for certain you will find that I have again and again committed the very faults I am protesting against. By this morning's post I have received a pamphlet dealing with conditions in Germany. The author tells me that he "felt impelled" to write it. I open it at random, and here is almost the first sentence that I see: "[The Allies] have an opportunity not only of achieving a radical transformation of Germany's social and political structure in such a way as to avoid a nationalistic reaction in Germany itself, but at the same time of laying the foundations of a co-operative and unified Europe." You see, he "feels impelled" to write—feels, presumably, that he has something new to say—and yet his words, like cavalry horses answering the bugle, group themselves automatically into the familiar dreary pattern. This invasion of one's mind by ready-made phrases (*lay the foundations, achieve a radical transformation*) can only be prevented if one is constantly on guard against them, and every such phrase anaesthetizes a portion of one's brain.

I said earlier that the decadence of our language is probably curable. Those who deny this would argue, if they produced an argument at all, that language merely reflects existing social conditions, and that we cannot influence its development by any direct tinkering with words and constructions.

So far as the general tone or spirit of a language goes, this may be true, but it is not true in detail. Silly words and expressions have often disappeared, not through any evolutionary process but owing to the conscious action of a minority. Two recent examples were *explore every avenue* and *leave no stone unturned,* which were killed by the jeers of a few journalists. There is a long list of flyblown metaphors which could similarly be got rid of if enough people would interest themselves in the job; and it should also be possible to laugh the *not un-* formation out of existence[3] to reduce the amount of Latin and Greek in the average sentence, to drive out foreign phrases and strayed scientific words, and, in general, to make pretentiousness unfashionable. But all these are minor points. The defense of the English language implies more than this, and perhaps it is best to start by saying what it does *not* imply.

To begin with it has nothing to do with archaism, with the salvaging of obsolete words and turns of speech, or with the setting up of a "standard English" which must never be departed from. On the contrary, it is especially concerned with the scrapping of every word or idiom which has outworn its usefulness. It has nothing to do with correct grammar and syntax, which are of no importance so long as one makes one's meaning clear, or with the avoidance of Americanisms, or with having what is called a "good prose style." On the other hand it is not concerned with fake simplicity and the attempt to make written English colloquial. Nor does it even imply in every case preferring the Saxon word to the Latin one, though it does imply using the fewest and shortest words that will cover one's meaning. What is above all needed is to let the meaning choose the word, and not the other way about. In prose, the worst thing one can do with words is to surrender to them. When you think of a concrete object, you think wordlessly, and then, if you want to describe the thing you have been visualizing you probably hunt about till you find the exact words that seem to fit it. When you think of something abstract you are more inclined to use words from the start, and unless you make a conscious effort to prevent it, the existing dialect will come rushing in and do the job for you, at the expense of blurring or even changing your meaning. Probably it is better to put off using words as long as possible and get one's meaning as clear as one can through pictures or sensations. Afterward one can choose—not simply *accept*—the phrases that will best cover the meaning, and then switch round and decide what impression one's words are likely to make on another person. This last effort of the mind cuts out all stale or mixed images, all prefabricated phrases, needless repetitions, and humbug and vagueness generally. But one can often be in doubt about the effect of a word or a phrase, and one needs rules that one can rely on when instinct fails. I think the following rules will cover most cases:

(i) Never use a metaphor, simile, or other figure of speech which you are used to seeing in print.

(ii) Never use a long word where a short one will do.

[3] One can cure oneself of the *not un-* formation by memorizing this sentence: *A not unblack dog was chasing a not unsmall rabbit across a not ungreen field.*

(iii) If it is possible to cut a word out, always cut it out.

(iv) Never use the passive where you can use the active.

(v) Never use a foreign phrase, a scientific word, or a jargon word if you can think of an everyday English equivalent.

(vi) Break any of these rules sooner than say anything outright barbarous.

These rules sound elementary, and so they are, but they demand a deep change of attitude in anyone who has grown used to writing in the style now fashionable. One could keep all of them and still write bad English, but one could not write the kind of stuff that I quoted in those five specimens at the beginning of this article.

I have not here been considering the literary use of language, but merely language as an instrument for expressing and not for concealing or preventing thought. Stuart Chase and others have come near to claiming that all abstract words are meaningless, and have used this as a pretext for advocating a kind of political quietism. Since you don't know what Fascism is, how can you struggle against Fascism? One need not swallow such absurdities as this, but one ought to recognize that the present political chaos is connected with the decay of language, and that one can probably bring about some improvement by starting at the verbal end. If you simplify your English, you are freed from the worst follies of orthodoxy. You cannot speak any of the necessary dialects, and when you make a stupid remark its stupidity will be obvious, even to yourself. Political language—and with variations this is true of all political parties, from Conservatives to Anarchists—is designed to make lies sound truthful and murder respectable, and to give an appearance of solidity to pure wind. One cannot change this all in a moment, but one can at least change one's own habits, and from time to time one can even, if one jeers loudly enough, send some worn-out and useless phrase—some *jackboot, Archilles' heel, hotbed, melting pot, acid test, veritable inferno,* or other lump of verbal refuse—into the dustbin where it belongs.

"NEXT TO OF COURSE GOD AMERICA I

E. E. Cummings

"next to of course god america i
love you land of the pilgrims' and so forth oh
say can you see by the dawn's early my
country 'tis of centuries come and go
and are no more what of it we should worry

in every language even deafanddumb
thy sons acclaim your glorious name by gorry
by jingo by gee by gosh by gum
why talk of beauty what could be more beautiful than these heroic happy dead
who rushed like lions to the roaring slaughter
they did not stop to think they died instead
then shall the voice of liberty be mute?"

He spoke.   And drank rapidly a glass of water

THE PRINCIPLES OF NEWSPEAK

George Orwell

Newspeak was the official language of Oceania and had been devised to meet the ideological needs of Ingsoc, or English Socialism. In the year 1984 there was not as yet anyone who used Newspeak as his sole means of communication, either in speech or writing. The leading articles in the *Times* were written in it, but this was a tour de force which could only be carried out by a specialist. It was expected that Newspeak would have finally superseded Oldspeak (or Standard English, as we should call it) by about the year 2050. Meanwhile it gained ground steadily, all Party members tending to use Newspeak words and grammatical constructions more and more in their everyday speech. The version in use in 1984, and embodied in the Ninth and Tenth Editions of the Newspeak dictionary, was a provisional one, and contained many superfluous words and archaic formations which were due to be suppressed later. It is with the final, perfected version, as embodied in the Eleventh Edition of the dictionary, that we are concerned here.

The purpose of Newspeak was not only to provide a medium of expression for the world-view and mental habits proper to the devotees of Ingsoc, but to make all other modes of thought impossible. It was intended that when Newspeak had been adopted once and for all and Oldspeak forgotten, a heretical thought—that is, a thought diverging from the principles of Ingsoc—should be literally unthinkable, at least so far as thought is dependent on words. Its vocabulary was so constructed as to give exact and often very subtle expression to every meaning that a Party member could properly wish to express, while excluding all other meanings and also the possibility of arriving at them by indirect methods. This was done partly by the invention of new words, but chiefly by eliminating undesirable words and by stripping such words as remained of unorthodox meanings, and so far as possible of all secondary meanings whatever. To give a simple example. The word *free* still existed in Newspeak, but it could only be used in such statements as "This dog is free from lice" or "This field is free from weeds." It could not be used in its old sense of "politically free" or "intellectually free," since political and intellectual freedom no longer existed even as concepts, and were therefore of necessity nameless. Quite apart from the suppression of definitely heretical words, reduction of vocabulary was regarded as an end in itself, and no word that could be dispensed with was allowed to survive. Newspeak was designated not to extend but to *diminish* the range of thought, and this purpose was indirectly assisted by cutting the choice of words down to a minimum.

Newspeak was founded on the English language as we now know it, through many Newspeak sentences, even when not containing newly created words, would be barely intelligible to an English-speaker of our own day. Newspeak words were divided into three distinct classes, known as the A vocabulary, the B vocabulary (also called compound words), and the C vocabulary. It will be simpler to discuss each class separately, but the grammatical peculiarities of the language can be dealt with in the section devoted to the A vocabulary, since the same rules held good for all three categories.

The A vocabulary. The A vocabulary consisted of the words needed for the business of everyday life—for such things as eating, drinking, working, putting on one's clothes, going up and down stairs, riding in vehicles, gardening, cooking, and the like. It was composed almost entirely of words that we already possess—words like *hit, run, dog, tree, sugar, house, field*—but in comparison with the present-day English vocabulary, their number was extremely small, while their meanings were far more rigidly defined. All ambiguities and shades of meaning had been purged out of them. So far as it could be achieved, a Newspeak word of this class was simply a staccato sound expressing *one* clearly understood concept. It would have been quite impossible to use the A vocabulary for literary purposes or for political or philosophical discussion. It was intended only to express simple, purposive thoughts, usually involving concrete objects or physical actions.

The grammar of Newspeak had two outstanding peculiarities. The first of these was an almost complete interchangeability between different parts of speech. Any word in the language (in principle this applied even to very abstract words such as *if* or *when*) could be used either as verb, noun, adjective, or adverb. Between the verb and the noun form, when they were of the same root, there was never any variation, this rule of itself involving the destruction of many archaic forms. The word *thought,* for example, did not exist in Newspeak. Its place was taken by *think,* which did duty for both noun and verb. No etymological principle was followed here; in some cases it was the original noun that was chosen for retention, in other cases the verb. Even where a noun and verb of kindred meaning were not etymologically connected, one or other of them was frequently suppressed. There was, for example, no such word as *cut,* its meaning being sufficiently covered by the noun-verb *knife.* Adjectives were formed by adding the suffix *-ful* to the noun-verb, and adverbs by adding *-wise.* Thus, for example, *speedful* meant "rapid" and *speedwise* meant "quickly." Certain of our present-day adjectives, such as *good, strong, big, black, soft,* were retained, but their total number was very small. There was little need for them, since almost any adjectival meaning could be arrived at by adding *-ful* to a noun-verb. None of the now-existing adverbs was retained, except for a very few already ending in *-wise;* the *-wise* termination was invariable. The word *well,* for example, was replaced by *goodwise.*

In addition, any word—this again applied in principle to every word in the language—could be negatived by adding the affix *un-,* or could be strengthened by the affix, *plus-,* or, for still greater emphasis, *doubleplus-.* Thus, for example, *uncold* meant "warm," while *pluscold* and *doubleplus-cold* meant, respectively, "very cold" and "superlatively cold." It was also possible, as in present-day English, to modify the meaning of almost any word by prepositional affixes such as *ante-, post-, up-, down-,* etc. By such methods it was found possible to bring about an enormous diminution of vocabulary. Given, for instance, the word *good,* there was no need for such a word as *bad,* since the required meaning was equally well—indeed, bette —expressed by *ungood.* All that was necessary, in any case where two words formed a natural pair of opposites, was to decide which of them to suppress. *Dark,* for example, could be replaced by *unlight,* or *light* by *undark,* according to preference.

The second distinguishing mark of Newspeak grammar was its regularity. Subject to a few exceptions which are mentioned below, all inflections followed the same rules. Thus, in all verbs the preterite and the past participle were the same and ended in *-ed.* The preterite of *steal* was *stealed,* the preterite of *think* was *thinked,* and so on throughout the language, all such forms as *swam, gave, brought, spoke, taken,* etc., being abolished. All plurals were made by adding *-s* or *-es* as the case might be. The plurals of *man, ox, life* were *mans, oxes, lifes.* Comparisons of adjectives was invariably made by adding *-er, -est* (*good, gooder, goodest*), irregular forms and the *more, most* formation being suppressed.

The only classes of words that were still allowed to inflect irregularly were the pronouns, the relatives, the demonstrative adjectives, and the auxiliary verbs. All of these followed their ancient usage, except that *whom* had been scrapped as unnecessary, and the *shall, should* tenses had been dropped, all their uses being covered by *will* and *would.* There were also certain irregularities in word-forming arising out of the need for rapid and easy speech. A word which was difficult to utter, or was liable to be incorrectly heard, was held to be ipso facto a bad word; occasionally, therefore, for the sake of euphony, extra letters were inserted into a word or an archaic formation was retained. But this need made itself felt chiefly in connection with the B vocabulary. *Why* so great an importance was attached to ease of pronunciation will be made clear later in this essay.

The B vocabulary. The B vocabulary consisted of words that had been deliberately constructed for political purposes: words, that is to say, which not only had in every case a political implication, but were intended to impose a desirable mental attitude upon the person using them. Without a full understanding of the principles of Ingsoc it was difficult to use these words correctly. In some cases they could be translated into Oldspeak, or even into words taken from the A vocabulary, but this usually demanded a long paraphrase and always involved the loss of certain overtones. The B words were a sort of verbal shorthand, often packing whole ranges of ideas into a few syllables, and at the same time more accurate and forcible than ordinary language.

The B words were in all cases compound words.[4] They consisted of two or more words, or portions of words, welded together in an easily pronounceable form. The resulting amalgam was always a noun-verb, and inflected according to the ordinary rules. To take a single example: the word *goodthink,* meaning, very roughly, "orthodoxy," or, if one chose to regard it as a verb, "to think in an orthodox manner." This inflected as follows: noun-verb, *goodthink;* past tense and past participle, *goodthinked;* present participle, *goodthinking;* adjective, *goodthinkful;* adverb, *goodthinkwise;* verbal noun, *goodthinker.*

The B words were not constructed on any etymological plan. The words of which they were made up could be any parts of speech, and could be placed in any order and mutilated in any way which made them easy to pronounce while indicating their derivation. In the word *crimethink* (thoughtcrime), for instance, the *think* came second, whereas in *thinkpol* (Thought Police) it came first, and in the latter word *police* had lost its second syllable. Because of the greater difficulty in securing euphony, irregular formations were commoner in the B vocabulary than in the A vocabulary. For example, the adjectival forms of *Minitrue, Minipax,* and *Miniluv* were, respectively, *Minitruthful, Minipeaceful,* and *Minilovely,* simply because *-trueful, -paxful,* and *-loveful* were slightly awkward to pronounce. In principle, however, all B words could inflect, and all inflected in exactly the same way.

Some of the B words had highly subtilized meanings, barely intelligible to anyone who had not mastered the language as a whole. Consider, for example, such a typical sentence from a *Times* leading article as *Oldthinkers unbellyfeel Ingsoc.* The shortest rendering that one could make of this in Oldspeak would be: "Those whose ideas were formed before the Revolution cannot have a full emotional understanding of the principles of English Socialism." But this is not an adequate translation. To begin with, in order to grasp the full meaning of the Newspeak sentence quoted above, one would have to have a clear idea of what is meant by *Ingsoc.* And, in addition, only a person thoroughly grounded in Ingsoc could appreciate the full force of the word *bellyfeel,* which implied a blind, enthusiastic acceptance

---

[4] Compound words, such as *speakwrite,* were of course to be found in the A vocabulary, but these were merely convenient abbreviations and had no special ideological color.

difficult to imagine today; or of the word *oldthink,* which was inextricably mixed up with the idea of wickedness and decadence. But the special function of certain Newspeak words, of which *oldthink* was one, was not so much to express meanings as to destroy them. These words, necessarily few in number, had had their meanings extended until they contained within themselves whole batteries of words which, as they were sufficiently covered by a single comprehensive term, could now be scrapped and forgotten. The greatest difficulty facing the compilers of the Newspeak dictionary was not to invent new words, but, having invented them, to make sure what they meant: to make sure, that is to say, what ranges of words they canceled by their existence.

As we have already seen in the case of the word *free,* words which had once borne a heretical meaning were sometimes retained for the sake of convenience, but only with the undesirable meanings purged out of them. Countless other words such as *honor, justice, morality, internationalism, democracy, science,* and *religion* had simply ceased to exist. A few blanket words covered them, and, in covering them, abolished them. All words grouping themselves round the concepts of liberty and equality, for instance, were contained in the single word *crimethink,* while all words grouping themselves round the concepts of objectivity and rationalism were contained in the single word *oldthink.* Greater precision would have been dangerous. What was required in a Party member was an outlook similar to that of the ancient Hebrew who knew, without knowing much else, that all nations other than his own worshiped "false gods." He did not need to know that these gods were called Baal, Osiris, Moloch, Ashtaroth, and the like; probably the less he knew about them the better for his orthodoxy. He knew Jehovah and the commandments of Jehovah; he knew, therefore, that all gods with other names or other attributes were false gods. In somewhat the same way, the Party member knew what constituted right conduct, and in exceedingly vague, generalized terms he knew what kinds of departure from it were possible. His sexual life, for example, was entirely regulated by the two Newspeak words *sexcrime* (sexual immorality) and *goodsex* (chastity). *Sexcrime* covered all sexual misdeeds whatever. It covered fornication, adultery, homosexuality, and other perversions, and, in addition, normal intercourse practiced for its own sake. There was no need to enumerate them separately, since they were all equally culpable, and, in principle, all punishable by death. In the C vocabulary, which consisted of scientific and technical words, it might be necessary to give specialized names to certain sexual aberrations, but the ordinary citizen had no need of them. He knew what was meant by *goodsex*—that is to say, normal intercourse between man and wife, for the sole purpose of begetting children, and without physical pleasure on the part of the woman; all else was *sexcrime.* In Newspeak it was seldom possible to follow a heretical thought further than the perception that it *was* heretical; beyond that point the necessary words were nonexistent.

No word in the B vocabulary was ideologically neutral. A great many were euphemisms. Such words, for instance, as *joycamp* (forced-labor camp) or *Minipax* (Ministry of Peace, i.e., Ministry of War) meant almost the exact opposite of what they appeared to mean. Some words, on the other hand, displayed a frank and contemptuous understanding of the real nature of Oceanic society. An example was *prolefeed,* meaning the rubbishy entertainment and spurious news which the Party handed out to the masses. Other words, again, were ambivalent, having the connotation "good" when applied to the Party and "bad" when applied to its enemies. But in addition there were great numbers of words which at first sight appeared to be mere abbreviations and which derived their ideological color not from their meaning but from their structure.

So far as it could be contrived, everything that had or might have political significance of any kind was fitted into the B vocabulary. The name of every organization, or body of people, or doctrine, or country, or institution, or public building, was invariably cut down into the familiar shape; that is, a single easily pronounced word with the smallest number of syllables that would preserve the original derivation. In the Ministry of Truth, for example, the Records Department, in which Winston Smith worked, was called *Recdep,* the Fiction Department was called *Ficdep,* the Teleprograms Department was called *Teledep,* and so on. This was done solely with the object of saving time. Even in the early decades of the twentieth century, telescoped words and phrases had been one of the characteristic features of political language; and it had been noticed that the tendency to use abbreviations of this kind was most marked in totalitarian countries and totalitarian organizations. Examples were such words as *Nazi, Gestapo, Comintern, Inprecorr, Agitprop.* In the beginning the practice had been adopted as it were instinctively, but in Newspeak it was used with a conscious purpose. It was perceived that in thus abbreviating a name one narrowed and subtly altered its meaning, by cutting out most of the associations that would otherwise cling to it. The words *Communist International,* for instance, call up a composite picture of universal human brotherhood, red flags, barricades, Karl Marx, and the Paris Commune. The word Comintern, on the other hand, suggests merely a tightly knit organization and a well-defined body of doctrine. It refers to something almost as easily recognized, and as limited in purpose, as a chair or a table. *Comintern* is a word that can be uttered almost without taking thought, whereas *Communist International* is a phrase over which one is obliged to linger at least momentarily. In the same way, the associations called up by a word like *Minitrue* are fewer and more controllable than those called up by *Ministry of Truth.* This accounted not only for the habit of abbreviating whenever possible, but also for the almost exaggerated care that was taken to make every word easily pronounceable.

In Newspeak, euphony outweighed every consideration other than exactitude of meaning. Regularity of grammar was always sacrificed to it when it seemed necessary. And rightly so, since what was required, above all for political purposes, were short clipped words of unmistakable meaning which could be uttered rapidly and which roused the minimum of echoes in the speaker's mind. The words of the B vocabulary even gained in force from the fact that nearly all of them were very much alike. Almost invariably these words—*goodthink, Minipax, prolefeed, sexcrime, joycamp, Ingsoc, bellyfeel, thinkpol,* and countless others—were words of two or three syllables, with the stress distributed equally between the first syllable and the last. The use of them encouraged a gabbling style of speech, at once staccato and monotonous. And this was exactly what was aimed at. The intention was to make speech, and especially speech on any subject not ideologically neutral, as nearly as possible independent of consciousness. For the purposes of everyday life it was no doubt necessary, or sometimes necessary, to reflect before speaking, but a Party member called upon to make a political or ethical judgment should be able to spray forth the correct opinions as automatically as a machine gun spraying forth bullets. His training fitted him to do this, the language gave him an almost foolproof instrument, and the texture of the words, with their harsh sound and a certain willful ugliness which was in accord with the spirit of Ingsoc, assisted the process still further.

So did the fact of having very few words to choose from. Relative to our own, the Newspeak vocabulary was tiny, and new ways of reducing it were constantly being devised. Newspeak, indeed, differed from almost all other languages in that its vocabulary grew smaller instead of larger every year. Each reduction was a gain, since the smaller the area of choice, the smaller the temptation to take thought. Ultimately it was hoped to make articulate speech issue from the larynx without involving the higher brain centers at all. This aim was frankly admitted in the Newspeak word *duckspeak,* meaning "to quack like a duck." Like various other words in the B vocabulary, *duckspeak* was ambivalent in meaning. Provided that the opinions which were quacked out were orthodox ones, it implied nothing but praise, and when the *Times* referred to one of the orators of the Party as a *doubleplusgood duckspeaker* it was paying a warm and valued compliment.

The C vocabulary. The C vocabulary was supplementary to the others and consisted entirely of scientific and technical terms. These resembled the scientific terms in use today, and were constructed from the same roots, but the usual care was taken to define them rigidly and strip them of undesirable meanings. They followed the same grammatical rules as the words in the other two vocabularies. Very few of the C words had any currency either in everyday speech or in political speech. Any scientific worker or technician could find all the words he needed in the list devoted to his own specialty, but he seldom had more than a smattering of the words occurring in the other lists. Only a very few words were common to all lists, and there was no vocabulary expressing the function of Science as a habit of mind, or a method of thought, irrespective of its particular branches. There was, indeed, no word for "Science," any meaning that it could possibly bear being already sufficiently covered by the word *Ingsoc.*

From the foregoing account it will be seen that in Newspeak the expression of unorthodox opinions, above a very low level, was well-nigh impossible. It was of course possible to utter heresies of a very crude kind, a species of blasphemy. It would have been possible, for example, to say *Big Brother is ungood.* But this statement, which to an orthodox ear merely conveyed a self-evident absurdity, could not have been sustained by reasoned argument, because the necessary words were not available. Ideas inimical to Ingsoc could only be entertained in a vague wordless form, and could only be named in very broad terms which lumped together and condemned whole groups of heresies without defining them in doing so. One could, in fact, only use Newspeak for unorthodox purposes by illegitimately translating some of the words back into Oldspeak. For example, *All mans are equal* was a possible Newspeak sentence, but only in the same sense in which *All men are redhaired* is a possible Oldspeak sentence. It did not contain a grammatical error, but it expressed a palpable untruth, i.e., that all men are of equal size, weight, or strength. The concept of political equality no longer existed, and this secondary meaning had accordingly been purged out of the word *equal*. In 1984, when Oldspeak was still the normal means of communication, the danger theoretically existed that in using Newspeak words one might remember their original meanings. In practice it was not difficult for any person well grounded in *doublethink* to avoid doing this, but within a couple of generations even the possibility of such a lapse would have vanished. A person growing up with Newspeak as his sole language would no more know that *equal* had once had the secondary meaning of "politically equal," or that *free* had once meant "intellectually free," than, for instance, a person who had never heard of chess would be aware of the secondary meanings attached to *queen* and *rook*. There would be many crimes and errors which it would be beyond his power to commit, simply because they were nameless and therefore unimaginable. And it was to be foreseen that with the passage of time the distinguishing characteristics of Newspeak would become more and more pronounced—its words growing fewer and fewer, their meanings more and more rigid, and the chance of putting them to improper uses always diminishing.

When Oldspeak had been once and for all superseded, the last link with the past would have been severed. History had already been rewritten, but fragments of the literature of the past survived here and there, imperfectly censored, and so long as one retained one's knowledge of Oldspeak it was possible to read them. In the future such fragments, even if they chanced to survive, would be unintelligible and untranslatable. It was impossible to translate any passage of Oldspeak into Newspeak unless it either referred to some technical process or some very simple everyday action, or was already orthodox (*goodthinkful* would be the Newspeak expression) in tendency. In practice this meant that no book written before approximately 1960 could be translated as a whole. Prerevolutionary literature could only be subjected to ideological translation—that is, alteration in sense as well as language. Take for example the well-known passage from the Declaration of Independence:

> We hold these truths to be self-evident, that all men are created equal,
> that they are endowed by their Creator with certain inalienable rights, that

among these are life, liberty and the pursuit of happiness. That to secure these rights, Governments are instituted among men, deriving their powers from the consent of the governed. That whenever any form of Government becomes destructive of those ends, it is the right of the People to alter or abolish it, and to institute new Government . . .

It would have been quite impossible to render this into Newspeak while keeping to the sense of the original. The nearest one could come to doing so would be to swallow the whole passage up in the single word *crimethink*. A full translation could only be an ideological translation, whereby Jefferson's words would be changed into a panegyric on absolute government.

A good deal of the literature of the past was, indeed, already being transformed in this way. Considerations of prestige made it desirable to preserve the memory of certain historical figures, while at the same time bringing their achievements into line with the philosophy of Ingsoc. Various writers, such as Shakespeare, Milton, Swift, Byron, Dickens and some others were therefore in process of translation; when the task had been completed, their original writings, with all else that survived of the literature of the past, would be destroyed. These translations were a slow and difficult business, and it was not expected that they would be finished before the first or second decade of the twenty-first century. There were also large quantities of merely utilitarian literature—indispensable technical manuals and the like—that had to be treated in the same way. It was chiefly in order to allow time for the preliminary work of translation that the final adoption of Newspeak had been fixed for so late a date as 2050.

THE HOLLOW MIRACLE

George Steiner

Agreed: post-war Germany is a miracle. But it is a very queer miracle. There is a superb frenzy of life on the surface; but at the heart, there is a queer stillness. Go there: look away for a moment from the marvel of the production lines; close your ears momentarily to the rush of the motors.

The thing that has gone dead is the German language. Open the daily papers, the magazines, the flood of popular and learned books pouring off the new printing presses; go to hear a new German play, listen to the language as it is spoken over the radio or in the Bundestag. It is no longer the language of Goethe, Heine, and Nietzsche. It is not even that of Thomas Mann. Something immensely destructive has happened to it. It makes noise. It even communicates, but it creates no sense of communion.

Languages are living organisms. Infinitely complex, but organisms never-theless. They have in them a certain life-force, and certain powers of ab-sorption and growth. But they can decay and they can die.

A language shows that it has in it the germ of dissolution in several ways. Actions of the mind that were once spontaneous become mechanical, frozen habits (dead metaphors, stock similes, slogans). Words grow longer and more ambiguous. Instead of style, there is rhetoric. Instead of precise com-mon usage, there is jargon. Foreign roots and burrowings are no longer absorbed into the blood stream of the native tongue. They are merely swal-lowed and remain an alien intrusion. All these technical failures accumulate to the essential failure: the language no longer sharpens thought but blurs it. Instead of charging every expression with the greatest available energy and directness, it loosens and disperses the intensity of feeling. The language is no longer adventure (and a live language is the highest adventure of which the human brain is capable). In short, the language is no longer lived; it is merely spoken.

That condition can last for a very long time; observe how Latin remained in use long after the springs of life in Roman civilization had run dry. But where it has happened, something essential in a civilization will not recover. And it has happened in Germany. That is why there is at the center of the miracle of Germany's material resurrection such a profound deadness of spirit, such an inescapable sense of triviality and dissimulation.

What brought death to the German language? That is a fascinating and complicated piece of history. It begins with the paradoxical fact that German was most alive before there was a unified German state. The poetic genius of Luther, Goethe, Schiller, Kleist, Heine, and in part that of Nietzsche, pre-dates the establishment of the German nation. The masters of German prose and poetry were men not caught up in the dynamism of Prussian-Germanic national consciousness as it developed after the foundation of modern Ger-many in 1870. They were, like Goethe, citizens of Europe, living in princely states too petty to solicit the emotions of nationalism. Or, like Heine and Nietzsche, they wrote from outside Germany. And this has remained true of the finest German literature even in recent times. Kafka wrote in Prague, Rilke in Prague, Paris, and Duino.

The official language and literature of Bismarck's Germany already had in them the elements of dissolution. It is the golden age of the militant histor-ians, of the philologists and the incomprehensible metaphysicians. These mandarins of the new Prussian empire produced that fearful composite of grammatical ingenuity and humorlessness which made the word "Germanic" an equivalent for dead weight. Those who escaped the Prussianizing of the language were the mutineers and the exiles, like those Jews who founded a brilliant journalistic tradition, or Nietzsche, who wrote from abroad.

For to the academicism and ponderousness of German as it was written by the pillars of learning and society between 1870 and the First World War, the imperial regime added its own gifts of pomp and mystification. The "Potsdam style" practiced in the chancelleries and bureaucracy of the new empire was a mixture of grossness ("the honest speech of soldiers") and high flights of romantic grandeur (the Wagnerian note). Thus university, officialdom, army, and court combined to drill into the German language habits no less dangerous than those they drilled into the German people: a terrible weakness for slogans and pompous clichés (*Lebensraum*, "the yellow peril," "the Nordic virtues"); an automatic reverence before the long word or the loud voice; a fatal taste for saccharine pathos (*Gemütlichkeit*) beneath which to conceal any amount of rawness or deception. In this drill, the justly renowned school of German philology played a curious and complex role. Philology places words in a context of older or related words, not in that of moral purpose and conduct. It gives to language formality, not form. It cannot be a mere accident that the essentially philological structure of German education yielded such loyal servants to Prussia and the Nazi Reich. The finest record of how the drill call of the classroom led to that of the barracks is contained in the novels of Heinrich Mann, particularly in *Der Untertan.*

When the soldiers marched off to the 1914 war, so did the words. The surviving soldiers came back, four years later, harrowed and beaten. In a real sense, the words did not. They remained at the front and built between the German mind and the facts a wall of myth. They launched the first of those big lies on which so much of modern Germany has been nurtured: the lie of "the stab in the back." The heroic German armies had not been defeated; they had been stabbed in the back by "traitors, degenerates, and Bolsheviks." The Treaty of Versailles was not an awkward attempt by a ravaged Europe to pick up some of the pieces but a scheme of cruel vengeance imposed on Germany by its greedy foes. The responsibility for unleashing war lay with Russia or Austria or the colonial machinations of "perfidious England," not with Prussian Germany.

There were many Germans who knew that these were myths and who knew something of the part that German militarism and race arrogance had played in bringing on the holocaust. They said so in the political cabarets of the 1920's, in the experimental theater of Brecht, in the writings of the Mann brothers, in the graphic art of Käthe Kollwitz and George Grosz. The German language leapt to life as it had not done since the Junkers and the philologists had taken command of it. It was a brilliant, mutinous period. Brecht gave back to German prose its Lutheran simplicity and Thomas Mann brought into his style the supple, luminous elegance of the classic and Mediterranean tradition. These years, 1920–1930, were the *anni mirabiles* of the modern German spirit. Rilke composed the *Duino Elegies* and the *Sonnets to Orpheus* in 1922, giving to German verse a wing-stroke and music it had not known since Hölderlin. *The Magic Mountain* appeared in 1924, Kafka's *Castle* in 1926. *The Three-Penny Opera* had its premiere in 1928, and in 1930 the German cinema produced *The Blue Angel*. The same year appeared the first volume of Robert Musil's strange and vast meditation on the decline of Western values, *The Man Without Qualities*. During this glorious decade, German literature and art shared in that great surge of the Western imagination which encompassed Faulkner, Hemingway, Joyce, Eliot, Proust, D. H. Lawrence, Picasso, Schoenberg, and Stravinsky.

But it was a brief noontime. The obscurantism and hatreds built into the German temper since 1870 were too deep-rooted. In an uncannily prophetic "Letter from Germany," Lawrence noted how "the old, bristling, savage spirit has set in." He saw the country turning away "from contact with western Europe, ebbing to the deserts of the east." Brecht, Kafta, and Thomas Mann did not succeed in mastering their own culture, in imposing on it the humane sobriety of their talent. They found themselves first the eccentrics, then the hunted. New linguists were at hand to make of the German language a political weapon more total and effective than any history had known, and to degrade the dignity of human speech to the level of baying wolves.

For let us keep one fact clearly in mind: the German language was not innocent of the horrors of Nazism. It is not merely that a Hitler, a Goebbels, and a Himmler happened to speak German. Nazism found in the language precisely what it needed to give voice to its savagery. Hitler heard inside his native tongue the latent hysteria, the confusion, the quality of hypnotic trance. He plunged unerringly into the undergrowth of language, into those zones of darkness and outcry which are the infancy of articulate speech, and which come before words have grown mellow and provisional to the touch of the mind. He sensed in German another music than that of Goethe, Heine, and Mann; a rasping cadence, half nebulous jargon, half obscenity. And instead of turning away in nauseated disbelief, the German people gave massive echo to the man's bellowing. It bellowed back out of a million throats and smashed-down boots. A Hitler would have found reservoirs of venom and moral illiteracy in any language. But by virtue of recent history, they were nowhere else so ready and so near the very surface of common speech. A language in which one can write a "Horst Wessel Lied" is ready to give hell a native tongue. (How should the word *"spritzen"* recover a sane meaning after having signified to millions the "spurting" of Jewish blood from knife points?)

And that is what happened under the Reich. Not silence or evasion, but an immense outpouring of precise, serviceable words. It was one of the peculiar horrors of the Nazi era that all that happened was recorded, catalogued, chronicled, set down; that words were committed to saying things no human mouth should ever have said and no paper made by man should ever have been inscribed with. It is nauseating and nearly unbearable to recall what was done and spoken, but one must. In the Gestapo cellars, stenographers (usually women) took down carefully the noises of fear and agony wrenched, burned, or beaten out of the human voice. The tortures and experiments carried out on live beings at Belsen and Matthausen were exactly recorded. The regulations governing the number of blows to be meted out on the flogging blocks at Dachau were set down in writing. When Polish rabbis were compelled to shovel out open latrines with their hands and mouths, there were German officers there to record the fact, to photograph it, and to label the photographs. When the SS elite guards separated mothers from children at the entrance to the death camps, they did not proceed in silence. They proclaimed the imminent horrors in loud jeers: *"Heida, heida, juchheisassa, Scheissjuden in den Schornstein!"*

The unspeakable being said, over and over, for twelve years. The unthinkable being written down, indexed, filed for reference. The men who poured quicklime down the openings of the sewers in Warsaw to kill the living and stifle the stink of the dead wrote home about it. They spoke of having to "liquidate vermin." In letters asking for family snapshots or sending season's greetings. Silent night, holy night, *Gemütlichkeit*. A language being used to run hell, getting the habits of hell into its syntax. Being used to destroy what there is in man of man and to restore to governance what there is of beast. Gradually, words lost their original meaning and acquired nightmarish definitions. *Jude, Pole, Russe* came to mean two-legged lice, putrid vermin which good Aryans must squash, as a party manual said, "like roaches on a dirty wall." "Final solution," *endgültige Lösung,* came to signify the death of six million human beings in gas ovens.

The language was infected not only with these great bestialities. It was called upon to enforce innumerable falsehoods, to persuade the Germans that the war was just and everywhere victorious. As defeat began closing in on the thousand-year Reich, the lies thickened to a constant snowdrift. The language was turned upside down to say "light" where there was blackness and "victory" where there was disaster. Gottfried Benn, one of the few decent writers to stay inside Nazi Germany, noted some of the new definitions from the dictionary of Hitler German:

> In December 1943, that is to say at a time when the Russians had driven us before them for 1,500 kilometers, and had pierced our front in a dozen places, a first lieutenant, small as a hummingbird and gentle as a puppy, remarked: "The main thing is that the swine are not breaking through." "Break through," "roll back," "clean up," "flexible, fluid lines of combat" —what positive and negative power such words have; they can bluff or they can conceal. Stalingrad—tragic accident. The defeat of the U-boats—a small, accidental technical discovery by the British. Montgomery chasing Rommel 4,000 kilometers from El Alamein to Naples—treason of the Badoglio clique.

And as the circle of vengeance closed in on Germany, this snowdrift of lies thickened to a frantic blizzard. Over the radio, between the interruptions caused by air-raid warnings, Goebbels' voice assured the German people that "titanic secret weapons" were about to be launched. On one of the very last days of Götterdämmerung, Hitler came out of his bunker to inspect a row of ashen-faced fifteen-year-old boys recruited for a last-ditch defense of Berlin. The order of the day spoke of "volunteers" and elite units gathered invincibly around the Führer. The nightmare fizzled out on a shameless lie. The *Herrenvolk* was solemnly told that Hitler was in the front-line trenches, defending the heart of his capital against Red beasts. Actually, the buffoon lay dead with his mistress, deep in the safety of his concrete lair.

Languages have great reserves of life. They can absorb masses of hysteria, illiteracy, and cheapness (George Orwell showed how English is doing so today). But there comes a breaking point. Use a language to conceive, organize, and justify Belsen; use it to make out specifications for gas ovens; use it to dehumanize man during twelve years of calculated bestiality. Something will happen to it. Make of words what Hitler and Goebbels and the hundred thousand *Untersturmführer* made: conveyors of terror and falsehood. Something will happen to the words. Something of the lies and sadism will settle in the marrow of the language. Imperceptibly at first, like the poisons of radiation sifting silently into the bone. But the cancer will begin, and the deep-set destruction. The language will no longer grow and freshen. It will no longer perform, quite as well as it used to, its two principal functions: the conveyance of humane order which we call law, and the communication of the quick of the human spirit which we call grace. In an anguished note in his diary of 1940, Klaus Mann observed that he could no longer read new German books: "Can it be that Hitler has polluted the language of Nietzsche and Hölderlin?" It can.

But what happened to those who are the guardians of a language, the keepers of its conscience? What happened to the German writers? A number were killed in the concentration camps; others, such as Walter Benjamin, killed themselves before the Gestapo could get at them to obliterate what little there is in a man of God's image. But the major writers went into exile. The best playwrights: Brecht and Zuckmayer. The most important novelists: Thomas Mann, Werfel, Feuchtwanger, Heinrich Mann, Stefan Zweig, Hermann Broch.

This exodus is of the first importance if we are to understand what has happened to the German language and to the soul of which it is the voice. Some of these writers fled for their lives, being Jews or Marxists or otherwise "undesirable vermin." But many could have stayed as honored Aryan guests of the régime. The Nazi were only too anxious to secure the luster of Thomas Mann's presence and the prestige that mere presence would have given to the cultural life of the Reich. But Mann would not stay. And the reason was that he knew exactly what was being done to the German language and that he felt that only in exile might that language be kept from final ruin. When he emigrated, the sycophantic academics of the University of Bonn deprived him of his honorary doctorate. In his famous open letter to the dean, Mann explained how a man using German to communicate truth or humane values could not remain in Hitler's Reich:

> The mystery of language is a great one; the responsibility for a language and for its purity is of a symbolic and spiritual kind; this responsibility does not have merely an aesthetic sense. The responsibility for language is, in essence, human responsibility. . . . Should a German writer, made responsible through his habitual use of language, remain silent, quite silent, in the face of all the irreparable evil which has been committed daily, and is being committed in my country, against body, soul and spirit, against justice and truth, against men and man?

Mann was right, of course. But the cost of such integrity is immense for a writer.

The German writers suffered different degrees of deprivation and reacted in different ways. A very few were fortunate enough to find asylum in Switzerland, where they could remain inside the living stream of their own tongue. Others, like Werfel, Feuchtwanger, and Heinrich Mann, settled near each other to form islands of native speech in their new homeland. Stefan Zweig, safely arrived in Latin America, tried to resume his craft. But despair overcame him. He was convinced that the Nazis would turn German into inhuman gibberish. He saw no future for a man dedicated to the integrity of German letters and killed himself. Others stopped writing altogether. Only the very tough or most richly gifted were able to transform their cruel condition into art.

Pursued by the Nazis from refuge to refuge, Brecht made of each of his new plays a brilliant rear-guard action. *Mother Courage* was first produced in Zurich in the dark spring of 1941. The further he was hounded, the clearer and stronger became Brecht's German. The language seemed to be that of a primer spelling out the ABC of truth. Doubtless, Brecht was helped by his politics. Being a Marxist, he felt himself a citizen of a community larger than Germany and a participant in the forward march of history. He was prepared to accept the desecration and ruin of the German heritage as a necessary tragic prelude to the foundation of a new society. In his tract "Five Difficulties Encountered When Writing the Truth," Brecht envisioned a new German language, capable of matching the word to the fact and the fact to the dignity of man.

Another writer who made of exile an enrichment was Hermann Broch. *The Death of Virgil* is not only one of the most important novels European literature has produced since Joyce and Proust; it is a specific treatment of the tragic condition of a man of words in an age of brute power. The novel turns on Virgil's decision, at the hour of his death, to destroy the manuscript of the *Aeneid*. He now realizes that the beauty and truth of language are inadequate to cope with human suffering and the advance of barbarism. Man must find a poetry more immediate and helpful to man than that of words: a poetry of action. Broch, moreover, carried grammar and speech beyond their traditional confines, as if these had become too small to contain the weight of grief and insight forced upon a writer by the inhumanity of our times. Toward the close of his rather solitary life (he died in New Haven, nearly unknown), he felt increasingly that communication might lie in modes other than language, perhaps in mathematics, that other face of silence.

Of all the exiles, Thomas Mann fared best. He had always been a citizen of the world, receptive to the genius of other languages and cultures. In the last part of the *Joseph* cycle, there seemed to enter into Mann's style certain tonalities of English, the language in the midst of which he was now living. The German remains that of the master, but now and again an alien light shines through it. In *Doctor Faustus,* Mann addressed himself directly to the ruin of the German spirit. The novel is shaped by the contrast between the language of the narrator and the events which he recounts. The language is that of a classical humanist, a touch laborious and old-fashioned, but always open to the voices of reason, skepticism, and tolerance. The story of Leverkühn's life, on the other hand, is a parable of unreason and disaster. Leverkühn's personal tragedy prefigures the greater madness of the German people. Even as the narrator sets down his pedantic but humane testimony to the wild destruction of a man of genius, the Reich is shown plunging to bloody chaos. In *Doctor Faustus* there is also a direct consideration of the roles of language and music in the German soul. Mann seems to be saying that the deepest energies of the German soul were always expressed in music rather than in words. And the history of Adrian Leverkühn suggests that this is a fact fraught with danger. For there are in music possibilities of complete irrationalism and hypnosis. Unaccustomed to finding in language any ultimate standard of meaning, the Germans were ready for the sub-human jargon of Nazism. And behind the jargon sounded the great dark chords of Wagnerian ecstasy. In *The Holy Sinner,* one of his last works, Mann returned to the problem of the German language by way of parody and pastiche. The tale is written in elaborate imitation of medieval German, as if to remove it as far as possible from the German of the present.

But for all their accomplishment, the German writers in exile could not safeguard their heritage from self-destruction. By leaving Germany, they could protect their own integrity. They witnessed the beginnings of the catastrophe, not its full unfolding. As one who stayed behind wrote: "You did not pay with the price of your own dignity. How, then, can you communicate with those who did?" The books that Mann, Hesse, and Broch wrote in Switzerland or California or Princeton are read in Germany today, but mainly as valuable proof that a privileged world had lived on "somewhere else," outside Hitler's reach.

What, then, of those writers who did stay behind? Some became lackeys in the official whorehouse of "Aryan culture," the *Reichsschrifttumskammer.* Others equivocated till they had lost the faculty of saying anything clear or meaningful even to themselves. Klaus Mann gives a brief sketch of how Gerhart Hauptmann, the old lion of realism, came to terms with the new realities:

"Hitler . . . after all, . . . My dear friends! . . . no hard feelings! . . . Let's try to be . . . No, if you please, allow me . . . objective . . . May I refill my glass? This champagne . . . very remarkable, indeed—the man Hitler, I mean . . . The champagne too, for that matter . . . Most extraordinary development . . . German youth . . . About seven million votes . . . As I often said to my Jewish friends . . . Those Germans . . . incalculable nation . . . very mysterious indeed . . . cosmic impulses . . . Goethe . . . Nibelungen Saga . . . Hitler, in a sense, expresses . . . As I tried to explain to my Jewish friends . . . dynamic tendencies . . . elementary, irresistible. . . ."

Some, like Gottfried Benn and Ernst Jünger, took refuge in what Benn called "the aristocratic form of emigration." They entered the German Army, thinking they might escape the tide of pollution and serve their country in the "old, honorable ways" of the officer corps. Jünger wrote an account of the victorious campaign in France. It is a lyric, elegant little book, entitled *Gärten und Strassen.* Not a rude note in it. An old-style officer taking fatherly care of his French prisoners and entertaining "correct" and even gracious relations with his new subjects. Behind his staff car come the trucks of the Gestapo and the elite guards fresh from Warsaw. Jünger does not mention any such unpleasantness. He writes of gardens.

Benn saw more clearly, and withdrew first into obscurity of style, then into silence. But the sheer fact of his presence in Nazi Germany seemed to destroy his hold on reality. After the war, he set down some of his recollections of the time of night. Among them, we find an incredible sentence. Speaking of pressures put on him by the régime, Benn says: "I describe the foregoing not out of resentment against National Socialism. The latter is now overthrown, and I am not one to drag Hector's body in the dust." One's imagination dizzies at the amount of confusion it must have taken to make a decent writer write that. Using an old academic cliché, he makes Nazism the equivalent of the noblest of Homeric heroes. Being dead, the language turns to lies.

A handful of writers stayed in Germany to wage a covert resistance. One of these very few was Ernst Wiechert. He spent some time in Buchenwald and remained in partial seclusion throughout the war. What he wrote he buried in his garden. He stayed on in constant peril, for he felt that Germany should not be allowed to perish in voiceless suffering. He remained so that an honest man should record for those who had fled and for those who might survive what it had been like. In *The Forest of the Dead* he gave a brief, tranquil account of what he saw in the concentration camp. Tranquil, because he wished the horror of the facts to cry out in the nakedness of truth. He saw Jews being tortured to death under vast loads of stone or wood (they were flogged each time they stopped to breathe until they fell dead). When Wiechert's arm developed running sores, he was given a bandage and survived. The camp medical officer would not touch Jews or Gypsies even with his glove "lest the oder of their flesh infect him." So they died, screaming with gangrene or hunted by the police dogs. Wiechert saw and remembered. At the end of the war he dug the manuscript out of his garden, and in 1948 published it. But it was already too late.

In the three years immediately following the end of the war, many Germans tried to arrive at a realistic insight into the events of the Hitler era. Under the shadow of the ruins and of economic misery, they considered the monstrous evil Nazism had loosed on them and on the world. Long rows of men and women filed past the bone heaps in the death camps. Returned soldiers admitted to something of what the occupation of Norway or Poland or France or Yugoslavia had been like—the mass shootings of hostages, the torture, the looting. The churches raised their voice. It was a period of moral scrutiny and grief. Words were spoken that had not been pronounced in twelve years. But the moment of truth was rather short.

The turning point seems to have come in 1948. With the establishment of the new Deutschmark, Germany began a miraculous ascent to renewed economic power. The country literally drugged itself with hard work. Those were the years in which men spent half the night in their rebuilt factories because their homes were not yet viable. And with the upward leap of material energy came a new myth. Millions of Germans began saying to themselves and to any foreigner gullible enough to listen that the past had somehow not happened, that the horrors had been grossly exaggerated by Allied propaganda and sensation-mongering journalists. Yes, there were some concentration camps, and *reportedly* a number of Jews and other unfortunates were exterminated. "But not six million, *lieber Freund,* nowhere near that many. That's just propaganda, you know." Doubtless, there had been some regrettable brutalities carried out on foreign territory by units of the S.S. and S.A. "But those fellows were *Lumpenhunde,* lower-class ruffians. The regular army did nothing of the kind. Not our honorable German Army. And, really, on the Eastern Front our boys were not up against normal human beings. The Russians are mad dogs, *lieber Freund,* mad dogs! And what of the bombing of Dresden?" Wherever one traveled in Germany, one heard such arguments. The Germans themselves began believing them with fervor. But there was worse to come.

Germans in every walk of life began declaring that they had not known about the atrocities of the Nazi régime. "We did not know what was going on. No one told us about Dachau, Belsen, or Auschwitz. How should we have found out? Don't blame us." It is obviously difficult to disprove such a claim to ignorance. There *were* numerous Germans who had only a dim notion of what might be happening outside their own backyard. Rural districts and the smaller, more remote communities were made aware of reality only in the last months of the war, when the battle actually drew near them. But an immense number *did* know. Wiechert describes his long journey to Buchenwald in the comparatively idyllic days of 1938. He tells how crowds gathered at various stops to jeer and spit at the Jews and political prisoners chained inside the Gestapo van. When the death trains started rolling across Germany during the war, the air grew thick with the sound and stench of agony. The trains waited on sidings at Munich before heading for Dachau, a short distance away. Inside the sealed cars, men, women, and children were going mad with fear and thirst. They screamed for air and water. They screamed all night. People in Munich heard them and told others. On the way to Belsen, a train was halted somewhere in southern Germany. The prisoners were made to run up and down the platform and a Gestapo man loosed his dog on them with the cry: "Man, get those dogs!" A crowd of Germans stood by watching the sport. Countless such cases are on record.

Most Germans probably did not know the actual details of liquidation. They may not have known about the mechanics of the gas ovens (one official Nazi historian called them "the anus of the world"). But when the house next door was emptied overnight of its tenants, or when Jews, with their yellow star sewn on their coats, were barred from the air-raid shelters and made to cower in the open, burning streets, only a blind cretin could not have known.

Yet the myth did its work. True, German audiences were moved not long ago by the dramatization of *The Diary of Anne Frank.* But even the terror of the *Diary* has been an exceptional reminder. And it does not show what happened to Anne *inside* the camp. There is little market for such things in Germany. Forget the past. Work. Get prosperous. The new Germany belongs to the future. When recently asked what the name Hitler meant to them, a large number of German schoolchildren replied that he was a man who had built the *Autobahnen* and had done away with unemployment. Had they heard that he was a bad man? Yes, but they did not really know why. Teachers who tried to tell them about the history of the Nazi period had been told from official quarters that such matters were not suitable for children. Some few who persisted had been removed or put under strong pressure by parents and colleagues. Why rake up the past?

Here and there, in fact, the old faces are back. On the court benches sit some of the judges who meted out Hitler's blood laws. On many professorial chairs sit scholars who were first promoted when their Jewish or Socialist teachers had been done to death. In a number of German and Austrian universities, the bullies swagger again with their caps, ribbons, dueling scars, and "pure Germanic" ideals. "Let us forget" is the litany of the new German age. Even those who cannot, urge others to do so. One of the very few pieces of high literature to concern itself with the full horror of the past is Albrecht Goes's *The Burnt Offering*. Told by a Gestapo official that there will be no time to have her baby where *she* is going, a Jewish woman leaves her baby carriage to a decent Aryan shopkeeper's wife. The next day she is deported to the ovens. The empty carriage brings home to the narrator the full sum of what is being committed. She resolves to give up her own life as a burnt offering to God. It is a superb story. But at the outset, Goes hesitates whether it should be told: "One has forgotten. And there must be forgetting, for how could a man live who had not forgotten?" Better, perhaps.

Everything forgets. But not a language. When it has been injected with falsehood, only the most drastic truth can cleanse it. Instead, the post-war history of the German language has been one of dissimulation and deliberate forgetting. The remembrance of horrors past has been largely uprooted. But at a high cost. And German literature is paying it right now. There are gifted younger writers and a number of minor poets of some distinction. But the major part of what is published as serious literature is flat and shoddy. It has in it no flame of life.[1] Compare the best of current journalism with an average number of the *Frankfurter Zeitung* of pre-Hitler days; it is at times difficult to believe that both are written in German.

This does not mean that the German genius is mute. There is a brilliant musical life, and nowhere is modern experimental music assured of a fairer hearing. There is, once again, a surge of activity in mathematics and the natural sciences. But music and mathematics are "languages" other than language. Purer, perhaps; less sullied with past implications; abler, possibly, to deal with the new age of automation and electronic control. But not language. And so far, in history, it is language that has been the vessel of human grace and the prime carrier of civilization.

[1] This statement was valid in 1959; not today. It is precisely by turning to face the past that German drama and fiction have resumed a violent, often journalistic, but undeniable force of life.

PART THREE

Toward Oneness

Man is born and man dies—and these, it seems, are the only certainties, the only truths upon which all men can agree. But man cannot rest with these alone. There must be other truths which can reveal to him who he is, where he came from and where he will eventually go, truths which can define his nature, explain the workings of his world, and thereby provide guidelines by which he can live. In short, man must somehow make sense of the myriad experiences which comprise human life and in so doing, endow his existence with purpose and meaning.

Few men, even the most sophisticated or cynical, doubt the existence of such truths. Differences arise over what they are, where they are to be found, and how to go about discovering them, but a belief in their existence seems essential to the human spirit.

Beginning with the tangible realities of birth and death, a creation myth is born. "Creation myths," Joseph Campbell tells us in 'Out of the Void— Space,' "are pervaded with a sense of the doom that is continually recalling all created shapes to the imperishable out of which they first emerged." Man cannot deny death. But as he is the only animal capable of contemplating his own death, he attempts to make his mortality bearable by aligning himself with a greater power, something beyond himself which destroys death as a terminus. The creation myth, then, is more than a story; it is an imaginative projection of man's aspirations, desires, and fears, reflecting values and priorities that remain long after the particulars of a given myth have been reasoned out of existence.

A mythology, then, which in its broadest sense can be considered the framework in which man conducts his search for higher truths (even the various political ideologies have decidedly mythic characteristics), can be a fluid and living thing as long as it remains flexible and allows for individual perceptions of reality. "Mythology is defeated," Campbell tells us, "when the mind rests solemnly with its favorite or traditional images, defending them as though they themselves were the message that they communicate." Thus Don C. Talayesva, in "The Return to the Old Gods," is resentful of a dominant Christian society which seeks to validate itself by denying his experience. ". . . Jesus Christ might do for modern whites in a good climate," he

139

believes, "but . . . the Hopi gods had brought success to us in the desert ever since the world begun."

When a culture ossifies, then, abandoning the search for higher truths by turning the symbols into the "truth" itself, it breeds discontent among those of its members who would continue the search. The final result is often violence, as was the case with the various Indian messianic movements and with Jewish messianism which, as a response to Roman oppression, gave rise to Christianity.

Thus, openness, fluidity, a responsiveness to the diverse perceptions of its members seems to be required of a society. There is a need for men like Thomas Merton, the Catholic monk whom the compassionate Buddha can eulogize, a man who unites all insight in his search for truth. The *Isā,* holiest of the Hindu *Upanisads,* tells us, "The truth lies beyond,/Beyond knowledge of knowledge and knowledge of ignorance."

OUT OF THE VOID—SPACE

Joseph Campbell

Saint Thomas Aquinas declares: "The name of being wise is reserved to him alone whose consideration is about the end of the universe, which end is also the beginning of the universe." The basic principle of all mythology is this of the beginning in the end. Creation myths are pervaded with a sense of the doom that is continually recalling all creation shapes to the imperishable out of which they first emerged. The forms go forth powerfully, but inevitably reach their apogee, break, and return. Mythology, in this sense, is tragic in its view. But in the sense that it places our true being not in the forms that shatter but in the imperishable out of which they again immediately bubble forth, mythology is eminently untragical. Indeed, wherever the mythological mood prevails, tragedy is impossible. A quality rather of dream prevails. True being, meanwhile, is not in the shapes but in the dreamer.

As in dream, the images range from the sublime to the ridiculous. The mind is not permitted to rest with its normal evaluations, but is continually insulted and shocked out of the assurance that now, at last, it has understood. Mythology is defeated when the mind rests solemnly with its favorite or traditional images, defending them as though they themselves were the message that they communicate. These images are to be regarded as no more than shadows from the unfathomable reach beyond, where the eye goeth not, speech goeth not, nor the mind, nor even piety. Like the trivialities of dream, those of myth are big with meaning.

The first phase of the cosmogonic cycle describes the breaking of formlessness into form, as in the following creation chant of the Maoris of New Zealand:

> Te Kore (The Void)
> Te Kore-tua-tahi (The First Void)
> Te Kore-tua-rua (The Second Void)
> Te Kore-nui (The Vast Void)
> Te Kore-roa (The Far-Extending Void)
> Te Kore-para (The Sere Void)
> Te Kore-whiwhia (The Unpossessing Void)
> Te Kore-rawea (The Delightful Void)
> Te Kore-te-tamaua (The Void Fast Bound)
> Te Po (The Night)
> Te Po-teki (The Hanging Night)

> Te Po-terea (The Drifting Night)
> Te Po-whawha (The Moaning Night)
> Hine-make-moe (The Daughter of Troubled Sleep)
> Te Ata (The Dawn)
> Te Au-tu-roa (The Abiding Day)
> Te Ao-marama (The Bright Day)
> Whai-tua (Space).

In space were evolved two existences without shape:

> Maku (Moisture [a male])
> Mahora-nui-a-rangi (Great Expanse of Heaven [a female]).

From these sprang:

> Rangi-potiki (The Heavens [a male])
> Papa (Earth [a female]).

Rangi-potiki and Papa were the parents of the gods.

From the void beyond all voids unfold the world-sustaining emanations, plantlike, mysterious. The tenth of the above series is night; the eighteenth, space or ether, the frame of the visible world; the nineteenth is the male-female polarity; the twentieth is the universe we see. Such a series suggests the depth beyond depth of the mystery of being. The levels correspond to the profundities sounded by the hero in his world-fathoming adventure; they number the spiritual strata known to the mind introverted in meditation. They represent the bottomlessness of the dark night of the soul.[1]

The Hebrew cabala represents the process of creation as a series of emanations out of the I AM of The Great Face. The first is the head itself, in profile, and from this proceed "nine splendid lights." The emanations are represented also as the branches of a cosmic tree, which is upside down, rooted in "the inscrutable height." The world that we see is the reverse image of that tree.

According to the Indian Samkhya philosophers of the eighth century B.C., the void condenses into the element ether or space. From this, air is precipitated. From air comes fire, from fire water, and from water the element earth. With each element evolves a sense-function capable of perceiving it: hearing, touch, sight, taste, and smell respectively.

An amusing Chinese myth personifies these emanating elements as five venerable sages, who come stepping out of a ball of chaos, suspended in the void:

"Before heaven and earth had become separated from each other, everything was a great ball of mist, called chaos. At that time, the spirits of the five elements took shape, and then developed into five ancients. The first was called the Yellow Ancient, and he was the master of earth. The second was called the Red Ancient, and he was the master of fire. The third was called the Dark Ancient, and he was the master of water. The fourth was called the

---

[1] In the sacred writings of Mahayana Buddhism, eighteen "voidnesses" or degrees of the void are enumerated and described. These are experienced by the yogi and by the soul as it passes into death. See Evans-Wentz, *Tibetan Yoga and Secret Doctrine,* pp. 206, 239 f.

Wood Prince, and he was the master of wood. The fifth was called the Metal Mother, and she was the mistress of metals.

"Now each of these five ancients set in motion the primordial spirit from which he had proceeded, so that water and earth sank downward; the heavens soared aloft and the earth became fast in the depths. Then the water gathered into rivers and lakes, and the mountains and plains appeared. The heavens cleared and the earth divided; then there were sun, moon, and all the stars, sand, clouds, rain, and dew. The Yellow Ancient gave play to the purest power of the earth, and to this were added the operations of fire and water. Then there sprang into being the grasses and trees, birds and animals, and the generations of the snakes and insects, and fishes and turtles. The Wood Prince and the Metal Mother brought light and darkness together and thereby created the human race, as man and woman. Thus gradually appeared the world. . . ."[2]

MYTH OF CREATION

Osage

Way beyond, a part of the Wazha'zhe lived in the sky. They desired to know their origin, the source from which they came into existence. They went to the sun. He told them that they were his children. Then they wandered still farther and came to the moon. She told them that she gave birth to them, and that the sun was their father. She told them that they must leave their present abode and go down to the earth and dwell there. They came to the earth, but found it covered with water. They could not return to the place they had left, so they wept, but no answer came to them from anywhere. They floated about in the air, seeking in every direction for help from some god; but they found none. The animals were with them, and of all these the elk was the finest and most stately, and inspired all the creatures with confidence; so they appealed to the elk for help. He dropped into the water and began to sink. Then he called to the winds, and the winds came from all quarters and blew until the waters went upward as in a mist.

At first rocks only were exposed, and the people traveled on the rocky places that produced no plants, and there was nothing to eat. Then the waters began to go down until the soft earth was exposed. When this happened, the elk in his joy rolled over and over on the soft earth, and all his loose hairs clung to the soil. The hairs grew, and from them sprang beans, corns, potatoes, and wild turnips, and then all the grasses and trees.

[2] The five elements according to the Chinese system are earth, fire, water, wood, and gold.

CREATION MYTH

Zuni

The Genesis of the Worlds, or the Beginning of Newness

Before the beginning of the new-making, Áwonawílona (the Maker and Container of All, the All-father Father), solely had being. There was nothing else whatsoever throughout the great space of the ages save everywhere black darkness in it, and everywhere void desolation.

In the beginning of the new-made, Áwonawílona conceived within himself and thought outward in space, whereby mists of increase, steams potent of growth, were evolved and uplifted. Thus, by means of his innate knowledge, the All-container made himself in person and form of the Sun whom we hold to be our father and who thus came to exist and appear. With his appearance came the brightening of the spaces with light, and with the brightening of the spaces the great mist-clouds were thickened together and fell, whereby was evolved water in water; yea, and the world-holding sea.

With his substance of flesh (*yépnane*) outdrawn from the surface of his person, the Sun-father formed the seed-stuff of twain worlds, impregnating therewith the great waters, and lo! in the heat of his light these waters of the sea grew green and scums (*k'yanashótsiyallawe*) rose upon them, waxing wide and weighty until, behold! they became Áwitelin Tsíta, the "Fourfold Containing Mother-earth," and Ápoyan Tä'chu, the "All-covering Father-sky."

The Genesis of Men and the Creatures

From the lying together of these twain upon the great world waters, so vitalizing, terrestrial life was conceived; whence began all beings of earth, men and the creatures, in the Four-fold womb of the World (Áwiten Téhu-'hlnakwi).

Thereupon the Earth-mother repulsed the Sky-father, growing big and sinking deep into the embrace of the waters below, thus separating from the Sky-father in the embrace of the waters above. As a woman forebodes evil for her first-born ere born, even so did the Earth-mother forebode, long withholding from birth her myriad progeny and meantime seeking counsel with the Sky-father. "How," said they to one another, "shall our children, when brought forth, know one place from another, even by the white light of the Sun-father?"

Now like all the surpassing beings (*píkwaiyin áhâi*) the Earth-mother and the Sky-father were 'hlímna (changeable), even as smoke in the wind; transmutable at thought, manifesting themselves in any form at will, like as dancers may by mask-making.

Thus, as a man and woman, spake they, one to the other. "Behold!" said the Earth-mother as a great terraced bowl appeared at hand and within it water, "this is as upon me the homes of my tiny children shall be. On the rim of each world-country they wander in, terraced mountains shall stand, making in one region many, whereby country shall be known from country, and within each, place from place. Behold, again!" said she as she spat on the water and rapidly smote and stirred it with her fingers. Foam formed, gathering about the terraced rim, mounting higher and higher. "Yea," said she, "and from my bosom they shall draw nourishment, for in such as this shall they find the substance of life whence we were ourselves sustained, for see!" Then with her warm breath she blew across the terraces; white flecks of the foam broke away, and, floating over above the water, were shattered by the cold breath of the Sky-father attending, and forthwith shed downward abundantly fine mist and spray! "Even so, shall white clouds float up from the great waters at the borders of the world, and clustering about the mountain terraces of the horizons be borne aloft and abroad by the breaths of the surpassing of soul-beings, and of the children, and shall hardened and broken be by thy cold, shedding downward, in rain-spray, the water of life, even into the hollow places of my lap! For therein chiefly shall nestle our children mankind and creature-kind, for warmth in thy coldness."

Lo! even the trees on high mountains near the clouds and the Sky-father crouch low toward the Earth-mother for warmth and protection! Warm is the Earth-mother, cold the Sky-father, even as woman is the warm, man the cold being!

"Even so!" said the Sky-father; "Yet not alone shalt *thou* helpful be unto our children, for behold!" and he spread his hand abroad with the palm downward and into all the wrinkles and crevices thereof he set the semblance of shining yellow corn-grains; in the dark of the early world-dawn they gleamed like sparks of fire, and moved as his hand was moved over the bowl, shining up from and also moving in the depths of the water therein. "See!" said he, pointing to the seven grains clasped by his thumb and four fingers, "by such shall our children be guided; for behold, when the Sun-father is not nigh, and thy terraces are as the dark itself (being all hidden therein), then shall our children be guided by lights—like to these lights of all the six regions turning round the midmost one—as in and around the midmost place, where these our children shall abide, lie all the other regions of space! Yea! and even as these grains gleam up from the water, so shall seed-grains like to them, yet numberless, spring up from thy bosom when touched by my waters, to nourish our children." Thus and in other ways many devised they for their offspring.

THE STORY OF THE CREATION

The Old Testament

Book of Genesis

Chapter 1

1 In the beginning God created the heaven and the earth.

2 And the earth was without form, and void; and darkness *was* upon the face of the deep. And the Spirit of God moved upon the face of the waters.

3 And God said, Let there be light: and there was light.

4 And God saw the light, that *it was* good: and God divided the light from the darkness.

5 And God called the light Day, and the darkness he called Night. And the evening and the morning were the first day.

6 ¶ And God said, Let there be a firmament in the midst of the waters, and let it divide the waters from the waters.

7 And God made the firmament, and divided the waters which *were* under the firmament from the waters which *were* above the firmament: and it was so.

8 And God called the firmament Heaven. And the evening and the morning were the second day.

9 ¶ And God said, Let the waters under the heaven be gathered together unto one place, and let the dry *land* appear: and it was so.

10 And God called the dry *land* Earth; and the gathering together of the waters called he Seas: and God saw that *it was* good.

11 And God said, Let the earth bring forth grass, the herb yielding seed, *and* the fruit tree yielding fruit after his kind, whose seed *is* in itself, upon the earth: and it was so.

12 And the earth brought forth grass, *and* herb yielding seed after his kind, and the tree yielding fruit, whose seed *was* in itself, after his kind: and God saw that *it was* good.

13 And the evening and the morning were the third day.

14 ¶ And God said, Let there be lights in the firmament of the heaven to divide the day from the night; and let them be for signs, and for seasons, and for days, and years:

15 And let them be for lights in the firmament of the heaven to give light upon the earth: and it was so.

16 And God made two great lights; the greater light to rule the day, and the lesser light to rule the night: *he made* the stars also.

17 And God set them in the firmament of the heaven to give light upon the earth.

18   And to rule over the day and over the night, and to divide the light from the darkness: and God saw that *it was* good.

19   And the evening and the morning were the fourth day.

20   And God said, Let the waters bring forth abundantly the moving creature that hath life, and fowl *that* may fly above the earth in the open firmament of heaven.

21   And God created great whales, and every living creature that moveth, which the waters brought forth abundantly, after their kind, and every winged fowl after his kind: and God saw that *it was* good.

22   And God blessed them, saying, Be fruitful, and multiply, and fill the waters in the seas, and let fowl multiply in the earth.

23   And the evening and the morning were the fifth day.

24   ¶ And God said, Let the earth bring forth the living creature after his kind, cattle, and creeping thing, and beast of the earth after his kind: and it was so.

25   And God made the beast of the earth after his kind, and cattle after their kind, and every thing that creepeth upon the earth after his kind: and God saw that *it was* good.

26   ¶ And God said, Let us make man in our image, after our likeness: and let them have dominion over the fish of the sea, and over the fowl of the air, and over the cattle, and over all the earth, and over every creeping thing that creepeth upon the earth.

27   So God created man in his *own* image, in the image of God created he him; male and female created he them.

28   And God blessed them, and God said unto them, Be fruitful, and multiply, and replenish the earth, and subdue it: and have dominion over the fish of the sea, and over the fowl of the air, and over every living thing that moveth upon the earth.

29   ¶ And God said, Behold, I have given you every herb bearing seed, which *is* upon the face of all the earth, and every tree, in the which *is* the fruit of a tree yielding seed; to you it shall be for meat.

30   And to every beast of the earth, and to every fowl of the air, and to every thing that creepeth upon the earth, wherein *there is* life, *I have given* every green herb for meat: and it was so.

31   And God saw every thing that he had made, and, behold, *it was* very good. And the evening and the morning were the sixth day.

Chapter 2

1   Thus the heavens and the earth were finished, and all the host of them.

2   And on the seventh day God ended his work which he had made; and he rested on the seventh day from all his work which he had made.

3   And God blessed the seventh day, and sanctified it: because that in it he had rested from all his work which God created and made.

4   ¶ These *are* the generations of the heavens and of the earth when they were created, in the day that the Lord God made the earth and the heavens,

5   And every plant of the field before it was in the earth, and every herb of the field before it grew: for the LORD God had not caused it to rain upon the earth, and *there was* not a man to till the ground.

6   But there went up a mist from the earth, and watered the whole face of the ground.

7   And the LORD God formed man *of* the dust of the ground, and breathed into his nostrils the breath of life; and man became a living soul.

8   ¶ And the LORD God planted a garden eastward in Ē′-dĕn; and there he put the man whom he had formed.

9   And out of the ground made the LORD God to grow every tree that is pleasant to the sight, and good for food; the tree of life also in the midst of the garden, and the tree of knowledge of good and evil.

10   And a river went out of Ē′-dĕn to water the garden; and from thence it was parted, and became into four heads.

11   The name of the first *is* Pī′-sŏn: that *is* it which compasseth the whole land of Hăv′-i-läh, where *there is* gold;

12   And the gold of that land *is* good: there *is* bdellium and the onyx stone.

13   And the name of the second river *is* Gī′-hon: the same *is* it that compasseth the whole land of Ē-thi-ō′-pĭ-ă.

14   And the name of the third river *is* Hĭd′dĕ-kĕl: that *is* it which goeth toward the east of Ăs-sўr′-ĭ-ă. And the fourth river is ĔÛ-phrā′-tēs.

15   And the LORD God took the man, and put him into the garden of Ē′-dĕn to dress it and to keep it.

16   And the LORD God commanded the man, saying, Of every tree of the garden thou mayest freely eat:

17   But of the tree of the knowledge of good and evil, thou shalt not eat of it: for in the day that thou eatest thereof thou shalt surely die.

18   ¶ And the LORD God said, *It is* not good that the man should be alone; I will make him an help meet for him.

19   And out of the ground the LORD God formed every beast of the field, and every fowl of the air; and brought *them* unto Ăd′-ăm to see what he would call them: and whatsoever Ăd′-ăm called every living creature, that *was* the name thereof.

20   And Ăd′-ăm gave names to all cattle and to the fowl of the air, and to every beast of the field; but for Ăd′-ăm there was not found an help meet for him.

21   And the LORD God caused a deep sleep to fall upon Ăd′-ăm, and he slept and he took one of his ribs, and closed up the flesh instead thereof;

22   And the rib, which the LORD God had taken from man, made he a woman and brought her unto the man.

23   And Ăd′-ăm said, This *is* now bone of my bones, and flesh of my flesh: she shall be called Woman, because she was taken out of Man.

24   Therefore shall a man leave his father and his mother, and shall cleave unto his wife: and they shall be one flesh.

25   And they were both naked, the man and his wife, and were not ashamed.

Chapter 3

Now the serpent was more subtil than any beast of the field which the LORD God had made. And he said unto the woman, Yea, hath God said, Ye shall not eat of every tree of the garden?

2   And the woman said unto the serpent, We may eat of the fruit of the trees of the garden:

3   But of the fruit of the tree which *is* in the midst of the garden, God hath said Ye shall not eat of it, neither shall ye touch it, lest ye die.

4   And the serpent said unto the woman, Ye shall not surely die:

5   For God doth know that in the day ye eat thereof, then your eyes shall be opened, and ye shall be as gods, knowing good and evil.

6   And when the woman saw that the tree *was* good for food, and that it *was* pleasant to the eyes, and a tree to be desired to make *one* wise, she took of the fruit thereof, and did eat, and gave also unto her husband with her; and he did eat.

7   And the eyes of them both were opened, and they knew that they *were* naked; and they sewed fig leaves together, and made themselves aprons.

8   And they heard the voice of the LORD God walking in the garden in the cool of the day: and Ăd′-ăm and his wife hid themselves from the presence of the LORD God amongst the trees of the garden.

9   And the LORD God called unto Ăd′-ăm, and said unto him, Where *art* thou?

10   And he said, I heard thy voice in the garden, and I was afraid, because I *was* naked; and I hid myself.

11   And he said, Who told thee that thou *wast* naked? Hast thou eaten of the tree, whereof I commanded thee that thou shouldest not eat?

12   And the man said, The woman whom thou gavest *to be* with me, she gave me of the tree, and I did eat.

13   And the LORD God said unto the woman, What *is* this *that* thou hast done? And the woman said, The serpent beguiled me, and I did eat.

14   And the LORD God said unto the serpent, Because thou hast done this, thou *art* cursed above all cattle, and above every beast of the field; upon thy belly shalt thou go, and dust shalt thou eat all the days of thy life:

15   And I will put enmity between thee and the woman, and between thy seed and her seed; it shall bruise thy head, and thou shalt bruise his heel.

16   Unto the woman he said, I will greatly multiply thy sorrow and thy conception, in sorrow thou shalt bring forth children; and thy desire *shall be* to thy husband, and he shall rule over thee.

17   And unto Ad′-ăm he said, Because thou has hearkened unto the voice of thy wife, and hast eaten of the tree, of which I commanded thee, saying, Thou shalt not eat of it: cursed *is* the ground for thy sake; in sorrow shalt thou eat *of* it all the days of thy life; . . .

RAPPACCINI'S DAUGHTER

from *The Writings of Aubépine*

Nathaniel Hawthorne

We do not remember to have seen any translated specimens of the productions of M. de l'Aubépine,—a fact the less to be wondered at, as his very name is unknown to many of his own countrymen as well as to the student of foreign literature. As a writer, he seems to occupy an unfortunate position between the Transcendentalists (who, under one name or another, have their share in all the current literature of the world) and the great body of pen-and-ink men who address the intellect and sympathies of the multitude. If not too refined, at all events too remote, too shadowy and unsubstantial in his modes of development, to suit the taste of the latter class, and yet too popular to satisfy the spiritual or metaphysical requisitions of the former, he must necessarily find himself without an audience, except here and there an individual or possibly an isolated clique. His writings, to do them justice, are not altogether destitute of fancy and originality; they might have won him greater reputation but for an inveterate love of allegory, which is apt to invest his plots and characters with the aspect of scenery and people in the clouds, and to steal away the human warmth out of his conceptions. His fictions are sometimes historical, sometimes of the present day, and sometimes, so far as can be discovered, have little or no reference either to time or space. In any case, he generally contents himself with a very slight embroidery of outward manners,—the faintest possible counterfeit of real life, and endeavors to create an interest by some less obvious peculiarity of the subject. Occasionally a breath of Nature, a raindrop of pathos and tenderness, or a gleam of humor, will find its way into the midst of his fantastic imagery, and make us feel as if, after all, we were yet within the limits of our native earth. We will only add to this very cursory notice that M. de l'Aubépine's productions, if the reader chance to take them in precisely the proper point of view, may amuse a leisure hour as well as those of a brigher man; if otherwise, they can hardly fail to look excessively like nonsense.

Our author is voluminous; he continues to write and publish with as much praiseworthy and indefatigable prolixity as if his efforts were crowned with the brilliant success that so justly attends those of Eugene Sue. His first appearance was by a collection of stories in a long series of volumes entitled "Contes deux fois racontées." The titles of some of his more recent works (we quote from memory) are as follows: "Le Voyage Céleste à Chemin de Fer," 3 tom., 1838; "Le nouveau Père Adam et la nouvelle Mère Eve," 2 tom., 1839; "Roderic; ou le Serpent à l'estomac," 2 tom., 1840; "Le Culte du Feu," a folio volume of ponderous research into the religion and ritual of the old Persian Ghebers, published in 1841; "La Soirée du Chateau en Espagne," 1 tom., 8vo., 1842; and "L'Artiste du Beau; ou le Papillon Mécanique," 5 tom., 4to., 1843. Our somewhat wearisome perusal of this startling catalogue of volumes has left behind it a certain personal affection and sympathy, though by no means admiration, for M. de l'Aubépine; and we would fain do the little in our power towards introducing him favorably to the American public. The ensuing tale is a translation of his "Beatrice; ou la Belle Empoisonneuse," recently published in La Revue Anti-Aristo- cratique. *This journal, edited by the Comte de Bearhaven, has for some years past led the defence of liberal principles and popular rights with a faithfulness and ability worthy of all praise.*

A young man, named Giovanni Guasconti, came, very long ago, from the more southern region of Italy, to pursue his studies at the University of Padua. Giovanni, who had but a scanty supply of gold ducats in his pocket, took lodgings in a high and gloomy chamber of an old edifice which looked not unworthy to have been the palace of a Paduan noble, and which, in fact, exhibited over its entrance the armorial bearings of a family long since extinct. The younger stranger, who was not unstudied in the great poem of his country, recollected that one of the ancestors of this family, and perhaps an occupant of this very mansion, had been pictured by Dante as a partaker of the immortal agonies of his Inferno. These reminiscences and associations, together with the tendency to heartbreak natural to a young man for the first time out of his native sphere, caused Giovanni to sigh heavily as he looked around the desolate and ill-furnished apartment.

"Holy Virgin, signor!" cried old Dame Lisabetta, who, won by the youth's remarkable beauty of person, was kindly endeavoring to give the chamber a habitable air, "what a sigh was that to come out of a young man's heart! Do you find this old mansion gloomy? For the love of Heaven, then, put your head out of the window, and you will see as bright sunshine as you have left in Naples."

Guasconti mechanically did as the old woman advised, but could not quite agree with her that Paduan sunshine was as cheerful as that of southern Italy. Such as it was, however, it fell upon a garden beneath the window, and expended its fostering influences on a variety of plants, which seemed to have been cultivated with exceeding care.

"Does this garden belong to the house?" asked Giovanni.

"Heaven forbid, signor, unless it were fruitful of better pot herbs than any that grow there now," answered old Lisabetta. "No; that garden is cultivated by the own hands of Signor Giacomo Rappaccini, the famous doctor, who, I warrant him, has been heard of as far as Naples. It is said that he distills these plants into medicines that are as potent as a charm. Oftentimes you may see the signor doctor at work, and perchance the signora, his daughter, too, gathering the strange flowers that grow in the garden."

The old woman had now done what she could for the aspect of the chamber; and, commending the young man to the protection of the saints, took her departure.

Giovanni still found no better occupation than to look down into the garden beneath his window. From its appearance, he judged it to be one of those botanic gardens which were of earlier date in Padua than elsewhere in Italy, or in the world. Or, not improbably, it might once have been the pleasure-place of an opulent family; for there was the ruin of a marble fountain in the centre, sculptured with rare art, but so wofully shattered that it was impossible to trace the original design from the chaos of remaining fragments. The water, however, continued to gush and sparkle into the sunbeams as cheerfully as ever. A little gurgling sound ascended to the young man's window, and made him feel as if the fountain were an immortal spirit that sung its song unceasingly and without heeding the vicissitudes around it, while one century embodied it in marble and another scattered the perishable garniture on the soil. All about the pool into which the water subsided grew various plants, that seemed to require a plentiful supply of moisture for the nourishment of gigantic leaves, and, in some instances, flowers gorgeously magnificent. There was one shrub in particular, set in a marble vase in the midst of the pool, that bore a profusion of purple blossoms, each of which had the lustre and richness of a gem; and the whole together made a show so resplendent that it seemed enough to illuminate the garden, even had there been no sunshine. Every portion of the soil was peopled with plants and herbs, which, if less beautiful, still bore tokens of assiduous care, as if all had their individual virtues, known to the scientific mind that fostered them. Some were placed in urns, rich with old carving, and others in common garden pots; some crept serpent-like along the ground or climbed on high, using whatever means of ascent was offered them. One plant had wreathed itself round a statue of Vertumnus, which was thus quite veiled and shrouded in a drapery of hanging foliage, so happily arranged that it might have served a sculptor for a study.

While Giovanni stood at the window he heard a rustling behind a screen of leaves, and became aware that a person was at work in the garden. His figure soon emerged into view, and showed itself to be that of no common laborer, but a tall, emaciated, sallow, and sickly-looking man, dressed in a scholar's garb of black. He was beyond the middle term of life, with gray hair, a thin, gray beard, and a face singularly marked with intellect and cultivation, but which could never, even in his more youthful days, have expressed much warmth of heart.

Nothing could exceed the intentness with which this scientific gardener examined every shrub which grew in his path: it seemed as if he was looking into their inmost nature, making observations in regard to their creative essence, and discovering why one leaf grew in this shape and another in that, and wherefore such and such flowers differed among themselves in hue and perfume. Nevertheless, in spite of this deep intelligence on his part, there was no approach to intimacy between himself and these vegetable existences. On the contrary, he avoided their actual touch or the direct inhaling of their odors with a caution that impressed Giovanni most disagreeably; for the man's demeanor was that of one walking among malignant influences, such as savage beasts, or deadly snakes, or evil spirits, which, should he allow them one moment of license, would wreak upon him some terrible fatality. It was strangely frightful to the young man's imagination to see this air of insecurity in a person cultivating a garden, that most simple and innocent of human toils, and which had been alike the joy and labor of the unfallen parents of the race. Was this garden, then, the Eden of the present world? And this man, with such a perception of harm in what his own hands caused to grow,—was he the Adam?

The distrustful gardener, while plucking away the dead leaves or pruning the too luxuriant growth of the shrubs, defended his hands with a pair of thick gloves. Nor were these his only armor. When, in his walk through the garden, he came to the magnificent plant that hung its purple gems beside the marble fountain, he placed a kind of mask over his mouth and nostrils, as if all this beauty did but conceal a deadlier malice; but, finding his task still too dangerous, he drew back, removed the mask, and called loudly, but in the infirm voice of a person affected with inward disease.

"Beatrice! Beatrice!"

"Here am I, father. What would you?" cried a rich and youthful voice from the window of the opposite house—a voice as rich as a tropical sunset, and which made Giovanni, though he knew not why, think of deep hues of purple or crimson and of perfumes heavily delectable. "Are you in the garden?"

"Yes, Beatrice," answered the gardener, "and I need your help."

Soon there emerged from under a sculptured portal the figure of a young girl, arrayed with as much richness of taste as the most splendid of the flowers, beautiful as the day, and with a bloom so deep and vivid that one shade more would have been too much. She looked redundant with life, health, and energy; all of which attributes were bound down and compressed, as it were, and girdled tensely, in their luxuriance, by her virgin zone. Yet Giovanni's fancy must have grown morbid while he looked down into the garden; for the impression which the fair stranger made upon him was as if here was another flower, the human sister of those vegetable ones, as beautiful as they, more beautiful than the richest of them, but still to be touched only with a glove, nor to be approached without a mask. As Beatrice came down the garden path, it was observable that she handled and inhaled the odor of several of the plants which her father had most sedulously avoided.

"Here, Beatrice," said the latter, "see how many needful offices require to be done to our chief treasure. Yet, shattered as I am, my life might pay the penalty of approaching it so closely as circumstances demand. Henceforth, I fear, this plant must be consigned to your sole charge."

"And gladly will I undertake it," cried again the rich tones of the young lady, as she bent towards the magnificent plant and opened her arms as if to embrace it. "Yes, my sister, my splendor, it shall be Beatrice's task to nurse and serve thee; and thou shalt reward her with thy kisses and perfumed breath, which to her is as the breath of life."

Then, with all the tenderness in her manner that was so strikingly expressed in her words, she busied herself with such attentions as the plant seemed to require; and Giovanni, at his lofty window, rubbed his eyes and almost doubted whether it were a girl tending her favorite flower, or one sister performing the duties of affection to another.

The scene soon terminated. Whether Dr. Rappaccini had finished his labors in the garden or that his watchful eye had caught the stranger's face, he now took his daughter's arm and retired. Night was already closing in; oppressive exhalations seemed to proceed from the plants and steal upward past the open window; and Giovanni, closing the lattice, went to his couch and dreamed of a rich flower and beautiful girl. Flower and maiden were different, and yet the same, and fraught with some strange peril in either shape.

But there is an influence in the light of morning that tends to rectify whatever errors of fancy, or even of judgment, we may have incurred during the sun's decline, or among the shadows of the night, or in the less wholesome glow of moonshine. Giovanni's first movement, on starting from sleep, was to throw open the window and gaze down into the garden which his dreams had made so fertile of mysteries. He was surprised and a little ashamed to find how real and matter-of-fact an affair it proved to be, in the first rays of the sun which gilded the dew-drops that hung upon leaf and blossom, and, while giving a brighter beauty to each rare flower, brought everything within the limits of ordinary experience. The young man rejoiced that, in the heart of the barren city, he had the privilege of overlooking this spot of lovely and luxuriant vegetation. It would serve, he said to himself, as a symbolic language to keep him in communion with Nature. Neither the sickly and thought-worn Dr. Giacomo Rappaccini, it is true, nor his brilliant daughter, were now visible; so that Giovanni could not determine how much of the singularity which he attributed to both was due to their own qualities and how much to his wonder-working fancy; but he was inclined to take a most rational view of the whole matter.

In the course of the day he paid his respects to Signor Pietro Baglioni, professor of medicine in the university, a physician of eminent repute, to whom Giovanni had brought a letter of introduction. The professor was an elderly personage, apparently of genial nature, and habits that might almost be called jovial. He kept the young man to dinner, and made himself very agreeable by the freedom and liveliness of his conversation, especially when warmed by a flask or two of Tuscan wine. Giovanni, conceiving that men of science, inhabitants of the same city, must needs be on familiar terms with one another, took an opportunity to mention the name of Dr. Rappaccini. But the professor did not respond with so much cordiality as he had anticipated.

"Ill would it become a teacher of the divine art of medicine," said Professor Pietro Baglioni, in answer to a question of Giovanni, "to withhold due and well-considered praise of a physician so eminently skilled as Rappaccini; but, on the other hand, I should answer it but scantily to my conscience were I to permit a worthy youth like yourself, Signor Giovanni, the son of an ancient friend, to imbibe erroneous ideas respecting a man who might here-

after chance to hold your life and death in his hands. The truth is, our worshipful Dr. Rappaccini has as much science as any member of the faculty—
with perhaps one single exception—in Padua, or all Italy; but there are certain grave objections to his professional character."

"And what are they?" asked the young man.

"Has my friend Giovanni any disease of body or heart, that he is so in-
quisitive about physicians?" said the professor, with a smile. "But as for
Rappaccini, it is said of him—and I, who know the man well, can answer
for its truth—that he cares infinitely more for science than for mankind. His
patients are interesting to him only as subjects for some new experiment. He
would sacrifice human life, his own among the rest, or whatever else was
dearest to him, for the sake of adding so much as a grain of mustard seed to
the great heap of his accumulated knowledge."

"Methinks he is an awful man indeed," remarked Guasconti, mentally recalling the cold and purely intellectual aspects of Rappaccini. "And yet,
worshipful professor, is it not a noble spirit? Are there many men capable of
so spiritual a love of science?"

"God forbid," answered the professor, somewhat testily; "at least, unless
they take sounder views of the healing art than those adopted by Rappaccini.
It is his theory that all medicinal virtues are comprised within those substances which we term vegetable poisons. These he cultivates with his own
hands, and is said even to have produced new varieties of poison, more horribly deleterious than Nature, without the assistance of this learned person,
would ever have plagued the world withal. That the signor doctor does less
mischief than might be expected with such dangerous substances is undeniable. Now and then, it must be owned, he has effected, or seemed to effect,
a marvellous cure; but, to tell you my private mind, Signor Giovanni, he
should receive little credit for such instances of success,—they being probably the work of chance,—but should be held strictly accountable for his
failures, which may justly be considered his own work."

The youth might have taken Baglioni's opinions with many grains of al-
lowance had he known that there was a professional warfare of long continuance between him and Dr. Rappaccini, in which the latter was generally
thought to have gained the advantage. If the reader be inclined to judge for
himself, we refer him to certain black-letter tracts on both sides, preserved
in the medical department of the University of Padua.

"I know not, most learned professor," returned Giovanni, after musing on
what had been said of Rappaccini's exclusive zeal for science,—"I know not
how dearly this physician may love his art; but surely there is one object
more dear to him. He has a daughter."

"Aha!" cried the professor, with a laugh. "So now our friend Giovanni's
secret is out. You have heard of this daughter, whom all the young men in
Padua are wild about, though not half a dozen have ever had the good hap
to see her face. I know little of the Signora Beatrice save that Rappaccini is
said to have instructed her deeply in his science, and that, young and beautiful as fame reports her, she is already qualified to fill a professor's chair. Perchance her father destines her for mine! Other absurd rumors there be, not

worth talking about or listening to. So now, Signor Giovanni, drink off your glass of lachryma."

Guasconti returned to his lodgings somewhat heated with the wine he had quaffed, and which caused his brain to swim with strange fantasies in reference to Dr. Rappaccini and the beautiful Beatrice. On his way, happening to pass by a florist's, he bought a fresh bouquet of flowers.

Ascending to his chamber, he seated himself near the window, but within the shadow thrown by the depth of the wall, so that he could look down into the garden with little risk of being discovered. All beneath his eye was a solitude. The strange plants were basking in the sunshine, and now and then nodding gently to one another, as if in acknowledgment of sympathy and kindred. In the midst, by the shattered fountain, grew the magnificent shrub, with its purple gems clustering all over it; they glowed in the air, and gleamed back again out of the depths of the pool, which thus seemed to overflow with colored radiance from the rich reflection that was steeped in it. At first, as we have said, the garden was a solitude. Soon, however,—as Giovanni had half hoped, half feared, would be the case,—a figure appeared beneath the antique sculptured portal, and came down between the rows of plants, inhaling their various perfumes as if she were one of those beings of old classic fable that lived upon sweet odors. On again beholding Beatrice, the young man was even startled to perceive how much her beauty exceeded his recollection of it; so brilliant, so vivid, was its character, that she glowed amid the sunlight, and, as Giovanni whispered to himself, positively illuminated the more shadowy intervals of the garden path. Her face being now more revealed than on the former occasion, he was struck by its expression of simplicity and sweetness,—qualities that had not entered into his idea of her character, and which made him ask anew what manner of mortal she might be. Nor did he fail again to observe, or imagine, an analogy between the beautiful girl and the gorgeous shrub that hung its gemlike flowers over the fountain,—a resemblance which Beatrice seemed to have indulged a fantastic humor in heightening, both by the arrangement of her dress and the selection of its hues.

Approaching the shrub, she threw open her arms, as with a passionate ardor, and drew its branches into an intimate embrace—so intimate that her features were hidden in its leafy bosom and her glistening ringlets all intermingled with the flowers.

"Give me thy breath, my sister," exclaimed Beatrice; "for I am faint with common air. And give me this flower of thine, which I separate with gentlest fingers from the stem and place it close beside my heart."

With these words the beautiful daughter of Rappaccini plucked one of the richest blossoms of the shrub, and was about to fasten it in her bosom. But now, unless Giovanni's draughts of wine had bewildered his senses, a singular incident occurred. A small orange-colored reptile, of the lizard or chameleon species, chanced to be creeping along the path, just at the feet of Beatrice. It appeared to Giovanni,—but, at the distance from which he gazed, he could scarcely have seen anything so minute,—it appeared to him, however, that a drop or two of moisture from the broken stem of the flower descended upon the lizard's head. For an instant the reptile contorted itself violently, and then lay motionless in the sunshine. Beatrice observed this remarkable phenomenon, and crossed herself, sadly, but without surprise; nor did she therefore hesitate to arrange the fatal flower in her bosom. There it blushed, and almost glimmered with the dazzling effect of a precious stone, adding to her dress and aspect the one appropriate charm which nothing else in the world could have supplied. But Giovanni, out of the shadow of his window, bent forward and shrank back, and murmured and trembled.

"Am I awake? Have I my senses?" said he to himself. "What is this being? Beautiful shall I call her, or inexpressibly terrible?"

Beatrice now strayed carelessly through the garden, approaching closer beneath Giovanni's window, so that he was compelled to thrust his head quite out of its concealment in order to gratify the intense and painful curiosity which she excited. At this moment there came a beautiful insect over the garden wall; it had, perhaps, wandered through the city and found no flowers or verdure among those antique haunts of men until the heavy perfumes of Dr. Rappaccini's shrubs had lured it from afar. Without alighting on the flowers, this winged brightness seemed to be attracted by Beatrice, and lingered in the air and fluttered about her head. Now, here it could not be but that Giovanni Guasconti's eyes deceived him. Be that as it might, he fancied that, while Beatrice was gazing at the insect with childish delight, it grew faint and fell at her feet; its bright wings shivered; it was dead—from no cause that he could discern, unless it were the atmosphere of her breath. Again Beatrice crossed herself and sighed heavily as she bent over the dead insect.

An impulsive movement of Giovanni drew her eyes to the window. There she beheld the beautiful head of the young man—rather a Grecian than an Italian head, with fair, regular features, and a glistening of gold among his ringlets—gazing down upon her like a being that hovered in mid air. Scarcely knowing what he did, Giovanni threw down the bouquet which he had hitherto held in his hand.

"Signora," said he, "there are pure and healthful flowers. Wear them for the sake of Giovanni Guasconti."

"Thanks, signor," replied Beatrice, with her rich voice, that came forth as it were like a gush of music, and with a mirthful expression half childish and half woman-like. "I accept your gift, and would fain recompense it with this precious purple flower; but if I toss it into the air it will not reach you. So Signor Guasconti must even content himself with my thanks."

She lifted the bouquet from the ground, and then, as if inwardly ashamed at having stepped aside from her maidenly reserve to respond to a stranger's greeting, passed swiftly homeward through the garden. But few as the moments were, it seemed to Giovanni, when she was on the point of vanishing beneath the sculptured portal, that his beautiful bouquet was already beginning to wither in her grasp. It was an idle thought; there could be no possibility of distinguishing a faded flower from a fresh one at so great a distance.

For many days after this incident the young man avoided the window that looked into Dr. Rappaccini's garden, as if something ugly and monstrous would have blasted his eyesight had he been betrayed into a glance. He felt conscious of having put himself, to a certain extent, within the influence of an unintelligible power by the communication which he had opened with Beatrice. The wisest course would have been, if his heart were in any real danger, to quit his lodgings and Padua itself at once; the next wiser, to have accustomed himself, as far as possible, to the familiar and daylight view of Beatrice,—thus bringing her rigidly and systematically within the limits of ordinary experience. Least of all, while avoiding her sight, ought Giovanni to have remained so near this extraordinary being that the proximity and possibility even of intercourse should give a kind of substance and reality to the wild vagaries which his imagination ran riot continually in producing. Guasconti had not a deep heart—or, at all events, its depths were not sounded now; but he had a quick fancy, and an ardent southern temperament, which rose every instant to a higher fever pitch. Whether or no Beatrice possessed those terrible attributes, that fatal breath, the affinity with those so beautiful and deadly flowers which were indicated by what Giovanni had witnessed, she had at least instilled a fierce and subtle poison into his system. It was not love, although her rich beauty was a madness to him; nor horror, even while he fancied her spirit to be imbued with the same baneful essence that seemed to pervade her physical frame; but a wild offspring of both love and horror that had each parent in it, and burned like one and shivered like the other. Giovanni knew not what to dread; still less did he know what to hope; yet hope and dread kept a continual warfare in his breast, alternately vanquishing one another and starting up afresh to renew the contest. Blessed are all simple emotions, be they dark or bright! It is the lurid intermixture of the two that produces the illuminating blaze of the infernal regions.

Sometimes he endeavored to assuage the fever of his spirit by a rapid walk through the streets of Padua or beyond its gates: his footsteps kept time with the throbbings of his brain, so that the walk was apt to accelerate itself to a race. One day he found himself arrested; his arm was seized by a portly personage who had turned back on recognizing the young man and expended much breath in overtaking him.

"Signor Giovanni! Stay, my young friend!" cried he. "Have you forgotten me? That might well be the case if I were as much altered as yourself."

It was Baglioni, whom Giovanni had avoided ever since their first meeting, from a doubt that the professor's sagacity would look too deeply into his secrets. Endeavoring to recover himself, he stared forth wildly from his inner world into the outer one and spoke like a man in a dream.

"Yes; I am Giovanni Guasconti. You are Professor Pietro Baglioni. Now let me pass!"

"Not yet, not yet, Signor Giovanni Guasconti," said the professor, smiling, but at the same time scrutinizing the youth with an earnest glance. "What! Did I grow up side by side with your father? and shall his son pass me like a stranger in these old streets of Padua? Stand still, Signor Giovanni; for we must have a word or two before we part."

"Speedily, then, most worshipful professor, speedily," said Giovanni, with feverish impatience. "Does not your worship see that I am in haste?"

Now, while he was speaking there came a man in black along the street, stooping and moving feebly like a person in inferior health. His face was all overspread with a most sickly and sallow hue, but yet so pervaded with an expression of piercing and active intellect that an observer might easily have overlooked the merely physical attributes and have seen only this wonderful energy. As he passed, this person exchanged a cold and distant salutation with Baglioni, but fixed his eyes upon Giovanni with an intentness that seemed to bring out whatever was within him worthy of notice. Nevertheless, there was a peculiar quietness in the look, as if taking merely a speculative, not a human, interest in the young man.

"It is Dr. Rappaccini!" whispered the professor, when the stranger had passed. "Has he ever seen your face before?"

"Not that I know," answered Giovanni, starting at the name.

"He *has* seen you! he must have seen you!" said Baglioni hastily. "For some purpose or other, this man of science is making a study of you. I know that look of his! It is the same that coldly illuminates his face as he bends over a bird, a mouse, or a butterfly, which, in pursuance of some experiment, he has killed by the perfume of a flower; a look as deep as Nature itself, but without Nature's warmth of love. Signor Giovanni, I will stake my life upon it, you are the subject of one of Rappaccini's experiments!"

"Will you make a fool of me?" cried Giovanni passionately. "*That,* signor professor, were an untoward experiment."

"Patience, patience!" replied the imperturable professor. "I tell thee, my poor Giovanni, that Rappaccini has a scientific interest in thee. Thou has fallen into fearful hands! And the Signora Beatrice,—what part does she act in this mystery?"

But Guasconti, finding Baglioni's pertinacity intolerable, here broke away, and was gone before the professor could again seize his arm. He looked after the young man intently and shook his head.

"This must not be," said Baglioni to himself. "The youth is the son of my old friend, and shall not come to any harm from which the arcana of medical science can preserve him. Besides, it is too insufferable an impertinence in Rappaccini, thus to snatch the lad out of my own hands, as I may say, and make use of him for his infernal experiments. This daughter of his! It shall be looked to. Perchance, most learned Rappaccini, I may foil you where you little dream of it!"

Meanwhile, Giovanni had pursued a circuitous route, and at length found himself at the door of his lodgings. As he crossed the threshold he was met by old Lisabetta, who smirked and smiled, and was evidently desirous to attract his attention; vainly, however, as the ebullition of his feelings had momentarily subsided into a cold and dull vacuity. He turned his eyes full upon the withered face that was puckering itself into a smile, but seemed to behold it not. The old dame, therefore, laid her grasp upon his cloak.

"Signor! signor!" whispered she, still with a smile over the whole breadth of her visage, so that it looked not unlike a grotesque carving in wood, darkened by centuries, "Listen, signor! There is a private entrance into the garden!"

"What do you say?" exclaimed Giovanni, turning quickly about, as if an inanimate thing should start into feverish life. "A private entrance into Dr. Rappaccini's garden?"

"Hush! hush! Not so loud!" whispered Lisabetta, putting her hand over his mouth. "Yes; into the worshipful doctor's garden, where you may see all his fine shrubbery. Many a young man in Padua would give gold to be admitted among those flowers."

Giovanni put a piece of gold into her hand.

"Show me the way," said he.

A surmise, probably excited by his conversation with Baglioni, crossed his mind, that this interposition of old Lisabetta might perchance be connected with the intrigue, whatever were its nature, in which the professor seemed to suppose that Dr. Rappaccini was involving him. But such a suspicion, though it disturbed Giovanni, was inadequate to restrain him. The instant that he was aware of the possibility of approaching Beatrice, it seemed an absolute necessity of his existence to do so. It mattered not whether she were angel or demon; he was irrevocably within her sphere, and must obey the law that whirled him onward, in ever lessening circles, towards a result which he did not attempt to foreshadow; and yet, strange to say, there came across him a sudden doubt whether this intense interest on his part were not delusory; whether it were really of so deep and positive a nature as to justify him in now thrusting himself into an incalculable position; whether it were not merely the fantasy of a young man's brain, only slightly or not at all connected with his heart.

He paused, hesitated, turned half about, but again went on. His withered guide led him along several obscure passages, and finally undid a door, through which, as it was opened, there came the sight and sound of rustling leaves, with the broken sunshine glimmering among them. Giovanni stepped forth, and, forcing himself through the entanglement of a shrub that wreathed its tendrils over the hidden entrance, stood beneath his own window in the open area of Dr. Rappaccini's garden.

How often is it the case that, when impossibilities have come to pass and dreams have condensed their misty substance into tangible realities, we find ourselves calm, and even coldly self-possessed, amid circumstances which it would have been a delirium of joy or agony to anticipate! Fate delights to thwart us thus. Passion will choose his own time to rush upon the scene, and lingers sluggishly behind when an appropriate adjustment of events would seem to summon his appearance. So was it now with Giovanni. Day after day his pulses had throbbed with feverish blood at the improbable idea of an interview with Beatrice, and of standing with her, face to face, in this very garden, basking in the Oriental sunshine of her beauty, and snatching from her full gaze the mystery which he deemed the riddle of his own existence. But now there was a singular and untimely equanimity within his breast. He threw a glance around the garden to discover if Beatrice or her father were present, and, perceiving that he was alone, began a critical observation of the plants.

The aspect of one and all of them dissatisfied him; their gorgeousness seemed fierce, passionate, and even unnatural. There was hardly an individual shrub which a wanderer, straying by himself through a forest, would not have been startled to find growing wild, as if an unearthly face had glared at him out of the thicket. Several also would have shocked a delicate instinct by an appearance of artificialness indicating that there had been such commixture, and, as it were, adultery, of various vegetable species, that the production was no longer of God's making, but the monstrous offspring of man's depraved fancy, glowing with only an evil mockery of beauty. They were probably the result of experiment, which in one or two cases had succeeded in mingling plants individually lovely into a compound possessing the questionable and ominous character that distinguished the whole growth of the garden. In fine, Giovanni recognized but two or three plants in the collection, and those of a kind that he well knew to be poisonous. While busy with these contemplations he heard the rustling of a silken garment, and, turning, beheld Beatrice emerging from beneath the sculptured portal.

Giovanni had not considered with himself what should be his deportment; whether he should apologize for his intrusion into the garden, or assume that he was there with the privity at least, if not by the desire, of Dr. Rappaccini or his daughter; but Beatrice's manner placed him at his ease, though leaving him still in doubt by what agency he had gained admittance. She came lightly along the path and met him near the broken fountain. There was surprise in her face, but brightened by a simple and kind expression of pleasure.

"You are a connoisseur in flowers, signor," said Beatrice, with a smile, alluding to the bouquet which he had flung her from the window. "It is no marvel, therefore, if the sight of my father's rare collection has tempted you to take a nearer view. If he were here, he could tell you many strange and interesting facts as to the nature and habits of these shrubs; for he has spent a lifetime in such studies, and this garden is his world."

"And yourself, lady," observed Giovanni, "if fame says true,—you likewise are deeply skilled in the virtues indicated by these rich blossoms and these spicy perfumes. Would you deign to be my instructress, I should prove an apter scholar than if taught by Signor Rappaccini himself."

"Are there such idle rumors?" asked Beatrice, with the music of a pleasant laugh. "Do people say that I am skilled in my father's science of plants? What a jest is there! No; though I have grown up among these flowers, I know no more of them than their hues and perfume; and sometimes methinks I would fain rid myself of even that small knowledge. There are many flowers here, and those not the least brilliant, that shock and offend me when they meet my eye. But pray, signor, do not believe these stories about my science. Believe nothing of me save what you see with your own eyes."

"And must I believe all that I have seen with my own eyes?" asked Giovanni, pointedly, while the recollection of former scenes made him shrink. "No, signora; you demand too little of me. Bid me believe nothing save what comes from your own lips."

It would appear that Beatrice understood him. There came a deep flush to her cheek, but she looked full into Giovanni's eyes and responded to his gaze of uneasy suspicion with a queenlike haughtiness.

"I do so bid you, signor," she replied. "Forget whatever you may have fancied in regard to me. If true to the outward senses, still it may be false in its essence; but the words of Beatrice Rappaccini's lips are true from the depths of the heart outward. Those you may believe."

A fervor glowed in her whole aspect and beamed upon Giovanni's consciousness like the light of truth itself; but while she spoke there was a fragrance in the atmosphere around her, rich and delightful, though evanescent, yet which the young man, from an indefinable reluctance, scarcely dared to draw into his lungs. It might be the odor of the flowers. Could it be Beatrice's breath which thus embalmed her words with a strange richness, as if by steeping them in her heart? A faintness passed like a shadow over Giovanni and flitted away; he seemed to gaze through the beautiful girl's eyes into her transparent soul, and felt no more doubt or fear.

The tinge of passion that had colored Beatrice's manner vanished; she became gay, and appeared to derive a pure delight from her communion with the youth not unlike what the maiden of a lonely island might have felt conversing with a voyager from the civilized world. Evidently her experience of life had been confined within the limits of that garden. She talked now about matters as simple as the daylight or summer clouds, and now asked questions in reference to the city, or Giovanni's distant home, his friends, his mother, and his sisters—questions indicating such seclusion, and such lack of familiarity with modes and forms, that Giovanni responded as if to an infant. Her spirit gushed out before him like a fresh rill that was just catching its first glimpse of the sunlight and wondering at the reflections of earth and sky which were flung into its bosom. There came thoughts, too, from a deep source, and fantasies of a gemlike brilliancy, as if diamonds and rubies sparkled upward among the bubbles of the fountain. Ever and anon there gleamed across the young man's mind a sense of wonder that he should be walking side by side with the being who had so wrought upon his imagination, whom he had idealized in such hues of terror, in whom he had positively witnessed such manifestations of dreadful attributes,—that he should be conversing with Beatrice like a brother, and should find her so human and so maidenlike. But such reflections were only momentary; the effect of her character was too real not to make itself familiar at once.

In this free intercourse they had strayed through the garden, and now, after many turns among its avenues, were come to the shattered fountain, beside which grew the magnificent shrub with its treasury of glowing blossoms. A fragrance was diffused from it which Giovanni recognized as identical with that which he had attributed to Beatrice's breath, but incomparably more powerful. As her eyes fell upon it, Giovanni beheld her press her hand to her bosom, as if her heart were throbbing suddenly and painfully.

"For the first time in my life," murmured she, addressing the shrub, "I had forgotten thee."

"I remember, signora," said Giovanni, "that you once promised to reward me with one of these living gems for the bouquet which I had the happy boldness to fling to your feet. Permit me now to pluck it as a memorial of this interview."

He made a step toward the shrub with extended hand; but Beatrice darted forward, uttering a shriek that went through his heart like a dagger. She caught his hand and drew it back with the whole force of her slender figure. Giovanni felt her touch thrilling through his fibres.

"Touch it not!" exclaimed she, in a voice of agony. "Not for thy life! It is fatal!"

Then, hiding her face, she fled from him and vanished beneath the sculptured portal. As Giovanni followed her with his eyes, he beheld the emaciated figure and pale intelligence of Dr. Rappaccini, who had been watching the scene, he knew not how long, within the shadow of the entrance.

No sooner was Guasconti alone in his chamber than the image of Beatrice came back to his passionate musings, invested with all the witchery that had been gathering around it ever since his first glimpse of her, and now likewise imbued with a tender warmth of girlish womanhood. She was human; her nature was endowed with all gentle and feminine qualities; she was worthiest to be worshipped; she was capable, surely, on her part, of the height and heroism of love. Those tokens which he had hitherto considered as proofs of a frightful peculiarity in her physical and moral system were now either forgotten, or, by the subtle sophistry of passion transmuted into a golden crown of enchantment, rendering Beatrice the more admirable by so much as she was the more unique. Whatever had looked ugly was now beautiful; or, if incapable of such a change, it stole away and hid itself among those shapeless half ideas which throng the dim region beyond the daylight of our perfect consciousness.

Thus did he spend the night, nor fell asleep until the dawn had begun to awake the slumbering flowers in Dr. Rappaccini's garden, whither Giovanni's dreams doubtless led him. Up rose the sun in his due season, and, flinging his beams upon the young man's eyelids, awoke him to a sense of pain. When thoroughly aroused, he became sensible of a burning and tingling agony in his hand—in his right hand—the very hand which Beatrice had grasped in her own when he was on the point of plucking one of the gemlike flowers. On the back of that hand there was now a purple print like that of four small fingers, and the likeness of a slender thumb upon his wrist.

Oh, how stubbornly does love,—or even that cunning semblance of love which flourishes in the imagination, but strikes no depth of root into the heart,—how stubbornly does it hold its faith until the moment comes when it is doomed to vanish into thin mist! Giovanni wrapped a handkerchief about his hand and wondered what evil thing had stung him, and soon forgot his pain in a reverie of Beatrice.

After the first interview, a second was in the inevitable course of what we call fate. A third; a fourth; and a meeting with Beatrice in the garden was no longer an incident in Giovanni's daily life, but the whole space in which he might be said to live; for the anticipation and memory of that ecstatic hour made up the remainder. Nor was it otherwise with the daughter of Rappaccini. She watched for the youth's appearance, and flew to his side with confidence as unreserved as if they had been playmates from early infancy— as if they were such playmates still. If, by any unwonted chance, he failed to come at the appointed moment, she stood beneath the window and sent up the rich sweetness of her tones to float around him in his chamber and echo and reverberate throughout his heart: "Giovanni! Giovanni! Why tarriest thou? Come down!" And he hastened into that Eden of poisonous flowers.

But, with all this intimate familiarity, there was still a reserve in Beatrice's demeanor, so rigidly and invariably sustained that the idea of infringing it scarcely occurred to his imagination. By all appreciable signs, they loved; they had looked love with eyes that conveyed the holy secret from the depths of one soul into the depths of the other, as if it were too sacred to be whispered by the way; they had even spoken love in those gushes of passion when their spirits darted forth in articulated breath like tongues of long-hidden flame; and yet there had been no seal of lips, no clasp of hands, nor any slightest caress such as love claims and hallows. He had never touched one of the gleaming ringlets of her hair; her garment—so marked was the physical barrier between them—had never been waved against him by a breeze. On the few occasions when Giovanni had seemed tempted to overstep the limit, Beatrice grew so sad, so stern, and withal wore such a look of desolate separation, shuddering at itself, that not a spoken word was requisite to repel him. At such times he was startled at the horrible suspicions that rose, monster-like, out of the caverns of his heart and stared him in the face; his love grew thin and faint as the morning mist; his doubts alone had substance. But, when Beatrice's face brightened again after the momentary shadow, she was transformed at once from the mysterious, questionable being whom he had watched with so much awe and horror; she was now the beautiful and unsophisticated girl whom he felt that his spirit knew with a certainty beyond all other knowledge.

A considerable time had now passed since Giovanni's last meeting with Baglioni. One morning, however, he was diagreeably surprised by a visit from the professor, whom he had scarcely thought of for whole weeks, and would willingly have forgotten still longer. Given up as he had long been to a pervading excitement, he could tolerate no companions except upon condition of their perfect sympathy with his present state of feeling. Such sympathy was not to be expected from Professor Baglioni.

The visitor chatted carelessly for a few moments about the gossip of the city and the university, and then took up another topic.

"I have been reading an old classic author lately," said he, "and met with a story that strangely interested me. Possibly you may remember it. It is of an Indian prince, who sent a beautiful woman as a present to Alexander the Great. She was as lovely as the dawn and gorgeous as the sunset; but what especially distinguished her was a certain rich perfume in her breath—richer than a garden of Persian roses. Alexander, as was natural to a youthful conqueror, fell in love at first sight with this magnificent stranger; but a certain sage physician, happening to be present, discovered a terrible secret in regard to her."

"And what was that?" asked Giovanni, turning his eyes downward to avoid those of the professor.

"That this lovely woman," cotinued Baglioni, with emphasis, "had been nourished with poisons from her birth upward, until her whole nature was so imbued with them that she herself had become the deadliest poison in existence. Poison was her element of life. With that rich perfume of her breath she blasted the very air. Her love would have been poison—her embrace death. Is not this a marvelous tale?"

"A childish fable," answered Giovanni, nervously starting from his chair. "I marvel how your worship finds time to read such nonsense among your graver studies."

"By the by," said the professor, looking uneasily about him, "what singular fragrance is this in your apartment? Is it the perfume of your gloves? It is faint, but delicious; and yet, after all, by no means agreeable. Were I to breathe it long, methinks it would make me ill. It is like the breath of a flower; but I see no flowers in the chamber. "

"Nor are there any," replied Giovanni, who had turned pale as the professor spoke; "nor, I think, is there any fragrance except in your worship's imagination. Odors, being a sort of element combined of the sensual and the spiritual, are apt to deceive us in this manner. The recollection of a perfume, the bare idea of it, may easily be mistaken for a present reality."

"Ay; but my sober imagination does not often play such tricks," said Baglioni; "and, were I to fancy any kind of odor, it would be that of some vile apothecary drug, wherewith my fingers are likely enough to be imbued. Our worshipful friend Rappaccini, as I have heard, tinctures his medicaments with odors richer than those of Araby. Doubtless, likewise, the fair and learned Signora Beatrice would minister to her patients with draughts as sweet as a maiden's breath; but woe to him that sips them!"

Giovanni's face evinced many contending emotions. The tone in which the professor alluded to the pure and lovely daughter of Rappaccini was a torture to his soul; and yet the intimation of a view of her character, opposite to his own, gave instantaneous distinctness to a thousand dim suspicions, which now grinned at him like so many demons. But he strove hard to quell them and to respond to Baglioni with a true lover's perfect faith.

"Signor professor," said he, "you were my father's friend; perchance, too, it is your purpose to act a friendly part towards his son. I would fain feel nothing towards you save respect and deference; but I pray you to observe, signor, that there is one subject on which we must not speak. You know not the Signora Beatrice. You cannot, therefore, estimate the wrong—the blasphemy, I may even say—that is offered to her character by a light or injurious word."

"Giovanni! my poor Giovanni!" answered the professor, with a calm expression of pity, "I know this wretched girl far better than yourself. You shall hear the truth in respect to the poisoner Rappaccini and his poisonous daughter; yes, poisonous as she is beautiful. Listen; for, even should you do violence to my gray hairs, it shall not silence me. That old fable of the Indian woman has become a truth by the deep and deadly science of Rappaccini and in the person of the lovely Beatrice."

Giovanni groaned and hid his face.

"Her father," continued Baglioni, "was not restrained by natural affection from offering up his child in this horrible manner as the victim of his insane zeal for science; for, let us do him justice, he is as true a man of science as ever distilled his own heart in an alembic. What, then, will be your fate? Beyond a doubt you are selected as the material of some new experiment. Perhaps the result is to be death; perhaps a fate more awful still. Rappaccini, with what he calls the interest of science before his eyes, will hesitate at nothing."

"It is a dream," muttered Giovanni to himself; "surely it is a dream."

"But," resumed the professor, "be of good cheer, son of my friend. It is not yet too late for the rescue. Possibly we may even succeed in bringing back this miserable child within the limits of ordinary nature, from which her father's madness has estranged her. Behold this little silver vase! It was wrought by the hands of the renowned Benvenuto Cellini, and is well worthy to be a love gift to the fairest dame in Italy. But its contents are invaluable. One little sip of this antidote would have rendered the most virulent poisons of the Borgias innocuous. Doubt not that it will be as efficacious against those of Rappaccini. Bestow the vase, and the precious liquid within it, on your Beatrice, and hopefully await the result."

Baglioni laid a small, exquisitely wrought silver vial on the table and withdrew, leaving what he had said to produce its effect upon the young man's mind.

"We will thwart Rappaccini yet," thought he, chuckling to himself, as he descended the stairs; "but, let us confess the truth of him, he is a wonderful man—a wonderful man indeed; a vile empiric, however, in his practice, and therefore not to be tolerated by those who respect the good old rules of the medical profession."

Throughout Giovanni's whole acquaintance with Beatrice, he had occasionally, as we have said, been haunted by dark surmises as to her character; yet so thoroughly had she made herself felt by him as a simple, natural, most affectionate, and guileless creature, that the image now held up by Professor Baglioni looked as strange and incredible as if it were not in accordance with his own original conception. True, there were ugly recollections connected with his first glimpses of the beautiful girl; he could not quite forget the bouquet that withered in her grasp, and the insect that perished amid the sunny air, by no ostensible agency save the fragrance of her breath. These incidents, however, dissolving in the pure light of her character, had no longer the efficacy of facts, but were acknowledged as mistaken fantasies, by whatever testimony of the senses they might appear to be substantiated. There is something truer and more real than what we can see with the eyes and touch with the finger. On such better evidence had Giovanni founded his confidence in Beatrice, though rather by the necessary force of her high attributes than by any deep and generous faith on his part. But now his spirit was incapable of sustaining itself at the height to which the early enthusiasm of passion had exalted it; he fell down, grovelling among earthly doubts, and defiled therewith the pure whiteness of Beatrice's image. Not that he gave her up; he did but distrust. He resolved to institute some decisive test that should satisfy him, once for all, whether there were those dreadful peculiarities in her physical nature which could not be supposed to exist without some corresponding monstrosity of soul. His eyes, gazing down afar, might have deceived him as to the lizard, the insect, and the flowers; but if he could witness, at the distance of a few paces, the sudden blight of one fresh and healthful flower in Beatrice's hand, there would be room for no further question. With this idea he hastened to the florist's and purchased a bouquet that was still gemmed with the morning dew-drops.

It was now the customary hour of his daily interview with Beatrice. Before descending into the garden, Giovanni failed not to look at his figure in the mirror,—a vanity to be expected in a beautiful young man, yet, as displaying itself at that troubled and feverish moment, the token of a certain shallowness of feeling and insincerity of character. He did gaze, however, and said to himself that his features had never before possessed so rich a grace, nor his eyes such vivacity, nor his cheeks so warm a hue of superabundant life.

"At least," thought he, "her poison has not yet insinuated itself into my system. I am no flower to perish in her grasp."

With that thought he turned his eyes on the bouquet, which he had never once laid aside from his hand. A thrill of indefinable horror shot through his frame on perceiving that those dewy flowers were already beginning to droop; they wore the aspect of things that had been fresh and lovely yesterday. Giovanni grew white as marble, and stood motionless before the mirror, staring at his own reflection there as at the likeness of something frightful. He remembered Baglioni's remark about the fragrance that seemed to pervade the chamber. It must have been the poison in his breath! Then he shuddered—shuddered at himself. Recovering from his stupor, he began to watch with curious eye a spider that was busily at work hanging its web from the antique cornice of the apartment, crossing and recrossing the artful system of interwoven lines—as vigorous and active a spider as ever dangled from an old ceiling. Giovanni bent towards the insect, and emitted a deep, long breath. The spider suddenly ceased its toil; the web vibrated with a tremor originating in the body of the small artisan. Again Giovanni sent forth a breath, deeper, longer, and imbued with a venomous feeling out of his heart; he knew not whether he were wicked or only desperate. The spider made a convulsive gripe with his limbs and hung dead across the window.

"Accursed! accursed!" muttered Giovanni, addressing himself, "Hast thou grown so poisonous that this deadly insect perishes by thy breath?"

At that moment a rich, sweet voice came floating up from the garden.

"Giovanni! Giovanni! It is past the hour! Why tarriest thou? Come down!"

"Yes," muttered Giovanni again. "She is the only being whom my breath may not slay! Would that it might!"

He rushed down, and in an instant was standing before the bright and loving eyes of Beatrice. A moment ago his wrath and despair had been so fierce that he could have desired nothing so much as to wither her by a glance; but with her actual presence there came influences which had too real an existence to be at once shaken off: recollections of the delicate and benign power of her feminine nature, which had so often enveloped him in a religious calm; recollections of many a holy and passionate outgush of her heart, when the pure fountain had been unsealed from its depths and made visible in its transparency to his mental eye; recollections which, had Giovanni known how to estimate them, would have assured him that all this ugly mystery was but an earthly illusion, and that, whatever mist of evil might seem to have gathered over her, the real Beatrice was a heavenly angel. Incapable as he was of such high faith, still her presence had not utterly lost its magic. Giovanni's rage was quelled into an aspect of sullen insensibility. Beatrice, with a quick spiritual sense, immediately felt that there was a gulf of blackness between them which neither he nor she could pass. They walked on together, sad and silent, and came thus to the marble fountain and to its pool of water on the ground, in the midst of which grew the shrub that bore gemlike blossoms. Giovanni was affrighted at the eager enjoyment—the appetite, as it were—with which he found himself inhaling the fragrance of the flowers.

"Beatrice," asked he, abruptly, "whence came this shrub?"

"My father created it," answered she, with simplicity.

"Created it! created it!" repeated Giovanni. "What mean you, Beatrice?"

"He is a man fearfully acquainted with the secrets of Nature," replied Beatrice; "and at the hour when I first drew breath this plant sprang from the soil, the offspring of his science, of his intellect, while I was but his earthly child. Approach it not!" continued she, observing with terror that Giovanni was drawing nearer to the shrub. "It has qualities that you little dream of. But I, dearest Giovanni,—I grew up and blossomed with the plant and was nourished with its breath. It was my sister, and I loved it with a human affection; for, alas!—hast thou not suspected it?—there was an awful doom."

Here Giovanni frowned so darkly upon her that Beatrice paused and trembled. But her faith in his tenderness reassured her, and made her blush that she had doubted for an instant.

"There was an awful doom," she continued, "the effect of my father's fatal love of science, which estranged me from all society of my kind. Until Heaven sent thee, dearest Giovanni, oh, how lonely was thy poor Beatrice!"

"Was it a hard doom?" asked Giovanni, fixing his eyes upon her.

"Only of late have I known how hard it was," answered she, tenderly. "Oh, yes; but my heart was torpid, and therefore quiet."

Giovanni's rage broke forth from his sullen gloom like a lightning-flash out of a dark cloud.

"Accursed one!" cried he, with venomous scorn and anger. "And, finding thy solitude wearisome, thou hast severed me likewise from all the warmth of life and enticed me into thy region of unspeakable horror!"

"Giovanni!" exclaimed Beatrice, turning her large bright eyes upon his face. The force of his words had not found its way into her mind; she was merely thunderstruck.

"Yes, poisonous thing!" repeated Giovanni, beside himself with passion. "Thou hast done it! Thou hast blasted me! Thou hast filled my veins with poison! Thou hast made me as hateful, as ugly, as loathsome and deadly a creature as thyself—a world's wonder of hideous monstrosity! Now, if our breath be happily as fatal to ourselves as to all others, let us join our lips in one kiss of unutterable hatred, and so die!"

"What has befallen me?" murmured Beatrice, with a low moan out of her heart. "Holy Virgin, pity me, a poor heart-broken child!"

"Thou,—dost thou pray?" cried Giovanni, still with the same fiendish scorn. "Thy very prayers, as they come from thy lips, taint the atmosphere with death. Yes, yes; let us pray! Let us to church and dip our fingers in the holy water at the portal! They that come after us will perish as by a pestilence! Let us sign crosses in the air! It will be scattering curses abroad in the likeness of holy symbols!"

"Giovanni," said Beatrice calmly, for her grief was beyond passion, "why dost thou join thyself with me thus in those terrible words? I, it is true, am the horrible thing thou namest me. But thou,—what hast thou to do, save with one other shudder at my hideous misery to go forth out of the garden and mingle with thy race, and forget that there ever crawled on earth such a monster as poor Beatrice?"

"Dost thou pretend ignorance?" asked Giovanni, scowling upon her. "Behold! this power have I gained from the pure daughter of Rappaccini."

There was a swarm of summer insects flitting through the air in search of the food promised by the flower odors of the fatal garden. They circled round Giovanni's head, and were evidently attracted towards him by the same influence which had drawn them for an instant within the sphere of several of the shrubs. He sent forth a breath among them, and smiled bitterly at Beatrice as at least a score of the insects fell dead upon the ground.

"I see it! I see it!" shrieked Beatrice. "It is my father's fatal science! No, no, Giovanni; it was not I! Never, never! I dreamed only to love thee and be with thee a little time, and so to let thee pass away, leaving but thine image in mine heart. For, Giovanni, believe it, though my body be nourished with poison, my spirit is God's creature, and craves love as its daily food. But my father,—he has united us in this fearful sympathy. Yes; spurn me, tread upon me, kill me! Oh, what is death after such words as thine? But it was not I. Not for a world of bliss would I have done it."

Giovanni's passion had exhausted itself in its outburst from his lips. There now came across him a sense, mournful, and not without tenderness, of the intimate and peculiar relationship between Beatrice and himself. They stood, as it were, in an utter solitude, which would be made none the less solitary by the densest throng of human life. Ought not, then, the desert of humanity around them to press this insulated pair closer together? If they should be cruel to one another, who was there to be kind to them? Besides, thought Giovanni, might there not still be a hope of his returning within the limits of ordinary nature, and leading Beatrice, the redeemed Beatrice, by the hand? Oh, weak, and selfish, and unworthy spirit, that could dream of an earthly union and earthly happiness as possible after such deep love had been so bitterly wronged as was Beatrice's love by Giovanni's blighting words! No, no; there could be no such hope. She must pass heavily, with that broken heart, across the borders of Time—she must bathe her hurts in some fount of paradise, and forget her grief in the light of immortality, and *there* be well.

But Giovanni did not know it.

"Dear Beatrice," said he, approaching her, while she shrank away as always at his approach, but now with a different impulse, "dearest Beatrice, our fate is not yet so desperate. Behold! there is a medicine, potent, as a wise physician has assured me, and almost divine in its efficacy. It is composed of ingredients the most opposite to those by which thy awful father has brought this calamity upon thee and me. It is distilled of blessed herbs. Shall we not quaff it together, and thus be purified from evil?"

"Give it me!" said Beatrice, extending her hand to receive the little silver vial which Giovanni took from his bosom. She added, with a peculiar emphasis, "I will drink; but do thou await the result."

She put Baglioni's antidote to her lips; and, at the same moment, the figure of Rappaccini emerged from the portal and came slowly towards the marble fountain. As he drew near, the pale man of science seemed to gaze with a triumphant expression at the beautiful youth and maiden, as might an artist who should spend his life in achieving a picture or a group of statuary and finally be satisfied with his success. He paused; his bent form grew erect with conscious power; he spread out his hands over them in the attitude of a father imploring a blessing upon his children; but those were the same hands that had thrown poison into the stream of their lives. Giovanni trembled. Beatrice shuddered nervously, and pressed her hand upon her heart.

"My daughter," said Rappaccini, "thou art no longer lonely in the world. Pluck one of those precious gems from thy sister shrub and bid thy bridegroom wear it in his bosom. It will not harm him now. My science and the sympathy between thee and him have so wrought within his system that he now stands apart from common men, as thou dost, daughter of my pride and triumph, from ordinary women. Pass on, then, through the world, most dear to one another and dreadful to all besides!"

"My father," said Beatrice, feebly,—and still as she spoke she kept her hand upon her heart,—"wherefore didst thou inflict this miserable doom upon thy child?"

"Miserable!" exclaimed Rappaccini. "What mean you, foolish girl? Dost thou deem it misery to be endowed with marvelous gifts against which no power nor strength could avail an enemy—misery, to be able to quell the mightiest with a breath—misery, to be as terrible as thou art beautiful? Wouldst thou, then, have preferred the condition of a weak woman, exposed to all evil and capable of none?"

"I would fain have been loved, not feared," murmured Beatrice, sinking down upon the ground. "But now it matters not. I am going, father, where the evil which thou hast striven to mingle with my being will pass away like a dream—like the fragrance of these poisonous flowers, which will no longer taint my breath among the flowers of Eden. Farewell, Giovanni! Thy words of hatred are like lead within my heart; but they, too, will fall away as I ascend. Oh, was there not, from the first, more poison in thy nature than in mine?"

To Beatrice,—so radically had her earthly part been wrought upon by Rappaccini's skill,—as poison had been life, so the powerful antidote was death; and thus the poor victim of man's ingenuity and of thwarted nature, and of the fatality that attends all such efforts of perverted wisdom, perished there, at the feet of her father and Giovanni.

Just at that moment Professor Pietro Baglioni looked forth from the window, and called loudly, in a tone of triumph mixed with horror, to the thunderstricken man of science.

"Rappaccini! Rappaccini! And is *this* the upshot of your experiment!"

HOW RELIGION AROSE, AND WHY IT FLOURISHED

C. E. M. Joad

An honest God is the noblest work of man.

Anon.

. . . In discussing the need for religion, I use the words "origin and nature" deliberately, because the conjunction of these two words seems to me to mask a fallacy which it is important to bring to light. The fallacy is to assume that to lay bare the origins of a thing is tantamount to describing its present nature.

. . . This is very far from being the case . . . yet we more often assume that it is, especially if we are of a scientific turn, than we are commonly aware, and the assumption is nowhere more prevalent than in regard to religion. By most of us, indeed, it is not even realised that an assumption is involved. We take it for granted that to demonstrate that religion began as witchcraft, totemism, or exogamy, is to prove that it is in essence no more than witchcraft, totemism, and exogamy now, although we should never dream of asserting that the fact that the savage can only count on the fingers of one hand, coupled with the demonstration that arithmetic began with and developed from such counting, invalidates the multiplication table. To show how a belief arises is not to describe, still less to discredit it, and, unless we are to deny to religion the kind of growth which we are prepared to concede to other expressions of the human spirit, it is obvious that there must be more in the religious consciousness to-day than in the savage fears and flatteries from which it may be shown to have arisen. And, if there is, it will be for just that "more" that an account of religion in terms of its origin and history will fail to make provision. The point is of importance because the interpretation of religion in terms of its origin is often used to prove that religion is not a permanent and necessary need of the human spirit; savage in inception, it will, it is urged, disappear when we have finally left our savagery behind us. Religion, it is often said, belongs to the childhood of the race, and will one day be outgrown, together with war and other savage habits, such as the habit of imprisoning men for punishment and animals for show, or the habit of decking the bodies of women with fragments of stone, lumps of metal, and portions of dead birds.

For myself, I do not hold this view. . . . Let us see what the explanations of religions in terms of origin involve.

They are advanced chiefly by anthropologists, who visit remote Melanesian islands for the purpose of observing the religious practices of the natives. Recording them, they conclude that primitive religion is the offspring of human fear and human conceit; it springs from the desire to propitiate the alien forces of nature, to invest human life with significance in face of the vast indifference of the universe, and to secure the support of an immensely powerful and ferocious personage for the individual, the tribe, or the nation. This general attitude to religion, by ascribing it to a subjective need of human nature, robs it of objective validity. Religion, if this account is correct, is not a revelation of reality, but a symptom of a state of mind; it is an expression of what man is like. To say that there is God is not to say anything more than that we need to think that there is, and the need is in no sense a guarantee of the existence of that which satisfies it. Thus the great religions of the world are not theology, but psychology; witnesses, not to the attributes of God, but to the inventive faculty of man. God is not a real being; He is the image of man, projected, enlarged, upon the empty canvas of the universe.

This view of religion as subjective expresses itself in different forms, according to the nature of the primitive feelings upon which it lays stress. I will take three as examples.

(1) The argument from man's feeling of loneliness and insecurity may be summarised as follows: Human life is immensely insignificant. It is an accidental development of matter, the chance product of forces, an accident unplanned and unforeseen in the history of the planet. A casual and unwanted passenger, it struggles across a fundamentally alien and hostile environment, in which the material and the brutal on all sides condition and determine the spiritual and the vital. One day it will finish its pointless journey with as little noise and significance as, in the person of the amœba, it began it. Until this consummation occurs, man will fare naked and forlorn through an indifferent universe, a puppet twitched into love and war by an indifferent showman who pulls the strings. His destiny is swayed by an inescapable fate; his fortunes are at the mercy of an irresponsible chance. He is a mere target for the shafts of doom.

These things we know, yet the knowledge is intolerable to us. We cannot bear to be without significance in the universe; we long to feel that we count, that somehow and to something we matter. And so we invent an immensely powerful and important personage called God, to whom we matter enormously.

By making ourselves important to a person who is Himself so enormously important, we achieve the desired significance, and the more powerful God is conceived to be, the more significant do we, His chief concern, become. So tremendously does He care about us that He has made the material universe for our benefit, this world rightly regarded being merely a school for human nature, in which it is trained and educated for life elsewhere; while by making Him in our own image we secure His special interest in the human race. The creation of the brute beasts to sustain our bodies and obey our orders is a token of that interest.

Interested as He is in the human species as a whole, He is quite specially interested in the particular race, nation or tribe to which we happen to belong; so that, whatever the quarrel upon which the nation or tribe may happen to be engaged, it may rest assured of His support, since He is guaranteed to take the same view of the rights and wrongs of it as we do ourselves.

Among polytheistic peoples this concept causes no difficulty; each has its own deity or set of deities, and the strongest gods win. But where there is one God, and only one, who sustains the worship and is the repository of the prayers of opposed nations, the zeal of His adherents tends to place the Almighty in a dilemma.

> To God the embattled nations sing and shout,
>   "God sträfe England" and "God save the King,"
> God this, God that and God the other thing.
>   "Good God!" said God, "I've got my work cut out."

But it is easy to provide for God's solution of the difficulty by invoking His omnipotence.

Interested in the nation or tribe to which we happen to belong, He is quite specially interested in ourselves; interested in and favorable towards, assisting us against those who seek to humiliate us, and generally discomfiting our enemies. This is a world in which the good man is notoriously oppressed, while the wicked flourish like a green bay-tree. The arrangement offends our sense of justice, and, what is more, since we are good men ourselves, it is unfair to us personally. Very well, then, we invent another world in which the good man flourishes eternally and the bad one is eternally punished. Thus the fundamental rightness of things is vindicated, and we incidentally benefit in the process.

But in order that the system may work, it is necessary that the good man and the bad man should be under continual observation, that neither the unrequited goodness of the one nor the unchastised badness of the other may go unregistered. This function is admirably performed by the vertical or upstairs-God. Thoughtfully accommodated with an abode in the skies, a position admirably adapted for purposes of espionage, He keeps a dossier of each individual, recognising in us the worth that others unaccountably fail to recognise, and observing the wickedness and hypocrisy of those whom the world equally unaccountably exalts. These things are carefully noted, and in the next world all is made right. Immensely important, admired and envied—for are we not the favoured children of Omnipotence?—we live happily ever afterwards; scorned and hated, our enemies are convincingly humiliated. Assuredly an admirable arrangement! It is difficult to see how it could be improved upon. But God is essential to its proper working, and God flourishes accordingly.

God, then, on this view, is at once the product of human terror and the prop of human pride. He comforts our wretchedness, calms our fears, gives us an assurance of justice, and makes us feel important. "Religious ideas," says Freud, "have sprung from the same need as all the other achievements of culture; from the necessity for defending oneself against the crushing supremacy of nature."

(2) But though Freud recognises one of the sources of religion in man's subjection to the forces of nature, he finds its chief root in his relationship to society. Hence his main account of the origin of religion is rather different from that just summarised.

This account will be found in Freud's book, *The Future of an Illusion,* which appeared in 1928. It is not very original, but it is typical of a certain attitude to religion, and may be taken as fairly representative of the view of many educated people, especially psychological and scientific workers today. Freud proceeds upon the basis of what is, in effect, a social contract theory of the origin of society. This theory is admirably stated early in the second book of Plato's *Republic.* Essential to it is the conception of primitive man as a completely non-moral animal; as such his natural inclination is to get his own way at all costs, without thought of the consequences to his neighbours. If his neighbour annoys him, he knocks him on the head; if his neighbour's wife attracts him, he makes off with her. Thus every man has, as Glaucon puts it in the *Republic,* a *natural* tendency to do injustice to his fellows. Admirable in theory, this system, or lack of system, has one serious drawback in practice; the right of every man to do injustice to his neighbours carries with it a corresponding right on the part of his neighbours to do injustice to him. He is one, but his neighbours are many, with the result that, where his hand is against every man and every man's hand is against him, he tends to get the worst of the bargain. His existence is intolerably insecure, he must be perpetually on his guard, and he has no secure enjoyment of his possessions. In the days before society was formed man's life, as the philosopher Hobbes puts it, was "nasty, brutish, and short." Finding the situation intolerable, men ended it by making a compact known as the social contract.

The compact was to form society. Consenting to live in society, man surrendered his natural right to do what he pleased to his fellows, on condition that they made a similar concession as regards himself. Social relations were regulated by public opinion, which later crystallised into law, and man for the future restrained his natural instincts lest he incur the social displeasure of his fellows. Thus was society formed, and from its formation

springs the system of inhibitions and restraints which men call morality. To
act morally is thus . . . the reverse of acting naturally and implies a victory
over the "natural man"; we obey the law, and keep our hands off our
neighbours' wife and property, not because we are by nature moral, but in
fear of the penalties with which society has proscribed actions which violate
the contract upon which it was formed. In other words, we do right only
through fear of the consequences of doing wrong. Remove this fear of consequences, as, for example, by endowing the individual with the gift of
invisibility at will, and the social man would immediately relapse into the
natural man, with the result that no property would be safe, no wife invio-
lable. The conclusion is that morality, which is simply the habit of acting in
a manner of which other people approve, is not natural to man; on the
contrary, it runs counter to his natural interests, frustrates his natural
desires, and requires him to surrender his natural rights.

Now, man is not born social. He only becomes so at the cost of suffering
and repression. Every child is born "natural," endowed with an egotism
that bids him tyrannise over his world. Seeking to impose his imperious
will upon his environment, he is surprised when his environment fails to
respond, pained when it begins to resent. For a creature who starts with this
"natural" endowment the business of growing up into a social adult who
knows the lawful limits that must be set upon his desires is, it is obvious,
a formidable one, so formidable that, according to Freud, it is seldom more
than partially achieved, and never achieved without suffering and injury.
To assist him in the difficult process of social adjustment the individual
invokes the aid of religion. Hence the essence of religion, according to
Freud, is compensation. It is compensation for man's loneliness in face of
the vast indifference of the universe; it is also, and more importantly, compensation for the renunciations which he must undertake at the bidding of
society.

> Wherein [asks Freud] lies the peculiar virtue of religious ideas? We have
> spoken of the hostility to culture produced by the pressure it exercises and
> the instinctual renunciations that it demands. If one imagined its prohibi-
> tions removed, then one could choose any woman who took one's fancy as
> one's sexual object, one could kill without hesitation one's rival or whoever
> interfered with one in any other way, and one could seize what one wanted
> of another man's goods without asking his leave: how splendid, what a
> succession of delights life would be!

Forgo these delights, we must, if we are to achieve civilisation. And, for-
going them, we demand that the gods shall reward us for our sacrifice.
Hence religion is the force that reconciles man to the burden of civilisation.
It is the most important of the compensations that civilisation offers to its
citizens; so important that only by offering it does civilisation become possible. When we have learned as by second nature to refrain from incest,
murder, torture, and arson, when we "pass right along the car, please," adjust our dress before leaving, and take our places at the end of the queue,
without thinking whether we want to do these things or not, the external
restrictions which society imposes have become instinctive habits, the primi-

tive child has become the civilised adult, and social adjustment has been achieved. But achieved only by the aid of religion. Had we no God to whom to turn for comfort and consolation, to whom to tell the unfulfilled wishes and thwarted ambitions, to whom to pray for fortitude to suffer and strength to forbear, the task would be too great for us.

With the very dawn of consciousness, the need for a father confessor makes itself felt.

> Thus little by little I became conscious where I was, and to have a wish to express my wishes to those who could content them; and I could not; for the wishes were within me and they without; nor could they, by any sense of theirs, enter within my spirit.

Thus St. Augustine, who proceeds to tell how he sought and found in God the confidant whom the world denied.

Nor is it only from others that we need a refuge. There is the riot of our desires, there are the prickings of our consciences; there is the sting of remorse. For, though manhood is achieved, the adjustment to society is not yet complete; still, though with decreasing vigour as the individual grows older and society more civilised, the natural man raises his head and rebels. When the rebellion comes into the open, when we refuse to pass down the car, take the head of the queue, or insist upon our inalienable privilege of driving upon the right-hand side of the road, society has little difficulty in quelling us. There are policemen, there are law courts, there are prisons, there are even scaffolds. But sometimes the rebellion stays underground, or, though it comes to the surface, goes undetected.

Against these hidden revolts society must protect itself, and devolves accordingly a system of espionage. There is a spy within the individual citadel itself, a spy in the service of society. This is our old Victorian acquaintance, the conscience, the policeman of society, stationed within the individual to see that social interests are duly observed. Directly we go wrong, directly, that is to say, we cease to act in a way of which society approves, conscience begins to nag. Like a dog that does not stop us from passing, but that we cannot prevent from barking, conscience voices the disapproval of society. The voice of conscience is an unpleasant one, causing us grave discomfort, and in extreme cases driving us to madness. Some refuge from the stings of conscience we must find, and we duly find it—in religion. Stricken by remorse, we demand that our sins be forgiven us. Who can forgive sin but God? Fouled by our sins of wrong-doing, we demand to be made clean. How can we be cleansed save by bathing in the blood of Jesus? And so we come to a new function of religion, a new use for God. Again religion takes the form of an insurance. We deny ourselves the minor luxuries, abstain from the grosser forms of vice, and submit to a little boredom on Sunday, and in return we are guaranteed against discomfort from the stings of conscience in the present and possible discomfort at the hands of the Almighty in the hereafter.

In all these ways and in many others religion seeks to compensate us for the strain and stress of living in society.

Freud traces the gradual evolution of religion to perform this function and the success with which it has, in fact, performed it. He distinguishes various stages in the growth of religion, determined by the nature of the need which at each successive stage it has been chiefly invoked to satisfy. Initially, the chief use of the gods is to protect man from the capriciousness of nature; but, as man progressed, the discoveries of science introduced order into disorder, and substituted law for caprice. At the same time, the growing complexity of civilisation increases the strain of social adjustment. Less needed in the physical world, God becomes an indispensable refuge for the harassed soul of man. Thus history records a decline in the physical and a growth in the moral attributes of the gods.

> In the course of time the first observations of law and order in natural phenomena are made, and therewith the forces of nature lose their human traits. But men's helplessness remains, and with it their father-longing and the gods. . . . And the more autonomous nature becomes and the more the gods withdraw from her, the more earnestly are all expectations concentrated on the third task assigned to them and the more does morality become their real domain. It now becomes the business of the gods to adjust the defects and evils of culture, to attend to the sufferings that men inflict on each other in their communal life, and to see that the laws of culture, which men obey so ill, are carried out. The laws of culture themselves are claimed to be of divine origin, they are elevated to a position above human society, and they are extended over nature and the universe.

Thus Freud records the progress of religion, and summarises the different functions which it performs. Nor is his account singular. On the contrary, it is one to which, with minor modifications, most psychologists and anthropologists would subscribe. The more we learn about our mental, the more we learn about our bodily natures, the more, it is said, do we lay bare the roots of religion in the fundamental needs of our natures. Psychologists derive the doctrine of original sin from the sense of man's impotence in the face of chance and destiny, physiologists from the transgressions of his passionate body against the taboos of society. From our infancy we walk between a fear and a fear, between ruthless Nature and restricting culture, crying, like Bunyan's Pilgrim, "What shall I do to be saved?" And, demanding salvation at all costs, we create God to save us.

Thus religion is the consolation of mankind, and as such its appeal is universal.

(3) But we now come to a more limited, but scarcely less important, function which religion has played in the history of man. To its successful performance of this function its growth and vigour in more modern times is mainly attributable.

There are evils which are the common heritage of all men; they are death, disease, the ingratitude of man to man, the malevolence of destiny. These are no respecters of persons, and bear with impartial severity upon us all. But there are others which do not belong to the essential conditions of human life, but are incidental to the way in which man has chosen collectively to organise his life. For men, equal in the eyes of God, are far from equal in the eyes of society. There are, and always have been, rulers and ruled, oppressors and oppressed, rich and poor; according to many authorities, there always will be. Society, moreover, is based upon force, which its rulers employ to maintain and perpetuate the inequalities on which they thrive. To make their task easier they invoke the assistance of religion. For religion is not only a means of reconciling the individual to society; it is also, and more particularly, a device for inducing the poor and oppressed to tolerate the particular order of society which impoverishes and oppresses them. Thus religion becomes the instrument of the rich and the bridle of the poor. How is the oracle worked?

It is significant, in the first place, that most religions extol the virtues appropriate to slaves—namely, meekness, humility, unselfishness, and contentment, and censure as the vices of pride and presumption the virtues of courage, originality, and independence, and that passionate resentment at injustice and wrong which are characteristic of those who aspire to rise above their servitude. The Christian religion goes further, and makes a virtue of poverty. It is only, we are assured, with the greatest difficulty that the rich man shall enter the Kingdom of Heaven, which opens its gates to the humble and needy. Poverty and insignificance are not, therefore, as they appear to be, and as the world insists on regarding them, disabilities to be avoided at all costs; they are passports to celestial bliss. As such they are rightly to be welcomed. The Christian religion, indeed, expressly encourages us to cultivate them, exhorting us to worldly improvidence and inertia by bidding us take no thought for the morrow and to be content with that state of life into which it has pleased God to call us.

As it has pleased Him to call ninety-nine out of every hundred of us to an extremely lowly state, religion, in so far as it is taken seriously, assists in keeping us where we are. Assists whom? Those who benefit by our remaining where we are—namely, our rulers. For the governing classes have been quick to seize the chance religion has offered them of not only subduing their inferiors, but of representing their subjection as a positive asset to their subjects. Ever since an early governing-class realist slipped the parable about Lazarus into the text of the Gospel of St. Luke, the priest and the parson, seeking to persuade the poor that it was only by remaining poor that they would go to heaven, have been able to produce good scriptural backing for their propaganda. The poor, on the whole, have been only too ready to agree, and have gladly embraced the promise of celestial bliss in the next world as a compensation for the champagne and cigars they were missing in this one. Since the celestial bliss was known to be of indefinite continuance, while the champagne and cigars could not last at most for more than a beggarly fifty years (as a matter of fact, they often lasted less, God having from time to time seen fit to punish the excesses of the worldly by dulling their palates and depriving them of their appetites in the present as an earnest of His intentions for the future[1]), the poor—it is obvious—have the best of the bargain. If it has ever occurred to them to wonder why the rich and powerful should recklessly jeopardise the chances which they have so

---

[1] More recently, of course, He has added cancer to the list of penalities.

freely proffered and warmly recommended to their poorer brethren, they may possibly have comforted themselves with the reflection that *quem deus vult perdere prius dementit.** Possibly, but not probably, for, on the whole, the poor and oppressed have been too much engaged with their poverty and oppression to reflect upon the motives of their betters.

Religion, from this point of view, is a gigantic social hoax, a hoax which has been, on the whole, remarkably successful, so much so, indeed, that from time to time one or another of the rulers of mankind, franker or more secure than the rest, has not scrupled to show how the trick was worked. Thus Napoléon, a notorious sceptic, taxed with the protection which he afforded to a religion in which he did not believe, and stoutly refusing to be drawn into anti-Christian or anti-clerical legislation:

> "What is it," he asked his critics, "that makes the poor man think it quite natural that there are fires in my palace while he is dying of cold? that I have ten coats in my wardrobe while he goes naked? that at each of my meals enough is served to feed his family for a week? It is simply religion, which tells him that in another life I shall be only his equal, and that he actually has more chance of being happy there than I. Yes, we must see to it that the doors of the churches are open to all, and that it does not cost the poor man much to have prayers said on his tomb."

Napoléon was right. The poor have a need for religion which the rich do not feel, and it is not surprising, therefore, to find that, while scepticism and atheism have on occasion flourished among the rich, religion has uniformly been embraced with eagerness by the poor. The growth of disbelief in governing-class circles, while it may have evoked the censure of society—the rich have always thought it prudent to keep up religious observances—has rarely called down the penalties of the law. Thus governing-class writers of the eighteenth century, Gibbon, Voltaire, or the Encyclopædists, for example, who were notoriously irreligious or hostile to religion, went comparatively scathless. Naturally, since they wrote for the educated upper, not for the ignorant lower, classes. Most of the early rationalists, again, were academic people whose books were too difficult or too dull to command a popular circulation. Excepting Woolston, they escaped unpunished. But Peter Annett, a schoolmaster who tried to popularise free thought and held forth on the village green, was sentenced to the pillory and hard labour in 1763. "If we take the cases in which the civil authorities have intervened to repress the publication of unorthodox opinions during the last two centuries," says Professor Burry, "we find that the object has always been to prevent the spread of free thought among the masses."

On the whole, however, the governing classes have thought it wiser themselves to profess allegiance to the religion which they cultivated for the benefit of others. Nor has the profession been always insincere. Using religion as an instrument, they have nevertheless revered it.

In the nineteenth century, as the danger to society from the new proletariat first made itself felt, the beliefs of the governing classes, it is interesting

---

* Whom the gods would destroy, they first make mad.

to note, become more pronounced as their religious example becomes more edifying. It was most important that the wage slaves of the industrial revolution should learn to know God, and in knowing Him to respect their betters. Their betters, then, should show them the way. This they proceeded to do.

The *Annual Register* for 1798 remarks:

> It was a wonder to the lower orders throughout all parts of England to see the avenues to the churches filled with carriages. This novel appearance prompted the simple country people to enquire what was the matter.

Soon afterwards Wilberforce managed to get the first day of meeting of the House of Commons put off to Tuesday, lest the re-assembling of Parliament on a Monday might cause members to travel and to be seen travelling through London on a Sunday. For the same reason the opening of the Newmarket Races was changed from Easter Monday to Tuesday. "In the old times the villages on the route used to turn out on Easter Sunday to admire the procession of rich revellers, and their gay colours and equipment. The Duke of York, in answer to remonstrances, said that it was true he travelled to the races on a Sunday, but he always had a Bible and a Prayer Book in his carriage."

The moral of all this is sufficiently obvious. It was, indeed, put succinctly enough by one Arthur Young, who, in *An Enquiry into the State of Mind Among the Lower Classes,* written in 1798, says:

> A stranger would think our churches were built, as indeed they are, only for the rich. Under such arrangement where are the lower classes to hear the Word of God, that Gospel which in our Saviour's time was preached more particularly to the poor? Where are they to learn the doctrines of that truly excellent religion which exhorts to content and to submission to the higher powers? . . .
>
> Twenty years later, one Englishman out of seven being at that time a pauper, Parliament voted a million of public money for the construction of churches to preach submission to the higher powers. In the debates in the House of Lords, in May 1818, Lord Liverpool laid stress on the social importance of guiding by this means the opinions of those who were beginning to receive education.

That the position remains radically unaltered is shown by the following dialogue between Cusins and Undershaft from Shaw's *Major Barbara,* a dialogue which has become a classic.

> CUSINS (*in a white fury*): Do I understand you to imply that you can buy Barbara?
>
> UNDERSHAFT: No; but I can buy the Salvation Army.
>
> CUSINS: Quite impossible.
>
> UNDERSHAFT: You shall see. All religious organisations exist by selling themselves to the rich.
>
> CUSINS: Not the Army. That is the Church of the poor.
>
> UNDERSHAFT: All the more reason for buying it.
>
> CUSINS: I don't think you quite know what the Army does for the poor.
>
> UNDERSHAFT: Oh yes, I do. It draws their teeth: that is enough for me— as a man of business——

CUSINS: Nonsense! It makes them sober——
UNDERSHAFT: I prefer sober workmen. The profits are larger.
CUSINS: —honest——
UNDERSHAFT: Honest workmen are the most economical.
CUSINS:—attached to their homes——
UNDERSHAFT: So much the better: they will put up with anything sooner than change their shop.
CUSINS: —happy——
UNDERSHAFT: An invaluable safeguard against revolution.
CUSINS: —unselfish——
UNDERSHAFT: Indifferent to their own interests, which suits me exactly.
CUSINS: —with their thoughts on heavenly things——
UNDERSHAFT (*rising*): And not on Trade Unionism nor Socialism. Excellent.
CUSINS (revolted): You really are an infernal old rascal.

Summing up, we may note that this conception of the special function of religion as the instrument of the rich and the bridle of the poor follows logically from its main social function considered above. I have already summarised Freud's account of religion as man's compensation for the renunciations which society demands of him. This may be described as the general social function of religion. It is the part which religion has been called upon to play in the lives of tribal and civilised men, because they live in tribes and societies. But in addition to the general there is a special social function of religion, which is to render the inequalities of society tolerable to the masses. Civilisation, requiring of the many poor far greater instinctive renunciations than it demands of the rich, has given them far fewer material compensations. It is essential, therefore, if they are to acquiesce in a state of society which on the material side demands so much while giving so little, that they should receive some compensation of the spirit, a compensation which brings comfort in the present and gives hope for the future. Such compensation is afforded by an ingeniously devised and richly satisfying religious system, which, while making a virtue of humility, feeds the fires of self-esteem, lest, revolting against their insignificance, the poor and the many should turn against society and destroy it. This, then, is one of the functions which religion, and especially the Christian religion, has performed in civilised societies; it has taken the revolutionary sting from poverty and blunted the edge of present discontent with promises of future well-being. Performing this function, religion has been sedulously exploited and used by the rich as an instrument of class domination. God, it has been found, is cheaper than a living wage. Very well, then, let us invest in Him! Religion is a show to keep the poor amused. Very well, then, let us build churches in the slums! For this reason Socialists have tended to be hostile to religion, and the Bolshevik Government veers between reluctant toleration and covert persecution.

 . . . I have endeavoured briefly to summarise a number of different accounts of the origin, the growth, and the function of religion. These accounts dominate the modern psychological and sociological treatment of the subject, which is, on the whole, markedly hostile to religion. There are, admittedly, differences on points of detail and different writers put the emphasis differently according to the purposes which their account is intended to serve and the aspect of religion with which it is chiefly concerned. But all the accounts which I have summarised are in fundamental agreement in interpreting religion on subjectivist lines.

On this one fundamental point they concur. When faced with the question, "Why is there religion?" they answer unanimously, "Because man wants it." When asked, "Whence does religion rise?" their reply is, "From the needs of man's nature." Pressed for an explanation of its authority and appeal, they represent it as a "rationalisation of his instinctive wishes." Thus all these accounts are in their different ways subjectivist. They affirm that religion enables man to accommodate himself to this world, that it expresses a human need, and that it is, therefore, pleasant and consoling; they do not say that it represents an objective fact, that it points forward to a different world, and that it is therefore true. With most of what they assert I am largely, if not entirely, in agreement. I think that the interpretations they give of the origin of religion in terms of the needs which it fulfils, and of the ground of its appeal in terms of the wishes that it rationalises, are in the main true. But I do not think that they are complete. They are, that is to say, interpretations in terms of origin only, and they take no account of the conception of end or purpose. They ask how religion began and why it flourished; they do not ask what it may become. Both conceptions are, I am convinced, necessary to an adequate description of the status of religion in the present, and a reasoned estimate of its chance of survival in the future. . . .

DOVER BEACH

Matthew Arnold

The sea is calm to-night.
The tide is full, the moon lies fair
Upon the straits;—on the French coast the light
Gleams and is gone; the cliffs of England stand,
Glimmering and vast, out in the tranquil bay.
Come to the window, sweet is the night-air!
Only, from the long line of spray
Where the sea meets the moon-blanch'd land,
Listen! you hear the grating roar
Of pebbles which the waves draw back, and fling,

At their return, up the high strand,
Begin, and cease, and then again begin,
With tremulous cadence slow, and bring
The eternal note of sadness in.

Sophocles long ago
Heard it on the Ægæan, and it brought
Into his mind the turbid ebb and flow
Of human misery; we
Find also in the sound a thought,
Hearing it by this distant northern sea.

The Sea of Faith
Was once, too, at the full, and round earth's shore
Lay like the folds of a bright girdle furl'd.
But now I only hear
Its melancholy, long, withdrawing roar,
Retreating, to the breath
Of the night-wind, down the vast edges drear
And naked shingles of the world.

Ah, love, let us be true
To one another! for the world, which seems
To lie before us like a land of dreams,
So various, so beautiful, so new,
Hath really neither joy, nor love, nor light,
Nor certitude, nor peace, nor help for pain;
And we are here as on a darkling plain
Swept with confused alarms of struggle and flight,
Where ignorant armies clash by night.

MAN AGAINST DARKNESS

W. T. Stace

I

The Catholic bishops of America recently issued a statement in which they said that the chaotic and bewildered state of the modern world is due to man's loss of faith, his abandonment of God and religion. For my part I believe in no religion at all. Yet I entirely agree with the bishops. It is no doubt an oversimplification to speak of *the* cause of so complex a state of affairs as the tortured condition of the world today. Its causes are doubtless multitudinous. Yet allowing for some element of oversimplification, I say that the bishops' assertion is substantially true.

M. Jean-Paul Sartre, the French existentialist philosopher, labels himself an atheist. Yet his views seem to me plainly to support the statement of the bishops. So long as there was believed to be a God in the sky, he says, men could regard him as the source of their moral ideals. The universe, created and governed by a fatherly God, was a friendly habitation for man. We could be sure that, however great the evil in the world, good in the end would triumph and the forces of evil would be routed. With the disappearance of God from the sky all this has changed. Since the world is not ruled by a spiritual being, but rather by blind forces, there cannot be any ideals, moral or otherwise, in the universe outside us. Our ideals, therefore, must proceed only from our own minds; they are our own inventions. Thus the world which surrounds us is nothing but an immense spiritual emptiness. It is a dead universe. We do not live in a universe which is on the side of our values. It is completely indifferent to them.

Years ago Mr. Bertrand Russell, in his essay *A Free Man's Worship,* said much the same thing.

> Such in outline, but even more purposeless, more void of meaning, is the world which Science presents for our belief. Amid such a world, if anywhere, our ideals henceforward must find a home. . . . Blind to good and evil, reckless of destruction, omnipotent matter rolls on its relentless way; for man, condemned today to lose his dearest, tomorrow himself to pass through the gate of darkness, it remains only to cherish, ere yet the blow falls, the lofty thoughts that ennoble his little day; . . . to worship at the shrine his own hands have built; . . . to sustain alone, a weary but unyielding Atlas, the world that his own ideals have fashioned despite the trampling march of unconscious power.

It is true that Mr. Russell's personal attitude to the disappearance of religion is quite different from either that of M. Sarte or the bishops or myself. The bishops think it a calamity. So do I. M. Sartre finds it "very distressing." And he berates as shallow the attitude of those who think that without God the world can go on just the same as before, as if nothing had happened. This creates for mankind, he thinks, a terrible crisis. And in this I agree with him. Mr. Russell, on the other hand, seems to believe that religion has done more harm than good in the world, and that its disappearance will be a blessing. But his picture of the world, and of the modern mind, is the same as that of M. Sartre. He stresses the *purposelessness* of the universe, the facts that man's ideals are his own creations, that the universe outside him in no way supports them, that man is alone and friendless in the world.

Mr. Russell notes that it is science which has produced this situation. There is no doubt that this is correct. But the way in which it has come about is not generally understood. There is a popular belief that some particular scientific discoveries or theories, such as the Darwinian theory of evolution, or the views of geologists about the age of the earth, or a series of such discoveries, have done the damage. It would be foolish to deny that these discoveries have had a great effect in undermining religious dogmas. But this account does not at all go to the root of the matter. Religion can probably outlive any scientific discoveries which could be made. It can accommodate itself to them. The root cause of the decay of faith has not been any particular discovery of science, but rather the general spirit of science and certain basic assumptions upon which modern science, from the seventeenth century onwards, has proceeded.

II

It was Galileo and Newton—notwithstanding that Newton himself was a deeply religious man—who destroyed the old comfortable picture of a friendly universe governed by spiritual values. And this was effected, not by Newton's discovery of the law of gravitation nor by any of Galileo's brilliant investigations, but by the general picture of the world which these men and others of their time made the basis of the science, not only of their own day, but of all succeeding generations down to the present. That is why the century immediately following Newton, the eighteenth century, was notoriously an age of religious skepticism. Skepticism did not have to wait for the discoveries of Darwin and the geologists in the nineteenth century. It flooded the world immediately after the age of the rise of science.

Neither the Copernican hypothesis nor any of Newton's or Galileo's particular discoveries were the real causes. Religious faith might well have accommodated itself to the new astronomy. The real turning point between the medieval age of faith and the modern age of unfaith came when the scientists of the seventeenth century turned their backs upon what used to be called "final causes." The final cause of a thing or event meant the purpose which it was supposed to serve in the universe, its cosmic purpose. What lay back of this was the presupposition that there is a cosmic order or plan and that everything which exists could in the last analysis be explained in terms of its place in this cosmic plan, that is, in terms of its purpose.

Plato and Aristotle believed this, and so did the whole medieval Christian world. For instance, if it were true that the sun and the moon were created and exist for the purpose of giving light to man, then this fact would explain why the sun and the moon exist. We might not be able to discover the purpose of everything, but everything must have a purpose. Belief in final causes thus amounted to a belief that the world is governed by purposes, presumably the purposes of some overruling mind. This belief was not the invention of Christianity. It was basic to the whole of Western civilization, whether in the ancient pagan world or in Christendom, from the time of Socrates to the rise of science in the seventeenth century.

The founders of modern science—for instance, Galileo, Kelper, and Newton—were mostly pious men who did not doubt God's purposes. Nevertheless they took the revolutionary step of consciously and deliberately expelling the idea of purpose as controlling nature from their new science of nature. They did this on the ground that inquiry into purposes is useless for what science aims at: namely, the prediction and control of events. To predict an eclipse, what you have to know is not its purpose but its causes. Hence science from the seventeenth century onwards became exclusively an inquiry into causes. The conception of purpose in the world was ignored and frowned on. This, though silent and almost unnoticed, was the greatest revolution in human history, far outweighing in importance any of the political revolutions whose thunder has reverberated through the world.

For it came about in this way that for the past three hundred years there has been growing up in men's minds, dominated as they are by science, a new imaginative picture of the world. The world, according to this new picture, is purposeless, senseless, meaningless. Nature is nothing but matter in motion. The motions of matter are governed, not by any purpose, but by blind forces and laws. Nature on this view, says Whitehead—to whose writings I am indebted in this part of my paper—is "merely the hurrying of material, endlessly, meaninglessly." You can draw a sharp line across the history of Europe dividing it into two epochs of very unequal length. The line passes through the lifetime of Galileo. European man before Galileo—whether ancient pagan or more recent Christian—thought of the world as controlled by plan and purpose. After Galileo European man thinks of it as utterly purposeless. This is the great revolution of which I spoke.

It is this which has killed religion. Religion could survive the discoveries that the sun, not the earth, is the center; that men are descended from simian ancestors; that the earth is hundreds of millions of years old. These discoveries may render out of date some of the details of older theological dogmas, may force their restatement in new intellectual frameworks. But they do not touch the essence of the religious vision itself, which is the faith that there is plan and purpose in the world, that the world is a moral order, that in the end all things are for the best. This faith may express itself through many different intellectual dogmas, those of Christianity, of Hinduism, of Islam. All and any of these intellectual dogmas may be destroyed without destroying the essential religious spirit. But that spirit cannot survive destruction of belief in a plan and purpose of the world, for that is the very heart of it. Religion can get on with any sort of astronomy, geology, biology, physics. But it cannot get on with a purposeless and meaningless universe.

If the scheme of things is purposeless and meaningless, then the life of man is purposeless and meaningless too. Everything is futile, all effort is in the end worthless. A man may, of course, still pursue disconnected ends, money, fame, art, science, and may gain pleasure from them. But his life is hollow at the center. Hence the dissatisfied, disillusioned, restless, spirit of modern man.

The picture of a meaningless world, and a meaningless human life, is, I think, the basic theme of much modern art and literature. Certainly it is the theme of modern philosophy. According to the most characteristic philosophies of the modern period from Hume in the eighteenth century to the so-called positivists of today, the world is just what it is, and that is the end of all inquiry. There is no reason for its being what it is. Everything might just as well have been quite different, and there would have been no reason for that either. When you have stated what things are, what things the world contains, there is nothing more which could be said, even by an omniscient being. To ask any question about *why* things are thus, or what purpose their being so serves, is to ask a senseless question, because they serve no purpose at all. For instance, there is for modern philosophy no such thing as the ancient problem of evil. For this once famous question presupposes that pain and misery, though they seem so inexpicable and irrational to us, must ultimately subserve some rational purpose, must have their places in the cosmic plan. But this is nonsense. There is no such overruling rationality in the universe. Belief in the ultimate irrationality of everything is the quintessence of what is called the modern mind.

It is true that, parallel with these philosophies which are typical of the modern mind, preaching the meaninglessness of the world, there has run a line of idealistic philosophies whose contention is that the world is after all spiritual in nature and that moral ideals and values are inherent in its structure. But most of these idealisms were simply philosophical expressions of romanticism, which was itself no more than an unsuccessful counterattack of the religious against the scientific view of things. They perished, along with romanticism in literature and art, about the beginning of the present century, though of course they still have a few adherents.

At the bottom these idealistic systems of thought were rationalizations of man's wishful thinking. They were born of the refusal of men to admit the cosmic darkness. They were comforting illusions within the warm glow of which the more tender-minded intellectuals sought to shelter themselves from the icy winds of the universe. They lasted a little while. But they are shattered now, and we return once more to the vision of a purposeless world.

III

Along with the ruin of the religious vision there went the ruin of moral principles and indeed of all values. If there is a cosmic purpose, if there is in the nature of things a drive towards goodness, then our moral systems will derive their validity from this. But if our moral rules do not proceed from something outside us in the nature of the universe—whether we say it is God or simply the universe itself—then they must be our own inventions. Thus it came to be believed that moral rules must be merely an expression of our own likes and dislikes. But likes and dislikes are notoriously variable. What pleases one man, people, or culture displeases another. Therefore morals are wholly relative.

This obvious conclusion from the idea of a purposeless world made its appearance in Europe immediately after the rise of science, for instance in the philosophy of Hobbes. Hobbes saw at once that if there is no purpose in the world there are no values either. "Good and evil," he writes, "are names that signify our appetites and aversions; which in different tempers, customs, and doctrines of men are different. . . . Every man calleth that which pleaseth him, good; and that which displeaseth him, evil."

This doctrine of the relativity of morals, though it has recently received an impetus from the studies of anthropologists, was thus really implicit in the whole scientific mentality. It is disastrous for morals because it destroys their entire traditional foundation. That is why philosophers who see the danger signals, from the time at least of Kant, have been trying to give to morals a new foundation, that is, a secular or nonreligious foundation. This attempt may very well be intellectually successful. Such a foundation, independent of the religious view of the world, might well be found. But the question is whether it can ever be a *practical* success, that is, whether apart from its logical validity and its influence with intellectuals, it can ever replace among the masses of men the lost religious foundation. On that question hangs perhaps the future of civilization. But meanwhile disaster is overtaking us.

The widespread belief in "ethical relativity" among philosophers, psychologists, ethnologists, and sociologists is the theoretical counterpart of the repudiation of principle which we see all around us, especially in international affairs, the field in which morals have always had the weakest foothold. No one any longer effectively believes in moral principles except as the private prejudices either of individual men or of nations or cultures. This is the inevitable consequence of the doctrine of ethical relativity, which in turn is the inevitable consequence of believing in a purposeless world.

Another characteristic of our spiritual state is loss of belief in the freedom of the will. This also is a fruit of the scientific spirit, though not of any particular scientific discovery. Science has been built up on the basis of determinism, which is the belief that every event is completely determined by a chain of causes and is therefore theoretically predictable beforehand. It is true that recent physics seems to challenge this. But so far as its practical consequences are concerned, the damage has long ago been done. A man's actions, it was argued, are as much events in the natural world as is an eclipse of the sun. It follows that men's actions are as theoretically predictable as an eclipse. But if it is certain now that John Smith will murder Joseph Jones at 2.15 P.M. on January 1, 1963, what possible meaning can it have to say that when that time comes John Smith will be *free* to choose whether he will commit the murder or not? And if he is not free, how can he be held responsible?

It is true that the whole of this argument can be shown by a competent philosopher to be a tissue of fallacies—or at least I claim that it can. But the point is that the analysis required to show this is much too subtle to be understood by the average entirely unphilosophical man. Because of this, the argument against free will is generally swallowed whole by the unphilosophical. Hence the thought that man is not free, that he is the helpless plaything of forces over which he has no control, has deeply penetrated the modern mind. We hear of economic determinism, cultural determinism, historical determinism. We are not responsible for what we do because our glands control us, or because we are the products of environment or heredity. Not moral self-control, but the doctor, the psychiatrist, the educationist, must save us from doing evil. Pills and injections in the future are to do what Christ and the prophets have failed to do. Of course I do not mean to deny that doctors and educationists can and must help. And I do not mean in any way to belittle their efforts. But I do wish to draw attention to the weakening of moral controls, the greater or less repudiation of personal responsibility which, in the popular thinking of the day, result from these tendencies of thought.

IV

What, then, is to be done? Where are we to look for salvation from the evils of our time? All the remedies I have seen suggested so far are, in my opinion, useless. Let us look at some of them.

Philosophers and intellectuals generally can, I believe, genuinely do something to help. But it is extremely little. What philosophers can do is to show that neither the relativity of morals nor the denial of free will really follows from the grounds which have been supposed to support them. They can also try to discover a genuine secular basis for morals to replace the religious basis which has disappeared. Some of us are trying to do these things. But in the first place philosophers unfortunately are not agreed about these matters, and their disputes are utterly confusing to the non-philosophers. And in the second place their influence is practically negligible because their analyses necessarily take place on a level on which the masses are totally unable to follow them.

The bishops, of course, propose as remedy a return to belief in God and in the doctrines of the Christian religion. Others think that a new religion is what is needed. Those who make these proposals fail to realize that the crisis in man's spiritual condition is something unique in history for which there is no sort of analogy in the past. They are thinking perhaps of the collapse of the ancient Greek and Roman religions. The vacuum then created was easily filled by Christianity, and it might have been filled by Mithraism if Christianity had not appeared. By analogy they think that Christianity might now be replaced by a new religion, or even that Christianity itself, if revivified, might bring back health to men's lives.

But I believe that there is no analogy at all between our present state and that of the European peoples at the time of the fall of paganism. Man had at that time lost their belief only in particular dogmas, particular embodiments of the religious view of the world. It had no doubt become incredible that Zeus and the other gods were living on the top of Mount Olympus. You could go to the top and find no trace of them. But the imaginative picture of a world governed by purpose, a world driving towards the good—which is the inner spirit of religion—had at that time received no serious shock. It had merely to re-embody itself in new dogmas, those of Christianity or some other religion. Religion itself was not dead in the world, only a particular form of it.

But now the situation is quite different. It is not merely that particular dogmas, like that of the virgin birth, are unacceptable to the modern mind. That is true, but it constitutes a very superficial diagnosis of the present situation of religion. Modern skepticism is of a wholly different order from that of the intellectuals of the ancient world. It has attacked and destroyed not merely the outward forms of the religious spirit, its particularized dog-mas, but the very essence of that spirit itself, belief in a meaningful and pur-poseful world. For the founding of a new religion a new Jesus Christ or Buddha would have to appear, in itself a most unlikely event and one for which in any case we cannot afford to sit and wait. But even if a new prophet and a new religion did appear, we may predict that they would fail in the modern world. No one for long would believe in them, for modern men have lost the vision, basic to all religion, of an ordered plan and purpose of the world. They have before their minds the picture of a purposeless universe, and such a world-picture must be fatal to any religion at all, not merely to Christianity.

We must not be misled by occasional appearances of a revival of the re-ligious spirit. Men, we are told, in their disgust and disillusionment at the emptiness of their lives, are turning once more to religion, or are searching for a new message. It may be so. We must expect such wistful yearnings of the spirit. We must expect men to wish back again the light that is gone, and to try to bring it back. But however they may wish and try, the light will not shine again,—not at least in the civilization to which we belong.

Another remedy commonly proposed is that we should turn to science itself, or the scientific spirit, for our salvation. Mr. Russell and Professor Dewey both make this proposal, though in somewhat different ways. Pro-fessor Dewey seems to believe that discoveries in sociology, the application of scientific method to social and political problems, will rescue us. This seems to me to be utterly naïve. It is not likely that science, which is basically the cause of our spiritual troubles, is likely also to produce the cure for them. Also it lies in the nature of science that, though it can teach us the best means for achieving our ends, it can never tell us what ends to pursue. It cannot give us any ideals. And our trouble is about ideals and ends, not about the means for reaching them.

V

No civilization can live without ideals, or to put it in another way, without a firm faith in moral ideas. Our ideals and moral ideas have in the past been rooted in religion. But the religious basis of our ideals has been undermined, and the superstructure of ideals is plainly tottering. None of the commonly suggested remedies on examination seems likely to succeed. It would there-fore look as if the early death of our civilization were inevitable.

Of course we know that it is perfectly possible for individual men, very highly educated men, philosophers, scientists, intellectuals in general, to live moral lives without any religious convictions. But the question is whether a whole civilizaton, a whole family of peoples, composed almost entirely of relatively uneducated men and women, can do this.

It follows, of course, that if we could make the vast majority of men as highly educated as the very few are now, we might save the situation. And we are already moving slowly in that direction through the techniques of mass education. But the critical question seems to concern the time-lag. Perhaps in a few hundred years most of the population will, at the present rate, be sufficiently highly educated and civilized to combine high ideals with an absence of religion. But long before we reach any such stage, the collapse of our civilization may have come about. How are we to live through the intervening period?

I am sure that the first thing we have to do is to face the truth, however bleak it may be, and then next we have to learn to live with it. Let me say a word about each of these two points. What I am urging as regards the first is complete honesty. Those who wish to resurrect Christian dogmas are not, of course, consciously dishonest. But they have that kind of unconscious dishonesty which consists in lulling oneself with opiates and dreams. Those who talk of a new religion are merely hoping for a new opiate. Both alike refuse to face the truth that there is, in the universe outside man, no spirituality, no regard for values, no friend in the sky, no help or comfort for man of any sort. To be perfectly honest in the admission of this fact, not to seek shelter in new or old illusions, not to indulge in wishful dreams about this matter, this is the first thing we shall have to do.

I do not urge this course out of any special regard for the sanctity of truth in the abstract. It is not self-evident to me that truth is the supreme value to which all else must be sacrificed. Might not the discoverer of a truth which would be fatal to mankind be justified in suppressing it, even in teaching men a falsehood? Is truth more valuable than goodness and beauty and happiness? To think so is to invent yet another absolute, another religious delusion in which Truth with a capital T is substituted for God. The reason why we must now boldly and honestly face the truth that the universe is nonspiritual and indifferent to goodness, beauty, happiness, or truth is not that it would be wicked to suppress it, but simply that it is too late to do so, so that in the end we cannot do anything else but face it. Yet we stand on the brink, dreading the icy plunge. We need courage. We need honesty.

Now about the other point, the necessity of learning to live with the truth. This means learning to live virtuously and happily, or at least contentedly, without illusions. And this is going to be extremely difficult because what we have now begun dimly to perceive is that human life in the past, or at least human happiness, has almost wholly depended upon illusions. It has been said that man lives by truth, and that the truth will make us free. Nearly the opposite seems to me to be the case. Mankind has managed to live only by means of lies, and the truth may very well destroy us. If one were a Bergsonian one might believe that nature deliberately puts illusions into our souls in order to induce us to go on living.

The illusions by which men have lived seem to be of two kinds. First, there is what one may perhaps call the Great Illusion—I mean the religious illusion that the universe is moral and good, that it follows a wise and noble plan, that it is gradually generating some supreme value, that goodness is bound to triumph in it. Secondly, there is a whole host of minor illusions on which human happiness nourishes itself. How much of human happiness notoriously comes from the illusions of the lover about his beloved? Then again we work and strive because of the illusions connected with fame, glory, power, or money. Banners of all kinds, flags, emblems, insignia, cere-monials, and rituals are invariably symbols of some illusion or other. The British Empire, the connection between mother country and dominions, is partly kept going by illusions surrounding the notion of kingship. Or think of the vast amount of human happiness which is derived from the illusion of supposing that if some nonsense syllable, such as "sir" or "count" or "lord" is pronounced in conjunction with our names, we belong to a superior order of people.

There is plenty of evidence that human happiness is almost wholly based upon illusions of one kind or another. But the scientific spirit, or the spirit of truth, is the enemy of illusions and therefore the enemy of human happiness. That is why it is going to be so difficult to live with the truth.

There is no reason why we should have to give up the host of minor il-lusions which render life supportable. There is no reason why the lover should be scientific about the loved one. Even the illusions of fame and glory may persist. But without the Great Illusion, the illusion of a good, kindly, and purposeful universe, we shall *have* to learn to live. And to ask this is really no more than to ask that we become genuinely civilized beings and not merely sham civilized beings.

I can best explain the difference by a reminiscence. I remember a fellow student in my college days, an ardent Christian, who told me that if he did not believe in a future life, in heaven and hell, he would rape, murder, steal, and be a drunkard. That is what I call being a sham civilized being. On the other hand, not only could a Huxley, a John Stuart Mill, a David Hume, live great and fine lives without any religion, but a great many others of us, quite obscure persons, can at least live decent lives without it.

To be genuinely civilized means to be able to walk straightly and to live honorably without the props and crutches of one or another of the childish dreams which have so far supported men. That such a life is likely to be ecstatically happy I will not claim. But that it can be lived in quiet content, accepting resignedly what cannot be helped, not expecting the impossible, and thankful for small mercies, this I would maintain. That it will be difficult for men in general to learn this lesson I do not deny. But that it will be im-possible I would not admit since so many have learned it already.

Man has not yet grown up. He is not adult. Like a child he cries for the moon and lives in a world of fantasies. And the race as a whole has perhaps reached the great crisis of its life. Can it grow up as a race in the same sense as individual men grow up? Can man put away childish things and adoles-cent dreams? Can he grasp the real world as it actually is, stark and bleak, without its romantic or religious halo, and still retain his ideals, striving for great ends and noble achievements? If he can, all may yet be well. If he can-not, he will probably sink back into the savagery and brutality from which he came, taking a humble place once more among the lower animals.

WHAT CHRISTIANS BELIEVE

C. S. Lewis

I have been asked to tell you what Christians believe, and I am going to begin by telling you one thing that Christians don't need to believe. If you are a Christian you don't have to believe that all the other religions are simply wrong all through. If you are an atheist you do have to believe that the main point in all the religions of the whole world is simply one huge mistake. If you are a Christian, you are free to think that all these religions, even the queerest ones, contain at least some hint of the truth. When I was an atheist I had to try to persuade myself that the whole human race were pretty good fools until about one hundred years ago; when I became a Christian I was able to take a more liberal view. But, of course, being a Christian does mean thinking that where Christianity differs from other religions, Christianity is right and they are wrong. Like in arithmetic—there's only one right answer to a sum, and all other answers are wrong: but some of the wrong answers are much nearer being right than others.

The first big division of humanity is into the majority, who believe in some kind of God or gods, and the minority who don't. On this point, Christianity lines up with the majority—lines up with ancient Greeks and Romans, modern savages, Stoics, Platonists, Hindoos, Mohammedans, etc., against the modern Western European materialist. There are all sorts of different reasons for believing in God, and here I'll mention only one. It is this. Supposing there was no intelligence behind the universe, no creative mind. In that case nobody designed my brain for the purpose of thinking. It is merely that when the atoms inside my skull happen for physical or chemical reasons to arrange themselves in a certain way, this gives me, as a by-product, the sensation I call thought. But if so, how can I trust my own thinking to be true? It's like upsetting a milk-jug and hoping that the way the splash arranges itself will give you a map of London. But if I can't trust my own thinking, of course I can't trust the arguments leading to atheism, and therefore have no reason to be an atheist, or anything else. Unless I believe in God, I can't believe in thought: so I can never use thought to disbelieve in God.

Now I go on to the next big division. People who all believe in God can be divided according to the sort of God they believe in. There are two very different ideas on this subject. One of them is the idea that He is beyond good and evil. *We* call one thing good and another thing bad. But according to some people that's merely our human point of view. These people would say that the wiser you become the less you'd want to call anything good or bad, and the more clearly you'd see that everything is good in one way and bad in another, and that nothing could have been different. Consequently, these people think that long before you got anywhere near the divine point of view the distinction would have disappeared altogether. We call a cancer bad, they'd say, because it kills a man; but you might just as well call a successful surgeon bad because he kills a cancer. It all depends on the point of view. The other and opposite idea is that God is quite definitely "good" or "righteous," a God who takes sides, who loves love and hates hatred, who wants us to behave in one way and not in another. The first of these views— the one that thinks God beyond good and evil—is called Pantheism. It was held by the great Prussian philosopher Hegel and, as far as I can understand them, by the Hindoos. The other view is held by Jews, Mohammedans, and Christians.

And with this big difference between Pantheism and the Christian idea of God, there usually goes another. Pantheists usually believe that God, so to speak, animates the universe as you animate your body: that the universe almost *is* God, so that if it didn't exist He wouldn't exist either, and anything you find in the universe is a part of God. The Christian idea is quite different. They think God *made* the universe—like a man making a picture or composing a tune. A painter isn't a picture, and he doesn't die if his picture is destroyed. You may say, "He's put a lot of himself into it," but that only means that all its beauty and interest have come out of his head. His skill isn't in the picture in the same way that it's in his head, or even in his hands. I expect you see how this difference between Pantheists and Christians hangs together with the other one. If you don't take the distinction between good and bad very seriously, then it's easy to say that anything you find in this world is a part of God. But, of course, if you think some things really bad, and God really good, then you can't talk like that. You must believe that God is separate from the world and that some of the things we see in it are contrary to His will. Confronted with a cancer or a slum the Pantheist can say, "If you could only see it from the divine point of view, you would realise that this also is God." The Christian replies, "Don't talk damned nonsense."[1] For Christianity is a fighting religion. It thinks God made the world—that space and time, heat and cold, and all the colours and tastes, and all the animals and vegetables, are things that God "made up out of His head" as a man makes up a story. But it also thinks that a great many things have gone wrong with the world that God made and that God insists, and insists very loudly, on our putting them right again.

And, of course, that raises a very big question. If a good God made the world why has it gone wrong? And for many years I simply wouldn't listen to the Christian answers to this question, because I kept on feeling "whatever you say, and however clever your arguments are, isn't it much simpler and easier to say that the world was *not* made by any intelligent power? Aren't all your arguments simply a complicated attempt to avoid the ob-

---

[1] One listener complained of the word *damned* as frivolous swearing. But I mean exactly what I say—nonsense that is *damned* is under God's curse, and will (apart from God's grace) lead those who believe it to eternal death.

vious?" But then that threw me back into those difficulties about atheism which I spoke of a moment ago. And soon I saw another difficulty.

My argument against God was that the universe seemed so cruel and unjust. But how had I got this idea of *just* and *unjust?* A man doesn't call a line crooked unless he has some idea of a straight line. What was I comparing this universe with when I called it unjust? If the whole show was bad and senseless from A to Z, so to speak, why did I, who was supposed to be part of the show, find myself in such violent reaction against it? A man feels wet when he falls into water, because man isn't a water animal: a fish wouldn't feel wet. Of course I could have given up my idea of justice by saying it was nothing but a private idea of my own. But if I did that then my argument against God collapsed too—for the argument depended on saying that the world was really unjust, not that it just didn't happen to please my private fancies. Thus in the very act of trying to prove that God didn't exist—in other words, that the whole of reality was senseless—I found I was forced to assume that one part of reality—namely my idea of justice—was full of sense. Consequently atheism turns out to be too simple. If the whole universe has no meaning, we should never have found out that it has no meaning: just as if there were no light in the universe and therefore no creatures with eyes we should never know it was dark. *Dark* would be a word without meaning.

II

Very well then, theism is too simple. And I'll tell you another view that is also too simple. It's the view I call Christianity-and-water, the view that just says there's a good God in Heaven and everything is all right—leaving out all the difficult and terrible doctrines about sin and hell and the devil, and the redemption. Both these are boys' philosophies.

It is no good asking for a simple religion. After all, real things *aren't* simple. They *look* simple, but they're not. The table I'm sitting at looks simple: but ask a scientist to tell you what it's really made of—all about the atoms and how the light waves rebound from them and hit my eye and what they do to the optic nerve and what it does to my brain—and, of course, you find that what we call "seeing a table" lands you in mysteries and complications which you can hardly get to the end of. A child, saying a child's prayer, looks simple. And if you're content to stop here, well and good. But if you're not—and the modern world usually isn't—if you want to go on and ask what's really happening—then you must be prepared for something difficult. If we ask for something more than simplicity, it's silly then to complain that the something more isn't simple. Another thing I've noticed about reality is that, besides being difficult, it's odd: it isn't neat, it isn't what you expect. I mean, when you've grasped that the earth and the other planets all go round the sun, you'd naturally expect that all the planets were made to match—all at equal distances from each other, say, or distances that regularly increased, or all the same size, or else getting bigger or smaller as you go further from the sun. In fact, you find no rhyme or reason (that we can see) about either the sizes or the distances; and some of them have one moon, one has four, one has two, some have none, and one has a ring. Reality, in fact, is always something you couldn't have guessed. That's one of the reasons I believe Christianity. It's a religion you couldn't have guessed. If it offered us just the kind of universe we'd always expected, I'd feel we were making it up. But, in fact, it's not the sort of thing anyone would have made up. It has just the queer twist about it that real things have. So let's leave behind all these boys' philosophies—these over-simple answers. The problem isn't simple and the answer isn't going to be simple either.

What is the problem? A universe that contains much that is obviously bad and apparently meaningless, but containing creatures like ourselves who know that it is bad and meaningless. There are only two views that face all the facts. One is the Christian view that this is a good world that has gone wrong, but still retains the memory of what it ought to have been. The other is the view called Dualism. Dualism means the belief that there are two equal and independent powers at the back of everything, one of them good and the other bad, and that this universe is the battlefield in which they fight out an endless war. I personally think that next to Christianity Dualism is the manliest and most sensible creed on the market. But it has a catch in it.

The two powers, or spirits, or gods—the good one and the bad one—are supposed to be quite independent. They both existed from all eternity. Neither of them made the other, neither of them has any more right than the other to call itself God. Each presumably thinks it is good and thinks the other bad. One of them likes hatred and cruelty, the other likes love and mercy, and each backs its own view. Now what do we mean when we call one of them the Good Power and the other the Bad Power? Either we're merely saying that we happen to prefer the one to the other—like preferring beer to cider—or else we're saying that, whatever *they* say about it, and whichever *we* happen to like, one of them is actually wrong, actually mistaken, in regarding itself as good. Now if we mean merely that we happen to prefer the first, then we must give up talking about good and evil at all. For good means what you ought to prefer quite regardless of what you happen to like at any given moment. If "being good" meant simply joining the side you happened to fancy, for no real reason, then good wouldn't *be* good. So we must mean that one of the two powers is actually wrong and the other actually right.

But the moment you say that, you are putting into the universe a third thing in addition to the two Powers: some law or standard or rule of good which one of the powers conforms to and the other fails to conform to. But since the two powers are judged by this standard, then this standard, or the being who made this standard, is farther back and higher up than either of them, and He will be the real God. In fact, what we meant by calling them good and bad turns out to be that one of them is in a right relation to the real ultimate God and the other in a wrong relation to Him.

The same point can be made in a different way. If Dualism is true, then the Bad Power must be a being who likes badness for its own sake. But in reality we have no experience of anyone liking badness just because it is bad. The nearest we can get to it is in cruelty. But in real life people are cruel for one of two reasons—either because they are sadists, that is, because they have a sexual perversion which makes cruelty a cause of sensual pleasure to them, or else for the sake of something they are going to get out of it—money, or power, or safety. But pleasure, money, power, and safety are all, as far as they go, good things. The badness consists in pursuing them by the wrong method, or in the wrong way, or too much. I don't mean, of course, that the people who do this aren't desperately wicked. I do mean that wickedness, when you examine it, turns out to be the pursuit of some good in the wrong way. You can be good for the mere sake of goodness: you can't be bad for the mere sake of badness. You can do a kind action when you're not feeling kind and when it gives you no pleasure, simply because kindness is right; but no one ever did a cruel action simply because cruelty is wrong —only because cruelty was pleasant or useful to him. In other words, badness can't succeed even in being bad *in the same way* in which goodness is good. Goodness is, so to speak, itself: badness is only spoiled goodness. And there must be something good first before it can be spoiled. We called sadism a sexual perversion; but you must first have the idea of a normal sexuality before you can talk of it being perverted; and you can see which is the perversion, because you can explain the perverted from the normal, and can't explain the normal from the perverted. It follows that the Bad Power, who is supposed to be on an equal footing with the Good Power, and to love badness in the same way as the good one loves goodness, is a mere bogey. In order to be bad he must have good things to want and then to pursue in the wrong way: he must have impulses which were originally good in order to be able to pervert them. But if he is bad he can't supply himself either with good things to desire or with good impulses to pervert. He must be getting both from the Good Power. And if so, then he is not independent. He is part of the Good Power's world: he was made either by the Good Power or by some power above them both.

Put it more simply still. To be bad, he must exist and have intelligence and will. But existence, intelligence, and will are in themselves good. Therefore he must be getting them from the Good Power: even to be bad he must borrow or steal from his opponent. And do you now begin to see why Christianity has always said that the devil is a fallen angel? That isn't a mere story for the children. It's a real recognition of the fact that evil is a parasite, not an original thing. The powers which enable evil to carry on are powers given it by goodness. All the things which enable a bad man to be effectively bad are in themselves good things—resolution, cleverness, good looks, existence itself. That's why Dualism, in a strict sense, won't work.

But I want to say that real Christianity (as distinct from Christianity-and-water) goes much nearer to Dualism than people think. One of the things that surprised me when I first read the New Testament seriously was that it was always talking about a Dark Power in the universe—a mighty evil spirit who was held to be the Power behind death and disease, and sin. The difference is that Christianity thinks this Dark Power was created by God, and was good when he was created, and went wrong. Christianity agrees with

Dualism that this universe is at war. But it doesn't think this is a war between independent powers. It thinks it's a civil war, a rebellion, and that we are living in a part of the universe occupied by the rebel.

Enemy-occupied territory—that's what this world is. Christianity is the story of how the rightful kind has landed, you might say landed in disguise, and is calling us all to take part in a great campaign of sabotage. When you go to church you're really listening in to the secret wireless from our friends: that's why the enemy is so anxious to prevent us going. He does it by playing on our conceit and laziness and intellectual snobbery. I know someone will ask me, "Do you really mean, at this time of day, to re-introduce our old friend the devil—hoofs and horns and all?" Well, what the time of day has to do with it I don't know. And I'm not particular about the hoofs and horns. But in other respects my answer is, "Yes, I do." I don't claim to know anything about his personal appearance. If anybody really wants to know him better I'd say to that person, "Don't worry. If you really want to, you will. Whether you'll like it when you do is another question."

III

Christians, then, believe that an evil power has made himself for the present the Prince of this World. And, of course, that raises problems. Is this state of affairs in accordance with God's will or not? If it is, He's a strange God, you'll say: and if it isn't, how *can* anything happen contrary to the will of a being with absolute power?

But anyone who has been in authority knows how a thing can be in accordance with your will in one way and not in another. It may be quite sensible for a mother to say to the children, "I'm not going to go and make you tidy the school-room every night. You've got to learn to keep it tidy on your own." Then she goes up one night and finds the Teddy bear and the ink and the French Grammar all lying in the grate. That's against her will. She would prefer the children to be tidy. But on the other hand, it is her will which has left the children free to be untidy. The same thing arises in any regiment, or trades union, or school. You make a thing voluntary and then half the people don't do it. That isn't what you willed, but your will has made it possible.

It's probably the same in the universe. God created things which had free will. That means creatures which can go wrong *or* right. Some people think they can imagine a creature which was free but had no possibility of going wrong, but I can't. If a thing is free to be good it's also free to be bad. And free will is what has made evil possible. Why, then, did God give them free will? Because free will, though it makes evil possible, is also the only thing that makes possible any love or goodness or joy worth having. A world of automata—of creatures that worked like machines—would hardly be worth creating. The happiness which God designs for His higher creatures is the happiness of being freely, voluntarily united to Him and to each other in an ecstasy of love and delight compared with which the most rapturous love between a man and a woman on this earth is *mere milk and water*. And for that they've got to be free.

Of course God knew that would happen if they used their freedom the wrong way: apparently He thought it worth the risk. Perhaps we feel inclined to disagree with Him. But there's a difficulty about disagreeing with God. He is the source from which all your reasoning power comes: you couldn't be right and He wrong any more than a stream can rise higher than its own source. When you are arguing against Him you're arguing against the very power that makes you able to argue at all: it's like cutting off the branch you're sitting on. If God thinks this state of war in the universe a price worth paying for free will—that is, for making a *real* world in which creatures can do real good or harm and something of real importance can happen, instead of a toy world which only moves when He pulls the strings—then we may take it it *is* worth paying.

When we've understood about free will, we shall see how silly it is to ask, as somebody once asked me: "Why did God make a creature of such rotten stuff that it went wrong?" The better stuff a creature is made of—the cleverer and stronger and freer it is—then the better it will be if it goes right, but also the worse it will be if it goes wrong. A cow can't be very good or very bad; a dog can be both better and worse; a child better and worse still; an ordinary man, still more so; a man of genius, still more so; a superhuman spirit best—or worst—of all.

How did the Dark Power go wrong? Well, the moment you have a self at all, there is a possibility of putting yourself first—wanting to be the centre —wanting to *be* God, in fact. That was the sin of Satan: and that was the sin he taught the human race. Some people think the fall of man had something to do with sex, but that's a mistake. What Satan put into the heads of our remote ancestors was the idea that they could "be like gods"—could set up on their own as if they had created themselves—be their own masters—invent some sort of happiness for themselves outside God, apart from God. And out of that hopeless attempt has come nearly all that we call human history—money, poverty, ambition, war, prostitution, classes, empires, slavery—the long terrible story of man trying to find something other than God which will make him happy.

The reason why it can never succeed is this. God made us: invented us as a man invents an engine. A car is made to run on petrol, and it won't run properly on anything else. Now God designed the human machine to run on Himself. He Himself is the fuel our spirits were designed to burn, or the food our spirits were designed to feed on. There isn't any other. That's why it's just no good asking God to make us happy in our own way without bothering about religion. God can't give us a happiness and peace apart from Himself, because it isn't there. There's no such thing.

That is the key to history. Terrific energy is expended—civilisations are built up—excellent institutions devised; but each time something goes wrong. Some fatal flaw always brings the selfish and cruel people to the top and it all slides back into misery and ruin. In fact, the machine konks. It seems to start up all right and runs a few yards, and then it breaks down. They're trying to run it on the wrong juice. That's what Satan has done to us humans.

And what did God do? First of all He left us conscience, the sense of right and wrong: and all through history there have been people trying (some of them very hard) to obey it. None of them ever quite succeeded. Secondly, He sent the human race what I call good dreams: I mean those queer stories scattered all through the heathen religions about a god who dies and comes to life again and, by his death, has somehow given new life to men. Thirdly, He selected one particular people and spent several centuries hammering into their heads the sort of God He was—that there was only one of Him and that He cared about right conduct. Those people were the Jews, and the Old Testament gives an account of the hammering process.

Then comes the real shock. Among these Jews there suddenly turns up a man who goes about talking as if He was God. He claims to forgive sins. He says He has always existed. He says He is coming to judge the world at the end of time. Now let us get this clear. Among Pantheists, like the Indians, anyone might say that he was a part of God, or one with God: there'd be nothing very odd about it. But this man, since He was a Jew, couldn't mean that kind of God. God, in their language, meant the Being outside the world Who had made it and was infinitely different from anything else. And when you've grasped that, you will see that what this man said was, quite simply, the most shocking thing that has ever been uttered by human lips.

I'm trying here to prevent anyone from saying the really silly thing that people often say about Him: "I'm ready to accept Jesus as a great moral teacher, but I don't accept His claim to be God." That's the one thing we mustn't say. A man who was merely a man and said the sort of things Jesus said wouldn't be a great moral teacher. He'd either be a lunatic—on a level with the man who says he's a poached egg—or else he'd be the Devil of Hell. You must make your choice. Either this man was, and is, the Son of God; or else a madman or something worse. You can shut Him up for a fool; you can spit at Him and kill Him as a demon; or you can fall at His feet and call Him Lord and God. But don't let us come with any patronising nonsense about His being a great human teacher. He hasn't left that open to us. He didn't intend to.

RED JACKET AND THE MISSIONARY

Seneca

In the summer of 1805, a number of the principal Chiefs and Warriors of the Six Nations, principally Senecas, assembled at Buffalo Creek, in the state of New York, at the particular request of Rev. Mr. Cram, a Missionary from the state of Massachusetts. The Missionary being furnished with an Interpreter, and accompanied by the Agent of the United States for Indian affairs, met the Indians in Council, when the following talk took place:

First, By the Agent:

"*Brothers of the Six Nations;* I rejoice to meet you at this time, and thank the Great Spirit, that he has preserved you in health, and given me another opportunity of taking you by the hand.

"*Brothers;* The person who sits by me, is a friend who has come a great distance to hold a talk with you. He will inform you what his business is, and it is my request that you would listen with attention to his words."

Missionary:

"*My Friends;* I am thankful for the opportunity afforded us of uniting together at this time. I had a great desire to see you, and inquire into your state and welfare; for this purpose I have travelled a great distance, being sent by your old friends, the Boston Missionary Society. You will recollect they formerly sent missionaries among you, to instruct you in religion, and labor for your good. Although they have not heard from you for a long time, yet they have not forgotten their brothers the Six Nations, and are still anxious to do you good.

"*Brothers;* I have not come to get your lands or your money, but to enlighten your minds, and to instruct you how to worship the Great Spirit agreeably to his mind and will, and to preach to you the gospel of his son Jesus Christ. There is but one religion, and but one way to serve God, and if you do not embrace the right way, you cannot be happy hereafter. You have never worshipped the Great Spirit in a manner acceptable to him; but have, all your lives, been in great errors and darkness. To endeavor to remove these errors, and open your eyes, so that you might see clearly, is my business with you.

"*Brothers;* I wish to talk with you as one friend talks with another; and, if you have any objections to receive the religion which I preach, I wish you to state them; and I will endeavor to satisfy your minds, and remove the objections.

"*Brothers;* I want you to speak your minds freely; for I wish to reason with you on the subject, and, if possible, remove all doubts, if there be any on your minds. The subject is an important one, and it is of consequence that you give it an early attention while the offer is made you. Your friends, the Boston Missionary Society, will continue to send you good and faithful ministers, to instruct and strengthen you in religion, if, on your part, you are willing to receive them.

"*Brothers;* Since I have been in this part of the country, I have visited some of your small villages, and talked with your people. They appear willing to receive instructions, but, as they look up to you as their older brothers in council, they want first to know your opinion on the subject.

"You have now heard what I have to propose at present. I hope you will take it into consideration, and give me an answer before we part."

After about two hours consulation among themselves, the Chief, commonly called by the white people, Red Jacket, (whose Indian name is Sagu-yu-what-hah, which interpreted is *Keeper awake*) rose and spoke as follows:

"Friend and Brother; It was the will of the Great Spirit that we should meet together this day. He orders all things, and has given us a fine day for our Council. He has taken his garment from before the sun, and caused it to shine with brightness upon us. Our eyes are opened, that we see clearly; our ears are unstopped, that we have been able to hear distinctly the words you have spoken. For all these favors we thank the Great Spirit; and Him *only*.

"Brother; This council fire was kindled by you. It was at your request that we came together at this time. We have listened with attention to what you have said. You requested us to speak our minds freely. This gives us great joy; for we now consider that we stand upright before you, and can speak what we think. All have heard your voice, and all speak to you now as one man. Our minds are agreed.

"Brother; you want an answer to your talk before you leave this place. It is right you should have one, as you are a great distance from home, and we do not wish to detain you. But we will first look back a little, and tell you what our fathers have told us, and what we have heard from the white people.

"Brother; Listen to what we say.

"There was a time when our forefathers owned this great island. Their seats extended from the rising to the setting sun. The Great Spirit had made it for the use of Indians. He had created the buffalo, the deer, and other animals for food. He had made the bear and the beaver. Their skins served us for clothing. He had scattered them over the country, and taught us how to take them. He had caused the earth to produce corn for bread. All this He had done for his red children, because He loved them. If we had some disputes about our hunting ground, they were generally settled without the shedding of much blood. But an evil day came upon us. Your forefathers crossed the great water, and landed on this island. Their numbers were small. They found friends and not enemies. They told us they had fled from their country for fear of wicked men, and had come here to enjoy their religion. They asked for a small seat. We took pity on them, granted their request; and they sat down amongst us. We gave them corn and meat, they gave us poison (alluding, it is supposed, to ardent spirits) in return.

"The white people had now found our country. Tidings were carried back, and more came amongst us. Yet we did not fear them. We took them to be friends. They called us brothers. We believed them, and gave them a larger seat. At length their numbers had greatly increased. They wanted more land; they wanted our country. Our eyes were opened, and our minds became uneasy. Wars took place. Indians were hired to fight against Indians, and many of our people were destroyed. They also brought strong liquor amongst us. It was strong and powerful, and has slain thousands.

"Brother; Our seats were once large and yours were small. You have now become a great people, and we have scarcely a place left to spread our blankets. You have got our country, but are not satisfied; you want to force your religion upon us.

"Brother; Continue to listen.

"You say that you are sent to instruct us how to worship the Great Spirit agreeably to his mind, and, if we do not take hold of the religion which you white people teach, we shall be unhappy hereafter. You say that you are right and we are lost. How do we know this to be true? We understand that your religion is written in a book. If it was intended for us as well as you, why has not the Great Spirit given to us, and not only to us, but why did he not give our forefathers, the knowledge of that book, with the means of understanding it rightly? We only know what you tell us about it. How shall we know when to believe, being so often deceived by the white people?

"*Brother;* You say there is but one way to worship and serve the Great Spirit. If there is but one religion; why do you white people differ so much about it? Why not all agreed, as you can all read the book?

"*Brother;* We do not understand these things.

"We are told that your religion was given to your forefathers, and has been handed down from father to son. We also have a religion, which was given to our forefathers, and has been handed down to us their children. We worship in that way. It teaches us to be thankful for all the favors we receive; to love each other, and to be united. We never quarrel about religion.

"*Brother;* The Great Spirit has made us all, but he has made a great difference between his white and red children. He has given us different complexions and different customs. To you He has given the arts. To these He has not opened our eyes. We know these things to be true. Since He has made so great a difference between us in other things; why may we not conclude that He has given us a different religion according to our understanding? The Great Spirit does right. He knows what is best for his children; we are satisfied.

"*Brother;* We do not wish to destroy your religion, or take it from you. We only want to enjoy our own.

"*Brother;* We are told that you have been preaching to the white people in this place. These people are our neighbors. We are acquainted with them. We will wait a little while, and see what effect your preaching has upon them. If we find it does them good, makes them honest and less disposed to cheat Indians; we will then consider again of what you have said.

"*Brother;* You have now heard our answer to your talk, and this is all we have to say at present.

"As we are going to part, we will come and take you by the hand, and hope the Great Spirit will protect you on your journey, and return you safe to your friends."

As the Indians began to approach the missionary, he rose hastily from his seat and replied, that he could not take them by the hand; that there was no fellowship between the religion of God and the works of the devil.

This being interpreted to the Indians, they smiled, and retired in a peaceable manner.

It being afterwards suggested to the missionary that his reply to the Indians was rather indiscreet; he observed, that he supposed the ceremony of shaking hands would be received by them as a token that he assented to what they had said. Being otherwise informed, he said he was sorry for the expressions.

THE RETURN TO THE OLD GODS

Don C. Talayesva

Hopi

My earliest memories of my real grandfather, Homikniwa, are full of kind feelings. I slept with him much of the time. In the morning before sunrise he sang to me and told me stories. He took me to his fields, where I helped him to work or slept under a peach tree. Whenever he saw me make a circle he stepped cautiously around it, saying that he had to watch me lest I block his path with my antelope power. He kept reminding me of this power. He also took me through the fields to collect healing herbs. I watched him sprinkle corn meal and pray to the Sun God before picking up leaves or berries or digging medicine roots. Whenever mothers brought their sick children to our house, I watched him take their pinches of meal, step outside, pray, and sprinkle them to the Sun God, Moon, or the stars, and to his special medicine god. Then he would return to the patient, blow upon his hands, and begin his treatment. He was respected by all. Even Mr. Voth, the missionary, came to him to learn about plants and herbs. He taught the white man many things. He also taught me almost all I ever learned about plants. He advised me to keep bad thoughts out of my mind, to face the east, look to the bright side of life, and learn to show a shining face even when unhappy.

Mr. Voth and the Christians came to Oraibi and preached Jesus in the plaza where the Katcinas danced. The old people paid no attention, but we children were told to receive any gifts and clothing. Mr. Voth never preached Christ to me alone but talked to us in groups. He said that Jesus Christ was our Saviour and suffered for our sins. He told us that Jesus was a good shepherd and that we were sheep or goats. We were to ask Jesus for whatever we wanted. Oranges and candy looked pretty good to me so I prayed for them. I said, "Jesus, give me some oranges and candy." Then I looked up into the sky, but I never saw him throw down anything to me. Mr. Voth claimed that our gods were not good but the old people pointed out to us that when the Katcinas danced in the Plaza, it often rained. Even as a child I was taught that the missionaries had no business condemning our gods and that it might cause droughts and famine.

One winter morning in February I saw a tall, strange Katcina coming into the village, blowing a bone whistle and uttering a long-drawn *"Hu-hu-huhuhu."* When he entered the Plaza women and children threw pinches of corn meal upon him and took sprigs of green corn and of spruce boughs from his tray. Two other Katcinas joined him near the kiva, where they were holding a ceremony, blew tobacco smoke on the backs of the Katcinas, and sprinkled them with corn meal. A number of different Katcinas, some running cross-legged, came through the streets handing out gifts. Some of us received bows, arrows, rattles, and Katcina dolls. Other Katcinas came into the village bringing bean sprouts in their baskets. We were in the Plaza watching them. Suddenly my mother threw a blanket over my head. When she uncovered me the Katcinas were all gone and the people were looking up in the sky and watching them fly about—they said. I looked up but could see nothing. My mother laughed and said that I must be blind.

I later saw some giantlike Katcinas stalking into the village with long black bills and big sawlike teeth. One carried a rope to lasso disobedient children. He stopped at a certain house and called for a boy. "You have been naughty," he scolded. "You fight with other children. You kill chickens. You pay no attention to the old people. We have come to get you and eat you." The boy cried and promised to behave better. The giants became angrier and threatened to tie him up and take him away. But the boy's parents begged for his life and offered fresh meat in his place. The giant reached out his hand as if to grab the boy but took the meat instead. Placing it in his basket, he warned the boy that he would get just one chance to change his conduct. I was frightened and got out of sight. I heard that sometimes these giants captured boys and really ate them.

By the time I was six . . . I had learned to find my way about the mesa and to avoid graves, shrines, and harmful plants, to size up people, and to watch out for witches. I was above average height and in good health. My hair was clipped just above the eyes, but left long in back and tied in a knot at the nape of my neck. I had almost lost an eye. I wore silver earrings, a missionary shirt or one made of a flour sack, and was always bare-legged, except for a blanket in cold weather. When no whites were present, I went naked. I slept out on the housetop in summer and sometimes in the kiva with other boys in winter. I could help plant and weed, went out herding with my father, and was a kiva trader. I owned a dog and a cat, a small bow made by my father, and a few good arrows. Sometimes I carried stolen matches tucked in the hem of my shirt collar. I could ride a tame burro, kill a kangaroo rat, and catch small birds, but I could not make fire with a drill and I was not a good runner like the other fellows. But I had made a name for myself by healing people; and I had almost stopped running after my mother for her milk. . . .

On June the fourteenth my father came for me and we returned home, riding burros and bringing presents of calico, lamps, shovels, axes, and other tools. It was a joy to get home again, to see all my folks, and to tell about my experiences at school. I had learned many English words and could recite part of the Ten Commandments. I knew how to sleep on a bed, pray to Jesus, comb my hair, eat with a knife and fork, and use a toilet. I had learned that the world is round instead of flat, that it is indecent to go naked in the presence of girls. I had also learned that a person thinks with his head instead of his heart. . . .

As I lay on my blanket I thought about my school days and all that I had learned. I could talk like a gentleman, read, write, and cipher. I could name all the states in the Union with their capitals, repeat the names of all the books in the Bible, quote a hundred verses of Scripture, sing more than two dozens of Christian hymns and patriotic songs, debate, shout football yells, swing my partners in square dances, bake bread, sew well enough to make a pair of trousers, and tell dirty Dutchman stories by the hour. It was important that I had learned how to get along with white men and earn money by helping them. But my death experience had taught me that I had a Hopi Spirit Guide whom I must follow if I wished to live. I wanted to become a real Hopi again, to sing the good old Katcina songs, and to feel free to make love without fear of sin or a rawhide.

I had learned a great lesson and now knew that the ceremonies handed down by our fathers mean life and security, both now and hereafter. I regretted that I had ever joined the Y.M.C.A. and decided to set myself against Christianity once and for all. I could see that the old people were right when they insisted that Jesus Christ might do for modern whites in a good climate, but that the Hopi gods had brought success to us in the desert ever since the world begun.

With marriage I began a life of toil and discovered that education had spoiled me for making a living in the desert. I was not hardened to heavy work in the heat and dust, and I did not know how to get rain, control winds, or even predict good and bad weather, I could not grow young plants in dry, wind-beaten, and worm-infested sand drifts; nor could I shepherd a flock of sheep through storm, drought, and disease. . . .

"Talayesva," my uncles and fathers said, "you must stay home and work hard like the rest of us. Modern ways help a little; but the whites come and go, while we Hopi stay on forever. Corn is our mother—and only the Cloud People can send rain to make it grow. . . . They come from the six directions to examine our hearts. If they are good they gather above us in cotton masks and white robes and drop rain to quench our thirst and nourish our plants. . . . Keep bad thoughts behind you and face the rising sun with a cheerful spirit, as did our ancestors in the days of plenty. Then rain fell on all the land." . . .

I thought I would be willing to go back to the very beginning of Hopi life, wear native clothes, and hunt wild deer. I let my hair grow long, tied it in a knot at the nape of my neck, and stored my citizen's clothes in a gunnysack. I ate old Hopi foods, practiced the Katcina and Wowochim songs, and brought sand up the mesa in my blanket to start a bean crop in the kiva.

I joined herds with . . . three old men—and had to go out and herd in the worst weather—in sleet, snow, and rain when it was too cold to ride a horse, and when shepherd and flock had to run to keep warm. Strong winds drove sand into my face and eyes, filled my ears and nose, and made it difficult to eat my lunch without catching mouthfuls of grit. My clothes were often heavy with sand and chafed me as I walked. . . . Dust and snowstorms scattered my flock and forced me to search days for stray animals. . . . Storms frequently caught sheep in labor or drove them from newborn lambs. These young things were beaten about and often killed by hail, water, and wind. I would gather wet, shivering lambs in my arms and bury them up to their eyes in warm, dry sand from a sheltered bank, I studied clouds and paid close attention to my dreams in order to escape being trapped by storms too far from shelter.

In July I was happy to bring a few sweet-corn stalks into the village for the Niman Dance. I made dolls and tied them to cattail stems while my mother prepared little plaques three inches across. We took these things up on the roof and presented them to the hawks on the day of Niman. We feasted and danced all day and presented sweet corn, dolls, and other gifts to the children. The Katcinas were sent away at sunset with urgent prayers for rain upon our drooping crops. Nearly every man broke off a spruce bough to plant in his cornfield. Next morning we choked the hawks to send them home, plucked their feathers, tied *pahos* to their necks, wings, and feet, took them out in the direction whence they came, and buried them with corn meal. We told them to hasten home and send us rain. I then took a spruce bough to my cornfield, set it in the sand, held meal in my right hand, and prayed silently to the sun, moon, and stars for a good crop. I also sprinkled a path of corn meal and wished for rain, taking care not to step on the meal. When it did rain, the ceremonial officer said that it was proof that our prayers had reached the Six Point Cloud People.

The land was very dry, the crops suffered, and even the Snake Dance failed to bring much rain. We tried to discover the reason for our plight, and remembered the Rev. Voth who had stolen so many of our ceremonial secrets and had even carried off sacred images and altars to equip a museum and become a rich man. When he had worked here in my boyhood, the Hopi were afraid of him and dared not lay their hands on him or any other missionary, lest they be jailed by the whites. During the ceremonies this wicked man would force his way into the kiva and write down everything he saw. He wore shoes with solid heels, and when the Hopis tried to put him out of the kiva he would kick them. He came back to Oraibi on a visit and took down many more names. Now I was grown, educated in the whites' school, and had no fear of this man. When I heard that he was in my mother's house I went over and told him to get out. I said: "You break the commandments of your own God. He has ordered you never to steal or to have any other Gods before him. He has told you to avoid all graven images; but you have stolen ours, and set them up in your museum. This makes you a thief and an idolator who can never go to heaven." I knew the Hopi Cloud People despised this man, and even though he was now old and wore a long beard I had a strong desire to seize him by the collar and kick him off the mesa.

One day I visited Kalnimptewa, my father's old blind brother, and said: "Father, as I stood in my door I saw a Hopi missionary preaching to you from a Bible." "Yes," the old man answered, "he talked a great deal, but his words failed to touch me. He warned me that it would not be long before Jesus Christ would come down from the sky, say a few sharp words, and destroy all disbelievers. He said that my only chance to escape destruction was to confess and pray to his holy God. He urged me to hurry before it was too late, for a great flood was coming to Oraibi. I told him that I had prayed for rain all my life and nobody expected a flood in Oraibi. I also said that I was an old man and would not live very long, so he could not frighten me that way. . . ." He concluded: "Now, Talayesva, my son, you are a full-grown man, a herder and a farmer who supports a family, and such work means a happy life. When our ceremonies come round, pray faithfully to our Gods, and increase the good life of your family, and in this way you will stay happy." I thanked him and went home feeling confident that I would never pay any serious attention to the Christians. Other Gods may help some people, but my only chance for a good life is with the Gods of my fathers. I will never forsake them, even though their ceremonies die out before my eyes and all their shrines are neglected.

OUTCAST

Claude McKay

For the dim regions whence my fathers came
My spirit, bondaged by the body, longs.
Words felt, but never heard, my lips would frame;
My soul would sing forgotten jungle songs.
I would go back to darkness and to peace,
But the great western world holds me in fee,
And I may never hope for full release
While to its alien gods I bend my knee.
Something in me is lost, forever lost,

Some vital thing has gone out of my heart,
And I must walk the way of life a ghost
Among the sons of earth, a thing apart.

For I was born, far from my native clime,
Under the white man's menace, out of time.

MESSIAHS: INDIAN AND OTHERS

Peter Farb

Several decades ago, reproductions in miniature of a sculpture called "The End of the Trail," which depicted a doleful Indian horseman, were commonly seen in White American living rooms. They seemed to signify the final victory over the vanishing Red man. In the years since, the Indian has not only refused to vanish, but has, thanks to the various messianic movements, managed to find a way to survive in a White world and to salvage a part of his native culture.

The scene of messianic movements has now switched from North America to other frontiers of the world—to South America, to Africa and Asia, and to the islands of the Pacific. Since the Second World War, with much of the world in turmoil, with the emergence of new nations and the spread of White influence, new messianic movements have sprung up vigorously, even within the context of such well-established religions as Islam, Buddhism, and Taoism. The dozens of messianic movements that have arisen among North American Indians can shed light on how and why they originate, the course they take, and the response Whites make to them.

Every messianic movement known to history has arisen in a society that has been subjected to the severe stress of contact with an alien culture—involving military defeat, epidemic, and acculturation. The bewildered search for ways to counteract the threat may actually increase the stress, arousing anxiety over whether new solutions will be any better than the old. Once doubts arise about any aspect of the ancestral cultural system, there is yet increased stress due to fear that the entire cultural system may prove inadequate. At this point, the culture as a whole begins to break down, manifested by widespread alcoholism, apathy, disregard of kinship obligations and marriage rules, and intragroup violence.

Such behavior comes at the very time when the culture is least able to cope with it, and so the intensity of the stress increases still more. Ultimately, the inadequacy of the culture becomes apparent even to the most conservative of its members, and the culture may deteriorate to such an extent that it literally dies. The birth rate drops and the death rate rises; the society no longer possesses the will to resist, and it is fallen upon by predatory neighbors; the few survivors scatter and either gradually die out or are absorbed by other groups. The collapse may be forestalled or even averted if a revitalization or messianic movement arises that is acceptable to the culture. Such a movement depends upon the appearance of a particular personality at a certain precise time in the disintegration of the culture.

Almost every messianic movement known around the world came into being as the result of the hallucinatory visions of a prophet. One point must be emphasized about the prophet of the messianic movement: He is not a schizophrenic, as was so long assumed. A schizophrenic with religious paranoia will state that he is God, Jesus, the Great Spirit, or some other supernatural being. The prophet, on the other hand, never states that he is supernatural—only that he is or has been in contact with supernatural powers. (Of course, after his death, his disciples tend to deify him or at least to give him saintly status.)

Invariably the prophet emerges from his hallucinatory vision bearing a message from the supernatural that makes certain promises: the return of the bison herds, a happy hunting ground, or peace on earth and good will to men. Whatever the specific promises, the prophet offers a new power, a revitalization of the whole society. But to obtain these promises, the prophet says that certain rituals must be followed. These rituals may include dancing around a ghost pole or being baptized in water, but usually numerous other duties must be attended to day after day. At the same time that the prophet offers promises to the faithful, he also threatens punishment and catastrophe, such as world destruction or everlasting damnation. The prophet now declares the old ways dead and shifts attention to a new way or to a revised conception of an old part of the culture. To spread the word of what he has learned from his visions, he gathers about him disciples and missionaries.

The various prophets known to world history differed in their preaching methods, just as the American Indian prophets differed from each other. Some prophets spoke emotionally to large crowds, whereas others addressed themselves to small groups and left it to their disciples to carry the message. Some, like the Qumran sect that copied out the Dead Sea scrolls, appealed to a religious elite of particularly devout people, whereas others concerned themselves only with the downtrodden and exploited who shall inherit the earth.

What most impresses the people around the prophet is the personality change he has undergone during this time. In most cases, he lived in obscurity until he suddenly emerged as a prophet; the Indian prophets became cured of previous spiritual apathy, and those who had been alcoholics gave up the habit. The sudden transformation in personality may be due to changes produced in the body under physical and emotional stress, although more research on this point is needed. It is known, though, that individuals vary a great deal in the reaction of their metabolisms to stress. That alone would explain why, when stress reaches a certain intensity in the culture, only certain individuals feel called forth to become prophets while most do not. In any event, the prophet has emerged in a new cultural role, and his personality is liberated from the stress that called his response into being in the first place. Immune to the stress under which his brethren still suffer, he must to them appear supernatural.

The disciples who gather around the prophet also, like him, undergo a revitalizing personality change—as did Peter, to name one very familiar example. The prophet continues his spiritual leadership, but the disciples take upon themselves the practical tasks of organizing the campaign to establish the new movement. They convert large numbers of people, who in turn also undergo revitalizing personality transformations. If the messianic movement has been allowed to survive to this point by the oppressive, dominant culture that called it into being in the first place, a vital step must now be taken. The prophet must emphasize that he is only the intermediary between the converts and the supernatural being whose message he has been spreading. This step is essential, for it ensures the continuity of the new movement after its founding prophet dies. The prophet puts the converts and the supernatural being into close touch with each other by calling for certain symbolic duties the faithful must perform toward the supernatural being, such as eating peyote or partaking of bread and wine.

The new movement often has to resist both the oppressive alien culture and the opposition of factions within itself. The successful messianic movement meets this resistance by resorting to any one of a number of adaptations. It may change its teachings, as did the early Christians who gradually gave up Jewish rituals, such as circumcision. It may resort to political maneuvering and compromise. Most messianic movements, though, make the disastrous mistake that almost all Jewish and American Indian messianic movements did: They choose to fight. Islam alone succeeded by force of arms, whereas the success of the early Christians was their choice of universal peace as their weapon.

Once the messianic movement has won a large following, a new culture begins to emerge out of the death of the old—not only in religious affairs but in all aspects of economic, social, and political life as well. An organization with a secular and a sacerdotal hierarchy arises to perpetuate the new doctrine. The religion in that way becomes routinized in a stable culture. All routinized religions today (whether they be the Native American Church, Mohammedanism, Judaism, or Christianity) are successful descendants of what originated as messianic movements—that is, one personality's vision of a new way of life for a culture under extreme stress.

These steps apply equally to the messianic movement in Soviet Russia, even though it denies belief in the supernatural. Czarist Russia in 1917 was a society under extreme stress, disintegrating both on the war front and at home; in the previous decade it had suffered a humiliating defeat by the Japanese. There was unrest, and repressive measures were stern. A prophet, Lenin, arose; and he made a miraculous return from exile in Switzerland in a railroad car that traversed enemy territory. He preached his vision of Utopia, and he referred constantly to a revered, almost supernatural being named Karl Marx. The missionary fervor excited Lenin's close followers, and they in turn won adherents even among their former enemies in society. One element of the population in particular—the economically downtrodden—was appealed to, and it was promised a reward here on earth. But first these people had to perform certain rituals: convert to the new doctrine of Marx–Lenin; change the economic way of life; publicly confess errors, even if such confession resulted in martyrdom. After the prophet's death, a political organization of key disciples (Stalin, Trotsky, and others) continued his teachings and prepared a complex doctrine that admitted of no revisionism or deviation. The prophet himself was deified after death, as demonstrated today by the people paying homage at Lenin's tomb to the embalmed cadaver that, miraculously, is not heir to the flesh's corruption.

From THE PASSOVER PLOT

Hugh J. Schonfield

1. The Last Times

Christianity is rooted in Palestine in a Jewish environment and in the historical circumstances of a plainly dated period. This assuredly requires no argument. To this time and place we are therefore bound to go for the elucidation of Christian Origins.

But it is by no means easy to relate the life of Jesus and the activities of his original followers, known as Nazoreans (Nazarenes), to the contemporary situation. This is largely due to the character of the New Testament and the paucity of external evidences about the beginnings of Christianity. To reach conclusions which can fairly be regarded as corresponding as nearly as possible to the reality entails a vast amount of analysis and comparison, the patient piecing together of a host of hints and scraps of tradition, and in particular a sympathetic involvement in the affairs of the Jewish people and detachment from considerations of Christian theology.

Because of what the Church has taught for so many centuries it has been extremely difficult for Christian scholars to undertake such an investigation objectively. Those who have embarked upon it and produced most valuable results merit the highest praise. One pioneer, Professor F. C. Burkitt of Cambridge, whom the writer was privileged to know personally, advisedly used these cautionary words: 'We must be prepared to find the whole drama of the rise of Christianity more confused, more secular, in a word more appropriate to the limitations of its own age, than we should gather from the epic selectiveness of the Creeds and the theological manuals.' Such language is necessary, and should be heeded by those theologians who feel quite at liberty to expound Christianity as if it owed little or nothing to its original background of thought. The Bishop of Woolwich, to quote a recent instance, can freely employ key words like Christ and Gospel without apparent concern for their primary meaning and implications. Christ is the Greek translation of the Hebrew term Messiah, meaning the Anointed One, and the Gospel, from the Greek Evangel, translating the Hebrew word for Good News, was initially the information that the Messiah expected by the Jews had appeared.

It makes all the difference to our understanding of Christianity if we are enabled to apprehend that it did not begin as a new religion but as a movement of monotheistic Jews who held Jesus to be their God-sent king and deliverer. Here, in a sentence, is what it is imperative to know about the origins of Christianity. Here we have the essential clue to the activities of Jesus and his first followers which helps to compensate for many material facts which are beyond recovery. Armed with this information we can get Christianity in correct perspective, and trace clearly and simply in the light of what is ascertainable how it was transformed into what it afterwards became.

It is often said that Christianity is founded upon a person. That is true. But it is only part of the historical truth. What, so to speak, was the person founded upon? The answer is that he was founded upon an idea, a strange idea current among the Jews of his time, an idea alien to Western thought which many non-Jewish theologians still find very inconvenient, the idea of Messianism. It was Messianism which made the life of Jesus what it was and so brought Christianity into being. It was Messianism, as accepted by Gentile believers, which contributed towards making the deification of Jesus inevitable. It was Messianism which provided the spiritual impulse behind the Jewish war with Rome which broke out in A.D. 66, resulting in the destruction of much authoritative testimony about Jesus and the substantial separation of Gentile from Jewish Christianity.

The fundamental teaching of Christianity, then, was that in Jesus the Messiah (the Christ) had come. There can be not the shadow of a doubt about this. It is the ultimate conviction on which the whole edifice of Christianity rests, the historical fact on which all the Gospels are agreed. This teaching was the gospel, underlying all the Gospels, the one thing which gave them the right to be so called. The faith of the earliest believers in Jesus was that which voiced itself in the declaration of Peter, as recorded in Mark, 'You are the Messiah', simply this without any qualification. The persuasion they had was built upon what Jesus had said and done. It was he who had given them cause to conclude that he was the Messiah, and he had done so quite deliberately. But what the Gospels do not tell us is what in the first instance had persuaded *him*. Unless we can discover why Jesus held himself to be the Messiah, what current teaching about the Messiah he applied to himself, we are not in possession of the key to the mystery of his life and death.

We have no right to say that while Jesus accepted the designation of Messiah he did so in a sense quite different from any expectations entertained in his time. It would be unthinkable for him to do this, firstly because being the Messiah meant answering to certain prophetic requirements which for him were divinely inspired, and secondly because he would consciously have been depriving his people of any possibility of acknowledging him: he would be inviting them to reject him as a false Messiah.

We have to take the view that Jesus believed it to be his calling and destiny to fulfil the Messianic Hope, and to do so in a manner which would conform with the predictions he accepted as authoritative. Our business is to find out the conditions with which Jesus felt he had to comply, and on this basis to follow the course of his actions. Obviously we have to divorce the issue altogether from the paganised doctrine of the incarnation of the Godhead with which for Christians it has become intermingled, since expectation did not identify the Messiah with God, and, indeed, the nature of Jewish monotheism wholly excluded such an idea. Jesus as much as any other Jew would have regarded as blasphemous the manner in which he is depicted, for instance, in the Fourth Gospel.

Taking the Gospels together, and these are the chief source of our information about Jesus, we have in them an epitome of the process by which the traditions about him grew and expanded with the changing needs and fortunes of succeeding generations of believers, Jewish and Gentile, so that Jesus as he appears in them is a composite and somewhat contradictory figure. His image is like the idol of Nebuchadnezzar's dream in the book of Daniel, part gold, part silver, part bronze, part iron and part clay. The gold is there to be extracted, but we cannot take hold of it unalloyed without knowledge of the influences and circumstances to which Jesus himself had responded. It is not enough to look back to him through the minds of much later believers not of Jewish origin: we have imperatively to look forward to him through the pre-Christian development of Messianism.

The coming of the Messiah was not something fortuitous: it was closely linked with a period of history prophetically anticipated, the Last Times or End of the Days, which would precede the inauguration of the Kingdom of God. The Messiah could not appear at any time, but only at the End of the Days, at a time of testing and great tribulation for Israel.

The conception of the Last Times drew upon Biblical predictions relating to the Latter Days and the Day of the Lord, which became combined with Babylonian and Persian ideas of a succession of Ages. During the Ages the forces of Good and Evil would contend with one another, and the struggle would reach its climax in the penultimate Age, being followed by the final Age of peace and bliss, the Kingdom of God. The Last Times would thus be the closing period of the old order, when the assaults of Evil would reach their most malevolent intensity, bringing great misery to humanity and persecution and suffering to the Elect of Israel. When these signs appeared then the Messiah was to be expected.

According to those who studied these matters, it could not be known how long the Last Times would endure, but it could be known approximately when they would begin. For this a basis of calculation had to be available, and it was found in the book of Daniel in the prophecy of the Seventy Weeks, later understood to mean seventy weeks of years (490 years). The

Last Times could be expected to begin after the lapse of 490 years 'from the going forth of the commandment [of Cyrus] to restore and build Jerusalem', that is to say, after about 46 B.C. Those who believed in this interpretation, and were living in the reign of Herod the Gread (37–4 B.C.), could accept that the Last Times had now begun, and that therefore before very long the coming of the Messiah was to be expected. This explains why a strong messianic excitement manifested itself among the Jews from this time onward, and why no one before this had claimed to be the Messiah.

The part of the book of Daniel in which the prophecy occurs has been dated about 164 B.C. The author is assuming the name of a man supposed to be living near the end of the sixth century B.C. From other visions of his he appears to have expected the Era of Righteousness would come not very long after his actual time. Some thought it had come in the reign of John Hyrcanus I (137–3 B.C.). We do not know much about earlier calculations, and the one to which we have referred was worked out later when the hopes entertained of the Hasmoneans had been grievously disappointed. It is after 100 B.C. that the literature we have reveals a mounting interest in the Last Times and in the advent of messianic personalities. By the first century of our era it had become quite feverish, and had engendered a state of near hysteria among the people. It was wholly in keeping with the circumstances that a figure like John the Baptist should now appear proclaiming that the Kingdom of God was at hand, and calling upon the people to repent and save themselves from the Wrath to Come. It was no less appropriate that a man like Jesus should be convinced he was the Messiah and announce that 'the Time is fulfilled'. The calculations of pious scribes confirmed the time, but what was more the conditions of the time reinforced the calculations.

Messianism was a product of the Jewish spirit. It was inspired by the Hebrew reading of the riddle of the creation and destiny of mankind. Though some of its features did not originate with the Hebrews, they absorbed them and brought them into relationship with a great vision of the ultimate Brotherhood of Man under the rule of the One God and Father of all men. The vision was not simply a cherished ideal: it was associated with a plan for its realisation. According to this plan God had chosen and set apart one nation among the nations of the world, neither numerous nor powerful, to be the recipient of his laws, and by observing them to offer a universal example. The Theocracy of Israel would be the persuasive illustration of a World Theocracy: it would be 'a kingdom of priests and a holy nation' witnessing to all nations. Manifestly, according to this view, the redemption of humanity waited upon the attainment by Israel of a state of perfect obedience to the will of God. By so much as Israel failed to meet the Divine requirements, by so much was the peace and well-being of mankind retarded.

The history of Israel, seen in this light, was a prolonged schooling, national disposition to go astray having to be corrected by the infliction of appropriate punishments, conquest and oppression by foreigners, pestilence and famine, exile. Internally much depended on the guidance of rulers, priests and kings. These too were judged by whether they 'did right in the sight of the Lord.' Their failures called for an additional activity by messengers of God in a succession of prophets.

Eventually, it began to be despaired of that the whole people could be brought to the necessary state of perfection. Hopes were pinned on an elect remnant of faithful souls, by whose obedience the redemption would be hastened. They would be the élite of the final World Order, entitled to its highest honours by their loyalty and by their sufferings in this present world. The Messianic Hope became concentrated upon the determined efforts of the pious, the Saints, to observe the Law, thus justifying God in acting speedily. If the time was greatly prolonged even the Elect might prove unequal to the strain. It was imperative for the pious themselves to search out what Divine guidance had been given to set a term to their endurance, what signs were to be expected to intimate that the End of the Days had arrived. The last stage of the evolution of the Messianic Hope envisaged the intervention of God by means of the Anointed Ones, ideal figures, a Prophet like Moses, a perfect Priest, a righteous King of the line of David. These would come in the End of the Days as God's highest appointed representatives to transform the whole scene and usher in the Kingdom of God.

The scheme of the Messianic Hope, as outlined here, must be understood to be composite and not fully comprehensive. Many ingredients went into the framing of the Hope. Different aspects were emphasised at different times and by different groups. It was accentuated as certain historical situations arose, particularly after the return from the Babylonian Exile, and was not consciously present in the thinking of the Jewish people all the time. Concern with the coming of messianic persons was part of the later expression of the Hope, especially from the second century B.C. onward, though it was nourished on ideas and predictions hundreds of years older, not excluding popular folklore and mystology.

We may select three circumstances as contributing importantly to making the Messianic Hope the powerful influence it became in the first century B.C. One of these was a change in attitude towards the Bible. The Hebrew Bible consists of three divisions; the Law, the Prophets (Joshua to Malachi), and the Writings (beginning with the Psalms and including the book of Daniel). The divisions represent stages of acceptance into canonicity. The Law, as consisting of the five books of Moses, had binding force by the fifth century B.C., or not much later. The Prophets did not acquire their force until about the third century B.C. The Psalms and some other books soon formed the basis of the third division, which was finally settled at the end of the first century A.D. The effects of the recognition of the Law and the Prophets, with the Psalms, as a corpus of sacred Scriptures were far-reaching. It opened the way for a new development, the treatment of these books as the Oracles of God. They became subject to all kinds of interpretation to draw out of them hidden meanings and prognostications.

A second circumstance was the worst calamity which had befallen the Jews since the destruction of the Kingdom of Judah and the loss of the

Temple at the beginning of the sixth century B.C. The new calamity was seen by pious Jews to be impending as a consequence of the attractions of Hellenism, which since the time of Alexander the Great had made increasing inroads into Jewish life and thought, fostering moral laxity and apostasy. The judgement of God must surely fall upon the nation as it had done in the past. It fully confirmed this opinion when the Seleucid king Antiochus Epiphanes (175–62 B.C.) decreed the abolition of the Jewish religion and converted the Temple at Jerusalem into a shrine of Zeus Olympius. Throughout the country there was great persecution, until resistance was organised by the sons of the aged priest Mattathias of Modin. One son, Judas Maccabaeus, led the revolt in the name of God, and after a series of remarkable successes cleansed and rededicated the defiled Temple. One of the products of this testing time was the book of Daniel. Its apocalyptic dreams and visions were to exercise a major influence on messianic thinking and prediction.

The third circumstance to which we must draw attention is Jewish sectarianism. The experiences of the nation in the time of Antiochus and his immediate successors had administered a severe shock. The people became much more devout. There was revived in them a sense of destiny, of belonging to God in a special way, which demanded faithfulness to the Law revealed to them through Moses. They saw in the victories of the Maccabees the hand of God, outstretched for their deliverance when they were obedient to his commandments. The Messianic Hope comes out strongly in Daniel, where the people of the Saints of the Most High (likened to a Son of Man compared with the Beast figures representing the predatory heathen Empires) are entrusted with God's everlasting kingdom, when all rulers will serve and obey him. It began to matter very much to the more spiritually sensitive that the Divine laws should be observed meticulously, and this inevitably gave rise to sectarianism, to competition in holiness. From this period three ways of life in particular are made known to us, those of the Sadducees, Pharisees and Essenes. They were minority movements, numbering only a few thousands in each case, but they were nevertheless extremely influential and gave impetus to the exposition of the Messianic Hope. Unfortunately, as regards the first two, they were also involved in a power-struggle for control of the political affairs of the nation.

From 160 B.C. we are in a new age, an age of extraordinary fervour and religiosity, in which almost every event, political, social and economic, was seized upon, scrutinised and analysed, to discover how and in what way it represented a Sign of the Times and threw light on the approach of the End of the Days. The whole condition of the Jewish people was psychologically abnormal. The strangest tales and imaginings could find ready credence. A new pseudonymous literature came into being, part moral exhortation and part apocalyptic prophecy, a kind of messianic science-fiction. People were on edge, neurotic. There were hot disputes, rivalries and recriminations.

The essence of the Messianic Hope, as we have seen, was the establishment of the Kingdom of God on earth, for which the prerequisite was a righteous Israel, or at least a righteous remnant of Israel. There must be a return to the relationship with God initiated at the Covenant of Sinai. Of this the prophecies of Jeremiah spoke, when he had said:

'Behold, the days come, saith the Lord, that I will make a New Covenant with the house of Israel, and with the house of Judah . . . After those days, saith the Lord, I will put my Law in their inward parts, and write it in their hearts; and I will be their God, and they shall be my people. And they shall teach no more every man his neighbour, and every man his brother, saying, Know the Lord; for they shall all know me, from the least of them to the greatest of them, saith the Lord: for I will forgive their iniquity, and I will remember their sin no more.'

Here it was promised that the spiritual infirmity of Israel would be helped by the intervention of God. To become worthy of this interposition was imperative. The three movements to which we have referred, and there were others, were fundamentally responses to this conviction. The Sadducees emphasised a strict and literal adherence to the Laws of Moses and the cultivation of ethics. The Pharisees aimed at the sanctification of the whole of daily life, and formulated new rules which extended the application of the Law to cover all contingencies. The Essenes, determined to be even more faultless, formed close communities from which contamination and impurity could be excluded, and where the utmost simplicity of living and rigid discipline could overcome material and fleshly temptations.

These movements reveal in themselves how deadly serious had become the desire to merit God's intervention. We should be out of tune with the temper of the time if we did not realise this. It was the study of the manner of the redemptive intervention which now accented the advent of messianic figures. The Sadducees, proving everything from express statements in the Law, looked for the coming of the Prophet like Moses. The Pharisees and Essenes ranged more widely and brought into prominence the perpetual covenants with Levi and David. The prophecies of Jeremiah had further contained this promise:

'Behold, the days come, saith the Lord, that I will perform that good thing which I have promised unto the house of Israel and to the house of Judah. In those days, and at that time, will I cause the Branch of Righteousness to grow up unto David; and he shall execute judgement and righteousness in the land. In those days shall Judah be saved, and Jerusalem shall dwell safely . . . For thus saith the Lord; David shall never want a man to sit upon the throne of the house of Israel; neither shall the priests the Levites want a man to offer burnt offerings, and to kindle meat offerings, and to do sacrifice continually.'

Therefore, it was held, God would intervene by means of Anointed Ones (Messiahs) of the tribes of Levi and Judah. One writer declares: 'And now, my children, obey Levi and Judah, and be not lifted up against these two tribes, for from them shall arise unto you the salvation of God. For the Lord shall raise up from Levi as it were a High Priest, and from Judah as it were a King; he shall save all the race of Israel.'

For the Essenes the Priestly Messiah would be the superior of the Royal

Messiah, while for the Pharisees, who became disillusioned with hierarchical government, the Messiah *par excellence* would be the ideal king of the line of David. But they admitted the priority of a Levitical messianic personality to the extent that the Davidic Messiah would be preceded by a priestly forerunner in the form of the returned Prophet Elijah, whom they held to have been a priest.

For a brief period in the latter part of the second century B.C. the greatest hopes were entertained as a result of the victories of the Hasmonean ruler John Hyrcanus I, under whom the Jews not only regained complete independence, but also a territory larger than any under Jewish rule since the reign of Solomon son of David. Not a few were ready to see in John one who combined all the messianic offices, being Prophet, Priest and King. But John Hyrcanus was no paragon, and his successors proved to be thoroughly unsatisfactory rulers, despotic, ambitious and unjust. Instead of the Kingdom of God there was war in Israel, and the Essenes had justification for their view that Satan had been let loose on the country.

From this time national affairs played an increasing part in the exposition of the Messianic Hope. It acquired a more personal and political colouring. The cry was raised, 'Behold, O Lord, and raise up unto them their king, the Son of David, in the time which thou, O God, knowest, that he may reign over Israel thy servant; and gird him with strength that he may break in pieces them that rule unjustly.'

The change of emphasis in messianic expectations caused much thought to be given to the conditions which the Scriptures indicated would prevail when the Messiah would be revealed. There would be wars and tumults, public strife and divided families, pestilence and famine, persecution of the saints, a host of tribulations. These would be the Woes of the Last Times, presaging the coming of the Messiah. As Jewish affairs went from bad to worse by so much more were messianic convictions intensified. Those who looked for signs could find them in abundance. In 63 B.C. the Romans were called upon to aid John Hyrcanus II against his ambitious brother Aristobulus. There was internecine conflict, the siege and capture of Jerusalem, with the Roman general Pompey committing the enormity of entering the Holy of Holies in the Temple. The Jews lost their brief independence, and their land became a vassal state of Rome. Once more Israel was subject to the heathen, and finally forced to accept at Roman hands a king, who, though he was a professing Jew, was of alien Idumean origin.

The reign of Herod the Great (37–4 B.C.) was from the beginning attended by disorders. Not only had he to preserve his throne by adroit manœuvre and political intrigue in relation to the struggle then going on in the Roman world, he had to govern a people intensely hostile to his regime, only too willing to see in him a manifestation of diabolical sovereignty.

Herod was an ambitious man and a clever one, brave, with regal bearing and qualities of leadership, but he was impulsive and had neurotic tendencies which the circumstances of his reign so aggravated as to convert him into something like the raging ruthless monster his apocalyptic-minded subjects believed him to be. With real and imagined plots against him he could not feel secure until he had destroyed the Hasmoneans around whom popular support could still gather. First to be got rid of was Antigonus, then the boy Aristobulus whom he had made high priest at the age of sixteen, and then the aged former high priest and king, the inoffensive Hyrcanus II. Later the Hasmonean princess Mariamne, whom he had married and genuinely loved, was executed, followed by her mother Alexandra; and to the end of his days the king's fear of conspiracy by family and friends led him on to the destruction even of his own children.

Successfully switching his allegiance from the vanquished Marc Antony to the victorious Octavian, afterwards the Emperor Augustus, Herod reached a height of political power and prestige. But as the friend of Caesar, devoted to the Romans and to the Hellenic way of life, he made himself ever more noxious to his people, who would not be placated even by his grandiose rebuilding of the Temple. They hated and feared him, and were kept from revolt only by the strongly manned fortresses which Herod constructed at strategic points and by his conversion of the country into what we would now call a police state. The pious attributed to the wrath of God the great earthquake in Judea in the seventh year of his reign and the persistent droughts followed by pestilence in the thirteenth year of his reign. Such calamities seemed like the plagues of Egypt, and Herod appeared as another Pharaoh of the Oppression. The signs seemed certainly to confirm the current interpretation of the prohecies that the Last Times had begun.

For the extreme pietists these days were 'the Period of the Wrath.' Many abandoned the cities and took to the wilderness. Sectarian communities, like that of Qumran by the Dead Sea, flourished as fresh recruits joined them. Such communities had long existed on the eastern fringe of the country; but now they were multiplied and increased in variety, holding themselves to be the faithful Elect of the Last Times.

Through the sources of information at our command we obtain a picture of the situation in Palestine towards the close of the first century b.c. which, if it could be put on canvas, would seem to be the work of a madman, or of a drug addict. A whole nation was in the grip of delirium. The king on this throne was a sick and gloomy tyrant. His embittered subjects feared and detested him to an extent that was almost maniacal. Religious fanatics fasted and prayed, and preached wrath and judgement. Obsessed with conviction that the Last Times had come, terror and superstition overcame all reason among the people. Self-recrimination accompanied messianic fervour. No wonder that when Herod died all hell was let loose.

At first a cry of relief went up throughout the land, and then in a moment all was tumult and disorder. Soldiers went on the rampage. Bands of brigands plundered. In the name of liberty from Rome and the Herodians various leaders set themselves up as king and readily got together a multitude of armed followers. 'And thus', writes Josephus, 'did a great and wild fury spread itself over the nation, because they had no king to keep the masses in good order; and because those foreigners, who came to reduce the seditious to sobriety, did, on the contrary, set them more in a flame, because of the injuries they offered them, and the avaricious management of their affairs.' In punitive actions by the Romans thousands were killed in different parts of the country, and at Jerusalem two thousand were crucified.

2. *He that should Come*

The circumstances we have outlined, which used, perhaps, to be more familiar to previous generations of Christians than they are today, have an obvious bearing on the understanding of the life of Jesus, and must be allowed their full weight in any attempt to comprehend him. We have seen what strange imaginings had gripped the Jewish people at this time, the time Jesus came into the world, fed by those who interpreted the Scriptures to them. According to many preachers, the eleventh hour had come, the Last Times had begun, the Kingdom of God was at hand. The world was on the eve of Wrath and Judgement. The Messiah would appear.

Christianity affirms that Jesus was this Messiah, whose advent fulfilled the prophecies, but singularly fails to concentrate on the implications as the effective means of becoming better acquainted with his character and activities. The Messiahship of Jesus is asserted, and then side-stepped in order to disclose him in a light more congenial to Hellenic rather than Jewish concepts. Quite commonly, for instance, quite apart from the claim that Jesus was God, the view is expressed that the Jews of the time of Jesus were expecting a Warrior Messiah, one who would win military victories over the enemies of Israel, and in this way accomplish the deliverance. The Jews rejected Jesus because he was a man of peace, who represented the love of God.

But what authority is there for such a view? Had this been the contemporary opinion of those who studied the Scriptures, certainly Jesus could never have thought of himself as the Messiah. But in fact in references to the Messiah up to the time of Jesus the conception of a Warrior Messiah does not appear. Among the peasantry of Palestine many did entertain such a notion, because conditions were so bad that violence seemed to offer the natural remedy. Living under alien domination, oppressed and ill-used, who is to blame them if they did? To the desperate the niceties of prophecy mattered little. Anyone would serve as Messiah, whether descended from David or not, if he was bold, courageous, a leader of men. There were plenty of people with little to lose, who were ready for any adventure which promised food and drink, and the destruction of the enemies, and who often quite sincerely would believe themselves to be fighting the battles of God. Such people over a thousand years later joined the Crusades. But we must not judge the Messianic Hope by such as they. Those who took things into their own hands, the violent ones, who resorted to militancy, were strongly criticised and denounced by the Pharisees, who were the chief spiritual instructors of the masses.

Of the Branch of David for whom pious Jews waited it was written: 'With righteousness shall he judge the poor, and reprove with equity for the meek of the earth: and he shall smite the earth *with the rod of his mouth,* and *with the breath of his lips* shall he slay the wicked.' The sharp two-edged sword of the Messiah would be no physical weapon, but justice and right-eousness.

Dating from the first century B.C. we have an exposition of the kind of Messiah who was expected, based on the passage from Isaiah just quoted.

'And a righteous king and taught of God is he that reigneth over them; and there shall be no iniquity in his days in their midst, for all shall be holy and their king is the Lord Messiah. For he shall not put his trust in horse and rider and bow, nor shall he multiply unto himself gold and silver for war, nor by ships shall he gather confidence for the day of battle . . . For he shall smite the earth with the word of his mouth even for evermore . . . He himself also is pure from sin, so that he may rule a mighty people, and rebuke princes and overthrow sinners by the might of his word. And he shall not faint all his days, because he leaneth upon his God: for God shall cause him to be mighty through the spirit of holiness, and wise through the counsel of understanding, with might and righteousness.'

The Son of David who was to come would be holy and just, 'the Messiah of righteousness', as he is called in the Dead Sea Scrolls, living in close communion with God and obedient to his will. It is by the word of truth that he will convict and defeat his adversaries.

That the Messiah should have such a character fully accords with what we have brought out about the nature of the Messianic Hope. The goal was the universal rule of God acknowledged by all men, when war, strife and wickedness should cease. To reach that goal it was required that Israel should be 'a kingdom of priests and a holy nation.' How much more must the Messiah, who would come in God's name, be the perfect Israelite? To him would apply the words of the Psalmist: 'Thou lovest righteousness, and hatest wickedness: therefore God, even thy God, hath anointed thee with the oil of gladness above thy fellows . . . Then said I, Lo I come: in the volume of the book it is written of me, I delight to do thy will, O my God: yea thy law is within my heart.'

This was the likeness to which the Messiah was expected to conform, and this is what Christians should have been taught. It was said of him:

'And he shall gather together a holy people, whom he shall lead in right-eousness: and shall judge the tribes of the people that hath been sanctified by the Lord his God. And he shall not suffer iniquity to lodge in their midst; and none that knoweth wickedness shall dwell with him. For he shall take knowledge of them that they be all sons of their God, and shall divide them upon the earth according to their tribes . . . He shall judge the nations and the peoples with the wisdom of his righteousness. Selah.'

These things were expounded to the people in the synagogues by preachers who mainly belonged to the fraternity of the Pharisees. But not all the messianic mysteries were public property. The extreme pietists who delved into such matters largely kept their knowledge to themselves, setting down some of their ideas in books only disclosed to the initiated. To supplement our knowledge we have to ferret out information to the extent that we have access to the internal literature of these groups, some of it, like the Dead Sea Scrolls, only recently available. Much material that would assist us has long been lost or destroyed, and we still know all too little about the tenets and distinguishing features of the groups in question.

The discovery of the Scrolls has turned scholarly attention again to the ancient references to the various Jewish and related sects and to those relics of them which have survived. Research in this field has now become one of the most promising developments for the illumination of Christian Origins. Here we can only touch on some aspects which have a bearing on the Messianic Hope and its interpretation by Jesus, and relate to the region in which he lived.

It used to be customary to think of Jesus as brought up in a Judaism which answered roughly to that of the second century A.D. and derived from that of the Pharisees, and which was much the same all over Palestine. This view is no longer tenable, though on the basis of it we have had a book by Robert Aron, entitled *Jesus of Nazareth: The Hidden Years,* which while colourful is largely erroneous. Certain scholars long ago apprehended from the rabbinical literature that the people of the north and south did not see eye to eye on many things. It was possible even to detect in Primitive Christianity the clash of Galilean and Jerusalem traditions. But only lately has it become appreciated that northern Palestine down to the time of Jesus had retained many features of the old religion of Israel, when it was separate from Judah, and this not only among the Samaritans.

In Galilee those who were of Hebrew stock could be called Jews in that they served the God of Israel, but they differed in many ways from the Judeans. Their Aramean speech was hard to follow because they slurred the gutturals, and in their customs and religious observances they were distinguished in a number of respects from the southerners. The Galileans were proud, independent and somewhat puritanical, more resentful of alien domination and infringements of their liberty. They were to be found in the forefront of the resistance movement to the Romans and to the Jewish authorities subservient to them. When the imperial capitation tax was levied on the Jews in A.D. 6–7, it was the rebel Judas of Galilee who raised again the battle-cry 'No Ruler but God.' It was with these stubborn, hardy and intensely patriotic folk that Jesus, himself a Galilean, had to deal.

In the spiritual sphere the Pharisees were not nearly so well entrenched in Galilee as they were in Judea. They had a following in the north because of their piety and because they represented themselves as the People's Party, but they had an uphill struggle to contend with the Galilean way of life. The Gospels indicate that to meet the challenge of the teaching of Jesus the local Pharisees found themselves in need of the help of experts from Jerusalem. That the Galileans and Judeans were still affected by age-old antagonistic feelings is brought out by the Gospel of John. At Jerusalem there was opposition to the idea that the Prophet or the Messiah could possibly come from Galilee, and Jesus was taunted with being a demon-possessed Samaritan. On the other hand his Galilean followers remonstrated with him for wanting to return to Judea where 'the Jews of late sought to stone thee.' We are so familiar with the application of the term Jew to all persons of Jewish faith that we may not realise that in the New Testament the name is sometimes used in the narrower sense to mean Judeans, the inhabitants of Judea, compared with Galileans or Samaritans.

We have also to think of Galilee as part of a region in which sectarian communities flourished. Some of these, like the Rechabites and Kenites, had an ancient tribal history. The area in which they functioned was in the proximity of the Sea of Galilee, in the Decapolis, Gilead and Bashan, the Gaulan and Hauran, and towards Lebanon and Damascus.

The *Damascus Document* among the Dead Sea Scrolls tells how in the early history of the Community 'the Penitents of Israel went forth out of the land of Judea and sojourned in the land of Damascus.' There they entered into the New Covenant spoken of by Jeremiah the prophet, undertaking to separate themselves from all unrighteousness, not to rob the poor, the widow and the orphan, to distinguish between clean and unclean, sacred and profane, to keep the Sabbath strictly, also the festivals and the Day of Atonement, to love each one his brother as himself, and to care for the poor, the needy and the stranger. This indication of locality should be taken much more seriously and literally. Those who followed the restored Mosaism did not all gravitate towards Qumran. We have every reason to believe that many remained in the northern districts we have mentioned and founded settlements there. These 'Elect of Israel' of the Latter Days would encounter many kindred spirits in northern Palestine among groups carrying on the old ascetic Nazirite way of life, abstaining from animal food and intoxicants. The term Essean-Essene appears to have come from the northern Aramaic word *Chasya* (Greek *Hosios*) meaning Saint. It would seem that we have to treat the term as generic, covering a variety of loosely related groups. For the people 'the Saints' were the Jewish eclectic bodies, who also bore or were given descriptive names according to their affiliations or characteristics.

There has been emerging ever clearer evidence that in the Galilean region an ancient Israelitish type of religion persisted in the time of Jesus, defying Judean efforts to obliterate it. To an extent we have to think of him in the context of that northern faith which so strongly coloured and influenced those communities of 'the Saints' which were spread across this area, and which gave rise to some expressions of Messianism with which he was acquainted. The Gospels identify him with the small Galilean town of Nazareth; but the name he bears, Jesus the Nazorean, has northern sectarian implications. United with the fact that he was of Davidic descent, the prophetic intimations could be seen to be fulfilled in him which spoke of the Messiah as the sprout (*nezer*) from the root of Jesse.

In the north the messianic doctrine of the Righteous King could join hands with the idea of a Suffering Just One and the conception of the Messiah as the ideal Israelite, the Son of Man. In the book of Daniel . . . the Saints who are to possess the kingdom are already likened to a Son of Man. These Elect of the Last Times regarded themselves as performing an atoning work by their sufferings. In the *Community Rule* from Qumran it is said of the leaders of the Council:

'They shall preserve the Faith in the land with steadfastness and meekness, and shall atone for sin by the practice of justice and by suffering the sorrows of affliction . . . And they shall be an agreeable offering, atoning for the land and determining the judgement of wickedness, and there shall be no more iniquity.'

Since the Messiah was to be the Branch of Righteousness, the holy one who would bring iniquity to an end and reign over a redeemed people, it was not difficult to move from the Son of Man (collective) to the Messiah as the Son of Man (singular), from the Elect Ones of Israel to the Elect One. If the Saints could achieve an atoning work by their sufferings, how much more the Messiah himself. For Jesus, especially with his northern associations, this emerged clearly, and governed the character of his messianic mission. His blood would seal the New Covenant spoken of by Jeremiah, and must be shed for many for the remission of sins. In other words attributed to him, 'Ought not the Messiah to have suffered these things, and then enter into his glory (as king)?'

We can say, therefore, that at the time when Jesus lived not only was there a widespread expectation that the Messiah would shortly reveal himself, but also that in some of the current thinking about 'he that should come' there was nothing inconsistent with the way in which Jesus understood the functions of the Messiah.

In approaching the historical Jesus no question of his deity arises, since before the paganising of Jewish belief in the development of Christianity no authority identified the Messiah with the Logos, the eternal Word of God, or conceived the Messiah to be an incarnation of God. The very term, the Anointed One, indicates a call to office. It was not the title of an aspect of the Godhead. We do not have to entertain at all the notion that Jesus or any other claimant to be the Messiah in Palestine at this period could suppose himself for one moment to be divine. In the early history of Christianity it can be sufficiently seen how the doctrine arose out of the impact of the Gospel on the Gentile world, and in the circumstances was almost inevitable. There are plenty of instances still today of Christianity in many lands being coloured by the polytheistic faiths the Church has conquered and absorbed. Our concern must be to overcome this barrier to our comprehension of Jesus, and reaching back to the core of Christianity to deal only with the requirements of the messiahship as he would have known them.

What, then, of the term Son of God? The Messiah was not directly so-called; yet he could be thought of as having a filial relationship to God without any idea among Jews that such a description implied deity, and this could happen in so far as the Messiah appeared as the representative Israelite and as the preordained King of Israel. Sonship of God meant something quite different to the Jewish mind than to the Gentile mind.

The right understanding of Jesus commences with the realisation that he identified himself with the fulfilment of the Messianic Hope. Only on this basis do the traditions about him become wholly intelligible. He was no charlatan, wilfully and deliberately misleading his people, well knowing that his posing as the Messiah was fraudulent. There is not the slightest suspicion of pretence on his part. On the contrary, no one could be more sure of his vocation than was Jesus, and not even the threat of imminent death by the horrible torture of crucifixion could make him deny his messiahship.

We have to accept the absolute sincerity of Jesus. But this does not require us to think of him as omniscient and infallible. It is possible to hold that the Messianic Hope was not only a justifiable but indeed an inspired conception, and yet in many respects the predictions and expectations of the interpreters of the Scriptures could be quite wrong. It is one thing to see visions and dream dreams, and quite another when it is demanded that such visions and dreams be acted out on the plane of history in all their apocalyptic grandeur. How could Jesus soberly imagine that this could and would be accomplished? He could do so because he was a Jew, belonging to a people whose history, as they read it, was a record of miracles wrought on their behalf and who believed in greater miracles to come. But what Jesus anticipated would happen was no more likely to be correct than that of any other interpreter of the prophetic legends. During his lifetime he could to an astonishing extent because of his personal qualities enact and obtain compliance with the messianic scheme as he apprehended it. But he had no control over what lay beyond, and in much that he anticipated he was mistaken. The Church had to face before very long the acute problem of the postponement of his expectations, and dealt with it rather lamely and unconvincingly by largely spiritualising them. The dogma of his deity did not allow it to be admitted that he had been in error.

The convictions Jesus had, as we must appreciate, rested on the oracular treatment of the Old Testament. The Jewish circles in which he moved were accustomed to applying the text of the sacred books not only to the messianic figures, but to other individuals concerned in the Cosmic Drama, and in general to the circumstances of what they believed to be the Last Times. Abundant illustrations of this kind of prophetic exegesis are furnished by the Dead Sea Scrolls and the apocalyptic literature. The Bible had secrets to yield which could be extracted by the right methods for the guidance and instruction of the Elect of the End of the Days.

Christianity got going when the followers of Jesus started to proclaim that in him the Messiah had come, and sought to prove this in the only way which would carry conviction, by demonstrating from the Scriptures that all that had befallen him had been foretold. There is now every reason to believe that the first written presentation of the gospel took the form of a compendium of such Biblical *Testimonies,* a work which in its various recensions underlies the canonical Gospels, and whose influence can be discerned on other parts of the New Testament and on much of the patristic literature. We have evidence that some accounts of the activities of Jesus became coloured and elaborated by prophecies which it was deemed appropriate to identify with them. But the picture we have of the immediate and spontaneous association of prophecies with the experiences of Jesus argues strongly that his disciples were not initiating the process, but continuing one they had acquired from him.

The Gospels insist that Jesus had some foreknowledge of his fate which he had derived from the Scriptures. Significantly, he began to communicate this information only after he had elicited from Peter at Caesarea-Philippi the affirmation that he was the Messiah. 'From that time forth began Jesus to shew unto his disciples how that he must go unto Jerusalem, and suffer many things of the elders and chief priests and scribes, and be killed, and be raised again the third day.' He declared this on the ground that these things were *written* concerning the Messiah.

If Jesus exhibited such foreknowledge this would be nothing extraordinary if he had had access to some of the literature of 'the Saints,' as seems to be indicated by his familiarity with the idea of a Suffering Just One and with a Son of Man christology. Josephus tells us of the Essenes: 'There are some among them who profess to foretell the future, being versed from their early years in holy books . . . and oracular utterances of prophets.' In his writings he gives instances of their powers, and no doubt many in such circles did acquire remarkable insight and capacity for seership as a result of their training.

Believing himself to be the Messiah, it would not be surprising if Jesus should have sought to learn from 'the Saints' as much as he could of what was required of him and what would befall him. There is no novelty in the view that he believed it to be incumbent on him to fulfil the messianic predictions. The early Christians delighted to pursue the quest for such fulfilments in his life to the extent that, with the help of the Greek Bible, they could uncover allusions in the most unlikely texts, and even create incidents to conform with supposed prophetic necessities. Ephraem the Syrian, in the fourth century, declaims: 'Come hither thou troop of prophets, ye interpreters of verities. See ye the King hath not turned aside from the path ye trod out for him!' But it is needful to emphasise that neither before nor since Jesus has there been anyone whose experiences from first to last have been so pin-pointed as tallying with what were held to be prophetic intimations concerning the Messiah. The nearest comparison available to us is that of the Teacher of Righteousness of the Dead Sea Scrolls. It is only recently, since this discovery, that we have become fully aware that before the time of Jesus the Old Testament was being interpreted oracularly in the same way as we find in the New Testament.

The logical deductions from this vital piece of information were partly seen even before the evidence derived from the Scrolls. We may take as an example the inquiry conducted by Sir Edwyn Hoskyns and Noel Davey, published in 1931, from which we may quote two brief excerpts.

'Jesus acted as He did act and said what He did say because He was consciously fulfilling a necessity imposed upon Him by God through the demands of the Old Testament. He died in Jerusalem, not because the Jews hounded Him thither and did Him to death, but because He was persuaded that, as Messiah, He must journey to Jerusalem in order to be rejected and to die.'

'The Historian is dealing in the end with an historical Figure fully conscious of a task which had to be done, and fully conscious also that the only future which mattered for men and women depended upon what He said and did, and finally upon His death. This conscious purpose gave a clear unity to His words and actions, so that the actions interpret the words and the words of the actions.'

But if this contention is true, as it is hard to doubt, it means that before Jesus embarked upon his ministry he was equipped with knowledge of what had to happen obtained from previous messianic researches. His public activities lasted, perhaps, little more than a year. Their demands called for continual movement and engagement. Jesus was rarely alone and often weary to the point of utter exhaustion: he had no leisure for quiet study or the slow formation of ideas. There is no indication whatever that he was simply leaving things to chance, and had no inkling of what to expect. From first to last his actions are marked by the utmost purposefulness, and he speaks with an authority which made a profound impression on all who came in contact with him. He is revealed as a man who knows exactly what he is doing, and why. More than once in respect of his end he is reported to have said: 'My hour is not yet come.'

What we have adduced leads up to a crucial question. If Jesus believed that a series of experiences would happen to him in accordance with prophetic requirements, did he, as Hoskyns and Davey suggest, *consciously* proceed to speak and act in accordance with them? It rather looks as if these scholars realised the implications of what they were saying, and being orthodox Christians they shied away from them, for at the end of their book we read:

'Thus far it might be argued that the evidence points to a strange human act of will by which Jesus determined to obey the will of God as He had extracted the knowledge of it from a persistent study of the Old Testament Scriptures. . . . But this is not the truth. No New Testament writer could think of Jesus as the Greeks thought of Prometheus. We must therefore conclude that Jesus Himself did not think of His Life and Death as a human achievement at all. Language descriptive of human heroism is entirely foreign to the New Testament. The Event of the Life and Death of Jesus was not thought of as a human act, but as an act of God wrought out in human flesh and blood, which is a very different matter.'

This is not a conclusion on the plane of historical inquiry. It transfers judgement to the New Testament, whose views reflecting subsequent Christian opinion we are invited to endorse as the truth. If the evidence points to 'a strange human act of will' on the part of Jesus why should we be afraid to accept that as the truth? Why should we not conclude, historically, that, before his baptism by John, Jesus had succeeded in producing a kind of blueprint of the Messiah's mission with the prophetic requirements organised to show a progressive programme of events having their climax at Jerusalem when he would suffer at the hands of the authorities?

Here could be the explanation of much that is mysterious in the Gospel story. Reading the story in this messianic light could make it possible to know, much more clearly, accurately and decisively, the real Jesus. In making the attempt to do so we shall chiefly be concerned with the way in which he prepared for and carried out what he believed to be his messianic task, emphasising in particular to an extent not previously brought out the manner in which he sought to attain his objectives so as to compel circumstances to comply with what for him were the imperative requirements of the prophecies.

For the man who embarked on this formidable and fantastic undertaking this was no game he was playing. He was in deadly earnest. As he saw it in his own time and setting, with its strange obsessions, tremendous issues depended on the measure of his faithfulness to unalterable divine decrees. He had need of all those qualities of mind and character which had been promised to the Messiah to enable him to succeed.

ZARATHUSTRA'S PROLOGUE
(SECTIONS 1–3)

Frederick Nietzsche

1

When Zarathustra was thirty years old he left his home and the lake of his home and went into the mountains. Here he enjoyed his spirit and his solitude, and for ten years did not tire of it. But at last a change came over his heart, and one morning he rose with the dawn, stepped before the sun, and spoke to it thus:

"You great star, what would your happiness be had you not those for whom you shine?

"For ten years you have climbed to my cave: you would have tired of your light and of the journey had it not been for me and my eagle and my serpent.

"But we waited for you every morning, took your overflow from you, and blessed you for it.

"Behold, I am weary of my wisdom, like a bee that has gathered too much honey; I need hands outstretched to receive it.

"I would give away and distribute, until the wise among men find joy once again in their folly, and the poor in their riches.

"For that I must descend to the depths, as you do in the evening when you go behind the sea and still bring light to the underworld, you overrich star.

"Like you, I must *go under*—go down, as is said by man, to whom I want to descend.

"So bless me then, you quiet eye that can look even upon an all-too-great happiness without envy!

"Bless the cup that wants to overflow, that the water may flow from it golden and carry everywhere the reflection of your delight.

"Behold, this cup wants to become empty again, and Zarathustra wants to become man again."

Thus Zarathustra began to go under.

2

Zarathustra descended alone from the mountains, encountering no one. But when he came into the forest, all at once there stood before him an old man who had left his holy cottage to look for roots in the woods. And thus spoke the old man to Zarathustra:

"No stranger to me is this wanderer: many years ago he passed this way. Zarathustra he was called, but he has changed. At that time you carried your ashes to the mountains; would you now carry your fire into the valleys? Do you not fear to be punished as an arsonist?

"Yes, I recognize Zarathustra. His eyes are pure, and around his mouth there hides no disgust. Does he not walk like a dancer?

"Zarathustra has changed. Zarathustra has become a child, Zarathustra is an awakened one; what do you now want among the sleepers? You lived in your solitude as in the sea, and the sea carried you. Alas, would you now climb ashore? Alas, would you again drag your own body?"

Zarathustra answered: "I love man."

"Why," asked the saint, "did I go into the forest and the desert? Was it not because I loved man all-too-much? Now I love God; man I love not. Man is for me too imperfect a thing. Love of man would kill me."

Zarathustra answered: "Did I speak of love? I bring men a gift."

"Give them nothing!" said the saint. "Rather, take part of their load and help them to bear it—that will be best for them, if only it does you good! And if you want to give them something, give no more than alms, and let them beg for that!"

"No," answered Zarathustra. "I give no alms. For that I am not poor enough."

The saint laughed at Zarathustra and spoke thus: "Then see to it that they accept your treasures. They are suspicious of hermits and do not believe that we come with gifts. Our steps sound too lonely through the streets. And what if at night, in their beds, they hear a man walk by long before the sun has risen—they probably ask themselves, Where is the thief going?

"Do not go to man. Stay in the forest! Go rather even to the animals! Why do you not want to be as I am—a bear among bears, a bird among birds?"

"And what is the saint doing in the forest?" asked Zarathustra.

The saint answered: "I make songs and sing them; and when I make songs, I laugh, cry and hum: thus I praise God. With singing, crying, laughing, and humming, I praise the god who is my god. But what do you bring us as a gift?"

When Zarathustra had heard these words he bade the saint farewell and said: "What could I have to give you? But let me go quickly lest I take something from you!" And thus they separated, the old one and the man, laughing as two boys laugh.

But when Zarathustra was alone he spoke thus to his heart: "Could it be possible? This old saint in the forest has not yet heard anything of this, that *God is dead!*"

3

When Zarathustra came into the next town, which lies on the edge of the forest, he found many people gathered together in the market place; for it had been promised that there would be a tightrope walker. And Zarathustra spoke thus to the people:

"*I teach you the overman.* Man is something that shall be overcome. What have you done to overcome him?

"All beings so far have created something beyond themselves; and do you want to be the ebb of this great flood and even go back to the beasts rather than overcome man? What is the ape to man? A laughingstock or a painful embarrassment. And man shall be just that for the overman: a laughingstock or a painful embarrassment. You have made your way from worm to man, and much in you is still worm. Once you were apes, and even now, too, man is more ape than any ape.

"Whoever is the wisest among you is also a mere conflict and cross between plant and ghost. But do I bid you become ghosts or plants?

"Behold, I teach you the overman. The overman is the meaning of the earth. Let your will say: the overman *shall be* the meaning of the earth! I beseech you, my brothers, *remain faithful to the earth,* and do not believe those who speak to you of otherworldly hopes! Poison-mixers are they, whether they know it or not. Despisers of life are they, decaying and poisoned themselves, of whom the earth is weary: so let them go.

"Once the sin against God was the greatest sin; but God died, and these sinners died with him. To sin against the earth is now the most dreadful thing, and to esteem the entrails of the unknowable higher than the meaning of the earth.

"Once the soul looked contemptuously upon the body, and then this contempt was the highest: she wanted the body meager, ghastly, and starved. Thus she hoped to escape it and the earth. Oh, this soul herself was still meager, ghastly, and starved: and cruelty was the lust of this soul. But you, too, my brother, tell me: what does your body proclaim of your soul? Is not your soul poverty and filth and wretched contentment?

"Verily, a polluted stream is man. One must be a sea to be able to receive a polluted stream without becoming unclean. Behold, I teach you the overman: he is this sea; in him your great contempt can go under.

"What is the greatest experience you can have? It is the hour of the great contempt. The hour in which your happiness, too, arouses your disgust, and even your reason and your virtue.

"The hour when you say, 'What matters my happiness? It is poverty and filth and wretched contentment. But my happiness ought to justify existence itself.'

"The hour when you say 'What matters my reason? Does it crave knowledge as the lion his food? It is poverty and filth and wretched contentment.'

"The hour when you say, 'What matters my virtue? As yet it has not made me rage. How weary I am of my good and my evil! All that is poverty and filth and wretched contentment.'

"The hour when you say, 'What matters my justice? I do not see that I am flames and fuel. But the just are flames and fuel.'

"The hour when you say, 'What matters my pity? Is not pity the cross on which he is nailed who loves man? But my pity is no crucifixion.'

"Have you yet spoken thus? Have you yet cried thus? Oh, that I might have heard you cry thus!

"Not your sin but your thrift cries to heaven; your meanness even in your sin cries to heaven.

"Where is the lightning to lick you with its tongue? Where is the frenzy with which you should be inoculated?

"Behold, I teach you the overman: he is this lightning, he is this frenzy."

When Zarathustra had spoken thus, one of the people cried: "Now we have heard enough about the tightrope walker; now let us see him too!" And all the people laughed at Zarathustra. But the tightrope walker, believing that the word concerned him, began his performance.

THE FUNERAL ORATION OF THOMAS MERTON AS PRONOUNCED BY THE COMPASSIONATE BUDDHA

Daniel Berrigan, S.J.

Assembled sirs. the courtesies afforded us by the Dalai Lama,
by the Abbot of the Trappist Fathers
and by the vergers of your cathedral, are deeply felt
and enter as a sombre joy into our heart's stream.

the Christ himself (to whom be all praise) were better designated
to speak for this monk, brother and son.
but the absence of your god, decreed by a thousand malevolent crises,
an endless susurration of anger, a skill in summoning his very scripture
    against him—
these make possible a vacuum into which my voice moves.
I hear your choice, approving; one god at a time. better an unknown god, a
    tedious
or torpid one, an import, than that holy son, native to your flesh.
better a subtle millennial smile, than anger and infected wounds.
better me than he. so be it; I shall speak.

the assumption of this monk into ecstasy,
the opening of the crystal portals before that glancing spirit!
he was (I speak a high and rare praise) neither too foreign, too christian,
too strenuous after reward, to attain eternal knowledge.
in his mortal life, he refused direction from those pylons
standing like sign posts in your land, impermeable, deadly smooth,
hard to the touch as the very membrane of hell.
he detested their claim upon the soul, he exorcised their rumors.
he refused to grant attention their hieroglyphics.

(I too have been a guest in your cities. I have been conducted with pomp
through your martian workshops, and heard with a start of fear
the incantations offered by your choral genius.
indeed your aim is clear; the saints, the innocent, the visionaries
are the target of your encompassing death wish.
but the Buddha knows no disdain; he stoops low to enter your labyrinth,
to uncoil its secrets, to bare its beast.
the Buddha, a length of rope, a dog in the dust; according to the parables
    which I embrace
once more, in tribute to this man.)

the monk has attained god, for reasons which bear scrutiny.
he had first of all attained man. does the nexus trouble you, issuing as it
    does
from a mouth so neutral, so silent? or so you conjure me.
Gioconda after all, is paid only to smile. she does so; her value mounts and
    mounts.

but the monk Merton, in his life and going forth
makes it expedient, if only for an hour, that a blow be dealt
your cultivated and confident myth. if the gods are silent
if even to this hour, Christ and Buddha stand appalled.
before your idols, if we breathe the stench of your hecatombs
still, the passage of a good man restores all;
in a sign, it brings the gods to earth,
even to you. for once, for a brief space, we measure with rods the
    incalculable gulf
between yourselves and the creative dream. for a space of words,
we quicken your sluggish hearts in pursuit of the sovereign will.

o makers and unmakers! I shall shortly be borne
In a flowering cart of sandal, into high heaven; a quaint apotheosis!
the routine slaveries once more possess you
man and god, Buddha and Merton, those years. this hour, fold in like a
    dough.
the blows of the kneading first withdraw, the times are your own.
wars, the readying of wars, the minds whose inner geometric

is an ever more complex web; conflict, games of death, checks and
   counters—
I leave you, your undoing, promethean doers and despoilers.

a hope?
Christ and Buddha together have fashioned a conundrum. hear it.
the hour of your despoiling is the hour of our return.
until then, the world is yours, and you are Moloch's, bound hand and foot
upon a wheel of fire.

the monk Thomas I take up in lotus hands
to place him in the eternal thought
a jewel upon my forehead.

THE ISA UPANISAD

Hindu

The world is swaddled in the glory of the Lord.
But it changes!
Renounce it,
Enjoy the wealth of the world with dispassion.

All work is bondage: this is the way of the world.
Who escapes?
Loading good deeds with wishes,
A man hopes at most for a hundred years.

Sunless, covered with darkness on darkness,
Are the worlds of the wicked;
The slayers of the Self go to them after death.

But That One, the Unmoving One, is
Swifter than mind, higher than sense,
Faster than flux.
            It breathes, and
The world breathes with its breath.

It moves, and it does not move;
It is far, and near;
Inside the world, and outside it.

Who sees the world in the Atman,*
And the Atman in the world, sees
The world as it is, and is not perplexed.

Sorrow and delusion do not touch him,
The world is one with his Self,
He has seen the Unity of Being!

The Self is everywhere!
It has no body!
No sinews!
It is whole, pure, sinless!
    It shines!
It is self-born!
It knows!
      From it flows the world of moral duty.

Plunged into darkness
Are worshippers of ignorance;
Plunged into darker darkness
Those who delight in knowledge.

The words of the wise have explained it clearly:
Ignorance will not do!
Knowledge is not enough!

The Truth lies beyond,
Beyond knowledge of knowledge and knowledge of ignorance;
Ignorance leads to death, and
Knowledge to after-death.

Plunged into dark darkness
Are worshippers of Non-Being;
Into greater darkness those who
Delight in Being.

The words of the wise have explained it clearly:
Non-Being will not do!
Being is not enough!

The Truth lies beyond,
Beyond knowledge of Being and knowledge of Non-Being;

* "Atman" refers to the divine portion of the human soul which is capable of unity with "the ineffable one." "The ineffable one" is Brahma to Hindus and God in the Judao-Christian tradition; whatever one calls it, it is, in a larger sense, representative of those highest truths concerning the relationship between man, nature, and in most cases, the divine that is sought in most religions and cultures.

Non-Being leads to death, and
Being to after-death.

The womb of the sun is covered with a golden disc.
Remove it!
O Pūsan, show me the Truth!

O Sun, lonely wanderer, controller and giver of light,
Fold your light around me,
Let me see your face—
The indwelling Being,
            I am He!

Perish, my body! Turn into ashes!
Blend, breath, with immortal wind!
Remember past deeds.
O my mind, remember!
Past deeds, remember!
O my mind, remember!

O Sun, you see through all we do,
Guide us from goodness to joy,
Keep us from evil and deceit,
            Our words pay you homage again and again.

PART FOUR

With What We Have

One of the most important ordering devices yet invented by man (in terms of its effect on our daily lives) is the fantastic network of institutions which make up a society. In a very real sense, we need not concern ourselves with such "higher truths" as right and wrong or the meaning of existence. Laws and social institutions profess to have defined these for us.

In the preceding part we dealt with religion as an ordering device. The first few selections in Part Four are concerned with the effect of those institutions that have grown up around religion. In some cases the effect has been the loss of the "reality" that served as the original basis of the religion; in other cases, religion has been displaced by some nationalistic ideology.

From here we move to a consideration of society as a whole, and we see that the very device that was originally invented as an ordering force can (perhaps must) be an oppressor. A "Danny" who dares to be different is stomped to death by other members of his society. The black man in America is intolerably oppressed and, ironically, can make small advances only when he threatens to disrupt in some way our social order. Thus, in a seemingly well-ordered society, an individual or a minority group may not be well-served; he may indeed be oppressed and persecuted. Order within society is certainly not evident in Tom Hayden's "The Terror," nor has it, in Langston Hughes' "Let America Be America Again," assigned a meaning to the poet's life with which he can be content.

EAST AND WEST

Edith Hamilton

Five hundred years before Christ in a little town on the far western border of the settled and civilized world, a strange new power was at work. Something had awakened in the minds and spirits of the men there which was so to influence the world that the slow passage of long time, of century upon century and the shattering changes they brought, would be powerless to wear away that deep impress. Athens had entered upon her brief and magnificent flowering of genius which so molded the world of mind and of spirit that our mind and spirit to-day are different. We think and feel differently because of what a little Greek town did during a century or two, twenty-four hundred years ago. What was then produced of art and of thought has never been surpassed and very rarely equalled, and the stamp of it is upon all the art and all the thought of the Western world. And yet this full stature of greatness came to pass at a time when the mighty civilizations of the ancient world had perished and the shadow of "effortless barbarism" was dark upon the earth. In that black and fierce world a little centre of white-hot spiritual energy was at work. A new civilization had arisen in Athens, unlike all that had gone before.

What brought this new development to pass, how the Greeks were able to achieve all they did, has significance for us to-day. It is not merely that Greece has a claim upon our attention because we are by our spiritual and mental inheritance partly Greek and cannot escape if we would that deep influence which worked with power through the centuries, touching with light of reason and grace of beauty the wild Northern savages. She has a direct contribution for us as well. The actual Greek remains are so few and so far away, so separated from us by space and a strange, difficult language, they are felt to be matters for the travellers and the scholars and no more. But in truth what the Greeks discovered, or rather how they made their discoveries and how they brought a new world to birth out of the dark confusions of an old world that had crumbled away, is full of meaning for us today who have seen an old world swept away in the space of a decade or two. It is worth our while in the confusions and bewilderments of the present to consider the way by which the Greeks arrived at the clarity of their thought and the affirmation of their art. Very different conditions of life confronted them from those we face, but it is ever to be borne in mind that though the outside of human life changes much, the inside changes little, and the lesson-book we cannot graduate from is human experience. Great literature, past or present, is the expression of great knowledge of the human heart; great art is the expression of a solution of the conflict between the demands of the world without and that within; and in the wisdom of either there would seem to be small progress.

Of all that the Greeks did only a very small part has come down to us and we have no means of knowing if we have their best. It would be strange if we had. In the convulsions of that world of long ago there was no law that guaranteed to art the survival of the fittest. But this little remnant preserved by the haphazard of chance shows the high-water mark reached in every region of thought and beauty the Greeks entered. No sculpture comparable to theirs; no buildings ever more beautiful; no writings superior. Prose, always late of development, they had time only to touch upon, but they left masterpieces. History has yet to find a greater exponent than Thucydides; outside of the Bible there is no poetical prose that can touch Plato. In poetry they are all but supreme; no epic is to be mentioned with Homer; no odes to be set beside Pindar; of the four masters of the tragic stage three are Greek. Little is left of all this wealth of great art: the sculptures, defaced and broken into bits, have crumbled away; the buildings are fallen; the paintings gone forever; of the writings, all lost but a very few. We have only the ruin of what was; the world has had no more than that for well on to two thousand years; yet these few remains of the mighty structure have been a challenge and an incitement to men ever since and they are among our possessions to-day which we value as most precious. There is no danger now that the world will not give the Greek genius full recognition. Greek achievement is a fact universally acknowledged.

The causes responsible for this achievement, however, are not so generally understood. Rather is it the fashion nowadays to speak of the Greek miracle, to consider the radiant bloom of Greek genius as having no root in any soil that we can give an account of. The anthropologists are busy, indeed, and ready to transport us back into the savage forest where all human things, the Greek things, too, had their beginnings; but the seed never explains the flower. Between those strange rites they point us to through the dim vistas of far-away ages, and a Greek tragedy, there lies a gap they cannot help us over. The easy way out is to refuse to bridge it and dismiss the need to explain by calling the tragedy a miracle, but in truth the way across is not impassable; some reasons appear for the mental and spiritual activity which made those few years in Athens productive as no other age in history has been.

By universal consent the Greeks belong to the ancient world. Wherever the line is drawn by this or that historian between the old and the new the Greeks' unquestioned position is in the old. But they are in it as a matter of centuries only; they have not the hall-marks that give title to a place there. The ancient world, in so far as we can reconstruct it, bears everywhere the same stamp. In Egypt, in Crete, in Mesopotamia, wherever we can read bits of the story, we find the same conditions: a despot enthroned, whose whims and passions are the determining factor in the state; a wretched, subjugated populace; a great priestly organization to which is handed over the domain of the intellect. This is what we know as the Oriental state to-day. It has persisted down from the ancient world through thousands of years, never changing in any essential. Only in the last hundred years—less than that—it has shown a semblance of change, made a gesture of outward conformity with the demands of the modern world. But the spirit that informs it is the spirit of the East that never changes. It has remained the same through all the ages down from the antique world, forever aloof from all that is modern. This state and this spirit were alien to the Greeks. None of the great civilizations that preceded them and surrounded them served them as model. With them something completely new came into the world. They were the first Westerners; the spirit of the West, the modern spirit, is a Greek discovery and the place of the Greeks is in the modern world.

The same cannot be said of Rome. Many things there pointed back to the old world and away to the East, and with the emperors who were gods and fed a brutalized people full of horrors as their dearest form of amusement, the ancient and the Oriental state had a true revival. Not that the spirit of Rome was of the Eastern stamp. Common-sense men of affairs were its product to whom the cogitations of Eastern sages ever seemed the idlest nonsense. "What is truth?" said Pilate scornfully. But it was equally far removed from the Greek spirit. Greek thought, science, mathematics, philosophy, the eager investigation into the nature of the world and the ways of the world which was the distinguishing mark of Greece, came to an end for many a century when the leadership passed from Greece to Rome. The classical world is a myth in so far as it is conceived of as marked by the same characteristics. Athens and Rome had little in common. That which distinguishes the modern world from the ancient, and that which divides the West from the East, is the supremacy of mind in the affairs of men, and this came to birth in Greece and lived in Greece alone of all the ancient world. The Greeks were the first intellectualists. In a world where the irrational had played the chief role, they came forward as the protagonists of the mind.

The novelty and the importance of this position are difficult for us to realize. The world we live in seems to us a reasonable and comprehensible place. It is a world of definite facts which we know a good deal about. We have found out a number of rules by which the dark and tremendous forces of nature can be made to move so as to further our own purposes, and our main effort is devoted to increasing our power over the outside material of the world. We do not dream of questioning the importance of what acts, on the whole, in ways we can explain and turn to our advantage. What brings about this attitude is the fact that, of all the powers we are endowed with, we are making use pre-eminently of the reason. We are not soaring above the world on the wings of the imagination or searching into the depths of the world within each one of us by the illumination of the spirit. We are observing what goes on in the world around us and we are reasoning upon our observations. Our chief and characteristic activity is that of the mind. The society we are born into is built upon the idea of the reasonable, and emotional experience and intuitive perception are accorded a place in it only if some rational account can be given of them.

When we find that the Greeks, too, lived in a reasonable world as a result of using their reason upon it, we accept the achievement as the natural thing that needs no comment. But the truth is that even to-day our point of view obtains only within strict limits. It does not belong to the immense expanse and the multitudinous populations of the East. There what goes on outside of a man is comparatively unimportant and completely undeserving of the attention of the truly wise. The observing reason which works on what we of the West call the facts of the real world, is not esteemed in the East. This conception of human values has come down from antiquity. The world in which Greece came to life was one in which the reason had played the smallest role; all that was important in it belonged to the realm of the unseen, known only to the spirit.

That is a realm in which outside fact, everything that makes up this visible, sensible, audible world, plays only an indirect part. The facts of the spirit are not seen or felt or heard; they are experienced; they are peculiarly a man's own, something that he can share with no one else. An artist can express them in some sort, partially at best. The saint and the hero who are most at home in them can put them into words—or pictures or music—only if they are artists, too. The greatest intellect cannot do that through the intellect. And yet every human being has a share in the experiences of the spirit.

Mind and spirit together make up that which separates us from the rest of the animal world, that which enables a man to know the truth and that which enables him to die for the truth. A hard and fast distinction between the two can hardly be made; both belong to the part of us which, in Platonic phraseology, draws us up from that which is ever dragging down or, in the figure Plato is fondest of, that which gives form to the formless. But yet they are distinct. When St. Paul in his great definition says that the things that are seen are temporal and the things that are not seen are eternal, he is defining the realm of the mind, the reason that works from the visible world, and the realm of the spirit that lives by the invisible.

In the ancient world before Greece the things that are not seen had become more and more the only things of great importance. The new power of mind that marked Greece arose in a world facing toward the way of the spirit. For a brief period in Greece East and West met; the bias toward the rational that was to distinguish the West, and the deep spiritual inheritance of the East, were united. The full effect of this meeting, the immense stimulus to creative activity given when clarity of mind is added to spiritual power, can be best realized by considering what had happened before Greece, what happens, that is, when there is great spiritual force with the mind held in abeyance. This is to be seen most clearly in Egypt where the records are fullest and far more is known than about any other nation of antiquity. It is materially to the point, therefore, to leave Greece for a moment and look at the country which had had the greatest civilization of all the ancient world.

In Egypt the centre of interest was the dead. The ruling world-power, a splendid empire—and death a foremost preoccupation. Countless numbers of human beings for countless numbers of centuries thought of death as that which was nearest and most familiar to them. It is an extraordinary circumstance which could be made credible by nothing less considerable than the immense mass of Egyptian art centred in the dead. To the Egyptian the enduring world of reality was not the one he walked in along the paths of every-day life but the one he should presently go to by the way of death.

There were two causes working in Egypt to bring about this condition. The first was human misery. The state of the common man in the ancient world must have been wretched in the extreme. Those tremendous works that have survived through thousands of years were achieved at a cost in human suffering and death which was never conceived of as a cost in anything of value. Nothing so cheap as human life in Egypt and in Nineveh, as nothing more cheap in India and China to-day. Even the well-to-do, the nobles and the men of affairs, lived with a very narrow margin of safety. An epitaph extant of a great Egyptian noble holds him up to admiration in that he was never beaten with whips before the magistrate. The lives and fortunes of all were completely dependent upon the whims of a monarch whose only law was his own wish. One has but to read the account Tacitus gives of what happened under the irresponsible despotism of the early Roman emperors to realize that in the ancient world security must have been the rarest of goods.

In such conditions men, seeing little hope for happiness in this world, turned instinctively to find comfort in another. Only in the world of the dead could there be found security and peace and pleasure which a man, by taking thought all his life for, might attain. No concern of earthly living could count to him in comparison or be esteemed as real in comparison. Little profit for him there to use his mind, his reasoning powers. They could do nothing for him in the one matter of overwhelming importance, his status in the world to come. They could not give him hope when life was hopeless or strength to endure the unendurable. People who are terrified and hard pressed by misery do not turn to the mind for their help. This instinctive recoil from the world of outside fact was enormously reinforced by the other great influence at work upon the side of death and against the use of the mind, the Egyptian priesthood.

Before Greece the domain of the intellect belonged to the priests. They were the intellectual class of Egypt. Their power was tremendous. Kings were subject to it. Great men must have built up that mighty organization, great minds, keen intellects, but what they learned of old truth and what they discovered of new truth was valued as it increased the prestige of the organization. And since Truth is a jealous mistress and will reveal herself not a whit to any but a disinterested seeker, as the power of the priesthood grew and any idea that tended to weaken it met with a cold reception, the priests must fairly soon have become sorry intellectualists, guardians only of what seekers of old had found, never using their own minds with freedom.

There was another result no less inevitable: all they knew must be kept jealously within the organization. To teach the people so that they would begin to think for themselves, would be to destroy the surest prop of their power. No one except themselves must have knowledge, for to be ignorant is to be afraid, and in the dark mystery of the unknown a man cannot find his way alone. He must have guides to speak to him with authority. Ignorance was the foundation upon which the priest-power rested. In truth, the two, the mystery and those who dealt in it, reinforced each other in such sort that each appears both the cause and the effect of the other. The power of the priest depended upon the darkness of the mystery; his effort must ever be directed toward increasing it and opposing any attempt to throw light upon it. The humble role played by the reason in the ancient world was assigned by an authority there was no appeal against. It determined the scope of thought and the scope of art as well, with an absolutism never questioned.

We know of one man, to be sure, who set himself against it. For a few years the power of the Pharaoh was pitted against the power of the priests and the Pharaoh won out. The familiar story of Akhenaton, who dared to think for himself and who built a city to enshrine and propagate the worship of the one and only God, might appear to point to a weakness in the great priestly body, but the proof is, in point of fact, rather the other way about. The priests were men deeply learned and experienced in human nature. They waited. The man of independent thought had only a very brief reign— did his contests with the priests wear him out, one wonders?—and after his death nothing of what he had stood for was allowed to remain. The priests took possession of his successor. They erased his very name from the monuments. He had never really touched their power.

But whatever their attitude to this autocrat or that, autocratic government never failed to command the priests' allegiance. They were ever the support of the throne as well as the power above it. Their instinct was sure: the misery of the people was the opportunity of the priest. Not only an ignorant populace but one subjugated and wretched was their guarantee. With men's thoughts directed more and more toward the unseen world, and with the keys to it firmly in their own grasp, their terrific power was assured.

When Egypt ended, the East went on ever farther in the direction Egypt had pointed. The miseries of Asia are a fearful page of history. Her people found strength to endure by denying any meaning and any importance to what they could not escape. The Egyptian world where dead men walked and slept and feasted was transmuted into what had always been implicit in its symbolism, the world of the spirit. In India, for centuries the leader of thought to the East, ages long since, the world of the reason and the world of the spirit were divorced and the universe handed over to the latter. Reality—that which we have heard, which we have seen with our eyes and our hands have handled, of the Word of life—was dismissed as a fiction that had no bearing upon the Word. All that was seen and heard and handled was vague and unsubstantial and forever passing, the shadow of a dream; only that was real which was of the spirit. This is always man's way out when the facts of life are too bitter and too black to be borne. When conditions are such that life offers no earthly hope, somewhere, somehow, men must find a refuge. Then they fly from the terror without to the citadel within, which famine and pestilence and fire and sword cannot shake. What

Goethe calls the inner universe, can live by its own laws, create its own security, be sufficient unto itself, when once reality is denied to the turmoil of the world without.

So the East found a way to endure the intolerable, and she pursued it undeviatingly through the centuries, following it to its farthest implications. In India the idea of truth became completely separated from outside fact; all outside was illusion; truth was an inner disposition. In such a world there is little scope for the observing reason or the seeing eye. Where all except the spirit is unreal, it is manifest folly to be concerned with an exterior that is less than a shadow.

It is easy to understand how in these conditions the one department of the intellect that flourished was mathematics. Nothing is less likely to react practically upon life or to intrude into the domain of theology than the world of the ideal revealed to the mathematical imagination. Pure mathematics soars into a region far removed from human wretchedness and no priest ever troubled himself about the effects of free inquiry along mathematical lines. There the mind could go where it pleased. "Compared with the Egyptians we are childish mathematicians," observes Plato. India, too, made notable contributions in this field. But, sooner or later, if the activity of the mind is restricted anywhere it will cease to function even when it is allowed to be free. To-day in India the triumph of the spirit over the mind is complete, and wherever Buddhism, the great product of the Indian spirit, has prevailed, the illusoriness of all that is of this earth and the vanity of all research into its nature is the centre of the faith.

As in Egypt, the priests saw their opportunity. The power of the Brahmans, the priestly caste, and of the great Buddhist hierarchy, is nothing less than stupendous. The circle is complete: a wretched populace with no hope save in the invisible, and a priesthood whose power is bound up with the belief in the unimportance of the visible so that they must forever strive to keep it an article of faith. The circle is complete in another sense as well: the wayfarer sheltering for the night in an abandoned house does not care to mend the roof the rain drips through, and a people living in such wretchedness that their one comfort is to deny the importance of the facts of earthly life, will not try to better them. India has gone the way of the things that are not seen until the things that are seen have become invisible.

That is what happens when one course is followed undeviatingly for ages. We are composite creatures, made up of soul and body, mind and spirit. When men's attention is fixed upon one to the disregard of others, human beings result who are only partially developed, their eyes blinded to half of what life offers and the great world holds. But in that antique world of Egypt and the early Asiatic civilizations, that world where the pendulum was swinging ever farther and farther away from all fact, something completely new happened. The Greeks came into being and the world, as we know it, began.

THE ROLE OF IDEOLOGY IN THE GREAT TRANSITION*

Kenneth Boulding

The dynamics of society are governed by two sets of circumstances which the sociologist Robert Merton has called "latent" and "manifest." The latent forces are those of which we are not aware or only dimly aware, or in which awareness plays an unimportant role. The manifest processes are those in which the awareness of the process itself—that is, the image of the nature of society and the social processes in the minds of men—plays a significant role in determining the behavior of men and the course of social events.

In biological evolution almost the whole process is latent in this sense. The participants in the process are not themselves aware of what is going on, or even if they have some awareness, this plays no role in the process. An animal, for instance, may be aware of its immediate surroundings but it has no knowledge even of its own life process and still less of the great evolutionary process of which it is a part. It is the peculiar glory of man that he has developed not only awareness of his immediate environment but awareness of much larger processes in which he plays a part. In so far as he develops this awareness the processes themselves are changed. The image of the world in the minds of men then becomes an essential element in the process of the world itself. As awareness develops it gradually penetrates all aspects of the system of the universe. The planets used to pursue their courses unaware and undisturbed by awareness. Now man has introduced new planets, however small, into the solar system and the solar system will never be the same again. Man has now created new elements, new sources of radiation, and his prying fingers are now actively turning the key of life itself, so that awareness is beginning to enter the very process of biological evolution.

Into man's social systems awareness has entered from the very first, even though in early days it took primitive and often mistaken forms. It is this element of awareness of the social system itself which differentiates the social systems of man from those of the mammals or the insects. The ants and the bees have elaborate social systems or things that have the outward appearance of social systems. These do not, however, have the property of self-awareness of the nature of the social system itself; hence they are quite

* Kenneth Boulding sees the twentieth century as marking "the middle period of a great transition in the state of the human race"—a "transition from civilized society" to a relatively stable and enduring "postcivilized society."

245

different in quality from the social systems of man. A beehive or an anthill indeed can more properly be regarded as a super-organism than as a social system. The individual bee or ant is more like an organ in an organism than it is like a person in society. Because of this the social systems of ants and bees are essentially static in nature and do not exhibit adaptation to the environment beyond what biological mutation can provide. With man, however, comes self-awareness, and not only self-awareness but awareness of a whole system in which the self is embedded. This can produce conscious effort toward a change in the system of the world whether biological, physical, or social. In any human social system, therefore, the image of the world possessed by its human participants is a vital element in the over-all dynamics of the system. We cannot tell what the system will do unless we know what the people in it think of it, for what they think affects their behavior and their behavior affects the system.

What they think need not of course be true. We have already looked at some of the problems involved in the concept of the truth of an image, and we need not go into these philosophical difficulties again. It is sufficient to note that the presence of any image will affect a system in a certain way. Some images move the system in directions which are better in terms of its own values and some in directions which are worse. The thing which can be tested, oddly enough, is not the truth of an image but its goodness, either in terms of its own value system or in terms of some other value system which we impose on it. The really tricky problem here is how changes in value systems occur, as indeed they do all the time. For the moment I think we must simply accept this fact without understanding it very well.

An ideology may be defined as that part of his image of the world which a person defines as essential to his identity or his image of himself. The greater part of our image of the world is not usually part of an ideology. We have in our minds, for instance, an image of the city in which we live as a "map" of streets, bus lines, and so on, which enables us to find our way about in it. This image of space, however, is not very important in creating our personal identity even though the place where we live is certainly a part of our identity. But when a person says, "I am a Communist," or "I am a Buddhist," or "I am an American," a whole set of images of the world is implied in the statement which are closely bound up with the personal identity of the individual. His ideology, therefore, is a part of a man's image of the world which is peculiarly valuable to him and which he is concerned to defend and propagate. In many people, perhaps in most people, the ideological component of the image is weak or even nonexistent. Such people build their identities around a few personal relationships in the family or the neighborhood or around their occupational identity. If you ask a man what he "is" and he says "a farmer" or if a woman says "just a housewife," the inference is that the ideological component is weak. As we get nearer to positions of power, however, especially political or ecclesiastical power, the ideological component is likely to be stronger, and for this reason if for no other the ideological tides which have swept across the face of history have had profound consequences for mankind. The history of social systems indeed is largely written in terms of these ideological tides. Buddhism, Christianity, Islam, Communism, and various nationalisms and imperialisms that have swept over parts of the world from time to time, have retreated and advanced, and have profoundly affected the lives of men.

At some periods of history, ideologies have exhibited sharp geographical boundaries and have been dominant in certain areas and almost absent outside them. When this has been the case the competition among ideologies has almost invariably been dangerous and costly, for the commonest way to change a boundary is through war. By contrast, in periods when ideologies have been geographically diffused so that their adherents were geographically intermingled, toleration has generally been forced on them by the sheer fact of physical coexistence, and the conflict among them has been relatively mild. A good example of this proposition can be seen in the conflict between Catholicism and Protestantism. In the fifteenth to sixteenth centuries, when these ideologies were associated with particular nations and states, the conflict between them was costly and bloody indeed. After the peace of Westphalia in 1648 a pattern of coexistence gradually developed until now these ideologies engage mainly in peaceful competition, even though there are some states predominantly Catholic and others predominantly Protestant. In many countries Protestants and Catholics mix in the same society and there are no sharp geographical boundaries which divide them.

We can see immediately that the sharp geographical separation between the Communist world or the socialist camp, as the Communists call themselves, and the self-styled free world presents a grave danger under the present circumstances. Each ideology becomes highly intolerant of the other, and the adherents of each ideology form an alienated minority on one side of the boundary and the dominant power on the other. The danger that ideological conflict may degenerate into war under these circumstances is very great, and as we have seen, war presents the most immediate threat to the achievement of the great transition. Anything which therefore can mitigate or moderate ideological conflict in the present circumstances is so much gain, and anything which intensifies it is a threat to man's future. Therefore an understanding of ideologies, of man's need for them, and of the circumstances under which they can be modified is a crucial component in the achievement of the great transition.

What is it, then, that gives to an image of the world power over a man's mind and that leads him to build his personal identity around it? The answer seems to be that an image of the world becomes an ideology if it creates in the mind of the person holding it a role for himself which he values highly. New ideologies are therefore likely to arise if people feel that the roles which they occupy in the existing society are unsatisfactory to them or despised by others. To create a role, however, an ideology must create a drama. The first essential characteristic of an ideology is then an interpretation of history sufficiently dramatic and convincing so that the individual feels that he can identify with it and which in turn can give the individual a role in the drama it portrays.

Thus Christianity portrays history as a grand drama of the salvation of man by the intervention of God in Christ. The individual by becoming a Christian identifies with this drama and accepts a role in it. Communism likewise portrays history as a great drama of class struggle in which the ultimate triumph of the proletariat will see the end of this process and the establishment of justice upon earth. In becoming a Communist an individual likewise sees himself as performing a role in a drama of large dimensions. It is indeed a smaller scale version of the cosmic drama of the Christian faith.

Going along with an interpretation of history is usually some view of the nature of reality and the sources of knowledge from which the interpretation of history is derived. Furthermore if the individual is to play a role, there must be a value system capable of developing principles of moral action and a standard for the criticism of behavior. The individual must be able to judge when he is performing the role well and when he is performing it badly. An interpretation of history applied to social systems also implies a value system applied to political behavior and decisions. The possessor of an ideology eats of the fruit of the tree of knowledge and is thereby able to distinguish good from evil; he knows who is a bad guy and who is a good guy, and, of course, he is allied with the good guys! Every ideology must have all these elements present to some degree, though there are some ideologies which lay more stress on the interpretation of history and others which lay more stress on the personal role.

An ideology is therefore likely to be a syndrome in the image of the world, if one may borrow a term from medicine. A syndrome is a set of reinforcing symptoms and conditions all of which tend to go together. Similarly in an ideology each part will reinforce the other with an internal logic and consistency. This has a powerful effect in reinforcing belief, for as an individual thinks of one part of ideology his belief in other parts is reinforced. Thus an ideology which states that the world is essentially meaningless but that we ought to strive, suffer, and fight for it is unlikely to be powerful because of the essential contradiction among its components. If an interpretation of history says the world is meaningless, then our value system is likely to be pure hedonism—"Eat, drink, and be merry, for tomorrow we die"—or else one of apathy or stoic resignation.

An ideology by contrast which has a clear image of a significant and exciting future and a clear view of what people have to do in order to achieve this future is likely to be powerful whether or not it is true. There is a great deal indeed in the suggestion made by Fred Polak[1] that the ability of an ideology to organize society depends in large measure on the optimistic or pessimistic quality of its images of the future and on whether it holds that the future can be changed by human activity.

On the other hand if an image of the world is too rational and too consistent it does not become an ideology simply because it does not differentiate the identity of the person holding it from that of anybody else. It would

[1] Fred Polak, *The Image of the Future,* New York, Oceana Press, 1960.

be hard to build an ideology around the multiplication table, for nobody would be against it. Images of the world involving truths which are obvious to all do not become ideologies. It is the half truth, or at least the insecure truth, which appeals to some but not to others, which is the best candidate to set up an ideology. It is frequently the symbols toward which we are ambivalent that have the greatest power over us. The obviously bad we simply reject. The obviously good we simply accept. But it is the things which attract and repel us at the same time that hold us as it were in a bind. The power of Communism among its followers, for instance, arises in part because it combines on the one hand a lofty idealism and a genuine concern for the welfare of mankind, along with the most unprincipled deceit, chicanery, violence, and coercion. The appeal of nationalism likewise rests on a similar ambivalence. The nation is at the same time the protector of widows and the roaster of children—social security and Hiroshima combined in a single body.

An important element in the dynamics of ideological interaction is the ability of an ideology to change without collapsing. Ideologies are always under pressure of some kind, if only because of the contradictions and ambivalences which seem necessarily connected with them. If, for instance, the expectations which it produces are persistently disappointed, the truth of the ideology will be suspect, and once this happens the power of the ideology is bound to wane. It has been said indeed, rather cynically, that an ideology goes through three stages. At first people believe in it, then they believe in believing in it, and then they cease to believe in it. The second stage, however, can last a long time. An ideology which has been successful in organizing a society, and which is associated in the minds of its adherents with persons or events which they admire for reasons quite unconnected with the ideology, may have a long life in the second stage even though the original fire may have gone out of it. There is evidence, for instance, that Communism in Russia has already reached this stage whereas in China it has certainly not.

Sometimes ideologies collapse dramatically. The British imperial ideology, for instance, as represented by Rudyard Kipling, collapsed dramatically between 1910 and 1920—perhaps as a result of the First World War. The *laissez faire* ideology in the United States suffered a certain collapse as a result of the great depression of 1929–33. On the other hand the change of an ideology is not the same thing as the collapse of a society or even of the death of the organization embodied in it. The ideology of both nations and churches change continually, but the organizations continue. This can happen under a legitimate and necessary process of reality testing.

Ideologies in society can also change slowly without collapse and without destructive conflicts. This might be called the process of the dialogue as opposed to the dialectic. In a dialogue or a conversation the image of each participant is continually modified in response to information received from the other. Nobody "wins" a conversation and yet the images of the world may be profoundly modified in it. Therefore the more we can establish dialogue among ideologies the less dangerous the ideological conflict becomes, and the more likely is it to be fruitful and to develop into a true learning process.

The danger of ideology is that it suppresses the learning process. If a man has an ideology which explains everything that happens to him, it relieves him of the necessity for learning. He knows everything already! The great dilemma of ideology therefore is that while it is capable of resolving internal conflict both in the individual and in the society and therefore of generating substantial power and motive force, in the course of generating this powerful engine it is likely to destroy the steering wheel and the compass. That is, it injures the learning process and the process of reality testing which are the only true guides to the *direction* of development. The ideal of course is to combine the powerful engine with the sensitive compass, and develop an image of the world which can provide motivation without impairing the capacity for learning about what is the best direction of change.

With these considerations in mind let us then turn to the ideological struggle of the present day, that between the socialist camp led by the Soviet Union and the market economies led by the United States. Even within these two camps there is of course a great variety of ideological belief and expression. This variety has increased in recent years, especially within the socialist camp, but still there is a great gulf even between the socialist capitalism of Scandinavia and the capitalist socialism of Yugoslavia.

The ideological rift is deep and real, producing societies which are very different in style, flavor, and quality of human life. In the socialist camp, ideology is more clearly formulated and is more an official part of the society. Ideology in the West is vaguer and much more diffused. In this respect the West is "Protestant" whereas the East is "Catholic." From the point of view of the impact of ideology on individual life, the Soviet Union is much more like Spain than it is like the United States. On the other hand, in terms of the practical disposition of its resources and the general character of its people, the Soviet Union is more like the United States than it is like Spain, simply because it is further along toward the great transition.

In view of the immense literature on the subject, it seems presumptuous to attempt to summarize the differences between the two ideologies in a few paragraphs. The essential differences, however, seem to me relatively simple. We shall find indeed that at the level of ultimate values and objectives the two ideologies are much more similar than appears at first sight. The differences arise mainly because of differences in the image of society and social causation, and differences in the assessment of certain instrumental values and institutional arrangements. As we noticed earlier, either ideological disagreements can be at the level of basic values, in which case they are extremely difficult to resolve, or they can be at the level of instrumental values—that is, things which are valued because they are believed to be necessary in order to achieve the basic values. In this latter case the dispute should be much more amenable to scientific testing.

One basic value common to both East and West today might be described as disalienation—that is, the development of a society from which no one will feel or be excluded or alien and in which all will have equal rights and equal privileges, in one at least of the many senses of the word equality. It is only in the backwaters of Western society such as South Africa, Alabama, or Portugal that one finds today any conscious defenders of a society of immobile castes and class stratification. The ethical principle which is at the base of much socialist ideology and which gives it much of its power might be called familism: the idea that all members of society and ultimately all members of the human race are part of a single family and therefore each has responsibility for all. However, this is neither more nor less than the idea of the brotherhood of man long preached and little practiced by all the great world religions. It is a vital part of whatever passes for ideology in the West as well as in the East.

At the instrumental level, however, the ideologies then proceed to divide. The Communist regards the class struggle as the key to history, culminating in the final triumph of the proletariat and the establishment of the classless society under the leadership of an elite and socially aware party. For the Communist it is the private ownership of the means of production which creates the fundamental alienation of the proletariat from the society which is run by the propertied and for the propertied. The only remedy in their eye, therefore, is violent revolution in which the propertied classes are dispossessed and the state as the representative of whole society takes over the ownership and administration of the means of production.

Fitting closely into this interpretation of history is an instrumental ethic which denies all legitimacy to private property, private profit, and the private ownership of capital, an ethic which is given a pseudoscientific sanction by Karl Marx's theory of surplus value. By denying the legitimacy of private profit the socialists largely cut themselves off from the possibility of organizing society through the institution of the market. They are forced then to organize the society through the institution of the national budget or plan. The socialist society then becomes a one-firm state in which the control of all economic activity is concentrated in a single massive organization.

This ideology seems to have very little appeal in the developed countries of the West, where it is confined for the most part to rather small sectarian groups. As development proceeds, the class structure of a society becomes more complex, and the Marxian prediction that the rich will get richer and the poor poorer has been completely falsified. The ownership of property in such a society becomes very widespread even though the bulk of ownership is still concentrated in about 10 per cent of the population. Under these circumstances the class war in Marx's sense becomes rather meaningless, and the political conflicts in society tend to be between occupational or regional groups rather than between classes. The working class indeed becomes a fiction which has no reality either in a common sentiment or common organization. The working class is fragmented into innumerable regional and occupational groups, and national consciousness becomes stronger than class consciousness. The movement toward the classless society or at least toward the integrated society then takes place not through revolution, or indeed through any dialectical process, but through a process of political dialogue, compromise, and the sheer working out of the social consequences of a long-continued process of economic growth. In the developed capitalist countries a true proletariat still exists, but it has become a minority, and furthermore, unfortunately, an impotent minority.

Under these circumstances Marx's interpretation of history simply ceases to have much meaning, and the attempt to force history into a dialectical form results merely in hairsplitting and intellectual dishonesty. The Communist party discredits itself simply because it does not speak to the needs of the society around it. It is working with a model of society which may be applicable in some times and places but which is by no means universal, and which is particularly inapplicable to the circumstances of a society enjoying rapid development under the market institutions.

Just as the class struggle and the dialectical interpretation of history evoke little response in a society which is obviously going another way, so the theory of surplus value and the attack on profit as such, or on private ownership in the means of production as such, fall on deaf ears. The organized working class perceives that its main line of advancement is through the exercise of market power. This is the essence of what is called business unionism. The industrial worker indeed, who was seen by Marx as the man of the future, rapidly becomes the man of the past. Every increase in technological efficiency reduces the proportion of population in this category and increases the proportion in professional, managerial, and service occupations. The industrial worker therefore gets too rich and scarce to function as the Marxian proletariat, and has very little incentive or opportunity to foment a revolution. If, however, he perceives his main avenue to advancement as a rise in wages, he becomes committed to the market system, and the market system is unworkable without private property and private profit. The labor movement therefore becomes a conservative force and a strong defender of the market economy, even to the extent of supporting the basic institutions of capitalism.

Under the circumstances where the market economy is obviously providing constantly increasing real income for all, the "one-firm state" of the socialist then looks like a monstrous concentration of economic and political power designed mainly to exploit the working class in the interest of the state itself, and completely defenseless against capture by ruthless dictators. Marx's description of the state as a committee of the bourgeoisie seems fantastically inappropriate to, say, the American federal government as we know it in the twentieth century. Popular nationalism indeed has turned out to be a far more powerful integrating force in society than either the unity of the working class under socialism (or for that matter Christianity or any other religion) as indeed the current split between Russia and China demonstrates. The Soviet Union was simply not prepared to sacrifice its own development for the sake of assisting Chinese development. The unity of the working class is clearly a myth, even within the socialist camp. Had it really existed the Soviet Union would have made massive sacrifices in order to assist the Chinese in their development. As it was, all the Soviet Union did for China was to grant a loan—at interest—amounting to about ten cents per Chinese per year, and to send a few technicians who were suddenly withdrawn with disastrous consequences in 1960. The Russians are Russians and the Chinese are Chinese long before they are either proletarian or socialist. The gap between the rich countries and the poor is much wider and more important than any gap between the rich and the poor within any one country, especially within any one developed country.

The successes of Communism are due to an aspect of its ideology which is quite separable from the foregoing. This is its explicit recognition of the nature of economic development and its self-conscious orientation toward it. The great transition in the West has taken place as a result largely of ecological forces, and without much conscious planning until recently. The Industrial Revolution in England certainly began and got under way not as a result of any conscious efforts on the part of the government or even of any individual who participated in it, but because of the interaction of individual decisions and certain latent forces in the society.

Following the publication of the *Wealth of Nations* by Adam Smith in 1776 the Western European countries and especially the United States became more self-conscious about the process of economic development, and indeed from that point on the development of these countries is much less accidental than it might look at first sight. The development of the United States especially was guided throughout by a policy which was quite self-conscious in its emphasis on the role of the market mechanism and also was not adverse to interfering with that mechanism by protective tariffs in the supposed interest of economic development. Nevertheless it is fair to say that the Communists have been more self-conscious about economic development than the countries of the West, and that the success of Communism where it has been successful is mainly a result of the willingness of these societies to put large amounts of resources into the growth industries, especially into education and capital goods. This has often been done inefficiently, and with great human cost, mainly because of the prejudice which these societies have against the market mechanism. If a society puts a lot of resources into growth, however, even though it does this very inefficiently, it is bound to grow.

The point at issue here is whether the market mechanism or the budget mechanism is the more developed form of social organization, and this seems to be a clear case in which dialogue is much more fruitful than a dialectical confrontation. The ideological crystallization into the two camps tends to prevent rational discussion of this problem on both sides of the real issue—which is that of the optimum mix of the market and budget mechanism in any particular society. The extreme positions on both sides seem to be untenable. The claim of the extreme advocates of *laissez faire* that the market mechanism is sufficient to do all the jobs required of society has been clearly discredited by many occasions on which the market machinery has proved inadequate. There are some wants, like that for sexual satisfaction, in which the market machinery is regarded as illegitimate; there are public goods for the provision of which the market machinery is inappropriate; and there is a basic necessity in society for supervising the market machinery to see that it does not get out of hand and give us depressions, inflations, or unacceptable distributions of income. Furthermore the demands of familistic ethics even in a market society require the existence of a grants economy to provide for both people and functions for which the market does not make adequate provision.

On the other hand the socialist economies are severely handicapped by their refusal to make rational use of the price system and of private property and private profit. The grudging acceptance of these institutions at the margins of a society, for instance in the New Economic Policy of the 1920's, or in the peasant plots and city markets of the later periods, unquestionably contributed to the survival of the Soviet society, but the prejudices of the ideology prohibit any rational examination of the proper social role of free markets. In what might be called the halfhearted socialist societies like Ceylon, Burma, and Indonesia, the "mix" seems to be almost the worst possible, combining the socialist disorganization of the market economy with *laissez faire* in the matter of allocating resources to growth!

In the light of the great transition the whole ideological struggle between capitalism and socialism takes on a certain air of irrelevance. It is clear by this time that development can take place under socialism. It is equally clear that it can also take place under capitalism, and that if it does take place successfully under capitalism, socialism becomes largely irrelevant to these societies at least in the sense of totalitarian socialism as we know it in the Communist countries. I have expressed this in what I call the doctrine of the missed bus. The bus for socialism comes along only at one stage of economic development. This is the early stage of capitalist development, when there is still a large proletarian working class, when there are still large inequalities of income, when development perhaps is concentrated in certain cities or areas of the society so that sharp disparities of income appear between the developed sectors and the undeveloped sectors, and when there are enough remains of feudal institutions and attitudes around to make the concept of class structure and class war look fairly realistic. Under these circumstances the Marxist ideology has a considerable appeal, and if this appeal has been heard by a small group of intellectuals who form a party, then especially if there is some internal upheaval such as a war or a spontaneous revolution, the party can capture the revolution, push the society into the socialist bus, and off it goes. Once in the socialist bus it is pretty hard for the society to get off it, and its development will follow a rather different path from then on.

If, however, the society misses the bus for one reason or another, either because a revolutionary situation never develops, or because it develops before the self-conscious party has developed, and if then the society enjoys a successful process of capitalist or market development, the socialist bus never comes by again, and the socialist solution becomes less and less relevant. In the Western European countries 1848 may well have been the moment at which, if there had been a Communist party, it might have taken over. This, however, was too early. The Communist Manifesto was not enough to create a party. This had to wait for *Das Kapital* and almost two generations of socialist atheologians. In the United States it is doubtful whether the bus ever came by at all. There was that moment in 1932 when it might also have been seen far down the street. Even then, at the height of depression, the Communists never became more than a modest threat. They failed to capture the imagination of the Negroes, with whom some success might have been expected, and their behavior gradually discredited them in the labor movement, from which they have been eventually expelled.

The ideological struggle is so dangerous today mainly because a large part of the world is still at the stage where the socialist bus has not yet come along, and the question is therefore open as to whether these societies will proceed in their development along totalitarian socialist lines or along the lines of what might be called the guided market economy. If the choice is between totalitarian socialist development and development under a successfully guided market economy the answer would be pretty clear. Totalitarian social development is a very high-cost form. It has a high cost in terms of refugees, in terms of terror and violence, in terms of propaganda, manipulation, lies, and the corruption of artistic and intellectual life. A nontotalitarian socialist development is not inconceivable. The closest approximation of this is unquestionably Poland, where a great deal of intellectual and artistic liberty coexists with socialist planning. Up to now, however, the brute fact is that almost all socialist development has been totalitarian and has been made at a very high cost in human suffering and human corruption.

We must not blind ourselves, however, to the fact that all development has a cost, and that unsuccessful capitalist development of the sort that can be seen in Africa, Asia, or some Latin American countries likewise has a high human cost—as high as, if not higher than, the human cost of totalitarian socialism. On the whole I am inclined to think of these cases as totalitarian capitalist development, and all the evidence points to the fact that it is the totalitarian element in the society, the reliance on the short cut of violence and coercion, which leads to the high cost. The sensible thing to look for, however, is development at least cost, and what the least cost is in any society is likely to be a function of its previous institutions. We cannot lay down any hard and fast rules as to what the mix should be between market and budget elements. I am inclined to the paradox that in a society in which the noneconomic elements in life have a strong familistic or socialist character the institutions of capitalism and the market economy will work very well because they are constantly guided and checked by the "socialist" ethic. I would cite the United States as a good case in point. On the other hand in societies where the sense of community is weak and where the sense of the responsibility of each for all is poorly developed, the institutions of capitalism can be quite corrupting. China before the revolution may well be an example. If we are to achieve a least-cost transition we must stop dichotomizing the world and develop a pragmatic, indeed a social scientific approach to the problem.

Therefore, if there is any ideology peculiarly appropriate to the achievement of the transition it is neither capitalism nor socialism but the scientific ideology itself applied to society. An ideology for the great transition must then be a strategy rather than an ideology. . . .

MENDING WALL

Robert Frost

Something there is that doesn't love a wall,
That sends the frozen-ground-swell under it
And spills the upper boulders in the sun,
And makes gaps even two can pass abreast.
The work of hunters is another thing:
I have come after them and made repair
Where they have left not one stone on a stone,
But they would have the rabbit out of hiding,
To please the yelping dogs. The gaps I mean,
No one has seen them made or heard them made,
But at spring mending-time we find them there.
I let my neighbor know beyond the hill;
And on a day we meet to walk the line
And set the wall between us once again.
We keep the wall between us as we go.
To each the boulders that have fallen to each.
And some are loaves and some so nearly balls
We have to use a spell to make them balance:
"Stay where you are until our backs are turned!"
We wear our fingers rough with handling them.
Oh, just another kind of outdoor game,
One on a side. It comes to little more:
There where it is we do not need the wall:
He is all pine and I am apple orchard.
My apple trees will never get across
And eat the cones under his pines, I tell him.
He only says, "Good fences make good neighbors."
Spring is the mischief in me, and I wonder
If I could put a notion in his head:
"*Why* do they make good neighbors? Isn't it
Where there are cows? But here there are no cows.
Before I built a wall I'd ask to know

What I was walling in or walling out,
And to whom I was like to give offense.
Something there is that doesn't love a wall,
That wants it down." I could say "Elves" to him,
But it's not elves exactly, and I'd rather
He said it for himself. I see him there,
Bringing a stone grasped firmly by the top
In each hand, like an old-stone savage armed.
He moves in darkness as it seems to me,
Not of woods only and the shade of trees.
He will not go behind his father's saying,
And he likes having thought of it so well
He says again, "Good fences make good neighbors."

HUMAN SACRIFICES FOR THE CROPS

Sir James G. Frazer

The Indians of Guayaquil, in Ecuador, used to sacrifice human blood and the hearts of men when they sowed their fields. The people of Cañar (now Cuenca in Ecuador) used to sacrifice a hundred children annually at harvest. The kings of Quito, the Incas of Peru, and for a long time the Spaniards were unable to suppress the bloody rite. At a Mexican harvest-festival, when the first-fruits of the season were offered to the sun, a criminal was placed between two immense stones, balanced opposite each other, and was crushed by them as they fell together. His remains were buried, and a feast and dance followed. This sacrifice was known as "the meeting of the stones." We have seen that the ancient Mexicans also sacrificed human beings at all the various stages in the growth of the maize, the age of the victims corresponding to the age of the corn; for they sacrificed new-born babes at sowing, older children when the grain had sprouted, and so on till it was fully ripe, when they sacrificed old men. No doubt the correspondence between the ages of the victims and the state of the corn was supposed to enhance the efficacy of the sacrifice.

The Pawnees annually sacrificed a human victim in spring when they sowed their fields. The sacrifice was believed to have been enjoined on them by the Morning Star, or by a certain bird which the Morning Star had sent to them as its messenger. The bird was stuffed and preserved as a powerful talisman. They thought that an omission of this sacrifice would be followed by the total failure of the crops of maize, beans, and pumpkins. The victim was a captive of either sex. He was clad in the gayest and most costly attire, was fattened on the choicest food, and carefully kept in ignorance of his doom. When he was fat enough, they bound him to a cross in the presence of the multitude, danced a solemn dance, then cleft his head with a tomahawk and shot him with arrows. According to one trader, the squaws then cut pieces of flesh from the victim's body, with which they greased their hoes; but this was denied by another trader who had been present at the ceremony. Immediately after the sacrifice the people proceeded to plant their fields. A particular account has been preserved of the sacrifice of a Sioux girl by the Pawnees in April 1837 or 1838. The girl was fourteen or fifteen years old and had been kept for six months and well treated. Two days before the sacrifice she was led from wigwam to wigwam, accompanied by the whole council of chiefs and warriors. At each lodge she received a small billet of wood and a little paint, which she handed to the warrior next to her. In this way she called at every wigwam, receiving at each the same present of wood and paint. On the twenty-second of April she was taken out to be sacrificed, attended by the warriors, each of whom carried two pieces of wood which he had received from her hands. Her body having been painted half red and half black, she was attached to a sort of gibbet and roasted for some time over a slow fire, then shot to death with arrows. The chief sacrificer next tore out her heart and devoured it. While her flesh was still warm it was cut in small pieces from the bones, put in little baskets, and taken to a neighbouring corn-field. There the head chief took a piece of the flesh from a basket and squeezed a drop of blood upon the newly-deposited grains of corn. His example was followed by the rest, till all the seed had been sprinkled with the blood; it was then covered up with earth. According to one account the body of the victim was reduced to a kind of paste, which was rubbed or sprinkled not only on the maize but also on the potatoes, the beans, and other seeds to fertilise them. By this sacrifice they hoped to obtain plentiful crops.

A West African queen used to sacrifice a man and a woman in the month of March. They were killed with spades and hoes, and their bodies buried in the middle of a field which had just been tilled. At Lagos in Guinea it was the custom annually to impale a young girl alive soon after the spring equinox in order to secure good crops. Along with her were sacrificed sheep and goats, which, with yams, heads of maize, and plantains, were hung on stakes on each side of her. The victims were bred up for the purpose in the king's seraglio, and their minds had been so powerfully wrought upon by the fetish men that they went cheerfully to their fate. A similar sacrifice used to be annually offered at Benin, in Guinea. The Marimos, a Bechuana tribe, sacrifice a human being for the crops. The victim chosen is generally a short, stout man. He is seized by violence or intoxicated and taken to the fields, where he is killed amongst the wheat to serve as "seed" (so they phrase it). After his blood has coagulated in the sun, it is burned along with the frontal bone, the flesh attached to it, and the brain; the ashes are then scattered over the ground to fertilise it. The rest of the body is eaten.

The Bagobos of Mindanao, one of the Philippine Islands, offer a human sacrifice before they sow their rice. The victim is a slave, who is hewn to pieces in the forest. The natives of Bontoc in the interior of Luzon, one of the Philippine Islands, are passionate head-hunters. Their principal seasons for head-hunting are the times of planting and reaping the rice. In order that the crop may turn out well, every farm must get at least one human head at planting and one at sowing. The head-hunters go out in twos and threes, lie in wait for the victim, whether man or woman, cut off his or her head, hands, and feet, and bring them back in haste to the village, where they are received with great rejoicings. The skulls are at first exposed on the branches of two or three dead trees which stand in an open space of every village surrounded by large stones which serve as seats. The people then dance round them and feast and get drunk. When the flesh has decayed from the head, the man who cut it off takes it home and preserves it as a relic, while his companions do the same with the hands and the feet. Similar customs are observed by the Apoyaos, another tribe in the interior of Luzon.

Among the Lhota Naga, one of the many savage tribes who inhabit the deep rugged labyrinthine glens which wind into the mountains from the rich valley of Brahmapootra, it used to be a common custom to chop off the heads, hands, and feet of people they met with, and then to stick up the severed extremities in their fields to ensure a good crop of grain. They bore no ill-will whatever to the persons upon whom they operated in this unceremonious fashion. Once they flayed a boy alive, carved him in pieces, and distributed the flesh among all the villagers, who put it into their corn-bins to avert bad luck and ensure plentiful crops of grain. The Gonds of India, a Dravidian race, kidnapped Brahman boys, and kept them as victims to be sacrificed on various occasions. At sowing and reaping, after a triumphal procession, one of the lads was slain by being punctured with a poisoned arrow. His blood was then sprinkled over the ploughed field or the ripe crop, and his flesh was devoured. The Oraons or Uraons of Chota Nagpur worship a goddess called Anna Kuari, who can give good crops and make a man rich, but to induce her to do so it is necessary to offer human sacrifices. In spite of the vigilance of the British Government these sacrifices are said to be still secretly perpetrated. The victims are poor waifs and strays whose disappearance attracts no notice. April and May are the months when the catchpoles are out on the prowl. At that time strangers will not go about the country alone, and parents will not let their children enter the jungle or herd the cattle. When a catchpole has found a victim, he cuts his throat and carries away the upper part of the ring finger and the nose. The goddess takes up her abode in the house of any man who has offered her a sacrifice, and from that time his fields yield a double harvest. The form she assumes in the house is that of a small child. When the householder brings in his unhusked rice, he takes the goddess and rolls her over the heap to double its size. But she soon grows restless and can only be pacified with the blood of fresh human victims.

But the best known case of human sacrifices, systematically offered to ensure good crops, is supplied by the Khonds or Kandhs, another Dravidian race in Bengal. Our knowledge of them is derived from the accounts written by British officers who, about the middle of the nineteenth century, were engaged in putting them down. The sacrifices were offered to the Earth Goddess, Tari Pennu or Bera Pennu, and were believed to ensure good crops and immunity from all disease and accidents. In particular, they were considered necessary in the cultivation of turmeric, the Khonds arguing that the turmeric could not have a deep red colour without the shedding of blood. The victim or Meriah, as he was called, was acceptable to the goddess only if he had been purchased, or had been born a victim—that is, the son of a victim father, or had been devoted as a child by his father or guardian. Khonds in distress often sold their children for victims, "considering the beatification of their souls certain, and their death, for the benefit of mankind, the most honourable possible." A man of the Panua tribe was once seen to load a Khond with curses, and finally to spit in his face, because the Khond had sold for a victim his own child whom the Panua had wished to marry. A party of Khonds, who saw this, immediately pressed forward to comfort the seller of his child, saying, "Your child has died that all the world may live, and the Earth Goddess herself will wipe the spittle from your face." The victims were often kept for years before they were sacrificed. Being regarded as consecrated beings, they were treated with extreme affection, mingled with deference, and were welcomed wherever they went. A Meriah youth, on attaining maturity, was generally given a wife, who was herself usually a Meriah or victim; and with her he received a portion of land and farm-stock. Their offspring were also victims. Human sacrifices were offered to the Earth Goddess by tribes, branches of tribes, or villages, both at periodical festivals and on extraordinary occasions. The periodical sacrifices were generally so arranged by tribes and divisions of tribes that each head of a family was enabled, at least once a year, to procure a shred of flesh for his fields, generally about the time his chief crop was laid down.

The mode of performing these tribal sacrifices was as follows. Ten or twelve days before the sacrifice, the victim was devoted by cutting off his hair, which, until then, had been kept unshorn. Crowds of men and women assembled to witness the sacrifice; none might be excluded, since the sacrifice was declared to be for all mankind. It was preceded by several days of wild revelry and gross debauchery. On the days before the sacrifice the victim, dressed in a new garment, was led forth from the village in solemn procession, with music and dancing, to the Meriah grove, a clump of high forest trees standing a little way from the village and untouched by the axe. There they tied him to a post, which was sometimes placed between two plants of the sankissar shrub. He was then anointed with oil, ghee, and turmeric, and adorned with flowers; and "a species of reverence, which it is not easy to distinguish from adoration," was paid to him throughout the day. A great struggle now arose to obtain the smallest relic from his person; a particle of the turmeric paste with which he was smeared, or a drop of his spittle, was esteemed of sovereign virtue, especially by the women. The crowd danced round the post to music, and, addressing the earth, said, "O God, we offer this sacrifice to you; give us good crops, seasons, and health"; then speaking to the victim they said, "We bought you with a price, and did not seize you; now we sacrifice you according to custom, and no sin rests with us."

On the last morning the orgies, which had been scarcely interrupted during the night, were resumed, and continued till noon, when they ceased, and the assembly proceeded to consummate the sacrifice. The victim was again anointed with oil, and each person touched the anointed part, and wiped the oil on his own head. In some places they took the victim in procession round the village, from door to door, where some plucked hair from his head, and others begged for a drop of his spittle, with which they anointed their heads. As the victim might not be bound nor make any show of resistance, the bones of his arms and, if necessary, his legs were broken; but often this precaution was rendered unnecessary by stupefying him with opium. The mode of putting him to death varied in different places. One of the commonest modes seems to have been strangulation, or squeezing to death. The branch of a green tree was cleft several feet down the middle; the victim's neck (in other places, his chest) was inserted in the cleft, which the priest, aided by his assistants, strove with all his force to close. Then he wounded the victim slightly with his axe, whereupon the crowd rushed at the wretch and hewed the flesh from the bones, leaving the head and bowels untouched. Sometimes he was cut up alive. In Chinna Kimedy he was dragged along the fields, surrounded by the crowd, who, avoiding his head and intestines, hacked the flesh from his body with their knives till he died. Another very common mode of sacrifice in the same district was to fasten the victim to the proboscis of a wooden elephant, which revolved on a stout post, and, as it whirled round, the crowd cut the flesh from the victim while life remained. In some villages Major Campbell found as many as fourteen of these wooden elephants, which had been used at sacrifices. In one district the victim was put to death slowly by fire. A low stage was formed, sloping on either side like a roof; upon it they laid the victim, his limbs wound round with cords to confine his struggles. Fires were then lighted and hot brands applied, to make him roll up and down the slopes of the stage as long as possible; for the more tears he shed the more abundant would be the supply of rain. Next day the body was cut to pieces.

The flesh cut from the victim was instantly taken home by the persons who had been deputed by each village to bring it. To secure its rapid arrival, it was sometimes forwarded by relays of men, and conveyed with postal fleetness fifty or sixty miles. In each village all who stayed at home fasted rigidly until the flesh arrived. The bearer deposited it in the place of public assembly, where it was received by the priest and the heads of families. The priest divided it into two portions, one of which he offered to the Earth Goddess by burying it in a hole in the ground with his back turned, and without looking. Then each man added a little earth to bury it, and the priest poured water on the spot from a hill gourd. The other portion of flesh he divided into as many shares as there were heads of houses present. Each head of a house rolled his shred of flesh in leaves, and buried it in his favourite field, placing it in the earth behind his back without looking. In some places each man carried his portion of flesh to the stream which watered his fields, and there hung it on a pole. For three days thereafter no house was swept; and, in one district, strict silence was observed, no fire might be given out, no wood cut, and no strangers received. The remains of the human victim (namely, the head, bowels, and bones) were watched by strong parties the night after the sacrifice; and next morning they were burned, along with a whole sheep, on a funeral pile. The ashes were scattered over the fields, laid as paste over the houses and granaries, or mixed with the new corn to preserve it from insects. Sometimes, however, the head and bones were buried, not burnt. After the suppression of the human sacrifices, inferior victims were substituted in some places; for instance, in the capital of Chinna Kimedy a goat took the place of the human victim. Others sacrifice a buffalo. They tie it to a wooden post in a sacred grove, dance wildly round it with brandished knives, then, falling on the living animal, hack it to shreds and tatters in a few minutes, fighting and struggling with each other for every particle of flesh. As soon as a man has secured a piece he makes off with it at full speed to bury it in his fields, according to ancient custom, before the sun has set, and as some of them have far to go they must run very fast. All the women throw clods of earth at the rapidly retreating figures of the men, some of them taking very good aim. Soon the sacred grove, so lately a scene of tumult, is silent and deserted except for a few people who remain to guard all that is left of the buffalo, to wit, the head, the bones, and the stomach, which are burned with ceremony at the foot of the stake.

In these Khond sacrifices the Meriahs are represented by our authorities as victims offered to propitiate the Earth Goddess. But from the treatment of the victims both before and after death it appears that the custom cannot be explained as merely a propitiatory sacrifice. A part of the flesh certainly was offered to the Earth Goddess, but the rest was buried by each householder in his fields, and the ashes of the other parts of the body were scattered over the fields, laid as paste on the granaries, or mixed with the new corn. These latter customs imply that to the body of the Meriah there was ascribed a direct or intrinsic power of making the crops to grow, quite independent of the indirect efficacy which it might have as an offering to secure the good-will of the deity. In other words, the flesh and ashes of the victim were believed to be endowed with a magical or physical power of fertilising the land. The same intrinsic power was ascribed to the blood and tears of the Meriah, his blood causing the redness of the turmeric and his tears producing rain; for it can hardly be doubted that, originally at least, the tears were supposed to bring down the rain, not merely to prognosticate it. Similarly the custom of pouring water on the buried flesh of the Meriah was no doubt a rain-charm. Again, magical power as an attribute of the Meriah appears in the sovereign virtue believed to reside in anything that came from his person, as his hair or spittle. The ascription of such power to the Meriah indicates that he was much more than a mere man sacrificed to propitiate a deity. Once more, the extreme reverence paid him points to the same conclusion. Major Campbell speaks of the Meriah as "being regarded as something more than mortal," and Major Macpherson says, "A species of reverence, which it is not easy to distinguish from adoration, is paid to him." In short, the Meriah seems to have been regarded as divine. As such, he may originally have represented the Earth Goddess or, perhaps, a deity of vegetation; though in later times he came to be regarded rather as a victim offered to a deity than as himself an incarnate god. This later view of the Meriah as a victim rather than a divinity may perhaps have received undue emphasis from the European writers who have described the Khond religion. Habituated to the later idea of sacrifice as an offering made to a god for the purpose of conciliating his favour, European observers are apt to interpret all religious slaughter in this sense, and to suppose that wherever such slaughter takes places, there must necessarily be a deity to whom the carnage is believed by the slayers to be acceptable. Thus their preconceived ideas may unconsciously colour and warp their descriptions of savage rites.

The same custom of killing the representative of a god, of which strong traces appear in the Khond sacrifices, may perhaps be detected in some of the other human sacrifices described above. Thus the ashes of the slaughtered Marimo were scattered over the fields; the blood of the Brahman lad was put on the crop and field; the flesh of the slain Naga was stowed in the corn-bin; and the blood of the Sioux girl was allowed to trickle on the seed. Again, the identification of the victim with the corn, in other words, the view that he is an embodiment or spirit of the corn, is brought out in the pains which seem to be taken to secure a physical correspondence between him and the natural object which he embodies or represents. Thus the Mexicans killed young victims for the young corn and old ones for the ripe corn; the Marimos sacrifice, as "seed," a short, fat man, the shortness of his stature corresponding to that of the young corn, his fatness to the condition which it is desired that the crops may attain; and the Pawnees fattened their victims probably with the same view. Again, the identification of the victim with the corn comes out in the African custom of killing him with spades and hoes, and the Mexican custom of grinding him, like corn, between two stones.

One more point in these savage customs deserves to be noted. The Pawnee chief devoured the heart of the Sioux girl, and the Marimos and Gonds ate the victim's flesh. If, as we suppose, the victim was regarded as divine, it follows that in eating his flesh his worshippers believed themselves to be partaking of the body of their god.

THE LOTTERY

Shirley Jackson

The morning of June 27th was clear and sunny, with the fresh warmth of a full-summer day; the flowers were blossoming profusely and the grass was richly green. The people of the village began to gather in the square, between the post office and the bank, around ten o'clock; in some towns there were so many people that the lottery took two days and had to be started on June 26th, but in this village, where there were only about three hundred people, the whole lottery took less than two hours, so it could begin at ten o'clock in the morning and still be through in time to allow the villagers to get home for noon dinner.

The children assembled first, of course. School was recently over for the summer, and the feeling of liberty sat uneasily on most of them; they tended to gather together quietly for a while before they broke into boisterous play, and their talk was still of the classroom and the teacher, of books and reprimands. Bobby Martin had already stuffed his pockets full of stones, and the other boys soon followed his example, selecting the smoothest and roundest stones; Bobby and Harry Jones and Dickie Delacroix—the villagers pronounced this name "Dellacroy"—eventually made a great pile of stones in one corner of the square and guarded it against the raids of the other boys. The girls stood aside, talking among themselves, looking over their shoulders at the boys, and the very small children rolled in the dust or clung to the hands of their older brothers or sisters.

Soon the men began to gather, surveying their own children, speaking of planting and rain, tractors and taxes. They stood together, away from the pile of stones in the corner, and their jokes were quiet and they smiled rather than laughed. The women, wearing faded house dresses and sweaters, came shortly after their menfolk. They greeted one another and exchanged bits of gossip as they went to join their husbands. Soon the women, standing by their husbands, began to call to their children, and the children came reluctantly, having to be called four or five times. Bobby Martin ducked under his mother's grasping hand and ran, laughing, back to the pile of stones. His father spoke up sharply, and Bobby came quickly and took his place between his father and his oldest brother.

The lottery was conducted—as were the square dances, the teen-age club, the Halloween program—by Mr. Summers, who had time and energy to devote to civic activities. He was a round-faced, jovial man and he ran the coal business, and people were sorry for him, because he had no children and his wife was a scold. When he arrived in the square, carrying the black wooden box, there was a murmur of conversation among the villagers, and he waved and called, "Little late today, folks." The postmaster, Mr. Graves followed him, carrying a three-legged stool, and the stool was put in the center of the square and Mr. Summers set the black box down on it. The villagers kept their distance, leaving a space between themselves and the stool, and when Mr. Summers said, "Some of you fellows want to give me a hand?" there was a hesitation before two men, Mr. Martin and his oldest son, Baxter, came forward to hold the box steady on the stool while Mr. Summers stirred up the papers inside it.

The original paraphernalia for the lottery had been lost long ago, and the black box now resting on the stool had been put into use even before Old Man Warner, the oldest man in town, was born. Mr. Summers spoke frequently to the villagers about making a new box, but no one liked to upset even as much tradition as was represented by the black box. There was a story that the present box had been made with some pieces of the box that had preceded it, the one that had been constructed when the first people settled down to make a village here. Every year, after the lottery, Mr. Summers began talking again about a new box, but every year the subject was allowed to fade off without anything's being done. The black box grew shabbier each year; by now it was no longer completely black but splintered badly along one side to show the original wood color, and in some places faded or stained.

Mr. Martin and his oldest son, Baxter, held the black box securely on the stool until Mr. Summers had stirred the papers thoroughly with his hand. Because so much of the ritual had been forgotten or discarded, Mr. Summers had been successful in having slips of paper substituted for the chips of wood that had been used for generations. Chips of wood, Mr. Summers had argued, had been all very well when the village was tiny, but now that the population was more than three hundred and likely to keep on growing, it was necessary to use something that would fit more easily into the black box. The night before the lottery, Mr. Summers and Mr. Graves made up the slips of paper and put them in the box, and it was then taken to the safe of Mr. Summers' coal company and locked up until Mr. Summers was ready to take it to the square next morning. The rest of the year, the box was put away, sometimes one place, sometimes another; it had spent one year in Mr. Graves's barn and another year underfoot in the post office, and sometimes it was set on a shelf in the Martin grocery and left there.

There was a great deal of fussing to be done before Mr. Summers declared the lottery open. There were the lists to make up—of heads of families, heads of households in each family, members of each household in each family. There was the proper swearing-in of Mr. Summers by the postmaster as the official of the lottery; at one time, some people remembered, there had been a recital of some sort, performed by the official of the lottery, a perfunctory, tuneless chant that had been rattled off duly each year; some people believed that the official of the lottery used to stand just so when he said or sang it, others believed that he was supposed to walk among the people, but years and years ago this part of the ritual had been allowed to lapse. There had been, also, a ritual salute, which the official of the lottery had had to use in addressing each person who came up to draw from the box, but this also had changed with time, until now it was felt necessary only for the official to speak to each person approaching. Mr. Summers was very good at all this; in his clean white shirt and blue jeans, with one hand resting carelessly on the black box, he seemed very proper and important as he talked interminably to Mr. Graves and the Martins.

Just as Mr. Summers finally left off talking and turned to the assembled villagers, Mrs. Hutchinson came hurriedly along the path to the square, her sweater thrown over her shoulders, and slid into place in the back of the crowd. "Clean forgot what day it was," she said to Mrs. Delacroix, who stood next to her, and they both laughed softly. "Thought my old man was out back stacking wood," Mrs. Hutchinson went on, "and then I looked out the window and the kids were gone, and then I remembered it was the twenty-seventh and came a-running." She dried her hands on her apron, and Mrs. Delacroix said, "You're in time, though. They're still talking away up there."

Mrs. Hutchinson craned her neck to see through the crowd and found her husband and children standing near the front. She tapped Mrs. Delacroix on the arm as a farewell and began to make her way through the crowd. The people separated good-humoredly to let her through; two or three people said, in voices just loud enough to be heard across the crowd, "Here comes your Missus, Hutchinson," and "Bill, she made it after all." Mrs. Hutchinson reached her husband, and Mr. Summers, who had been waiting, said cheerfully, "Thought we were going to have to get on without you, Tessie." Mrs. Hutchinson said, grinning, "Wouldn't have me leave m'dishes in the sink, now, would you, Joe?" and soft laughter ran through the crowd as the people stirred back into position after Mrs. Hutchinson's arrival.

"Well, now," Mr. Summers said soberly, "guess we better get started, get this over with, so's we can go back to work. Anybody ain't here?"

"Dunbar," several people said. "Dunbar, Dunbar."

Mr. Summers consulted his list. "Clyde Dunbar," he said. "That's right. He's broke his leg, hasn't he? Who's drawing for him?"

"Me, I guess," a woman said, and Mr. Summers turned to look at her. "Wife draws for her husband," Mr. Summers said. "Don't you have a grown boy to do it for you, Janey?" Although Mr. Summers and everyone else in the village knew the answer perfectly well, it was the business of the official of the lottery to ask such questions formally. Mr. Summers waited with an expression of polite interest while Mrs. Dunbar answered.

"Horace's not but sixteen yet," Mrs. Dunbar said regretfully. "Guess I gotta fill in for the old man this year."

"Right," Mr. Summers said. He made a note on the list he was holding. Then he asked, "Watson boy drawing this year?"

A tall boy in the crowd raised his hand. "Here," he said. "I'm drawing for m'mother and me." He blinked his eyes nervously and ducked his head as several voices in the crowd said things like "Good fellow, Jack," and "Glad to see your mother's got a man to do it."

"Well," Mr. Summers said, "guess that's everyone. Old Man Warner make it?"

"Here," a voice said, and Mr. Summers nodded.

A sudden hush fell on the crowd as Mr. Summers cleared his throat and looked at the list. "All ready?" he called. "Now, I'll read the names—heads of families first—and the men come up and take a paper out of the box. Keep the paper folded in your hand without looking at it until everyone has had a turn. Everything clear?"

The people had done it so many times that they only half listened to the directions; most of them were quiet, wetting their lips, not looking around. Then Mr. Summers raised one hand high and said, "Adams." A man disengaged himself from the crowd and came forward. "Hi, Steve," Mr. Summers said, and Mr. Adams said, "Hi, Joe." They grinned at one another humorlessly and nervously. Then Mr. Adams reached into the black box and took out a folded paper. He held it firmly by one corner as he turned and went hastily back to his place in the crowd, where he stood a little apart from his family, not looking down at his hand.

"Allen," Mr. Summers said. "Anderson . . . Bentham."

"Seems like there's no time at all between lotteries any more," Mrs. Delacroix said to Mrs. Graves in the back row. "Seems like we got through with the last one only last week."

"Time sure goes fast," Mrs. Graves said.

"Clark . . . Delacroix."

"There goes my old man," Mrs. Delacroix said. She held her breath while her husband went forward.

"Dunbar," Mr. Summer and Mrs. Dunbar went steadily to the box while one of the women said, "Go on, Janey," and another said, "There she goes."

"We're next," Mrs. Graves said. She watched while Mr. Graves came around from the side of the box, greeted Mr. Summers gravely, and selected a slip of paper from the box. By now, all through the crowd there were men holding the small folded papers in their large hands, turning them over and over nervously. Mrs. Dunbar and her two sons stood together, Mrs. Dunbar holding the slip of paper.

"Harburt . . . Hutchinson."

"Get up there, Bill," Mrs. Hutchinson said, and the people near her laughed.

"Jones."

"They do say," Mr. Adams said to Old Man Warner, who stood next to him, "that over in the north village they're talking of giving up the lottery."

Old Man Warner snorted. "Pack of crazy fools," he said. "Listening to the young folks, nothing's good enough for *them*. Next thing you know, they'll be wanting to go back to living in caves, nobody work any more, live that way for a while. Used to be a saying about 'Lottery in June, corn be heavy soon.' First thing you know, we'd all be eating stewed chickweed and acorns. There's *always* been a lottery," he added petulantly. "Bad enough to see young Joe Summers up there joking with everybody."

"Some places have already quit lotteries," Mrs. Adams said.

"Nothing but trouble in *that,*" Old Man Warner said stoutly. "Pack of young fools."

"Martin." And Bobby Martin watched his father go forward. "Overdyke . . . Percy."

"I wish they'd hurry," Mrs. Dunbar said to her older son. "I wish they'd hurry."

"They're almost through," her son said.

"You get ready to run tell Dad," Mrs. Dunbar said.

Mr. Summers called his own name and then stepped forward precisely and selected a slip from the box. Then he called, "Warner."

"Seventy-seventh year I been in the lottery," Old Man Warner said as he went through the crowd. "Seventy-seventh time."

"Watson." The tall boy came awkwardly through the crowd. Someone said, "Don't be nervous, Jack," and Mr. Summers said, "Take your time, son."

"Zanini."

After that, there was a long pause, a breathless pause, until Mr. Summers, holding his slip of paper in the air, said, "All right, fellows." For a minute, no one moved, and then all the slips of paper were opened. Suddenly, all the women began to speak at once, saying, "Who is it?" "Who's got it?" "Is it the Dunbars?" "Is it the Watsons?" Then the voices began to say, "It's Hutchinson. It's Bill," "Bill Hutchinson's got it."

"Go tell your father," Mrs. Dunbar said to her older son.

People began to look around to see the Hutchinsons. Bill Hutchinson was standing quiet, staring down at the paper in his hand. Suddenly, Tessie Hutchinson shouted to Mr. Summers, "You didn't give him time enough to take any paper he wanted. I saw you. It wasn't fair."

"Be a good sport, Tessie," Mrs. Delacroix called, and Mrs. Graves said, "All of us took the same chance."

"Shut up, Tessie," Bill Hutchinson said.

"Well, everyone," Mr. Summers said, "that was done pretty fast, and now we've got to be hurrying a little more to get done in time." He consulted his next list. "Bill," he said, "you draw for the Hutchinson family. You got any other households in the Hutchinsons?"

"There's Don and Eva," Mrs. Hutchinson yelled. "Make *them* take their chance!"

"Daughters draw with their husbands' families, Tessie," Mr. Summers said gently. "You know that as well as anyone else."

"It wasn't *fair,*" Tessie said.

"I guess not, Joe," Bill Hutchinson said regretfully. "My daughter draws with her husband's family, that's only fair. And I've got no other family except the kids."

"Then, as far as drawing for families is concerned, it's you," Mr. Summers said in explanation, "and as far as drawing households is concerned, that's you, too. Right?"

"Right," Bill Hutchinson said.

"How many kids, Bill?" Mr. Summers asked formally.

"Three," Bill Hutchinson said. "There's Bill, Jr., and Nancy, and little Dave. And Tessie and me."

"All right, then," Mr. Summers said. "Harry, you got their tickets back?"

Mr. Graves nodded and held up the slips of paper. "Put them in the box, then," Mr. Summers directed. "Take Bill's and put it in."

"I think we ought to start over," Mrs. Hutchinson said, as quietly as she could. "I tell you it wasn't *fair.* You didn't give him time enough to choose. *Every*body saw that."

Mr. Graves had selected the five slips and put them in the box, and he dropped all the papers but those onto the ground, where the breeze caught them and lifted them off.

"Listen, everybody," Mrs. Hutchinson was saying to the people around her.

"Ready, Bill?" Mr. Summers asked, and Bill Hutchinson, with one quick glance around at his wife and children, nodded.

"Remember," Mr. Summers said, "take the slips and keep them folded until each person has taken one. Harry, you help little Dave." Mr. Graves took the hand of the little boy, who came willingly with him up to the box. "Take a paper out of the box, Davy," Mr. Summers said. Davy put his hand into the box and laughed. "Take just *one* paper," Mr. Summers said. "Harry, you hold it for him." Mr. Graves took the child's hand and re-moved the folded paper from the tight fist and held it while little Dave stood next to him and looked up at him wonderingly.

"Nancy next," Mr. Summers said. Nancy was twelve, and her school friends breathed heavily as she went forward, switching her skirt, and took a slip daintily from the box. "Bill, Jr.," Mr. Summers said, and Billy, his face red and his feet over-large, nearly knocked the box over as he got a paper out. "Tessie," Mr. Summers said. She hesitated for a minute, looking around defiantly, and then set her lips and went up to the box. She snatched a paper out and held it behind her.

"Bill," Mr. Summers said, and Bill Hutchinson reached into the box and felt around, bringing his hand out at last with the slip of paper in it.

The crowd was quiet. A girl whispered, "I hope it's not Nancy," and the sound of the whisper reached the edges of the crowd.

"It's not the way it used to be," Old Man Warner said clearly. "People ain't the way they used to be."

"All right," Mr. Summers said. "Open the papers. Harry, you open little Dave's."

Mr. Graves opened the slip of paper and there was a general sigh through the crowd as he held it up and everyone could see that it was blank. Nancy and Bill, Jr., opened theirs at the same time, and both beamed and laughed, turning around to the crowd and holding their slips of paper above their heads.

"Tessie," Mr. Summers said. There was a pause, and then Mr. Summers looked at Bill Hutchinson, and Bill unfolded his paper and showed it. It was blank.

"It's Tessie," Mr. Summers said, and his voice was hushed. "Show us her paper, Bill."

Bill Hutchinson went over to his wife and forced the slip of paper out of her hand. It had a black spot on it, the black spot Mr. Summers had made the night before with the heavy pencil in the coal-company office. Bill Hutchinson held it up, and there was a stir in the crowd.

"All right, folks," Mr. Summers said. "Let's finish quickly."

Although the villagers had forgotten the ritual and lost the original black box, they still remembered to use stones. The pile of stones the boys had made earlier was ready; there were stones on the ground with the blowing scraps of paper that had come out of the box. Mrs. Delacroix selected a stone so large she had to pick it up with both hands and turned to Mrs. Dunbar. "Come on," she said. "Hurry up."

Mrs. Dunbar had small stones in both hands, and she said, gasping for breath, "I can't run at all. You'll have to go ahead and I'll catch up with you."

The children had stones already, and someone gave little Davy Hutchinson a few pebbles.

Tessie Hutchinson was in the center of a cleared space by now, and she held her hands out desperately as the villagers moved in on her. "It isn't fair," she said. A stone hit her on the side of the head.

Old Man Warner was saying, "Come on, come on, everyone." Steve Adams was in the front of the crowd of villagers, with Mrs. Graves beside him.

"It isn't fair, it isn't right," Mrs. Hutchinson screamed, and then they were upon her.

ON THE NEW IDOL

Frederick Nietzsche

Somewhere there are still peoples and herds, but not where we live, my brothers: here there are states. State? What is that? Well then, open your ears to me, for now I shall speak to you about the death of peoples.

State is the name of the coldest of all cold monsters. Coldly it tells lies too; and this lie crawls out of its mouth: "I, the state, am the people." That is a lie! It was creators who created peoples and hung a faith and a love over them: thus they served life.

It is annihilators who set traps for the many and call them "state": they hang a sword and a hundred appetites over them.

Where there is still a people, it does not understand the state and hates it as the evil eye and the sin against customs and rights.

This sign I give you: every people speaks its tongue of good and evil, which the neighbor does not understand. It has invented its own language of customs and rights. But the state tells lies in all the tongues of good and evil; and whatever it says it lies—and whatever it has it has stolen. Everything about it is false; it bites with stolen teeth, and bites easily. Even its entrails are false. Confusion of tongues of good and evil: this sign I give you as the sign of the state. Verily, this sign signifies the will to death. Verily, it beckons to the preachers of death.

All-too-many are born: for the superfluous the state was invented.

Behold, how it lures them, the all-too-many—and how it devours them, chews them, and ruminates!

"On earth there is nothing greater than I: the ordering finger of God am I"—thus roars the monster. And it is not only the long-eared and short-sighted who sink to their knees. Alas, to you too, you great souls, it whispers its dark lies. Alas, it detects the rich hearts which like to squander themselves. Indeed, it detects you too, you vanquishers of the old god. You have grown weary with fighting, and now your weariness still serves the new idol. With heroes and honorable men it would surround itself, the new idol! It likes to bask in the sunshine of good consciences—the cold monster!

It will give you everything if you will adore it, this new idol: thus it buys the splendor of your virtues and the look of your proud eyes. It would use you as bait for the all-too-many.

Indeed, a hellish artifice was invented there, a horse of death, clattering in the finery of divine honors. Indeed, a dying for many was invented there, which praises itself as life: verily, a great service to all preachers of death!

State I call it where all drink poison, the good and the wicked, state, where all lose themselves, the good and the wicked; state, where the slow suicide of all is called "life."

Behold the superfluous! They steal the works of the inventors and the treasures of the sages for themselves; "education" they call their theft—and everything turns to sickness and misfortune for them.

Behold the superfluous! They are always sick; they vomit their gall and call it a newspaper. They devour each other and cannot even digest themselves.

Behold the superfluous! They gather riches and become poorer with them. They want power and first the lever of power, much money—the impotent paupers!

Watch them clamber, these swift monkeys! They clamber over one another and thus drag one another into the mud and the depth. They all want to get to the throne: that is their madness—as if happiness sat on the throne. Often mud sits on the throne—and often also the throne on mud. Mad they all appear to me, clambering monkeys and overardent. Foul smells their idol, the cold monster: foul they smell to me altogether, these idolators.

My brothers, do you want to suffocate in the fumes of their snouts and appetites? Rather break the windows and leap to freedom.

Escape from the bad smell! Escape from the idolatry of the superfluous!

Escape from the bad smell! Escape from the steam of these human sacrifices!

The earth is free even now for great souls. There are still many empty seats for the lonesome and the twosome, fanned by the fragrance of silent seas.

A free life is still free for great souls. Verily, whoever possesses little is possessed that much less: praised be a little poverty!

Only where the state ends, there begins the human being who is not superfluous: there begins the song of necessity, the unique and inimitable tune.

Where the state *ends*—look there, my brothers! Do you not see it, the rainbow and the bridges of the overman?

Thus spoke Zarathustra.

LONDON

William Blake

I wander thro' each charter'd street,
Near where the charter'd Thames does flow,
And mark in every face I meet
Marks of weakness, marks of woe.

In every cry of every Man,
In every Infant's cry of fear,
In every voice, in every ban,
The mind-forg'd manacles I hear.

How the Chimney-sweeper's cry
Every black'ning Church appalls;
And the hapless Soldier's sigh
Runs in blood down Palace walls.

But most thro' midnight streets I hear
How the youthful Harlot's curse
Blasts the new born Infant's tear,
And blights with plagues the Marriage hearse.

I, THE FAKE MAD BOMBER AND WALKING IT HOME AGAIN

Byron Black

First comes the cold,
and puffing as classes change
fast as the frames of a film
and dried old sarcophagi of professors reel on
trot placidly Latin with its dust and their rot.

Then dives the red sun
crashes like the stock market, in black
"the day was fine" as Wm. says
and the Tower stands impudent, one wants to slap it down
before the blast-off into stone-gray space.

Brisk bright day
Wm. and I walking fast,
we smile at lurid tales which shock like adders

Dark people with the faces of bulldogs
gruffly waddle past, Chryslers with the scream of a rocket
charge us jousting, we hurry fast
to the flap and claw of the Night Hawk

where dark hamburgers from the heart of a living vulture
are served by an Aztec princess
"the hamburger don't come with onions"
(pimples as jewels, and the pop of gum)
And the white bourgeois, slimy smiles
slide in with assuredness of talkative slugs, to music of the bank

outside the brightwork of their gaudy Cadillacs
wails like a chrome banshee toward the cool evening, and sad glass eyes,
And I thanking Wm. we part
he for home
and I full of cheer and good meat

head for my place, legs flashing
the power of wet muscles

273

sends an electric orgasm,
and as approaching Red River, now dry
beside the stadium where Christians are devourers
the night breaks
I know myself as the Fake Mad Bomber
and light a black cigar in the dark to prove it.

THE HERO TODAY

Joseph Campbell

... The democratic ideal of the self-determining individual, the invention of the power-driven machine, and the development of the scientific method of research, have so transformed human life that the long-inherited, timeless universe of symbols has collapsed. In the fateful, epoch-announcing words of Nietzsche's Zarathustra: "Dead are all the gods."[1] One knows the tale; it has been told a thousand ways. It is the hero-cycle of the modern age, the wonder-story of mankind's coming to maturity. The spell of the past, the bondage of tradition, was shattered with sure and mighty strokes. The dream-web of myth fell away; the mind opened to full waking consciousness; and modern man emerged from ancient ignorance, like a butterfly from its cocoon, or like the sun at dawn from the womb of mother night.

It is not only that there is no hiding place for the gods from the searching telescope and microscope; there is no such society any more as the gods once supported. The social unit is not a carrier of religious content, but an economic-political organization. Its ideals are not those of the hieratic pantomime, making visible on earth the forms of heaven, but of the secular state, in hard and unremitting competition for material supremacy and resources. Isolated societies, dream-bounded within a mythologically charged horizon, no longer exist except as areas to be exploited. And within the progressive societies themselves, every last vestige of the ancient human heritage of ritual, morality, and art is in full decay.

The problem of mankind today, therefore, is precisely the opposite to that of men in the comparatively stable periods of those great co-ordinating mythologies which now are known as lies. Then all meaning was in the group, in the great anonymous forms, none in the self-expressive individual; today no meaning is in the group—none in the world: all is in the individual. But there the meaning is absolutely unconscious. One does not know toward what one moves. One does not know by what one is propelled.

[1] Nietzsche, *Thus Spake Zarathustra,* 1.22.3.

The lines of communication between the conscious and the unconscious zones of the human psyche have all been cut, and we have been split in two.

The hero-deed to be wrought is not today what it was in the century of Galileo. Where then there was darkness, now there is light; but also, where light was, there now is darkness. The modern hero-deed must be that of questing to bring to light again the lost Atlantis of the co-ordinated soul.

Obviously, this work cannot be wrought by turning back, or away, from what has been accomplished by the modern revolution; for the problem is nothing if not that of rendering the modern world spiritually significant—or rather (phrasing the same principle the other way round) nothing if not that of making it possible for men and women to come to full human maturity through the conditions of contemporary life. Indeed, these conditions themselves are what have rendered the ancient formulae ineffective, misleading, and even pernicious. The community today is the planet, not the bounded nation; hence the patterns of projected aggression which formerly served to co-ordinate the in-group now can only break it into factions. The national idea, with the flag as totem, is today an aggrandizer of the nursery ego, not the annihilator of an infantile situation. Its parody-rituals of the parade ground serve the ends of Holdfast, the tyrant dragon, not the God in whom self-interest is annihilate. And the numerous saints of this anticult—namely the patriots whose ubiquitous photographs, draped with flags, serve as official icons—are precisely the local threshold guardians (our demon Sticky-hair) whom it is the first problem of the hero to surpass.

Nor can the great world religions, as at present understood, meet the requirement. For they have become associated with the causes of the factions, as instruments of propaganda and self-congratulation. (Even Buddhism has lately suffered this degradation, in reaction to the lessons of the West.) The universal triumph of the secular state has thrown all religious organizations into such a definitely secondary, and finally ineffectual, position that religious pantomime is hardly more today than a sanctimonious exercise for Sunday morning, whereas business ethics and patriotism stand for the remainder of the week. Such a monkey-holiness is not what the functioning world requires; rather, a transmutation of the whole social order is necessary, so that through every detail and act of secular life the vitalizing image of the universal god-man who is actually immanent and effective in all of us may be somehow made known to consciousness.

And this is not a work that consciousness itself can achieve. Consciousness can no more invent, or even predict, an effective symbol than foretell or control tonight's dream. The whole thing is being worked out on another level, through what is bound to be a long and very frightening process, not only in the depths of every living psyche in the modern world, but also on those titanic battlefields into which the whole planet has lately been converted. We are watching the terrible clash of the Symplegades, through which the soul must pass—identified with neither side.

But there is one thing we may know, namely, that as the new symbols become visible, they will not be identical in the various parts of the globe;

the circumstances of local life, race, and tradition must all be compounded in the effective forms. Therefore, it is necessary for men to understand, and be able to see, that through various symbols the same redemption is revealed. "Truth is one," we read in the Vedas; "the sages call it by many names." A single song is being inflected through all the colorations of the human choir. General propaganda for one or another of the local solutions, therefore, is superfluous—or much rather, a menace. The way to become human is to learn to recognize the lineaments of God in all of the wonderful modulations of the face of man.

With this we come to the final hint of what the specific orientation of the modern hero-task must be, and discover the real cause for the disintegration of all of our inherited religious formulae. The center of gravity, that is to say, of the realm of mystery and danger has definitely shifted. For the primitive hunting peoples of those remotest human millenniums when the sabertooth tiger, the mammoth, and the lesser presences of the animal kingdom were the primary manifestations of what was alien—the source at once of danger, and of sustenance—the great human problem was to become linked psychologically to the task of sharing the wilderness with these beings. An unconscious identification took place, and this was finally rendered conscious in the half-human, half-animal, figures of the mythological totem-ancestors. The animals became the tutors of humanity. Through acts of literal imitation—such as today appear only on the children's playground (or in the madhouse)—an effective annihilation of the human ego was accomplished and society achieved a cohesive organization. Similarly, the tribes supporting themselves on plant-food became cathected to the plant; the life-rituals of planting and reaping were identified with those of human procreation, birth, and progress to maturity. Both the plant and the animal worlds, however, were in the end brought under social control. Whereupon the great field of instructive wonder shifted—to the skies—and mankind enacted the great pantomime of the sacred moon-king, the sacred sun-king, the hieratic, planetary state, and the symbolic festivals of the world-regulating spheres.

Today all of these mysteries have lost their force; their symbols no longer interest our psyche. The notion of a cosmic law, which all existence serves and to which man himself must bend, has long since passed through the preliminary mystical stages represented in the old astrology, and is now simply accepted in mechanical terms as a matter of course. The descent of the Occidental sciences from the heavens to the earth (from seventeenth-century astronomy to nineteenth-century biology), and their concentration today, at last, on man himself (in twentieth-century anthropology and psychology), mark the path of a prodigious transfer of the focal point of human wonder. Not the animal world, not the plant world, not the miracle of the spheres, but man himself is now the crucial mystery. Man is that alien presence with whom the forces of egoism must come to terms, through whom the ego is to be crucified and resurrected, and in whose image society is to be reformed. Man, understood however not as "I" but as "Thou": for the ideals and temporal institutions of no tribe, race, continent, social class, or century, can be the measure of the inexhaustible and multifariously wonderful divine existence that is the life in all of us.

The modern hero, the modern individual who dares to heed the call and seek the mansion of that presence with whom it is our whole destiny to be atoned, cannot indeed must not, wait for his community to cast off its slough of pride, fear, rationalized avarice, and sanctified misunderstanding. "Live," Nietzsche says, "as though the day were here." It is not society that is to guide and save the creative hero, but precisely the reverse. And so every one of us shares the supreme ordeal—carries the cross of the redeemer—not in the bright moments of his tribe's great victories, but in the silences of his personal despair.

THE NEW HERO

Louis W. Cartwright

How do I feel about America, her education systems, her institutions, her people, her land, her me? What question could be more important for each of us to answer! Yet how can one sufficiently untangle oneself from the living and struggling of this vast human drama in order to answer it?

It is impossible for me to respond to a subject so consuming and elusive in the stride of a professional. I can't focus on one or two aspects, for I haven't yet become an expert in any one field. Nor, as I see it now, will I in the future specialize in order to be able to say that I know a few things. So, I begin this collection of feelings about America by saying that I don't know anything for sure. I don't think I have ever known anything for sure long enough to remember it. America is that way to me: every now and then I see her for an instant to be a certain country, definable and pin-pointable; but before I get my pen raised to plunge, she disappears in a cloud-twist of change.

Since there is no other proof of one's feelings than living according to them, I'd say mine are healthy. I've lived a quarter of a century and thus far haven't been put away. My wife doesn't run back to Mother and I'm finally through trying to get my father to tell me how to live. I'm punctual and pay my debts, and there is a good chance I'll instantly like anyone who is and does the same. I'd say I'm doing pretty well. If nothing accidental occurs I might even reach manhood and find out for myself what it's all about—providing I can endure the pace I've set for myself, blaming no one else for anything and not seeking salvation tomorrow but always today, now. All this without TV is fairly difficult, but I have faith.

The bomb frightened the daylight out of my life. For two years I didn't make one decision, one plan that bound more than two days together. I continued doing what I had been doing like a castrated bull pacing indifferently among the cows. How many nightmares did I die in? How many mornings did the sun crash into my bed like a surprise party! Finally, out of a desperation to live, I decided that the bomb didn't matter, that if it came today we wouldn't have to face dying the day after. I might as well make big plans, seeing as how nothing had changed. So I made big plans and still make them. But like hell it hasn't changed! I'm probably more religious now than the most devout Jehovah's Witness, but I have no one to pray to. I am devoted to life, health and future, to preserve these in the nowness of every thought, wish and dream. The only one left to believe in is Man, so I figure we've got to prepare him for the responsibilities of being God. And we've got to start with ourselves. Which means we have to start all over again, look at it all as if we had just arrived like children walking to school for the first time. To these ends, then, my life is a first attempt and my feelings are my only guide.

I trust myself at the intuitive level. Propaganda may be pulling me here and there, and it may not be; I don't know. I don't deal decisions out to distant realities like Vietnam. All I know is I don't have any reasons to kill anyone, and I'm the one who has to have them in order to do it. I can't be pushed or bullied into a war I don't understand. That goes for all things of that nature. The term civil rights means nothing to me, but a person getting unfairly shafted means everything. I'll just have to say I don't have time for sit-ins and marches; I'm too busy learning how to live. Besides, most sit-ins and marches are too popular to be effective; in a sense they've been wasted on too many little points. However, they might be the only method of resistance against the State for those of us who can't afford a lobby. I might be wrong not to march or sit, but I just haven't felt it yet. I might be committing huge mistakes that in two years will rise up and hurl a shadow over my life, force me into that corner from which the only escape is to the analyst or Mr. Tambourine Man. There are so many might-be's in my style of life, too many to waste my time in elaborate and absolute preparation. So I keep open to the front and worry only about my back.

I am not contemporary, popular, in the "new look" of the "Pepsi Generation," and I'm not frightened. This party has been going on so long now, that I think if someone announced that it was over nobody would leave. They'd have no place to go. I get the same feeling when I pass a bar at two o'clock and listen to the homeless begging not to be thrown out. If television were suddenly canceled what would people do? All that free time? Occasionally I feel trapped by the outstanding accomplishments of the Beatles, the overnight success of skateboards and hula hoops . . . I find myself trying to come up with a gimmick to make a million. Then I wake up and grab myself by the collar: What? You want to create another ride for them to spend their time on? Then I begin to blame these heroes who throw the people a bone for their money and model nothing but materialism to our children. But, hell, it isn't them. It's the potential in the situation that pays their type, and the situation has never been anything but a blueprint unraveling; it's we who create the morality from it; by morality I mean the way to be, and the way to be is to choose your hero and dress him in money, and it is still of the people. I guess I'm just lonely believing I got my morality from the Earth: the animal in me and at large is in stride with a higher truth than my intellect can handle. Morality is the intellect's attempt to protect itself against the animal, but it is only an aftereffect of life and the animal knows this. We Americans have always fought the animal by ignoring it. Our morality has been a blindfold to wear in the daytime and a sleeping pill to take at night. I've experimented at living without masks and pills and, no kidding, it's all right. We're pretty damn fine animals when we loosen up the cinch and remove the bit.

It's all a matter of fads and trends, of the short-run and the long-run, of the eternal trend of mankind; the rest is the Fourth of July and firecrackers, and anybody knows where to buy them. So you pop 'em off; I don't care.

America has seldom been more than a list of many moving spirits clashing, joining, splitting, some small and violent, others huge and bullying, but it has never been describable in terms of one spirit. (Although the Beatles might take some issue.) Today I see a spirit moving in America almost as widespread as the heavy silence following Kennedy's assassination; this is the spirit of uniformity. It seems to bulldoze everything unique and human down until the ground is flat enough for one hundred square miles of identical houses. And I don't have to wait for history to come along with its approval or condemnation of my opinion; I am the pen-point of history writing, my life is its ink. I am defining myself en route, knowing that before the ink is dry what I've written is already inaccurate, for I am a process of becoming different. And this gives me hope.

I am a rear-engine sports car, a Lotus or a Porsche pushing myself into the future of blind curves and diminishing left-handers. I am prepared for the unexpected, I lunge toward it with hunger, even though I've seen so much I seldom encounter a surprise; however, I am most near death when I begin believing I've seen it all. So I continuously doubt the future. My faith is behind me, not out in front: I am not drawn ahead by the apron strings of Heaven; I am pushing at crashing speeds into the unknowns, whether or not I interrupt any heavens. I've made no contract with God; his promises and threats do not interest or frighten me. A life after death is not separated by dying: I die into dream each night and am sifted or jolted back into life each morning. My power is in me, in all of us. Life is this power.

Self-reliance or -directedness is the first inevitable step out of alienation and solitude, and since solitude is such a shocking realization it leaves a scar or flaw in our subsequent adjustment to life. I call this scar a sense of privacy. You might look on it as a void in one's personality which he fills with his very own ideas of the universe; in here he writes philosophy for himself and his dependents. Here, then, is the factory of self-reliance. Others might look upon this void or room as a guest cottage for God, a place we go to pray, an island of insanity. Indirectly self-reliance is manufactured there no matter what you call it.

The obvious counterpart or concomitant of being self-directed is that I profoundly resent anyone interfering by ordering me to do something or go somewhere. Once my father directed my life; when I left home I took over; on occasion he will ask me to do something for him, but it is no longer an order and he has heard my refusal. The police and the selective service don't respect me and my sense of privacy. This is a real fact, and I know it, so it is again up to me to stay out of their way if I want to remain in charge of my doings. Needless to say, I have been negligent and have put myself in positions where they pushed me. You see, I keep forgetting that they no longer keep the peace; they enforce law and so disturb peace. I forget that they do not deal with humans as being human; they deal with humans as being law-breakers. I forget that one cannot be innocent or ignorant or have lapses into innocence because those states of being are illegal. I guess I forget because I want to. I don't want to recall that I grew up in a town where I was ordered to show a policeman my identification card three or four times a week. There's no excuse for me forgetting that! I should not take walks at night; I know better.

Also, I loathe the notion America is promoting that one has to go to college in order to "make it." How about those who don't want to? Those who have a couple of dreams of their own that they'd like to try out? When a notion like that becomes almost an unwritten law, a matter of course, then we defeat ourselves: we end up forcing pure character and imagination, our only chance for health and future, into systems of education that return to us a beast who is intelligent only because he has finally been trained to answer with the acceptable notions of our time. Once so potentially brilliant and eager to learn about life, they return to us predictably dull and bored under the oppressive weight of collections of information. We frustrate the creative mind into a desperate submission whereupon it closes up like a clam on the ocean floor and never feels good or free about life again. Some of our young blood isn't meant for college even though it can pass the entrance exams, but where else are they encouraged to go? Into the Army? The parent offers to send him to, and support him through, college only if he goes directly after high school and stays with it for a continuous four years (or is it six, now?). So they go, are never late, are never passionate, sit in classrooms, while the life they felt to be good quietly dies.

I first enrolled in college because I wanted to. This was two years after high school, after I had hitchhiked around America, after having cycled a year in Europe, and worked in a missile factory—after, I'd like to say, I felt that I had earned the readiness for learning. I wanted to learn all about the Greeks, especially Odysseus, for he, like me, had traveled. But I wasn't allowed to take Greek Mythology or study the Greek language; I had to take certain *preliminary* courses. I did manage to lie my way into a philosophy class. At the end of that year I felt that I had had enough; I knew that I could learn without having an examination date placed before me for discipline. I still liked learning. So I quit and returned to Europe. My father was astounded and hurt at my courteous refusal of the security of a college degree; he made me feel like I was cheating. But he wished me good luck and a quick return.

My first trip to Europe had been a magic carpet tour; I had enough money, and though I cycled I didn't need to work my way, didn't need to stay any place longer than it pleased me. The second trip was the yes-trip: it was yes to everything, and I was broke. I took jobs doing anything, lived anywhere, ate anything, and learned a great deal about freedom. For instance, I learned that you can cycle all day in the rain and not catch cold if you work hard (and if your clothes get washed). I didn't belong in school, anyone could see that. I needed to try myself in life, see if I could learn how to be. From where I was in the south of France, American middle-class security looked like a sickness, one that most got over. When I returned home, in spite of the particular mood I was in or my reason for returning, I was full of life and lean as a coyote. I wanted to sleep, then eat, then think.

"But he's got to finish college," I heard my father saying to my mother behind their door that night.

"Let him rest awhile," said mother.

"Hell, rest, he's twenty-one. When I was his age I was supporting my parents."

"We don't need support."

"I don't want his support, I want him to get to work. It's not healthy to sit and do nothing."

I listened to them. My father was right. So was I. He wouldn't give in and neither would I. The last favor I wanted of my parents was time, time to decide what I wanted to try next. Three months later I introduced him to my fiancée, and within a month, married, I left that time and place of my childhood forever.

A year later I wanted to return to school to pursue a new interest, and within a week I hated college. It was stuffy, crowded, tightly scheduled, fast, an authority center where questions were slaughtered quickly and efficiently with brilliant little answers. I had to put away my interests and get in line with the others. It wasn't learning; it was read, memorize and answer, and there wasn't any time for exceptions to the beautiful rules. It was terrible, but I had unwittingly promised myself that I would stick it out. I'd convinced myself that like climbing a long, steep grade, there is a personal benefit gained in reaching the top. So here fulfilling my promise was my only reason for remaining. Endurance.

My reason for enduring became a chant I whisper to myself when it gets worse than bad: you can make it, you made it over the Alps, you can do anything. Don't I have other reasons? Would I come to watch people? I'd rather stand on Market Street.[1] Would I come to learn from teachers? We all know how unnecessary and redundant many professors are, how they never quite come alive before their classes, as if the administration were controlling their oxygen supply. Most classrooms are holding a recital of the

[1] San Francisco's main business and shopping thoroughfare, running from the Ferry Building to Twin Peaks.

text you read last night. But every now and then, one man sneaks through and holds a class on his own that balances off the entire history of inadequate professors. Yes, for that chance (as long as it doesn't get any slimmer) I'd sign up for a full load and attend. But isn't it so very unfortunate that the clothesline of education droops so low between the occasional giants? To this point I append the twin to the statement that all of us shouldn't go to college: all of those who are teaching shouldn't be. Perhaps half of all who populate a campus should be in a trade school or on a ranch. I feel we have sacrificed learning for education, that, as with missiles, we are competing with Russia to graduate people, hit or miss. No! No no no no. We fail beneath the statistical affidavits of our success: there it is in black and white, but there it ain't in the people.

Another aspect of this swelling horror is the soul-shrinking speed at which we educate! Got to hurry, got to meet my future in four years, go go—college à go-go. I imagine an IBM computer graduating twenty thousand cards and there's no one there to claim them. What's the hurry? It reminds me of the Yiddish saying: *Sleep fast, we need the pillows.* Along with this preoccupation with speed develops the feeling that one is supposed to know a few things simply because he is nearing the exit. The poor beast, he knows all the right answers in his field and he is secure. Meantime, as Bob Dylan sings in one of his verses, life goes on all about him.

Nope. Our country wants our colleges to do more than they can honestly do, so it forces them to be dishonest. Do anything you have to do but make sure the statistics are ready in time to be published in the July 1 issue of Time. One million graduate this June!

I'm in no hurry and resent being shoved. A college or university should be slow and easy. It shouldn't have too clear of an idea what an educated man should know. There should be no such system as a major and a minor and so many of each kind of units to sign up for. Curiosity if left alone will fill out a healthy program. And professors should be paid enough to keep them from griping about salaries in the classroom. They sometimes remind me of the street performer who has to send his hat about the crowd.

College should be a free place with huge doors that swing open to whomever feels curious about what goes on inside. It shouldn't be a prerequisite to life; it is an aftereffect. I've learned and have been inspired more by my time spent in college bars and cafeterias with others than in the hours I've sat in classrooms. But I get no credit for that time. So maybe classes should be held in the college cafeteria. I want it to be that free and slow. The way I describe how a college should be, it becomes obvious that we have very few colleges in America. We have trade schools where one learns how to do psychology and engineering and creative writing, and where curiosity is called game playing and inefficient. After all, if you keep asking those questions, you'll never get out by June!

The university is not an ivory tower without a city to be ivory for; they are inseparable. But America separates them. The American student is in constant conflict between working to earn enough to go to school and studying to earn the grades to stay in school. And most often he can't get a job in the field of his studies. So combine work with school. Give him not only a salary but college credit for his time spent on the job, for isn't experience the best way to learn? The new work-study program sponsored by the government is a timid step in this direction. But it still doesn't reacquaint the city with the college, and this is essential.

America devises or chooses so many easy ways out. College is now an easy way out of worrying about becoming a success. You get a degree and they've got it all worked out for you on an easy-to-understand form which lists how long it will take to be earning twenty-five thousand a year. And this goes for all the other easy ways out.

Some afternoons a few of us would gather for coffee in the cafeteria and discuss our private lives and their progress toward freedom. One would describe his latest LSD trip, another would remind us that marijuana is still a good ride, and someone from another state would say, "Yeah, those are good but haven't you tried mushrooms or cactus?" On and on it would go. I was always the one who after a few rounds began to tell about my latest fishing or hunting trip. I would try to describe it vividly so as to remind them that life is still a pretty good trip. I would "trip out" discussing my trip (they called it "zooming," which means getting carried away). They often wondered what I was taking. After my story I tried to convince them that they didn't need pills to be free, that LSD is most often a pause, time out from facing reality as it will be when they return. However, there were always more of them than me, so I would lose, so to speak, to someone else's LSD vacation story. Oo! The colors! On those days I left school feeling so very lonely I didn't see why or how I could return.

If you take the pill, then chemically you are *forced* to look *freely* at yourself. It is as if we no longer have it within ourselves to reach out and touch the terrible truths, as if we haven't the faith and guts to get us there on our own. Where is America's confidence? The confidence that doesn't depend on pills and degrees and sunglasses, on the new look and the club card, and approval of the authority. Have our governments and schools done so much for us that we have completely forgotten that we can do some things on our own? Why do the majority of professors have to write out a lecture to read to their class? What happened to "off-the-cuff"?

Maybe it is my fault for not being able to see that we have reached a new level of life where only institutions can handle humanity and where the individual is the element of error that must be canceled out. If that is it then I don't want it. Progress can carry America wherever she wants to go, but I'm glad my feet are on the earth and I enjoy walking.

Whose America *is* this? I no longer feel a part of her. I am a stranger in her schools and indifferent to, or against, her goals (or the possible lack thereof). I've pulled my car off the circuit, quit the race to nowhere; now I drive where I want to, and it is up to me to keep out of her way if I want to keep free. (Isn't that ironic? I have to fight America for my freedom!)

My America is me alive and living, wading upstream, crashing through brush, chasing grunion, watching salmon leap, screeching my brakes on the freeway to watch a flight of Canadian geese, picking up a hitchhiker and asking him where he's going, having coffee with a trucker, finding an arrowhead, and being attacked by a blackbird because I passed too near her nest. America is me getting up tired and driving thirty miles to meet someone on time, or hiking up mountains just to do it. It's the whole country when you look around from a mountain fourteen thousand feet tall. It's feeling as if fences are merely spider webs that cling to your pants legs when you go roaming. It isn't a job at ten thousand a year, a club to drink in, a fast red car, and a pasteboard house; and it isn't going to be that ulcer at forty, either. Sometimes I think *I'm* America.

America: a big place, fragmented by rules into smaller places, further broken up by borders into smaller places, and finally, unfindable on a country map, my town, a peephole through which I interact with and spy on the world—if and when I choose to. If I choose not to, they will try to force me to, and though it would take sixty days for Washington's red paper snake to strike me into her army, I'd rather make them use it than submit like a good son. I'm no son of Washington.

Yep! America's a big place, but it barely has room for me. I live on its borders, up against its cultural limits at all times. The cost of living on the border is high: you've got to be wealthy, and wealth here is measured in terms of how little you need to live. How few possessions. I need so little I have to make up reasons for not retiring tomorrow. I'm lean. I'm a tramp playing dress-up. My possessions are souvenirs, they are not necessaries. I do not need the luxuries this country uses to bait its people toward progress. I've learned to despise that word.

For whenever we look about to see what it was we were working for, what do we see: a house that wasn't built well enough to raise our children, broken appliances in the garage, two cars falling apart while only one or two years old, furniture that was once so pretty you felt you had to cover it with plastic, an electric kitchen with a trash box full of TV dinner tins. Is this the only other way to avoid another crash: to build stuff so cheaply it will break down and have to be bought again and again? The other way to keep this economy going is to keep a war going. Is this all to build a home for the brave to preserve freedom? No, I'm afraid no one will buy that one any more. We all know that we don't know why we're doing all the things we do, that we don't like what we do, but we don't know what to do about it. Okay, it is easy to say what is happening, and it is easy to list a few reasons why. But what to do about it? What do we do?

It would be pointless to list ways we could alter this situation unless I thought we would do it, that is the sorrow that weighs me down: I don't think most Americans want to change; they have faith in these systems. Oh, they might argue this in the bar after work with their friends when it doesn't count, but be sure that the next morning they'll be back at the bench performing some push-button task that in some way supports the sicknesses of our time. Whether it's throwing together pasteboard houses, squeezing food into heat-and-serve tins, printing stories they know are just half-true, creating advertising to further confuse and take advantage of others like themselves who no longer know better. Each one plays a small-enough role so he doesn't feel accountable. It's *they* who are doing it, the owners, the board, the office. "Don't look at me, buddy, I just work here."

The other night my wife and I went to a drive-in movie. At the intermission I went in to get her an ice water and a coffee. I poured myself the coffee and asked the girl to please fix me an ice water. She turned to the boy cashier: "How much do we have to charge for the large cup?"

He didn't turn his head: "Twenty-five cents," he answered.

I couldn't believe I heard him right. "No," I said, "it's just a cup of ice water."

He turned smilingly: "I know, but it doesn't matter. The cups are on inventory. Everyone that goes out of here I have to get twenty-five cents for."

"Look," I said, "the cup probably cost three cents at best. How can you charge a quarter for it? I don't care about inventory."

"But the office made the inventory. It's a rule."

"Well, break the damn rule! It's ridiculous."

"How do I explain it to them? There's supposed to be a quarter for each cup."

"Tell them you stepped on one."

"Nah, I couldn't do that."

"Aren't you part of them?" I asked.

"No, I just work here."

"Oh, you're their slave, then?"

"What do you mean?" he asked.

"You are part of this company. All you'd have to do is leave a note for the inventory saying you sold one cup for a nickel."

"I can't do it, I'm sorry."

"Because of them?"

"Yes."

"You know, friend, you're dead. I don't know why anyone would ever want to talk to you. I couldn't stand behind a counter if I had to point blame to my "they" every time something different came up. Don't you realize that every time you shirk and shrug off responsibility you make yourself smaller? You've already shrunk to a pip-squeak."

He just smiled at me like a baby who thinks it's funny to see anger. So did all the people crowding around, but no one said anything or got too close. They wouldn't have done anything to stop me from killing the dead-boy.

"Look," I said with great tolerance, "I'll give you one more chance. You sell me the cup for twenty-five cents. I'll bring it back, wash it, and you give me twenty cents return on it, okay?"

"I can't do it. How would I explain the five cents extra in the drawer?"

"PUT IT IN YOUR POCKET!"

The speechless dead-boy stood expressionless, like he didn't understand a word I had said. I held his eyes sternly as I strode out of the refreshment room. No one said a word. They didn't even call me a nut behind my back. On the way back to the car I counted four empty cups blowing around in the wind.

I know that these kinds of Americans, the ones you'll never hear about unless they get killed in a spectacular accident, are not strong enough to begin a battle back to reality, to that state of knowing you are alone and that each person has his own idea of himself and you, and that beyond this we know nothing for sure. It is a state of dignity and responsibility to eternity which includes this moment. Some try to return to this state of awareness; they sink in despair at the odds with which they're faced. Others don't try; they sink silently into systems they don't understand. A few make it. They are put into institutions for safekeeping. But the dead-boy behind the counter sits safely inside a stockade made up of fears he doesn't look at. If he steps out in any direction he's afraid he'll be attacked. He's a nobody and an anybody. So what'll happen to him? Who'll help him? No one. So stay there and blame them, blame the boss who isn't here right now. So, each of us lives on that pinhead surrounded by others like ourselves who will point at us if we move. That doesn't stop some from moving but it stops most.

Therefore we needn't be surprised when we read that a woman was raped in a New York building in front of many witnesses, or that a man was killed in front of the same. It's the law that you are not supposed to interfere with the scene of an accident. So better drive by and be glad it wasn't you who careened off that embankment and are now crying in pain wishing some fragmented person like yourself would break the law and stop to help you. When the people of a country won't or can't help one another then it is no longer a country.

We won't help one another but we are herded off in battalions to help Vietnam! America, the big meat producer, has something wrong with her and she blames others for the whyness of the war that she needs to fight in order to keep her sick economy flowing. Why are the best of our youths devising huge gambles in order not to be drafted? Faking homosexuality, psychoses, and nervous breakdowns, or flatly refusing to go and thereby putting themselves in jail. They are doing this because they believe there is no longer any cause great enough to kill others for. They have become responsible to humanity, for all wars now have a red line, a point beyond which we cannot go and survive. In this respect the bomb is a blessing, for it gives us an unarguable reason not to try to prove our points in other countries, spilling blood of people who never heard of America.

When I think of war, of bombs startling children and splashing horror on faces of screaming mothers I nearly go mad with anger! While I'm sitting in the cafeteria having coffee or on a stream at dawn feeling very happy, all of a sudden the image of war goose-steps into my mind and I scream: Why? What for? Who for? A million pettinesses crawl quickly like ants to answer those questions. I know it isn't just America, that there have to be at least two to have a war, that the innocent always get it, and that others make money on it, and that others die in it, and that some don't care a damn about it. Okay, this is reality and I know it, but I'm not relieved of anger. I want to fight something, whatever it is, that creates war. But when I try to express my feelings someone nails me down to the hard facts of life as if these facts were the sacred Part Two of the Ten Commandments. I want to fight these facts.

When I fight I am like all neurotics who have waged a war alone. I have no one to compare myself to, no one out there to keep me honest, no one to tell me to go home when my opposition has disappeared. Often I feel like the kid who gets mad when a bunch of his friends playfully pile on top of him. The madness builds up as their laughter loudens, until it cannot be contained, and the boy explodes with unconquerable strength; he breaks loose and swings. He slugs everyone standing around. And he can't stop himself. America sometimes feels like a hundred bags labeled friendship being piled on top of me; I tear loose and rip them all open just to see them pour out. Of course I don't trust everyone. I trust about ten people, and I trust them to be just who they are, not me. But I don't trust America. It thinks friendship can be won during a party, or at least let's all forget about it and have a good time together. Well, that's it, I can't forget. I can't forget that America doesn't want to mean what it says, that it isn't fighting for freedom, that we are not the great home of the brave. And I can't forget that it is my fault, for the others do not care. I miss the America I dreamt about.

When I, the People, learn to remember, when I the People, use the lessons of yesterday and no longer forget who robbed me last year, who played me for a fool—then there will be no speaker in all the world to say the name: "The People," with any fleck of a sneer in his voice or any far-off smile of derision.[2]

I guess having been banged around by those bags of false friendship has made me sound pretty strong and angry. I even surprised myself. I said that I blame myself for everything and turned right around and began blaming others for not remembering, not having the strength to keep reality in focus long enough to become reacquainted with it. I must now state that I haven't written one sentence against America that was not first composed in self-disgust. At one time or another I, too, forgot about everything painful or challenging. I, too, used the word love as only a technique for snowing a girl into bed. I, too, passed the blame to the *They* of America. I didn't know any better. Oh, I felt different, but feelings aren't necessarily expedient. "You can't get anywhere being honest, Mac." The worst most unhealthy person I see today I wouldn't be able to understand unless I had at one time stood in his shoes. I recognize those shoes. I used to be very sick, and that was when I was considered by my elders to be most healthy. Now I am well and clean, and they consider me to be sick. There is not merely a matter of opinion, either.

Every time I kept quiet, put off something I felt for fear of endangering my standing in a group, I began to hate myself. This hate would build up, collect in some recess of my personality, until I was so divided against myself I would have to break open. If I was right I had to argue and fight. If I was wrong and knew it, I had to break down my old feelings and sweat it out forming new ones that were still strange to me. After about fifteen

---

[2] Carl Sandburg, from "I Am the People, the Mob," from *Chicago Poems,* Holt Rinehart and Winston, Inc., 1916.

years of this I have finally learned not to keep quiet, not to postpone, not to let someone else do it for fear of getting myself involved too deeply. I don't want to keep quiet any more, and I won't forget anything to make being noisy easier.

Let me backtrack a moment to pick up the points I've tried to make. First, I don't feel a part of America any more: I don't believe in her reasons; I don't learn from her schools; and her systems and laws have just about controlled the human element out of the experiment. Second, I can't forget the fullness of the world in order to make my life easier. Third, I have promised myself not to keep quiet any longer, for I feel to blame for everything, which makes me responsible. And fourth, I can't be pushed into a war or way of life I don't feel to be true. Death would be sweeter than a deadly lifetime, and I feel that is the goal of American progress, which leaves me out.

Why do I feel to blame?

It is simple: I am not part of the system, and the system's hopes, ends and means, but I am part of the people. I am responsible to them and the land. I am responsible to that part in each that each has forgotten, the dark side of their personalities' moon, their subconscious, their back-forgotten. I get along best with those of us we've locked up because we think we can't get along with them. The ones who can't hide any more because they have no place left to run to, the juvenile delinquents, the drunks, neurotics still at large, and other yet unclassified people who are trying to do what they want to do without causing too much of a disturbance. When I say "the people" I refer to those who still try to enrich their lives by seeking out reality, not evading it. The others who coast along from ride to ride with a pocketful of free passes are the dead weight who have to be awakened to the fact that they are being carried.

There are none living in America today who are more lonesome than the responsible. These are people who have made it their primary goal to form a functional overview of mankind and live within and nourish this view. I don't know who said so, or even if it has been announced yet, but every man has a duty to develop a philosophy that he would rule the world by if he were elected king. In a small way every father does this if he's worth a damn. Unfortunately for most of the children born since World War II, this duty has been sorrowfully neglected, purposively forgotten, ignored.

Bobby Dylan sings in one of his verses, that he hasn't anything to live for. I did. My father was a big, warm man, active and responsible, and he truly loved his sons. In the old style to some, in just plain style to me, he could make me believe there were fish in rain puddles. I had to live a long way up to reach and befriend him on that highest of all friendship planes—father and son. I felt it my duty to learn all that he knew. He was there. Behind him stood my mother.

Now he is not there (in the same way). Behind him stand the mountains. He now stands in me and I still have someone to live up to: myself.

Looking around I can find nothing that we need more than men who will fulfill the duty of king. We need fathers. We've plenty of mothers, too much mama. What does Dylan mean when he says; "I've got no one to live up to."

He's saying this, in the song, to his mother. He's saying there's nobody he respects more than himself, that he doesn't have any idea of a better man, no hero, nobody he would pattern his life after. I believe a boy needs this. He needs to see what becoming a man means, the same way a girl needs to see what mothering means. Children need models to aim their lives toward. Without them society stops growing, codes fall apart, lives begin to be lived from day to day and fad to fad, planning spans shorten, hopes shrink, discipline loses its value, nobility vanishes—all life loses its ability to endure.

I have an egocentric view of the universe; I know that man is the center no matter where he is. The father is the center of the family. He is a guide. He takes his son on trips into the world. He answers unanswerable questions by simply saying: "I don't know." He earns his son's respect by being respectable. In short, the father is there like the mother is there, and he doesn't close the door when he feels like screaming at God. He encourages strength and guts by being strong and persevering. He models his own image of man to his son. When the son grows strong enough to leave, the father is still there to model dignity of age. This is the greatest gift a father can give his son: the image of a strong, warm man. And a father can't give it if he doesn't have it, and he can't get it without learning what it means to be a man.

In all strong nations the father has been there in the center along with a strong mother—in rich balance. He is not in American culture today. He was once upon a time. The old heroes that haunt our deepest dreams and who confuse our decisions as to how and what to try for in our lives come from this era of America: the pioneer, the broad-minded Irish-American priest, the Gary Coopers of all the High Noons of life who face their enemies in the open, the individual politician who wouldn't be bought, the Elmer Gantrys who stumble pugnaciously into true religion—these heroes still walk tall through our dreams, but they're seldom encountered on the street, at work, at church, and on the speaker's platform. So we miss them. This is what I meant when I said that this is not the America I dreamt about.

I also said I didn't think that most Americans were strong enough to begin to walk back to the world—as it is. They don't have the guts to be that responsible, and they don't have it because they don't believe it is necessary in order for them to get along. But what about their children? I'm sure a man can sneak through life without getting touched, but I don't think that man's child can. We need models of the best make, models that reflect universes of possibility. We don't have them.

William Butler Yeats's poem *The Second Coming* paints the picture I'm trying to get at so vividly that I cite it here in full:

> Turning and turning in the widening gyre
> The falcon cannot hear the falconer;
> Things fall apart; the centre cannot hold;
> Mere anarchy is loosed upon the world,
> The blood-dimmed tide is loosed, and everywhere
> The ceremony of innocence is drowned;
> The best lack all conviction, while the worst

Are full of passionate intensity.
Surely some revelation is at hand;
Surely the Second Coming is at hand.
The Second Coming! Hardly are those words out
When a vast image out of *Spiritus Mundi*
Troubles my sight: somewhere in sands of the desert
A shape with lion body and the head of a man,
A gaze blank and pitiless as the sun,
Is moving its slow thighs, while all about it
Reel shadows of the indignant desert birds.
The darkness drops again; but now I know
That twenty centuries of stony sleep
Were vexed to nightmare by a rocking cradle
And what rough beast, its hour come round at last,
Slouches towards Bethlehem to be born?

America is big, so big a man doesn't know how to be any more. He doesn't know how to raise his children to be, either. Because he no longer knows what his country is. He, like the falcon, cannot hear it call to him to come this way or go that way. Truly, the center of America cannot hold us together, for no two of us know the same center. Therefore there is no center. Just as cities break up into shopping centers, our government has disassembled into bureaus in which no one man is responsible or accountable for anything—all is left up to the committee that is going to meet as soon as it has been formed. Which means that the only responsible item left is the system. This is America.

It is vague, big, impersonal, undefined, soft, sloppy. America is a slob. A thing that collects unemployment pay whenever it gets the chance. No one has to be true to anything: the system will take care of who is honest and who is not. The system is sick, and the people are without courage. The best have no confidence and the worst have too much.

But we still have a chance; all our seeds aren't bad. The few old hero-types who are left will be coming out more and more; they always do when things get bad. As a band of animals drives off the one of them that is sick, so these Americans will drive sick America out of business. They will beg for responsible positions and then gamble them against the truth and health of every little incident with which they have to deal. Professors who refuse to be bullied by administrators, personnel managers who refuse to be blinded by the degree, men who still search for personal character and strength— anyplace you find a person living by principles that grow in scope as he learns you find what I call an American. And yes, he looks primitive and ridiculous standing out there all alone. He is an old hero. And he will die nobly. But the others, the faceless gray murmur in every crowd, will need an expensive funeral, for contrast, so that their mourners will think that they had lived.

And where are the new heroes? Who are they? How do they live? Are they slouching beneath the shadows of the indignant dying American majority toward some Bethlehem to be born? Has Man been asleep for twenty centuries because he believed that Christ paid the price of wakefulness and that this price could be paid just once by one and not always by all? Then, what weird hero-child carries the nightmare of this two thousand years in his innocent and willing head?

When I ask, Who is the new hero? I'm not looking for a name, a celebrity, any one person. I'm looking for the image we have of our own best self. The new hero is one who is following after this image, but, unlike the donkey that follows after the farmer's carrot, he holds his own carrot out in front, and this keeps him honest. I'm not going to say that Zorba[3] is the hero, or that Bobby Dylan is the hero; but I would say that they and others have by example added to the portrait of a potential hero. You could say that potential is the hero, potential wherever it is found and expressed.

So I say the new hero is a world personality, for we are a potential world of men who require no corrals, who seek and enjoy freedom of being at ease among ourselves. If we can dream of a united world we can have one. All dreams are mirages of realities just beyond our present reach; tomorrow they will have a snow-cone stand in the middle of the Sahara!

He's new, not yet standing, "moving his slow thighs," but he's here. He's a rough beast to handle because he can't think in terms of discriminant groups, nations, cultures; he thinks in terms of *Man*. Patriotism is a part of the two-thousand-year-old nightmare he has; the definition of the word stymies him, for he has no feeling with which to fuel it. He's like the country boy who's gone to the city and now can't stand his small town, can't take a job in his father's firm. He pours sympathy into the gap between him and his father but he pumps his passion onto the world as a whole. He learns at least a few words in all the major languages, but he doesn't feel it necessary to hitch up a welcome wagon to meet a man from Zanzibar; rather, he'll meet a man and like him and drink coffee with him and in the stride of the encounter learn that Zanzibar is where he comes from. And he won't excitedly ask him to say something! He'd carry no flag to the moon. He'd walk into any church to pray, and he'd pray without thinking to whom. These are truths for the new hero, and by being so, they direct his stride not his strife. He isn't fighting for them; he's got them. Finally, because being a world personality is about as big as he can be, he has no one else to live up to and he doesn't need an identification card.

He deals with life in person, with persons in person; you know he's all there when you're with him. He's learned that he doesn't need anyone's seal of approval to continue in his first attempt at living life. He knows nobody knows and he isn't afraid of not knowing. He cherishes his innocence. He enjoys mystery and quarrels with most solutions like a puppy tugging at a sock until it is in threads. He has much hope in the future—and is sure we'd all like one another if we'd just bury our bombs.

He believes himself to be capable to endure at any level, therefore doesn't worry about losing a job, and therefore doesn't have to adopt a role to please a boss. He has dodged those great compromises by learning to love both alternatives: job, no job, it doesn't matter, for there will soon be another job, and in the meantime, he's a good gardener. He can get along anywhere;

---

[3] Nikos Kazantzakis, *Zorba the Greek*, New York, Simon and Schuster, 1952. Also the film by the same name.

he didn't specialize in anything except life and so he can still learn very quickly.

He's got just what everyone needs today and he can't help but give it to them: warmth and time. He's never too busy, but he always has something to do.

Those who have moved out of town, to a small village, have forgotten their TV, radio and newspaper subscriptions, but have brought their kazoos, marbles, tops, kites, jacks, and Monopoly and are attempting to get clean and simple. They are repairing their damaged personalities without America's help. I think these people know that they are living and going someplace and are excited. Disowned, suspended, kicked out, evicted—they've finally got the message that society don't want 'em subvertin' their program. They've gone, now, to live a life out of line. I've got a feeling they, too, are potential new heroes.

You see, it all comes back to what is possible for us to do in life, to accomplish, to create, to enjoy. When we systematize life we are saying that any other way outside of the system is impossible, for this and this and this will happen to you. We defend our systems by a stockade of consequences. And then somehow we forget that we created both the system and the consequences; we begin to believe the system is unchangeable, is absolute, is god. In any case, life becomes increasingly impossible outside of certain definitions, and increasingly miserable inside them. How about the exceptions, the human exceptions to the rules? For example, and this is not an extreme example even though it shocks some of us: a father wakes up in the night, his daughter is crying, he finds her suffering from some sickness, so he rushes her to the nearest, not the cheapest, hospital. At the desk they inquire: "Do you have insurance? Do you have any money? Well, I'm terribly sorry but you'll have to see our social welfare personnel and they won't be in until tomorrow morning. There's nothing I can do," she says. The twenty-five-cent paper cup. What would you do in his shoes? Or should I ask, what have you done, for I imagine all of us have run into these counter people. But most of us comply even though some rough beast is raging beneath our breath to break desks, rules and systems and more or less kidnap the help we need. But we comply, we wait for people to do it the system's way, and the clock ticks and we wait and the little girl dies in the man's arms.

And it happens all over on all levels from the grossest to the pettiest— exceptions to the rules are forced to comply. Now I put it to you, *what human being is not an exception to the rule?*

No system should ever become so rigid as to not be able to handle with ease the unexpected. Which is just another way of saying no system should not be able to handle life.

In conclusion, the new hero is out to prove to himself and others that there are ways to live where no *They* is ever blamed, where no rule is ever made that can't be unmade or changed, and where the exceptions make up the reality and beauty of being human.

THE UNKNOWN CITIZEN

W. H. Auden

(To JS|07|M|378
This Marble Monument
Is Erected by the State)

He was found by the Bureau of Statistics to be
One against whom there was no official complaint,
And all the reports on his conduct agree
That, in the modern sense of an old-fashioned word, he was a saint,
For in everything he did he served the Greater Community.
Except for the War till the day he retired
He worked in a factory and never got fired,
But satisfied his employers, Fudge Motors Inc.
Yet he wasn't a scab or odd in his views,
For his Union reports that he paid his dues,
(Our report on his Union shows it was sound)
And our Social Psychology workers found
That he was popular with his mates and liked a drink.
The Press are convinced that he bought a paper every day
And that his reactions to advertisements were normal in every way.
Policies taken out in his name prove that he was fully insured,
And his Health-card shows he was once in hospital but left it cured.
Both Producers Research and High-Grade Living declare
He was fully sensible to the advantages of the Instalment Plan
And had everything necessary to the Modern Man,
A phonograph, a radio, a car and a frigidaire.
Our researchers into Public Opinion are content
That he held the proper opinions for the time of year;
When there was peace, he was for peace; when there was war, he went.
He was married and added five children to the population,
Which our Eugenist says was the right number for a parent of his generation,
And our teachers report that he never interfered with their education.
Was he free? Was he happy? The question is absurd:
Had anything been wrong, we should certainly have heard.

A & P

John Updike

In walks these three girls in nothing but bathing suits. I'm in the third checkout slot, with my back to the door, so I don't see them until they're over by the bread. The one that caught my eye first was the one in the plaid green two-piece. She was a chunky kid, with a good tan and a sweet broad soft-looking can with those two crescents of white just under it, where the sun never seems to hit, at the top of the backs of her legs. I stood there with my hand on a box of HiHo crackers trying to remember if I rang it up or not. I ring it up again and the customer starts giving me hell. She's one of these cash-register-watchers, a witch about fifty with rouge on her cheekbones and no eyebrows, and I know it made her day to trip me up. She'd been watching cash registers for fifty years and probably never seen a mistake before.

By the time I got her feathers smoothed and her goodies into a bag—she gives me a little snort in passing, if she'd been born at the right time they would have burned her over in Salem—by the time I get her on her way the girls had circled around the bread and were coming back, without a pushcart, back my way along the counters, in the aisle between the checkouts and the Special bins. They didn't even have shoes on. There was this chunky one, with the two-piece—it was bright green and the seams on the bra were still sharp and her belly was still pretty pale so I guessed she just got it (the suit)—there was this one, with one of those chubby berry-faces, the lips all bunched together under her nose, this one, and a tall one, with black hair that hadn't quite frizzed right, and one of those sunburns right across under the eyes, and a chin that was too long—you know, the kind of girl other girls think is very "striking" and "attractive" but never quite makes it, as they very well know, which is why they like her so much—and then the third one, that wasn't quite so tall. She was the queen. She kind of led them, the other two peeking around and making their shoulders round. She didn't look around, not this queen, she just walked straight on slowly, on these long white prima-donna legs. She came down a little hard on her heels, as if she didn't walk in her bare feet that much, putting down her heels and then letting the weight move along to her toes as if she was testing the floor with every step, putting a little deliberate extra action into it. You never know for sure how girls' minds work (do you really think it's a mind in there or just a little buzz like a bee in a glass jar?) but you got the idea she had talked the other two into coming in here with her, and now she was showing them how to do it, walk slow and hold yourself straight.

She had on a kind of dirty-pink—beige maybe, I don't know—bathing suit with a little nubble all over it and, what got me, the straps were down. They were off her shoulders looped loose around the cool tops of her arms, and I guess as a result the suit had slipped a little on her, so all around the top of the cloth there was this shining rim. If it hadn't been there you wouldn't have known there could have been anything whiter than those shoulders. With the straps pushed off, there was nothing between the top of the suit and the top of her head except just *her,* this clean bare plane of the top of her chest down from the shoulder bones like a dented sheet of metal tilted in the light. I mean, it was more than pretty.

She had sort of oaky hair that the sun and salt had bleached, done up in a bun that was unravelling, and a kind of prim face. Walking into the A & P with your straps down, I suppose it's the only kind of face you *can* have. She held her head so high her neck, coming up out of those white shoulders, looked kind of stretched, but I didn't mind. The longer her neck was, the more of her there was.

She must have felt in the corner of her eye me and over my shoulder Stokesie in the second slot watching, but she didn't tip. Not this queen. She kept her eyes moving across the racks, and stopped, and turned so slow it made my stomach rub the inside of my apron, and buzzed to the other two, who kind of huddled against her for relief, and then they all three of them went up the cat-and-dog-food-breakfast-cereal-macaroni-rice-raisins-season-ings-spreads-spaghetti-soft-drinks-crackers-and-cookies aisle. From the third slot I look straight up this aisle to the meat counter, and I watched them all the way. The fat one with the tan sort of fumbled with the cookies, but on second thought she put the package back. The sheep pushing their carts down the aisle—the girls were walking against the usual traffic (not that we have one-way signs or anything)—were pretty hilarious. You could see them, when Queenie's white shoulders dawned on them, kind of jerk, or hop, or hiccup, but their eyes snapped back to their own baskets and on they pushed. I bet you could set off dynamite in an A & P and the people would by and large keep reaching and checking oatmeal off their lists and mut-tering "Let me see, there was a third thing, began with A, asparagus, no, ah, yes, applesauce!" or whatever it is they do mutter. But there was no doubt, this jiggled them. A few houseslaves in pin curlers even looked around after pushing their carts past to make sure what they had seen was correct.

You know, it's one thing to have a girl in a bathing suit down on the beach, where what with the glare nobody can look at each other much any-way, and another thing in the cool of the A & P, under the fluorescent lights, against all those stacked packages, with her feet paddling along naked over our checkerboard green-and-cream rubber-tile floor.

"Oh Daddy," Stokesie said beside me. "I feel so faint."

"Darling," I said. "Hold me tight." Stokesie's married, with two babies chalked up on her fuselage already, but as far as I can tell that's the only difference. He's twenty-two, and I was nineteen this April.

"Is it done?" he asks, the responsible married man finding his voice. I forgot to say he thinks he's going to be manager some sunny day, maybe in 1990 when it's called the Great Alexandrov and Petrooshki Tea Company or something.

What he meant was, our town is five miles from a beach, with a big summer colony out on the Point, but we're right in the middle of town, and the women generally put on a shirt or shorts or something before they get out of the car into the street. And anyway these are usually women with six children and varicose veins mapping their legs and nobody, including them, could care less. As I say, we're right in the middle of town, and if you stand at our front doors you can see two banks and the Congregational church and the newspaper store and three real-estate offices and about twenty-seven old freeloaders tearing up Central Street because the sewer broke again. It's not as if we're on the Cape; we're north of Boston and there's people in this town haven't seen the ocean for twenty years.

The girls had reached the meat counter and were asking McMahon something. He pointed, they pointed, and they shuffled out of sight behind a pyramid of Diet Delight peaches. All that was left for us to see was old McMahon patting his mouth and looking after them sizing up their joints. Poor kids, I began to feel sorry for them, they couldn't help it.

Now here comes the sad part of the story, at least my family says it's sad, but I don't think it's so sad myself. The store's pretty empty, it being Thursday afternoon, so there was nothing much to do except lean on the register and wait for the girls to show up again. The whole store was like a pinball machine and I didn't know which tunnel they'd come out of. After a while they come around out of the far aisle, around the light bulbs, records at discount of the Caribbean Six or Tony Martin Sings or some such gunk you wonder they waste the wax on, sixpacks of candy bars, and plastic toys done up in cellophane that fall apart when a kid looks at them anyway. Around they come, Queenie still leading the way, and holding a little gray jar in her hand. Slots Three through Seven are unmanned and I could see her wondering between Stokes and me, but Stokesie with his usual luck draws an old party in baggy gray pants who stumbles up with four giant cans of pineapple juice (what do these bums *do* with all that pineapple juice? I've often asked myself) so the girls come to me. Queenie puts down the jar and I take it into my fingers icy cold. Kingfish Fancy Herring Snacks in Pure Sour Cream: 49¢. Now her hands are empty, not a ring or a bracelet, bare as God made them, and I wonder where the money's coming from. Still with that prim look she lifts a folded dollar bill out of the hollow at the center of her nubbled pink top. The jar went heavy in my hand. Really, I thought that was so cute.

Then everybody's luck begins to run out. Lengel comes in from haggling with a truck full of cabbages on the lot and is about to scuttle into that door marked MANAGER behind which he hides all day when the girls touch his eye. Lengel's pretty dreary, teaches Sunday school and the rest, but he doesn't miss that much. He comes over and says, "Girls, this isn't the beach."

Queenie blushes, though maybe it's just a brush of sunburn I was noticing for the first time, now that she was so close. "My mother asked me to pick up a jar of herring snacks." Her voice kind of startled me, the way voices do when you see the people first, coming out so flat and dumb yet kind of tony, too, the way it ticked over "pick-up" and "snacks." All of a sudden I slid right down her voice into her living room. Her father and the other men were standing around in ice-cream coats and bow ties and the women were in sandals picking up herring snacks on toothpicks off a big glass plate and they were all holding drinks the color of water with olives and sprigs of mint in them. When my parents have somebody over they get lemonade and if it's a real racy affair Schlitz in tall glasses with "They'll Do It Every Time" cartoons stencilled on.

"That's all right," Lengel said. "But this isn't the beach." His repeating this struck me as funny, as if it had just occurred to him, and he had been thinking all these years the A & P was a great big dune and he was the head lifeguard. He didn't like my smiling—as I say he doesn't miss much—but he concentrates on giving the girls that sad Sunday-school-superintendent stare.

Queenie's blush is no sunburn now, and the plump one in plaid, that I liked better from the back—a really sweet can—pipes up, "We weren't doing any shopping. We just came in for the one thing."

"That makes no difference," Lengel tells her, and I could see from the way his eyes went that he hadn't noticed she was wearing a two-piece before. "We want you decently dressed when you come in here."

"We *are* decent," Queenie says suddenly, her lower lip pushing, getting sore now that she remembers her place, a place from which the crowd that runs the A & P must look pretty crummy. Fancy Herring Snacks flashed in her very blue eyes.

"Girls, I don't want to argue with you. After this come in here with your shoulders covered. It's our policy." He turns his back. That's policy for you. Policy is what the kingpins want. What the others want is juvenile delinquency.

All this while, the customers had been showing up with their carts but, you know, sheep, seeing a scene, they had all bunched up on Stokesie, who shook open a paper bag as gently as peeling a peach, not wanting to miss a word. I could feel in the silence everybody getting nervous, most of all Lengel, who asks me, "Sammy, have you rung up their purchase?"

I thought and said "No" but it wasn't about that I was thinking. I go through the punches, 4, 9, GROC, TOT—it's more complicated than you think, and after you do it often enough, it begins to make a little song, that you hear words to, in my case "Hello (*bing*) there, you (*gung*) hap-py *pee*-pul (*splat*)!"—the *splat* being the drawer flying out. I uncrease the bill, tenderly as you may imagine, it just having come from between the two smoothest scoops of vanilla I had ever known were there, and pass a half and a penny into her narrow pink palm, and nestle the herrings in a bag and twist its neck and hand it over, all the time thinking.

The girls, and who'd blame them, are in a hurry to get out, so I say "I quit" to Lengel quick enough for them to hear, hoping they'll stop and watch me, their unsuspected hero. They keep right on going, into the electric eye;

the door flies open and they flicker across the lot to their car, Queenie and Plaid and Big Tall Goony-Goony (not that as raw material she was so bad), leaving me with Lengel and a kink in his eyebrow.

"Did you say something, Sammy?"

"I said I quit."

"I thought you did."

"You didn't have to embarrass them."

"It was they who were embarrassing us."

I started to say something that come out "Fiddle-de-doo." It's a saying of my grandmother's, and I know she would have been pleased.

"I don't think you know what you're saying," Lengel said.

"I know you don't," I said. "But I do." I pull the bow at the back of my apron and start shrugging it off my shoulders. A couple customers that had been heading for my slot begin to knock against each other, like scared pigs in a chute.

Lengel sighs and begins to look very patient and old and gray. He's been a friend of my parents for years. "Sammy, you don't want to do this to your Mom and Dad," he tells me. It's true, I don't. But it seems to me that once you begin a gesture it's fatal not to go through with it. I fold the apron, "Sammy" stitched in red on the pocket, and put it on the counter, and drop the bow tie on top of it. The bow tie is theirs, if you've ever wondered. "You'll feel this for the rest of your life," Lengel says, and I know that's true, too, but remembering how he made that pretty girl blush makes me so scrunchy inside I punch the No Sale tab and the machine whirs "pee-pul" and the drawer splats out. One advantage to this scene taking place in summer, I can follow this up with a clean exit, there's no fumbling around getting your coat and galoshes, I just saunter into the electric eye in my white shirt that my mother ironed the night before, and the door heaves itself open, and outside the sunshine is skating around on the asphalt.

I look around for my girls, but they're gone, of course. There wasn't anybody but some young married screaming with her children about some candy they didn't get by the door of a powder-blue Falcon station wagon. Looking back in the big windows, over the bags of peat moss and aluminum lawn furniture stacked on the pavement, I could see Lengel in my place in the slot, checking the sheep through. His face was dark gray and his back stiff, as if he'd just had an injection of iron, and my stomach kind of fell as I felt how hard the world was going to be to me hereafter.

DANNY

J. M. Synge

One night a score of Erris men,
A score I'm told and nine,
Said, "We'll get shut of Danny's noise
Of girls and widows dyin'.

"There's not his like from Binghamstown
To Boyle and Ballycroy,
At playing hell on decent girls,
At beating man and boy.

"He's left two pairs of female twins
Beyond in Killacreest,
And twice in Crossmolina fair
He's struck the parish priest.

"But we'll come round him in the night
A mile beyond the Mullet;
Ten will quench his bloody eyes,
And ten will choke his gullet."

It wasn't long till Danny came,
From Bangor making way,
And he was damning moon and stars
And whistling grand and gay.

Till in a gap of hazel glen—
And not a hare in sight—
Out lepped the nine-and-twenty lads
Along his left and right.

Then Danny smashed the nose on Byrne,
He split the lips on three,
And bit across the right-hand thumb
On one Red Shawn Magee.

But seven tipped him up behind,
And seven kicked before,

And seven squeezed around his throat
Till Danny kicked no more.

Then some destroyed him with their heels,
Some tramped him in the mud,
Some stole his purse and timber pipe,
And some washed off his blood.

And when you're walking out the way
From Bangor to Belmullet,
You'll see a flat cross on a stone,
Where men choked Danny's gullet.

A MESSAGE

Huey P. Newton

The lower socio-economic Black male is a man of confusion. He faces a hostile environment and is not sure that it is not his own sins that have attracted the hostilities of society. All his life he has been taught (explicitly and implicitly) that he is an inferior approximation of humanity. As a man, he finds himself void of those things that bring respect and a feeling of worthiness. He looks around for something to blame for his situation, but because he is not sophisticated regarding the socio-economic teachings, he ultimately blames himself.

When he was a child, his parents told him that they were not affluent because "we didn't have the opportunity to become educated," or "we did not take advantage of the educational opportunities that were offered to us." They tell their children that things will be different for them if they are educated and skilled, but that there is absolutely nothing other than this occasional warning (and often not even this) to stimulate education. Black people are great worshippers of education, even the lower socio-economic Black person, but at the same time, they are afraid of exposing themselves to it. They are afraid because they are vulnerable to having their fears verified; perhaps they will find that they can't compete with white students. The Black person tells himself that he could have done much more if he had really wanted to. The fact is, of course, that the assumed educational opportunities were never available to the lower socio-economic Black person due to the unique position assigned him in life.

It is a two-headed monster that haunts this man. First, his attitude is that he lacks innate ability to cope with the socio-economic problems confronting him, and second, he tells himself that he has the ability but he simply has not felt strongly enough to try to acquire the skills needed to manipulate his environment. In a desperate effort to assume self-respect, he rationalizes that he is lethargic; in this way, he denies a possible lack of innate ability. If he openly attempts to discover his abilities, he and others may see him for what he is—or is not, and this is the real fear. He then withdraws into the world of the invisible, but not without a struggle. He may attempt to make himself visible by processing his hair, acquiring a "boss mop," or driving a long car, even though he can't afford it. He may father several illegitimate children by several different women in order to display his masculinity. But in the end, he realizes that he is ineffectual in his efforts.

Society responds to him as a thing, a beast, a nonentity, something to be ignored or stepped on. He is asked to respect laws that do not respect him. He is asked to digest a code of ethics that acts upon him but not for him. He is confused and in a constant state of rage, of shame and doubt. This psychological set permeates all his interpersonal relationships. It determines his view of the social system. His psychological set developments have been prematurely arrested. This doubt begins at a very early age and continues through his life. The parents pass it on to the child and the social system reinforces the fear, the shame, and the doubt.

In the third or fourth grade he may find that he shares the classroom with white students, but when the class is engaged in reading exercises, all the Black students find themselves in a group at a table reserved for slow readers. This may be quite an innocent effort on the part of the school system. The teacher may not realize that the Black students feared (in fact, feel certain) that Black means dumb and white means smart. The children do not realize that the head start the children got at home is what accounts for the situation. It is generally accepted that the child is the father of the man; this holds true for the lower socio-economic Black people.

With whom, with what can he, a man, identify? As a child he had no permanent male figure with whom to identify; as a man, he sees nothing in society with which he can identify as an extension of himself. His life is built on mistrust, shame, doubt, guilt, inferiority, role confusion, isolation and despair. He feels that he is something less than a man, and it is evident in his conversation: "the white man is 'THE MAN', he got everything, and he knows everything, and a nigger ain't nothing."

In a society where a man is valued according to occupation and material possessions, he is unskilled and more often than not, either marginally employed or unemployed. Often his wife (who is able to secure a job as a maid cleaning for white people) is the breadwinner. He is therefore viewed as quite worthless by his wife and children. He is ineffectual both in and out of the home. He cannot provide for or protect his family. He is invisible, a nonentity. Society will not acknowledge him as a man. He is a consumer and not a producer. He is dependent upon the white man ('THE MAN') to feed his family, to give him a job, educate his children, serve as the model that he tries to emulate. He is dependent and he hates 'THE MAN' and he hates himself. Who is he? Is he a very old adolescent or is he the slave he used to be?

What did he do to be so BLACK and blue?

BLACK RAGE

William H. Grier
Price M. Cobbs

History may well show that of all the men who lived during our fateful century none illustrated the breadth or the grand potential of man so magnificently as did Malcolm X. If, in future chronicles, America is regarded as the major nation of our day, and the rise of darker people from bondage as the major event, then no figure has appeared thus far who captures the spirit of our times as does Malcolm.

Malcolm is an authentic hero, indeed the only universal black hero. In his unrelenting opposition to the viciousness in America, he fired the imagination of black men all over the world.

If this black nobleman is a hero to black people in the United States and if his life reflects their aspirations, there can be no doubt of the universality of black rage.

Malcolm responded to his position in his world and to his blackness in the manner of so many black boys. He turned to crime. He was saved by a religious sect given to a strange, unhistorical explanation of the origin of black people and even stranger solutions to their problems. He rose to power in that group and outgrew it.

Feeding on his own strength, growing in response to his own commands, limited by no creed, he became a citizen of the world and an advocate of all oppressed people no matter their color or belief. Anticipating his death by an assassin, he distilled, in a book, the essence of his genius, his life. His autobiography thus is a legacy and, together with his speeches, illustrates the thrusting growth of the man—his evolution, rapid, propulsive, toward the man he might have been had he lived.

The essence of Malcolm X was growth, change, and a seeking after truth.

Alarmed white people saw him first as an eccentric and later as a dangerous radical—a revolutionary without troops who threatened to stir black people to riot and civil disobedience. Publicly, they treated him as a joke; privately, they were afraid of him.

After his death he was recognized by black people as the "black shining prince" and recordings of his speeches became treasured things. His autobiography was studied, his life marveled at. Out of this belated admiration came the philosophical basis for black activism and indeed the thrust of Black Power itself, away from integration and civil rights and into the "black bag."

Unlike Malcolm, however, the philosophical underpinnings of the new black militancy were static. They remained encased within the ideas of revolution and black nationhood, ideas Malcolm had outgrown by the time of his death. His stature has made even his earliest statements gospel and men now find themselves willing to die for words which in retrospect are only milestones in the growth of a fantastic man.

Many black men who today preach blackness seem headed blindly toward self-destruction, uncritical of anything "black" and damning the white man for diabolical wickedness. For a philosophical base they have turned to the words of Malcolm's youth.

This perversion of Malcolm's intellectual position will not, we submit, be held against him by history.

Malcolm's meaning for us lies in his fearless demand for truth and his evolution from a petty criminal to an international statesman—accomplished by a black man against odds of terrible magnitude—in America. His message was his life, not his words, and Malcolm knew it.

Black Power activism—thrust by default temporarily at the head of a powerful movement—is a conception that contributes in a significant way to the strength and unity of that movement but is unable to provide the mature vision for the mighty works ahead. It will pass and leave black people in this country prouder, stronger, more determined, but in need of grander princes with clearer vision.

We believe that the black masses will rise with a simple and eloquent demand to which new leaders must give tongue. They will say to America simply:

"Get Off Our Backs!"

The problem will be so simply defined.
What is the problem?
The white-man has crushed all but the life from blacks from the time they came to these shores to this very day.
What is the solution?
Get off their backs.
How?
By simply doing it—now.
This is no oversimplification. Greater changes than this in the relations of peoples have taken place before. The nation would benefit tremendously. Such a change might bring about a closer examination of our relations with foreign countries, a reconsideration of economic policies, and a re-examination if not a redefinition of nationhood. It might in fact be the only change which can prevent a degenerative decline from a powerful nation to a feeble, third-class, ex-colonialist country existing at the indulgence of stronger powers.

In spite of the profound shifts in power throughout the world in the past thirty years, the United States seems to have a domestic objective of "business as usual," with no change needed or in fact wanted.

All the nasty problems are overseas. At home the search is for bigger profits and smaller costs, better education and lower taxes, more vacation and less work, more for me and less for you. Problems at home are to be talked away, reasoned into nonexistence, and put to one side while we continue the great American game of greed.

There is, however, an inevitability built into the natural order of things. Cause and effect are in fact joined, and if you build a sufficient cause then not all the talk or all the tears in God's creation can prevent the effect from presenting itself one morning as the now ripened fruit of your labors.

America began building a cause when black men were first sold into bondage. When the first black mother killed her newborn rather than have him grow into a slave. When the first black man slew himself rather than submit to an organized system of man's feeding upon another's flesh. America had well begun a cause when all the rebels were either slain or broken and the nation set to the task of refining the system of slavery so that the maximum labor might be extracted from it.

The system achieved such refinement that the capital loss involved when a slave woman aborted could be set against the gain to be expected from forcing her into brutish labor while she was with child.

America began building a potent cause in its infancy as a nation.

It developed a way of life, an American ethos, a national life style which included the assumption that blacks are inferior and were born to hew wood and draw water. Newcomers to this land (if white) were immediately made to feel welcome and, among the bounty available, were given blacks to feel superior to. They were required to despise and deprecate them, abuse and exploit them, and one can only imagine how munificent this land must have seemed to the European—a land with built-in scapegoats.

The hatred of blacks has been so deeply bound up with being an American that it has been one of the first things new Americans learn and one of the last things old Americans forget. Such feelings have been elevated to a position of national character, so that individuals now no longer feel personal guilt or responsibility for the oppression of black people. The nation has incorporated this oppression into itself in the form of folkways and storied traditions, leaving the individual free to shrug his shoulders and say only: "That's our way of life."

This way of life is a heavy debt indeed, and one trembles for the debtor when payment comes due.

America has waxed rich and powerful in large measure on the backs of black laborers. It has become a violent, pitiless nation, hard and calculating, whose moments of generosity are only brief intervals in a ferocious narrative of life, bearing a ferocity and an aggression so strange in this tiny world where men die if they do not live together.

With the passing of the need for black laborers, black people have become useless; they are a drug on the market. There are not enough menial jobs. They live in a nation which has evolved a work force of skilled and semi-skilled workmen. A nation which chooses simultaneously to exclude all black men from this favored labor force and to deny them the one thing America has offered every other group—unlimited growth with a ceiling set only by one's native gifts.

The facts, however obfuscated, are simple. Since the demise of slavery black people have been expendable in a cruel and impatient land. The damage done to black people has been beyond reckoning. Only now are we beginning to sense the bridle placed on black children by a nation which does not want them to grow into mature human beings.

The most idealistic social reformer of our time, Martin Luther King, was not slain by one man; his murder grew out of that large body of violent bigotry America has always nurtured—that body of thinking which screams for the blood of the radical, or the conservative, or the villain, or the saint. To the extent that he stood in the way of bigotry, his life was in jeopardy, his saintly persuasion notwithstanding. To the extent that he was black and was calling America to account, his days were numbered by the nation he sought to save.

Men and women, even children, have been slain for no other earthly reason than their blackness. Property and goods have been stolen and the victims then harried and punished for their poverty. But such viciousness can at least be measured or counted.

Black men, however, have been so hurt in their manhood that they are now unsure and uneasy as they teach their sons to be men. Women have been so humiliated and used that they may regard womanhood as a curse and flee from it. Such pain, so deep, and such real jeopardy, that the fundamental protective function of the family has been denied. These injuries we have no way to measure.

Black men have stood so long in such peculiar jeopardy in America that a *black norm* has developed—a suspiciousness of one's environment which is necessary for survival. Black people, to a degree that approaches paranoia, must be ever alert to danger from their white fellow citizens. It is a cultural phenomenon peculiar to black Americans. And it is a posture so close to paranoid thinking that the mental disorder into which black people most frequently fall is paranoid psychosis.

Can we say that white men have driven black men mad?

An educated black woman had worked in an integrated setting for fifteen years. Compliant and deferential, she had earned promotions and pay increases by hard work and excellence. At no time had she been involved in black activism, and her only participation in the movement had been a yearly contribution to the N.A.A.C.P.

During a lull in the racial turmoil she sought psychiatric treatment. She explained that she had lately become alarmed at waves of rage that swept over her as she talked to white people or at times even as she looked at them. In view of her past history of compliance and passivity, she felt that something was wrong with her. If her controls slipped she might embarrass herself or lose her job.

A black man, a professional, had been a "nice guy" all his life. He was a hard-working non-militant who avoided discussions of race with his white colleagues. He smiled if their comments were harsh and remained unresponsive to racist statements. Lately he had experienced almost uncontrollable anger toward his white co-workers, and although he still manages to keep his feelings to himself, he confides that blacks and whites have been lying to each other. There is hatred and violence between them and he feels trapped. He too fears for himself if his controls should slip.

If these educated recipients of the white man's bounty find it hard to control their rage, what of their less fortunate kinsman who has less to protect, less to lose, and more scars to show for his journey in this land?

. . . The centuries of senseless cruelty and the permeation of the black man's character with the conviction of his own hatefulness and inferiority tell a sorry tale.

This dismal tone has been deliberate. It has been an attempt to evoke a certain quality of depression and hopelessness in the reader and to stir these feelings. These are the most common feelings tasted by black people in America.

The horror carries the endorsement of centuries and the entire lifespan of a nation. It is a way of life which reaches back to the beginnings of recorded time. And all the bestiality, wherever it occurs and however long it has been happening, is narrowed, focused, and refined to shine into a black child's eyes when first he views his world. All that has ever happened to black men and women he sees in the victims closest to him, his parents.

A life is an eternity and throughout all that eternity a black child has breathed the foul air of cruelty. He has grown up to find that his spirit was crushed before he knew there was need of it. His ambitions, even in their forming, showed him to have set his hand against his own. This is the desolation of black life in America.

Depression and grief are hatred turned on the self. It is instructive to pursue the relevance of this truth to the condition of black Americans.

Black people have shown a genius for surviving under the most deadly circumstances. They have survived because of their close attention to reality. A black dreamer would have a short life in Mississippi. They are of necessity bound to reality, chained to the facts of the times; historically the penalty for misjudging a situation involving white men has been death. The preoccupation with religion has been a willing adoption of fantasy to prod an otherwise reluctant mind to face another day.

We will even play tricks on ourselves if it helps us stay alive.

The psychological devices used to survive are reminiscent of the years of slavery, and it is no coincidence. The same devices are used because black men face the same danger now as then.

The grief and depression caused by the condition of black men in America is an unpopular reality to the sufferers. They would rather see themselves in a more heroic posture and chide a disconsolate brother. They would like to point to their achievements (which in fact have been staggering); they would rather point to virtue (which has been shown in magnificent form by some blacks); they would point to bravery, fidelity, prudence, brilliance, creativity, all of which dark men have shown in abundance. But the overriding experience of the black American has been grief and sorrow and no man can change that fact.

His grief has been realistic and appropriate. What people have so earned a period of mourning?

We want to emphasize yet again the depth of the grief for slain sons and ravished daughters, how deep and lingering it is.

If the depth of this sorrow is felt, we can then consider what can be made of this emotion.

As grief lifts and the sufferer moves toward health, the hatred he had turned on himself is redirected toward his tormentors, and the fury of his attack on the one who caused him pain is in direct proportion to the depth of his grief. When the mourner lashes out in anger, it is a relief to those who love him, for they know he has now returned to health.

Observe that the amount of rage the oppressed turns on his tormentor is a direct function of the depth of his grief, and consider the intensity of black men's grief.

Slip for a moment into the soul of a black girl whose womanhood is blighted, not because she is ugly, but because she is black and by definition all blacks are ugly.

Become for a moment a black citizen of Birmingham, Alabama, and try to understand his grief and dismay when innocent children are slain while they worship, for no other reason than that they are black.

Imagine how an impoverished mother feels as she watches the light of creativity snuffed out in her children by schools which dull the mind and environs which rot the soul.

For a moment make yourself the black father whose son went innocently to war and there was slain—for whom, for what?

For a moment be any black person, anywhere, and you will feel the waves of hopelessness that engulfed black men and women when Martin Luther King was murdered. All black people understood the tide of anarchy that followed his death.

It is the transformation of this quantum of grief into aggression of which we now speak. As a sapling bent low stores energy for a violent backswing, blacks bent double by oppression have stored energy which will be released in the form of rage—black rage, apocalyptic and final.

White Americans have developed a high skill in the art of misunderstanding black people. It must have seemed to slaveholders that slavery would last through all eternity, for surely their misunderstanding of black bondsmen suggested it. If the slaves were eventually to be released from bondage, what could be the purpose of creating the fiction of their subhumanity?

It must have seemed to white men during the period 1865 to 1945 that black men would always be a passive, compliant lot. If not, why would they have stoked the flames of hatred with such deliberately barbarous treatment?

White Americans today deal with "racial incidents" from summer to summer as if such minor turbulence will always remain minor and one need only keep the blacks busy till fall to have made it through another troubled season.

Today it is the young men who are fighting the battles, and, for now, their elders, though they have given their approval, have not joined in. The time seems near, however, for the full range of the black masses to put down the broom and buckle on the sword. And it grows nearer day by day. Now we see skirmishes, sputtering erratically, evidence if you will that the young men are in a warlike mood. But evidence as well that the elders are watching closely and may soon join the battle.

Even these minor flurries have alarmed the country and have resulted in a spate of generally senseless programs designed to give *temporary summer jobs!* More interesting in its long-range prospects has been the apparent eagerness to draft black men for military service. If in fact this is a deliberate design to place black men in uniform in order to get them off the street, it may be the most curious "instant cure" for a serious disease this nation has yet attempted. Young black men are learning the most modern techniques for killing—techniques which may be used against *any* enemy.

But it is all speculation. The issue finally rests with the black masses. When the servile men and women stand up, we had all better duck.

We should ask what is likely to galvanize the masses into aggression against the whites.

Will it be some grotesque atrocity against black people which at last causes one-tenth of the nation to rise up in indignation and crush the monstrosity?

Will it be the example of black people outside the United States who have gained dignity through their own liberation movement?

Will it be by the heroic action of a small group of blacks which by its wisdom and courage commands action in a way that cannot be denied?

Or will it be by blacks, finally and in an unpredictable way, simply getting fed up with the bumbling stupid racism of this country? Fired not so much by any one incident as by the gradual accretion of stupidity into fixtures of national policy.

All are possible, or any one, or something yet unthought. It seems certain only that on the course the nation now is headed it will happen.

One might consider the possibility that, if the national direction remains unchanged, such a conflagration simply might not come about. Might not black people remain where they are, as they did for a hundred years during slavery?

Such seems truly inconceivable. Not because blacks are so naturally warlike or rebellious, but because they are filled with such grief, such sorrow, such bitterness, and such hatred. It seems now delicately poised, not yet risen to the flashpoint, but rising rapidly nonetheless. No matter what repressive measures are invoked against the blacks, they will never swallow their rage and go back to blind hopelessness.

If existing oppressions and humiliating disenfranchisements are to be lifted, they will have to be lifted most speedily, or catastrophe will follow.

For there are no more psychological tricks blacks can play upon themselves to make it possible to exist in dreadful circumstances. No more lies can they tell themselves. No more dreams to fix on. No more opiates to dull the pain. No more patience. No more thought. No more reason. Only a welling tide risen out of all those terrible years of grief, now a tidal wave of fury and rage, and all black, black as night.

THE AMERICAN INDIAN: CITIZEN IN CAPTIVITY

Biloine W. Young

The school board of a city in the Southwest bordering an Indian reservation had been looking for a tract of land to acquire as a site for a new public high school. The acreage finally selected was owned by a Mrs. Yazzi, a Navajo (the name is fictitious, but the incident isn't). When the superintendent of schools opened negotiations to purchase the land he learned that he would not be dealing with Mrs. Yazzi, nor with her attorney, but with the realty agent for the Bureau of Indian Affairs of the Navajo Agency. This agent would do the negotiating, make all of the decisions (including whether or not to sell the land), and would stipulate the terms of the sale. If the sale is consummated, the income derived will not be given to Mrs. Yazzi but will be invested for her by the Bureau realty officer.

The federal government has intervened in the sale of the Yazzi land for one reason alone: Mrs. Yazzi is an American Indian. Although she is an adult, mentally competent, a citizen of the United States, a speaker of English, Mrs. Yazzi cannot, without permission from the Secretary of the Interior, enter into a contract with an attorney to sell her land for her. Nor can she sell, lease, rent, or give it away herself without authorization from the Department of the Interior. Ever since its establishment in 1824, the Bureau of Indian Affairs has operated under a set of paternalistic assumptions about the Indians that have resulted not in a participating citizenship for them (as they were surely designed to do) but in the perpetuation of isolation, dependence on government charity, and the illusion of self-government through a cluster of quasi-nations housed on government-granted enclaves throughout the country.

Overseeing the lives of most of the Indians in the United States is the Bureau of Indian Affairs, a vast agency under the Secretary of the Interior. The Bureau provides schooling, social services, jobs, and, through the Public Health Service, free medical and dental care for most of the 552,228 Indians living on 286 separate land units. Through the Bureau of Indian Affairs the federal government acts as a trustee "to protect the interests of minors and incompetents," to quote the expression used in the booklet *Answers to Questions About American Indians,* published by the Department of the Interior.

If the Bureau of Indian Affairs views its Indian trusts as "minors and incompetents" it is not surprising that a great many of the Indians have also come to accept this view of themselves. Many Indians now expect to be retarded in school. They expect to drink to excess (when an Indian alcoholic was asked why he drank, he replied, "Because I'm an Indian").

In their application for the Community Action Program (approved and funded March 3, 1965, by the Office of Economic Opportunity) the Navajo themselves identify these attitudes as being among their more severe problems. In their proposal they wrote, "One of the greatest needs existing today on the Navajo reservation lies in creating a feeling that the people in the isolated areas are important and that they do have an important role in determining their own future and destiny. . . . Many Navajos believe their future lies outside their control, and a dependency on either the Bureau of Indian Affairs or the Navajo Tribe has been substituted."

Although Mrs. Yazzi was present at the meeting between the Bureau officials and the school board to negotiate the sale of her land, she did not participate in the discussion. She, and everyone else, knew that she was only the figurehead owner of the land, that her presence at the meeting was only to perpetuate a fiction. She was not expected to take any part in the negotiations and so she did not.

The land owned by Mrs. Yazzi is known as "allotment land." There are currently about 4,185 allotments of 160 acres each still remaining in the Navajo country. These are similar in origin to homestead lands. Between 1907 and 1922 federal officers allotted 160 acres of land in the public domain to heads of Indian families and equal acreages for wives and each of the children. These allotments were made to protect Indians who were living on the public domain in the tenure of their land.

Although the Indians may have been under the impression that they held exclusive titles to their allotted land, they were mistaken. As the *Navajo Yearbook* explains it, "The United States Government holds, in trust for the Navajo Tribe, the title to the Reservation lands, including those areas purchased by the Tribe; and the United States government holds, in trust status for recipients of allotments or for their heirs, title to such areas of individual ownership. As trustee, the Federal Government is responsible for protection and management of property to which title is vested in Indian Tribes (or in individuals, in the case of trust allotments) and this responsibility is exercised, in part, by the Branch of Realty. The functions of this agency of the Federal Government include the sale, exchange, partition, patenting and leasing of Tribal and allotted lands. . . ."

Federal involvement with the Indians is divided into four major areas: land management, health services, education, and industrial development. The Bureau is also trying to teach the Indian how to govern himself through the establishment of various carefully controlled tribal organizations or pseudo-nations.

The paternalism of the government toward the Indians is nowhere better illustrated than in Public Law 474, passed by the Eighty-first Congress. Section 6 of the act authorizes the Navajo tribe to draw up a tribal constitution: "The constitution shall authorize the fullest possible participation of the Navajos in the administration of their affairs as approved by the Secretary of the Interior and shall become effective when approved by the Secretary. The constitution may be amended from time to time . . . and the Secretary of the Interior shall approve any amendment which in the opinion of the Secretary of the Interior advances the development of the Navajo people. . . ." Tribal funds may be spent only upon approval of the Secretary of the Interior. The tribe is also prohibited from entering into an agreement with an attorney involving tribal lands or funds.

The tragedy of the Indian is that, although he is an adult in the world of adults, he is still going through the adolescent play-acting of governing himself—playing at making decisions when, in reality, these decisions are being made for him by agents of the federal government. This federal trusteeship has not resulted, by and large, in the development of citizens who are particularly noted for their ability to make wise choices. The Navajo tribe, the largest single group of Indians in the United States (in 1960 they totaled 80,364 and, according to the Navajos, may have passed the 100,000 mark by now), has a birth rate that is one of the highest in the world, estimated at from 4.5 to 7 per cent annually; a rate of alcoholism that runs from an estimated 10 to 20 per cent of the adult population, topping that of almost any other group in the country; and a per capita income that is among the lowest in the nation. Problem drinking has long been associated with cultural stress. Gallup, New Mexico, known as the Indian capital, averages 750 arrests per month for drinking. Ninety per cent of those arrested are Indians. In 1958, 83 per cent of all the crimes committed by Navajos involved excessive drinking.

The Bureau of Indian Affairs in 1961 estimated the average per capita income among the Navajo at about $521. If each family contains five members, then the average family income would be approximately $2,600. When the value of free goods and services is included, the average per capita rises to about $645 and the average family income to about $3,225. This is 35.6 per cent of the comparable amount received by other citizens of New Mexico and only 29.8 per cent of the comparable amount received by fellow citizens of the United States.

The Indians themselves, however, declare their income to be far below the Bureau's estimates. In their application to the Office of Economic Opportunity for funds to initiate a Community Action Program, the Navajos estimated their average family income at $600 per year. Of 16,000 families now living on the reservation, 12,800 are listed as earning less than $1,000 per year. Of a total of 15,000 housing units extant, 13,000 are listed as substandard, with an average of six persons occupying each room.

The relationship between education and social and economic development has long been observed, and it is on education that the Bureau of Indian Affairs has spent the major portion of its budget, more than $121,000,000 for the current fiscal year. Despite these expenditures, the Indians continue to be retarded educationally. Of 9,751 elementary-level Navajo children whose records were analyzed in December 1957, only 6 per cent were up to grade level, 40 per cent were retarded at least one year, and 54 per cent were retarded two or more years.

Moreover, when the records of 100 Southwest Indians enrolled at the University of New Mexico between 1954 and 1958 were studied, they showed that 70 per cent dropped out of school with low grades, 20 per cent were currently enrolled, and 10 per cent obtained degrees. Of the 30 per cent who remained in school or obtained degrees, the majority were at some time placed on probation for inadequate scholarship. Of the thirty-one Indian students enrolled at the University of New Mexico in 1958, 84 per cent did not finish the first semester with a C average.

What holds back the Indian students? A lack of knowledge of English is the single most serious cause of Indian retardation in school, according to Dr. Anne Smith, of the Museum of New Mexico. Yet neither the Bureau of Indian Affairs nor the State Department of Education of New Mexico makes any requirement that elementary teachers in either the Bureau or public schools have training in the teaching of English as a second language.

A second factor in the retardation of Indian children is the segregated schooling provided by the Bureau of Indian Affairs. In Bureau schools, attended only by Indian children, the cultural and linguistic isolation of the reservation is institutionalized and perpetuated. Although the state policy of the Bureau is to place Indian children in public schools as rapidly as possible, Commissioner of Indian Affairs Philleo Nash, in a speech in June 1965, reported that contracts totaling more than $8,000,000 had been let for Indian school construction since the beginning of 1965—despite the fact that research indicates that Indian children perform better in public than in Bureau schools.

More than six years ago the Bureau agreed to place 1,000 Indian students in the Albuquerque school system, but to date it has placed only 339. Recently the Bureau announced plans to build a $13,000,000 boarding school in Albuquerque. The plan was temporarily dropped after an outcry from the New Mexico State Department of Education and public school superintendents in the state.

The experience of Dr. Charles Spain, late superintendent of the Albuquerque schools, is typical. Dr. Spain says, "The BIA [Bureau of Indian Affairs] has never contacted the schools to see if special classes could be arranged to better prepare more students for entering public schools. We've never been informed why the BIA isn't meeting its contractual obligations to send 1,000 students a year to the public schools." Dr. Spain adds that BIA has never approached the Albuquerque system to accept students at an earlier age, or to provide special remedial classes, to include them in planning for the Technical-Vocational Institute, or otherwise try to work out arrangements for incorporating more students in the schools. "We would be happy to work with the BIA to work out some of these problems. But they haven't asked us."

Segregated Bureau of Indian Affairs schools are continuing to be built, one within ten miles of Gallup, New Mexico.

Despite the Indian's economic and educational failures, and despite his alcoholic response to the stresses of living simultaneously in two cultures, he is showing signs of impatience with his role as a "minor and incompetent." Many are saying they want to manage their own affairs. Unfortunately, they must convince the Bureau of Indian Affairs that they are ready to do more than play at making their own decisions. The way it is now, the quiet Bureau agent who sits at the back of the Chapter House meetings can outvote the whole tribe. In subtle ways we still hold the Indian captive. Isn't it time we inaugurated a constructive program to set him free?

SMOHALLA SPEAKS

Nez Percé

My young men shall never work. Men who work cannot dream, and wisdom comes in dreams.

You ask me to plow the ground. Shall I take a knife and tear my mother's breast? Then when I die she will not take me to her bosom to rest.

You ask me to dig for stone. Shall I dig under her skin for bones? Then when I die I cannot enter her body to be born again.

You ask me to cut grass and make hay and sell it, and be rich like white men. But how dare I cut off my mother's hair?

It is a bad law, and my people cannot obey it. I want my people to stay with me here. All the dead men will come to life again. We must wait here in the house of our fathers and be ready to meet them in the body of our mother.

THE CASE OF THE DEERSLAYER

Stan Steiner

In the quiet of the courthouse square the dark-skinned men sat under the leafless trees of spring, waiting. With brooding and ominous eyes they scrutinized the town. Hundreds of Indians squatted there with old pistols in their belts, or they leaned on the aged trees, eying their pickup trucks, where they had hidden their rifles.

A hunter was on trial for killing a deer. The deerslayer was a Cherokee named John Chewie.

Out of the windows of the dim courtroom the handful of small-town officials who had gathered watched the crowd of Indians with growing disquiet. Laughing, someone said it was a scalping party. The whispered rumor spread: "I hear the Cherokees got guns!" It was not to be believed, for it was safer not to believe it; after all, this was not the set of a shoot-'em-up on television, nor could anyone imagine an Indian uprising of the Old West resurrected on the docile Main Street of Jay in uneventful Oklahoma. This was the United States of America, spring, 1966.

313

Was the ancient Cherokee war chant to re-echo beneath the Coca-Cola signs on the town square?

> Hayi! Yu! Listen!
> Now instantly, we have lifted the red war club.
> Quickly his soul shall be without motion.
> There under the earth, where the black war clubs shall be
>   moving like ballsticks in a game,
>   there his soul shall be,
>   never to reappear.
> We cause it to be so.[1]

That morning, and the night before, the young men and the old men of the Cherokee villages had been coming out of the hills. Into the town they came, past the GET RIGHT WITH GOD sign on the roadway, the gas stations, the hot dog stands, and the neon-lit bars that were the outposts of civilization.

In twos and threes they came walking along the roadway, with their rifles in their fists, in pickup trucks hunched down to duck the night winds, in old cars that rattled along like farm wagons.

> I am rising to seek the warpath,
> The earth and the sky beside me;
> I walk in the day and in the night,
> The star of the evening guides me.

Jay, Oklahoma, is a little town, population 1,120. Not much more need be said of it. In eastern Oklahoma, deep in the wooded hills of the Ozarks near the Arkansas line, the town is surrounded by fields where game birds gather and rough stands of woods where the tracks of deer and possum are visible to the myopic eye, and mountain brooks. Hunters say the region is a paradise; perhaps it is. It is as well the county seat of Delaware County, a "depressed area," where the hills are crowded with full-blooded Indians.

Hostile in a way so ingrained that no one needs to say anything about it, the town is not off bounds to the Indians. But they rarely come into town, unless they have to. Except, of course, on Saturday nights. It was unheard of for so many to come. One could feel the tension.

The courthouse in the town square is a fortlike building of no particular architecture. It looks like any other county courthouse in rural Oklahoma.

In the corridors of the courthouse there was a residue of exhausted air. The judicial chambers opened upon rows of gnarled and initialed benches. The benches might have been mistaken for the pews of an ascetic church. The pedestal of the judge who sat in judgment on the boredom that passes

---

[1] These religious chants, or sacred formulas, of the Cherokee are reprinted from *Sacred Formulas of the Cherokees* by James Mooney, 7th Annual Report of the Bureau of American Ethnology, Washington, D.C., 1891. Mooney wrote that he had translated them from writings, in the Cherokee language, by religious men of the tribe who had transcribed them "for their own use."

Cherokees believe it is sacrilegious for a non-Cherokee to publish, print, or use these sacred formulas. In deference to these fine, deeply religious people I therefore wish to explain that I have merely reprinted them from James Mooney, as he reprinted them from the writing of the Cherokees of the nineteenth century.

for sin in a small town was like a pulpit. The jailhouse, an ugly structure of heavy stones, was visible from the courtroom; a reminder of the swift justice that was a tradition of the Old West. The prisoners, on the Ozark frontier, were mostly Indians. John Chewie had waited in this jailhouse.

And still they came, the silent Indians with their silent weapons. "When Cherokees go armed, they generally carry pistols. They may be of almost any type, from ancient .45 caliber 'hot legs,' to modern compact automatics," said a man in nearby Tahlequah. "Pistols tucked under the waistband of pants, in the deep back pocket of overalls, or in a coat pocket. Pistols in the glove compartments of cars, or behind the seat of a pickup. Rifles, too, are 'kept handy' in a nearby car or pickup."

"There were four hundred armed Cherokees in Jay ready to use them if that man was prosecuted," said the principal of a rural Delaware County school, Harold Wade, who was in town that day.

In a town of little more than one thousand, the sudden appearance of four hundred armed Indians was frightening. In any town if that many men, bearing loaded guns, were to appear at city hall to surround the town square, not demonstrating but sitting silently, with rifles and pistols cocked, there would be reason to fear. But in Jay these Indians could have occupied the town in hours.

Were it to happen in New York City's Harlem, whose Negro population is about equal to that of the American Indians, or in Los Angeles' Watts, as it almost did, the alarm would ring out, on the wire services, "Insurrection! Call out the National Guard! And the *Life* photographers!" But the armed Indians were met with silence. Not with the National Guard; not even with the television cameras. The newspapers, except for the local press, ignored the threat of the armed uprising in the hills.

Was it incomprehensible to the townspeople that the stoic Indians, the long-suffering and eternally enduring, the apostles of patience, were so violently angry? The Indians were the town joke, as they were the national joke. They were not to be taken too seriously.

"Lo, the Poor Indian," mocked the Tulsa *Tribune* in an editorial of fatherly disapproval. And yet the newspaper at the oil capital was somewhat apprehensive too. The reports of rifle-toting redskins would have been easier to laugh off if it hadn't been for scare words like "Red Power" that some of the young Indians were using. The *Tribune* sensed that the rebellion of the Red Muslims, as the new Indian leaders themselves called it, was not being staged for laughs.

The Tulsa *Tribune* feared that "Then would come a militant separatist movement, such as the French-Canadians have in Quebec, and we're back to the Little Big Horn."

In Tahlequah, back in the hills, Clyde Warrior laughed at these words. The young Indian intellectual was one of the angriest of the angry young men of the hills. Not a Cherokee, he had no part in the uprising. But he was its uninhibited, fiery voice to other tribes.

"We have a Southern social structure in eastern Oklahoma," Warrior said. "The only way you change that structure is to smash it. You turn it over sideways. And stomp on it. It appears to me that's what will happen around here. I think violence will come about. And as far as I am concerned the sooner the better."

> Ho, you young men, warriors!
> Bear your arms to the place of battle!

Indeed, something had to be done. That winter, under the cold clouds of discontent, the envoys from Washington had been holding councils of peace. It was tumultuous enough with the urban Negroes once again threatening to disquiet the summer solstice with cries of "Black Power" without rural Indians threatening to do the same with hunting rifles. Quietly, behind the scenes, the emissaries of the Justice Department, the agents of the F.B.I., the mediators of the Interior Department, and the lawyers of the Attorney General's office in Oklahoma City had gone into the hills surreptitiously, to confer with the armed Cherokees. "To calm the natives down," said Clyde Warrior.

Was all of this because John Chewie had gone hunting? Chewie, an ex-Marine, known as a hard drinker and a hungry hunter, had indeed gone hunting. He had, by killing a deer, become the symbol of the Red Nationalist rebellion.

The rangers of the Oklahoma Department of Wildlife had arrested him for possession of deer meat in his car out of season, and for hunting without a license. He did not deny the charges. He had shot the deer, he said, in the Kenwood Reserve, a region of woodland held in trust by the U.S. Government for the Cherokee Tribe. He was a full-blooded Cherokee and he would not apologize for hunting on land that rightfully belonged to his people; nor did he have to be licensed like a dog by the state. He had hunted because he was hungry, he told the court; to feed himself and his family. It had been the dead of winter and they had to eat.

In the hunter's behalf, Robert Thomas, a sardonic Cherokee anthropologist, testified at the court hearing that these Indians believed that God had put the wild game on earth for the sustenance of man. Were they, believing that, to obtain hunting licenses from God?

Thomas, who directed the Carnegie Corporation's Cross Cultural Project on the Cherokee culture and language in Tahlequah, told the court that the per capita annual income of the Indians in Delaware County was $500. Hardly enough to starve on, he said. He implied that the religious beliefs of the Indians were neither wholly metaphysical nor legally fatuous, but necessary for survival. The diet was simply inadequate, testified Albert Wahrhaftig, the junior anthropologist with the Carnegie Project. So poor was the economic condition of the Indians, he said, that without wild game to supplement their meager food supplies they would have no meat at all.

"I seen my father suffer. I seen my aunt, my own aunt, die of starvation. I seen old womens suffer. I seen the childrens buried in the county coffins." The mourner was a rural Indian, a backwoods dirt church preacher of the

Indian Baptists among the Creeks of Oklahoma, the Reverend Clifton Hill, who shepherded a rebellious movement of his own people in a neighboring county. "Sometimes I goes to funerals, and see the poor Indians, I mean *poor* Indians, who don't have a thing they own, lying in the county coffin. And you don't know what I feel when I see that.

"Go down to the depths of the Creek Nation. We have shabby houses. It's nothing like compared in the city. It's worse. When I talk about poor, I mean *poor*."

> Here on my breast I have bled!
> See! See! My battle scars!
> You mountains tremble at my yell!
> I strike for life!

"These are very poor people in the midst of a land of plenty," said Finis Smith, one of the religious leaders of the Cherokees and the descendant of Chief Redbird Smith. He believed the "exploitation is accelerating." So was the anger of his people.

"In eastern Oklahoma we have a system of peonage," said Clyde Warrior. "The local politicians and local businessmen find it very profitable to keep these Indians in a state of peonage. They work for people as slave labor; they rent from people off their welfare checks. It has been going on for several years; it is just now coming to a head; the anger, you might say, of the Indian people."

"The life of most Oklahoma Indians is very, very bad," said Warrior, "the sickest, poorest people in the country." Because they were so low economically, and felt so low psychologically, the "Oklahoma Indians had no way of relating to urban America," he said, "just like any other poor people."

The weed roots of poverty in the Indian villages were dug up statistically by Graham Holmes, the former Bureau of Indian Affairs area director for the Five Civilized Tribes of Oklahoma. In a survey prepared for Congressman Wayne Aspinall of the House Interior and Insular Affairs Committee in 1962, Holmes laconically noted:

> Of 19,000 adult Indians in eastern Oklahoma, between the ages of 18 and 55, an estimated 10,000, or 52.6 percent, were unemployed;
> Of the 10,000 jobless adult Indians well over half received no unemployment insurance, or any other welfare assistance—whatsoever;
> Of young Indians, when he was queried "How many Indians 16 or 17 [years old] are now employed? Full time?" the succinct official replied: "Very few, if any."

Yet, having tabulated these statistics of poverty, Holme's document ended happily. He dryly assured the Congress that all was well:
Question: "How is the morale of the Indian people?"
Reply: "Good."
Question: "Are there any evidences of unusual concern by the Indians?"
Reply: "No."

In rural Oklahoma there is little work for the Indian to do. The economic exodus from the rural towns long since left nothing but a residue of odd jobs and seasonal farm work for those who refused to become city Indians.

John Chewie was a farm laborer. He worked in the strawberry and vegetable crops, when there was work. Most of the time he was unemployed. Hands were more numerous than jobs. Like his neighbors, he hoed a hard row. He was a poor backwoods Indian. A friend in Tahlequah said of him: "He is very Indian looking, with a perpetual scared and timid look on his face. He has no ideological axes to grind. He is a hell of a nice guy, with a great sense of humor, but he is the least likely guy in the world to be in the forefront of an Indians'-rights push that you can imagine. I call him 'The Reluctant Hero.'

"But he is all man," the friend added, "and he doesn't like to be shoved around, bribed, and threatened. So he has gotten real angry about this case. He just wants to hunt."

Hunting to an Indian like John Chewie is not a sport. He does not go hunting and fishing to recapture his lost innocence with mass-produced moose-mating horns. The woodsy disguises of the suburbanite in search of a pseudo-primitive manliness are not for him. Nor is he escaping from the office routine. Like most of the Cherokee hunters, he seeks to escape from the statistics of unemployment. It is not escape into nothingness, but into Indianness. The woods, the hunt, the wild game, the earth represent dignity and pride in the Indian ways. Cherokee tribes hunt to reaffirm their way of life, their oneness with nature, the uniqueness of their Indianness, their treaty rights as an Indian nation. And to eat meat.

Hunting has become a symbol of the new tribalism. Wherever the new Indians gather to reaffirm their rights, the Deerslayer reappears. His rifle echoes and re-echoes throughout Indian country.

Up on the high mountain mesas of the Pueblos of the Hopis the traditional chiefs would not buy hunting licenses for young hunters of the tribe. "We are still a sovereign nation. We have never abandoned our sovereignty to any foreign power or government," they said. Chippewas of Wisconsin's Lake Superior shores demanded their "earth right," as a tribal official phrased it, to fish and to harvest wild rice, without interference, or "okay from outside." The fishermen of the Yakima Indians of Washington State patrolled the banks of the Columbia River with rifles to safeguard their tribal nets and to enforce their treaty rights. In New York State, the Iroquois, the "native nationalists" that Edmund Wilson wrote of in his book *Apology to the Iroquois,* restated their old religious beliefs by an unfettered and free return of tribal hunting bands to the eastern forests. Deep in the Everglades of Florida the Seminoles were doing the same, while the Red Lake Band of Chippewas in Minnesota fought for and won their "ancestral right" to hunt wild ducks without licenses from the state or the United States.

But why had the movement of tribal nationalism taken on so seemingly archaic a form? Why, of all things, hunting rights?

The wild duck hunters of the Chippewas may offer the clue. For generations the tribe hunted wild ducks on the shores of Red Lake. They ran afoul of game wardens with warrants in their jodhpurs, who arrested the Indians in flocks for not buying migratory bird hunting stamps.

Lo, the poor wild duck became a *cause célèbre*. His unstamped death was fought in the corridors of the Interior Department, until one judicious day the then Acting Commissioner of Indian Affairs, H. Rex Lee, consulted with the wise men of the legal staff and declared: "In an opinion dated June 30, 1936 the Solicitor of this Department pointed out that, while the various treaties between the United States and the Chippewa Indians did not reserve the right to the Indians to hunt and fish within unceded lands of the Red Lake Reservation, it was not necessary to reserve such rights because of the larger rights possessed by the Indians in land occupied and used by them, and such rights remained in the Indians unless granted away.

"In view of the foregoing, it is our view that members of the Red Lake Band of Chippewa Indians are not required to obtain a Migratory Bird Hunting Stamp to hunt wild ducks on the Reservation."

Whether to buy or not to buy a migratory bird hunting stamp? It may not have seemed of historic importance. But it was. The Indians by defying the proclaimed rights of the states were proclaiming their right to govern themselves. And they were protecting their ancient way of tribal life, with rifles ready. The Chippewas and the Yakimas and the Cherokees were issuing declarations of independence.

The Navajo Tribe had spoken of this independence when one Fourth of July in the early sixties their tribal newspaper editorialized: "Perhaps, for the Indian, the celebration is a bit premature. . . . The day will come, and it is rapidly approaching, all the time, when the part of Webster's definition of Independence which reads 'self-maintenance' will become a reality. We call it self-determination in Navajoland, but it means the same thing."

In any event, the defiance of Stamp Acts ought to have had a familiar ring. In the Boston Tea Party of 1773, when the liberty-minded colonials fought the King's Stamp Act, they masqueraded as Indians. Now the Indians were taking off their masks of timidity and defying the latter-day Stamp Acts that denied them their independence.

In the definitive *Handbook of Federal Indian Law* the late Felix S. Cohen had recognized that "tribal rights of hunting and fishing have received judicial recognition and protection against state and private interference, and even against interference by Federal administrative officials." But the words did not persuade the deeds. At the Chicago Conference of American Indians held at the University of Chicago in 1961, a resolution on "Hunting and Fishing Rights" noted the "increasing concern" of the tribes that state governments were "encroaching on the rights of individual [Indians] hunting, fishing, trapping, and harvesting wild rice on Indian reservations." The four hundred Indians from fifty tribes who gathered at that anthropological powwow petitioned the Secretary of Interior for "a favorable ruling on the rights of Indians to hunt, fish, trap and harvest wild rice, and other vegetation on their own lands."

John Chewie had hunted for more than deer meat. He had hunted for his self-respect and for self-determination in his tribal way of life.

He had not gone into the woods by himself. The men of fifty villages in the hills had come together that winter and talked of their hungers for food and pride. Led by Finis Smith, these men had secretly met in snowbound cabins and in backwoods towns. They founded the Five County Cherokee Movement, a society of full-bloods—the silent men with rifles. And in the dark of winter, yet unheard in the noisy towns, they voiced what was to be their declaration of independence—the Declaration of the Five County Cherokees:

> We meet in a time of darkness to seek the path to the light. We come together, just as our fathers have always done, to do these things. . . .
>
> We, the Five County Cherokees, are one people. We stand united in the sight of God, our creator. We are joined by love and concern for each other and for all men. . . .
>
> We offer ourselves as the voice of the Cherokee people. For many years our people have not spoken and have not been heard. Now we gather as brothers and sisters. . . .
>
> We use our right to freedom of speech. This right is the ancient custom of our people. This right is guaranteed by the Constitution of the United States of America. We insist on equality under the laws of these United States. We act now, peaceably but firmly, to carry out the wish of our people. . . .
>
> We do this for the benefit of all Cherokees. We do this as a good example to all men. Already we have gathered to protect our rights to harvest fish and game to feed ourselves and our children. . . .

These men went into the woods together. In bands of hunters as in the old days, they hunted for game as their fathers had. Chewie was one of many. He was caught, but he was not alone. The hundreds who stood by his side with their rifles on the day of his trial were his blood brothers. In their tribal oath they had pledged to one another:

"We will go on until our lands and our homes are safe. Until we live within the full and just protection of the law. Until we live as the American authors of the Constitution and the Declaration of Independence intended each of the nationalities in this country to live. As dignified men. As free men. As men equal to all other men.

"From this beginning we will go on until the job is done. . . ."

> O Great Terrestrial Hunter, I come to the edge of your spittle, where you repose.
> Give me the wind.
> Give me the breeze.
> Yu!

Inside the courtroom the hearing itself was dull. Hardly was there need of legal evidence to determine what had happened. Even the cross-examination was mostly repartee:

PROSECUTOR: "How many times have you been arrested?"
DEFENDANT: "I don't know. I haven't counted."
PROSECUTOR: "John, do you drink whiskey?"
DEFENDANT: "Don't you?"

Jokingly the State of Oklahoma's Assistant Attorney General, D. L. Cook, invoked his constitutional right not to answer under the Fifth Amendment. The laughter in the courtroom was, on this cue, more polite than prolonged; it was somewhat nervous.

One of the defense attorneys, Stuart Trapp, who had come from Memphis, Tennessee, to represent the American Civil Liberties Union, then took the stand. He did so, the lawyer said, because he sensed that the tension in the town of Jay was about to flare into bloodshed, unless the Case of the Deerslayer were taken out of the State of Oklahoma's jurisdiction. It ought to be judged by the federal courts. The courthouse square was "an unhappy place of considerable tension," Trapp said. He had listened to the Indians talk of injustices for hours, while fingering their rifles.

In deference to the rifles of the silent, and uninvited, witnesses, the Case of the Deerslayer was held over for the federal courts. And, as quietly as they had come, the Indians withdrew from the town.

Once again the town was peaceable. There had been no violence. No shooting. No riot. Not a window shattered. No shouting. No slogans. The young men with rifles had gathered up their rifles and slipped away. It was as though they had never come. By their silence they indicated their disdain of the whole proceeding.

"The Cherokees and the Creeks are a very legal-minded people. They want to try everything that is right and proper," Clyde Warrior said, "because they believe that if they do everything that is legal and proper then justice will prevail. What they fail to see is that in the American system nothing is done legally, honestly, and truthfully. Now, when they find that out, they are going to be pretty damn mad. If that [the legal way] fails, then violence will take place. The country should take heed."

His wrath voiced the frustrations of not only the young, educated Indians. In the hills the country Indians were more and more vocal. And their pent-up angers, so long frustrated by their feelings of hopelessness, upset the rural calm. "These people are becoming more and more aggressive. I do not use the term 'aggressive' lightly. In many areas it is on the verge of militancy," Warrior said.

These views provoked much headshaking among the local officials, especially since the views were supported by hundreds of rifles. In the cities community leaders were troubled.

When the Council of the Five Civilized Tribes of Oklahoma met to discuss the uprising in the hills, there was much dismay. The Reverend James L. Partridge, a Creek tribal councilman of Sapulpa, advocated that the U.S. Congress and the State Legislature pass laws to "stop all this marching and all this violence." It ought to be a federal offense "to lead an act of violence," Reverend Partridge said.

W. W. Keeler, the principal chief of the Cherokee Nation, was more conciliatory. One of the distinguished Indian citizens of Oklahoma and vice president of Phillips Petroleum, Keeler had been a spokesman of the "task force" on Indian Affairs appointed by the late President Kennedy. He thought it wiser to soothe, rather than restrict, the dissident full-bloods. "Now is the time to forget these differences" and past "mistakes," Keeler said; let the Cherokees "join hands and work together."

The principal chief was appointed by the President of the United States; he was not elected by the tribe. In the hills they called him "the President's chief"; he was rudely rebuffed by the full-bloods. He was a "white Indian" to the backwoods, dirt-farm rebels.

Finis Smith, the leader of the Five County Cherokee Movement, was blunt: "We do not need to be called to assemblies to be berated for not cooperating in our own destruction. In a strict sense, there are no alternatives to Indian wants. There is no alternative to having control of our own destiny and having our voices heard and taken seriously. . . . We certainly need to strike bargains with the general society, but we do not need to help whites become big shots in Indian affairs [by being] 'good little Indians.' "

The old tribal leader talked in a tone different from that of a young "hotblood" like Warrior. But his goals differed little.

"The 'best of all possible worlds' for the Cherokee people would have been for the Cherokee Nation to have continued up to the present," Smith said; "for the Cherokee people to live as an *independent republic of Indians,* closely tied and friendly to the United States, under the treaties—as a *modern Indian state* of small communities of kinfolk, taking part in the present industrialized economy of the world, but with a Cherokee government, and legal system in the Cherokee language, with lands held in common, and educational system in the Cherokee language, and with industrial work as an addition to farming and hunting.

"However, we are willing to compromise and modify our aspirations to accommodate to the presence of our white brothers who now live among us."

> You have brought me down the white road.
> There in mid-earth you have placed me.
> I shall stand erect upon the earth.

In the words with which Finis Smith described the old Cherokee Nation there was a description of the tribal nationalism of the new Indians. What had been forgotten, or merely suppressed, was no longer spoken of as the past. It was to be enlarged to a "Greater Indian America."

Finis Smith, being a traditional chief, had a power in his words that the younger man did not. Wherever one went in the hills of eastern Oklahoma, asking what was happening, people said, "Have you talked to Finis? You have to talk to Finis." The merchants of the hill towns whispered that he was "the redskinned Malcolm X"; to the local newspapers he was a "dupe" who was used "by outside agitators." He was a "menace to the peace of the community," said a police officer. "He is working the Indians up to no good," complained a small-town mayor in Cherokee County. "But if you quote me, don't use my name. I got Indian voters." The Reverend Lindy Waters, himself a cousin of Smith's, talked of "his brilliant mind [that] is being channeled in the wrong direction."

The man was revered and reviled, heard and feared. Yet no one talked of him in the old stereotype of the taciturn, the inscrutable, the enigmatic Indian.

He was an old Indian. But he was an outspoken new Indian. In the personnel files of the local office of the Bureau of Indian Affairs the folder on Finis Smith revealed that he had lost several jobs for "trying to stir up Indian workers to stand up for their rights"—as a government clerk confided. Smith had been fired from the Tinker Air Force Base, in Oklahoma City, for what was said to be organizing activity among the Indians.

"We do *all* the compromising, and our white brothers have drawn the arena and made the rules by which life must be lived, and we have no choice but to go along, whether we like it or not," Smith said. "But a compromise must go both ways. To begin with, whites must recognize our existence as a modern and permanent part of Oklahoma; as a *people.* . . . It follows that whites must be willing to modify many Oklahoma institutions, laws, and procedures so that we can participate in a common society with them."

> You have put me in the white house.
> I shall be in it as it moves about.

"The Cherokees have always led the way in every revolutionary concept [in] Indian affairs. Whatever happens in eastern Oklahoma will have a terrific impact on all Indian tribes," said Clyde Warrior. "I've heard it said that whatever the Cherokees do, that's what everyone else will do. I've heard it said, in my travels around the country, that Indians are just waiting for the Cherokees to do something. And then it will be like a snowball rolling down a hill."

The Indian tribes throughout the country were waiting to see what would happen to the Cherokees, Smith thought. It had traditionally been true. History supported this belief, wrote John Collier, the former Commissioner of Indian Affairs, in *Indians of the Americas:* "More than any other tribe, the Cherokee Nation furnished the crystallizing thread of the United States government policy and action in Indian affairs."

It may have been with this vision of the past and the future in mind that the Declaration of the Five County Cherokees was written. For it beautifully and prophetically and simply said what the new Indians, everywhere, believed:

> Now, we shall not rest until we have regained our rightful place. We shall tell our young people what we know. We shall send them to the corners of the earth to learn more. They shall lead us.
>
> Now, we have much to do. When our task is done, we will be ready to rest.
>
> In these days, intruders, named without our consent, speak for the Cherokees. When the Cherokee government is the Cherokee people, we shall rest.
>
> In these days, we are informed of the decisions other people have made about our destiny. When we control our destiny, we shall rest.
>
> In these days, the high courts of the United States listen to people who have been wronged. When our wrongs have been judged in these courts, and the illegalities of the past have been corrected, we shall rest.

In these days, there are countless ways by which people make their grievances known to all Americans. When we have learned these new ways that
bring strength and power, and we have used them, we shall rest.

In these days, we are losing our homes and our children's homes. When
our homeland is protected, for ourselves and for the generations to follow,
we shall rest.

In the vision of our creator, we declare ourselves ready to stand proudly
among the nationalities of these United States of America.

> I stand with my face toward the Sun Land.
> No one is ever lonely with me.
> Wherever I go
> No one is ever lonely with me.

And so in the hills of Oklahoma the Indians hold on to their rifles. They
sit in their wooded villages, in their highway shanty-towns, in their forest
cabins, with their rifles between their knees, waiting to hear if justice will
absolve them from the burden of blood that the white man's inhumanity
and greed have cast upon them. They wait to see if the white man's democracy and rich abundance, taken from their lands, will be shared with the
Indian.

They sit silently, doubting and waiting. They squat, and they clean their
rifles. They have waited patiently for a long time, but they are no longer
patient.

Somewhere in the hills Clyde Warrior, the Ponca, spoke: "I say there will
be an uprising that will make Kenyatta's Mau Mau movement look like a
Sunday-school picnic."

Clyde Warrior grinned. He, too, was waiting.

WATTS

Alvin A. Saxon, Jr.

1

From what great sleep
lightning jumps from an amber sky
causing famine,
assassinating tin people and whole grass-blades?

Senile edifices crying like lumberjacks: "Timber!"
Streets of dwellings wrapped in cellophane
of negligence,
where old wine-winded wisemen in oversized coats
and baggy trousers soliloquize a jungle futility.

And a baby warbles a milk-dry cry
to a mother's wiry ear who sits ice-eyed
with frozen pain like icicles in her heart.

What great sleep,
resonant with nightmares,
causes a man to awaken gap-eyed?

2

Diogenes came with a burning lamp
searching for honest men, but his beautiful light
fell only upon the shadow people
and those who found meaning in the penumbral days
meted out in marijuana's fantasy
and the half-bliss of the prostitute's bed.

Socrates came with nebulous knowledge
to make a liar of the Oracle of Delphi,
but found only
schoolrooms of metal and wood carvings
and those who escape into
some kind of intoxicant—running from
some too-true truth.

Against what false fantasy
the children ball on their golden slides,
bouncing balls, and putty clay—
and Socrates, horrid-eyed, gulped the hemlock
while weeping Diogenes hurled his flame
to the barren soil.

THE TERROR

Tom Hayden

We will never know the full story of how these troops and the police hurt the black people of Newark. But there is now sufficient evidence to establish the main features of their behavior.

The military forces called in to put down the black rebellion were nearly all white. Virtually none of the 250 Negro Newark policemen took part directly in the violent suppression. Only 1.2 per cent of the New Jersey National Guard is black and, according to columnists Evans and Novak on July 22, the organization is "highly social in nature—much like the local chapter of the Moose or Elks. Few Negroes ever try to join." There are five Negroes among 1200 New Jersey state troopers, and many of the white majority are from conservative South Jersey towns where the troopers act as local police. It was understandable that these men would bring into the ghetto racist attitudes that would soon support outright sadism. A captain who commanded helicopter-borne infantry told a *New York Times* reporter on July 14: "They put us here because we're the toughest and the best . . . If anybody throws things down our necks, then it's shoot to kill, it's either them or us, and it ain't going to be us."

On Saturday the 15th, troopers charged up the stairs of the Hayes Homes, shouting, "Get back, you black niggers!" There was shooting up each flight of stairs as they charged. Later, an officer pumped more than thirty bullets into the body of a fallen teen-ager while shouting, "Die, bastard, die!" A Guardsman asked a witness, "What do you want us to do, kill all you Negroes?" A Newark policeman chipped in, "We are going to do it anyway, so we might as well take care of these three now."

These are not isolated examples, but a selection from innumerable incidents of the kind that were reported throughout the riots. From them, we can draw three conclusions about the soldiers and the police.

Trigger-Happiness Because of Fear, Confusion and Exhaustion

Many of the troops were assigned to round-the-clock duty. During that duty they were under conditions of extreme tension. They were kept moving about by incidents or reports of looting, burning and shooting. They drove at speeds of more than 50 miles per hour; they ran continually along the streets after people. They were surrounded by unfamiliar and hostile faces. There were no foxholes or other shelters from attack. The troopers and Guardsmen knew little or nothing about the terrain. They often were unable to tell the direction of shooting. The New York *Daily News* of July summarized:

> Reporters in the riot area feared the random shots of the guardsmen far more than the shots from snipers . . . Once a frantic voice shouted [over the radio], "Tell those Guardsmen to stop shooting at the roof. Those men they're firing at are policemen." . . . "They were completely out of their depth," said one reporter. "It was like giving your kid brother a new toy. They were firing at anything and everything."

In a report on police behavior for the *New York Times* July 20, Peter Khiss quoted the police radio on Sunday night to this effect: Newark police, hold your fire! State police, hold your fire! . . . You're shooting at each other! National Guardsmen, you're shooting at buildings and sparks fly so we think there are snipers! Be sure of your targets! Khiss adds: "After these appeals, there seemed to be a decrease in sniper alarms."

General and Deliberate Violence Employed Against the Whole Community

On Friday night 10 Negroes were killed, 100 suffered gunshot wounds, 500 were "treated" at City Hospital, and at least as many were arrested or held. By Sunday night another 10 were dead, at least 50 more had gunshot wounds, and another 500 were in jail. People were stopped indiscriminately in the streets, shoved, cursed, and beaten and shot. On Thursday, Joe Price, a veteran of the Korean war and an employee of ITT for fifteen years, was beaten on the head, arms, stomach and legs by five Newark policemen inside the Fourth Precinct. He had protested police harassment of neighborhood teen-agers earlier in the day. Later, Jerry Berfet, walking peacefully on a sidewalk with two women, was stopped by the police who told him to strip, ripped off his clothes, and forced him to run naked down the street. No charges were entered against either man. A Negro professional worker was arrested while driving on a quiet street after the 10 P.M. curfew, beaten unconscious, and then forced to perform what his lawyer describes as "degrading acts" when he revived in the police station.

Troops fired freely and wildly up streets and into buildings at real or imagined enemies.

On Saturday before darkness fell, three women were killed in their homes by police fire. Rebecca Brown, a twenty-nine-year-old nurse's aide, was cut nearly in half as she tried to rescue her two-year-old child by the window. Hattie Gainer, an elderly twenty-year resident of her neighborhood, was shot at her window in view of her three grandchildren. Eloise Spellman was shot through the neck in her Hayes apartment with three of her eleven children present.

A child in Scudder Homes lost his ear and eye to a bullet. A man was shot while fixing his car as police charged after a crowd. When another man told police he was shot in the side, the officer knocked him down and kicked him in the ribs.

The most obvious act of deliberate aggression was the police destruction of perhaps a hundred Negro-owned stores Saturday and Sunday. One witness followed police down Bergen Street for fifteen blocks watching them shoot into windows marked "soul brother." Another store owner observed a systematic pattern. On his block three white-owned stores were looted Thursday night; no Negro stores were damaged. There were no other disturbances on his block until well after midnight Saturday when he received calls that troopers were shooting into the Negro-owned stores or were breaking windows with the butts of their guns.

Was it because the police hated black people indiscriminately? Was it because the police wanted to teach middle-class Negroes that they must take responsibility for what "criminal" Negroes do? Or because the police wanted to prevent Negro-operated stores from gaining an advantage over the looted white merchants? Whatever the reason, the result was summed up clearly by Gustav Heningburg, a Negro who is a lay official of the Episcopal Church. He told the Newark *News* of July 17 that "the nonrioting Negroes are more afraid of the police than the rioters" because the police were retaliating instead of protecting.

Governor Hughes said on Sunday that all reports of excessive behavior would be handled by the troopers' own investigative unit. If charges were proved true, "and after all the police are only human," the Governor was sure that "justice will be done." As for himself, "I felt a thrill of pride in the way our state police and National Guardsmen have conducted themselves."

Cold-Blooded Murder

An evaluation of the deaths so far reported suggests that the military forces killed people for the purposes of terror and intimidation. Nearly all the dead were killed by police, troopers, and Guardsmen. The "crimes" of the victims were petty, vague, or unproven. None were accused by police of being snipers; only one so far is alleged to have been carrying a gun. Several of the dead were engaged in small-scale looting at most. The majority were observers; ten, in fact, were killed inside or just outside their homes. Many were killed in daylight. Nearly all the dead had families and jobs; only a few had previous criminal records. Seven of the dead were women, two were young boys. Of those known to be dead, 5 were killed between Thursday night and dawn Friday: 1 in a hit-and-run car, 1 allegedly shot by mistake by a sniper, 3 others by Newark police. On Friday and Friday night 9 were slain; 9 between Saturday afternoon and late Sunday; 1 on Monday night. All but one or two of these seemed to be police victims.

The July 28th issue of *Life* magazine carried a photo-essay on the death of William Furr. On Saturday afternoon Furr and a few others were carrying cases of beer out of a store that had been looted the previous night. Furr appears in the *Life* photos in the act of looting. The *Life* reporter even shared a can of stolen beer, and was warned by Furr to "get rid of it and run like hell" if the police appeared. Suddenly the police raced up with their sirens off, jumped out of the car with shotguns. Furr, according to the *Life* article, had "part of a six-pack in his left hand." With the *Life* photographer's camera shutter snapping, William Furr ran halfway down the block before two shots from behind dropped him. He died almost immediately, and a twelve-year-old boy, Joe Bass, was severely wounded while standing at the end of the block. A few minutes before Furr had told the *Life* reporter, "When the police treat us like people instead of treating us like animals, then the riots will stop."

The killing of nineteen-year-old James Rutledge will not soon be forgotten in Newark. On Sunday afternoon, he was inside a looted tavern with several other teen-agers hiding from the fire of troopers and police. According to a witness, the troopers burst into the tavern shooting and yelling, "Come out you dirty fucks." James Rutledge agreed to come out from behind a cigarette machine. He was frisked against the wall. Then:

> The two troopers . . . looked at each other. Then one trooper who had a rifle shot Jimmy from about three feet away . . . While Jimmy lay on the

floor, the same trooper started to shoot Jimmy some more with the rifle. As he fired . . . he yelled "Die, you dirty bastard, die you dirty nigger, die die . . ." At this point a Newark policeman walked in and asked what happened. I saw the troopers look at each other and smile . . .

The trooper who shot Jimmy remained . . . took a knife out of his own pocket and put it in Jimmy's hand.

Shortly after three men came in with a stretcher. One said, "they really laid some lead on his ass" . . . He asked the state trooper what happened. The trooper said, "he came at me with a knife" . . .

[We remained where we were] for about fifteen minutes, then I got up and walked to the window and knocked a board down.——and——came over to the window. One state trooper and two National Guardsmen came to the window and said, "Come out or we are going to start shooting" . . .

A National Guardsman said, "What do you want us to do, kill all you Negroes?" I saw a Newark policeman say: "We are going to do it anyway, we might as well take care of these three now." I saw the Newark policeman go over to——point a pistol at his head and say: "How do you feel?" Then he started laughing . . .

For anyone who wonders whether this is an exaggerated youthful horror story, the photographs of James Rutledge's chest and head are available from his mother. There were forty-five bulletholes in his head and body.

Clearly the evidence points to a military massacre and suppression in Newark rather than to a two-sided war. This was not only the conclusion of the Negroes in the ghetto but of private Newark lawyers, professors of constitutional law and representatives of the state American Civil Liberties Union. They have charged that the police were the instrument of a conspiracy "to engage in a pattern of systematic violence, terror, abuse, intimidation, and humiliation" to keep Negroes second-class citizens. The police, according to the lawyers' statement, "seized on the initial disorders as an opportunity and pretext to perpetrate the most horrendous and widespread killing, violence, torture, and intimidation, not in response to any crime or civilian disorder, but as violent demonstration of the powerlessness of the plaintiffs and their class . . ."

Thus it seems to many that the military, especially the Newark police, not only triggered the riot by beating a cab-driver but then created a climate of opinion that supported the use of all necessary force to suppress the riot. The force used by police was not in response to snipers, looting, and burning, but in retaliation against the successful uprising of Wednesday and Thursday nights.

The action of the troops was supported by civilian authority, which turned the legal and judicial process into an anti-riot weapon. "New Jersey will show its abhorrence of these criminal activities and society will protect itself by fair, speedy and retributive justice," the Governor declared. Not counting hundred of Negroes swept up by police, held for hours, and released without being charged, 1400 altogether were arrested and detained in jail. Of 829 adults and 144 juveniles interviewed in jail by lawyers during the riot period, more than 80 per cent were charged with looting. Nearly all the other arrests were for minor offenses such as curfew violation. Almost none were for shooting, bombing or arson.[1] Only 85 "dangerous weapons" were confiscated, according to final police reports, and of these only 51 were guns. About 675 of the arrested people—not quite half of them—were reported to have criminal records. But *Life* magazine called this figure "somewhat loaded" since city officials admitted that in half the 675 cases, the "criminal records" consisted of arrests but not convictions. The evidence is that most of the prisoners were adults with jobs and families; holding them for several days created serious problems for each.

High bail prevented prisoners from being able to get out of jail. Minimum bond was set at $1,000 for curfew and loitering charges, $2,500 for looting, $5,000 for possession of a gun, $10,000 to $25,000 for other weapons charges. Chief Magistrate James Del Mauro, replying to criticism of the high bail cost, declared in the July 14 Newark *News:* "If they can't afford it, let them stay in jail." As Henry diSuvero of the state American Civil Liberties Union pointed out, this meant that the concept of "innocent until proven guilty" and the constitutional provision against "excessive bail" was discarded. Thus people were kept off the streets and, in diSuvero's view, held as "hostages" in the conflict.

During this mass detention no one with the exception of about 150 juveniles, was fed until Saturday and many not until Sunday, even when food was brought to the jails by friends and relatives of the prisoners. As the court pens filled up, prisoners were sent to the Newark Street Jail (condemned as uninhabitable in the 1930s), federal detention facilities, a state prison, and the armory where Hughes and the troops were headquartered. Some of the prisoners were beaten in their cells.

Prisoners were not permitted to receive visitors or make telephone calls for legal assistance, nor were they allowed to notify friends and relatives. The right to preliminary hearings was denied. This right, provided for in New Jersey law, compels the prosecutor to demonstrate to the judge there is "probable cause" to hold the accused; it permits the defendant to discover the state's case against himself as well. Thus, merely the word of the arresting officer became sufficient to hold people without determination of probable cause.

Municipal Court judges started arraigning prisoners at round-the-clock sessions. One prisoner passed through court every three minutes, according to the *Star-Ledger* of July 16. Pleas by attorneys for the reduction of bail were ignored except in rare instances.

---

[1] An earlier, preliminary, breakdown of arrests revealed the following: 473 arrested for breaking and entering (looting, larceny); 50 for curfew violation; 47 for possession or receiving stolen goods; 40 for concealed weapons or possession of weapons; 12 for assault and battery on police, troopers, or guards; 14 for assault and battery (presumably against civilians); 9 for disorderly conduct; 14 for loitering; 3 for failure to give good account of self; 3 for resisting arrest; 3 for resisting arrest after curfew; 1 for unlawfully eluding police; 3 for auto theft; 3 for malicious damage; 3 for possession of marijuana; 2 for failure to obey a policeman; 1 for shooting wife; 1 for impersonating a member of the armed forces; 1 as a material witness; 1 for possession of a gas bomb; 1 for attempted armed robbery; 1 for discharging weapon; 3 for attempted arson; 1 for arson.

Starting Monday two Grand Juries heard felony charges and returned, by week's end, some 500 indictments. With the handing down of an indictment, which itself is a finding of probable cause, the prisoners lost forever their right to preliminary hearing. Thus, by agreeing to rush presentations, the Grand Jury acted more as a rubber stamp for the prosecutors' requests than a body to ensure an objective check on evidence. The ACLU charge that Hughes was using the judiciary as a weapon to restore order is supported by this post-riot statement the Governor gave to *US News & World Report:* "The full measure of the criminal law should be exacted in these cases. I have insisted on that from the beginning. I went to the extent of arranging with the appropriate courts for the immediate impaneling of grand juries and presentation of cases to them."

But the attitude of the courts was perhaps better indicated on July 21 when Newark's Chief Magistrate Del Mauro rejected the attempt by cab-driver Smith's attorney, Harris David, to file criminal complaints against the two police who arrested Smith. According to the *Times,* Del Mauro's words were:

> In these times of stress, with all the havoc and destruction, a policeman killed, a fireman killed, more than twenty people killed and $15 million of damage, *I am not accepting a complaint against the police.*
>
> It was this particular man, if I recall from reading the papers, that originally caused the rioting, when he was arrested and rumors swept through the colored community that he had been killed. He has been paroled . . . he is alive and there is nothing wrong with him.

"Mr. Smith," the *Times* reported the next day, "wore a six-inch-wide bandage wrapped tightly around his rib cage" and declined any comment on the advice of his lawyer.

One of the riot's lessons was that the white community, at the highest official levels, gave support to this entire military operation. The Governor stated the necessity of "drawing the line" for all America in Newark; the Governor commented he was "thrilled" by the performance of the troops; the Governor dismissed police brutality charges as "standard operating procedure." City officials were just as implicated. The *Washington Post* of July 24 reported: "There was massive destruction of property—but no deaths —until Newark Mayor Hugh J. Addonizio instructed the city police to use any means necessary to put down the riot . . ." During the height of bloodshed, when Richard Taliaferro was shot in the back on South 8th Street Friday night (the police claimed Taliaferro exchanged shots with them), the Mayor told a Newark *News* reporter: "That's a good show of force in quick time." From the streets to the court room, Negroes' rights were secondary.

In the aftermath of the riot it became clear that substantial citizens of Newark were aware of the magnitude of the police brutality issue. A Committee of Concern, including the Episcopal Bishop, the dean of Rutgers' Newark branch and the dean of Rutgers' Law School, the vice-presidents of the Prudential Insurance Company and of Newark's largest department store, declared that one of the major causes of the riot was the feeling among Negroes that the police are the "single continuously lawless element operating in the community." The solid citizens agreed that this Negro view had merit; indeed, they said "independent observers" agreed with it. Since their statement implied a prior awareness of the problem, the question could be asked why they had taken no action previously to solve the problem. If *Life* magazine could express worry that the Negro community did not turn in the snipers in its midst, would it not be proper to worry why the white community never turned in the violent element in its midst?

The riot made clear that if something is not done about the police immediately, the fears of white society will be transformed into reality: whites will be facing a black society that will not only harbor, but welcome and employ snipers. The troops did not instill fear so much as a fighting hatred in the community. Many people, of every age and background, cursed the soldiers. Women spit at armored cars. Five-year-old kids clenched bottles in their hands. If the troops made a violent move, the primitive missiles were loosed at them. People openly talked of the riot turning into a showdown and, while a great many were afraid, few were willing to be pushed around by the troops. All told there were more than 3000 people arrested, injured, or killed; thousands more witnessed these incidents. From this kind of violence, which touches people personally, springs a commitment to fight back. By the end of the weekend many people spoke of a willingness to die.

Jimmy Cannon was one such person. He was the uncle riding with ten-year-old Eddie Moss when the Guardsmen shot through the car and the young boy's head was ripped open. Jimmy put the car, blood, bullet-holes and all, into a private garage as proof of what happened. Then he was beaten on the street corner by police who found him there. Jimmy learned how to fight during four years in the Marines. "I don't hold any grudges against you," he told a white person who interviewed him. "I'm just for rights, not for violence. This thing is wrong. I've faced a lot of things, but this is bad, and I just don't care anymore. I am to the point where I just don't care."

LET AMERICA BE AMERICA AGAIN

Langston Hughes

Let America be America again.
Let it be the dream it used to be.
Let it be the pioneer on the plain
Seeking a home where he himself is free.

(America never was America to me.)

Let America be the dream the dreamers dreamed—
Let it be that great strong land of love
Where never kings connive nor tyrants scheme
That any man be crushed by one above.

(It never was America to me.)

O, let my land be a land where Liberty
Is crowned with no false patriotic wreath,
But opportunity is real, and life is free,
Equality is in the air we breathe.

(There's never been equality for me,
Nor freedom in this "homeland of the free.")

Say who are you that mumbles in the dark?
And who are you that draws your veil across the stars?

I am the poor white, fooled and pushed apart,
I am the red man driven from the land.
I am the refugee clutching the hope I seek—
But finding only the same old stupid plan
Of dog eat dog, of mighty crush the weak.
I am the Negro, "problem" to you all.
I am the people, humble, hungry, mean—
Hungry yet today despite the dream.
Beaten yet today—O, Pioneers!
I am the man who never got ahead,
The poorest worker bartered through the years.
Yet I'm the one who dreamt our basic dream
In that Old World while still a serf of kings,
Who dreamt a dream so strong, so brave, so true,
That even yet its mighty daring sings
In every brick and stone, in every furrow turned
That's made America the land it has become.
O, I'm the man who sailed those early seas
In search of what I meant to be my home—
For I'm the one who left dark Ireland's shore,
And Poland's plain, and England's grassy lea,
And torn from Black Africa's strand I came
To build a "homeland of the free."

The free?
Who said the free? Not me?

Surely not me? The millions on relief today?
The millions who have nothing for our pay
For all the dreams we've dreamed
And all the songs we've sung
And all the hopes we've held
And all the flags we've hung,
The millions who have nothing for our pay—
Except the dream we keep alive today.

O, let America be America again—
The land that never has been yet—
And yet must be—the land where *every* man is free.
The land that's mine—the poor man's, Indian's, Negro's, ME—
Who made America,
Whose sweat and blood, whose faith and pain,
Whose hand at the foundry, whose plow in the rain,
Must bring back our mighty dream again.

O, yes,
I say it plain,
America never was America to me,
And yet I swear this oath—
America will be!

PART FIVE

A Return to Vision

There have been many attempts to define art, and none of them has yet proved to be quite adequate. Some definitions are offered in the selections which follow, and perhaps the reader will arrive at some of his own from his reading of the selections. The purpose here, however, is not to simply define; it is, rather, to examine some of the uses of art in the context of the issues explored in this book.

We have been dealing, directly and indirectly, with man's need to perceive order in his universe, to find meaning in his life. This, then, is one of the two basic functions of art as expressed in S. I. Hayakawa's "Art and Tension," the first selection reprinted in this part. Art is one medium through which order is imposed on life. It also serves, according to Hayakawa, as a means of relieving tensions, tensions like those expressed in Part Four by Langston Hughes, Tom Hayden, and others. Robinson Jeffers expresses very nearly the same thoughts about art in his poem, "Apology for Bad Dreams" —a work of art about the nature of art.

In Thomas DeQuincey's essay, "The Literature of Knowledge and the Literature of Power," art is assigned yet another function. It has the power, says DeQuincey, to elevate our thoughts, to help us arrive at a higher reality, the kind of reality seen by the boy in E. M. Forster's "The Celestial Omnibus," and tragically misunderstood by the snob, Mr. Bons.

The remaining selections here deal specifically with the artist himself, and the nature of his obligation to himself and to society, but, as in "Sonny's Blues," the artist seems always in the final analysis to be ". . . dealing with the roar rising from the void and imposing order on it as it hits the air."

ART AND TENSION

S. I. Hayakawa

Bearing the Unbearable

Animals know their environment by direct experience only; man crystallizes his knowledge and his feelings in phonetic symbolic representations; by written symbols he accumulates knowledge and passes it on to further generations of men. Animals feed themselves where they find food, but man, coordinating his efforts with the efforts of others by linguistic means, feeds himself abundantly and with food prepared by a hundred hands and brought great distances. Animals exercise but limited control over each other, but man, again by employing symbols, establishes laws and ethical systems, which are linguistic means of imposing order and predictability upon human conduct. Acquiring knowledge, securing food, establishing social order—these activities make sense to the biologist because they contribute to survival. For human beings, each of these activities involves a symbolic dimension—a dimension of which lower animals have no inkling.

Let us attempt to state the functions of literature in scientifically verifiable terms—in other words, in terms of biological "survival value." Granted that this is a difficult task in the present state of psychological knowledge, it is necessary that we try to do so, since most explanations of the necessity or value of literature (or the other arts) take the form of purr-words—which are really no explanations at all. For example, Wordsworth speaks of poetry as "the breath and finer spirit of all knowledge"; Coleridge speaks of it as "the best words in the best order." The explanations of literature given by many teachers and critics follow a similar purr-word pattern, usually reducible to "You should read great literature because it is very, very great." If we are to give a scientific account of the functions of literature, we shall have to do better than that.

Having included under the term "literature" all the affective uses of language, we are helped in our inquiry by recent psychological and psychiatric investigations, as well as by the insights of critics and students of literature. These sources indicate that, from the point of view of the utterer, one of the most important functions of the utterance is the relieving of *tensions*. We have all known the relief that comes from uttering a long and resounding series of impolite vocables under the stress of great irritation. The same releasing of psychological tensions—Aristotle called it *catharsis*—appears to be effected at all levels of affective utterance, if we are to believe what writers themselves have said about the creative process. The novel, the drama, the poem, like the oath or the expletive, arise, at least in part, out of internal necessity when the organism experiences a serious tension, whether resulting from joy, grief, disturbance, or frustration. And as a result of the

336

utterances made, the tension is, to a greater or lesser degree—perhaps only momentarily—mitigated.

A frustrated or unhappy animal can do relatively little about its tensions.[1] A human being, however, with an extra dimension (the world of symbols) to move around in, not only undergoes experience, but also *symbolizes his experience to himself.* Our states of tension—especially the unhappy tensions—*become tolerable* as we manage to *state what is wrong—to get it said* —whether to a sympathetic friend, or on paper to a hypothetical sympathetic reader, or even to oneself.[2] If our symbolizations are adequate and sufficiently skillful, our tensions are brought *symbolically under control.* To achieve this control, we may employ what Kenneth Burke has called "symbolic strategies"—that is, ways of reclassifying our experiences so that they are "encompassed" and easier to bear.[3] Whether by processes of "pouring out our hearts" or by "symbolic strategies" or by other means, we may employ symbolizations as mechanisms of relief when the pressures of a situation become intolerable.

As we all know, language is social, and for every speaker there may be hearers. An utterance that relieves a tension for the speaker can relieve a similar tension, should one happen to exist, in the hearer. And because human experience remains fairly constant, this process is possible even when speaker and hearer are separated by centuries or by different cultures. The symbolic manipulation by which John Donne "encompassed" his feelings of guilt in one of his Holy Sonnets enables us too, at another time and under another set of circumstances, to encompass our feelings of guilt about, in all probability, a different set of sins.

William Ernest Henley confronted the fact of his chronic invalidism— he had been ill since childhood and had spent long periods of his life in hospitals—by stating, in his well-known poem "Invictus," his refusal to be defeated:

> Out of the night that covers me,
> Black as the pit from pole to pole,

[1] See the account of "substitutive, or symbolic" behavior among cats under conditions of experimentally induced neurosis in Jules Masserman's *Behavior and Neurosis* (1943). It can hardly be denied, in the face of Dr. Masserman's evidence, that an extremely rudimentary form of what might be called "pre-poetic" behavior, analogous to the treasuring of a lock of a loved one's hair, is to be found even among cats. The cats, when hungry, fondle the push-button that *used to* trip a mechanism that brought them food, although they appear to know (since they no longer move to the food box after touching the button) that it no longer works.

[2] An indication of the importance of "getting it said" is given in the research of Charles W. Slack of the Harvard Psychological Clinic. Dr. Slack "hired," at modest hourly wages, unemployed young men hanging around street corners in Cambridge. He asked them to be "research consultants" to help inquire into the question of "how guys foul up." Their task was to talk into tape-recorders about themselves and their problems. A dramatic improvement in behavior was shown by almost all the boys who took part in the project: they got jobs and held them; the number of arrests among them dropped by half.

[3] See Kenneth Burke, *Philosophy of Literary Form* (1941). An infielder for the Chicago White Sox some years ago made four errors in four consecutive chances. Naturally, he found his performance difficult to face. His "symbolic strategy" was reported by a Chicago *Times* writer who quoted the infielder as saying, "Anyway, I bet it's a *record!*"

I thank whatever gods may be
  For my unconquerable soul.

In the fell clutch of circumstance
  I have not winced nor cried aloud.
Under the bludgeonings of chance
  My head is bloody, but unbowed.

Beyond this place of wrath and tears
  Looms but the horror of the shade,
And yet the menace of the years
  Finds, and shall find me, unafraid.

It matters not how strait the gate,
  How charged with punishments the scroll,
I am the master of my fate:
  I am the captain of my soul.

How, at a different time and under different circumstances, other people can use Henley's utterance to take arms against a different sea of troubles is shown by the fact that this poem is one of the favorite poems of American Negroes and is sometimes recited or sung chorally by Negro organizations. The extra meaning of the word "black" in the second line when the poem is said by Negroes makes it perhaps an even more pointed utterance for the Negro reader than it was for the original author. Indeed, the entire poem takes on different meanings depending on what a reader, putting himself into the role of the speaker of the poem, projects into the words "the night that covers me."[4]

Poetry has often been spoken of as an aid to sanity. Kenneth Burke calls it "equipment for living." It would appear that we can take these statements seriously and work out their implications in many directions. What are, for example, some of the kinds of symbolic manipulation by which we attempt to equip ourselves in the face of the constant succession of difficulties and tensions, great and small, that confront us day by day? Of course, the stimulus of social tension is not necessary for all literature, but unquestionably it is often a significant spur to creation.

Some "Symbolic Strategies"

First of all, of course, there is what is called literary "escape"—a tremendous source of literature, poetry, drama, comic strips, and other forms of

---

[4] Anyone saying, as the present writer does, that a poem may mean different things to different people, lays himself open to the charge that his relativistic position makes it impossible "to distinguish between right and wrong readings of a poem." It is perhaps necessary, therefore, to clarify what is asserted here: saying that a poem may have different meanings for different people is *not* the same as saying that a poem can mean anything at all.

Incidentally, another example of a poem acquiring a changed meaning in a changed context is provided by the Freedom Riders who "sat in" and refused to budge from segregated premises. They responded to threats with the old hymn, "We shall not be, we shall not be moved," endowing the words with a meaning not found when sung in church.

affective communication. Edgar Rice Burroughs, confined to a sickbed, symbolically traipsed through the jungle, in the person of Tarzan, in a series of breath-taking and triumphant adventures—and by means of this symbolic compensation made his sickbed endurable. At the same time he made life endurable for millions of undersized, frustrated, and feeble people. One may not think much of the author and the readers of the Tarzan stories; still, it is to be emphasized that in order to derive what relief they offer from pain or boredom, it takes, both in the telling and in the reading of such stories, the symbolic process, and hence a *human* nervous system.

Let us take another example of symbolic strategy. When a disgruntled employee calls his employer a "half-pint Hitler," is he not using a "strategy" which, by means of introducing his employer (a petty tyrant) into a perspective which includes Hitler (a great tyrant), symbolically reduces his employer to what Kenneth Burke calls manageable proportions? And did not Dante likewise, unable to punish his enemies as they deserved to be punished, symbolically put them in their places in the most uncomfortable quarters in Hell? There is a world of difference between the completeness and adequacy of such a simple epithet as "half-pint Hitler" and Dante's way of disposing of his enemies—and Dante accomplished many more things in his poem besides symbolically punishing his enemies—but are they not both symbolic manipulations by means of which the utterers derive a measure of relief or relaxation of psychological tensions?

Let us take another example. Upton Sinclair was deeply disturbed by the stockyards as they were in 1906. He could have tried to forget them; he could have buried himself in reading or writing about other things, such as idyllic lands long ago and far away or entirely nonexistent—as do the readers and writers of escape literature. He could have tried, by a different symbolic manipulation, to show that present evil was part of greater good "in God's omniscient plan." This has been the strategy of many religions as well as of many authors. Still another possibility would have been actually to reform conditions at the stockyards so that he could contemplate them with equanimity—but he would have had to be an important official in a packing company or in the government to initiate a change in conditions. What he did, therefore, was to *socialize his discontent*—pass it on to others —on the very good theory that if enough people felt angry or disgusted with the situation, they could collectively change the stockyards in such a way that one could adjust oneself to them. Sinclair's novel, *The Jungle,* upset so many people that it led to a federal investigation of the meat industry and to the enactment of legislation controlling some of its practices.

As is now well known, when tensions are experienced constantly, and permitted to accumulate, they may lead to more or less serious psychological maladjustment. Adjustment, as modern psychology sees the process, is no static condition of unreflective bliss that comes from neither knowing nor caring what is wrong with the world. It is a dynamic, day-to-day, moment-to-moment process, and it involves changing the environment to suit one's personality as much as it involves adapting one's feelings to existing conditions. The greater resources one has for achieving and maintaining adjustment, the more successful will the process be. Literature appears to be one of the available resources.

Both the production and enjoyment of literature, then, being human symbolic devices employed in the day-to-day process of equipping ourselves for living, appear to be extensions of our adjustment mechanism beyond those provided for us by that part of our biological equipment which we have in common with lower animals. If a man were to spend years of his life trying to discover the chemical constituency of salt water without bothering to find out what has already been said on the subject in any elementary chemistry book, we should say that he was making very imperfect use of the resources which our symbolic systems have made available to us. Similarly, can it not be said that people, worrying themselves sick over their individual frustrations, constantly suffering from petty irritations and hypertensions, are making extremely imperfect use of the available human resources of adjustment when they fail to strengthen and quiet themselves through contact with literature and the other arts?

What all this boils down to, then, is that poetry (along with the other arts), whether it be good or bad and at whatever level of crudity or refinement, exists to fulfill a necessary biological function for a symbol-using class of life, that of *helping us to maintain psychological health and equilibrium.*

"Equipment for Living"

Psychiatrists recognize no distinct classes of the "sane" and the "unsane." Sanity is a matter of degree, and "sane" people are all capable of becoming more sane, or less, according to the experiences they encounter and the strength and flexibility of the internal equipment with which they meet them. Even as one's physical health has to be maintained by food and exercise, it would appear that one's psychological health too has to be maintained in the very course of living by "nourishment" at the level of affective symbols: literature that introduces us to new sources of delight; literature that makes us feel that we are not alone in our misery; literature that shows us our own problems in a new light; literature that suggests new possibilities to us and opens new areas of possible experience; literature that offers us a variety of "symbolic strategies" by means of which we can "encompass" our situations.

But there are certain kinds of literature, like certain kinds of processed food, which look very much like nourishment but contain none of the essential vitamin ingredients, so that great quantities can be consumed without affecting one's spiritual undernourishment.[5] (One could mean by "essential vitamin ingredients" in this context, "maps" of actual "territories" of human experience, directives that are both realistic and helpful, and so on.) Certain kinds of popular fiction claim to throw light on given problems in life— stories with such titles as "The Office Wife—Was She Playing Fair?"—but,

---

[5] Wendell Johnson of the University of Iowa refers to television-viewing, reading the Sunday papers, and similar diversions as "semantic thumb-sucking": you go through the motions of getting nourishment without getting any.

like patent medicines, these offer apparent soothing to surface symptoms, and ignore underlying causes. Other kinds of fiction, like drugs and liquor, offer escape from pain, and again leave causes untouched, so that the more of them you take the more you need. Fantasy-living—which is one of the important characteristics of schizophrenia—can be aggravated by the consumption of too much of this narcotic literature. Still other kinds of fiction, movies, television programs, and the like, give a false, prettified picture of the world—a world that can be adjusted to *without effort*. But readers who adjust themselves to this unreal world naturally become progressively less adjusted to the world as it is. Such "adjustment to unreality" must lead to an enormous amount of disappointment and heartbreak among the young and unsophisticated, when they discover that the world is not as it was depicted in romantic tales.

On the other hand, it will not do to apply too crudely the principle of literature as an aid to sanity. Some might be tempted to say that, if literature is an instrument for maintaining sanity, the writings of many not-too-sane geniuses will have to be thrown out as unhealthy. It would seem, on the contrary, that the symbolic strategies devised by extremely tortured people like Dostoyevsky or Donne or Shelley for the encompassing of their situations are valuable in the extreme. They mixed themselves powerful medicines against their ills, and their medicines not only help us to encompass whatever similar tortures we may be suffering from, but may serve also as antitoxins for future sufferings.

Furthermore, when a work of literature is said to be "permanent," "lasting," or "great," does it not mean that the symbolic strategy by which the author encompassed his disturbance (achieved his equilibrium) works for other people troubled by other disturbances at other times and places? Is it possible, for example, to read Sinclair's strategic handling of the Chicago stockyards without awareness that it applies more or less adequately to other people's disturbances about factory conditions in Turin, or Manchester, or Kobe, or Montreal? And if it applies especially well to, say, Detroit, does not the Detroiter regard Sinclair's book as having lasting value? And if, under changing conditions, there are no longer social situations which arouse similar tensions, or if the strategies seem no longer adequate, do we not consider the author to be "dated," if not "dead"?[6] But if an author has adequately dealt with tensions that people in all times and under all conditions

---

[6] *The Jungle* is, in the writer's opinion, very much dated in most respects, although still powerful in some. Working people in the United States (and in many other parts of the world as well) are simply not treated as badly as they are in this novel, partly because of unionization, of course, and also partly because of advances in technology and a more highly developed public conscience. But ever since its publication in 1906, it has been widely read by working classes all over the world: few American books have been translated into so many languages.

The symbolic strategies of works of great literary art, unlike those of *The Jungle*, are usually too complex and subtle for such a rough analysis as has been attempted here. *The Jungle* has been chosen for discussion because books like this, which are far from being great masterpieces and yet give a great deal of profoundly felt insight into segments of human experience, are especially helpful in the understanding of the theories of literature proposed in this chapter. The strategies, being not too subtle, can be clearly seen and described.

appear to experience, do we not call his writings "universal" and "undying"?

The relationship between literature and life is a subject about which little is known scientifically at the present time. Nevertheless, in an unorganized way, we all feel that we know something about that relationship, since we have all felt the effects of some kind of literature at some time in our lives. Most of us have felt, even if we have not been able to prove, that harmful consequences can arise from the consumption of such literary fare as is offered in many movies, in popular magazines, and in the so-called comic books. But the imperfection of our scientific knowledge is revealed by the fact that, when there is widespread argument as to whether or not comic books should be banned, equally imposing authorities on both sides are able to "prove" their cases; some say that comic books stimulate children's imaginations in unhealthy ways and lead them into crime, while others say that the crimes are committed by psychopathic children who would have committed them anyway, and that comic books, by offering to normal children a symbolic release of their aggressive tendencies, actually help to calm them down. It appears to be anybody's guess.

Because no one yet has answers to such questions, it would seem to be extremely desirable for students of literature and of psychology to work together. If they do, perhaps they will some day be able to state, in the interests of everyday sanity, what kinds of literature contribute to maturity and what kinds help to keep us permanently infantile and immature in our evaluations.

Art as Order

At least one other important element enters into our pleasure both in the writing and reading of literature—but about this there is still less available scientific knowledge. It pertains to what are called the artistic or esthetic values of a work of the imagination.

[In a preceding chapter] we spoke of the relationships, for example in a novel, of the incidents and characters to each other—that is, the meaningful arrangement of experiences that makes a novel different from a jumbled narrative. Before we speak of a narrative as a "novel" and therefore as a "work of art," we must be satisfied that, regardless of whether or not we could "live the story" through imaginative identification with the characters, the incidents are arranged in some kind of *order*. Even when we don't happen to like the story, if we find a complex, but discernible and interesting, order to the incidents in a novel, we are able to say, "It certainly is beautifully put together." Indeed, sometimes the internal order and neat relationships of the parts to each other in a novel may be so impressive that we enjoy it in spite of a lack of sympathy with the kinds of incidents or people portrayed. Why is order interesting almost of itself?

The writer would suggest that if an answer is found to this question, it will have to be found in terms of human symbolic processes and the fact that symbols of symbols, symbols of symbols of symbols, and so on, can be manufactured indefinitely by the human nervous system. This fact can be given a special application that may enable us to understand the functions of literature.

Animals, as we have remarked, live in the extensional world—they have no symbolic world to speak of. There would seem to be no more "order" in an animal's existence than the order of physical events as they impinge on its life. Man, however, both *lives* (at the extensional level) and *talks about his life to himself* (at the symbolic level, either with words or, in the case of painters and musicians and dancers, with nonverbal symbols). A human being is not satisfied simply to know his way around extensionally; he can hardly help talking to himself about what he has seen and felt and done.

The data of experience, when talked about, are full of contradictions. Mrs. Robinson loves her children, but ruins them through misdirected love; the illiterate peasants of a Chinese village show greater social and personal wisdom than the educated people of great cities; people say crime doesn't pay, but in some cases it pays extremely well; a young man who is by temperament a scholar and a poet feels compelled to commit a political murder; a faithful wife of twenty years deserts her husband for no apparent reason; a ne'er-do-well acts courageously in a dangerous situation—these and a thousand other contradictions confront us in the course of our lives. Unordered, and bearing no relationship to each other, our statements about experience are not only disconnected, but they are difficult to use.

Insofar as we are aware of these contradictions, this disorder among our statements is itself a source of tension. Such contradictions provide us with no guide to action; hence they leave us with the tensions of indecision and bewilderment. These tensions are not resolved until we have, *by talking to ourselves about our talking* (symbolizing our symbols), "fitted things together," so that, as we say, things don't seem to be "meaningless" any more. Religions, philosophies, science, and art are equally, and through different methods, ways of resolving the tensions produced by the contradictory data of experience by talking about our talking, then talking about our talking about our talking, and so on, until some kind of *order* has been established among the data.

Talking about things, talking about talking, talking about talking about talking, etc., represent what we shall call talking at different *levels of abstraction*. The imposition of order upon our pictures of the world is, it appears, what we mean by "understanding." When we say that a scientist "understands" something, does it not mean that he has ordered his observations at the objective, descriptive, and higher inferential levels of abstraction into a workable system in which all levels are related to other levels in terms of a few powerful generalizations? When a great religious leader or philosopher is said to "understand" life, does it not mean that he has also ordered his observations into a set of attitudes, often crystallized into exceedingly general and powerful directives? And when a novelist is said to "understand" the life of any segment of humanity (or humanity as a whole), has he not also ordered his observations at many different levels of abstraction—the particular and concrete, the general, and the more general? (Fuller explanation of "levels of abstraction" will be found in [a following chapter].) However, the novelist presents that order not in a scientific, ethical, or philosophical system of highly abstract generalizations, but in a set of symbolic experiences at the descriptive level of affective reports, involving the reader's feelings through the mechanism of identification. And these symbolic experiences, in the work of any competent novelist, are woven together to frame a consistent set of attitudes, whether of scorn, or compassion, or admiration of courage, or sympathy with the downtrodden, or a sense of futility, depending on his outlook.

Some of the ways of organizing a set of experiences for literary purposes are purely mechanical and external: these are the "rules" governing the proper construction of the novel, the play, the short story, the sonnet, and so on. But more important are the ways of organization suggested by the materials of the literary work—the experiences which the writer wishes to organize. When the materials of a story do not fit into the conventional pattern of a novel, the novelist may create a new organization altogether, more suited to the presentation of his experiences than the conventional patterns. In such a case, critics speak of the materials as "creating their own form." In such a case, too, the order may seem like disorder at first—one thinks of Laurence Sterne's *Tristram Shandy* and James Joyce's *Ulysses*—because the principles of organization, being new, have to be discovered in the course of reading. The reason a poem, novel, or play assumes the shape it ultimately does is the concern of the technical literary critic. He studies the interplay of external and internal demands which finally shape the materials into a "work of art."

To symbolize one's experiences adequately and then to order them into a coherent whole constitute an integrative act. The great novelist or dramatist or poet is one who has successfully integrated and given coherence to vast areas of human experience. Literary greatness requires, therefore, great extensional awareness of the range of human experience as well as great powers of ordering that experience meaningfully. This is why the discipline of the creative artist is endless: there is always more to learn, both about human experience (which is the material to be ordered) and about the techniques of his craft (which are the means of ordering).

From the point of view of the reader, the fact that language is social is again of central importance. The ordering of experiences and attitudes accomplished linguistically by the writer produces, in the reader, some ordering of his own experiences and attitudes. The reader becomes, as a result of this ordering, somewhat better organized himself. That's what art is for.

APOLOGY FOR BAD DREAMS

Robinson Jeffers

I

In the purple light, heavy with redwood, the slopes drop seaward,
Headlong convexities of forest, drawn in together to the step ravine. Below, on the sea-cliff,
A lonely clearing; a little field of corn by the streamside; a roof under spared trees. Then the ocean
Like a great stone someone has cut to a sharp edge and polished to shining. Beyond it the fountain
And furnace of incredible light flowing up from the sunk sun. In the little clearing a woman
Is punishing a horse; she had tied the halter to a sapling at the edge of the wood, but when the great whip
Clung to the flanks the creature kicked so hard she feared he would snap the halter; she called from the house
The young man her son; who fetched a chain tie-rope, they working together
Noosed the small rusty links round the horse's tongue
And tied him by the swollen tongue to the tree.
Seen from this height they are shrunk to insect size.
Out of all human relation. You cannot distinguish
The blood dripping from where the chain is fastened,
The beast shuddering; but the thrust neck and the legs
Far apart. You can see the whip fall on the flanks . . .
The gesture of the arm. You cannot see the face of the woman.
The enormous light beats up out of the west across the cloudbars of the trade-wind. The ocean
Darkens, the high clouds brighten, the hills darken together. Unbridled and unbelievable beauty
Covers the evening world . . . not covers, grows apparent out of it, as Venus down there grows out
From the lit sky. What said the prophet? "I create good: and I create evil: I am the Lord."

II

This coast crying out for tragedy like all beautiful places,
(The quiet ones ask for quieter suffering: but here the granite cliff the gaunt cypresses crown

345

Demands what victim? The dykes of red lava and black what Titan? The
hills like pointed flames
Beyond Soberanes, the terrible peaks of the bare hills under the sun, what
immolation?)
This coast crying out for tragedy like all beautiful places: and like the pas-
sionate spirit of humanity
Pain for its bread: God's many victims', the painful deaths, the horrible
transfigurements: I said in my heart,
"Better invent than suffer: imagine victims
Lest your own flesh be chosen the agonist, or you
Martyr some creature to the beauty of the place." And I said,
"Burn sacrifices once a year to magic
Horror away from the house, this little house here
You have built over the ocean with your own hands
Beside the standing boulders: for what are we,
The beast that walks upright, with speaking lips
And little hair, to think we should always be fed,
Sheltered, intact, and self-controlled? We sooner more liable
Than the other animals. Pain and terror, the insanities of desire; not acci-
dents but essential,
And crowd up from the core:" I imagined victims for those wolves, I made
them phantoms to follow,
They have hunted the phantoms and missed the house.
It is not good to forget over what gulfs the spirit
Of the beauty of humanity, the petal of a lost flower blown seaward by the
night-wind, floats to its quietness.

III

Boulders blunted like an old bear's teeth break up from the headland; below
them
All the soil is thick with shells, the tide-rock feasts of a dead people.
Here the granite flanks are scarred with ancient fire, the ghosts of the tribe
Crouch in the nights beside the ghost of a fire, they try to remember the sun-
light,
Light has died out of their skies. These have paid something for the future
Luck of the country, while we living keep old griefs in memory: though
God's
Envy is not a likely fountain of ruin, to forget evils calls down
Sudden reminders from the cloud: remembered deaths be our redeemers;
Imagined victims our salvation: white as the half moon at midnight
Someone flamelike passed me, saying, "I am Tamar Cauldwell, I have my
desire,"
Then the voice of the sea returned, when she had gone by, the stars to their
towers.
. . . Beautiful country burn again, Point Pinos down to the Sur Rivers
Burn as before with bitter wonders, land and ocean and the Carmel water.

IV

He brays humanity in a mortar to bring the savor
From the bruised root: a man having bad dreams, who invents victims, is
    only the ape of that God.
He washes it out with tears and many waters, calcines it with fire in the red
    crucible,
Deforms it, makes it horrible to itself: the spirit flies out and stands naked,
    he sees the spirit,
He takes it in the naked ecstasy; it breaks in his hand, the atom is broken,
    the power that massed it
Cries to the power that moves the stars, "I have come home to myself, be-
    hold me.
I bruised myself in the flint mortar and burnt me
In the red shell, I tortured myself, I flew forth,
Stood naked of myself and broke me in fragments,
And here am I moving the stars that are me."
I have seen these ways of God: I know of no reason
For fire and change and torture and the old returnings.
He being sufficient might be still. I think they admit no reason; they are the
    ways of my love.
Unmeasured power, incredible passion, enormous craft: no thought appar-
    ent but burns darkly
Smothered with its own smoke in the human brain-vault: no thought out-
    side: a certain measure in phenomena:
The fountains of the boiling stars, the flowers on the foreland, the ever-re-
    turning roses of dawn.

THE LITERATURE OF KNOWLEDGE
AND THE LITERATURE OF POWER

Thomas DeQuincey

What is it that we mean by *literature?* Popularly, and amongst the
thoughtless, it is held to include everything that is printed in a book. Little
logic is required to disturb *that* definition; the most thoughtless person is
easily made aware that in the idea of *literature* one essential element is—
some relation to a general and common interest of man, so that what applies only to a local—or professional—or merely personal interest, even
though presenting itself in the shape of a book, will not belong to literature.
So far the definition is easily narrowed; and it is as easily expanded. For not

only is much that takes a station in books not literature; but inversely, much that really *is* literature never reaches a station in books. The weekly sermons of Christendom, that vast pulpit literature which acts so extensively upon the popular mind—to warn, to uphold, to renew, to comfort, to alarm, does not attain the sanctuary of libraries in the ten thousandth part of its extent. The drama again, as, for instance, the finest of Shakspere's plays in England, and all leading Athenian plays in the noontide of the Attic stage, operated as a literature on the public mind, and were (according to the strictest letter of that term) *published* through the audiences that witnessed[1] their repre-sentation some time before they were published as things to be read; and they were published in this scenical mode of publication with much more effect than they could have had as books, during ages of costly copying or of costly printing.

Books, therefore, do not suggest an idea co-extensive and interchangeable with the idea of literature; since much literature, scenic, forensic, or didactic, (as from lecturers and public orators,) may never come into books; and much that *does* come into books, may connect itself with no literary interest. But a far more important correction, applicable to the common vague idea of literature, is to be sought—not so much in a better definition of literature, as in a sharper distinction of the two functions which it fulfils. In that great social organ, which collectively we call literature, there may be distinguished two separate offices that may blend and often *do* so, but capable severally of a severe insulation, and naturally fitted for reciprocal repulsion. There is first the literature of *knowledge,* and secondly, the literature of *power.* The function of the first is—to *teach;* the function of the second is—to *move:* the first is a rudder, the second an oar or a sail. The first speaks to the *mere* discursive understanding; the second speaks ultimately it may happen to the higher understanding or reason, but always *through* affections of pleasure and sympathy. Remotely, it may travel towards an object seated in what Lord Bacon calls *dry* light; but proximately it does and must operate, else it ceases to be a literature of *power,* on and through that *humid* light which clothes itself in the mists and glittering *iris* of human passions, desires, and genial emotions. Men have so little reflected on the higher functions of literature, as to find it a paradox if one should describe it as a mean or subordinate purpose of books to give information. But this is a paradox only in the sense which makes it honourable to be paradoxical. Whenever we talk in ordinary language of seeking information or gaining knowledge, we understand the words as connected with something of absolute novelty. But it is the grandeur of all truth which *can* occupy a very high place in human interests, that it is never absolutely novel to the meanest of minds: it exists eternally by way of germ or latent principle in the lowest as in the highest, needing to be developed but never to be planted. To be capable of transplantation is the immediate criterion of a truth that

---

[1] Charles I, for example, when Prince of Wales, and many others in his father's court, gained their known familiarity with Shakspere—not through the original quartos, so slenderly diffused, nor through the first folio of 1623, but through the court representations of his chief dramas at Whitehall.

ranges on a lower scale. Besides which, there is a rarer thing than truth, namely, *power* or deep sympathy with truth. What is the effect, for instance, upon society—of children? By the pity, by the tenderness, and by the peculiar modes of admiration, which connect themselves with the helplessness, with the innocence, and with the simplicity of children, not only are the primal affections strengthened and continually renewed, but the qualities which are dearest in the sight of heaven—the frailty for instance, which appeals to forebearance, the innocence which symbolizes the heavenly, and the simplicity which is most alien from the worldly, are kept up in perpetual remembrance, and their ideals are continually refreshed. A purpose of the same nature is answered by the higher literature, viz. the literature of power. What do you learn from Paradise Lost? Nothing at all. What do you learn from a cookery-book? Something new, something that you did not know before, in every paragraph. But would you therefore put the wretched cookery-book on a higher level of estimation than the divine poem? What you owe to Milton is not any knowledge, of which a million separate items are still but a million of advancing steps on the same earthly level; what you owe—is *power,* that is, exercise and expansion to your own latent capacity of sympathy with the infinite, where every pulse and each separate influx is a step upwards—a step ascending as upon a Jacob's ladder from earth to mysterious altitudes above the earth. *All* the steps of knowledge, from first to last, carry you farther on the same plane, but could never raise you one foot above your ancient level of earth: whereas, the very *first* step in power is a flight—is an ascending into another element where earth is forgotten.

Were it not that human sensibilities are ventilated and continually called out into exercise by the great phenomena of infancy, or of real life as it moves through chance and change, or of literature as it recombines these elements in the mimicries of poetry, romance, &c., it is certain that, like any animal power or muscular energy falling into disuse, all such sensibilities would gradually droop and dwindle. It is in relation to these great *moral* capacities of man that the literature of power, as contradistinguished from that of knowledge, lives and has its field of action. It is concerned with what is highest in man: for the Scriptures themselves never condescend to deal by suggestion or co-operation, with the mere discursive understanding: when speaking of man in his intellectual capacity, the Scriptures speak not of the understanding, but of *"the understanding heart,"*—making the heart, *i. e.,* the great *intuitive* (or non-discursive) organ, to be the interchangeable formula for man in his highest state of capacity for the infinite. Tragedy, romance, fairy-tale, or epopee, all alike restore to man's mind the ideals of justice, of hope, of truth, of mercy, of retribution, which else, (left to the support of daily life in its realities,) would languish for want of sufficient illustration. What is meant for instance by *poetic justice?*—It does not mean a justice that differs by its object from the ordinary justice of human jurisprudence; for then it must be confessedly a very bad kind of justice; but it means a justice that differs from common forensic justice by the degree in which it *attains* its object, a justice that is more omnipotent over its own ends, as dealing—not with the refractory elements of earthly life—but with elements of its own creation, and with materials flexible to its own purest preconceptions. It is certain that, were it not for the literature of power, these ideals would often remain amongst us as mere arid notional forms; whereas, by the creative forces of man put forth in literature, they gain a vernal life of restoration, and germinate into vital activities. The commonest novel, by moving in alliance with human fears and hopes, with human instincts of wrong and right, sustains and quickens those affections. Calling them into action, it rescues them from torpor. And hence the pre-eminency over all authors that merely *teach,* of the meanest that moves; or that teaches, if at all, indirectly *by* moving. The very highest work that has ever existed in the literature of knowledge, is but a *provisional* work: a book upon trial and sufferance, and *quamdiu bene se gesserit.* Let its teaching be even partially revised, let it be but expanded, nay, even let its teaching be but placed in a better order, and instantly it is superseded. Whereas the feeblest works in the literature of power, surviving at all, survive as finished and unalterable amongst men. For instance, the *Principia* of Sir Isaac Newton was a book *militant* on earth from the first. In all stages of its progress it would have to fight for its existence: 1*st,* as regards absolute truth; 2*dly,* when that combat is over, as regards its form or mode of presenting the truth. And as soon as a La Place, or anybody else, builds higher upon the foundations laid by this book, effectually he throws it out of the sunshine into decay and darkness; by weapons won from this book he superannuates and destroys this book, so that soon the name of Newton remains, as a mere *nominis umbra,* but his book, as a living power, has transmigrated into other forms. Now, on the contrary, the Iliad, the Prometheus of Æschylus,—the Othello or King Lear,—the Hamlet or Macbeth,—and the Paradise Lost, are not militant but triumphant for ever as long as the languages exist in which they speak or can be taught to speak. They never *can* transmigrate into new incarnations. To reproduce *these* in new forms, or variations, even if in some things they should be improved, would be to plagiarize. A good steam-engine is properly superseded by a better. But one lovely pastoral valley is not superseded by another, nor a statue of Praxiteles by a statue of Michael Angelo. These things are not separated by imparity, but by disparity. They are not thought of as unequal under the same standard, but as differing in *kind,* and as equal under a different standard. Human works of immortal beauty and works of nature in one respect stand on the same footing: they never absolutely repeat each other: never approach so near as not to differ; and they differ not as better and worse, or simply by more and less: they differ by undecipherable and incommunicable differences, that cannot be caught by mimicries, nor be reflected in the mirror of copies, nor become ponderable in the scales of vulgar comparison.

Applying these principles to Pope, as a representative of fine literature in general, we would wish to remark the claim which he has, or which any equal writer has, to the attention and jealous winnowing of those critics in particular who watch over public morals. Clergymen, and all the organs of public criticism put in motion by clergymen, are more especially concerned in the just appreciation of such writers, if the two canons are remembered, which we have endeavoured to illustrate, viz., that all works in this class, as opposed to those in the literature of knowledge, 1*st,* work by far deeper agencies; and, 2*dly,* are more permanent; in the strictest sense they are κτηματα ες αει [possessions forever]: and what evil they do, or what good they do, is commensurate with the national language, sometimes long after the nation has departed. At this hour, 500 years since their creation, the tales of Chaucer,[2] never equalled on this earth for tenderness, and for life of picturesqueness, are read familiarly by many in the charming language of their natal day, and by others in the modernizations of Dryden, of Pope, and Wordsworth. At this hour, 1800 years since their creation, the Pagan tales of Ovid, never equalled on this earth for the gaiety of their movement and the capricious graces of their narrative, are read by all Christendom. This man's people and their monuments are dust: but *he* is alive: he has survived them, as he told us that he had it in his commission to do, by a thousand years; "and *shall* a thousand more."

All the literature of knowledge builds only ground-nests, that are swept away by floods, or confounded by the plough; but the literature of power builds nests in aerial altitudes of temples sacred from violation, or of forests inaccessible to fraud. *This* is a great prerogative of the *power* literature: and it is a greater which lies in the mode of its influence. The *knowledge* literature, like the fashion of this world, passeth away. An Encyclopædia is its abstract; and, in this respect, it may be taken for its speaking symbol—that, before one generation has passed, an Encyclopædia is superannuated; for it speaks through the dead memory and unimpassioned understanding, which have not the *rest* of higher faculties, but are continually enlarging and varying their phylacteries. But all literature, properly so called—literature κατ' εξοχην [i.e., great literature], for the very same reason that it is so much more durable than the literature of knowledge, is (and by the very same proportion it is) more intense and electrically searching in its impressions. The directions in which the tragedy of this planet has trained our human feelings to play, and the combinations into which the poetry of this planet has thrown our human passions of love and hatred, of admiration and contempt, exercises a power bad or good over human life, that cannot be contemplated when seen stretching through many generations, without a sentiment allied to awe.[3] And of this let every one be assured—that he owes to the impassioned books which he has read, many a thousand more of emotions than he can consciously trace back to them. Dim by their origination, these emotions yet arise in him, and mould him through life like the forgotten incidents of childhood.

[2] The Canterbury Tales were not made public until 1380 or thereabouts: but the composition must have cost 30 or more years; not to mention that the work had probably been finished for some years before it was divulged.

[3] The reason why the broad distinctions between the two literatures of power and knowledge so little fix the attention, lies in the fact, that a vast proportion of books—history, biography, travels, miscellaneous essays, &c., lying in a middle zone, confound these distinctions by interblending them. All that we call "amusement" or "entertainment," is a diluted form of the power belonging to passion, and also a mixed form; and where threads of direct *instruction* intermingle in the texture with these threads of *power*, this absorption of the duality into one representative *nuance* neutralises the separate perception of either. Fused into a *tertium quid,* or neutral state, they disappear to the popular eye as the repelling forces, which in fact they are.

THE CELESTIAL OMNIBUS

E. M. Forster

The boy who resided at Agathox Lodge, 28, Buckingham Park Road, Surbiton, had often been puzzled by the old sign-post that stood almost opposite. He asked his mother about it, and she replied that it was a joke, and not a very nice one, which had been made many years back by some naughty young men, and that the police ought to remove it. For there were two strange things about this sign-post: firstly, it pointed up a blank alley, and, secondly, it had painted on it, in faded characters, the words, "To Heaven."

"What kind of young men were they?" he asked.

"I think your father told me that one of them wrote verses, and was expelled from the University and came to grief in other ways. Still, it was a long time ago. You must ask your father about it. He will say the same as I do, that it was put up as a joke."

"So it doesn't mean anything at all?"

She sent him up-stairs to put on his best things, for the Bonses were coming to tea, and he was to hand the cake-stand.

It struck him, as he wrenched on his tightening trousers, that he might do worse than ask Mr. Bons about the sign-post. His father, though very kind, always laughed at him—shrieked with laughter whenever he or any other child asked a question or spoke. But Mr. Bons was serious as well as kind. He had a beautiful house and lent one books, he was a churchwarden, and a candidate for the County Council; he had donated to the Free Library enormously, he presided over the Literary Society, and had Members of Parliament to stop with him—in short, he was probably the wisest person alive.

Yet even Mr. Bons could only say that the sign-post was a joke—the joke of a person named Shelley.

"Of course!" cried the mother; "I told you so, dear. That was the name."

"Had you never heard of Shelley?" asked Mr. Bons.

"No," said the boy, and hung his head.

"But is there no Shelley in the house?"

"Why, yes!" exclaimed the lady, in much agitation. "Dear Mr. Bons, we aren't such Philistines as that. Two at the least. One a wedding present, and the other, smaller print, in one of the spare rooms."

"I believe we have seven Shelleys," said Mr. Bons, with a slow smile. Then he brushed the cake crumbs off his stomach, and, together with his daughter, rose to go.

The boy, obeying a wink from his mother, saw them all the way to the garden gate, and when they had gone he did not at once return to the house, but gazed for a little up and down Buckingham Park Road.

His parents lived at the right end of it. After No. 39 the quality of the houses dropped very suddenly, and 64 had not even a separate servants' entrance. But at the present moment the whole road looked rather pretty, for the sun had just set in splendour, and the inequalities of rent were drowned in saffron afterglow. Small birds twittered, and the breadwinners' train shrieked musically down through the cutting—that wonderful cutting which has drawn to itself the whole beauty out of Surbiton, and clad itself, like any Alpine valley, with the glory of the fir and the silver birch and the primrose. It was this cutting that had first stirred desires within the boy—desires for something just a little different, he knew not what, desires that would return whenever things were sunlit, as they were this evening, running up and down inside him, up and down, up and down, till he would feel quite unusual all over, and as likely as not would want to cry. This evening he was even sillier, for he slipped across the road towards the sign-post and began to run up the blank alley.

The alley runs between high walls—the walls of the gardens of "Ivanhoe" and "Belle Vista" respectively. It smells a little all the way, and is scarcely twenty yards long, including the turn at the end. So not unnaturally the boy soon came to a standstill. "I'd like to kick that Shelley," he exclaimed, and glanced idly at a piece of paper which was pasted on the wall. Rather an odd piece of paper, and he read it carefully before he turned back. This is what he read:

S. AND C. R. C. C.
Alteration in Service.

Owing to lack of patronage the Company are regretfully compelled to suspend the hourly service, and to retain only the

Sunrise and Sunset Omnibuses,

which will run as usual. It is to be hoped that the public will patronize an arrangement which is intended for their convenience. As an extra inducement, the Company will, for the first time, now issue

Return Tickets!

(available one day only), which may be obtained of the driver. Passengers are again reminded that *no tickets are issued at the other end,* and that no complaints in this connection will receive consideration from the Company. Nor will the company be responsible for any negligence or stupidity on the part of Passengers, nor for Hailstorms, Lightning, Loss of Tickets, nor for any Act of God.

For the Direction.

Now he had never seen this notice before, nor could he imagine where the omnibus went to. S. of course was for Surbiton, and R.C.C. meant Road Car Company. But what was the meaning of the other C.? Coombe and Malden, perhaps, or possibly "City." Yet it could not hope to compete with the South-Western. The whole thing, the boy reflected, was run on hopelessly unbusiness-like lines. Why no tickets from the other end? And what an hour to start! Then he realized that unless the notice was a hoax, an omnibus must have been starting just as he was wishing the Bonses goodbye. He peered at the ground through the gathering dusk, and there he saw what might or might not be the marks of wheels. Yet nothing had come out of the alley. And he had never seen an omnibus at any time in the Buckingham Park Road. No: it must be a hoax, like the sign-posts, like the fairy tales, like the dreams upon which he would wake suddenly in the night. And with a sigh he stepped from the alley—right into the arms of his father.

Oh, how his father laughed! "Poor, poor Popsey!" he cried. "Diddums! Diddums! Diddums think he'd walky-palky up to Evvink!" And his mother, also convulsed with laughter, appeared on the steps of Agathox Lodge. "Don't, Bob!" she gasped. "Don't be so naughty! Oh, you'll kill me! Oh, leave the boy alone!"

But all that evening the joke was kept up. The father implored to be taken too. Was it a very tiring walk? Need one wipe one's shoes on the door-mat? And the boy went to bed feeling faint and sore, and thankful for only one thing—that he had not said a word about the omnibus. It was a hoax, yet through his dreams it grew more and more real, and the streets of Surbiton, through which he saw it driving, seemed instead to become hoaxes and shadows. And very early in the morning he woke with a cry, for he had had a glimpse of its destination.

He struck a match, and its light fell not only on his watch but also on his calendar, so that he knew it to be half-an-hour to sunrise. It was pitch dark, for the fog had come down from London in the night, and all Surbiton was wrapped in its embraces. Yet he sprang out and dressed himself, for he was determined to settle once for all which was real: the omnibus or the streets. "I shall be a fool one way or the other," he thought, "until I know." Soon he was shivering in the road under the gas lamp that guarded the entrance to the alley.

To enter the alley itself required some courage. Not only was it horribly dark, but he now realized that it was an impossible terminus for an omnibus. If it had not been for a policeman, whom he heard approaching through the fog, he would never have made the attempt. The next moment he had made the attempt and failed. Nothing. Nothing but a blank alley and a very silly boy gaping at its dirty floor. It *was* a hoax. "I'll tell papa and mamma," he decided. "I deserve it. I deserve that they should know. I am too silly to be alive." And he went back to the gate of Agathox Lodge.

There he remembered that his watch was fast. The sun was not risen; it would not rise for two minutes. "Give the bus every chance," he thought cynically, and returned into the alley.

But the omnibus was there.

It had two horses, whose sides were still smoking from their journey, and its two great lamps shone through the fog against the alley's walls, changing their cobwebs and moss into tissues of fairyland. The driver was huddled up in a cape. He faced the blank wall, and how he had managed to drive in so neatly and so silently was one of the many things that the boy never discovered. Nor could he imagine how ever he would drive out.

"Please," his voice quavered through the foul brown air. "Please, is that an omnibus?"

"Omnibus est," said the driver, without turning round. There was a moment's silence. The policeman passed, coughing, by the entrance of the alley. The boy crouched in the shadow, for he did not want to be found out. He was pretty sure, too, that it was a Pirate; nothing else, he reasoned, would go from such odd places and at such odd hours.

"About when do you start?" He tried to sound nonchalant.

"At sunrise."

"How far do you go?"

"The whole way."

"And can I have a return ticket which will bring me all the way back?"

"You can."

"Do you know, I half think I'll come." The driver made no answer. The sun must have risen, for he unhitched the brake. And scarcely had the boy jumped in before the omnibus was off.

How? Did it turn? There was no room. Did it go forward? There was a blank wall. Yet it was moving—moving at a stately pace through the fog, which had turned from brown to yellow. The thought of warm bed and warmer breakfast made the boy feel faint. He wished he had not come. His parents would not have approved. He would have gone back to them if the weather had not made it impossible. The solitude was terrible; he was the only passenger. And the omnibus, though well-built, was cold and somewhat musty. He drew his coat round him, and in so doing chanced to feel his pocket. It was empty. He had forgotten his purse.

"Stop!" he shouted. "Stop!" And then, being of a polite disposition, he glanced up at the painted notice-board so that he might call the driver by name. "Mr. Browne! stop; Oh, do please stop!"

Mr. Browne did not stop, but he opened a little window and looked in at the boy. His face was a surprise, so kind it was and modest.

"Mr. Browne, I've left my purse behind. I've not got a penny. I can't pay for the ticket. Will you take my watch, please? I am in the most awful hole."

"Tickets on this line," said the driver, "whether single or return, can be purchased by coinage from no terrene mint. And a chronometer, though it had solaced the vigils of Charlemagne, or measured the slumbers of Laura, can acquire by no mutation the double-cake that charms the fangless Cerberus of Heaven!" So saying, he handed in the necessary ticket, and, while the boy said "Thank you," continued: "Titular pretensions, I know it well, are vanity. Yet they merit no censure when uttered on a laughing lip, and in an homonymous world are in some sort useful, since they do serve to distinguish one Jack from his fellow. Remember me, therefore, as Sir Thomas Browne."

"Are you a Sir? Oh, sorry!" He had heard of these gentlemen drivers. "It *is* good of you about the ticket. But if you go on at this rate, however does your bus pay?"

"It does not pay. It was not intended to pay. Many are the faults of my equipage; it is compounded too curiously of foreign woods; its cushions tickle erudition rather than promote repose; and my horses are nourished not on the evergreen pastures of the moment, but on the dried bents and clovers of Latinity. But that it pays!—that error at all events was never intended and never attained."

"Sorry again," said the boy rather hopelessly. Sir Thomas looked sad, fearing that, even for a moment, he had been the cause of sadness. He invited the boy to come up and sit beside him on the box, and together they journeyed on through the fog, which was now changing from yellow to white. There were no houses by the road; so it must be either Putney Heath or Wimbledon Common.

"Have you been a driver always?"

"I was a physician once."

"But why did you stop? Weren't you good?"

"As a healer of bodies I had scant success, and several score of my patients preceded me. But as a healer of the spirit I have succeeded beyond my hopes and my deserts. For though my draughts were not better nor subtler than those of other men, yet, by reason of the cunning goblets wherein I offered them, the queasy soul was ofttimes tempted to sip and be refreshed."

"The queasy soul," he murmured; "if the sun sets with trees in front of it, and you suddenly come strange all over, is that a queasy soul?"

"Have you felt that?"

"Why yes."

After a pause he told the boy a little, a very little, about the journey's end. But they did not chatter much, for the boy, when he liked a person, would as soon sit silent in his company as speak, and this, he discovered, was also the mind of Sir Thomas Browne and of many others with whom he was to be acquainted. He heard, however, about the young man Shelley, who was now quite a famous person, with a carriage of his own, and about some of the other drivers who are in the service of the Company. Meanwhile the light grew stronger, though the fog did not disperse. It was now more like mist than fog, and at times would travel quickly across them, as if it was part of a cloud. They had been ascending, too, in a most puzzling way; for over two hours the horses had been pulling against the collar, and even if it were Richmond Hill they ought to have been at the top long ago. Perhaps it was Epsom, or even the North Downs; yet the air seemed keener than that which blows on either. And as to the name of their destination, Sir Thomas Browne was silent.

Crash!

"Thunder, by Jove!" said the boy, "and not so far off either. Listen to the echoes! It's more like mountains."

He thought, not very vividly, of his father and mother. He saw them sitting down to sausages and listening to the storm. He saw his own empty place. Then there would be questions, alarms, theories, jokes, consolations. They would expect him back at lunch. To lunch he would not come, nor to tea, but he would be in for dinner, and so his day's truancy would be over. If he had had his purse he would have bought them presents—not that he should have known what to get them.

Crash!

The peal and the lightening came together. The cloud quivered as if it were alive, and torn streamers of mist rushed past. "Are you afraid?" asked Sir Thomas Browne.

"What is there to be afraid of? Is it much farther?"

The horses of the omnibus stopped just as a ball of fire burst up and exploded with a ringing noise that was deafening but clear, like the noise of a blacksmith's forge. All the cloud was shattered.

"Oh, listen, Sir Thomas Browne! No, I mean look; we shall get a view at last. No, I mean listen; that sounds like a rainbow!"

The noise had died into the faintest murmur, beneath which another murmur grew, spreading stealthily, steadily, in a curve that widened but did not vary. And in widening curves a rainbow was spreading from the horses' feet into the dissolving mists.

"But how beautiful! What colours! Where will it stop? It is more like the rainbows you can tread on. More like dreams."

The colour and the sound grew together. The rainbow spanned an enormous gulf. Clouds rushed under it and were pierced by it, and still it grew, reaching forward, conquering the darkness, until it touched something that seemed more solid than a cloud.

The boy stood up. "What is that out there?" he called. "What does it rest on, out at that other end?"

In the morning sunshine a precipice shone forth beyond the gulf. A precipice—or was it a castle? The horses moved. They set their feet upon the rainbow.

"Oh, look!" the boy shouted. "Oh, listen! Those caves—or are they gateways? Oh, look between those cliffs at those ledges. I see people! I see trees!"

"Look also below," whispered Sir Thomas. "Neglect not the diviner Acheron."

The boy looked below, past the flames of the rainbow that licked against their wheels. The gulf also had cleared, and in its depths there flowed an everlasting river. One sunbeam entered and struck a green pool, and as they passed over he saw three maidens rise to the surface of the pool, singing, and playing with something that glistened like a ring.

"You down in the water—" he called.

They answered, "You up one the bridge—" There was a burst of music. "You up on the bridge, good luck to you. Truth in the depth, truth on the height."

"You down in the water, what are you doing?"

Sir Thomas Browne replied: "They sport in the mancipiary possession of their gold"; and the omnibus arrived.

The boy was in disgrace. He sat locked up in the nursery of Agathox Lodge, learning poetry for a punishment. His father had said, "My boy! I can pardon anything but untruthfulness," and had caned him, saying at each stroke, "There is *no* omnibus, *no* driver, *no* bridge, *no* mountain; you are a *truant*, a *gutter snipe*, a *liar*." His father could be very stern at times. His mother had begged him to say he was sorry. But he could not say that. It was the greatest day of his life, in spite of the caning and the poetry at the end of it.

He had returned punctually at sunset—driven not by Sir Thomas Browne, but by a maiden lady who was full of quiet fun. They had talked of omnibuses and also of barouche landaus. How far away her gentle voice seemed now! Yet it was scarcely three hours since he had left her up the alley.

His mother called through the door. "Dear, you are to come down and to bring your poetry with you."

He came down and found that Mr. Bons was in the smoking-room with his father. It had been a dinner party.

"Here is the great traveller!" said his father grimly. "Here is the young gentleman who drives in an omnibus over rainbows, while young ladies sing to him." Please with his wit, he laughed.

"After all," said Mr. Bons, smiling, "there is something a little like it in Wagner. It is odd how, in quite illiterate minds, you will find glimmers of Artistic Truth. The case interests me. Let me plead for the culprit. We have all romanced in our time, haven't we?"

"Hear how kind Mr. Bons is," said his mother, while his father said, "Very well. Let him say his Poem, and that will do. He is going away to my sister on Tuesday, and *she* will cure him of his alley-slopering." (Laughter.) "Say your Poem."

The boy began. " 'Standing aloof in giant ignorance.' "

His father laughed again—roared. "One for you, my son! Standing aloof in giant ignorance!' I never knew these poets talked sense. Just describes you. Here, Bons, you go in for poetry. Put him through it, will you, while I fetch up the whisky?"

"Yes, give me the Keats," said Mr. Bons. "Let him say his Keats to me."

So for a few moments the wise man and the ignorant boy were left alone in the smoking-room.

" 'Standing aloof in giant ignorance, of thee I dream and of the Cyclades, as one who sits ashore and longs perchance to visit—' "

"Quite right. To visit what?"

" 'To visit dolphin coral in deep seas,' " said the boy, and burst into tears.

"Come, come! why do you cry?"

"Because—because all these words that only rhymed before, now that I've come back they're me."

Mr. Bons laid the Keats down. The case was more interesting than he had expected. *"You?"* he exclaimed. "This sonnet, *you?"*

"Yes—and look further on: 'Aye, on the shores of darkness there is light, and precipices show untrodden green.' It *is* so, sir. All these things are true."

"I never doubted it" said Mr. Bons, with closed eyes.

"You—then you believe me? You believe in the omnibus and the driver and the storm and that return ticket I got for nothing and—"

"Tut, tut! No more of your yarns, my boy. I meant that I never doubted the essential truth of Poetry. Some day, when you have read more, you will understand what I mean."

"But Mr. Bons, it *is* so. There *is* light upon the shores of darkness. I have seen it coming. Light and a wind."

"Nonsense," said Mr. Bons.

"If I had stopped! They tempted me. They told me to give up my ticket —for you cannot come back if you lose your ticket. They called from the river for it, and indeed I was tempted, for I have never been so happy as among those precipices. But I thought of my mother and father, and that I must fetch them. Yet they will not come, though the road starts opposite our house. It has all happened as the people up there warned me, and Mr. Bons has disbelieved me like every one else. I have been caned. I shall never see that mountain again."

"What's that about me?" said Mr. Bons, sitting up in his chair very suddenly.

"I told them about you, and how clever you were, and how many books you had, and they said, 'Mr. Bons will certainly disbelieve you.' "

"Stuff and nonsense, my young friend. You grow impertinent. I—well— I will settle the matter. Not a word to your father. I will cure you. Tomorrow evening I will myself call here to take you for a walk, and at sunset we will go up this alley opposite and hunt for your omnibus, you silly little boy."

His face grew serious, for the boy was not disconcerted, but leapt about the room singing, "Joy! joy! I told them you would believe me. We will drive together over the rainbow. I told them that you would come." After all, could there be anything in the story? Wagner? Keats? Shelley? Sir Thomas Browne? Certainly the case was interesting.

And on the morrow evening, though it was pouring with rain, Mr. Bons did not omit to call at Agathox Lodge.

The boy was ready, bubbling with excitement, and skipping about in a way that rather vexed the President of the Literary Society. They took a turn down Buckingham Park Road, and then—having seen that no one was watching them—slipped up the alley. Naturally enough (for the sun was setting) they ran straight against the omnibus.

"Good heavens! exclaimed Mr. Bons. "Good gracious heavens!"

It was not the omnibus in which the boy had driven first, nor yet that in which he had returned. There were three horses—black, gray, and white, the gray being the finest. The driver, who turned round at the mention of goodness and of heaven, was a sallow man with terrifying jaws and sunken eyes. Mr. Bons, on seeing him, gave a cry as if of recognition, and began to tremble violently.

The boy jumped in.

"Is is possible?" cried Mr. Bons. "Is the impossible possible?"

"Sir; come in, sir. It is such a fine omnibus. Oh, here is his name—Dan some one."

Mr. Bons sprang in too. A blast of wind immediately slammed the omnibus door, and the shock jerked down all the omnibus blinds, which were very weak on their springs.

"Dan . . . Show me. Good gracious heavens! we're moving."

"Hooray!" said the boy.

Mr. Bons became flustered. He had not intended to be kidnapped. He could not find the door-handle, nor push up the blinds. The omnibus was quite dark, and by the time he had struck a match, night had come on outside also. They were moving rapidly.

"A strange, a memorable adventure," he said, surveying the interior of the omnibus, which was large, roomy, and constructed with extreme regularity, every part exactly answering to every other part. Over the door (the handle of which was outside) was written, "Lasciate ogni baldanza voi che entrate"—at least, that was what was written, but Mr. Bons said that it was Lashy arty something, and that baldanza was a mistake for speranza. His voice sounded as if he was in church. Meanwhile, the boy called to the cadaverous driver for two return tickets. They were handed in without a word. Mr. Bons covered his face with his hand and again trembled. "Do you know who that is!" he whispered, when the little window had shut upon them. "It is the impossible."

"Well, I don't like him as much as Sir Thomas Browne, though I shouldn't be surprised if he had even more in him."

"More in him?" He stamped irritably. "By accident you have made the greatest discovery of the century, and all you can say is that there is more in this man. Do you remember those vellum books in my library, stamped with red lilies? This—sit still, I bring you stupendous news!—*this is the man who wrote them.*"

The boy sat quite still. "I wonder if we shall see Mrs. Gamp?" he asked, after a civil pause.

"Mrs.—?"

"Mrs. Gamp and Mrs. Harris. I like Mrs. Harris. I came upon them quite suddenly. Mrs. Gamp's bandboxes have moved over the rainbow so badly. All the bottoms have fallen out, and two of the pippins off her bedstead tumbled into the stream."

"Out there sits the man who wrote my vellum books!" thundered Mr. Bons, "and you talk to me of Dickens and of Mrs. Gamp?"

"I know Mrs. Gamp so well," he apologized. "I could not help being glad to see her. I recognized her voice. She was telling Mrs. Harris about Mrs. Prig."

"Did you spend the whole day in her elevating company?"

"Oh, no. I raced. I met a man who took me out beyond to a race-course. You run, and there are dolphins out at sea."

"Indeed. Do you remember the man's name?"

"Achilles. No; he was later. Tom Jones."

Mr. Bons sighed heavily. "Well, my lad, you have made a miserable mess of it. Think of a cultured person with your opportunities! A cultured person would have known all these characters and known what to have said to each. He would not have wasted his time with a Mrs. Gamp or a Tom Jones. The creations of Homer, of Shakespeare, and of Him who drives us now, would alone have contented him. He would not have raced. He would have asked intelligent questions."

"But Mr. Bons," said the boy humbly, "you will be a cultured person. I told them so."

"True, true, and I beg of you not to disgrace me when we arrive. No gossiping. No running. Keep close to my side, and never speak to these Immortals unless they speak to you. Yes, and give me the return tickets. You will be losing them."

The boy surrendered the tickets, but felt a little sore. After all, he had found the way to this place. It was hard first to be disbelieved and then to be lectured. Meanwhile, the rain had stopped, and moonlight crept into the omnibus through the cracks in the blinds.

"But how is there to be a rainbow?" cried the boy.

"You distract me," snapped Mr. Bons. "I wish to meditate on beauty. I wish to goodness I was with a reverent and sympathetic person."

The lad bit his lip. He made a hundred good resolutions. He would imitate Mr. Bons all the visit. He would not laugh, or run, or sing, or do any of the vulgar things that must have disgusted his new friends last time. He would be very careful to pronounce their names properly, and to remember who knew whom. Achilles did not know Tom Jones—at least, so Mr. Bons said. The Duchess of Malfi was older than Mrs. Gamp—at least, so Mr. Bons said. He would be self-conscious, reticent, and prim. He would never say he liked any one. Yet, when the blind flew up at a chance touch of his head, all these good resolutions went to the winds, for the omnibus had reached the summit of a moonlit hill, and there was the chasm, and there, across it, stood the old precipices, dreaming, with their feet in the everlasting river. He exclaimed, "The mountain! Listen to the new tune in the water! Look at the camp fires in the ravines," and Mr. Bons, after a hasty glance, retorted, "Water? Camp fires? Ridiculous rubbish. Hold your tongue. There is nothing at all."

Yet, under his eyes, a rainbow formed, compounded not of sunlight and storm, but of moonlight and the spray of the river. The three horses put their feet upon it. He thought it the finest rainbow he had seen, but he did not dare to say so, since Mr. Bons said that nothing was there. He leant out—the window had opened—and sang the tune that rose from the sleeping waters.

"The prelude to Rhinegold?" said Mr. Bons suddenly. "Who taught you these *leit motifs*?" He, too, looked out of the window. Then he behaved very oddly. He gave a choking cry, and fell back on to the omnibus floor. He writhed and kicked. His face was green.

"Does the bridge make you dizzy?" the boy asked.

"Dizzy!" gasped Mr. Bons. "I want to go back. Tell the driver."

But the driver shook his head.

"We are nearly there," said the boy. "They are asleep. Shall I call? They will be so pleased to see you, for I have prepared them."

Mr. Bons moaned. They moved over the lunar rainbow, which ever and ever broke away behind their wheels. How still the night was! Who would be sentry at the Gate?

"I am coming," he shouted, again forgetting the hundred resolutions. "I am returning—I, the boy."

"The boy is returning," cried a voice to other voices, who repeated, "The boy is returning."

"I am bringing Mr. Bons with me."

Silence.

"I should have said Mr. Bons is bringing me with him."

Profound silence.

"Who stands sentry?"

"Achilles."

And on the rocky causeway, close to the springing of the rainbow bridge, he saw a young man who carried a wonderful shield.

"Mr. Bons, it is Achilles, armed."

"I want to go back," said Mr. Bons.

The last fragment of the rainbow melted, the wheels sang upon the living rock, the door of the omnibus burst open. Out leapt the boy—he could not resist—and sprang to meet the warrior, who, stooping suddenly, caught him on his shield.

"Achilles!" he cried, "let me get down, for I am ignorant and vulgar, and I must wait for that Mr. Bons of whom I told you yesterday."

But Achilles raised him aloft. He crouched on the wonderful shield, on heroes and burning cities, on vineyards grave in gold, on every dear passion, every joy, on the entire image of the Mountain that he had discovered, encircled, like it, with an everlasting stream. "No, no," he protested, "I am not worthy. It is Mr. Bons who must be up here."

But Mr. Bons was whimpering, and Achilles trumpeted and cried, "Stand upright upon my shield!"

"Sir, I did not mean to stand! something made me stand. Sir, why do you delay? Here is only the great Achilles, whom you knew."

Mr. Bons screamed, "I see no one. I see nothing. I want to go back." Then he cried to the driver, "Save me! Let me stop in your chariot. I have honoured you. I have quoted you. I have bound you in vellum. Take me back to my world."

The driver replied, "I am the means and not the end. I am the food and not the life. Stand by yourself, as that boy has stood. I cannot save you. For poetry is a spirit; and they that would worship it must worship in spirit and in truth."

Mr. Bons—he could not resist—crawled out of the beautiful omnibus. His face appeared, gaping horribly. His hands followed, one gripping the step, the other beating the air. Now his shoulders emerged, his chest, his stomach. With a shriek of "I see London," he fell—fell against the hard, moonlit rock, fell into it as if it were water, fell through it, vanished, and was seen by the boy no more.

"Where have you fallen to, Mr. Bons? Here is a procession arriving to honour you with music and torches. Here come the men and women whose names you know. The mountain is awake, the river is awake, over the race-

course the sea is awaking those dolphins, and it is all for you. They want
you——"

There was the touch of fresh leaves on his forehead. Some one had
crowned him.

ΤΕΛΟΣ

From the *Kingston Gazette, Surbiton Times, and
Raynes Park Observer.*

The body of Mr. Septimus Bons has been found in a shockingly mutilated
condition in the vicinity of the Bermondsey gas-works. The deceased's pockets contained a sovereign-purse, a silver cigar-case, a bijou pronouncing
dictionary, and a couple of omnibus tickets. The unfortunate gentleman had
apparently been hurled from a considerable height. Foul play is suspected,
and a thorough investigation is pending by the authorities.

THE ARTIST AS HERO
A DISCONSOLATE CHIMERA

R. P. Blackmur

The place where morals hit hardest on the arts is in the center, where the
hero is; or at least it seems to me we may think so when we remember how
often we identify the work of art with its chief character or with the role
which that character plays. It is the hero who becomes the symbol for all
the reality which has been made actual in the work of art, and if there is no
hero as such we give the hero's role to some feeling or emotion or theme
that runs through the work and find in it the symbolic form of all we value.
Morals is how we estimate the relation to life of what we value; not how
we find the value or change the value but how we estimate it. It is a secondary labor that must follow, and cannot precede, understanding and apprehension. With this in mind as an approach it should be an observation of
commanding interest that the hero of some of the most ambitious art of our
time should have become the artist himself and that in a vast amount of
other work the theme of the role of art should have become dominant in
value. Since this has never happened before, it will take a little fresh moral-
izing to make good morals out of our estimation of it; and that fresh moral-
izing, which I hope will halt short of stridency, is the task this paper is meant
to take hold of.

The subject is easier for me to handle in literature than in the other arts,
but as I see it there is nothing I can say about it in literature that does not

have its parallel in painting, sculpture, dancing, and music, and for all I know architecture as well; for all of these arts have had half a century's relation to the frame of mind and the habit of value called expressionism in the widest sense of that term. It is with the expressionistic hero that we have to do. But let us take the hero first, and see how far he has come, before we look at what expressionism has now done to his features.

There is no sense starting with the Greeks and Romans, lest we should merely find ourselves repeating them. But there is good sense starting in the Middle Ages, which is as far away from ourselves as we can get. In the literature of the Middle Ages the characteristic hero was the prince or the soldier, someone in high station, represented as a type by a poet nearly anonymous. The prince or the soldier was the conscience and the motive of the action. By the Renaissance both the artist and the hero had become somewhat more individualized, the motive and the conscience somewhat obscured. By the eighteenth century the artist was rooted for his inspiration in a relatively fixed national society; his heroes were descendants of the earlier breeds and had fallen in social position—they were the same heroes but were celebrated at a less heroic level. Motive and conscience had become easy. Here is the crisis in this sequence. With the romantic period, when the historical sense came in, a new decision was taken: the artist himself might be a hero, as Byron, Goethe, Hugo were themselves heroes greater than any of the heroes in their works; motive and conscience had got outside the works. But the day of this hero was short, though it has never been forgotten. Except for the virtuosi who did very well, the artist became the hero *manqué,* the *poète maudit,* and celebrated himself or prototypes of himself in his works. Then with the rise of symbolism and art for art's sake the heroes of a considerable body of work began to be portrayed as artists. The subject of the artist and the special sensibility of the artist began to be the heroic subject and the heroic sensibility which best expressed society itself. The hero was expression, without need either of motive or conscience.

I do not know how this long sequence came about, but it seems natural when looked at, especially its latter end. Arnold was making his claims that poetry might save the world by taking on the jobs of all the other functions of the mind. And Tolstoy was making the congruous claim that art could help Christian fundamentalism save the world—or it could if only it got rid of almost everything it ever had been. Between the two, art was to replace both motive and conscience.

Now this happened at the time of the great burst of population, the great expansion of education, and the profound (as it seems, final) division of the fields of knowledge. Man, as he became so many, seemed incompatible with his selves, and he entered upon the era of competition for theoretic supremacy among his isolated and opposed selves. Of these selves the most sympathetic to the artist was of course the artistic self; at once the most isolated and the most opposed, and in an excellent position, because of his work, that he was the higher example of and the only escape from the common predicament: as if somehow all the world had become professional and with nobody left to practice on. Hence it is that the problem of the artist became a version of the problem of man and that the proper human heroism was the heroism of the artist.

This sort of belief is a part of the behavior—it is as deep as that—of a major fraction of the thousands of fresh artists our system throws up every year into fuller isolation and with a more certain end in failure than ever before. But this belief has also been expressed articulately, with a kind of reason and critical power. I think of Delmore Schwartz's article (*Partisan Review,* Spring 1945) called "T. S. Eliot as the International Hero." The ultimate value of this article is apart from the argument about the hero—in the shrewd and illuminating remarks about the depth of the perceptions in Eliot's poetry; but it is with the argument that I am here concerned. The argument runs to the effect that the poetic method—an aesthetic knowledge —alone makes us aware of the nature of our own times by being alone capable of uniting them to themselves and to their history. This, Schwartz says, is a heroic method. It is at this point that I begin to suffer from the word hero; it has begun to mean too much other than itself; but I think Schwarz let a sound instinct guide him to the use of this term; for many will understand it in the isolation of their own natures and in the depths of their own behavior—which is where men if they do not understand each other at least imitate each other. Hero is the high name we give to those to whom we turn for strength in the effort to find ourselves a motive, or in the worse effort to create in ourselves a conscience. What Schwartz is arguing is that the role of poetry is the heroic role for our time: in which is expressed the heroism of the non-heroic: the defeated, the rejected, the impotent, the loveless.

Does it not appear on a mere moment's meditation that the role of this hero is expressionistic and that the one unanimity that this heroic act can reach is the residual unanimity, almost the accidental unanimity, under the babble of differences?

I do not share this view of the world; I regard it with terrified sympathy, like the horror of being about to fall; for this may be what people are getting to be like. It is the terror and the horror of contemplating the individual who, being without the strength of society, finds himself, in full motive and all conscience, committing gradual suicide. It is the predicament in which we turn to the radio or to the whole of literature each hour on the hour to see what has happened.

There is another view which I want to interpose for a moment before we return to the heroes of expressionism. My friend Robert Fitzgerald said recently in a seminar that Oedipus' answer to the Sphinx riddle was a silly answer and that the Sphinx must have died by falling over backward from a kind of shame at his impertinence. What is it that at first walks on four legs, then on two, and at last on three? When Oedipus said Man, he only proposed another riddle, as is clear if you read Sophocles' plays about him. What I propose, to represent a view not expressionistic, is that Oedipus might have answered the riddle thus: That animal which dares to become a man, and dares long enough, will end crippled. This is not to solve the riddle, but to rehearse it in the terms of another heroism than that of Oedipus or the expressionists.

So much for my intervention. What is this word *expression* when it takes on an extra syllable and becomes a mode of the mind? I rest on the dictionary which like faith is the substance of things hoped for. Here is what Webster has to say:

> *expressionism.* 1. The theory or practice of freely expressing one's inner, or subjective, emotions and sensations; a sense originally developed in painting. 2. In 20th-century literature and drama, such interpretation of life in stylized and distorted scenes and characters, symbolic of reality, usually presented so as to reflect the subjective state of the chief character. 3. Belief in, or advocacy or practice of, the free expression of one's individuality, especially as a means toward the acquirement of individual culture.

The order of these notions is interesting; number 2 includes and deforms number 1; number 3 includes and deforms numbers 1 and 2 so there is very nearly nothing left of either the individual or his culture. (Culture, if Eliot is right, is the incarnation of religion whether in the individual or his society: the motive at work in relation to the conscience.) These do not disappear, but are deformed. One thing all three have in common is the resolute avoidance of taking second thought or second sight except on matters of executive form or manners. There is no query and no scrutiny, of the inspiration: upon which we have been more often fooled than upon any other important matter.

Yet there is something wonderfully warm and tempting and heroic about these notions. Like every resort to the primitive they seem to recreate the innocent and to make one at home with the savage; the effect of destroying the burden of the individual while perfecting his freedom. They represent the incentive in a phrase of Maritain: "Art bitten by Poetry longs to be freed from Reason."

It is at this point—in this longing, in these *longueurs*—that all we mean by expressionism shows its warrant for being and the nature of its justification by works. If we think of these longings and how their release may be passionate, with a passion that may seem of universal scope, then I think we can see how great-spirited men have made great works by heroizing the longing to be freed from reason. The whole human world shares and expresses itself in this longing. Not only is the artist isolated and the hero of all his knowledge, but he finds that he has upon his hands the task of the deliberate creation of conscience in a conscienceless society. Especially has this been true in literature. Stephen Dedalus, in the *Portrait of the Artist As a Young Man,* goes forth to forge in the smithy of his soul the uncreated conscience of his race; and H. C. Earwicker in *Finnegans Wake* is, in his dream of the great soul of the world, the very smithy where, to the best of his ability, Joyce forged that conscience: in the ground, the soil, the chthonic home of behavior. Joyce is one of the peaks reached by the artist as hero;

in him, at the end, all the nostalgias have come home again in the great spreading stain of general expression from which he started.

In Henry James the motion is the same but he neither went so far nor started, consciously, so far back. I think the argument of his whole work is that art gives you all you have of conscience before official morals come in, and his tales of the artist—whether writer or painter—put up the artist as the characteristic impersonal hero of that enterprise: a scapegoat paying with life for art. That is what I mean by the creation of conscience in a conscienceless world. James himself put the matter best at the practical level. The theme of the artist remained interesting, he said, only so long as the artist was a failure, that is, so long as he remained a person. For if the artist succeeded, he went on, he disappeared into his work, and there was no person left. If there is something thin and meager about all James's fables of the artist's failure and success, there is also something haunting and demonic: all that fades in an embrace, and is yet there, all that is heroic in the artist who has disappeared into the hero.

If in James it is his impersonality that makes the artist the heroic form of conscience, in André Gide it is the other way round. In *The Counterfeiters* the personality contains almost everything that is at stake; the book is indeed an effort to create a personality for the author himself at the expense of anything that used to be called the individual, and it is a personality so frail and precarious that it is at the point of extinction and needs the food of some fresh adventure either in life, or in the classics expressionistically conceived, to keep it alive at all. You will remember that this book contains the journal of the novelist Edouard in which he both writes about the other characters with relation to another novel and also engorges them for his own sustenance: he eats what he expresses, he expresses what he eats, and he does both conscientiously. It only adds to the involvement in personality to remember that Gide also kept and published the journal of his own experience in writing *The Counterfeiters*—the journal of what it was like to express himself in the guise of Edouard. The conscience has become merely personal, and the motive an appetite. The final value is in the success of the artist, by the success of his art, in the struggle against the world: an expressionistic struggle toward individual culture, as the dictionary says, in which the old-style individual is sacrificed and demolished. This is the excruciating triumph of moralism which has lost its religion or the substance of its religion. It is also, I think, the characteristic triumph of expressionism. We have climbed the tower of Babel; we hear each voice make invocation of a private Pentecost; and we see what is merely possible masquerading as opaque prophecy.

Let me suggest that this comes about, because of what Gide did with Dostoevski's notion of fundamental caprice—the goat-like act of our underground natures—as animating so much of our behavior. Gide turned caprice into the free act—the *acte gratuit*—in which we create our natures and derive our behavior. If the word were in fashion I would say that Gide's form of expressionism operated on a diabolic aesthetic, but I should have to add that it is a protestant devil, withal scrupulous and deeply adventurous.

Gide's sensibility may or may not be diabolic; Thomas Mann's *Doctor Faustus* is avowedly an essay in humanistic diabolism. Its hero, Adrian Leverkühn, becomes a great composer by selling the humanity of his life to the devil; which was neither a capricious nor a free act, but historic, compulsive, fatal, done to raise the expressive irresponsibility of the artist to the breaking point of absolute responsibility: which is to say total, because unimplicated, response. Adrian Leverkühn's music is the naked human voice of the actual world and collapses at the apocalypse of the world to come.

Because that voice is given precise and independent form in the art of music it is so far separated from the world that it can act as the naked and intolerable conscience: the expressive judgment of the chaos of the German 'twenties and the horrible order of the German 'thirties and 'forties. Because that voice is still the human voice, Leverkühn's music in the very act of formalizing it discerns its motive. Conscience and motive together, in this case, lead to damnation. So much for the tragic role of the art of music as hero: it could be carried no further in accounting for the journey of the war, in which Dante tells us we are all engaged. What of the other war, the war of the pity, which must engage our contemplation? What of the hero Leverkühn who composed the heroic music?

Craving personality as much as any character of Gide, ambitious as any in Joyce, quite as willing as any in James to surrender himself to his art, his own adventure is carried, I think, a step further than any of these. He is not impersonal, he does not disappear into his work; he is cut off even from that; he is depersonalized humanity, depersonalized to the point where he becomes the anguished expressive parody of that very humanity of which his music created the conscience and revealed the motive. His first large work was the opera *Love's Labour's Lost,* which being interpreted here means, he could not do love's labors; without love, he had to live without faith and without reason. He knew only what they expressed: but he himself could only express it as parody, however heroic. I should like to think that *Doctor Faustus* is the last novel in which the artist as such is the hero. The hero of expressionism could go no further, in magnitude or depth.

THE ARTIST AND HIS TIME

Albert Camus

1. As an artist, have you chosen the role of witness?

This would take considerable presumption or a vocation I lack. Personally I don't ask for any role and I have but one real vocation. As a man, I have a preference for happiness; as an artist, it seems to me that I still have characters to bring to life without the help of wars or of law-courts. But I have been sought out, as each individual has been sought out. Artists of the past could at least keep silent in the face of tyranny. The tyrannies of today are improved; they no longer admit of silence or neutrality. One has to take a stand, be either for or against. Well, in that case, I am against.

But this does not amount to choosing the comfortable role of witness. It is merely accepting the time as it is, minding one's own business, in short. Moreover, you are forgetting that today judges, accused, and witnesses exchange positions with exemplary rapidity. My choice, if you think I am making one, would at least be never to sit on a judge's bench, or beneath it, like so many of our philosophers. Aside from that, there is no dearth of opportunities for action, in the relative. Trade-unionism is today the first, and the most fruitful among them.

II. Is not the quixotism that has been criticized in your recent works an idealistic and romantic definition of the artist's role?

However words are perverted, they provisionally keep their meaning. And it is clear to me that the romantic is the one who chooses the perpetual motion of history, the grandiose epic, and the announcement of a miraculous event at the end of time. If I have tried to define something, it is, on the contrary, simply the common existence of history and of man, everyday life with the most possible light thrown upon it, the dogged struggle against one's own degradation and that of others.

It is likewise idealism, and of the worse kind, to end up by hanging all action and all truth on a meaning of history that is not implicit in events and that, in any case, implies a mythical aim. Would it therefore be realism to take as the laws of history the future—in other words, just what is not yet history, something of whose nature we know nothing?

It seems to me, on the contrary, that I am arguing in favor of a true realism against a mythology that is both illogical and deadly, and against romantic nihilism whether it be bourgeois or allegedly revolutionary. To tell the truth, far from being romantic, I believe in the necessity of a rule and an order. I merely say that there can be no question of just any rule whatsoever. And that it would be surprising if the rule we need were given us by this disordered society, or, on the other hand, by those doctrinaires who declare themselves liberated from all rules and all scruples.

III. The Marxists and their followers likewise think they are humanists. But for them human nature will be formed in the classless society of the future.

To begin with, this proves that they reject at the present moment what we all are: those humanists are accusers of man. How can we be surprised that such a claim should have developed in the world of court trials? They reject the man of today in the name of the man of the future. That claim is religious in nature. Why should it be more justified than the one which announces the kingdom of heaven to come? In reality the end of history cannot have, within the limits of our condition, any definable significance. It can only be the object of a faith and of a new mystification. A mystification that today is no less great than the one that of old based colonial oppression on the necessity of saving the souls of infidels.

IV. Is not that what in reality separates you from the intellectuals of the left?

You mean that is what separates those intellectuals from the left? Traditionally the left has always been at war against injustice, obscurantism, and oppression. It always thought that those phenomena were interdependent. The idea that obscurantism can lead to justice, the national interest to liberty, is quite recent. The truth is that certain intellectuals of the left (not all, fortunately) are today hypnotized by force and efficacy as our intellectuals of the right were before and during the war. Their attitudes are different, but the act of resignation is the same. The first wanted to be realistic nationalists; the second want to be realistic socialists. In the end they betray nationalism and socialism alike in the name of a realism henceforth without content and adored as a pure, and illusory, technique of efficacy.

This is a temptation that can, after all, be understood. But still, however the question is looked at, the new position of the people who call themselves, or think themselves, leftists consists in saying: certain oppressions are justifiable because they follow the direction, which cannot be justified, of history. Hence there are presumably privileged executioners, and privileged by nothing. This is about what was said in another context by Joseph de Maistre, who has never been taken for an incendiary. But this is a thesis which, personally, I shall always reject. Allow me to set up against it the traditional point of view of what has been hitherto called the left: all executioners are of the same family.

V. What can the artist do in the world of today?

He is not asked either to write about co-operatives or, conversely, to lull to sleep in himself the sufferings endured by others throughout history. And since you have asked me to speak personally, I am going to do so as simply as I can. Considered as artists, we perhaps have no need to interfere in the affairs of the world. But considered as men, yes. The miner who is exploited or shot down, the slaves in the camps, those in the colonies, the legions of persecuted throughout the world—they need all those who can speak to communicate their silence and to keep in touch with them. I have not written, day after day, fighting articles and texts, I have not taken part in the common struggles because I desire the world to be covered with Greek statues and masterpieces. The man who has such a desire does exist in me. Except that he has something better to do in trying to instill life into the creatures of his imagination. But from my first articles to my latest book I have written so much, and perhaps too much, only because I cannot keep from being drawn toward everyday life, toward those, whoever they may be, who are humiliated and debased. They need to hope, and if all keep silent or if they are given a choice between two kinds of humiliation, they will be forever deprived of hope and we with them. It seems to me impossible to endure that idea, nor can he who cannot endure it lie down to sleep in his tower. Not through virtue, as you see, but through a sort of almost organic intolerance, which you feel or do not feel. Indeed, I see many who fail to feel it, but I cannot envy their sleep.

This does not mean, however, that we must sacrifice our artist's nature to some social preaching or other. I have said elsewhere why the artist was more than ever necessary. But if we intervene as men, that experience will have an effect upon our language. And if we are not artists in our language first of all, what sort of artists are we? Even if, militants in our lives, we speak in our works of deserts and of selfish love, the mere fact that our lives are militant causes a special tone of voice to people with men that desert and that love. I shall certainly not choose the moment when we are beginning to leave nihilism behind to stupidly deny the values of creation in favor of the values of humanity, or vice versa. In my mind neither one is ever separated from the other and I measure the greatness of an artist (Molière, Tolstoy, Melville) by the balance he managed to maintain between the two. Today, under the pressure of events, we are obliged to transport that tension into our lives likewise. This is why so many artists, bending under the burden, take refuge in the ivory tower or, conversely, in the social church. But as for me, I see in both choices a like act of resignation. We must simultaneously serve suffering and beauty. The long patience, the strength, the secret cunning such service calls for are the virtues that establish the very renascence we need.

One word more. This undertaking, I know, cannot be accomplished without dangers and bitterness. We must accept the dangers: the era of chairbound artists is over. But we must reject the bitterness. One of the temptations of the artist is to believe himself solitary, and in truth he hears this shouted at him with a certain base delight. But this is not true. He stands in the midst of all, in the same rank, neither higher nor lower, with all those who are working and struggling. His very vocation, in the face of oppression, is to open the prisons and to give a voice to the sorrows and joys of all. This is where art, against its enemies, justifies itself by proving precisely that it is no one's enemy. By itself art could probably not produce the renascence which implies justice and liberty. But without it, that renascence would be without forms and, consequently, would be nothing. Without culture, and the relative freedom it implies, society, even when perfect, is but a jungle. This is why any authentic creation is a gift to the future.

SONNY'S BLUES

James Baldwin

I read about it in the paper, in the subway, on my way to work. I read it, and I couldn't believe it, and I read it again. Then perhaps I just stared at it, at the newsprint spelling out his name, spelling out the story. I stared at it in the swinging lights of the subway car, and in the faces and bodies of the people, and in my own face, trapped in the darkness which roared outside.

It was not to be believed and I kept telling myself that, as I walked from the subway station to the high school. And at the same time I couldn't doubt it. I was scared, scared for Sonny. He became real to me again. A great block of ice got settled in my belly and kept melting there slowly all day long, while I taught my classes algebra. It was a special kind of ice. It kept melting, sending trickles of ice water all up and down my veins, but it never got less. Sometimes it hardened and seemed to expand until I felt my guts were going to come spilling out or that I was going to choke or scream. This would always be at a moment when I was remembering some specific thing Sonny had once said or done.

When he was about as old as the boys in my classes his face had been bright and open, there was a lot of copper in it; and he'd had wonderfully direct brown eyes, and great gentleness and privacy. I wondered what he looked like now. He had been picked up, the evening before, in a raid on an apartment downtown, for peddling and using heroin.

I couldn't believe it: but what I mean by that is that I couldn't find any room for it anywhere inside me. I had kept it outside me for a long time. I hadn't wanted to know. I had had suspicions, but I didn't name them, I kept putting them away. I told myself that Sonny was wild but he wasn't crazy. And he'd always been a good boy, he hadn't ever turned hard or evil or disrespectful, the way kids can, so quick, so quick, especially in Harlem. I didn't want to believe that I'd ever see my brother going down, coming to nothing, all that light in his face gone out, in the condition I'd already seen so many others. Yet it had happened and here I was, talking about algebra to a lot of boys who might, every one of them for all I knew, be popping off needles every time they went to the head. Maybe it did more for them than algebra could.

I was sure that the first time Sonny had ever had horse, he couldn't have been much older than these boys were now. These boys, now, were living as we'd been living then, they were growing up with a rush and their heads bumped abruptly against the low ceiling of their actual possibilities. They were filled with rage. All they really knew were two darknesses, the darkness of their lives, which was now closing in on them, and the darkness of the movies, which had blinded them to that other darkness, and in which they now, vindictively, dreamed, at once more together than they were at any other time, and more alone.

When the last bell rang, the last class ended, I let out my breath. It seemed I'd been holding it for all that time. My clothes were wet—I may have looked as though I'd been sitting in a steam bath, all dressed up, all afternoon. I sat alone in the classroom a long time. I listened to the boys outside, downstairs, shouting and cursing and laughing. Their laughter struck me for perhaps the first time. It was not the joyous laughter which—God knows why—one associates with children. It was mocking and insular, its intent was to denigrate. It was disenchanted, and in this, also, lay the authority of their curses. Perhaps I was listening to them because I was thinking about my brother and in them I heard my brother. And myself.

One boy was whistling a tune, at once very complicated and very simple, it seemed to be pouring out of him as though he were a bird, and it sounded very cool and moving through all that harsh, bright air, only just holding its own through all those other sounds.

I stood up and walked over to the window and looked down into the courtyard. It was the beginning of the spring and the sap was rising in the boys. A teacher passed through them every now and again, quickly, as though he or she couldn't wait to get out of that courtyard, to get those boys out of their sight and off their minds. I started collecting my stuff. I thought I'd better get home and talk to Isabel.

The courtyard was almost deserted by the time I got downstairs. I saw this boy standing in the shadow of a doorway, looking just like Sonny. I almost called his name. Then I saw that it wasn't Sonny, but somebody we used to know, a boy from around our block. He'd been Sonny's friend. He'd never been mine, having been too young for me, and, anyway, I'd never liked him. And now, even though he was a grown-up man, he still hung around that block, still spent hours on the street corners, was always high and raggy. I used to run into him from time to time and he'd often work around to asking me for a quarter or fifty cents. He always had some real good excuse, too, and I always gave it to him, I don't know why.

But now, abruptly, I hated him. I couldn't stand the way he looked at me, partly like a dog, partly like a cunning child. I wanted to ask him what the hell he was doing in the school courtyard.

He sort of shuffled over to me, and he said, "I see you got the papers. So you already know about it."

"You mean about Sonny? Yes, I already know about it. How come they didn't get you?"

He grinned. It made him repulsive and it also brought to mind what he'd looked like as a kid. "I wasn't there. I stay away from them people."

"Good for you." I offered him a cigarette and I watched him through the smoke. "You come all the way down here just to tell me about Sonny?"

"That's right." He was sort of shaking his head and his eyes looked strange, as though they were about to cross. The bright sun deadened his damp dark brown skin and it made his eyes look yellow and showed up the dirt in his kinked hair. He smelled funky. I moved a little away from him and I said, "Well, thanks. But I already know about it and I got to get home."

"I'll walk you a little ways," he said. We started walking. There were a couple of kids still loitering in the courtyard, and one of them said goodnight to me and looked strangely at the boy beside me.

"What're you going to do?" he asked me. "I mean, about Sonny?"

"Look. I haven't seen Sonny for over a year, I'm not sure I'm going to do anything. Anyway, what the hell *can* I do?"

"That's right," he said quickly, "ain't nothing you can do. Can't much help old Sonny no more, I guess."

It was what I was thinking and so it seemed to me he had no right to say it.

"I'm surprised at Sonny, though," he went on—he had a funny way of talking, he looked straight ahead as though he were talking to himself—"I thought Sonny was a smart boy, I thought he was too smart to get hung."

"I guess he thought so too," I said sharply, "and that's how he got hung. And now about you? You're pretty goddamn smart, I bet."

Then he looked directly at me, just for a minute. "I ain't smart," he said. "If I was smart, I'd have reached for a pistol a long time ago."

"Look. Don't tell *me* your sad story, if it was up to me, I'd give you one." Then I felt guilty—guilty, probably, for never having supposed that the poor bastard *had* a story of his own, much less a sad one, and I asked, quickly, "What's going to happen to him now?"

He didn't answer this. He was off by himself some place. "Funny thing," he said, and from his tone we might have been discussing the quickest way to get to Brooklyn, "when I saw the papers this morning, the first thing I asked myself was if I had anything to do with it. I felt sort of responsible."

I began to listen more carefully. The subway station was on the corner, just before us, and I stopped. He stopped, too. We were in front of a bar and he ducked slightly, peering in, but whoever he was looking for didn't seem to be there. The juke box was blasting away with something black and bouncy and I half watched the barmaid as she danced her way from the juke box to her place behind the bar. And I watched her face as she laughingly responded to something someone said to her, still keeping time to the music. When she smiled one saw a little girl, one sensed the doomed, still-struggling woman beneath the battered face of the semi-whore.

"I never *give* Sonny nothing," the boy said finally, "but a long time ago I come to school high and Sonny asked me how it felt." He paused, I couldn't bear to watch him, I watched the barmaid, and I listened to the music which seemed to be causing the pavement to shake. "I told him it felt great." The music stopped, the barmaid paused and watched the juke box until the music began again. "It did."

All this was carrying me some place I didn't want to go. I certainly didn't want to know how it felt. It filled everything, the people, the houses, the music, the dark, quicksilver barmaid, with menace; and this menace was their reality.

"What's going to happen to him now?" I asked again.

"They'll send him away some place and they'll try to cure him." He shook his head. "Maybe he'll even think he's kicked the habit. Then they'll let him loose"—he gestured, throwing his cigarette into the gutter. "That's all."

"What do you mean, that's *all?*"

But I knew what he meant.

"I *mean,* that's *all.*" He turned his head and looked at me, pulling down the corners of his mouth. "Don't you know what I mean?" he asked, softly.

"How the hell *would* I know what you mean?" I almost whispered it, I don't know why.

"That's right," he said to the air, "how would *he* know what I mean?" He turned toward me again, patient and calm, and yet I somehow felt him shaking, shaking as though he were going to fall apart. I felt that ice in my guts again, the dread I'd felt all afternoon; and again I watched the barmaid, moving about the bar, washing glasses, and singing. "Listen. They'll let him out and then it'll just start all over again. That's what I mean."

"You mean—they'll let him out. And then he'll just start working his way back in again. You mean he'll never kick the habit. Is that what you mean?"

"That's right," he said, cheerfully. "*You* see what I mean."

"Tell me," I said at last, "why does he want to die? He must want to die, he's killing himself, why does he want to die?"

He looked at me in surprise. He licked his lips. "He don't want to die. He wants to live. Don't nobody want to die, ever."

Then I wanted to ask him—too many things. He could not have answered, or if he had, I could not have borne the answers. I started walking. "Well, I guess it's none of my business."

"It's going to be rough on old Sonny," he said. We reached the subway station. "This is your station?" he asked. I nodded. I took one step down. "Damn!" he said, suddenly. I looked up at him. He grinned again. "Damn it if I didn't leave all my money home. You ain't got a dollar on you, have you? Just for a couple of days, is all."

All at once something inside gave and threatened to come pouring out of me. I didn't hate him any more. I felt that in another moment I'd start crying like a child.

"Sure," I said. "Don't sweat." I looked in my wallet and didn't have a dollar, I only had a five. "Here," I said. "That hold you?"

He didn't look at it—he didn't want to look at it. A terrible, closed look came over his face, as though he were keeping the number on the bill a secret from him and me. "Thanks," he said, and now he was dying to see me go. "Don't worry about Sonny. Maybe I'll write him or something."

"Sure," I said. "You do that. So long."

"Be seeing you," he said. I went on down the steps.

And I didn't write Sonny or send him anything for a long time. When I finally did, it was just after my little girl died; he wrote me back a letter which made me feel like a bastard.

Here's what he said:

Dear brother,

You don't know how much I needed to hear from you. I wanted to write you many a time but I dug how much I must have hurt you and so I didn't write. But now I feel like a man who's been trying to climb up out of some deep, real deep and funky hole and just saw the sun up there, outside. I got to get outside.

I can't tell you much about how I got here. I mean I don't know how to tell you. I guess I was afraid of something or I was trying to escape from something and you know I have never been very strong in the head (smile.). I'm glad Mama and Daddy are dead and can't see what's happened to their son and I swear if I'd known what I was doing I would never have hurt you so, you and a lot of other fine people who were nice to me and who believed in me.

I don't want you to think it had anything to do with me being a musician. It's more than that. Or maybe less than that. I can't get anything straight in my head down here and I try not to think about what's going to happen to me when I get outside again. Sometime I think I'm going to flip and *never* get outside and sometime I think I'll come straight back. I tell you one thing, though, I'd rather blow my brains out than go through this again. But that's what they all say, so they tell me. If I tell you when I'm coming to New York and if you could meet me, I sure would appreciate it. Give my love to Isabel and the kids and I was sure sorry to hear about little Gracie. I wish I could be like Mama and say the Lord's will be done, but I don't know it seems to me that trouble is the one thing that never does get stopped and I don't know what good it does to blame it on the Lord. But maybe does some good if you believe it.

> Your brother,
> SONNY

Then I kept in constant touch with him and I sent him whatever I could and I went to meet him when he came back to New York. When I saw him many things I thought I had forgotten came flooding back to me. This was because I had begun, finally, to wonder about Sonny, about the life that Sonny lived inside. This life, whatever it was, had made him older and thinner and it had deepened the distant stillness in which he had always moved. He looked very unlike my baby brother. Yet, when he smiled, when we shook hands, the baby brother I'd never known looked out from the depths of his private life, like an animal waiting to be coaxed into the light.

"How you been keeping?" he asked me.

"All right. And you?"

"Just fine." He was smiling all over his face. "It's good to see you again."

"It's good to see you."

The seven years' difference in our ages lay between us like a chasm: I wondered if these years would ever operate between us as a bridge. I was remembering, and it made it hard to catch my breath, that I had been there when he was born; and I had heard the first words he had ever spoken. When he started to walk, he walked from our mother straight to me. I caught him just before he fell when he took the first steps he ever took in this world.

"How's Isabel?"

"Just fine. She's dying to see you."

"And the boys?"

"They're fine, too. They're anxious to see their uncle."

"Oh, come on. You know they don't remember me."

"Are you kidding? Of course they remember you."

He grinned again. We got into a taxi. We had a lot to say to each other, far too much to know how to begin.

As the taxi began to move, I asked, "You still want to go to India?"

He laughed. "You still remember that. Hell no. This place is Indian enough for me."

"It used to belong to them," I said.

And he laughed again. "They damn sure knew what they were doing when they got rid of it."

Years ago, when he was around fourteen, he'd been hipped on the idea of going to India. He read books about people sitting on rocks, naked, in all kinds of weather, but mostly bad, naturally, and walking barefoot through hot coals and arriving at wisdom. I used to say that it sounded to me as though they were getting away from wisdom as fast as they could. I think he sort of looked down on me for that.

"Do you mind," he asked, "if we have the driver drive alongside the park? On the west side—I haven't seen the city in so long."

"Of course not," I said. I was afraid that I might sound as though I were humoring him, but I hoped he wouldn't take it that way.

So we drove along, between the green of the park and the stony, lifeless elegance of hotels and apartment buildings, toward the vivid, killing streets of our childhood. These streets hadn't changed, though housing projects jutted up out of them now like rocks in the middle of a boiling sea. Most of the houses in which we had grown up had vanished, as had the stores from which we had stolen, the basements in which we had first tried sex, the rooftops from which we had hurled tin cans and bricks. But houses exactly like the houses of our past yet dominated the landscape, boys exactly like the boys we once had been found themselves smothering in these houses, came down into the streets for light and air, and found themselves encircled by disaster. Some escaped the trap, most didn't. Those who got out always left something of themselves behind, as some animals amputate a leg and leave it in the trap. It might be said, perhaps, that I had escaped, after all, I was a school teacher; or that Sonny had, he hadn't lived in Harlem for years. Yet, as the cab moved uptown through streets which seemed, with the rush, to darken with dark people, and as I covertly studied Sonny's face, it came to me that what we both were seeking through our separate cab windows was that part of ourselves which had been left behind. It's always at the hour of trouble and confrontation that the missing member aches.

We hit 110th Street and started rolling up Lenox Avenue. And I'd known this avenue all my life, but it seemed to me again, as it had seemed on the day I'd first heard about Sonny's trouble, filled with a hidden menace which was its very breath of life.

"We almost there," said Sonny.

"Almost." We were both too nervous to say anything more.

We live in a housing project. It hasn't been up long. A few days after it was up it seemed uninhabitably new, now of course, it's already rundown. It looks like a parody of the good, clean, faceless life—God knows the people who live in it do their best to make it a parody. The beat-looking grass lying around isn't enough to make their lives green, the hedges will never hold out the streets, and they know it. The big windows fool no one, they aren't big enough to make space out of no space. They don't bother with the windows, they watch the TV screen instead. The playground is most popular with the children who don't play at jacks, or skip rope, or roller skate, or swing, and they can be found in it after dark. We moved in partly because it's not too far from where I teach, and partly for the kids; but it's really just like the houses in which Sonny and I grew up. The same things happen, they'll have the same things to remember. The moment Sonny and I started into the house I had the feeling that I was simply bringing him back into the danger he had almost died trying to escape.

Sonny has never been talkative. So I don't know why I was sure he'd be dying to talk to me when supper was over the first night. Everything went fine, the oldest boy remembered him, and the youngest boy liked him, and Sonny had remembered to bring something for each of them; and Isabel, who is really much nicer than I am, more open and giving, had gone to a lot of trouble about dinner and was genuinely glad to see him. And she's always been able to tease Sonny in a way that I haven't. It was nice to see her face so vivid again and to hear her laugh and watch her make Sonny laugh. She wasn't, or, anyway, she didn't seem to be, at all uneasy or embarrassed. She chatted as though there were no subject which had to be avoided and she got Sonny past his first, faint stiffness. And thank God she was there, for I was filled with that icy dread again. Everything I did seemed awkward to me, and everything I said sounded freighted with hidden meaning. I was trying to remember everything I'd heard about dope addiction and I couldn't help watching Sonny for signs. I wasn't doing it out of malice. I was trying to find out something about my brother. I was dying to hear him tell me he was safe.

"Safe!" my father grunted, whenever Mama suggested trying to move to a neighborhood which might be safer for children. "Safe, hell! Ain't no place safe for kids, nor nobody."

He always went on like this, but he wasn't, ever, really as bad as he sounded, not even on weekends, when he got drunk. As a matter of fact, he was always on the lookout for "something a little better," but he died before he found it. He died, suddenly, during a drunken weekend in the middle of the war, when Sonny was fifteen. He and Sonny hadn't ever got on too well. And this was partly because Sonny was the apple of his father's eye. It was because he loved Sonny so much and was frightened for him, that he was always fighting with him. It doesn't do any good to fight with Sonny. Sonny just moves back, inside himself, where he can't be reached. But the principal reason that they never hit it off is that they were so much alike. Daddy was big and rough and loud-talking, just the opposite of Sonny, but they both had—that same privacy.

Mama tried to tell me something about this, just after Daddy died. I was home on leave from the army.

This was the last time I ever saw my mother alive. Just the same, this picture gets all mixed up in my mind with pictures I had of her when she was younger. The way I always see her is the way she used to be on a Sunday afternoon, say, when the old folks were talking after the big Sunday dinner. I always see her wearing pale blue. She'd be sitting on the sofa. And my father would be sitting in the easy chair, not far from her. And the living room would be full of church folks and relatives. There they sit, in chairs all around the living room, and the night is creeping up outside, but nobody knows it yet. You can see the darkness growing against the windowpanes and you hear the street noises every now and again, or maybe the jangling beat of a tambourine from one of the churches close by, but it's real quiet in the room. For a moment nobody's talking, but every face looks darkening, like the sky outside. And my mother rocks a little from the waist, and my father's eyes are closed. Everyone is looking at something a child can't see. For a minute they've forgotten the children. Maybe a kid is lying on the rug, half asleep. Maybe somebody's got a kid in his lap and is absent-mindedly stroking the kid's head. Maybe there's a kid, quiet and big-eyed, curled up in a big chair in the corner. The silence, the darkness coming, and the darkness in the faces frightens the child obscurely. He hopes that the hand which strokes his forehead will never stop—will never die. He hopes that there will never come a time when the old folks won't be sitting around the living room, talking about where they've come from, and what they've seen, and what's happened to them and their kinfolk.

But something deep and watchful in the child knows that this is bound to end, is already ending. In a moment someone will get up and turn on the light. Then the old folks will remember the children and they won't talk any more that day. And when light fills the room, the child is filled with darkness. He knows that every time this happens he's moved just a little closer to that darkness outside. The darkness outside is what the old folks have been talking about. It's what they've come from. It's what they endure. The child knows that they won't talk any more because if he knows too much about what's happened to *them,* he'll know too much too soon, about what's going to happen to *him.*

The last time I talked to my mother, I remember I was restless. I wanted to get out and see Isabel. We weren't married then and we had a lot to straighten out between us.

There Mama sat, in black, by the window. She was humming an old church song, *Lord, you brought me from a long ways off.* Sonny was out somewhere. Mama kept watching the streets.

"I don't know," she said, "if I'll ever see you again, after you go off from here. But I hope you'll remember the things I tried to teach you."

"Don't talk like that," I said, and smiled. "You'll be here a long time yet."

She smiled, too, but she said nothing. She was quiet for a long time. And

I said, "Mama, don't you worry about nothing. I'll be writing all the time, and you be getting the checks. . . ."

"I want to talk to you about your brother," she said, suddenly. "If anything happens to me he ain't going to have nobody to look out for him."

"Mama," I said, "ain't nothing going to happen to you *or* Sonny. Sonny's all right. He's a good boy and he's got good sense."

"It ain't a question of his being a good boy," Mama said, "nor of his having good sense. It ain't only the bad ones, nor yet the dumb ones that gets sucked under." She stopped, looking at me. "Your Daddy once had a brother," she said, and she smiled in a way that made me feel she was in pain. "You didn't never know that, did you?"

"No," I said, "I never knew that," and I watched her face.

"Oh, yes," she said, "your Daddy had a brother." She looked out of the window again. "I know you never saw your Daddy cry. But *I* did—many a time, through all these years."

I asked her, "What happened to his brother? How come nobody's ever talked about him?"

This was the first time I ever saw my mother look old.

"His brother got killed," she said, "when he was just a little younger than you are now. I knew him. He was a fine boy. He was maybe a little full of the devil, but he didn't mean nobody no harm."

Then she stopped and the room was silent, exactly as it had sometimes been on those Sunday afternoons. Mama kept looking out into the streets.

"He used to have a job in the mill," she said, "and, like all young folks, he just liked to perform on Saturday nights. Saturday nights, him and your father would drift around to different places, go to dances and things like that, or just sit around with people they knew, and your father's brother would sing, he had a fine voice, and play along with himself on his guitar. Well, this particular Saturday night, him and your father was coming home from some place, and they were both a little drunk and there was a moon that night, it was bright like day. Your father's brother was feeling kind of good, and he was whistling to himself, and he had his guitar slung over his shoulder. They was coming down a hill and beneath them was a road that turned off from the highway. Well, your father's brother, being always kind of frisky, decided to run down this hill, and he did, with that guitar banging and clanging behind him, and he ran across the road, and he was making water behind a tree. And your father was sort of amused at him and he was still coming down the hill, kind of slow. Then he heard a car motor and that same minute his brother stepped from behind the tree, into the road, in the moonlight. And he started to cross the road. And your father started to run down the hill, he says he don't know why. This car was full of white men. They was all drunk, and when they seen your father's brother they let out a great whoop and holler and they aimed the car straight at him. They was having fun, they just wanted to scare him, the way they do sometimes, you know. But they was drunk. And I guess the boy, being drunk, too, and scared, kind of lost his head. By the time he jumped it was too late. Your father says he heard his brother scream when the car rolled over him, and he heard the wood of that guitar when it give, and he heard them strings go flying, and he heard them white men shouting, and the car kept on a-going and it ain't stopped till this day. And, time your father got down the hill, his brother weren't nothing but blood and pulp."

Tears were gleaming on my mother's face. There wasn't anything I could say.

"He never mentioned it," she said, "because I never let him mention it before you children. Your Daddy was like a crazy man that night and for many a night thereafter. He says he never in his life seen anything as dark as that road after the lights of that car had gone away. Weren't nothing, weren't nobody on that road, just your Daddy and his brother and that busted guitar. Oh, yes. Your Daddy never did really get right again. Till the day he died he weren't sure but that every white man he saw was the man that killed his brother."

She stopped and took out her handkerchief and dried her eyes and looked at me.

"I ain't telling you all this," she said, "to make you scared or bitter or to make you hate nobody. I'm telling you this because you got a brother. And the world ain't changed."

I guess I didn't want to believe this. I guess she saw this in my face. She turned away from me, toward the window again, searching those streets.

"But I praise my Redeemer," she said at last, "that He called your Daddy home before me. I ain't saying it to throw no flowers at myself, but, I declare, it keeps me from feeling too cast down to know I helped your father get safely through this world. Your father always acted like he was the roughest, strongest man on earth. And everybody took him to be like that. But if he hadn't had *me* there—to see his tears!"

She was crying again. Still, I couldn't move. I said, "Lord, Lord, Mama, I didn't know it was like that."

"Oh, honey," she said, "there's a lot that you don't know. But you are going to find it out." She stood up from the window and came over to me. "You got to hold on to your brother," she said, "and don't let him fall, no matter what it looks like is happening to him and no matter how evil you gets with him. You going to be evil with him many a time. But don't you forget what I told you, you hear?"

"I won't forget," I said. "Don't you worry, I won't forget. I won't let nothing happen to Sonny."

My mother smiled as though she were amused at something she saw in my face. Then, "You may not be able to stop nothing from happening. But you got to let him know you's *there*."

Two days later I was married, and then I was gone. And I had a lot of things on my mind and I pretty well forgot my promise to Mama until I got shipped home on a special furlough for her funeral.

And, after the funeral, with just Sonny and me alone in the empty kitchen, I tried to find out something about him.

"What do you want to do?" I asked him.

"I'm going to be a musician," he said.

For he had graduated, in the time I had been away, from dancing to the juke box to finding out who was playing what, and what they were doing with it, and he had bought himself a set of drums.

"You mean, you want to be a drummer?" I somehow had the feeling that being a drummer might be all right for other people but not for my brother Sonny.

"I don't think," he said, looking at me very gravely, "that I'll ever be a good drummer. But I think I can play a piano."

I frowned. I'd never played the role of the older brother quite so seriously before, had scarcely ever, in fact, *asked* Sonny a damn thing. I sensed myself in the presence of something I didn't really know how to handle, didn't understand. So I made my frown a little deeper as I asked: "What kind of musician do you want to be?"

He grinned. "How many kinds do you think there are?"

"Be *serious*," I said.

He laughed, throwing his head back, and then looked at me. "I *am* serious."

"Well, then, for Christ's sake, stop kidding around and answer a serious question. I mean, do you want to be a concert pianist, you want to play classical music and all that, or—or what?" Long before I finished he was laughing again. "For Christ's *sake*, Sonny!"

He sobered, but with difficulty. "I'm sorry. But you sound so—*scared!*" and he was off again.

"Well, you may think it's funny now, baby, but it's not going to be so funny when you have to make your living at it, let me tell you *that*." I was furious because I knew he was laughing at me and I didn't know why.

"No," he said, very sober now, and afraid, perhaps, that he'd hurt me, "I don't want to be a classical pianist. That isn't what interests me. I mean"—he paused, looking hard at me, as though his eyes would help me to understand, and then gestured helplessly, as though perhaps his hand would help—"I mean, I'll have a lot of studying to do, and I'll have to study *everything*, but, I mean, I want to play *with*—jazz musicians." He stopped. "I want to play jazz," he said.

Well, the word had never before sounded as heavy, as real, as it sounded that afternoon in Sonny's mouth. I just looked at him and I was probably frowning a real frown by this time. I simply couldn't see why on earth he'd want to spend his time hanging around nightclubs, clowning around on bandstands, while people pushed each other around a dance floor. It seemed —beneath him, somehow. I had never thought about it before, had never been forced to, but I suppose I had always put jazz musicians in a class with what Daddy called "good-time people."

"Are you *serious?*"

"Hell, *yes*, I'm serious."

He looked more helpless than ever, and annoyed, and deeply hurt.

I suggested, helpfully: "You mean—like Louis Armstrong?"

His face closed as though I'd struck him. "No, I'm not talking about none of that oldtime, down home crap."

"Well, look, Sonny, I'm sorry, don't get mad. I just don't altogether get it, that's all. Name somebody—you know, a jazz musician you admire."

"Bird."

"Who?"

"Bird! Charlie Parker! Don't they teach you nothing in the goddamn army?"

I lit a cigarette. I was surprised and then a little amused to discover that I was trembling. "I've been out of touch," I said. "You'll have to be patient with me. Now. Who's this Parker character?"

"He's just one of the greatest jazz musicians alive," said Sonny, sullenly, his hands in his pockets, his back to me. "Maybe *the* greatest," he added, bitterly, "that's probably why *you* never heard of him."

"All right," I said "I'm ignorant. I'm sorry. I'll go out and buy all the cat's records right away, all right?"

"It don't," said Sonny, with dignity, "make any difference to me. I don't care what you listen to. Don't do me no favors."

I was beginning to realize that I'd never seen him so upset before. With another part of my mind I was thinking that this would probably turn out to be one of those things kids go through and that I shouldn't make it seem important by pushing it too hard. Still, I didn't think it would do any harm to ask: "Doesn't all this take a lot of time? Can you make a living at it?"

He turned back to me and half leaned, half sat, on the kitchen table. "Everything takes time," he said, "and—well, yes, sure, I can make a living at it. But what I don't seem to be able to make you understand is that it's the only thing I want to do."

"Well, Sonny," I said gently, "you know people can't always do exactly what they *want* to do—"

"*No,* I don't know that," said Sonny, surprising me. "I think people *ought* to do what they want to do, what else are they alive for?"

"You getting to be a big boy," I said desperately, "it's time you started thinking about your future."

"I'm thinking about my future," said Sonny, grimly. "I think about it all the time."

I gave up. I decided, if he didn't change his mind, that we could always talk about it later. "In the meantime," I said, "you got to finish school." We had already decided that he'd have to move in with Isabel and her folks. I knew this wasn't the ideal arrangement because Isabel's folks are inclined to be dicty and they hadn't especially wanted Isabel to marry me. But I didn't know what else to do. "And we have to get you fixed up at Isabel's."

There was a long silence. He moved from the kitchen table to the window. "That's a terrible idea. You know it yourself."

"Do you have a *better* idea?"

He just walked up and down the kitchen for a minute. He was as tall as I was. He had started to shave. I suddenly had the feeling that I didn't know him at all.

He stopped at the kitchen table and picked up my cigarettes. Looking at me with a kind of mocking, amused defiance, he put one between his lips. "You mind?"

"You smoking already?"

He lit the cigarette and nodded, watching me through the smoke. "I just wanted to see if I'd have the courage to smoke in front of you." He grinned and blew a great cloud of smoke to the ceiling. "It was easy." He looked at my face. "Come on, now. I bet you was smoking at my age, tell the truth."

I didn't say anything but the truth was on my face, and he laughed. But now there was something very strained in his laugh. "Sure. And I bet that ain't all you was doing."

He was frightening me a little. "Cut the crap," I said. "We already decided that you was going to go and live at Isabel's. Now what's got into you all of a sudden?"

"*You* decided it," he pointed out. "*I* didn't decide nothing." He stopped in front of me, leaning against the stove, arms loosely folded. "Look, brother. I don't want to stay in Harlem no more, I really don't." He was very earnest. He looked at me, then over toward the kitchen window. There was something in his eyes I'd never seen before, some thoughfulness, some worry all his own. He rubbed the muscle of one arm. "It's time I was getting out of here."

"Where do you want to *go*, Sonny?"

"I want to join the army. Or the navy, I don't care. If I say I'm old enough, they'll believe me."

Then I got mad. It was because I was so scared. "You must be crazy. You goddamn fool, what the hell do you want to go and join the *army* for?"

"I just told you. To get out of Harlem."

"Sonny, you haven't even finished *school*. And if you really want to be a musician, how do you expect to study if you're in the *army?*"

He looked at me, trapped, and in anguish. "There's ways. I might be able to work out some kind of deal. Anyway, I'll have the G.I. Bill when I come out."

"*If* you come out." We stared at each other. "Sonny, please. Be reasonable. I know the setup is far from perfect. But we got to do the best we can."

"I ain't learning nothing in school," he said. "Even when I go." He turned away from me and opened the window and threw his cigarette out into the narrow alley. I watched his back. "At least, I ain't learning nothing you'd want me to learn." He slammed the window so hard I thought the glass would fly out, and turned back to me. "And I'm sick of the stink of these garbage cans!"

"Sonny," I said, "I know how you feel. But if you don't finish school now, you're going to be sorry later that you didn't." I grabbed him by the shoulders. "And you only got another year. It ain't so bad. And I'll come back and I swear I'll help you do *whatever* you want to do. Just try to put up with it till I come back. Will you please do that? For me?"

He didn't answer and he wouldn't look at me.

"Sonny. You hear me?"

He pulled away. "I hear you. But you never hear anything *I* say."

I didn't know what to say to that. He looked out of the window and then back at me. "OK," he said, and sighed. "I'll try."

Then I said, trying to cheer him up a little, "They got a piano at Isabel's. You can practice on it."

And as a matter of fact it did cheer him up for a minute. "That's right," he said to himself. "I forgot that." His face relaxed a little. But the worry, the thoughtfulness, played on it still, the way shadows play on a face which is staring into the fire.

But I thought I'd never hear the end of that piano. At first, Isabel would write me, saying how nice it was that Sonny was so serious about his music and how, as soon as he came in from school, or wherever he had been when he was supposed to be at school, he went straight to that piano and stayed there until suppertime. And, after supper, he went back to that piano and stayed there until everybody went to bed. He was at the piano all day Saturday and all day Sunday. Then he bought a record player and started playing records. He'd play one record over and over again, all day long sometimes, and he'd improvise along with it on the piano. Or he'd play one section of the record, one chord, one change, one progression, then he'd do it on the piano. Then back to the record. Then back to the piano.

Well, I really don't know how they stood it. Isabel finally confessed that it wasn't like living with a person at all, it was like living with sound. And the sound didn't make any sense to her, didn't make any sense to any of them—naturally. They began, in a way, to be afflicted by this presence that was living in their home. It was as though Sonny were some sort of god, or monster. He moved in an atmosphere which wasn't like theirs at all. They fed him and he ate, he washed himself, he walked in and out of their door; he certainly wasn't nasty or unpleasant or rude, Sonny isn't any of those things; but it was as though he were all wrapped up in some cloud, some fire, some vision all his own; and there wasn't any way to reach him.

At the same time, he wasn't really a man yet, he was still a child, and they had to watch out for him in all kinds of ways. They certainly couldn't throw him out. Neither did they dare to make a great scene about that piano because even they dimly sensed, as I sensed, from so many thousands of miles away, that Sonny was at that piano playing for his life.

But he hadn't been going to school. One day a letter came from the school board and Isabel's mother got it—there had, apparently, been other letters but Sonny had torn them up. This day, when Sonny came in, Isabel's mother showed him the letter and asked where he'd been spending his time. And she finally got it out of him that he'd been down in Greenwich Village, with musicians and other characters, in a white girl's apartment. And this scared her and she started to scream at him and what came up, once she began—though she denies it to this day—was what sacrifices they were making to give Sonny a decent home and how little he appreciated it.

Sonny didn't play the piano that day. By evening, Isabel's mother had calmed down but then there was the old man to deal with, and Isabel herself. Isabel says she did her best to be calm but she broke down and started crying. She says she just watched Sonny's face. She could tell, by watching him, what was happening with him. And what was happening was that they penetrated his cloud, they had reached him. Even if their fingers had been a thousand times more gentle than human fingers ever are, he could hardly help feeling that they had stripped him naked and were spitting on that nakedness. For he also had to see that his presence, that music, which was life or death to him, had been torture for them and that they had endured it, not at all for his sake, but only for mine. And Sonny couldn't take that. He can take it a little better today than he could then but he's still not very good at it and, frankly, I don't know anybody who is.

The silence of the next few days must have been louder than the sound of all the music ever played since time began. One morning, before she went to work, Isabel was in his room for something and she suddenly realized that all of his records were gone. And she knew for certain that he was gone. And he was. He went as far as the navy would carry him. He finally sent me a postcard from some place in Greece and that was the first I knew that Sonny was still alive. I didn't see him any more until we were both back in New York and the war had long been over.

He was a man by then, of course, but I wasn't willing to see it. He came by the house from time to time, but we fought almost every time we met. I didn't like the way he carried himself, loose and dreamlike all the time, and I didn't like his friends, and his music seemed to be merely an excuse for the life he led. It sounded just that weird and disordered.

Then we had a fight, a pretty awful fight, and I didn't see him for months. By and by I looked him up, where he was living, in a furnished room in the Village, and I tried to make it up. But there were lots of other people in the room and Sonny just lay on his bed, and he wouldn't come downstairs with me, and he treated these other people as though they were his family and I weren't. So I got mad and then he got mad, and then I told him that he might just as well be dead as live the way he was living. Then he stood up and he told me not to worry about him any more in life, that he *was* dead as far as I was concerned. Then he pushed me to the door and the other people looked on as though nothing were happening, and he slammed the door behind me. I stood in the hallway, staring at the door. I heard somebody laugh in the room and then the tears came to my eyes. I started down the steps, whistling to keep from crying. I kept whistling to myself, *You going to need me, baby, one of these cold, rainy days.*

I read about Sonny's trouble in the spring. Little Grace died in the fall. She was a beautiful little girl. But she only lived a little over two years. She died of polio and she suffered. She had a slight fever for a couple of days, but it didn't seem like anything and we just kept her in bed. And we would certainly have called the doctor, but the fever dropped, she seemed to be all right. So we thought it had just been a cold. Then, one day, she was up, playing, Isabel was in the kitchen fixing lunch for the two boys when they'd come in from school, and she heard Grace fall down in the living room. When you have a lot of children you don't always start running when one of them falls, unless they start screaming or something. And, this time, Grace was quiet. Yet, Isabel says that when she heard that *thump* and then that silence, something happened in her to make her afraid. And she ran to the living room and there was little Grace on the floor, all twisted up, and the reason she hadn't screamed was that she couldn't get her breath. And when she did scream, it was the worst sound, Isabel says, that she'd ever heard in all her life, and she still hears it sometimes in her dreams. Isabel will sometimes wake me up with a low, moaning, strangled sound and I have to be quick to awaken her and hold her to me and where Isabel is weeping against me seems a mortal wound.

I think I may have written Sonny the very day that little Grace was buried. I was sitting in the living room in the dark, by myself, and I suddenly thought of Sonny. My trouble made his real.

One Saturday afternoon, when Sonny had been living with us, or, anyway, been in our house, for nearly two weeks, I found myself wandering aimlessly about the living room, drinking from a can of beer, and trying to work up the courage to search Sonny's room. He was out, he was usually out whenever I was home, and Isabel had taken the children to see their grandparents. Suddenly I was standing still in front of the living-room window watching Seventh Avenue. The idea of searching Sonny's room made me still. I scarcely dared to admit to myself what I'd be searching for. I didn't know what I'd do if I found it. Or if I didn't.

On the sidewalk across from me, near the entrance to a barbecue joint, some people were holding an old-fashioned revival meeting. The barbecue cook, wearing a dirty white apron, his conked hair reddish and metallic in the pale sun, and a cigarette between his lips, stood in the doorway, watching them. Kids and older people paused in their errands and stood there, along with some older men and a couple of tough-looking women who watched everything that happened on the avenue, as though they owned it, or were maybe owned by it. Well, they were watching this, too. The revival was being carried on by three sisters in black, and a brother. All they had were their voices and their Bibles and a tambourine. The brother was testifying and while he testified two of the sisters stood together, seeming to say, amen, and the third sister walked around with the tambourine outstretched and a couple of people dropped coins into it. Then the brother's testimony ended and the sister who had been taking up the collection dumped the coins into her palm and transferred them to the pocket of her long black robe. Then she raised both hands, striking the tambourine against the air, and then against one hand, and she started to sing. And the two other sisters and the brother joined in.

It was strange, suddenly, to watch, though I had been seeing these street meetings all my life. So, of course, had everybody else down there. Yet, they paused and watched and listened and I stood at the window. " *'Tis the old ship of Zion,*" they sang, and the sister with the tambourine kept a steady, jangling beat, "*it has rescued many a thousand!*" Not a soul under the sound of their voices was hearing this song for the first time, not one of them had been rescued. Nor had they seen much in the way of rescue work being done around them. Neither did they especially believe in the holiness of the three sisters and the brother, they knew too much about them, knew where they lived, and how. The woman with the tambourine, whose voice dominated the air, whose face was bright with joy, was divided by very little from the woman who stood watching her, a cigarette between her heavy, chapped lips, her hair a cuckoo's nest, her face scarred and swollen from many beatings, and her black eyes glittering like coal. Perhaps they both knew this, which was why, when, as rarely, they addressed each other, they addressed each other as Sister. As the singing filled the air the watching, listening faces underwent a change, the eyes focusing on something within; the music seemed to soothe a poison out of them; and time seemed, nearly, to fall away from the sullen, belligerent, battered faces, as though they were fleeing back to their first condition, while dreaming of their last. The barbecue cook half shook his head and smiled, and dropped his cigarette and disappeared into his joint. A man fumbled in his pockets for change and stood holding it in his hand impatiently, as though he had just remembered a pressing appointment further up the avenue. He looked furious. Then I saw Sonny, standing on the edge of the crowd. He was carrying a wide, flat notebook with a green cover, and it made him look, from where I was standing, almost like a schoolboy. The coppery sun brought out the copper in his skin, he was very faintly smiling, standing very still. Then the singing stopped, the tambourine turned into a collection plate again. The furious man dropped in his coins and vanished, so did a couple of the women, and Sonny dropped some change in the plate, looking directly at the woman with a little smile. He started across the avenue, toward the house. He has a slow, loping walk, something like the way Harlem hipsters walk, only he's imposed on this his own half-beat. I had never really noticed it before.

I stayed at the window, both relieved and apprehensive. As Sonny disappeared from my sight, they began singing again. And they were still singing when his key turned in the lock.

"Hey," he said.

"Hey, yourself. You want some beer?"

"No. Well, maybe." But he came up to the window and stood beside me, looking out. "What a warm voice," he said.

They were singing *If I could only hear my mother pray again!*

"Yes," I said, "and she can sure beat that tambourine."

"But what a terrible song," he said, and laughed. He dropped his notebook on the sofa and disappeared into the kitchen. "Where's Isabel and the kids?"

"I think they went to see their grandparents. You hungry?"

"No." He came back into the living room with his can of beer. "You want to come some place with me tonight?"

I sensed, I don't know how, that I couldn't possibly say no. "Sure. Where?"

He sat down on the sofa and picked up his notebook and started leafing through it. "I'm going to sit in with some fellows in a joint in the Village."

"You mean, you're going to play, tonight?"

"That's right." He took a swallow of his beer and moved back to the window. He gave me a sidelong look. "If you can stand it."

"I'll try," I said.

He smiled to himself and we both watched as the meeting across the way broke up. The three sisters and the brother, heads bowed, were singing *God be with you till we meet again.* The faces around them were very quiet. Then the song ended. The small crowd dispersed. We watched the three women and the lone man walk slowly up the avenue.

"When she was singing before," said Sonny, abruptly, "her voice reminded me for a minute of what heroin feels like sometimes—when its in your veins. It makes you feel sort of warm and cool at the same time. And distant. And—and sure." He sipped his beer, very deliberately not looking at me. I watched his face. "It makes you feel—in control. Sometimes you've got to have that feeling."

"Do you?" I sat down slowly in the easy chair.

"Sometimes." He went to the sofa and picked up his notebook again. "Some people do."

"In order," I asked, "to play?" And my voice was very ugly, full of contempt and anger.

"Well"—he looked at me with great, troubled eyes, as though, in fact, he hoped his eyes would tell me things he could never otherwise say—"they *think* so. And *if* they think so—!"

And what do *you* think?" I asked.

He sat on the sofa and put his can of beer on the floor. "I don't know," he said, and I couldn't be sure if he were answering my question or pursuing his thoughts. His face didn't tell me. "It's not so much to *play.* It's to *stand* it, to be able to make it at all. On any level." He frowned and smiled: "In order to keep from shaking to pieces."

"But these friends of yours," I said, "they seem to shake themselves to pieces pretty goddamn fast."

"Maybe." He played with the notebook. And something told me that I should curb my tongue, that Sonny was doing his best to talk, that I should listen. "But of course you only know the ones that've gone to pieces. Some don't—or at least they haven't *yet* and that's just about all *any* of us can say." He paused. "And then there are some who just live, really, in hell, and they know it and they see what's happening and they go right on. I don't know." He sighed, dropped the notebook, folded his arms. "Some guys, you can tell from the way they play, they on something *all* the time. And you can see that, well, it makes something real for them. But of course," he picked up his beer from the floor and sipped it and put the can down again, "they *want* to, too, you've got to see that. Even some of them that say they don't—*some,* not all."

"And what about you?" I asked—I couldn't help it. "What about you? Do *you* want to?"

He stood up and walked to the window and remained silent for a long time. Then he sighed. "Me," he said. Then: "While I was downstairs before, on my way here, listening to that woman sing, it struck me all of a sudden how much suffering she must have had to go through—to sing like that. It's *repulsive* to think you have to suffer that much."

I said: "But there's no way not to suffer—is there, Sonny?"

"I believe not," he said and smiled, "but that's never stopped anyone from trying." He looked at me. "Has it?" I realized, with this mocking look, that there stood between us, forever, beyond the power of time or forgiveness, the fact that I had held silence—so long!—when he had needed human speech to help him. He turned back to the window. "No, there's no way not to suffer. But you try all kinds of ways to keep from drowning in it, to keep on top of it, and to make it seem—well, like *you*. Like you did something, all right, and now you're suffering for it. You know?" I said nothing. "Well you know," he said, impatiently, "why *do* people suffer? Maybe it's better to do something to give it a reason, *any* reason."

"But we just agreed," I said, "that there's no way not to suffer. Isn't it better, then, just to—take it?"

"But nobody just takes it," Sonny cried, "that's what I'm telling you! *Everybody* tries not to. You're just hung up on the *way* some people try—it's not *your* way!"

The hair on my face began to itch, my face felt wet. "That's not true," I said, "that's not true. I don't give a damn what other people do, I don't even care how they suffer. I just care how *you* suffer." And he looked at me. "Please believe me," I said, "I don't want to see you—die—trying not to suffer."

"I won't," he said, flatly, "die trying not to suffer. At least, not any faster than anybody else."

"But there's no need." I said, trying to laugh, "is there? in killing yourself."

I wanted to say more, but I couldn't. I wanted to talk about will power and how life could be—well, beautiful. I wanted to say that it was all within; but was it? or, rather, wasn't that exactly the trouble? And I wanted to promise that I would never fail him again. But it would all have sounded —empty words and lies.

So I made the promise to myself and prayed that I would keep it.

"It's terrible sometimes, inside," he said, "that's what's the trouble. You walk these streets, black and funky and cold, and there's not really a living ass to talk to, and there's nothing shaking, and there's no way of getting it out—that storm inside. You can't talk with it and can't make love with it, and when you finally try to get with it and play it, you realize *nobody's* listening. So *you've* got to listen. You got to find a way to listen."

And then he walked away from the window and sat down on the sofa again, as though all the wind had suddenly been knocked out of him. "Sometimes you'll do *anything* to play, even cut your mother's throat." He laughed and looked at me. "Or your brother's." Then he sobered. "Or your own." Then: "Don't worry, I'm all right now and I think I'll *be* all right. But I can't forget—where I've been. I don't mean just the physical place I've been, I mean where I've *been*. And *what* I've been."

"What have you been, Sonny?" I asked.

He smiled—but sat sideways on the sofa, his elbow resting on the back, his fingers playing with his mouth and chin, not looking at me. "I've been something I didn't recognize, didn't know I could be. Didn't know anybody could be." He stopped, looking inward, looking helplessly young, looking old. "I'm not talking about it now because I feel *guilty* or anything like that —maybe it would be better if I did, I don't know. Anyway, I can't really talk about it. Not to you, not to anybody," and now he turned and faced me. "Sometimes, you know, and it was actually when I was most *out* of the world, I felt that I was in it, that I was *with* it, really, and I could play or I didn't really have to *play,* it just came out of me, it was there. And I don't know how I played, thinking about it now, but I know I did awful things, those times, sometimes, to people. Or it wasn't that I *did* anything to them —it was that they weren't real." He picked up the beer can; it was empty; he rolled it between his palms: "And other times—well, I needed a fix, I needed to find a place to lean, I needed to clear a space to *listen*—and I couldn't find it, and I —went crazy, I did terrible things to *me,* I was terrible *for* me." He began pressing the beer can between his hands, I watched the metal begin to give. It glittered, as he played with it, like a knife, and I was afraid he would cut himself, but I said nothing. "Oh well. I can never tell you I was all by myself at the bottom of something, stinking and sweating and crying and shaking, and I smelled it, you know? *my* stink, and I thought I'd die if I couldn't get away from it and yet, all the same, I knew that everything I was doing was just locking me in with it. And I didn't know," he paused, still flattening the beer can, "I didn't know, I still *don't know,* something kept telling me that maybe it was good to smell your own stink, but I didn't think that *that* was what I'd been trying to do—and—who can stand it?" and he abruptly dropped the ruined beer can, looking at me with a small, still smile, and then rose, walking to the window as though it were the lodestone rock. I watched his face, he watched the avenue. "I couldn't tell you when Mama died—but the reason I wanted to leave Harlem so bad was to get away from drugs. And then, when I ran away, that's what I was running from—really. When I came back, nothing had changed, *I* hadn't changed, I was just—older." And he stopped, drumming with his fingers on the windowpane. The sun had vanished, soon darkness would fall. I watched his face. "It can come again," he said, almost as though speaking to himself. Then he turned to me. "It can come again," he repeated. "I just want you to know that."

"All right," I said, at last. "So it can come again. All right."

He smiled, but the smile was sorrowful. "I had to try to tell you," he said.

"Yes," I said. "I understand that."

"You're my brother," he said, looking straight at me, and not smiling at all.

"Yes," I repeated, "yes. I understand that."

He turned back to the window, looking out. "All that hatred down there," he said, "all that hatred and misery and love. It's a wonder it doesn't blow the avenue apart."

We went to the only nightclub on a short, dark street, downtown. We squeezed through the narrow, chattering, jam-packed bar to the entrance of the big room, where the bandstand was. And we stood there for a moment, for the lights were very dim in this room and we couldn't see. Then, "Hello, boy," said a voice and an enormous black man, much older than Sonny or myself, erupted out of all that atmospheric lighting and put an arm around Sonny's shoulder. "I been sitting right here," he said, "waiting for you."

He had a big voice, too, and heads in the darkness turned toward us.

Sonny grinned and pulled a little away, and said, "Creole, this is my brother. I told you about him."

Creole shook my hand. "I'm glad to meet you, son," he said, and it was clear that he was glad to meet me *there,* for Sonny's sake. And he smiled, "You got a real musician in *your* family," and he took his arm from Sonny's shoulder and slapped him, lightly, affectionately, with the back of his hand.

"Well. Now I've heard it all," said a voice behind us. This was another musician, and a friend of Sonny's, a coal-black, cheerful-looking man, built close to the ground. He immediately began confiding to me, at the top of his lungs, the most terrible things about Sonny, his teeth gleaming like a lighthouse and his laugh coming up out of him like the beginning of an earthquake. And it turned out that everyone at the bar knew Sonny, or almost everyone; some were musicians, working there, or nearby, or not working, some were simply hangers-on, and some were there to hear Sonny play. I was introduced to all of them and they were all very polite to me. Yet, it was clear that, for them, I was only Sonny's brother. Here, I was in Sonny's world. Or, rather: his kingdom. Here, it was not even a question that his veins bore royal blood.

They were going to play soon and Creole installed me, by myself, at a table in a dark corner. Then I watched them, Creole, and the little black man, and Sonny, and the others, while they horsed around, standing just below the bandstand. The light from the bandstand spilled just a little short of them and, watching them laughing and gesturing and moving about, I had the feeling that they, nevertheless, were being most careful not to step into that circle of light too suddenly: that if they moved into the light too suddenly, without thinking, they would perish in flame. Then, while I watched, one of them, the small, black man, moved into the light and crossed the bandstand and started fooling around with his drums. Then— being funny and being, also, extremely ceremonious—Creole took Sonny by the arm and led him to the piano. A woman's voice called Sonny's name and a few hands started clapping. And Sonny, also being funny and being ceremonious, and so touched, I think, that he could have cried, but neither hiding it nor showing it, riding it like a man, grinned, and put both hands to his heart and bowed from the waist.

Creole then went to the bass fiddle and a lean, very bright-skinned brown man jumped up on the bandstand and picked up his horn. So there they were, and the atmosphere on the bandstand and in the room began to change and tighten. Someone stepped up to the microphone and announced them. Then there were all kinds of murmurs. Some people at the bar shushed others. The waitress ran around, frantically getting in the last orders, guys and chicks got closer to each other, and the lights on the bandstand, on the quartet, turned to a kind of indigo. Then they all looked different there. Creole looked about him for the last time, as though he were making certain that all his chickens were in the coop, and then he—jumped and struck the fiddle. And there they were.

All I know about music is that not many people ever really hear it. And even then, on the rare occasions when something opens within, and the music enters, what we mainly hear, or hear corroborated, are personal, private, vanishing evocations. But the man who creates the music is hearing something else, is dealing with the roar rising from the void and imposing order on it as it hits the air. What is evoked in him, then, is of another order, more terrible because it has no words, and triumphant, too, for that same reason. And his triumph, when he triumphs, is ours. I just watched Sonny's face. His face was troubled, he was working hard, but he wasn't with it. And I had the feeling that, in a way, everyone on the bandstand was waiting for him, both waiting for him and pushing him along. But as I began to watch Creole, I realized that it was Creole who held them all back. He had them on a short rein. Up there, keeping the beat with his whole body, wailing on the fiddle, with his eyes half closed, he was listening to everything, but he was listening to Sonny. He was having a dialogue with Sonny. He wanted Sonny to leave the shoreline and strike out for the deep water. He was Sonny's witness that deep water and drowning were not the same thing—he had been there, and he knew. And he wanted Sonny to know. He was waiting for Sonny to do the things on the keys which would let Creole know that Sonny was in the water.

And, while Creole listened, Sonny moved, deep within, exactly like someone in torment. I had never before thought of how awful the relationship must be between the musician and his instrument. He has to fill it, this instrument, with the breath of life, his own. He has to make it do what he wants it to do. And a piano is just a piano. It's made out of so much wood and wires and little hammers and big ones, and ivory. While there's only so much you can do with it, the only way to find this out is to try; to try and make it do everything.

And Sonny hadn't been near a piano for over a year. And he wasn't on much better terms with his life, not the life that stretched before him now. He and the piano stammered, started one way, got scared, stopped; started another way, panicked, marked time, started again; then seemed to have found a direction, panicked again, got stuck. And the face I saw on Sonny I'd never seen before. Everything had been burned out of it, and, at the same time, things usually hidden were being burned in, by the fire and fury of the battle which was occurring in him up there.

Yet, watching Creole's face as they neared the end of the first set, I had the feeling that something had happened, something I hadn't heard. Then they finished, there was scattered applause, and then, without an instant's warning, Creole started into something else, it was almost sardonic, it was *Am I Blue*. And, as though he commanded, Sonny began to play. Something began to happen. And Creole let out the reins. The dry, low, black man said something awful on the drums. Creole answered, and the drums talked back. Then the horn insisted, sweet and high, slightly detached perhaps, and Creole listened, commenting now and then, dry, and driving, beautiful and calm and old. Then they all came together again, and Sonny was part of the family again. I could tell this from his face. He seemed to have found, right there beneath his fingers, a damn brand-new piano. It seemed that he couldn't get over it. Then, for awhile, just being happy with Sonny, they seemed to be agreeing with him that brand-new pianos certainly were a gas.

Then Creole stepped forward to remind them that what they were playing was the blues. He hit something in all of them, he hit something in me, myself, and the music tightened and deepened, apprehension began to beat the air. Creole began to tell us what the blues were all about. They were not about anything very new. He and his boys up there were keeping it new, at the risk of ruin, destruction, madness, and death, in order to find new ways to make us listen. For, while the tale of how we suffer, and how we are delighted, and how we may triumph is never new, it always must be heard. There isn't any other tale to tell, it's the only light we've got in all this darkness.

And this tale, according to that face, that body, those strong hands on those strings, has another aspect in every country, and a new depth in every generation. Listen, Creole seemed to be saying, listen. Now these are Sonny's blues. He made the little black man on the drums know it, and the bright, brown man on the horn. Creole wasn't trying any longer to get Sonny in the water. He was wishing him Godspeed. Then he stepped back, very slowly, filling the air with the immense suggestion that Sonny speak for himself.

Then they all gathered around Sonny and Sonny played. Every now and again one of them seemed to say, amen. Sonny's fingers filled the air with life, his life. But that life contained so many others. And Sonny went all the way back, he really began with the spare, flat statement of the opening phrase of the song. Then he began to make it his. It was very beautiful because it wasn't hurried and it was no longer a lament. I seemed to hear with what burning he had made it his, with what burning we had yet to make it ours, how we could cease lamenting. Freedom lurked around us and I understood, at last, that he could help us to be free if we would listen, that he would never be free until we did. Yet, there was no battle in his face now. I heard what he had gone through, and would continue to go through until he came to rest in earth. He had made it his: that long line, of which we knew only Mama and Daddy. And he was giving it back, as everything must be given back, so that, passing through death, it can live forever. I saw my mother's face again, and felt, for the first time, how the stones of the road she had walked on must have bruised her feet. I saw the moonlit road where my father's brother died. And it brought something else back to me, and carried me past it, I saw my little girl again and felt Isabel's tears again, and I felt my own tears begin to rise. And I was yet aware that this was only a moment, that the world waited outside, as hungry as a tiger, and that trouble stretched above us, longer than the sky.

Then it was over. Creole and Sonny let out their breath, both soaking wet, and grinning. There was a lot of applause and some of it was real. In the dark, the girl came by and I asked her to take drinks to the bandstand. There was a long pause, while they talked up there in the indigo light and after awhile I saw the girl put a Scotch and milk on top of the piano for Sonny. He didn't seem to notice it, but just before they started playing again, he sipped from it and looked toward me, and nodded. Then he put it back on top of the piano. For me, then, as they began to play again, it glowed and shook above by brother's head like the very cup of trembling.

SPEECH OF ACCEPTANCE UPON THE AWARD OF THE NOBEL PRIZE FOR LITERATURE

William Faulkner

I feel that this award was not made to me as a man, but to my work—a life's work in all the agony and sweat of the human spirit, not for glory and least of all for profit, but to create out of the materials of the human spirit something which did not exist before. So this award is only mine in trust. It will not be difficult to find a dedication for the money part of it commensurate with the purpose and significance of its origin. But I would like to do the same with the acclaim too, by using this moment as a pinnacle from which I might be listened to by the young men and women already dedicated to the same anguish and travail, among whom is already that one who will some day stand here where I am standing.

Our tragedy today is a general and universal physical fear so long sustained by now that we can even bear it. There are no longer problems of the spirit. There is only the question: When will I be blown up? Because of this, the young man or woman writing today has forgotten the problems of the human heart in conflict with itself which alone can make good writing because only that is worth writing about, worth the agony and the sweat.

He must learn them again. He must teach himself that the basest of all things is to be afraid; and, teaching himself that, forget it forever, leaving no room in his workshop for anything but the old verities and truths of the heart, the old universal truths lacking which any story is ephemeral and doomed—love and honor and pity and pride and compassion and sacrifice.

Until he does so, he labors under a curse. He writes not of love but of lust, of defeats in which nobody loses anything of value, of victories without hope and, worst of all, without pity or compassion. His griefs grieve on no universal bones, leaving no scars. He writes not of the heart but of the glands.

Until he relearns these things, he will write as though he stood among and watched the end of man. I decline to accept the end of man. It is easy enough to say that man is immortal simply because he will endure; that when the last ding-dong of doom has clanged and faded from the last worthless rock hanging tideless in the last red and dying evening, that even then there will still be one more sound: that of his puny inexhaustible voice, still talking. I refuse to accept this. I believe that man will not merely endure: he will prevail. He is immortal, not because he alone among creatures has an inexhaustible voice, but because he has a soul, a spirit capable of compassion and sacrifice and endurance. The poet's, the writer's, duty is to write about these things. It is his privilege to help man endure by lifting his heart, by reminding him of the courage and honor and hope and pride and compassion and pity and sacrifice which have been the glory of his past. The poet's voice need not merely be the record of man, it can be one of the props, the pillars to help him endure and prevail.

TO A FRIEND WHOSE WORK HAS COME TO NOTHING

William Butler Yeats

Now all the truth is out,
Be secret and take defeat
From any brazen throat,
For how can you compete,
Being honor bred, with one
Who, were it proved he lies,
Were neither shamed in his own
Nor in his neighbors' eyes?
Bred to a harder thing
Than Triumph, turn away
And like a laughing string
Whereon mad fingers play
Amid a place of stone,
Be secret and exult,
Because of all things known
That is most difficult.

Suggestions for Further Reading

Note: This is not intended to be a comprehensive bibliography; instead, the following titles are merely meant to be suggestive of the range of works related to the subjects dealt with in this book.

THE FEAR

Non-fiction Prose:

CABELL, JAMES BRANCH. *Beyond Life.* New York: Robert M. McBride & Co., 1927.
DUBOS, RENÉ. *So Human an Animal.* New York: Charles Scribner's Sons, 1968.
TOYNBEE, ARNOLD J. *Civilization on Trial.* New York: Oxford University Press, 1948.

Fiction, Poetry, Drama:

AMIS, KINGSLEY. *The Anti-Death League.*
ANDERSON, SHERWOOD. *Winesburg, Ohio.*
ANON. *Beowulf.*
AUDEN, W. H. *The Age of Anxiety.*
BECKETT, SAMUEL. *Endgame; Waiting for Godot.*
BIERCE, AMBROSE. *In the Midst of Life.*
CAMUS, ALBERT. *Caligula; The Plague.*
CONRAD, JOSEPH. *Heart of Darkness.*
CRANE, STEPHEN. *The Monster and Other Stories.*
DURRENMATT, FRIEDRICH. *The Pledge.*
ELIOT, T. S. "The Wasteland."
HARDY, THOMAS. *The Collected Poems of Thomas Hardy.*
HOUSMAN, A. E. *The Collected Poems of A. E. Housman.*
KAFKA, FRANZ. *The Penal Colony: Stories and Short Pieces; The Trial.*
O'NEILL, EUGENE. *The Emperor Jones; The Iceman Cometh.*
SARTRE, JEAN PAUL. *No Exit.*
SHAKESPEARE, WILLIAM. *Troilus and Cressida.*

THE WORD

Non-fiction Prose:

ASTROV, MARGOT, ed. *American Indian Prose and Poetry.* New York: Capricorn Books, 1962.
BLACK, MAX, ed. *The Importance of Language.* Englewood Cliffs, N. J.: Prentice-Hall, Inc., 1962.
FRANCIS, W. NELSON. *The English Language.* New York: W. W. Norton & Co., Inc., 1965.
HAYAKAWA, S. I. *Language in Thought and Action.* New York: Harcourt, Brace & World, Inc., 1964.
———, ed. *The Use and Misuse of Language.* New York: Fawcett, 1962.

JESPERSON, OTTO. *Language, Its Nature, Development, and Origin.* New York: W. W. Norton & Co., Inc., 1964.

SMITH, ARTHUR L. *Rhetoric of Black Revolution.* Boston: Allyn and Bacon, Inc., 1969.

STEINER, GEORGE. *Language and Silence.* New York: Atheneum, 1970.

Fiction, Poetry, Drama:

ALBEE, EDWARD. *The American Dream.*

SHAW, GEORGE BERNARD. *Pygmalion.*

SYNGE, JOHN MILLINGTON. *The Playboy of the Western World.*

TOWARD ONENESS

Non-fiction Prose:

ALEXANDER, HARTLEY BURR. *North American Mythology.* Cambridge: Cambridge University Press, 1916.

BRANDON, S. G. F. *The Judgement of the Dead.* New York: Scribner, 1969.

CAMPBELL, JOSEPH. *The Hero With a Thousand Faces.* New York: Bollingen Foundation, 1949.

FARB, PETER. *Man's Rise to Civilization as Shown by the Indians of North America from Primeval Times to the Coming of the Industrial State.* New York: E. P. Dutton, 1968.

FRAZER, SIR JAMES GEORGE. *The Golden Bough (abridged edition).* Toronto: The Macmillan Co., 1950.

HAMILTON, EDITH. *Mythology.* New York: The New American Library, Inc., 1942.

JOAD, C. E. M. *The Present and Future of Religion.* New York: The Macmillan Co., 1930.

KAUFMANN, WALTER, ed. *Existentialism from Dostoevsky to Sartre.* New York: Meridian, 1956.

———, ed. *Religion from Tolstoy to Camus.* New York: Harper & Row, 1964.

MERTON, THOMAS. *The Seven Storey Mountain,* New York: Harcourt, Brace & World, 1948.

MILLER, PERRY, ed. *The American Puritans.* Garden City, N. Y.: Doubleday, 1956.

RUSSELL, BERTRAND. *Religion and Science.* New York: Holt, 1935.

SCHONFIELD, HUGH J. *The Passover Plot.* New York: Bantam, 1967.

———. *Those Incredible Christians.* New York: Bantam, 1968.

WEBER, MAX. *The Protestant Ethic and the Spirit of Capitalism.* London: G. Allen & Unwin, 1930.

Fiction, Poetry, Drama:

BELLOW, SAUL. *Henderson the Rain King.*

BLAKE, WILLIAM. *The Complete Writings of William Blake.* Ed. Geoffrey Keynes. London: Oxford University Press, 1969.

CONRAD, JOSEPH. *Lord Jim.*

DOSTOYEVSKI, FYODOR. *The Brothers Karamazov; Crime and Punishment; The Idiot.*

ELIOT, T. S. *Murder in the Cathedral.*

FROST, ROBERT. *The Mask of Reason.*

HAWTHORNE, NATHANIEL. "Young Goodman Brown"; *The Scarlet Letter.*

HESSE, HERMAN. *Siddhartha.*

KAZANTZAKIS, NIKOS. *The Last Temptation of Christ; The Greek Passion.*

LEWIS, SINCLAIR. *Elmer Gantry.*

MACLEISH, ARCHIBALD. *J. B.*

MELVILLE, HERMAN. *Moby Dick.*

MILLER, ARTHUR. *The Crucible.*

NIETZSCHE, FREDERICK. *The Portable Nietzsche.* Ed. and tr. by Walter Kaufmann. New York: Viking, 1968.

SHAKESPEARE, WILLIAM. *Measure for Measure.*

SHAW, GEORGE BERNARD. St. Joan.

SYNGE, JOHN MILLINGTON. *Riders to the Sea.*

TWAIN, MARK. "The Mysterious Stranger"; *Letters from the Earth.*

YEATS, WILLIAM BUTLER. *Calvary; Purgatory.*

WITH WHAT WE HAVE

Non-fiction Prose:

ADAMS, HENRY. *The Education of Henry Adams.*

BOULDING, KENNETH. *The Meaning of the 20th Century.* New York: Harper & Row, 1964.

CLEAVER, ELDRIDGE. *Soul on Ice.* New York: Dell, 1968.

FARB, PETER. *Man's Rise to Civilization, etc.* New York: Dutton, 1968.

GRIER, WILLIAM H. and PRICE M. COBBS. *Black Rage.* New York: Bantam, 1968.

HAMILTON, EDITH. *The Greek Way.* New York: Norton, 1964.

HAYDEN, TOM. *Rebellion in Newark: Official Violence and Ghetto Response.* New York: Random House, 1967.

JONES, LEROI. *Home.* New York: William Morrow, 1966.

MAILER, NORMAN. *Miami and the Siege of Chicago.* New York: The New American Library, 1968.

MALCOLM X. *The Autobiography of Malcolm X.* New York: Grove Press, 1964.

PAINE, THOMAS. *Common Sense.*

STEINER, STAN. *The New Indians.* New York: Dell, 1968.

TALAYESVA, DON C. *Sun Chief, Autobiography of a Hopi.* Ed. Leo W. Simmons. New Haven: Yale University Press, 1942.

Fiction, Poetry, Drama:

AMIS, KINGSLEY. *Lucky Jim.*

BALDWIN, JAMES. *Going to Meet the Man.*

ELIOT, T. S. "The Love Song of J. Alfred Prufrock."

ELLISON, RALPH. *The Invisible Man.*

FAULKNER, WILLIAM. "Barn Burning."

FITZGERALD, F. SCOTT. *The Great Gatsby.*

GOLDING, WILLIAM. *Lord of the Flies.*

HUFFAKER, CLAIR. *Nobody Loves a Drunken Indian.*

HUXLEY, ALDOUS. *Brave New World; Brave New World Revisited.*

JONES, LEROI. *The Dutchman.*

JOYCE, JAMES. *Dubliners.*

KESEY, KEN. *One Flew Over the Cuckoo's Nest.*

KOESTLER, ARTHUR. *Darkness at Noon.*

LAWRENCE, JEROME and ROBERT E. LEE. *Inherit the Wind.*

MELVILLE, HERMAN. "Bartleby the Scrivener"; *Billy Budd.*

MILLER, ARTHUR. *Death of a Salesman.*

ORWELL, GEORGE. *Animal Farm; 1984.*

SHAKESPEARE, WILLIAM. *The Merchant of Venice.*

SHAW, GEORGE BERNARD. *Man and Superman; Major Barbara.*

STEINBECK, JOHN. *The Grapes of Wrath; The Winter of Our Discontent; The Long Valley.*

SWIFT, JONATHAN. *Gulliver's Travels.*

TWAIN, MARK. "The Man Who Corrupted Hadleyburg"; *Huckleberry Finn; Pudd'nhead Wilson.*

WARREN, ROBERT PENN. *All the King's Men.*

WOUK, HERMAN. *The Caine Mutiny.*

WRIGHT, RICHARD. *Native Son.*

A RETURN TO VISION

Non-fiction Prose:

BLACKMUR, R. P. *The Lion and the Honeycomb.* New York: Harcourt, Brace & World, 1955.

CAMUS, ALBERT. *The Myth of Sisyphus and Other Essays.* New York: Random House, 1955.

CARY, JOYCE. *Art and Reality.* Garden City, N. Y.: Doubleday.

STEINBECK, JOHN. *Travels With Charley.* New York: Bantam. 1964.

Fiction, Poetry, Drama:

CARY, JOYCE. *The Horse's Mouth.*

HAWTHORNE, NATHANIEL. "The Artist of the Beautiful."

JAMES, HENRY. "The Real Thing."

JOYCE, JAMES. *Portrait of the Artist as a Young Man.*

KAFKA, FRANZ. "The Hunger Artist."

KEATS, JOHN. "On First Looking into Chapman's Homer."

MANN, THOMAS. *Dr. Faustus.*

MAUGHAM, W. SOMERSET. *The Moon and Sixpence.*

SHELLEY, PERCY BYSSHE. "Ode to the West Wind."

THOMAS, DYLAN. "In My Craft or Sullen Art."

WILDE, OSCAR. *The Picture of Dorian Gray.*